Dependable Computing and Fault-Tolerant Systems

Edited by
A. Avižienis, H. Kopetz, J. C. Laprie

Volume 1

William C. Carter

A. Avižienis, H. Kopetz, J. C. Laprie (eds.)

The Evolution of Fault-Tolerant Computing

In the Honor of William C. Carter

Springer-Verlag Wien New York

Prof. Dr. Algirdas Avižienis, UCLA, Los Angeles, Calif., U.S.A.

Prof. Dr. Hermann Kopetz, Technical University, Wien, Austria

Dr. Jean-Claude Laprie, LAAS, Toulouse, France

With 52 Figures, 35 Portraits and 1 Frontispiece

Library of Congress Cataloging-in-Publication Data

The Evolution of fault-tolerant computing.

  (Dependable computing and fault-tolerant systems ; vol. I)
  "In the honor of William C. Carter.
  Bibliography: p.
  Includes index.
  1. Fault-tolerant computing. 2. Carter, William C.
(William Caswell) I. Carter, William C. (William
Caswell) II. Avižienis, Algirdas. III. Kopetz,
Hermann. IV. Laprie, J. C. (Jean-Claude)
V. Symposium on the Evolution of Fault-tolerant
Computing (1986 : Baden, Austria) VI. Series.
QA76.9.F38E96   1987   004.2   87-19110

ISBN-13:978-3-7091-8873-6 (U.S.)

ISSN 0932-5581
ISBN-13:978-3-7091-8873-6   e-ISBN-13:978-3-7091-8871-2
DOI: 10.1007/978-3-7091-8871-2

Foreword

For the editors of this book, as well as for many other researchers in the area of fault-tolerant computing, Dr. William Caswell Carter is one of the key figures in the formation and development of this important field. We felt that the IFIP Working Group 10.4 at Baden, Austria, in June 1986, which coincided with an important step in Bill's career, was an appropriate occasion to honor Bill's contributions and achievements by organizing a one-day "Symposium on the Evolution of Fault-Tolerant Computing" in the honor of William C. Carter.

The Symposium, held on June 30, 1986, brought together a group of eminent scientists from all over the world to discuss the evolution, the state of the art, and the future perspectives of the field of fault-tolerant computing. Historic developments in academia and industry were presented by individuals who themselves have actively been involved in bringing them about. The Symposium proved to be a unique historic event and these Proceedings, which contain the final versions of the papers presented at Baden, are an authentic reference document.

Vienna, May 1987

Algirdas Avižienis
Hermann Kopetz
Jean-Claude Laprie

IFIP Working Group WG 10.4:
"Reliable Computing and Fault Tolerance"

The Working Group WG 10.4 of IFIP, the International Federation for Information Processing, was established by the IFIP General Assembly in October 1980, and operates under IFIP Technical Committee TC-10, "Digital Systems Design". The charter of WG 10.4 states the aim and the scope of this Working Group as follows:

Aim: Correct design and reliable operation are basic goals for all classes of information processing systems (data processing, process control, telecommunications, etc.). The Aim of the Working Group is to promote and integrate the many diverse specialities of reliable computing (fault tolerance and fault avoidance) into a cohesive field of scientific and technical knowledge.

Scope: Specifically, the Working Group is concerned with progress in:

- understanding of faults (design faults, physical faults, human interaction faults, etc.) and their effects;
- development of specification and design methods for reliability, availability, maintainability, testability and verifiability;
- development of methods for fault detection and treatment;
- development of validation methods (testing, verification, evaluation);

The concept of WG 10.4 was formulated during the IFIP Working Conference on Reliable Computing and Fault Tolerance on September 27-29, 1979 in London, England, held in conjunction with the Euro-IFIP 79 Conference. Professor A. Avižienis of UCLA, Los Angeles, USA and Professor A. Costes of LAAS, Toulouse, France, who organized the London Conference and proposed the formation of the Working Group were appointed as Chairman and Vice Chairman, respectively, of the new WG 10.4 in 1980 and served until 1986, when Dr. J. C. Laprie (LAAS, Toulouse, France) succeeded to serve as Chairman, and Profs. J. Meyer (University of Michigan, USA), and Y. Tohma (Tokyo Institute of Technology, Japan) became Vice Chairmen of the Working Group.

The first meeting of the new WG 10.4 took place in Portland, Maine, USA, on June 22-23, 1981. In attendance were 29 founding members of the Working Group. Since then, the membership has grown to 50 members from 15 countries. Ten WG 10.4 meetings have been held from 1981 through 1986 in various locations, including USA (4 meetings), France (2), and Italy, Australia, Canada, Austria (1 each).

The main goal of WG 10.4 meetings is to conduct in-depth discussions of important technical topics. The principal theme since the first meeting has been the understanding and exposition of the fundamental concepts of fault-tolerant computing. Other major topics have been: distributed computing, real-time systems, certification of dependable systems, specification methods, and design diversity. Beside the key themes, research reports by members and guests are presented at every meeting, and business meetings are held to plan future activities.

In addition to group meetings, beginning in 1982 the WG 10.4 has served as a cooperating sponsor of the annual International Symposium on Fault-Tolerant Computing that is organized by the TC on Fault-Tolerant Computing of the IEEE Computer Society. Since 1983, the WG 10.4 also cooperates with the "Safety, Security, and Reliability" technical committee (TC 7) of EWICS, the European Workshop on Industrial Computer Systems, and other groups in sponsorship of the IFAC SAFECOMP Workshops.

This volume is first of a series of technical books that represent the efforts of the members of IFIP WG 10.4 and of their colleagues who cooperate with them or are guests at WG 10.4 meetings.

Table of Contents

Experiences in Fault Tolerant Computing, 1947 - 1971

W. C. Carter
Consultant
3 Shagbark Lane
Woodbury, CT 06798, USA

ABSTRACT

This essay is based upon my recollections pertinent to fault tolerant computing. The material included is determined by my interactions with talented and adventurous colleagues and with the general computing community. This means that many worthy and interesting projects will be slighted. I apologize to all who worked on these projects, and blame my memory. This essay begins with my work on the ENIAC, (modified to be a writable ROM microprogram controlled computer), and continues through my work helping with the design of dependable (for the period) data processing systems at Raytheon, Datamatic, and Honeywell. My report on work at IBM begins with HARVEST, includes S/360 and ends with my early work at IBM Research in fault tolerant computing, including projects started in the early 1970's, some of which were published later. After the founding of the IEEE FTTC and the Annual Fault Tolerant Computing Symposia in 1971 there is so much published material that I shall let the professional historians sort it out.

1. Apologia - A Poor Substitute for History

This essay is not history. To quote from Metropolis,(1980), 'The critic who investigates the inadequacies of the history of computing is at once faced with an embarrassment of riches. Computer scientists seem determined to confirm the judgement of professional historians that scientists should not be depended upon to produce the histories of their own fields.' Metropolis' article has a good bibliography of early efforts in electronic computing efforts, 93 references including references to books by professional historians. This article will contain recollections pertinent to fault tolerant computing based upon my experiences working with groups of talented engineers and scientists, and upon my interactions with the computing community at those times. References will be made to published material whenever possible, but no effort has been made to search for original sources. No attempt will be made to describe the development of systems or ideas with which I was not familiar at the time of their development. However, as in any scientific work, an honest effort has been made to find, read, understand, use, and refer to previous pertinent material. Much historical information is contained in the Annals of the History of Computing, 1979-, Brian Randell's book, (1973), the Encyclopedia of Computer Science, (Ralston 1976), and the IBM Journal of Research & Development, 25th Anniversary Issue, 1981.

This essay will end with a consideration of projects which started at about the time of the beginning of the IEEE Fault Tolerant Technical Committee, the initiation of the annual International Symposium on Fault Tolerant Computing, and the frequent appearance of Special Issues devoted to Fault Tolerant Computing in the IEEE Transactions on Computing. From then on, fault tolerant work has been well documented.

My personal feeling is that attacking the many new problems in fault tolerance and trying to conquer the host of difficulties is far more rewarding than studying in depth the usually parallel developments of previous pertinent hidden ideas.

This paper will use the terminology developed by the IFIP Working Group 10.4 on Reliability and Fault Tolerant Computing and the IEEE FTTC, (Laprie 1985). Computer system dependability is the quality of the delivered service such that reliance can justifiably be placed on this service. Fault tolerant computing is concerned with methods of achieving computer system dependability.

The first steps in fault tolerant computing were not the development of theories, but the day to day struggle with practical difficulties. How could you trust the answers given by these new complicated machines? These answers were to previously unsolved problems. Were the answers valid scientifically? Were they accurate? How could the answers be validated? Would computers really be useful in solving day to day real problems? My experience with these steps will be chronicled in this essay.

2. The Early Days - Or All Computing Was "Fault-Tolerant"

In 1947 if you wanted to run scientific problems on an electronic computer in the US, you went to Aberdeen Proving Ground (APG). The ENIAC was coming in March, 1948 ! The Ballistic Research Laboratories under the leadership of Col. Leslie Simon did the calculations for the Army Ballistic Tables, and other research work which needed computing resources. They had extensive practical operating computing systems; a modern differential analyzer and several Bell Relay Computers [BRC] (Harvard Proc. 1949). In relay computers, intermittent faults far outnumbered permanent faults (ERA 1950). For this reason, these systems used extensive dynamic checking (binary codes and proper finish of instructions). The success of the BRC's is evidenced by this quotation: 'starting with the Model III delivered to the Armed Forces in 1944, not one of our customers has reported their computers giving out a wrong answer as a result of a machine error (Harvard Proc. 1949). The BRC Model V at APG had two central processors. When one had to stop because of an error, the other would read the next problem from paper tape and begin its execution (ERA 1950). The model VI had an improvement - a 'second try' feature for retrying an operation immediately if it failed. These are good examples of the second of the two basic strategies employed in designing dependable computers (see Carter & Bouricius 1970, with a bibliography with 73 early references). The first technique is to increase the reliability through advances in component technology and simplicity of design; the second to use protective redundancy to permit correct performance (perhaps in a degraded mode) in the presence of component failures. The first technique assumes that simplicity of design will aid in serviceability; the second assumes that availability of information about the failure is preferable. Time has shown a fluctuation in the popularity of each strategy, based primarily on changes in technologies, applications, and costs.

Reliable the BRC's might be, but they were very slow and had limited capacity, the ENIAC was electronic and fast ! Following Metropolis (1980), the development of these early computers can be most easily understood in terms of the description of their modes of program control.

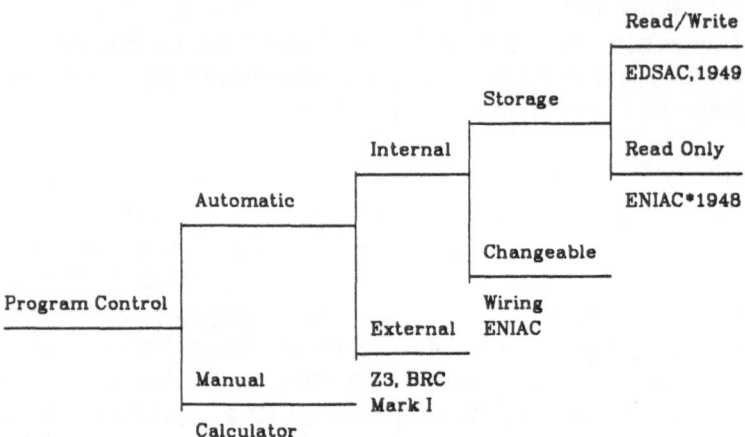

3. The ENIAC

The ENIAC, was built at the Moore School of EE (U. Penn.) by P. Eckert, J. Mauchly, and A. R. Burks under contract to the BRL with H. H. Goldstine as liason. It is well described in (Burks 1981). It used tubes and calculated artillery firing tables during the latter part of WW II. A rough intuitive description of the ENIAC is that it was essentially a data flow machine. There were about 20 'accumulators' each of which could add, subtract, clear or transfer 12 decimal digits of information onto the data transfer bus after receiving the appropriate signal from one of the signal transfer buses. There was also a unit which performed multiplication, division, and calculated square roots (MDSQ), with start also controlled by external signals. The ENIAC had a read only memory, the 'function tables' which could store 312 words of 12 decimal digit numbers each. Input information was read 6 words at a time from an IBM card into registers. Output was punched 6 words at a time onto an IBM card.

The signal transfer buses were essentially a distributed plug board using jack plugs and switches. Routines were programmed by determining in what sequence data would be available and needed, then ensuring that the signals on the signal transfer buses gave each independent unit the correct signal at the right time. In the late 40's such coding for a problem was a very difficult task. Remember that 'Planning and Coding Problems for an Electronic Computing Instrument' by Goldstine and von Neumann (1947), which introduced flow charts, had just been written and represented the extent of publically documented programming knowledge. However, the program to calculate firing tables worked very well, and a few steps were even done in parallel. Preparing the ENIAC for a new problem was very time consuming; doing the planning, making the physical set-up and getting the routine to work. After WW II it was planned to move the ENIAC to APG, and have it do more general scientific work. Improvements were needed.

4. The ENIAC Modified for User Microprogramming - the ENIAC*

R. F. Clippinger from APG (Metropolis 1980) suggested that the function tables might be used to store 6 two decimal digit instructions or one constant. Using a new program control unit and a constant setting of the data buses and distributed plug board and signal buses, up to 100 possible instructions could be decoded and implemented. R. Clippinger, J. von Neumann and E. Bartik (Head of Programming at the Moore School) and N. Metropolis (from Los Alamos) worked on the order code, choosing 84 instructions. A. Goldstine started a control implementation, finished by N. Metropolis and K. von Neumann (Metropolis 1980). The ENIAC was then moved, and the proposed changes made.

The modified ENIAC, denoted by ENIAC*, was essentially a register transfer level computer. It contained 18 general purpose registers for variable storage, an accumulator for addition and subtraction, the MDSQ, the 312 word function tables used for ROM instruction or data storage, and connections to the IBM card I/O equipment. The function table contents could be changed by physically setting up to 3744 10 position switches. To transfer data between registers and computation units 20 transfer instructions were used. The 19 addition operations were of the type 'Add the contents of register 1 to the accumulator'. The sign of the accumulator could be changed to permit subtraction. The branch and conditional branch functions could be implemented using the proper choice from 12 instructions. There were 20 shift instructions for number scaling. Multiply, divide, square root, STOP, 7 I/O and some miscellaneous instructions rounded out the 84 orders. The ENIAC* satisfied Brian Randell's criteria for a computer, (Burks 1981), by being able to compute values of data then do a conditional branch on the data value. A room full of IBM equipment; printer, sorter, comparer, and card punch provided necessary support.

N. Metropolis and K. von Neumann then used their AEC priority to run the first problem, the original Monte Carlo, on the ENIAC*. The disappointed low priority group, R. F. Clippinger, J. H. Giese and W. C. Carter, with programming support, were second in March 1948. To begin our work on supersonic compressible fluid flow around bodies of revolution we needed to calculate the conical flow along a characteristic at 960 points with 10 decimal digit accuracy. The differential equation is second order and non-linear. The problem is a two point boundary value problem with known conditions - the velocity and direction of the flow along the cone and the boundary conditions at the shock wave. To start, assume the angle at which the characteristic meets the cone, calculate along the assumed characteristic until the shock wave is met. Then the errors in the shockwave conditions are determined and used to adjust the angle at which the characteristic meets the cone. This procedure is iterated until the characteristic and its values are found.

Very simple - today. But then we were allowed to use the ENIAC* to solve this problem for 24 hours a day, 5 1/2 days a week, for 2 weeks. First, all you knew was that the ENIAC* had worked for the previous program. Enter your program and permanent data by setting up to 3,744 switches to their proper decimal values. Next read in your first card of parameters and begin, hoping that nothing has gone wrong. When the program doesn't work, start stepping through it, using your set of hand calculated values and looking at the register contents. Our programs were organized by flow charts, following Goldstine and von Neumann (1947), and each box had values listed step by step - but not all 18 of them as displayed by the register lights. There may be a program bug, or there may be a bad tube (there were 18,000) not used in the previous problem, or a tube may have failed, or the order code may not be completely debugged. Work until you have made the changes to get a running section of the program. You now have a test program and hardware diagnostic to run before starting to see if program is likely to run. You also have part of one step in the program debugged. This 'test' program could be run under marginal conditions to catch weak components. Our program was, we thought, the most computationally intensive program yet run on the ENIAC* or ENIAC. The maintenance personnel, with our help, weeded many bad tubes out of the ENIAC* using our test program, now a diagnostic. A tiresome error recreation process.

Now we could get some answers! However the tube error rate was so great that we could not complete the computation for a single trial characteristic. To check our progress we began punching an output card at the end of each step in the integration. This card contained the input data for the next step of the integration. By comparing the sets of completed cards using the external card comparator we checked the progress of each run. Then I had an idea - change the program so that it could start at any step, given the data for that step. Now run until failure, start again, check for duplicated values, and begin with the last duplicated values. By using this simple 'check point/restart' we were able to finish trial characteristics, iterate, and in two weeks depart with our desired correctly calculated data (the most accurate in the world).

Later we moved to our first goal, supersonic flow about cone cylinders. Now we had to solve non-linear second order hyperbolic partial differential equations using at least a second order approximation (for our planned computational accuracy). Debugging these programs was difficult, and the maintenance crew hated to see us come because of the latent errors we uncovered and the length of time to get a complicated application program debugged on a faulty machine.

Then R. Clippinger got the idea of changing the control wiring so that the data from an input card could be treated like the data from the function table under proper conditions. Now we could write test routines and run them from input to the card reader without changing the switches which defined the application program. An organized set of these diagnostic routines were soon being used regularly by the maintenance crew. However, when we ran our programs, we learned about partial test coverage, unit stress, and intermittent errors.

We tried one last wiring change. Make the IBM card-punch punch the contents of the card registers after each major cycle. Then change the programs so the values we wanted to track were sent to the card registers. This program trace was very useful. But the ENIAC* results were produced so rapidly that the IBM card punch ran at full speed for long periods of time. This caused serious maintenance problems, and we were ordered to stop.

In summary, after about 9 months the computing center that ran the ENIAC* was using periodic functional diagnostics for detecting and locating failures, and system validation before use. If the ENIAC* was stressed by an application program, some form of checkpoint/restart was used. The validity of such results was determined by duplication and comparison or other tests. These tests usually used the associated IBM equipment. As we did this, we surveyed the field for stored program computers, and planned for our new computers, the EDVAC and ORDVAC, which finally came in 1952, after my departure.

5. Early Stored Program Computers

The EDVAC was specified in 1945, and shortly thereafter contracts for it, the IAS computer (Estrin 1953) and the RAYDAC computer, (Block 1948) were given by the US government. At about the same time Northrop Aircraft, Inc. contracted with Eckery-Mauchly Inc. for the BINAC.

RAYDAC had the following features: a modulo 31 check was used for all arithmetic operations. Data transfer used a mod 15 check. The operand addresses and opcode execution were back checked for correctness, memory was checked for read errors, and logical operations were checked by repeated computation using DeMorgan's law. The data from magnetic tapes was checked by a 4 bit transfer weight count, as well as control checks. The 'problem preparation unit' was duplicated so input, and the appended weight counts, could be compared before use. R. M. Block explicitly stated this necessity for checking computer controls (Harvard Proc. 1949). The EDVAC and BINAC (Ralston 1976) used two arithmetic units and compared their results; data transfers and the memory were checked by parity. The IAC computer, (Weik 1955) started the hardware implementation of illegal result tests such as divide check and implemented a special instruction to take a check sum of part of memory. This latter instruction was also used to check I/O results by examining all data blocks after reading. The NORC, designed just a little later, was a decimal machine with modulo 9 arithmetic checking and modulo 3 data transfer checking.

Designing and getting these systems to work proved lengthy, since the sequential functions of the control units posed unexpected difficulties. Information about all designs and difficulties was freely exchanged. A second group of computers, containing the ILLIAC, SEAC, ORDVAC, MANIAC, OHRAC (Ralston 1976 & Weik 1955) were designed to be simple and use reliable circuits. Comparatively little checking - at most parity on data transfers - was used. All of these systems became operational at about the same time.

Just after these systems came the first 'large' computing systems, with 60-100 microsecond addition, 450 - 800 microsecond multiplication, slightly slower division, and 8-16 K byte storage. The first was UNIVAC I, designed for 'commercial data processing'. Like its predecessor the BINAC, the UNIVAC did arithmetic checking by duplication and comparison, and data transfer checking by parity. It stored data on metallic magnetic tapes, and read and wrote blocks. This data was checked by a block character count with automatic reread in case of error (Weik 1955). The IBM 650, (Hsiao 1981), had its data flow, magnetic drum memory, and arithmetic operations checked by a SED 2 out of 5 code. I/O units were checked by parity, and its control units were checked by ensuring that proper sequences of signals occurred, using some duplicated circuitry. There were 'program' checks for invalid opcodes, invalid addresses, and arithmetic overflow. The IBM 702 (Basche 1954) was designed for 'commercial data processing'. It handled variable length fields with parity checked bytes in both data transfer and arithmetic. It read blocks of data from magnetic tape files, with bit error detection for each character. I/O was provided by card readers and punches, or by directly connected line printers. The IBM 701 (Bucholz 1953) assumed sufficiently reliable components no checking was used.

These systems were kept running by customer engineers (CE). The field replaceable units (FRU's) consisted of packages with two or three tubes and associated passive components. The CE ws expected to have a comprehensive knowledge of the system logic as well as understanding logic circuits. He had a complete set of logic and electrical diagrams. In addition he had a set of computer self-test routines, functional diagnostics. The system was validated by running this set of functional diagnostics combined with marginal checking. Frequently customer or system programs which were known to stress the system were run as a final test. The first FORTRAN compiler was a favorite. To repair these computers, error recreation aided by the same functional diagnostics was used for fault location. The first technique for fault isolation was substitution of a spare FRU for the FRU suspected of being faulty, or swapping two FRU's to see if now the system would work. If this did not succeed, signal testing using an oscilloscope was necessary. The most difficult cases occurred when only the application program(s) failed. The usual saying was 'Nothing runs but the diagnostics'. Now a knowledge of the customer's operations (and often the programmer's aid) was necessary. In spite of ingenious routines like the 'Leap Frog' for memory (Wheeler 1953) and comprehensive attempts at coverage (Walters 1953) the consensus of users and vendors was that there were as yet no good general testing methods. Practices varied from one installation to another, and efficiency depended strongly upon the competence of the CE (Eachus 1953).

6. Using the Early Stored Program Computers

The responsibility for obtaining correct answers efficiently was thus left to the individual applications analyst. Clippinger Dimsdale and Levin (1953) published a description of their methods. They wrote independent routines to handle I/O and to perform checkpoint/restart for each individual application program. Checkpointing was done frequently on magnetic tapes, since in those days computer time was charged by the minute and repeating part of a program was expensive.

The theme of the 1953 Eastern Joint Computer Conference was 'Information Processing Systems-Reliability and Requirements'. W. Bouricius (1953) discussed operating experience with the Los

Alamos 701. His installation was run as a self-service center: the user was responsible for programming, debugging, and correctness of results. The installation provided subroutines and a simple Assembly program. Trace and memory dump routines were used for program debugging. For a 7 month period they had 74.9% good time, 19.5% scheduled maintenance, 3.3% downtime due to unscheduled maintenance, and 2.3% down time due to human errors.

R. Kopp (1953) discussed 18 months experience with the Air Force UNIVAC. They has 61% good time, 20% preventive maintenance, and 19% down time. The most desirable UNIVAC characteristic was the self checking feature. It aided in fault location, and it was agreed by the users that the UNIVAC never introduced a mistake into the computation. The greatest trouble maker was tubes, followed by the effects of heat on selenium rectifiers, then came diodes. The mercury memory proved very stable. They used their own personnel to do servicing and had 11 CE's for a 7 day week, 24 hours a day, operating schedule. It took 8 months to train a qualified electrical engineer or physicist to do maintenance. Another major difficulty was obtaining enough spare parts.

J. Weir (1953) discussed the reliability and characteristics of the ILLIAC electrostatic memory. The MTBF was measured to be between 11.5 and 16.6 hours, about as reliable as the rest of the machine. For fault location they used the 'Leap Frog' test, knowledge of the application program, or diagnostic routines written on the spot. Before running a problem they cleared memory. To quote, 'The all zeros opcode was invalid and not decoded, so if called it stopped the computer. Thus errors usually resulted in a machine halt or an endless loop. It often turned out to be a simple matter to locate the failure which caused this behavior'.

P. Shepe and R. Kirsch (1953) reviewed two years of SEAC experience. The machine had 70.7% good time, and the users spent 20.4% of total time doing program debugging. Users were made to take a check point every half hour. For standard maintenance they used prepared diagnostic tests with marginal testing, and the same tests augmented with tests prepared on the spot for fault location. They regarded maintenance procedures as very important. They used large scale removal of tubes and diodes (including some good components) to achieve improved system operational time.

L. Whitehead (1953) gave a summary of the reliability of military electronics equipment. Tubes caused 60-70% of failures, poor engineering 12-16%, other components 9-12%, operation and maintenance errors 6-8%, and manufacturing 3-4%.

F. Murray (1953) discussed the acceptance test for the Raytheon Hurricane computer (RAYDAC). This test gave a preliminary evaluation of RAYDAC's 'unusual features' (the checking described earlier). To quote, 'The checking circuits not only kept the computations free of error but because of their diagnostic effect, the machine itself was brought to a remarkable state of operational perfection. Thus a system difficulty which would occur about one time in a million repetitions of one specific order in one set of circumstances was detected and eliminated'.

J. Mauchly (1953) gave a heuristic appraisal of cost of built-in checking to the user. He pointed out that duplication of runs is the most expensive, periodic marginal testing does not detect transient errors, and programmed checks are hard to find for many problems. He concluded that for general purpose equipment hardware checking is least expensive for the user.

Fortunately, J. Forrester (1951) invented magnetic core memories, which greatly improved memory reliability. Then Bell Laboratories invented the transistor, so tubes were replaced by more reliable circuitry. The introduction of these inventions into the commercial computer market in the middle to late 1950's brought about a marked de-emphais on computer error checking and self-repair, especially for scientific computers. Their error detection centered primarily on memories and I/O equipment. However large scale business computers had to have checking because of accounting traditions. As reported by Davis (1953) reliable file storage on tape and disk was considered the most important unsolved problem by large commercial computer installations. Could accountants and auditors use and trust these new devices? The complexity of these systems, the accounting traditions of guarantees on accuracy, and the demands of difficult application areas like space, kept a small group of people working on reliability and fault tolerance.

7. Early Development of Theory

As the previous section shows, transistor circuits and core memories were not in wide use until the late 1950's. To determine which of the two methods of attaining reliability, good components or protective redundancy was more desirable, theoretical methods for analyzing checking, testing and reliability were needed. Good methods to ease the burden of program preparation, debugging and operation were also necessary. Finally, the structure of computer systems, and the relationship of the synchronous central computer and its asynchronous file storage and I/O had to be attacked.

The analysis of testing and checking were facilitated by two basic papers. The paper on symbolic analysis of relays and switching circuits by Shannon (1938) was rediscovered in the late 1940's. R. Hamming (1950) published his paper on coding theory when many people were interested in that problem.

The Raytheon computer department was one of the first to use Boolean algebraic statements to design computers. As the next experimental computer was being designed, the first question asked was about methods of checking. Should the RAYDAC methods be repeated? A new checking method was invented. Code the individual logic variables in a one bit Hamming code. Replace the Boolean variable x by the pair of values (x, x), called two rail logic, since each line is replaced by two lines. The original logic value 1 corresponds to (1,0) and 0 corresponds to (0,1). The combinations (0,0) and (1,1) indicate errors. The Boolean logic operators 'AND', 'OR', and 'NOT' are implemented using circuit logic operations 'and' and 'or' for each pair of lines as follows; x AND w by (xw, x or w), NOT x by interchanging the two lines, x OR w by (x or w, xw). This method considerably increased the amount of circuitry used, especially as there was no easy way to analyze error propagation and no cheap way to implement the EXCLUSIVE OR circuit which checks that the line values are correct. In the 1960's improved methods of error analysis and checking allowed the IBM S/360 model 40 to use this checking method for the ALU.

The next step at Raytheon was to develop alternating logic, using time redundancy instead of space redundancy (Bark 1953). If f(x) is a Boolean logic function, and S, T are the two timing pulses we devised methods to specify F(x,S,T) the corresponding self dual function. Since S and T are never both 1, circuit minimization can be done easily. A digital computer was planned and the design started. Once again a good cheap way of checking was not available. A one bit Hamming SEC/DED code (sequential TMR) was considered but dismissed as impractical.

To improve the reliability of the computer, diode logic was used for switching with tubes acting as drivers only. To make construction easier, several standard packages were chosen, and the system was to be built using only these packages, suitably interconnected. R. Eldred, J. Mekota and I had to plan test methods for these packages and the computer. Functional tests were easy to describe, but their fault locating ability was poor. Then we thought why not use the fact that the computer and the packages were designed using Boolean logic. Faulty lines have the wrong value, 1 instead of 0 and vice versa. If single faults are assumed, then one input to or the output from a Boolean connective will have the erroneous value. (Now called 'stuck-at' faults.) This model let us devise rules to predict the effect of faults. For these small packages, and the simple computer, determining error propagation until they could be detected was easy. Then devising tests was not hard. The engineers responsible for the computer firmly rejected this 'crazy mathematical idea' for testing. We reached a standoff - neither group had experimental evidence. We planned two sets of tests, and experiments, but the computer was never finished.

Reliability modeling applied specifically to computers was also beginning. The fact that component failure distributions followed the 'bathtub curve' was accepted, as was the exponential failure rate for operating components (Epstein 1953). Using the exponential failure rate for units was controversial, but the D. Davis (1952) analysis of experimental data was finally convincing. J. Mekota and I devised a model of computer reliability using these ideas (Carter 1954). Our analysis showed that system reliability was most sensitive to changes in repair rates, and, under reasonable assumptions for the amount of circuitry added, built-in checking would improve computer reliability. C. Creveling (1956) discussed further increasing the reliability of repairable computers by adding redundancy, as did E. Flehinger (1958).

Basic theory received a big boost, again principally due to van Neumann, with the publication of Automata Studies, Annals of Mathematics Studies number 34. This volume contained the famous article by von Neumann (1956) in which he proved that reliable organisms can be synthesized from unreliable components by using a majority organ sufficiently more reliable than the other components. In the same volume, Moore (1956) considered abstract testing experiments, and other papers by M. Minsky, C. Shannon, M. Davis, J. McCarthy and W. Ashby prepared the way for sequential machine theory. Moore and Shannon (1956) devised circuits to improve relay reliability by fault masking, and Tryon (1962) generalized this to quadded logic.

Ease of programming was a very important issue (Wilkes 1951). Should the computer be binary for hardware efficiency or decimal for ease of coding? How simple should the order structure be? How would subroutines be called, used, and organized into a library? Assembly routines, pioneered by Grace Hopper, settled most of these questions. Having the computer help prepare its own programs is as useful as having it help test itself. Basic control programs were devised for handling interrupts, loading programs and data, and assisting in debugging, testing, and basic system operation. Buffers and elementary channels helped reduce the mismatch between the internal synchronous computer and the slower and asynchronous file storage and I/O. The realization that computer system functions could be extended by such a layer with a more abstract interface freed both designers and users from many restrictions. The next step was the beginning of Higher Order Languages.

8. Contract and Commercial Systems - Second Generation

The first steps toward the complexity of current and projected computer systems are shown by the following special systems developed under specific contracts, all except one for the government. One of the first computer systems to be designed with truly high availability goals was IBM's AN/FSQ7 (SAGE) (Everett 1957). This system was used for real-time processing of radar data for air defense, as well as potential missle launching by the Air Force. The AN/FSQ8 was used in the combat center. Both systems used two complete tube computers with core memories, one operating on line and the other as a hot standby. The spare executed self-tests when not being updated. Each computer had an error detection scheme employing parity checks and elaborate software diagnostics. After error detection, the switchover and recovery was executed by software. In a national network, each computer system exchanged data over communication lines. The significance of the SAGE effort was that it demonstrated the feasibility of merging a network of computers and communications to provide system solutions for complex, real-time applications (Jarema 1981). In 1981, 5 SAGE installations were still operating, with an availability of more that 95%. Later versions, the AN/FSQ 31 and AN/FSQ 32 (Weik 1961) used transistorized circuitry, more inclusive checking, and the FIX concept of correcting single errors using software.

Remington Rand's Titan missle guidance computer, the Athena, (Raymond 1958) attained high availability by using carefully controlled construction and selection of its components. Manufacturing and assembly were done in the first 'White Room'. Remington Rand's LARC (Weik 1957) featured Hamming SEC codes for data transfers and storage. Arithmetic operations were checked by ALU duplication.

The STRETCH computer, (Bucholz 1963), used either parity, duplication and residue 3 checks on various of its arithmetic operations. The memories and data paths used a Hamming SEC/DED code. Address bounding registers were used for storage protection. When uncorrectable errors occurred, the machine was interrupted and a diagnostic 'logout' of pertinent data on punched cards was initiated. The STRETCH controls were checked by parity on various register fields, validity checks on clocking, and some duplication of circuitry. The magnetic tapes had bit error detection, and the disk used a SEC/DED code.

The HARVEST extension (Snyder 1980) added 2,048 words of very high speed memory, special 'Streaming' hardware to perform special statistical and complex logical operations (all checked). The main addition was a high speed Exchange connected to very large volume magnetic tape storage units which had automatic features for loading and accessing tape cartridges. An SEC/DED code was used for each 16 bit character. This large complicated system worked very well for 14 years.

Another interesting application was the Orbiting Astronomical Observatory (Anderson 1968). This unmanned vehicle was required to operate for one year in orbit. The processor used quad redundancy, and the large memory used TMR. The system was launched and operated without error for 4 years until shut down by command from the ground.

IBM's Saturn guidance computer had to meet a reliability specification of .99 for 250 hours. The computer processor was segmented into 7 functional modules which were then implemented in TMR/Simplex. Disagreement detectors were put across each pair of lines, and when an error occurred the TMR configuration was replaced by a simplex system using one of the remaining units. The simplex mode was necessary for adequate checkout before flight, and also improved the reliability (Dickinson 1964). The memory was duplexed with parity checking used to isolate the failed unit. The buses were parity checked and used 'alternate data retry' to correct solid errors.

The Apollo Guidance Computer (Alonso 1963) was a short word length von Neumann type computer with special features for number systems, addressing system, order code and multiple precision arithmetic.

Ground control systems for real-time computer complexes (RTCC) have very high availability requirements. The Gemini RTTC had to control two maneuverable spacecraft in orbit at the same time. It consisted of 5 IBM 7094 computers, interconnected through a switching network, and associated communications and display equipment (James 1981). It began operation in 1965, and its functions were extended to include simultaneous real-time processing of both telemetry and tracking data.

The SABRE system (Perry 1961), a commercial outgrowth of the SAGE concepts, used two IBM 7094's in on-line-standby roles and duplexed files, drums, and communication front ends supporting a network of airline terminals. The major improvement of this system over other early electronic reservations systems was that it handled not only the seat inventory but the passenger name records as well. The SABRE system also interconnected to other airlines via telegraphic facilities to automatically request space segments on their flights. The system became fully operational in 1964, connecting over 1100 agent terminals over 9 full-duplex leased lines. Innovations included a very efficient real-time operating system and a cooperative line testing program with A.T.& T. The rate for reliable transmission was raised from 1200 bps to 2400 bps on leased voice-grade channels.

These special systems showed that for high dependability very good recovery systems are necessary, beginning with excellent checking. These systems were all designed to do one type of job well, and took advantage of this to achieve simplicity. However, even these special tasks developed surprising complexity. The ground based and commercial systems soon faced the difficulties of adding new applications.

Because of the reliability advantages of transistor circuitry and core memories, most of the commercial systems simply continued using their previous types of checking and concentrated their work on previously very weak areas. Independent buffers and channels were added so that reading and writing of file and I/O data could proceed simultaneously with computing. Most effort went into improving the availability of file storage devices, both by improving components and by devising new checking systems.

There were exceptions. The Burroughs B5500 (Bock 1965) used two processors in duplex mode. The National Cash Register 304 (Shiowitz 1956) had two types of exception signals; one stopped the computer and the other initiated retry.

The IBM 7070 (Hsiao 1981) continued all IBM 650 checking and added address checking and validity checking for memory data. The new tape devices, in addition to technology improvements, had vertical redundancy and longitudinal redundancy checks for triple error detection (and detected most higher order errors). To make sure the recorded data was correct, a read-after-write check was implemented. For disk storage, the 1301 used a 16 bit polynomial code for burst error detection.

The Datamatic (now Honeywell) D-1000 (Carter 1957) used weight counts like its predecessor RAYDAC, but parity in the core memory. Its advances were in its test routines (hardware and software) and in its use of control programs. The 1000 FRU's contained OR-AND-OR diode switching trees with tubes as drivers. R. Eldred (1959), with Y. Yang's assistance, derived test patterns for stuck-at faults for every line in the computer. He then wrote a program which tested every line and ensured that if a single error occurred, the erroneous value was propagated to both a hardware test circuit and a program check condition. This time the computer was built, and experimental verification was quickly obtained. Cold soldered joints had been very difficult to find, until this routine was used, when their location was easy. Many engineers were convinced of the method's worth. The electrical as well as logical characteristics of the FRU's were tested by an independent unit.

The system programs delivered with the machine included a basic control program (100 words including 10 words of interrupt locations). Obeying console commands, this routine would read a designated program from a tape and prepare the computer for operation. During operation, system error interrupts were indicated to the user. This same program controlled the hardware and software testing routines.

The software debugging system tested batches of programs in sequence. For each application program to be tested the system first load data on tapes, as instructed by pseudocommands. Then the program to be debugged would be reassembled, with 'snapshot' or selective trace pseudocommands inserted. 'Snapshots' dumped the contents of designated memory locations on tape; selective traces traced the execution of instructions in an address range. All programs began on a background of words with invalid opcodes to cause an exception condition, if activated, and contained data including its address. The control program then ran the application program, executing the pseudocommands. After the batch run, an editor was called to print the results.

For hardware testing, the control program with utility routines enabled the CE's to load and execute their diagnostics and test programs, and control the devices used from the console (Carter 1958).

9. The Third Generation - General Commercial Use

The major users interested in highly available computers were the on-line or time-sharing, transaction oriented commercial computing facilities or the space missions. In the former, the customer wants high availability in the ever more complex computers needed to keep pace with the transaction demand. In the latter, the need is for fault tolerant computers capable of maintaining some minimum level of computing power with a very high probability for an extremely long mission time.

Because many present systems use parts of the dependability features introduced in S/360, this system will be discussed first, (Carter 1964). Basic modeling experiments (Ball 1969), and experience indicated that software tests have serious deficiencies. These are especially serious for large and complex systems, or for those with many asynchronous actions. The first deficiency is control of the elements being tested. The fraction of circuits accessible to direct control is small, so it is very difficult to write a software program to produce a desired test pattern to recreate a particular fault and error condition. The second deficiency is the state resolution problem, the interrogation of the results of applying the test patterns. Several instructions and many intermediate states and timing cycles have intervened. Finally, test coverage is practically unmeasurable, and control of the system of programs for a particular test or error situation for a particular machine is very difficult.

The IBM System/360 was designed to achieve better availability than that of previous systems by a significant improvement in serviceability. From the beginning the S/360 was developed as an integrated package of hardware, operating system programs, application program facilities, and maintenance procedures.

The major problems to be solved to gain this maintenance improvement and integration were (a) reducing the maximum duration of service calls; (b) reducing the median duration and mean duration of service calls; and (c) matching a single package of maintenance programs and procedures to a large variety of operational monitor programs, machine models, and customer situations.

These problems were attacked by supplementing standard servicing facilities (both hardware and program) with (a) the ability to record automatically the complete, detailed, system environment at the instant of error discovery; (b) the ability to initialize the CPU to any arbitrarily specified state (either "legal" or "illegal"), to advance from this state by a specified number of machine cycles, and to compare the new state with a precomputed result state, much of this using circuits that are independent of those required for program sequencing; (c) a system of programs that can be integrated with the S/360 Design Automation System to produce automatically the inputs, results, and location analyses that are required to exploit the capabilities described in (b); (d) a family of diagnostic program monitors that attack directly the problem of matching maintenance procedures to machine models and operational monitor programs; (e) programs to analyze the results of (a) to aid the diagnostic analysis of the customer engineer, when necessary; and (f) a good set of hardware checks and the facility to retry failing CPU operations at the instruction level in the larger models, in addition to the usual retry at the program segment level. Other special diagnostic hardware made storage, channel, and I/O control unit state latches accessible to CPU interrogation for easier and better fault location. Additional storage made channel 'wrap-around' tests possible.

A more complete summary, as well as an account of the further IBM developments, is given in Hsiao (1981). To quote this paper 'With the advent of S/360 and its supervisor program (OS), IBM was trying to do the whole difficult job of recovery and multiprocessing for the first time'. 'Logout', automatic error environment capture, is used as the basis for the Environmental Recording and Analysis Programs (OSVS2 1985). The error location error analysis has been improved to ED/FI, (Error Detection/ Field replaceable unit Isolation), (Bossen 1982). 'Scan-in, scan-out' has been adapted to LSI and VLSI and improved to Level Sensitive Scan Design, (LSSD), (Eichelberger 1977). Based on practical experience, the seminal papers on recovery were written early, Davies (1973) and Bjork (1973). Ideas described in these papers have been expanded, improved, and incorporated into many products.

The S/360 family had microprogrammed controls, which contained the controls for scan-in, scan-out, logout, and the reading of scan patterns from tape into memory. There were two types of scan, n step with one output pattern test for the synchronous case (Carter 1964) and a n step with n output pattern tests, 'sequential scan' for the channels and asynchronous units with no unique reset state (Preiss 1972). During design analyses, it soon became evident that these routines would be useful if they could be called by the CPU. With proper data acquisition, and scan-out interrogation, these routines could solve the accessibility and state resolution problems. Also, for example, testing memories using standard machine instructions meant that the memories did not operate continuously at top speed, so the tests were not stringent. The invention of the DIAGNOSE instruction solved both difficulties, and micro-diagnostics were invented (Hackl 1965). Soon console controls were changed so that a set of microdiagnostics was run when the computer was turned on. The DIAGNOSE instruction still is the only S/360-S/370 instruction which is model specific, since the internal structure and its interface with the program structure varies from model to model. However, the ability to have an interface between standard and micro instructions has proved useful in more ways than maintenance.

Sequential scan routines usually ran by executing pattern P1 then checking against its test T1; then executing P1, P2 and checking against T2; etc. They were effective, but difficult to generate because of finding T2. Their first use was to track down an intermittent error in the channel of the engineering model of the S/360 model 50. The standard diagnostics ran well. However, intermittently the channel would detect an error, but the rerun routines always worked properly. No analysis could find the fault.

Then sequential scan tests were finished, and tried. The second test was not satisfied. Examination showed that a package had never been installed. The logical function of this package was to regulate the channel input to prevent overload conditions, and it was used only then. The standard diagnostics had tried to run the channel with peak load, but had failed to achieve overload conditions. This is but one example of the usefulness of fault location tests in prototype and manufacturing system bring-up, Preiss (1965).

Since the S/360 was a program compatible family of computers, it was important to show that the first models, 30, 40. 50, 65, and 75 satisfied the same specifications. This was done by preparing a set of standard verification routines, using the formal description of S/360 on APL (Falkoff 1964) as the specification. The set of routines ran successfully on each of the original members of the S/360 family.

While the S/360 goals were met, and the techniques have been useful, the system was not a high availability system by the standards of that time. The usual commercial approach was to use a multi-processor configuration with redundant I/O and programs which could control 'graceful degradation'. The best known examples are Bell's Electronic Switching System, No. 1 ESS Issue, (1964); IBM's 9020 (Keeler 1967); Burrough's B-8500 (Gluck 1965); and the Univac 1108 Multiprocessor (Starga 1967). Such machines are typically organized with several memory units, CPU's, and I/O channels accessed from a common data bus. When the operating system, alerted by the checking and/or periodic diagnostic testing determined that a device had failed, that device, together with a maintenance subsystem, was configured out of the main system. The main system continued with performance degradation (if possible). After the failure was located and fixed, the subsystem was brought back into the main computation system. Very simple in conception; surprisingly difficult to do.

The A. T.& T. ESS systems are an extremely important set of dependable computer systems. They are described in detail in another chapter in this book, but the lessons they learned, and shared through their publications and presentations have been extremely valuable. We all owe them a debt of gratitude.

The IBM 9020 is the multiprocessing computer system that is the core of the FAA's National Airspace System for coordinated air-traffic control throughout the United States. In the 9020, from 3 to 5 S/360 model 65's serve as the CPU, and from 2 to 4 S/360 model 50's serve as programmable channel controllers. The system can recover from any error which causes a single unit to fail.

Because of the frequency of the repetitive radar input data, and its continuity, missing a few cycles causes a very small problem. Rapid repair of failures is necessary. The error environment states which are captured by logout immediately after error detection proved very difficult to analyze. So they were changed, (Lancto 1967). This analysis and reporting gives another example of the difficulties lurking in even the simplest appearing jobs connected with fault tolerance.

10. Reliability and Fault Tolerance Research in IBM, Before 1975

This section will be a survey of various research and advanced development efforts before the middle 1970's. Projects which began in the late 1960's will be considered, even though many of them finished late in the 70's. Some projects which began later but finished at the same time will be ignored. The development of on-board space computer total systems will not be considered further, for more information see Cooper, (1976). The 25th Anniversary Issue of the IBM Journal of Research and Development has much historical information scattered in various articles. IBM control computers are covered in Harrison (1981), communications by Jarema (1981), and reliability, availability, and serviceability by Hsiao (1981). The first two subjects will not be discussed and while there is some overlap with the third article, much of the information is disjoint.

An area of importance to chip and system manufacturing and to computer system maintenance and operations is circuit test generation. The problem is straightforward, for each fault at the node of the Boolean graph representing the circuit, determine a set of inputs which will propagate the effects of the fault to a circuit output where it can be observed. R. Forbes while at IBM Endicott with C. Stieglitz's help constructed the first automated test generation system. It could handle small systems and used the ideas of S. Seshu and J. P. Roth (Chang, 1970). The first large system applicable to computers was prepared by K. Maling and M. Evans under the direction of R. Preiss for S/360 (Carter 1964), (Preiss 1972). This routine would handle circuits with slightly over 1,000 gates and 125 inputs. These systems would extract circuit information from the logic design file, generate tests heuristically, determine the faults covered using a deductive fault simulator. The tests were arranged in a diagnostic tree, with one leaf indicating a good machine, and the others pointing to a fault location dictionary (Chang 1970). The S/360 test generator had about 80-90% stuck fault coverage.

P. Roth (1966) developed the D-calculus and proved that using this technique, a complete test generation routine could be written; if a test for the node fault exists, the routine will eventually find it. Roth's procedure is widely used. Such routines are more complicated than heuristic routines, but P. Schneider (1967) showed that they are necessary. Ibarra (1975) proved the procedure to be NP complete. However, in practice, these routines have a running time proportional to the square of the number of inputs. The Boolean difference (Sellers 1968) can be used to state the problem of test generation for a node as one of solving two sets of Boolean equations. P. Goel (1980) used this as a basis for his more efficient test generation program. D. Bossen and S. J. Hong (1971) developed basic criteria for multiple fault detection. F. Putzulu and J. P. Roth (1971) developed a reasonable heuristic test generation method for sequential circuits.

Hamming's paper (1950) defines codes which apply to the detection and correction of unrelated bit(s) in words. Reed-Solomon codes (Reed 1954) use finite field theory to detect and/or correct any of the possible errors in bytes with b bits. Berger (1961) devised codes which detect all unidirectional and multiple errors. Because of the fault and error characteristics of VLSI circuitry, Berger codes are now very important.

Codes are useful in fault tolerant computers only if their parity check matrix has been tailored to fit the specific physical faults and resulting error properties. Reliable memories are usually built so that only one bit in a word is read from a chip. The chip contains much addressing logic, but often power and other supporting modules at the board level serve b adjacent chips. In addition, the fault and error characteristics of the adjacent bus and switching circuitry between the store and its users must be considered.The focus of coding research at IBM has been to devise variants of theoretical codes so that the variants will efficiently detect and/or correct the errors caused by physical faults. Any parallel implementation of detection/correction circuits takes much circuitry and time. Methods of improving these are also very important.

Hsiao (1970) developed an optimum parity check matrix for Hamming SEC/DED codes by using a selection of columns with every column having an odd number of bits. Shortened codes can be chosen to detect classes of errors in addition to their normal correction and detection properties, by proper choice of their parity check matrix. The popular SEC/DED code for 64 bits will handle any number of bits between 57 and 120. Reorganizing Hsiao's generating matrix allows error patterns over b adjacent bits to be detected for b equal to 3 or 4 (Chen 1984).

Bossen (1970) simplified the potential detection/correction circuitry in Reed-Solomon codes by using the representation of the b elements in a finite field by a subset of the square matrices with b rows. This allows practical parallel detection/correction circuits to be built. In the French supercomputer Marianne, the 16 processors and 16 memories are connected by a 'perfect shuffle' network. When one switch element fails, errors may be introduced in 4 adjacent data bits. A modified S4EC code (Carter 1973) is used to allow 4 adjacent bit error correction as in Reed-Solomon codes, but in addition this code, using 9 check bits, is 50% D4ED and also detects more addressing errors (Arlat 1984).

Cyclic codes which detect and correct long burst errors are very useful for channels and I/O devices. Peterson (1961) gave a unified description of cyclic codes and algebraic coding theory. However, faults in channels also depend very much upon physical characteristics. Inter-symbol interference, literally the interference of adjacent 1's and 0's, present difficulties in high speed channels. Constrained coding places a restriction on the maximum and minimum number of 0's which can occur between consecutive 1's. The encoding takes into account the bit stream, the neighboring segments of information, and the code properties (Franaszek 1972). For tapes and disks, in addition to the cyclic BCH or Firc codes, rectangular codes, i.e. codes in which both dimensions of the data block are checked, are widely used. Combining a parity check and a cyclic redundancy check (Patel 1974) allows all errors in a single column to be corrected.

Maintenance analysis procedures are always important. For system continuation, replacement of critical functions must be performed. This process, and physical repair if possible, must be accurate and rapid. If the procedures to be carried out can not be specified, then automated procedures are obviously impossible and manual procedures will be very slow. Maintenance Analysis Procedures (Burnstine 1966) provided a step by step process to isolate the fault, and provided means to compare different procedures. This, with the S/360 maintenance features, permitted emphasis on an 'how-to-fix' method which lead to RETAIN (REmote Technical Access Information Network), Fitzsimons (1972) which allows a field engineer to access a data bank of solutions to difficult hardware and software problems as well as to talk to experts in the appropriate problem area.

Specific fault tolerance research at IBM Research began in 1966 with W. Bouricius, W. Carter, J.P. Roth and P. Schneider working on the ARC contract (Roth 1967). The goal of this study was to specify and do the preliminary design for a computer system which would have .99 reliability for a 2 year mission. We began by using our practical experience to agree that the best way to proceed was to develop a basic method of attacking the problem, then develop the support technology to allow us to use efficient design methods, then do the design. To determine the effect of errors it is necessary to treat formally the relationship between faults and errors. We planned to use the D calculus as it was developed and new improved circuit testing methods. To predict our results with some accuracy, we invented dependability evaluation directed computer system design. The first step was to invent a system modeling technique which would consider the total system design, including the effects of software controlled recovery. We defined the system parameter coverage to be the conditional probability that if an error exists the computer system will be able to recover. By a sensitivity analysis of coverage, we found that computer system designs, which must satisfy very high dependability criteria, are extremely sensitive to coverage. This sensitivity dictated the use of a careful, well planned modeling process during the early design process.

Then we had our first interim review. Our ideas went over like a lead balloon. The sponsors wanted progress in designing units. We wanted to predict what the unit characteristics should be before designing. It was a standoff. We continued our attack.

As we continued, this work emphasized that the particular models developed must be extremely useful in indicating those changes in key system parameters which result in the maximum increase in system dependability. It was emphasized that absolute numbers are not of prime importance; relative results are. This is dictated by a general uncertainty in the values of many parameters relating to system design. The first step was to determine the system model, then perform a sensitivity analysis to show the feasibility of the basic design. This was very time consuming unless we had an interactive dependability modeling program. We designed one using the first interactive version of APL. We used this tool and the fault modeling tool to monitor the design, reestimate parameters, and proceed from the system design to the design of units. This design can be best understood in terms of a general system model. To avoid repetition in descriptions of our later work, a slightly more general model than the one we first used will be given.

The basic uniprocessor configuration consists of partitioned subunits attached to a switching network with its own control. The basic subunits are memory and control, program control, recovery and monitoring unit, I/O and file processors, ALU and other specialized processing units. Each such unit has autonomous controls (including its local operating system) and sufficient local storage. The system consists of replicas of these basic subunits, with configuration control handled by a global operating system. The major problems are the designs for the interfaces, switching, and recovery to meet the constraints of various specific dependability conditions.

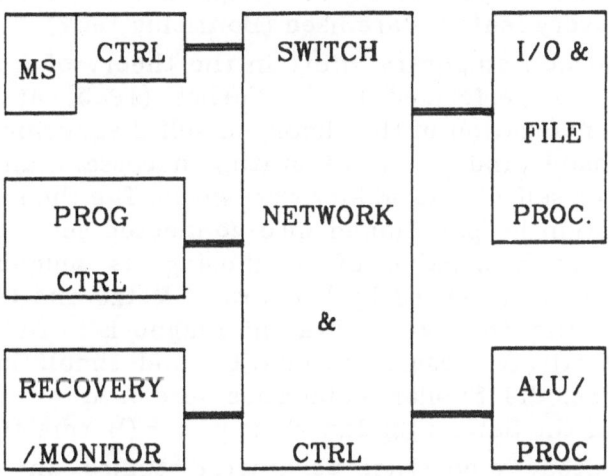

While working on this first ARC contract, we found that comparative measures of reliability provided the best design guidelines because they emphasized the difference in reliability between the two systems being repaired. The Mission Time Improvement, the ratio of the mission times for the same reliability for two designs gave us the most information.

The first work finished was the circuit testing (Roth 1966 & Bouricius 1971). The dependability modeling techniques, with coverage, including a description of the interactive program, was published later (Bouricius 1969). The design process indicated that the major design problems were those listed above, so we used evaluation directed unit design to develop solutions. The results are published in (Roth 1967, and Bouricius 1967). They are better described in four patents (Bouricius 1972). The first is on status switching, the second on storage protection, the third is on error tolerant ALU's and the fourth on triple modular redundancy with spares. The switching unit for TMR/Sparing with one spare has an elegant solution for controls. The final modeling study (Roth 1967) showed that reasonable systems with masking redundancy and attainable unit reliability were inadequate to meet the require- ment of .99 reliability for a mission time of 2 years, but that sys- tems using standby spares could meet this goal. Finally we found that using larger subunits, each efficiently designed to have the ability to recover from the effects of one or more permanent faults (as well as the ability to recover from transients) allowed more dependable systems to be designed than if smaller units without recovery features are used (Bouricius 1967).

A second contemporary effort in the theory of fault tolerant computers was performed by R. Forbes (1965) and R. Agnew (1967). A formalization of the theory of self-diagnosing digital sys- tems was made, and theorems stating necessary and sufficient conditions for self-diagnosability were given. The theorems require that the system be partitioned into connected sets of diagnostic subsystems, each capable of diagnosing its neighbors. These theorems were generalized by Preparata, Metze and Chien (1967) and started the theory of 'System Diagnosis'. To apply such theories effectively, design automation and simulation must be used, as Forbes did. Similar techniques were used for the checkout and design of the Saturn Guidance computer (Hardie 1967).

As indicated by coverage parameter studies, any fault toler- ance technique using protective redundancy depends upon the efficient design and placement of checking circuits and configuration control. The book by Sellers, 1968, discusses many unit designs. A general method for checking systems is to encode all input and output interfaces and extend each unit mapping function so that component failures produce faults whose results are in the detectable error space (Carter 1968) In this paper, W. Carter and P. Schneider began the study of the general models and design methods needed for the design of totally self checking systems. Until 1973 this effort was confined to IBM Research; in that year R. Anderson and G. Metze (1973) published a more for- mal set of definitions, and general interest increased. This by now well known set of definitions will not be repeated here. However, many such definitions have been made constantly more abstract, and show clearly the great similarity between hardware and software design. For example, 'Error detection functions (com- monly called checking circuits or checkers) are the implementa- tion of assertions which indicate that, during the monitored period of activity of a module, there has been no occurrence of an error attributable to the occurrence in the module of a fault in the class of faults modeled' (Carter 1985). Many discussions, especially with W. Heimerdinger, led to such a definition. As is well known, such checking circuits must have at least two outputs, and no output may take a constant value for code inputs. The usual outputs chosen are (0,1) and (1,0). Many methods have been published for designing such checking circuits. An interesting new extension to this technique is extending the model to sequential circuits (the realistic case) and examining error propagation (Smith 1983).

To return in time, at IBM Research and IBM FSD Huntsville work continued in the late 1960's on the NASA project MARCS (Modular Architecture for Reliable Computer Systems (Carter 1970). The design techniques described previously were extended, following our general method. The design constraints were that hardware must be designed to fit weight, power, size, performance, and dependability requirements. The tradeoffs we considered were hardware efficiency and potential system performance against: 1) specified system dependability goals; 2) simplification of the recovery process and other basic executive functions; 3) high failure coverage and ease of design validation; 4) ease of program validation; 5) programming convenience and diagnosability of external equipment; and 6) system flexibility.

The specific goals were first to make a more detailed evaluation of the constraints listed above and second to create at least a paper design for a totally self-checking computer. The tradeoff study was published as (Carter 1971).

The most error prone computer unit is the memory. To make it sufficiently fault tolerant the storage uses a SEC/DED code, while the data flow uses byte parity. The unit which performs error detection, correction, and code translation is large and error prone. To make this unit totally self-checking is difficult. The syndrome lines change state seldom, and they are inputs to the correction circuit and the function which signals a double error. The latter function changes state only after a double error. By experimentation, circuit logic fault analysis and diagnostic pattern evaluation by interactive fault simulation, a theory was discovered. A totally self checking SEC/DED translator was designed, beginning with Hsiao's parity check matrix (Carter 1970). The syndrome lines were replaced by two lines, with the usual coding. In analyzing the design, it was noticed that one output pair changed to the other at a rate determined by the values of the code space inputs. It was important to design the unit so all line changes occured frequently. Typically, a proof using the D-calculus was necessary to prove that each gate was tested and was fault secure, and that the classes of input values were such that all pairs of lines changed values frequently.

The checking circuit outputs are not the only lines which take constant values for very long periods in a computer. Exception and event signaling lines, and the lines determining protection control have this property (e.g. ALU, I/O, or storage exception signal lines, and inter-unit error control signal lines). The ALU exception lines were studied in A. Wadia's thesis (1970). Other exception lines were discovered in the generalization of the SEC/DED translator to a b-adjacent code translator (Carter 1973). Such lines were called semipassive in contrast to lines which change values often. A set of semipassive lines have some application as individual lines, but they are normally interconnected by logic operators to result in semipassive Boolean functions with inputs and outputs semipassive lines (e.g. the function which detects and signals a double error in a SEC/DED translator). Failures of these functions can mask errors, allowing them to go undetected with resulting data contamination and lack of fault tolerance for the computer system. W. Carter, A. Wadia, and D. Jessep (1971) showed that after replacing each semipassive line by a pair of lines encoded as checker outputs are encoded, the corresponding semipassive logic functions can be designed to be totally self-checking. Finally, in 1971, in a joint project with the IBM Boeblingen laboratory, a complete paper design of a S/360 processor was carried out (Carter 1977).

Under a NASA contract, W. Carter and C. McCarthy (1976) designed a memory with three spare planes and a totally self checking SEC/DED decoder and switching unit. They used a variant of the standard SEC/DED code so that double errors could be corrected using sequential decoding. The memory was built, delivered to NASA Marshall Space Flight Center, and tested for years. All double errors, both inserted and due to alpha particles, were corrected. Bossen and Hsiao (1980) designed another SEC/DED translator which uses sequential decoding to correct double errors. This translator is widely used in IBM computers.

Local as well as global recovery mechanisms were introduced into IBM computers for commercial applications at this time. The basic instruction retry mechanism patents were filed in 1966-68 (Hsiao 1981) and used first in the S/370 models 155 and 165. Hardware and microcode channel/channel unit retry was also introduced in the S/370 model 155. I/O path switching was introduced in the 2314 disk controllers in 1971 (Hsiao 1981). The improved availability MVS offers stems mainly from its ability to automatically reconfigure these hardware and software components after their errors, as well as handle errors in program tasks. The trend of adding hardware for error detection to aid recovery functions has continued.

A universal system service adapter was incorporated in the S/370 model 155, and this idea was extended to an independent processor for system monitoring (Fox 1975). The 308x processor controllers with their increased ED/FI functionality (Hsiao 1981) are an improved version. The efficient fault location analysis programs running in parallel with main computer operation are particularly important.

11. Conclusion

This early history shows that fault tolerance theory was developed as a result of difficulties which arose in practice. It was relatively easy to obtain data about the performance of discrete components operating synchronously and use this experimental data as a basis to build theory.

Present computer systems use asynchronous subunit operation and VLSI components. The difficulties discussed in the previous sections are still with us: testing, checking, fault location, recovery, system monitoring, validation, efficient coding techniques, maintenance, and configuration control. Now these difficulties are magnified by the effects of complexity and time. Errors still occur in system control, defined by the application and system programs which make a general purpose computer into a series of special purpose computers in order to solve problems. Very little is known about these and other design errors, and almost no data concerning them has been collected. Until enough data has been collected and analyzed so that we can understand such difficulties, more general and valid theories of fault tolerance can not be invented.

12. Bibliography

Agnew, R. W., et al, 1967: An Approach to Self-Repairing Computers, Dig. 1st IEEE Computer Group Conf., pp. 37-46.

Alonso, R. L., Blair-Smith H., Hopkins, A. L., 1963: Some Aspects of the Logical Design of a Control Computer: A Case Study, IEEE TEC, pp. 687-698.

Anderson, D. A., Metze G., 1973: Design of Totally Selfchecking Check Circuits for m-out-of-n Codes, IEEE TC, pp. 263-269.

Anderson, J. E., 1968: 7 Years of OAO, 1968 Product Assurance Conf., Hofstra University.

Arlat, J, Carter, W. C., 1984: Implementation and Evaluation of a (b,k)-Adjacent Error-Correcting/Detecting Scheme for Supercomputer Systems, IBM J. R&D, 28, No. 2, pp. 159-169.

Ball, M., Hardie, F., 1969: Effect & Detection of Intermittent Failures in Digital Systems, FJCC, V. 35, pp. 329-336.

Bark, A., Kinne, C. B., 1953: The Application of Pulse Position Modulation to Digital Computers, Proc. NEC, pp. 656-664.

Basche, C. J., Bucholz, W., Rochester, N., 1954: The BM 702, an Electronic Data Processing Machine for Business, JACM, V. 1, pp. 149-169.

Berger, J. M., 1961: A Note on Error Detection Codes for Asymmetric Channels, Info. & Control, pp. 68-73.

Bjork, L. A., 1973: Recovery Scenario for a DB/DC System, Proc. ACM Annual Conf., pp. 142-146.

Block, R. M. et al, 1948: The Logical Design of the Raytheon Computer, MTAC, Bu. Stds.

Bock, R. V., Toth, A. P., 1965: Hardware & Software for Maintenance in the B5500 Processor, IEEE Int. Conf. pp. 65-72.

Bossen, D. C., 1970: b-adjacent Error Correction, IBM J. R&D, V. 14, pp. 402-408.

Bossen, D. C., Hong, S. J., 1971: Cause Effect Analysis for Multiple Fault Detection in Combinational Networks, IEEE TC, C-20, No. 11, pp. 1252-1263.

Bossen, D. C., Hsiao, M. Y., 1980: A System Solution to the Memory Soft Error Problem, IBM J.R&D, No. 3, pp. 390-397.

Bossen, D. C., Hsiao, M. Y., 1982: Model for Transient and Permanent Error-detection & Fault-isolation Coverage, IBM J. J. R&D, 26, No. 1, pp. 67-77.

Bouricius, W. G., 1953: Operating Experience with the Los Alamos 701, EJCC, pp. 45-47.

Bouricius, W. G., et al, 1967: Investigations in the Design of an Automatically Repaired Computer, Dig. 1st IEEE Comp. Conf.

Bouricius, W. G., Carter, W. C., Schneider, P. R., 1969: Reliability Modeling Techniques for Self-Repairing Computer Systems, Proc. ACM Ann. Conf., pp. 295-309

Bouricius, W. G., et al, 1971: Algorithms for Detection of Faults in Logic Circuits, IEEE TC, C-20, pp. 1258-1264.

Bouricius, W. G., Carter, W. C., Roth, J. P., Schneider, P. R., 1972: US Patent No. 3,665,173; Triple Modular Redundancy/Sparing.

Bouricius, W. G., Carter, W. C., Roth, J. P., Schneider, P. R., 1972: US Patent No. 3,665,174; Error Tolerant ALU.

Bouricius, W. G., Carter, W. C., Roth, J. P., Schneider, P. R., 1972: US Patent No. 3,665,175; Dynamic Storage Address Blocking to Achieve Error Toleration in Addressing Circuitry.

Bouricius, W. G., Carter, W. C., Roth, J. P., Schneider, P. R., 1972: US Patent No. 3,665,418; Status Switching in an Automatically Repaired Computer.

Bucholz, W., 1953: The System Design of The IBM 701 Computer, Proc. IRE, 41, pp. 1262-1275.

Bucholz, W., Ed., 1962: Planning a Computer System (Project Stretch), McGraw Hill.

Burks, Burks, A.R., 1981: The ENIAC: First General Purpose Electronic Computer, Annals Hist. Comp., V.3, No. 4 pp. 310 - 399.

Burnstine, D. C., Eppard, W. H., 1966: Maintenance Strategy Diagramming Technique, 1966 Annual Symp. on Rel. pp. 75-83.

Carter, W. C., Mekota, J. E., 1954: Panel Discussion, Redundancy Checking for Small Digital Computers, EJCC, pp. 56-57.

Carter, W. C., 1957: A New Large Scale Data Handling System - DATAmatic 1000, ACM Symp. New Computers, A Report from the Manufacturers, pp. 36-57.

Carter, W. C., 1958: Automatic Machine and Program Testing Routines, 5th Annual Symp. on Comp. & Data Processing, U. Colorado, Boulder, Colorado.

Carter, W. C., et al, 1964: Design of Serviceability Features for the IBM System/360, IBM J R&D, V. 8, No. 4, pp. 115-126.

Carter, W. C., Schneider P. R., 1968: Design of Dynamically Checked Computer Systems, Inf. Proc. 68, IFIPS, pp. 878-883.

Carter, W. C., Jessep, D. C., Wadia, A. B., 1970a: Error-Free Decoding for Failure Tolerant Memories, Proc. 1st IEEE Comp. Group Conf. pp. 25-30.

Carter, W. C., et al, 1970b: Design Techniques for MARCS (Modular Architecture for Reliable Computer Systems), IBM RA12.

Carter, W. C., Bouricius W. G., 1971a: A Survey of Fault Tolerant Architecture and Its Evaluation, COMPUTER, Jan., pp. 10-16 (See Related Fault Tolerance papers in the issue).

Carter, W. C., Wadia, A. B., Jessep, D.C., 1971b: Implementation of Checkable Acyclic Automata by Morphic Boolean Functions, Pr. Smp. Cmp. & Auto. Poly. Tech. Inst. Brooklyn, pp. 466-482.

Carter, W. C., et al, 1971c: Logic Design for Dynamic and Interactive Recovery, IEEE TC, C-20, pp. 1300-1306.

Carter, W. C., Hsieh, E. P., Wadia, A. B., 1973: US Patent No. 3,766,521; Multiple b-Adjacent Group Correction and Detection Codes and Self-Checking Translators Therefor.

Carter, W. C., McCarthy, C. E., 1976: Implementation of an Experimental Fault-Tolerant Memory System, IEEE TC, pp. 557-568.

Carter, W. C., et al, 1977: Cost Effectiveness of Self-Checking Computer Design, Proc. FTCS-7, pp. 117-123.

Carter, W. C., Wadia, A. B., 1980: Design and Analysis of Codes and Their Self-checking Circuit Implementations for Correction and Detection of Multiple b-adjacent Errors, Proc. FTCS-10, pp. 35-40.

Carter, W. C., 1985: Chapter in Resilient Computing Systems, T. Anderson, Ed.

Chang, H. Y., E. Manning, Metze, G., 1970: Fault Diagnosis of Digital Systems, Wiley-Interscience, N.Y.

Chen, C. L., Hsiao, M. Y., 1984: Error-Correction Codes for Semiconductor Memory Applications: A State-of-the-Art Review, IBM J. R&D, 28, No. 2, pp. 124-134.

Clippinger, R. F., et al, 1953: The Programming of Stored Program Computers, SIAM Journal, V.1, Nos. 1,2,3.

Cooper, A. E., Chow, W. T., 1976: Development of Onboard Space Computers, IBM J. R&D, 20, pp. 5-19.

Creveling, C. J., 1956: Increasing the Reliability of Electronic Equipment by the Use of Redundant Circuits, Proc. IRE, V. 44, pp. 509-515.

Davies, C. T., 1973: Recovery Semantics for a DB/DC System, Proc. ACM Annual Conf. pp. 136-144.

Davis, D. J., 1952: An Analysis of Failure Data, J. Am. Stat. Soc., No. 5, pp. 104-135.

Davis, M. E., 1983: Use of the Electronic Data-Processing Systems in the Life Insurance Business, EJCC, pp. 11-17.

Dickinson, M. M., et al, 1964: Saturn V Launch Vehicle Digital Computer & Adapter, FJCC, V. 26, pp. 501-516.

Eachus, J. J., 1953: Group Discussion on Diagnostic Checks, EJCC, p. 119.

Eichelberger, E. B.,Williams, T. J., 1977: A Logic Design Structure for LSI Testability, Proc. D.A. Conf. pp. 462-468.

Eldred, R. D., 1959: Test Routines Based on Symbolic Logic Statements, JACM, V.6, No. 1, pp. 33-36

Epstein, B & M. Sobol,1953: Life Testing, Journal of American Statistical Assoc., V. 48, No. 263, pp. 486-502.

E.R.A., 1950: High Speed Computing Devices, McGraw-Hill.

Estrin, G., 1953: The Electronic Computer at the Institute for Advanced Study, MTAC, 7, pp. 108-110.

Everett, R. R., et al, 1957: SAGE - A Data-Processing System for Air Defense, EJCC, pp. 148-155.

Falkoff, A. D., et al, 1964: A Formal Description of System/360 IBM Sys. J. V.3, No. 3, pp. 193-262.

Fitzsimons, R. M., 1972: TRIDENT - A New Maintenance Weapon, Proc. FJCC, 41, pp. 255-267.

Flehinger, B. J., 1958: Reliability Improvement through Redundancy at Various System Levels, IBM J R&D, pp. 223-245.

Forbes, R. E., et al, 1965: A Self-Diagnosable Computer, FJCC, V. 27, Part 1, pp. 1073-1087.

Forrester, J. W., 1951: Digital Information Storage in Three Dimensions Using Magnetic Cores, J. Ap. Physics, pp. 44-48.

Fox, J. L., 1975: Availability Design of the S/370 Model 168 Multiprocessor, Proc. 2nd USA-Japan Comp. Conf. pp. 52-57.

Franaszek, P. E., 1972: US Patent No. 3,689,899; Run-length-limited Variable Length Coding with Error Propagation Limitation.

Gluck, S., 1965: Impact of Scratchpads in Design: Multifunctional Scratchpad Memories in the Burroughs B8500, FJCC, pp. 661-667.

Goel, P., 1980: An Implicit Enumeration Algorithm to Generate Tests for Combinational Logic Circuits, FTCS-10, pp. 145-151.

Goldberg, J., et al, 1972: Survey of Fault Tolerant Computing Systems, SRI Inc. Report.

Goldstine, H. H., von Neumann, J., 1947: Planning & Coding of Problems for an Electronic Computing Instrument, Inst. of Advanced Study, Princeton.

Griesmer, J. H., R. E. Miller, Roth, J. P., 1962: The Design of Digital Circuits to Eliminate Catastrophic Failures, Redundancy Tech. for Comp. Sys., Spartan Books.

Hackl, F. J., Shirk, R. W., 1965: An Integrated Approach to Automated Computer Maintenance, IEEE Conf. Rec. on Switching Theory & Logic Des., pp. 289-302.

Hamming, R. W.,1953: Error Detecting & Error Correcting Codes, BSTJ, 29, pp. 147-160.

Hardie, F., Suhocki, R. S., 1967: Design & Use of Fault Simulation for Saturn Computer Design, IEEE TC, pp. 412-429.

Harrison, T. J., et al, 1981: Evolution of Small Real-Time IBM Computer Systems, IBM J. R&D, V. 25, pp. 441-453.

Harvard Proc., 1949: Proc. of a 2nd Symp. on Large Scale Digital Calculating Machinery, Annals Comp. Lab., V. XXII.

Hsiao, M. Y., 1970: A Class of Optimal Minimum Odd-Weight-Column SEC/DED codes, IBM J R&D, V. 14, pp. 395-403.

Hsiao, M. Y., et al, 1981: Reliability, Availability, & Serviceability of IBM Computer Systems: A Quarter Century of Progress, IBM J R&D, V. 25, pp. 453-465.

Ibarra, O. H., Sahni, S. J., 1975: Polynomially Complete Fault Detection Problems, IEEE TC, C-24, pp. 242-253.

James, S. E., 1981: Evolution of Real-Time Computer Systems for Manned Spaceflight, IBM J. R&D, V. 25, pp. 417-429.

Jarema, D. R., Sussenguth, E. H., 1981: IBM Data Communications: A Quarter Century of Evolution & Progress, IBM J. R&D, V. 25, pp. 391-405.

Keeler, J., 1967: Special Issue on IBM 9020, IBM Sys. J. 6, No. 2.

Kopp, R., 1953: Experience with the Air Force UNIVAC, EJCC, pp. 62-67.

Lancto, D. C., Rockefeller, R. L. 1967: The Operational Error Analysis Program, IBM Sys. J., 6, No. 2, pp. 103-149.

Laprie, J.-C., 1985: Dependable Computing & Fault Tolerance: Concepts & Terminology, Proc. FTCS-15, pp. 2-14.

Mauchly, J. W., 1953: The Advantages of Built-In Checking, EJCC, pp, 99-101.

Metropolis, N., Worlton, J., 1980: A Trilogy on Errors in Computing History, Annals Hist. Comp., V. 2, No. 1, pp. 49-59. (Excellent list of 93 references).

Moore, E. F., 1956: Gedanken-Experiments on Sequential Machines, Automata Studies, Princeton, pp. 129-156.

Moore, E. F., Shannon, C. E., 1956: Reliable Circuits Using Less Reliable Relays, J. Franklin Inst., pp. 191-208;281-297.

Murray, F. J., 1953: Acceptance Test for the Raytheon Hurricane Computer, EJCC, pp. 48-52 (RAYDAC).

No. 1 ESS Issues, 1964: BSTJ, V. 43, No. 5, pp. 1831-2610.

OSVS2, 1985: OSVS2 MVS Overview, No. GC20-0954-0, IBM Brnch Of.

Patel, A. M., Hong, S. J., 1974: Optimal Rectangular Code for High Density Magnetic Tapes, IBM J. R&D, 18, pp. 579-588.

Perry, M. N., Plugge, W. P., 1961: American Airlines 'SABRE' Electronics Reservation System, WJCC, pp. 563-601.

Peterson, W. W., 1961: Error Correcting Codes, MIT Press.

Preiss, R. J., 1965: The Use of Fault Location Tests in Prototype Bring-up, Proc. IFIP65, pp. 511-517.

Preiss, R. J., 1972: Design Automation of Digital Systems, M. E. Breuer, Ed., V. 1, pp. 335-410.

Preparata, F. P., Metze, G., Chien, R. T., 1967: On the Connection Assignment Problem of Diagnosable Systems, IEEE TC, C-16, No. 6, pp. 848-854.

Proceedings of the ACM Conference, 1952: Pittsburgh, Pa. Several papers on the History of Computing, pp. 1-32.

Putzulu, G. R., Roth, J. P., 1971: An Heuristic Algorithm for the Testing of Asynchronous Circuits, IEEE TC, pp. 639-648.

Ralston, A., 1976: The Encyclopedia of Computer Science, McGraw-Hill, N.Y.

Randell, B., (Ed.) 1973: The Origins of Digital Computers, Springer-Verlag.

Randell, B., 1981: Comments on Burks, A. W., 1981.

Raymond, G. A., 1958: A Transistor-Circuit Chassis for High Reliability in Missle Guidance Systems, EJCC, pp. 132-135.

Reed, I. S., 1954: A Class of Multiple-error-correcting Codes and Their Decoding Scheme, Trans. IRE, IT-4, pp. 38-40.

Roth, J. P., 1966: Diagnosis of Automata Failures: A Calculus and a Method, IBM J. R&D, pp. 278-291.

Roth, J. P., Bouricius, W. G., Carter, W. C., Schneider, P. R., 1967: Phase II of an Architectural Study for a Self-Repairing Computer, SAMSO TR-67-106.

Schneider, P. R., 1967: On the Necessity to Examine D-Chains in Diagnostic Test Generation-An Example, IBM J. R&D, pp. 114.

Sellers, F. F., Hsiao, M. Y., Bearnson, L. W., 1968a: Error Detecting Logic for Digital Computers, McGraw-Hill, N.Y.

Sellers, F. F., Hsiao, M. Y., Bearnson, L. W., 1968b: Analyzing Errors with the Boolean Difference, IEEE TC, pp. 676-683.

Shannon, C., 1938: A Symbolic Analysis of Relay & Switching Circuits, AIEE Trans., 57, pp. 713-723.

Shepe, P. D. Jr., Kirsch, R. A., 1953: SEAC - Review of Three Years of Operation, EJCC, pp. 83-90.

Shiowitz, M., et al, 1956: Functional Description of the NCR 304 Data Processing System for Business Applications, EJCC, pp. 34-39.

Smith, J. E., Lam, P., 1983: A Theory of Totally Self-Checking System Design, IEEE TC, pp. 491-499.

Snyder, S. S., 1980: Computer Advances Pioneered by Cryptologic Organizations, Ann. Hist. Comp., V. 2, No. 1, pp. 60-71.

Stanga, D. C., 1967: UNIVAC 1108 Multiprocessor System, AFIPS, SJCC, pp. 45-51.

Tryon, J. G., 1962: Quadded Logic, Redundancy Techniques for Computing Systems, Spartan Books, pp. 205-228.

von Neumann, J., 1956: Probabilistic Logics & the Synthesis of Reliable Organisms from Unreliable Components, Automata Studies, Princeton, pp. 43-97.

Wadia, A. B., 1970: Investigation into the Design of Dynamically Checked Arithmetic Units, Ph. D. Thesis, Harvard.

Walters, L. R., 1953: Diagnostic Programming Techniques for the IBM Type 701 E. D. P. M., Conv. Rec., IRE Nat. Convention.

Weik, M. H., 1955: A Survey of Domestic Electronics Digital Computing Systems, BRL, Rpt. No. 971, Aberdeen Proving Ground, Md.

Weik, M. H., 1957: A 2nd Survey of Domestic Electronics Digital Computing Systems, BRL, Rpt. No. 971, Aberdeen Proving Ground, Md.

Weik, M. H., 1961: A 3rd Survey of Domestic Electronics Digital Computing Systems, BRL, Rpt. No. 971, Aberdeen Proving Ground, Md.

Weir, J. M., 1953: Reliability & Characteristics of the ILLIAC Electrostatic Memory, EJCC, pp. 72-77.

Wheeler, D.J., Robertson, J. E., 1953: Diagnostic Programs for the ILLIAC, Proc. IRE, V. 41, pp. 1320-1325.

Whitelock, L. D., 1953: Methods Used to Improve Reliability in Military Electronics Equipment, EJCC, pp. 31-33.

Wilkes, M. V., Wheeler, D. J., Gill, S., 1951: The Preparing of Programs for an Electronic Digital Computer, Addison-Wesley.

Evolution of Fault Tolerant Switching Systems in AT&T

George F. Clement
AT&T Bell Laboratories
Naperville, IL 60566
Telephone: 312/979-5966

Paul K. Giloth
AT&T Bell Laboratories
Naperville, IL 60566
Telephone: 312/979-3114

ABSTRACT

Fault tolerant hardware and software architectures
for analog/digital electronic telephone switching systems have evolved over the last 30 years at AT&T Bell
Laboratories and have been deployed extensively in
several generations of telephone switching and support
systems. Fault tolerance has been necessary as large
complex systems are never fault free. The techniques
employed detect errors, correct errors, reconfigure the
system, reinitialize the system automatically, and in
general provide for system integrity under all operating
and fault situations. The ultimate quality of performance depends on how well the fault tolerant techniques have been implemented. The fault tolerant
techniques developed for communication systems are
also useful in many other applications where real-time,
continuous system operation is mandatory. A summary
of these hardware and software fault tolerant

techniques are provided with application data to demonstrate effectiveness. As part of the maintenance strategy, "expert systems" were developed and deployed and have continued to evolve. They provide excellent automatic maintenance support for several thousand switching systems.

1. History

Fault tolerant techniques were used by AT&T in electromechanical switching systems for many years to obtain high quality performance before the advent of Stored Program Controlled (SPC) machines. The antecedents of the AT&T semiconductor SPC machines were the crossbar [1] and panel electromechanical machines. These switching systems made use of a Common Control System (CCS) which segregated the switching machine into a switching network and control units that could be used to quickly activate the various stages of setting up or taking down a call. The control units were shared by all calls during set up and breakdown. This contrasted to progressive systems, such as S x S, which tied up, not only the network, but also the control elements used in an individual call for the duration of the call. The CCS also made possible the introduction in the late 1920's of maintenance systems that could record the progress of a call and make note (and save) information on the data of failed calls. The systems were also capable of retrying a failed call using control units different from those used in the failed attempt.

The crossbar machines can be classed as a type of a distributed system. For example, in the crossbar system the switching network connections are controlled by markers [11]. A marker "marks" the end points of a path through the network. There are, in each system, a multiplicity of markers, any one of which can be used for a given call. The number of markers depends on the traffic a particular system is required to carry plus a number of spares. Progress of a given call is monitored and a record of troubles encountered shown on an office maintenance frame. A failed call, as mentioned above, automatically tries a second time, using different control units than were employed on the first attempt. Diagnosis of the trouble and repair were done manually when these systems were first deployed.

The techniques used to detect errors in call progress included timing, error codes, and self-checking. Reliable hardware design and redundancy was employed in the provisioning of control units and common circuits (e.g. senders that received and transmitted signaling data) so that retries of failed calls could be automatically activated. The configuration techniques employed in the electromechanical systems and the analysis of diagnostic data and identification of failed units were largely manual. These systems achieved high availability (3 min. per year down time) and had no more than .01 percent of telephone calls processed incorrectly.

When stored program controlled switching systems became feasible in the 1960's the stringent reliability requirements that had evolved during the electromechanical era had to be met along with the many requirements that had evolved for maintenance and administration. Furthermore, based on the technology of the late 1950's through the mid 60's, when the first commercial AT&T [1] ESS system was put in service, the feasible architecture for Electronic Switching Systems was hierarchical with a single high speed central processor providing the control functions. As a matter of fact, it has been only in the past 10 or so years with the advent of micro processors that a more distributed architecture has proved to be economically feasible. In either case, the same fundamental techniques are applied to achieve Fault Tolerant high quality performance.

To establish an ultra-reliable switching environment [10] redundancy of system components is used. Without redundance, single component failures have the potential of causing complete failure of the entire system. Essentially, duplication of all components except the switching fabric was employed in the 1ESS and some of the succeeding smaller switching developments. However, in 1A [10,11] and 4E [7], while duplication was used for the central control unit in the processor, N+m redundancy plans were used for most other components (e.g., stores, files, digital terminal units, etc.) In the statement N+m, N represents the number of units required operationally and m the number needed as spares to meet dependability objectives. A detailed discussion of fault tolerant techniques for 1, 1A, 2, 3, 4, and 5ESS systems is covered in reference material 2, 3, 4, 5, 6, 7, 8, 9, 10, and 11.

1.1. Causes of System Downtime

When 1 ESS was first introduced into the field (1965) and before the accumulation of large amounts of field data, total system outage was usually [10] assigned to hardware failures. However, as field data was accumulated it soon became apparent that the situation was more complex. As is shown in Fig. 1, [13] hardware failures are responsible for approximately 1/3 of such outages, procedural error 1/3, software 25% and other causes 5%. Procedural errors are those due to maintenance and administration personnel using wrong maintenance or operational procedures. These errors are responsible essentially equally with hardware and software in causing system outages. The lesson here is that the dependability requirements for the system must be allocated equally across these three failure causes. Incidentally, one important aspect of obtaining high dependability in a system is to continually examine the cause of each outage and correct the deficiency in either hardware, software, or human engineering that resulted in the outage.

2. Performance Requirements

During the last 30 years very sophisticated Stored Program Controlled switching systems have evolved. The hardware for these systems, include not only computers but also digital switching networks, digital terminal equipment, human machine interface units and off-line support systems. Modeling techniques have been developed to design the hardware to meet reliability requirements. Since the dominant role in hardware reliability is component failure, it has been possible to design hardware systems to meet performance requirements by using component failure rates, redundant equipment, matching, and conservative architecture. However, the ultimate reliability of the system depends on software to control the overall system and provide functional, administrative, and maintenance features.

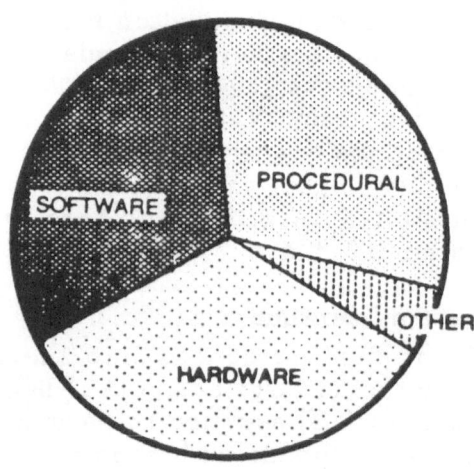

Fig. 1 Causes of major system failures

The design of the software systems for modern digital switching systems has also evolved over the years, but unfortunately it has not been possible to develop a design process which can be modeled and evaluated adequately before the design begins. Unlike hardware the dominant role in software failure are errors in design and implementation. Large reliable software systems (2 million lines of code) have been developed but the process is not very scientific. The conventional waterfall design process is a laborious, cumbersome, labor intensive, expensive process but can be used to develop extremely reliable software if supplemented by fault tolerant techniques suitable for the application.

2.1. Composition of Switching System Software

The hardware and software for switching systems must be designed to meet the requirements shown in Table 1.

Operation	• Continuous (20 years)
Time Shared Channels	• Thousands
Recovery Time	• Critical
Value of Reliability	• High 1 call per 100,000 call cut off
Downtime	• <3 minutes/yr.
Synchronization	• Network Sync
System Growth Data Base Changes Program Changes Maintenance	All must be done with the system on-line and operational

Table 1: System Requirements

The above list of requirements indicate that a switching system is very complex and includes all the major design problems that face software system designers. The balance of this paper will be devoted to reviewing the hardware and software techniques in Table 2 which are used to implement reliable switching systems. These have been applied for the most part to all AT&T switching systems (even the electromechanical switches). Their implementation has evolved over the years along with improved and new technology toward almost complete automation and certainly toward much shorter response times and higher effectiveness.

Configuration	• Redundancy
Error Tolerance	• Error Correction
Recovery Techniques	• Error Detection • Audits • Interrupts • Automatic Re-Start
Fault Location	• Automatic

Table 2: Fault Tolerant Techniques

3. Design Strategies for Dependable Hardware

All hardware is designed to fail at some rate. Therefore in the basic design, system operation in the face of failure must be considered. By the use of redundancy with rapid reconfiguration capability, hardware failures can be made transparent to system operation. The needed redundancy depends on the requirements of the system under design and the known component failure rates. For example, assume, as in Fig. 2, the switching system is represented by four layers of modules (L) each controlling access terminations of size N. The lower level, L4, affects one termination and the upper layer L1 affects all terminations.

A point (e.g., L3) represents the objective that a module of size N should be designed for T or less downtime caused by that level or higher in the control hierarchy. If a per trunk termination unavailability objective exists, 28 minutes per year is assumed in Fig. 1, a straight line connecting L1 and L4 downtime can be used to allocate portions of cumulative downtime to each of the modules in this case: L1 - 3 minute/year, L2 - 10 minute/year, L3 - 5 minute/year, and L4 - 10 minute/year. With this data the allocations can be further partitioned to allocate the objective for hardware failures as a percentage of the total for each module. Once the hardware allocation is determined standard modeling techniques considering failures in time, mean time to repair, automatic diagnostic techniques, and redundancy can be employed.

Control hierarchy represented by common control model

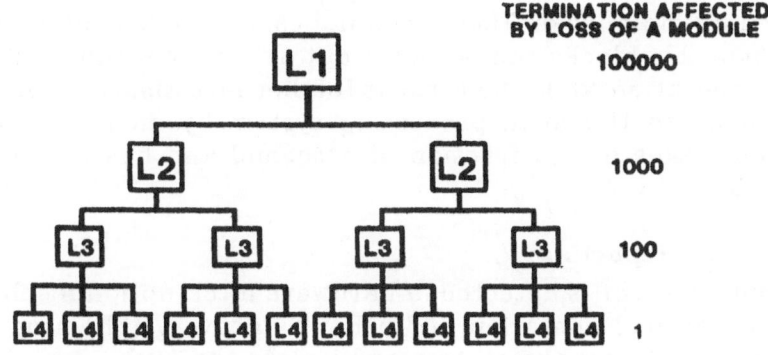

Toll office cumulative downtime objectives

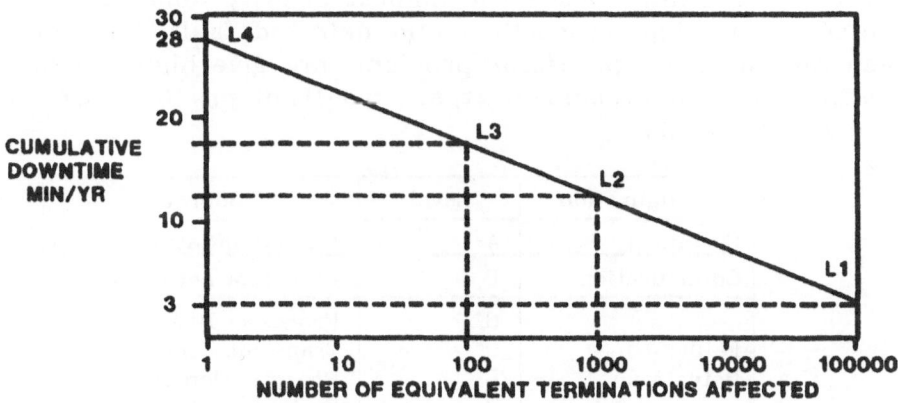

Fig. 2

3.1. Error Detection and Correction Architecture

In modern switching systems the control architecture may be hierarchically distributed, completely distributed or a combination of both. In any case many computer elements are used in addition to special hardware to perform switching, terminal, synchronization, and associated functions. In hardware, it is necessary to build in the capability for error detection, error reporting, fault recovery and the facility for fault location and repair.

3.1.1. Error Detection

The most useful techniques for error detection are matching, timing, error checking and correcting codes, partial self checking, and round trip checks. These techniques are implemented so that reconfigurable blocks can be taken out of service without affecting system operation while the error is further investigated. The error is reported to the main processing system by an interrupt. An interrupt takes only a fraction of a second and has no effect on system operation.

3.1.2. Error Reporting

When an error is detected, a hardware interruption mechanism suspends normal operation and a Fault Recovery (FR) program is used to reconfigure the system and isolate the fault. A hierarchical interruption mechanism is used to report failures to the control processor. In general, problems affecting the largest number of calls or circuits are given the highest priority. Priorities are set, for example, as shown in Table 3 where five categories are defined with system configuration the highest priority followed by fault detection, testing, processing, and deferred fault detection. In general, the main processor problems are give highest priority, peripheral problems come next, and per-trunk problems are set at the lowest priority.

Configuration	Level	Source
System	A	Manual Initiation
Configuration	B	Processor Activated
Fault Detection	C D E F	Processor Mismatch Transient Memory Program Memory Peripheral Units
Testing	G	Internal Timer
Processing	K	System Integrity
Deferred Fault Detection	Interject Base	High Priority Low Priority

Table 3: System Interrupt Mechanisms

Every interrupt is also recorded in disc memory with a complete record of appropriate error data and key unit register states. This data is analyzed by automated procedures to correlate and identify intermittent errors which cannot be found by normal diagnostics.

3.1.3. Fault Recovery (FR)

Almost all system reconfiguration and service restoral procedures are controlled by a system of automatic fault recovery
programs rather than dependence on manual hardware techniques. The accuracy and efficiency of these recovery programs
directly influence system reliability.

A typical recovery scenario following detection of a hardware
failure is as follows:

    a.   Normal operation is suspended and a FR program is exe-
cuted.

    b.   FR program identifies source of failure, saves critical data,
runs series of access tests, and classifies error.

    c.   Selects course of action which can include more than one
of the following actions.

       1.   system reconfiguration

       2.   data initialization

       3.   schedule diagnostics

    d.   If no trouble is found, unit is returned to system for
duplex configuration.

    e.   Hard fault cases are turned over for fault location and
repair.

    f.   Data on transient errors are sent to error analysis for
evaluation and use by the FR programs.

The FR programs are designed to achieve correct recovery
with minimum interrupts, disrupting occasionally a few calls, and
to prevent the propagation of errors. Incorrect actions should be
minimized since they can cause outages rather than
reconfigurations or can propagate into more serious system
outages. Experience to date shows that FR programs have been
eminently successful and are one of the key factors in making possible continuous operation of real-time systems.

3.1.4. Fault Location and Repair

Repair support is provided by a set of on-line diagnostic programs. These diagnostics are designed when the hardware unit is
designed so that the required access to logic functions and failure
nodes are made available. The diagnostic programs are provided
for each unit type and are subdivided into phases which are associated with defined blocks of hardware. Each diagnostic is
designed to resolve a hardware fault to a few replaceable modules

or circuit packs. This is accomplished by applying the raw data from the diagnostic program output to a Trouble Location Program (TLP). The TLP process is a unique on-line feature which is automatic and uses pattern recognition, correction information, and hardware arrays to produce a priority list of circuit packs to be replaced.

This automatic procedure has proved very effective and for systems now in use 98 percent of the faults can be detected automatically and 94 percent can be located to a replaceable unit. Faults that are not detected automatically or resolved by the TLP are found by manual backup methods such as interactive diagnostic execution, looping at specific addresses, and analysis of raw data.

3.2. Performance Measurements

There is a common saying in telecommunication that "If you cannot measure it you do not know what you are talking about". Therefore, modern switching systems need a comprehensive measurement system to measure automatically all important performance characteristics. Traffic volume and maintenance activity for each unit is recorded and available for analysis. Every incident of customer service failure is also recorded. This data is used to correct problems which could lead to system outages.

4. Design Strategies for Software Integrity

Current software technology is not advanced enough to allow the development of significant amounts of code without error or to determine and uncover all errors by analysis and test. In fact, in large software systems it is not economically feasible to uncover all possible program "bugs." Therefore, the software system must be designed to work in the presence of software "bugs."

Switching system programs can be divided into two broad categories. One category consists of those subsystems that are high usage and/or deal with closed algorithms. The second category consists of subsystems which are run infrequently and have many routes from one state to another. Table 4 illustrates the two types of subsystems:

High_Usage
Operating System
Call Processing
Common Channel Signaling
System Data Base
Automatic Message Accounting

Low_Usage
Network Management
Data Base On-Line Change
Fault Recovery
Diagnostic
Fault Location
System Integrity

Table 4: Software Subsystems

The subsystems in the first category lend themselves to definitive testing and because of their high usage rate are exercised frequently over a given period of calendar time. This results in a high probability of uncovering "bugs" in these subsystems. Unfortunately in switching systems the code in this category generally only comprises between 10 and 20 percent of the total code.

In the second category, and in particular for maintenance and recovery subsystems, if the system reliability comes even close to the range of the desired objectives (3 minutes per year downtime) the amount of time required to exercise the system thoroughly through all possible paths becomes prohibitive. Error tolerance to bugs is provided by error prevention and error correction techniques. Error prevention emphasizes quality, defensive coding techniques, methodology, and memory protection. Error correction emphasizes audits, software integrity monitors and software integrity control.

4.1. Defensive Programming Techniques

Two of the techniques used in error prevention are defensive coding and memory protection: defensive coding limits a program subsystems access of data such that it cannot inadvertently mutilate data in areas that it has no need to access. Specific techniques are check state codes, range checks, symbolic addressing, interpreting and accounting for *all* input stimuli, and linking by index (not by absolute address).

Memory protection also guards from data mutilation in critical areas by random writes. This protection is provided by special "unlocking" instructions that must be used to gain access to critical memory areas. This mechanism also restricts certain classes of programs from writing into forbidden program memory areas.

4.2. Software Error Detection and Recovery

The use of defensive programming techniques, particularly in program subsystems that fall in the high usage category, proves to be costly in real time consumption. Therefore these techniques are generally limited in applications to those cases where anomalies in processing cannot be tolerated. In many (in fact most) cases in real time systems while unavailability cannot be tolerated, occasional anomalies in processing can be (e.g., one interrupted call in 100,000 in a switching system or one piece of tracking data in 100 in an aircraft control system). Here detection and correction of software and hardware errors are adequate and can be provided by audits, integrity monitors, defensive checks and overload congestion monitors.

The basic philosophy of the audit system is to detect data inconsistences and when found to correct them. Audits rely on the fact that data in large software systems appears redundantly and each copy is usually in a different format. Audits verify that each redundant copy of the data is consistent. This can be accomplished by direct comparison, comparison by association (e.g., verifying proper layouts are linked, verifying that physical data is consistent with memory, format checking etc.). Individual audits are designed for each data structure including registers, timing structures, queues and lists. These audits are run automatically by a scheduler or on demand as needed or can be manually requested.

An integrity monitor is used to detect scheduling and cycling irregularities. An overall program sanity timer is used to make sure the system scheduler is working properly. Several additional monitors are used for checking the operation of subsystems. A test call program creates special calls which are looped around in the system to verify that the system is sane and is able to complete calls. Various additional defensive links and system overload indicators are used as inputs to a software integrity control program which receives information on errors and performs analysis.

4.3. System Initialization and Recovery

The highest level of corrective software action available in switching systems is automatic system initialization and automatic system recovery. These actions are system wide and affect all other system activity until finished. For each system a set of recovery levels are made available. The objective is to interfere as little as possible with system operation while correcting the problem. For example, in the 4ESS digital switching system, 4 levels or phases of recovery exist, each increasing in the severity of its corrective action.

These phases are triggered by specific system conditions as shown in Table 5 which are activated by a software integrity control program.

- Excessive Maintenance Interrupts
- Excessive Lower Level Phases
- Excessive Audit Requests
- Duplex Failure of A Duplicated Unit
- Mutilation of the Software Clock
- Invalid Entry to Interject Monitor
- Program Sanity Timer Timeout
- Excessive K-Level Interrupts
- Nonservice of Interject Level Programs
- Sanity Loss in Software Integrity
  Control

Table 5: Phase Triggers

Phases normally start with a Phase 1 and progress in sequence to Phase 3 if required. If a Phase 3 does not correct the problem a Phase 4 can be manually requested. Table 6 summarizes the phase structure in 4ESS System.

Phase	Action
1	Initialize Specific Transient Memory
D1	Initialize a Duplex Failed Peripheral Frame
2	Reconfigure All Peripheral Hardware Initialize All Transient Memory
3	Reconfigure and Initialize Whole System
4	Same As Phase 3 Except Initialize All Memory (Manual Request Only)

Table 6: Phase Structure

Phase 1 saves all calls. Phases D1, 2, and 3 save all stable calls. Phase 4 tears down all calls. Other modern systems have slightly different structures but meet the same intent.

The key to continuous reliable operation of complex systems is the ability to detect an error, correct it essentially in real time, and/or reconfigure the system to an operating state in a very short period of time. In some systems, such as 1ESS, this may be measured in tenths of seconds and in others with independent signal processors in seconds. Both response times have been achieved as appropriate in AT&T ESS systems.

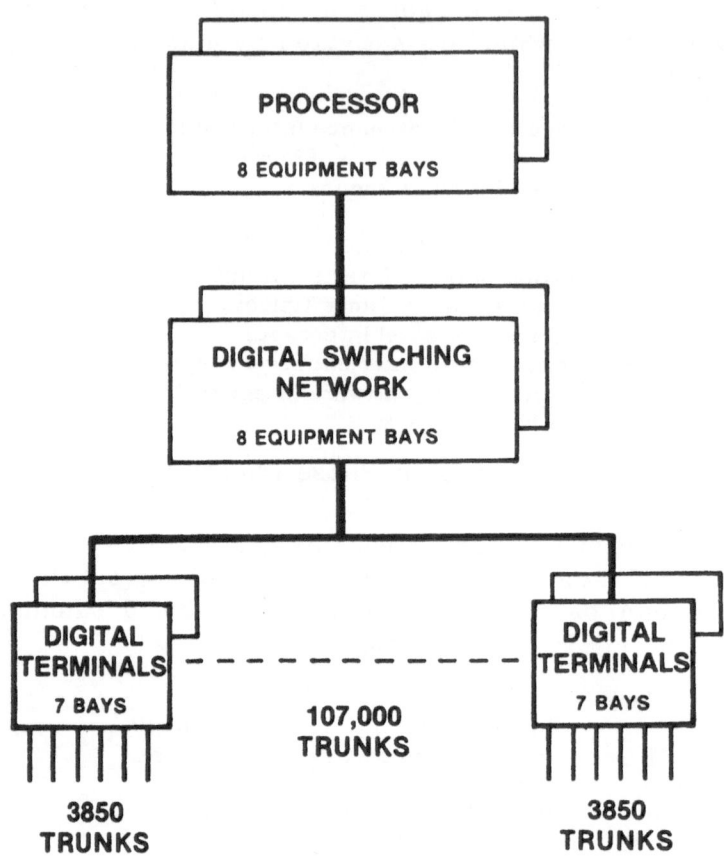

Fig. 3 4ESS *TM* stored program controlled switching system

5. Service Experience with 4ESS System

The 4ESS digital switch is an example of a switching system which has been designed using the fault tolerant techniques described in this paper. Fig. 3 is a block diagram of the 4ESS switching system. The switching system consists of a powerful central processor but many control functions have been distributed to the switching network and the digital terminals by the use of several hundred micro processors.

As shown in Fig. 3, the central processor (8 bays) makes up only a small part of the total system. The switching network for a typical 72,000 trunk office consists of 8 bays of logic equipment, and the digital terminals for 72,000 trunks require 126 bays of equipment. The equipment in the network and digital terminals use computer type components such as micro processors, memory and logic circuits. Therefore, the problem of continuous reliable operation is not just required in the 8 bay processor, but in the overall complex of 142 bays of highly complex VLSI and LSI circuitary.

There are now 130 4ESS systems in service in North America, Taiwan and Korea each capable of handling 700,000/hour. These systems terminate 5.0 million trunks and handle over 7.0 billion calls per month. The main software program for these systems is over 3.0 million lines of code and is being updated each year to include new system features and system improvements. Table 7 is a summary of performance measurements for 130 systems averaged over a 1-year period [13].

Hardware Interrupts	<15 per day
Software Audits	<20 per day
Automatic Initializations	<0.5 per month
Manual Initializations	<1.0 per 50 months
Mean Time To Restore System	32 seconds
Cut Off Calls	<5 per million
Denied Calls	<4 per million
Trunk Out of Service	<9 minutes per tr.yr
Mean Time To Failure (MTTF) (Major Outages)	50 months
System Downtime (Major Outages)	1.7 hour per 40 yr.
Circuit Pack Replacement	.04% per month
Billing Accuracy	<1 error per 100 K calls
Effect of Pack Failure	0.9% require Manual Procedures
System Trouble Escalation	2.2% of Failures Escalated to a central bureau of experts
Hardware Trouble Escalation	0.7% of Failures Escalated to a central bureau of experts
Mean Time to Repair (MTTR) Hard Faults	15 minutes
Intermittent Faults	2 hours

Table 7: 4ESS System Performance

The AT&T ESS systems have achieved the goals and requirements set for ultrareliable operation. From our early experience with 1ESS, we learned the desirability of remoting maintenance to a centralized location [10,12]. One of the problems experienced throughout the history of ESS is that members of the repair forces do not get an opportunity to use their skills often. Even in the early phases of introduction of new ESS systems when the unavailability objective of ≤ 3 minutes per year is not yet realized, the fact remains that serious failures do not occur often. So while the craft force may be highly skilled at the completion of training, these skills tend to be lost over a period of time because in any single office there is little chance to practice them. One way around this is to provide remote maintenance for a number of offices at a central location. This has been done with the introduction in 1974 of the Switching Control Center System (SCCS). This technique allows a select group of craft to maintain and sharpen their skills by working on failures from a large number of offices. Not only is this cost effective but it reduces outages due to human errors.

6. Conclusion

Experience with many stored programmed controlled switching systems has shown that the application of fault tolerant techniques in both hardware and software are necessary to meet the stringent communication performance requirements expected from high quality systems. A summary of technique and approximate introduction dates are shown in Appendix I.

The 4ESS digital switching system is a very large hardware and software complex which has been designed using extensive fault tolerant techniques and is a representative example of the high quality performance achieved in AT&T ESS systems. The reliability and excellent performance can be attributed to the incorporation of these techniques in the initial design and the dedicated effort to perfect these implementations. The excellent performance has shown that reliable large software systems can be implemented and made operational. Hardware and software in these large systems which are continually evolving will always have latent faults and therefore fault tolerant techniques are a necessity to keep the systems operating until fault or design errors can be corrected. The fault tolerant techniques used in switching systems are also applicable to other systems which have requirements for continuous real time operation. The key to continuous high quality operation of complex systems is the ability to detect an error, correct it essentially in real time, and/or reconfigure the system to an operating mode. Generally this is accomplished in less than a second.

7. Acknowledgements

This paper reports on the work of all the AT&T-BL switching development teams which have evolved the fault tolerant and maintenance techniques mentioned in the paper. It is not possible to list all the individual contributions, however, an extensive coverage is given in the references.

8. References

[1]   A. E. Joel, Jr., et al., "A History of Engineering and Science in the Bell System," Switching Technology (1925-1975), Bell Telephone Laboratories, Inc., 1982.

[2]   W. Keister, et al., "1 ESS," BSTJ, September, 1964, Vol. 43, No. 5, Part 1 and 2, pp. 1831-2592.

[3]   A. E. Spencer, et al., "No. 2ESS," BSTJ, October, 1969, Vol. 48, No. 8, pp. 2607-2896

[4]   J. C. Ewin, P. K. Giloth, et al., "No. 1ESS ADF," BSTJ, December, 1970, Vol. 49, No. 10, pp. 2733-3004.

[5]   R. J. Jaeger, Jr., et al., "TSPS No. 1," BSTJ, December, 1970, Vol. 49, No. 10, pp. 2417-2731.

[6]   R. E. Staehler, et al., "The 1A Processor," BSTJ, February, 1977, Vol. 56, No. 2, pp. 119-315.

[7]   A. E. Spencer, Jr., et al., "No. 4ESS," BSTJ, September, 1977, Vol. 56, No. 7, pp. 1015-1320.

[8]   K. E. Martersteck, et al., "4ESS System Evolution," BSTJ, July-August, 1981, Vol. 60, No. 6, Part 2, pp. 1041-1228.

[9]   K. E. Martersteck, A. E. Spencer, et al., "The 5ESS Switching System," AT&T Technical Journal, July-August, 1985, Vol. 64, No. 6, Part 2, pp. 1305-1564.

[10]   G. F. Clement, et al., "Recovery From Faults in the 1A Processor," International Symposium on Fault Tolerant Computing No. 4, 1974, pp. 5.2-5.7.

[11]   W. N. Toy, "Fault Tolerant Design of Local ESS Processors," Proceedings of the IEEE, October, 1978, pp. 1126-1145.

[12]   R. M. Averill, Jr., et al., "Centralized Maintenance Techniques for Electronic Switching Systems," International Switching Symposium Record, June, 1972, pp.304-312.

[13]   P. K. Giloth, "Reliability and Performance Assurance of the 4ESS Digital Switch - IEEE International Conference on Communications," June, 1985.

9. Appendix I

Dependability Techniques Introduced with AT&T Switching Systems

N+M Redundancy	late 1930's No. 1 Cross Bar
Error Correction Codes	late 1940's

Maching By Duplication

Watchdog Timers

Software Integrity Monitors

Audits

Link Lists

Overload Congestion Monitors   Introduced with
                                       Morris ESS Field
Automatic Recovery From Fault   Trial 1960

- Fault Detection
- Fault Testing
- Fault Processing

Dictionaries

- To Locate Fault By Error
  Signatures

Roll Back

Directed Fault Recovery	1967 No. 1 ESS
Duplicated Switching Network	1976 No. 4 ESS

Fault Tolerance in Tandem Computer Systems

Joel Bartlett
Jim Gray
Bob Horst

March 1986

ABSTRACT

Tandem builds single-fault-tolerant computer systems. At the hardware level, the system is designed as a loosely coupled multi-processor with fail-fast modules connected via dual paths. It is designed for online diagnosis and maintenance. A range of CPUs may be inter- connected via a hierarchical fault-tolerant local network. A variety of peripherals needed for online transaction processing are attached via dual ported controllers. A novel disc subsystem allows a choice between low cost-per-Mbyte and low cost-per-access. System software provides processes and messages as the basic structuring mechanism. Processes provide software modularity and fault isolation. Process pairs tolerate hardware and transient software failures. Applications are structured as requesting processes making remote procedure calls to server processes. Process server classes utilize multi-processors. The resulting process abstractions provide a distributed system which can utilize thousands of processors. Networking protocols such as SNA, OSI, and a proprietary network are built atop this base. A relational database provides distributed data and distributed transactions.

An application generator allows users to develop fault-tolerant applications as though the system were a conventional computer. The resulting system has price/performance competitive with conventional systems.

1. Introduction

Conventional well-managed transaction processing systems fail about once every two weeks for about an hour [Mourad], [Burman]. This translates to 99.7% availability. These systems tolerate some faults, but fail in case of a serious hardware, software or operations error.

When the sources of faults are examined in detail, a surprising picture emerges: Faults come from hardware, software, operations, maintenance and environment in about equal measure. Hardware may go for two months without giving problems and software may be equally reliable. The result is a one month MTBF. When one adds in operator errors, errors during maintenance, and power failures the MTBF sinks below two-weeks.

By contrast, it is possible to design systems which are single-fault-tolerant -- parts of the system may fail but the rest of the system tolerates the failures and continues delivering service. This paper reports on the structure and success of such a system -- the Tandem NonStop system. It has MTBF measured in years -- more than two orders of magnitude better than conventional designs.

2. Design Principles for Fault-Tolerant Systems

The key design principles of Tandem systems are:

Modularity: Both hardware and software are decomposed into fine- granularity modules which are units of service, failure, diagnosis, repair and growth.

Fail-Fast: Each module is self-checking. When it detects a fault, it stops.

Single Fault Tolerance: When a hardware or software module fails, its function is immediately taken over by another module -- giving a mean time to repair measured in milliseconds. For processors or processes this means a second processor or process exists. For storage modules, it means the storage and paths to it are duplexed.

On Line Maintenance: Hardware and software can be diagnosed and repaired while the rest of the system continues to deliver service. When hardware, programs, or data are repaired, they are reinte- grated without interrupting service.

Simplified User Interfaces: Complex programming and operations interfaces can be a major source of system failures. Every attempt is made to simplify or automate interfaces to the system.

This paper presents Tandem systems viewed from this perspective.

3. Hardware

3.1. Principles

Hardware fault tolerance requires multiple modules in order to tolerate module failures. From a fault tolerance standpoint, two modules of each type are generally sufficient since the probability of a second independent failure during the repair interval of the first is extremely low. For instance, if a processor has a mean time between failures of 10,000 hours (about a year) and a repair time of 4 hours, the MTBF of a dual system increases to about 10 million hours (about 1000 years). Added gains in reliability by adding more than two processors are minimal due to the much higher probability of software or system operations related system failures.

Modularity is important to fault-tolerant systems because individual modules must be replaceable online. Keeping modules independent also makes it less likely that a failure of one module will affect the operation of another module. Having a way to increase performance by adding modules allows the capacity of critical systems to be expanded without requiring major outages to upgrade equipment.

Fail-fast logic, defined as logic which either works properly, or stops, is required to prevent corruption of data in the event of a failure. Hardware checks including parity, coding, and selfchecking, as well as firmware and software consistency checks provide fail-fast operation.

Price and price-performance are frequently overlooked requirements for commercial fault-tolerant systems -- they must be competitive with non-fault-tolerant systems. Customers have evolved ad-hoc methods for coping with unreliable computers. For instance, financial applications usually have a paper-based fallback system in case the computer is down. As a result, most customers are not willing to pay double or triple for a system just because it is fault-tolerant. Commercial fault-tolerant vendors have the difficult task of designing systems which keep up with the state of the art in all aspects of traditional computer architecture and design, as well as solving the problems of fault tolerance, while incurring the extra costs of dual pathing and storage.

3.2. Tandem Architecture

The Tandem NonStop I was the introduced in 1976 as the first commercial fault-tolerant computer system. Fig. 1 is a diagram of its basic architecture. The system consists of 2 to 16 processors connected via dual 13 Mbyte/sec busses (the "Dynabus"). Each processor has its own memory in which its own copy of the operating system resides. All processor to processor communication is done by passing messages over the Dynabus.

Each processor has its own I/O bus. Controllers are dual ported and connect to I/O busses of two different CPUs. An ownership bit in each controller selects which of its ports is currently the "primary" path.

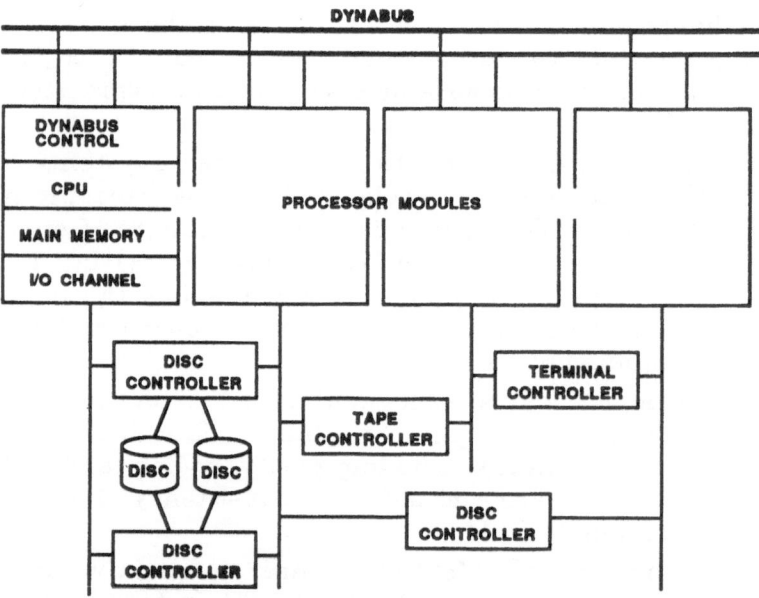

Fig. 1. The original Tandem architecture. Up to 16 CPUs are connected via the dual 13 Mbyte Dynabus. Each processor has its own main memory and copy of the distributed operating system. The system can continue operation despite the loss of any single component.

When a CPU or I/O bus failure occurs, all controllers which were primaried on that I/O bus switch to the backup. The controller configuration can be arranged so that in an N-processor system, the failure of a CPU causes the I/O workload of the failed CPU to be spread out over the remaining N-1 CPUs (see Figure 1.)

3.3. CPUs

In the Tandem architecture, the design of the CPU is not much different than any traditional processor. Each processor operates independently and asynchronously from the rest of the processors. The novel requirement is that the Dynabus interfaces must be engineered to prevent a single CPU failure from disabling both busses. This requirement boils down to the proper selection of a single part type - the buffer which drives the bus. This buffer must be "well behaved" when power is removed from the CPU to prevent glitches from being induced on both busses.

In order to make processors fail-fast, extensive error checking is incorporated in the design. Error detection in data paths is typically done by parity checking and parity prediction, while checking of control paths is done with parity, illegal state detection, and selfchecking.

Loosely coupling the processors relaxes the constraints on the error detection latency. A processor is only required to stop itself in time to avoid sending incorrect data over the I/O bus or Dynabus. In some cases, in order to avoid lengthening the processor cycle time, error detection is pipelined and does not stop the processor until several clocks after the error occurred. Several clocks of latency is not a problem in the Tandem architecture, but could not be tolerated in systems with locksteped processors or systems where several processors share a common memory.

Traditional mainframe computers have error detection hardware as well as hardware to allow instructions to be retried after a failure. This hardware is used both to improve availability and to reduce service costs. The Tandem architecture does not require instruction retry for availability. The VLX processor is the first to incorporate a kind of retry hardware, primarily to reduce service costs.

In the VLX, most of the data path and control circuitry is in high density gate arrays, which are extremely reliable. This leaves the high speed static RAMs in the cache and control store as the major contributors to processor unreliability. Both cache and control store are designed to retry intermittent errors, and both have spare RAMs which may be switched in to continue operating despite a hard RAM failure.

Since the cache is store-through, there is always a valid copy of cache data in main memory; a cache parity error just forces a cache miss, and the correct data is refetched from memory. The microcode keeps track of the parity error rate, and when it exceeds a threshold, switches in the spare.

The VLX control store has two identical copies to allow a two cycles access of each control store starting on alternate cycles. The second copy of control store is also used to retry an access in case of an intermittent failure in the first. Again, the microcode switches in a spare RAM online once the error threshold is reached.

Traditional instruction retry was not included due to its high cost and complexity relative to the small system MTBF improvement it would yield.

The power, packaging and cabling must also be carefully thought through. Parts of the system are redundantly powered through diode ORing of two different power supplies. In this way, I/O controllers and Dynabus controllers tolerate a power supply failure. Table 1 gives a summary of the evolution of Tandem CPUs.

	NonStopI	NonStopII	TXP	VLX
Year Introduced	1976	1981	1983	1986
MIPs	.7	.8	2.0	3.0
Cycle Time	100ns	100ns	83.3ns	83.3ns
Gates	20k	30k	58k	86k
CPU Boards	2	3	4	2
Integration	MSI	MSI	PALs	Gate Arrays
Virt Mem Addressing	512KB	1GB	1GB	1 GB
Phys Mem Addressing	2MB	16MB	16MB	256MB
Memory per board	64-384KB	512KB-2MB	2-8MB	8MB

Table 1: A summary of the evolution of Tandem CPUs.

The original Dynabus connected from 2 to 16 processors. This bus was "overdesigned" to allow for future improvements in CPU performance without redesign of the bus. The same bus was used on the NonStop II CPU, introduced in 1980, and the NonStop TXP, introduced in 1983. The II and the TXP can even plug into the same backplane as part of a single mixed system. A full 16 processor TXP system does not drive the bus near saturation. A new

Dynabus has been introduced on the VLX. This bus provides peak throughput of 40 MB/sec, relaxes the length constraints of the bus, and has a reduced manufacturing cost due to improvements in its clock distribution. It has again been overdesigned to accommodate the higher processing rates of future CPUs.

A fiber optic bus extension (FOX) was introduced in 1983 to extend the number of processors which could be applied to a single application. FOX allows up to 14 systems of 16 processors (224 processors total) to be linked in a ring structure. The distance between adjacent nodes was 1 Km on the original FOX, and is 4 Km with FOX II, which was introduced on the VLX. A single FOX ring may mix NonStop II, TXP and VLX processors.

Fox is actually four independent rings. This design can tolerate the failure of any Dynabus or any node and still connect all the remaining nodes with high bandwidth and low latency.

Transaction processing benchmarks have shown that the bandwidth of FOX is sufficient to allow linear performance growth in large multinode systems -- throughput increases proportionally as processors and peripherals are added [Horst 85].

Fault tolerant processors are viable only if their price-performance is competitive. Both the architecture and technology of Tandem processors have evolved to keep pace with trends in the computer industry. Architecture improvements include the expansion to 1 Gbyte of virtual memory (NonStop II), incorporation of cache memory (TXP), and expansion of physical memory addressability to 256 Mbyte (VLX). Technology improvements include the evolution from core memory to 4K, 16K, 64K and 256K dynamic RAMs, and the evolution from Shottky TTL (NonStop I, II) to Programmable Array Logic (TXP) to bipolar gate arrays (VLX) [Horst 84, Elect].

The Tandem multiprocessor architecture allows a single processor design to cover a wide range of processing power. Having processors of varying power adds another dimension to this flexibility. For instance, for approximately the same processing power, a customer may choose a four processor VLX, a six processor TXP, or a 16 processor NonStop II. The VLX has optimal price/performance, the TXP can provide better performance under failure conditions (losing 1/6 of the system instead of 1/4), and the NonStop II may be the best solution for customers who wish to upgrade an existing smaller system. Having a range of processors extends the spectrum of users from those sensitive to low entry price, to those with extremely high-volume processing needs.

While ease of expansion is a major design goal in midrange and high- end systems, low-end systems are more sensitive to entry cost. The entry cost includes not only the system itself, but also the costs of floorspace, air conditioning and computer room preparation.

To address low entry cost, Tandem introduced the EXT10 and EXT25. They are self contained fault tolerant systems which include modified NonStop II and NonStop TXP processors, respectively. Each has 2 processors, up to 8 125 Mbyte disks, a cartridge tape drive, and an integrated operation and service processor in a package about the size of two four-drawer file cabinets. The systems operate in a copier room environment with low audible noise and minimal power and air conditioning requirements.

3.4. Peripherals

In building a fault-tolerant system, the entire system, not just the CPU, must have the basic fault-tolerant properties of dual paths, modularity, fail-fast design, and good price/performance. Tandem peripherals and their attachment architecture have changed considerably over the last decade.

The basic architecture provides the ability to configure the I/O system to allow multiple paths to each I/O device. With dual port controllers and dual port peripherals, there are actually four paths to each device. When discs are mirrored, there are eight paths which can be used to read or write data.

The original architecture did not provide as rich an interconnection scheme for communications and terminals. The first asynchronous terminal controller was dual ported, and connected to 32 terminals. Since the terminals themselves are not dual ported, it was not possible to configure the system to withstand a terminal controller failure without disabling a large number of terminals. The solution for critical applications was to have two terminals nearby which were connected to different terminal controllers.

In 1982, Tandem introduced the 6100 communications subsystem which reduces the impact of a failure in the communications subsystem. The 6100 consists of two dual ported communications interface units (CIUs) which talk to I/O busses from two different processors. Individual Line Interface Units (LIUs) connect to both CIUs, and to the communication line or terminal line. With this arrangement, CIU failures are completely transparent, and LIU failures result in the loss only of the attached line(s). An added advantage is that each LIU may be downloaded with a different protocol in order to support different communications environments and to offload protocol interpretation from the main processors.

Dual pathing has also evolved in the support of system initialization and maintenance. NonStop I systems had only a set of lights and switches per processor for communicating error information and for resetting and loading processors. NonStop II and TXP systems added an Operations and Service Processor (OSP) to aid in system operation and repair. The OSP is a Z80 microcomputer system which communicates with all processors and a maintenance console. It can be used to remotely reset and load processors, and to display error information. The OSP is not fault-tolerant, but is not required to operate in order for the system to operate. Critical OSP functions such as processor reset, reload and memory dump can also be performed by the front panel switches.

In the VLX system, dual pathing and fault tolerance was also extended to a new maintenance system. This new system, called CHECK, consists of two 68000 based processors which communicate with each other and other subsystems via dual bit-serial maintenance busses. The CPUs, FOX II controllers, and power supply monitors all connect to the maintenance busses. Any unexpected event, such as a hardware failure, fan failure or power supply failure is logged by CHECK. CHECK communicates with an expert system running in the main CPUs which analyzes the event log to determine what corrective action should take place. The system also has dial-out and dial-in capability for notification of service personnel. A fault tolerant maintenance system can always be counted on to be functional, and critical operations can be done solely by the CHECK system. The front panel lights and switches were eliminated, and more functionality was incorporated into the CHECK system.

Modularity is standard in peripherals -- it is common to mix different types of peripherals to match the intended application. In online transaction processing in it is desirable to independently select increments of disc capacity and of disc performance. On-line transaction processing applications often require more disc arms per Mbyte than is provided by traditional 14 inch discs. This may result in customers buying more Mbytes of disc than they need in order to avoid queuing at the disc arm.

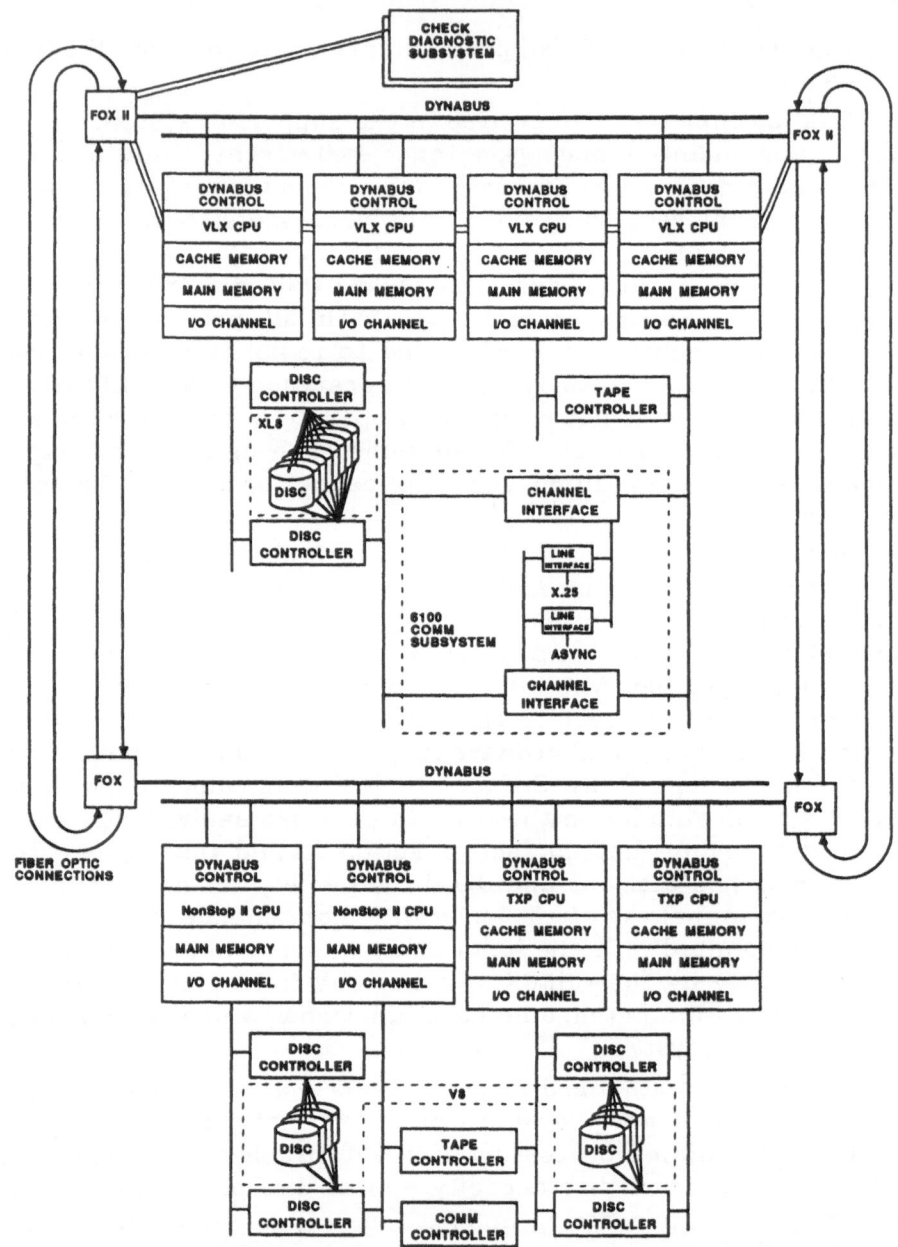

Fig. 2 shows the 1986 Tandem architecture. Up to 14 systems of 16 CPUs (224 processors) are connected at distances of up to 4Km in a fault-tolerant fiber-optic ring network. The network can include three different processor types - the .8 MIPs NonStop II, the 2 MIPs TXP and the 3 MIPs VLX. New architectures for communications, disc drives, and maintenance have also been introduced.

In 1984, Tandem departed from traditional disc architectures by introducing the V8 disc drive. The V8 is a single cabinet which contains up to eight 168 Mbyte eight-inch Winchester disc drives in six square feet of floor space. Using multiple eight-inch drives instead of a single 14-inch drive gives more access paths and less wasted capacity. The modular design is easily serviced, since individual drives may be removed and replaced online. In a mirrored configuration, system software automatically brings the replaced disc up to date while new transactions are underway.

Once a system is single fault-tolerant, the second order effects begin to become important in system failure rates. One category of compound faults is the combination of a hardware failure and a human fault during the consequent human activity of diagnosis and repair. The V8 made a contribution to reducing system failure rates by simplifying servicing and eliminating preventative maintenance which combine to reduce the likelyhood of such compound hardware-human failures.

Peripheral controllers have fail-fast requirements similar to processors, They must not corrupt data on both their I/O busses when they fail. If possible, they must return error information to the processor when they fail.

Tandem's contribution in peripheral fail-fast design has been to put added emphasis on error detection within the peripheral controllers. An example is Tandem's first VLSI tape controller. This controller uses dual locksteped 68000 processors with compare circuits to detect errors. It also contains totally selfchecked logic and selfchecking checkers to detect errors in the random logic portion of the controller.

Above this, the system software uses "end-to-end" checksums generated by the high-level software. These checksums are stored with the data and recomputed and rechecked when the data is reread.

In fault-tolerant systems design, keeping down the price of peripherals is even more important than in traditional systems. Some parts of the peripheral subsystem must be duplicated, yet they provide little or no added performance.

For disc mirroring, the two disc arms give better read performance than two single discs because the seeks are shorter and because the read work is spread evenly over the two servers. Writes on the other hand do cost twice as much channel and controller time. Mirroring does double the cost per Mbyte stored. In order to reduce the price per Mbyte of storage, Tandem introduced the XL8 disc drive in 1986. The XL8 has eight nine-inch Winchester discs in a single cabinet and has a total capacity of 4.2

Gbytes. As in the V8 drive, discs within the same cabinet may be mirrored, saving the costs of added cabinetry and floor space. Also like the V8, the reliable sealed media and modular replacement keep down maintenance costs.

Other efforts to reduce peripheral prices include the use of VLSI gate arrays in controllers to reduce part counts and improve reliability, and using VLSI to integrate the stand alone 6100 communications subsystem into a series of single board controllers.

Year	Product	Contribution
1976	NonStop I	Dual ported controllers, single fault tolerant I/O system
1977	NonStop I	Mirrored and dual ported discs
1982	InfoSat	Fault tolerant satellite communications
1983	6100	Fault tolerant communications subsystem
1983	FOX	Fault tolerant high speed fiber optic LAN
1984	V8 Disc Drive	Eight drive fault-tolerant disc subsystem
1985	3207 Tape Ctrl	Totally selfchecked VLSI tape controller
1985	XL8 Disc Drive	Eight drive high-capacity / low-cost disc
1986	CHECK	Fault tolerant maintenance system

Table 2. Tandem contributions to peripheral fault tolerance.

4. Systems Software

4.1. Processes and Messages

Processes are the software analog of processors. They are the units of software modularity, service, failure and repair. The operating system kernel running in each processor provides multiple processes, each with a one gigabyte virtual address space. Processes in a processor may share memory, but sharing of read-write memory among processes is frowned upon because it jeopardizes fault containment within a process. Rather, processes communicate via messages. They only share read-only code segments.

The kernel of the system performs the basic chores of priority dispatching, message transmission among processes, and reconfiguration in case of hardware failure.

The kernel sends messages among processes in a processor and also to kernels of other processors which in turn send the message to the destination process. The path taken by the message, memory-to-memory or across a local or long-haul network, is transparent to the sender and receiver. Only the kernel is concerned with the routing of the message. This is the software analog of multiple data paths. If a physical path fails, the message is retransmitted along another path.

The kernel is able to hide some hardware failures. For example, if a read-only page gets an uncorrectable memory error, then the page can be refreshed from disc. Similarly, a power failure is handled by storing the processor state to memory, quiescing the system and waiting for power restoration. Batteries carry the memory for several hours. Beyond that, an uninterruptable power supply is required. When power is restored, the system resumes operation. Fail-fast operation requires that some hardware and software faults cause the kernel to fail the processor. Such faults are predominately software bugs or operator errors -- the hardware is comparatively reliable [Gray 85].

When a processor stops, the other processors sense the failure by noticing that it has not sent an "I'm Alive" message lately (the latency is about 2 seconds). The remaining processors go through a "regroup" algorithm to decide who is up and who is down. This logic is fairly simple if the failure is simple, but can be complex in the presence of faulty processors or marginal power causing frequent failures. It has not been necessary to adopt the Byzantine Generals model of this problem [Lamport], rather the regroup algorithm assumes that each processor is dead, slow, or healthy. Based on that assumption, the processors exchange messages to decide who is up. After two broadcast rounds, the decision is made by all processors.

4.2. Process Pairs

When a process fails because of a transient software bug or a processor fault, single-fault tolerance requires that the application continue functioning. Process pairs are one approach to this. A process can have a "backup" process in another CPU. The backup process has the same program, logical address space and sessions as the primary. Together these two processes comprise a process pair [Bartlett].

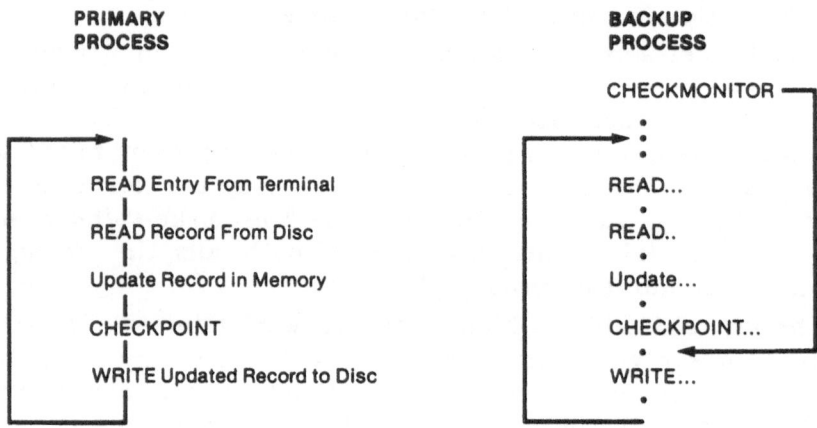

Fig. 3. Process pairs give reliable execution. They allow a program to continue execution even if a processor fails. The backup process executes CHECKMONITOR while the primary executes. If the primary fails, the backup begins execution as of the last CHECK-POINT of the primary process.

While the primary process executes, the backup is largely passive. At critical points, the primary process sends the backup "checkpoint" messages. These checkpoint messages can take many forms: they can be a "new state image" which the backup copies into its address space, a "delta" which the backup applies to its state, or even a function which the backup applies to its state. Gradually, Tandem is evolving to the delta and function approaches because they transmit less data and because errors in the primary process state are less likely to contaminate the backup's state [Borr 84].

When the primary process fails for some reason, the backup becomes the primary of the process pair. The kernels direct all current and future messages to the backup. Sequence numbers are used to regenerate duplicate responses to already-processed requests during the takeover. During normal operation, these sequence numbers are used for duplicate elimination and detection of lost messages in case of transmission error [Bartlett].

Process pairs give single-fault-tolerant program execution. They tolerate any single hardware fault and some transient software faults. We believe most faults in production software are transients (Heisenbugs). Process pairs allow fail-fast programs to continue execution in the backup when the software bug is transient [Gray 85].

4.3. Process Server Classes

To obtain software modularity, computations are broken into several processes. For example, a transaction arriving from a terminal passes through a line-handler process (say x.25), a protocol process (e.g. SNA), a presentation services process to do screen handling, an application process which has the database logic, and several disc processes which manage discs, disc buffer pools, locks and audit trails. This breaks the application into many small modules. These modules are units of service and of failure. If one fails, it's computation switches to its backup process.

If a process performs a particular service, for example managing a particular database, then as the system grows, traffic against this server is likely to grow. Gradually, the load on such a process will increase until it becomes a bottleneck. Such bottlenecks can be an impediment to linear growth in performance as processors are added. The concept of process server class is introduced to circumvent this problem. A server class is a collection of processes all of which perform the same function. These processes are typically spread over several processors. Requests are sent to the class rather than to individual members of the class. As the load increases, members are added to the class. If a member fails or if one of the processors fail, the server class migrates into the remaining processors. As the load decreases, the server class shrinks. Hence process server classes are a mechanism for fault tolerance and for load balancing in a distributed system [Tandem Pathway].

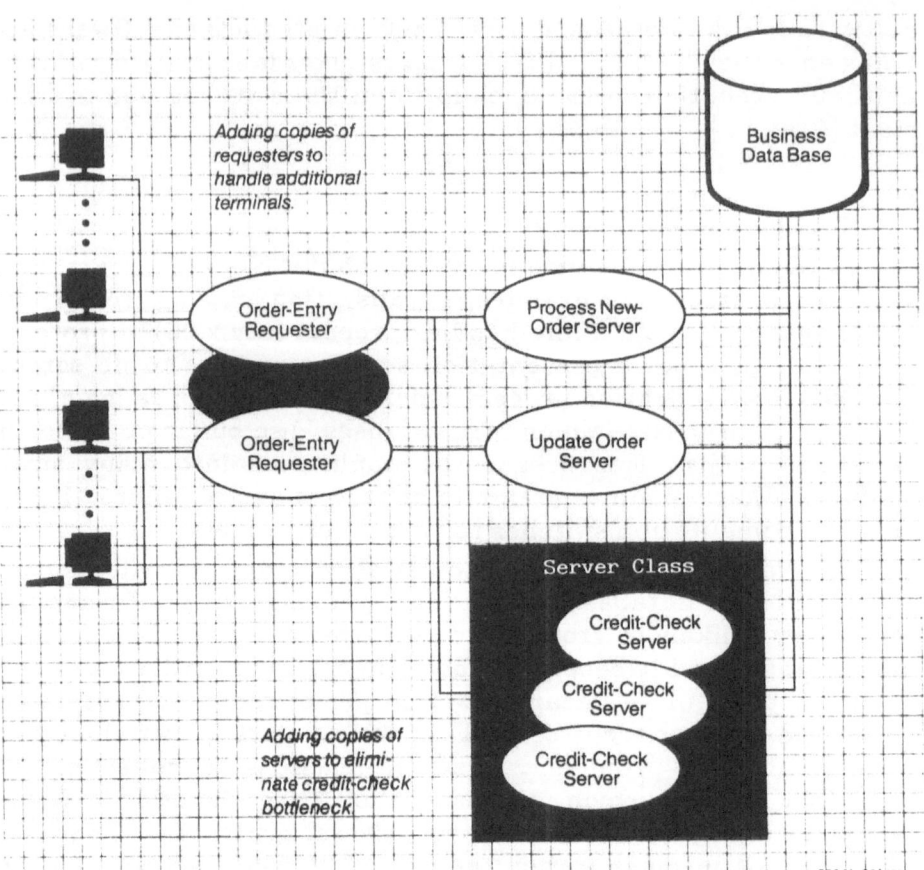

Fig. 4. Adding server classes and multiple requesters can utilize multiple processors and also avoid software bottlenecks.

4.4. Files

The data management system supports unstructured and structured (entry sequenced, relative, and key sequenced) files. Structured files may have multiple secondary indices. Files may be partitioned among discs distributed throughout the network. In addition, each file partition is mirrored on two discs. A class of process pairs manages each disc. Reads of a partition go to the primary class which maintains a cache of recently accessed disc pages. If the page is not in the disc cache, then the disc process reads it from the disc which is idle and which offers the shortest seek time. Because duplexed discs offer shorter seeks, they support higher read rates than two ordinary discs. Writes are a different matter. When a file is updated, it is updated on both of the mirrored discs -- so writes are twice as expensive.

Files may optionally be protected with a transaction audit trail of undo and redo records along with file-granularity and record-granularity locks to prevent concurrency anomalies. The disc process maintains file and record locks to avoid inconsistencies due to concurrent updates. The disc process also records the undo and redo audit records to allow transaction backout and transaction recovery in case of failure.

In the event of a hardware or software failure of the primary disc process server class, the backup server class in the other cpu assumes responsibility for that mirrored disc and continues service without service interruption or loss of data integrity.

4.5. Transactions

The work of a computation can be packaged as a unit by using the Transaction Monitoring Facility (TMF). TMF allows the application to obtain a transaction identifier (transid) for a particular job. All work done for that job is "tagged" with the transid. Locks are corollated to the transid. Undo and redo audit trail records are tagged by the transid. If the transaction commits, then all its effects are made durable, if it aborts, then all its effects are undone. For many applications, this is simpler than coding process pairs. In fact, most Tandem customers now use this transaction mechanism in lieu of process pairs to get application fault tolerance [Borr 81].

Device drivers and kernel software continue to need process pairs, because they are "below" the TMF interface. Indeed, process pairs are used to implement a non-blocking commit protocol in TMF and other basic systems features.

A process begins a transaction by invoking the BeginTransaction verb. This verb allocates a network-unique transaction identifier which will tag all messages and all database updates sent by this requester and by servers working on the transaction. Locks acquired by the transaction are tagged by the transaction identifier. In addition, disc processes generate log records (audit trail records) which allow the transaction to be undone in case it aborts or redone in case it commits and there is a later failure. When the requester is satisfied with the outcome, it can call CommitTransaction to commit all the work of the transaction. On the other hand, any process participating in the transaction can unilaterally abort it. This is implemented by the classic two-phase-locking and two-phase-commit protocols. They coordinate all the work done by the transaction at all the nodes of the local and long-haul network.

The transaction log combined with an archive copy of the database, allows the system to tolerate dual disc media failures as well as software and operations failures which damage both media of a pair. Such failures may result in temporary data unavailability, but the data is not lost or corrupted.

This multi-fault tolerance has paid off for several customers and is becoming standard -- although multiple faults are rare the consequent cost is very high. The transaction mechanism costs about 10% more and gives the customer considerably more peace of mind.

The newest fault-tolerance issue is disaster protection. Conventional disaster recovery schemes have mean time to repair of hours or days. There is increasing interest in distributing applications and data to multiple sites so that one site can take over for another in a matter of seconds or minutes with little or no lost transactions or lost data. The transaction log applied to a remote copy of the data can keep the database up-to-date. By having a symmetric network design and application design, customers can have two or more sites back one another up in case of disaster.

4.6. Networking

The process-message based kernel naturally generalized to a network operating system. By installing line handlers for a proprietary network, called Expand, Tandem was able to evolve the 16-processor design to a 4096 processor network. Expand uses a packet-switched hop-by-hop routing scheme to move messages among nodes, in essence it is a gateway among the individual 16-processor nodes. It is now widely used as a backbone for corporate networks, or as an intelligent network, acting as a gateway among other nets. The fault tolerance and modularity of the architecture make it a natural for these applications.

Increasingly, the system software is supporting standards such as SNA, OSI, MAP, SWIFT, etc. These protocols run on top of the kernel message system and appear to extend it [Tandem Expand].

5. Application Development Software

Application software provides a high-level interface for developing on line transaction processing applications to run on the low-level process-message-network system described above.

The basic principle is that the simpler the system, the less likely the user is to make mistakes.

For data communications, high-level interfaces are provided to "paint" screens for presentation services and a high-level interface is provided to SNA to simplify the applications programming task.

For data base, the relational data model is adopted and a relational query language integrated with a report writer allows quick development of ad hoc reports.

Systems programs are written in a Pascal-like language. Most commercial applications are written in Cobol or use the application generators. In addition, the system supports Fortran, Pascal, C, Basic, Mumps and other specialized languages. A binder allows modules from different languages to be combined into a single application, and a symbolic debugger allows the user to debug in the source programming language. The goal is to replace such conventional programming with application generators and higher level programming interfaces.

A menu-oriented application development system guides developers through the process of developing and maintaining applications. Where possible, it generates the application code for requesters and servers based on the contents of an integrated system dictionary.

Applications are structured as requester processes which read input from terminals, make one or more requests of various server processes, and then reply to the terminals. The transaction mechanism coordinates these multiple operations making them atomic, consistent, integral, and durable.

The application generator builds most requesters from the menu-oriented interface, although the user may tailor the requester by adding Cobol. The template for the servers is also automatically generated, but customers must add the semantics of the application -- generally using Cobol. Servers access the relational database either via Cobol record-at-a-time verbs or via set-oriented relational operators.

Using automatically generated requesters and the transaction mechanism, customers can build fault-tolerant distributed applications with no special programming.

As explained earlier, customers demand good price performance of fault-tolerant systems. Each VLX processor can process about ten standard transactions per second. Benchmarks have demonstrated that 32 processors have 16 times the transaction throughput of two processors: that is throughput grows linearly with the number of processors and the price per transaction declines slightly. We believe a 100 processor VLX system is capable of 1000 transactions per second. The price per transaction for a small system compares favorably with other full-function systems. This demonstrates that single-fault tolerance need not be an expensive proposition.

6. Operations and Maintenance

Operations errors are a major source of faults. Computer operators are often asked to make difficult decisions based on insufficient data or training. The Tandem system attempts to minimize operator actions and, where they are required, directs the operator to perform tasks and then checks his action for correctness.

Nevertheless, the operator is in charge, the computer must follow his orders. This poses a dilemma to the system designer -- how to limit the actions of the operator. First, all routine operations are handled by the system. For example, the system automatically reconfigures itself in case of a single fault. The operator is left with exception situations. Single-fault tolerance reduces the urgency of dealing with failures of single components. The operator can be leisurely about dealing with most single failures.

Increasingly, operators are given a simple and uniform high-level model of the system's behavior which deals in physical "real-world" entities such as discs, tapes, lines, terminals, applications, and so on rather than control blocks. The interface is organized in terms of actions and exception reports. The operator is prompted through diagnostic steps to localize and repair a failed component.

Maintenance problems are very similar to operations. Ideally, there would be no maintenance. Single fault tolerance allows hardware repair to be done on a scheduled basis rather than "as soon as possible", since the system continues to operate even if a module fails. This reduces the cost and stress of conventional maintenance. In practice, maintenance consists of diagnosing a fault and replacing a field replaceable unit (FRU). The failing FRU is sent back for remanufacture. Increasingly, the remote online maintenance system is used to diagnose and track the history of each FRU.

The hardware and software is extensively instrumented to generate exception reports. A rule-based system analyzes these reports and forms hypothesis on the cause of the fault. In some cases, it can predict a hard fault based on reports of transient faults prior to the hard fault. When a hard fault occurs or is predicted, a remote diagnostics center is contacted by the system. This center analyzes the situation and dispatches a service person along with the hardware or software fix.

The areas of single-fault-tolerant operations and single-fault tolerant maintenance are major topics of research at Tandem.

7. Summary and Conclusions

Single-fault tolerance is a good engineering tradeoff for commercial systems. For example, single discs are rated at a MTBF of 3 years. Duplexed discs, recording data on two mirrored discs and connecting them to dual controllers and dual cpus, raises the MTBF to 5000 years (theoretical) and 1500 years (measured). Triplexed discs would have theoretical MTBF of over one million years, but because operations and software errors dominate, the measured MTBF would probably be similar to that of duplexed discs.

Single-fault tolerance through the use of fail-fast modules and reconfiguration must be applied to both software and hardware.

Processes and messages are the key to structuring software into modules with good fault isolation. A side benefit of this design is that it can utilize multiple processors and lends itself to a distributed system design.

Modular growth of software and hardware is a side effect of fault tolerance. If the system can tolerate repair and reintegration of modules, then it can tolerate the addition of brand new modules.

In addition, systems must tolerate operations and environmental faults. Tolerating operations faults is our greatest challenge.

8. References

[Bartlett] Bartlett, J.,"A NonStop Kernel," Proceedings of the Eighth Symposium on Operating System Principles, pp. 22-29, Dec. 1981.

[Borr 81] Borr, A., "Transaction Monitoring in ENCOMPASS," Proc. 7Th VLDB, September 1981. Also Tandem Computers TR 81.2.

[Borr 84] Borr, A., "Robustness to Crash in a Distributed Database: A Non Shared-Memory Multi-processor Approach," Proc. 9th VLDB, Sept. 1984. Also Tandem Computers TR 84.2.

[Burman] Burman, M. "Aspects of a High Volume Production Online Banking System", Proc. Int. Workshop on High Performance Transaction Systems, Asilomar, Sept. 1985.

[Elect] Anon., "Tandem Makes a Good Thing Better", Electronics, pp. 34-38, April 14, 1986.

[Gray] Gray, J., "Why Do Computers Stop and What Can We Do About It?", Tandem Technical Report TR85.7, 1985, Cupertino, CA.

[Horst 84] Horst, R. and Metz, S., "New System Manages Hundreds of Transactions/Second." Electronics, pp. 147-151, April 19, 1984. Also Tandem Computers TR 84.1

[Horst 85] Horst, R., Chou, T., "The Hardware Architecture and Linear Expansion of Tandem NonStop Systems" Proceedings of 12th International Symposium on Computer Architecture, June 1985. or Tandem Technical Report 85.3

[Lamport] Lamport, L., Shostak, R., Pease, M., "Then Byzantine Generals Problem", ACM Transactions on Programming Languages and Systems, Vol. 4, No. 3, July 1982.

[Mourad] Mourad, S. and Andrews, D., "The Reliability of the IBM/XA̍ Operating System", Digest of 15th Annual Int. Sym. on Fault-Tolerant Computing, June 1985. IEEE Computer Society Press.

[Tandem] "Introduction to Tandem Computer Systems", Tandem Part No. 82503, March 1985, Cupertino, CA.

"System Description Manual", Tandem Part No. 82507, Cupertino, CA.

"Expand(tm) Reference Manual" Tandem Part No. 82370, Cupertino, CA.

"Introduction to Pathway", Tandem Computers Inc., Part No: 82339-A00, Cupertino, CA.

Evolution of Reliable Computing in Hitachi
and
Autonomous Decentralized System

Hirokazu Ihara
Kinji Mori
Shoji Miyamoto
Systems Development Laboratory, Hitachi Ltd.
1099 Ohzenji Asao Kawasaki Japan 215

ABSTRACT

The history of R/D activities of control computer system group at Hitachi is briefly overviewed from the reliability point of view in order to show the back ground of Autonomous Decentralized System.

The autonomous decentralized system concept and its applications to the computer control field are presented with a biological analogy in order to realize fault--tolerance, required extensibility and complete maintainability even during on--line operation such as the living things. The system properties derived from new concept are uniformity, equality and locality. They are applied to the system architecture, software and hardware.

1. Introduction

Reliability of the products is vital for manufacturing companies. Hitachi has been suppling a very wide line of important products to the society, such as thermal power plant, public utility

plant, transportation system, industrial plant, public communication system, banking information system. Many research and
development works related to the reliability of systems and components have been done by Hitachi's R/D groups based on one of
the company's most fundamental principles.

In this chapter, only the evolution of system reliability on control computer system is briefly overviewed prior to citing Autonomous Decentralized System. The development of the Hitachi's
control computer system was started in 1963 by industrial control
group independently of general purpose computer system group,
which delivered their computer systems since 1959. The reason
was greatly due to general lack of reliability of the computer when
it come to be applied as the real-time controller.

Three types of the control computers by germanium transistors or silicon transistors were delivered to the industry(IHA.67).
The main effective techniques which make them reliable were
derating usage and screening of their components.

In 1968, third generation control computer was delivered
mainly thanks to integrated circuits. Adaptation of ICs greatly
improved the system reliability and thus extended the sphere of
applications of computer control. However, since the cost of the
system was rather unacceptable to the small scale industry, the
leadership introducing computer control system was taken by
such big organizations as Iron and steel companies, utility supply
companies until mini- computer became popular(FUJ.68)(MOR.69).

In 1972, the COMTRAC system came successfully in operation
which managed and controlled the traffic of the bullet trains
"Shinkansen". The system operated in dual configuration in order
to avoid any failed output and its unexpected shutdown. This system was replaced by a three symmetric computer complex in 1975
when Shinkansen was extended. It can control trains almost all
time in dual operation because the third stand-by computer can
automatically take over the failed computer in dual
operation(IHA.78).

There were great difficulties in its replacement. It was prohibitive to debug whole program using the real trains on rail. Moreover, available time duration to replace was less than 3 hours in
the midnight.

The third computer played as the traffic simulator and as the
computer for adjusting programs to the change of the railway
configuration and traffic schedules.

Referring to the experiences of COMTRAC and other on-line
real time Systems, new control computer series were developed in
1975 by "consolidated modular engineering technology(COMET)".

The system has inherently a multiprocessor architecture connected by common memory. This COMET concept offered flexible system configurations such as dual, duplex, half duplex, shared, multi and distributed(KAM.78).

A more sophisticated COMTRAC system by COMET concept was completed as three symmetric processor complex in 1982 when new bullet railways were constructed in the northern part of Japan.

Advent of LSI and microcomputer technologies made it easier to implement not only multi-computer syetms but also distributed computer systems to increase computing ability and reliability in 1980's.

Most large scale and real-time control systems have three major characteristic requirements. The first is that the system can continue its operation through the fault occurrence in it, lest the unexpected shut down of the system should result in serious damage. The second is that the system is gradually constructed step by step and at any step the part of the system can start its operation even under the construction of the other part. The third is that the failed part of the system can be repaired during the operation of the system.

These needs imply that the large scale control system has three intrinsic requirements of fault tolerance, extensibility and maintainability. These three requirements cannot completely be satisfied in the centralized system such as COMTRAC and even in the conventional decentralized system. A new design philosophy for autonomous decentralized control system, based on a biological analogy, has been developed for structuring and controlli a distributed system which satisfies the before mentioned three requirements in consideration of the experiences on COMTRAC since 1977.

2. Analogy to Molecular Biology

We have grasped a biological organism as a system with the following attributes.

(1) The system always has faulty parts;
(2) It changes constantly, alternating between operation, maintenance, and growth; and
(3) It keeps accomplishing its objective almost completely.

The basic mechanism of all vital biological processes, including morphogenesis and physical movements, can be expressed by the digital code determined by the base sequence of deoxyribonucleic acid (DNA).

Genetic information causing this cell division produces identical clones, and immunoreaction is the mechanism by which different clones are identified and inhibited.

Molecular biologists determined that the entire mechanism of morphogenesis and the preservation of an organism is programmed by DNA information. In the case of human beings, the volume of nongenetic information--that acquired by learning and tradition--shows an explosive increase and covers the shortage of genetic information.

The information system, being the combination of processors and transmission lines, is like the system of neurons and synapses. Programs stored in a processor resemble the DNA of cells.

The process of regeneration by the reproduction of genetic information in cells resembles that of a computer program.

As for homeostasis, an abnormality processing program, such as the stability point search algorithm for reconfiguration and control at the time of system abnormality, corresponds to the receptor recorded in the DNA.

For hardware replacement, it is required to presuppose the direct portability of the former program, and no hardware is adopted if it does not permit it. The program is also replaced by degrees, according to changes in the required specifications. This can be compared to the shift toward dominant genes. In this case, the program(i.e. DNA) is apparently of vital importance, and the hardware is only its temporary pool.

3. The Autonomous Decentralization Concept

In molecular biology, which has recently made enormous progress, a living thing is viewed not as a whole unit but as a set of cells. The fundamental concept is that a cell intrinsically has all the genes necessary for its growth.

Cells are fundamental living subsystems having the same structure and the same information. Although there are no supervisory elements to control them integrally, those independent cells collectively perform the function of organs.

In the process of biological growth and metabolism, there are continuous operations of "repairing while being broken." Living systems carry out building, expansion, operation and maintenance not as separate processes, but as simultaneously advancing processes, to keep their reliability and flexibility.

Our concept has been introduced by this biological analogy, that is, a living thing is always renewed by metabolism and gradual growth. Therefore, it is quite normal for a system to have failed parts, in other words being faulty is normal. In this concept, it is assumed that a subsystem has its own control region and own objectives. Subsystems are not considered to be parts of a divided total system, and are considered to be required the following three properties:

(1) Autonomous Observability
Subsystems can observe their own territories in case of another subsystem's failure;

(2) Autonomous Controllability
Subsystems can control themselves in case of another subsystem's failure;

(3) Autonomous Coordinability
Subsystems can coordinate each other in case of other subsystem's failure.

Such an Autonomous Decentralized System(ADS) requires the constituent subsystems to have the following three conditions:

(1) Uniformity
In order to keep operating in spite of a fault in any subsystems, each subsystem has the same hardware and software structure;

(2) Equality
The hardware and software of each subsystem is equal to that of every other subsystems, that is, the system does not have any supervisory parts;

(3) Locality
Each subsystem controls itself based on local information without knowing the structure or status of the whole system.

4. Autonomous Decentralized System

Those properties suggest that the ADS structure is an aggregation of homogeneous, uniform subsystems, each having intelligence--with hardware and software systems not in the master-slave relation--and each being equivalent in capacity and performance.

4.1. System Structure

The system control and coordination of ADS are explained as the followings in Fig. 1. The axis of controllability indicates the controllability of the subsystems surviving against partial system failure. The controllability of surviving subsystems--that is, their resistance to faulty subsystems-- is greater for hierarchical distributed systems and ADS. For systems with low controllability, such as centralized and functional distributed systems, it is necessary to devise measures for preventing system failure (fault avoidance). If the system has high controllability, the subsystems surviving partial failure have large fault tolerance, or the capacity to function after failures.

The axis of coordinability indicates the coordinability of the subsystems surviving partial system failure. The coordinability of surviving subsystems-- that is, preventing the failure of any subsystem--is greater for ADS and functional distributed systems. For systems with low coordinability, such as hierarchical distributed and centralized systems, efforts are made to realize the highest cost performance of the entire system with the failure-free condition as the normal system state. If the system has high coordinability, efforts are made to realize functioning of all surviving subsystems against partial system failure(that is, increase the system functional performance), rather than to increase the cost performance of the entire system operating without any failure.

The information system in ADS can be summarized as follows:
(1) There is no priority given to any information or transmission.
(2) All information is transmitted consecutively to the subsystems adjoining to the generating point. Each subsystem picks up what it needs from the transmitted information and transmits all information to the adjoining subsystems.

Since these properties dispense with preprocessing and post-processing (required in conventional information transmission to maintain communication between senders and receivers), transmission control data is not exchanged; furthermore, there is no common controller that maintains the entire system. Most important, the control of data transmission is held by the receiver, not the sender: Each subsystem recognizes the information received and fetches only what it needs. The kind of information fetched varies according to the function of each subsystem and changes with the state of the subsystem or with its surrounding conditions. Information is transmitted from the generating point to each subsystem by the shortest route.

As information is transmitted to all subsystems at the time of its generation, a subsystem can fetch that information and can use it as needed without any time lag or concern for the condition of other subsystems. There is no need to establish priority transmission or to compensate for information loss due to system failure. Nor does transmission speed need to be increased to ensure immediate processing.

In conventional systems, the effective transmission volume is considerably lower than indicated, because it is reduced by the exchange of control data. In ADS, however, the effective transmission volume is approximately indicated because there is no flow of control data in the transmission line. Each subsystem must protect itself against subsystem abnormalities that threaten ADS. For this reason, each subsystem has a detection and prevention function for the failures of the other subsystems, which is based on the information of each subsystem and its vicinity. Using this function, each subsystem detects the abnormality of other subsystems, protects itself against the propagation of failure of other subsystems, and prevents propagation of its failure to other subsystems.

The supervisory and management functions for the entire systems have to be recognized as those of autonomous subsystems, since they are individual and independent.

4.2. Software Structure

A software system consists of subsystems, all of which satisfy the before- mentioned three properties.

They suggest that every software subsystem requires an intelligence to manage itself and to coordinate with other subsystems. That is, the software subsystem consists of not only the application modules but also its own management module, which is called the ACP(autonomous decentralized control processor) shown in Fig.2. Moreover, these properties do not permit a common resource among the software subsystems, because the fault of the common resource itself causes all the subsystems using it to operate incorrectly. Hence, a common file among the software subsystems is not acceptable in the autonomous decentralized software structure. For communicating and coordinating among the software subsystems without using the common file, the data field (DF) concept is proposed. Every software module is connected to the DF, in which every item of data circulates. All data is sent out to the DF as soon as it has been originated by the software module. The module does not continue to store the data without broadcasting it. The software modules copy the data in the DF with the support of the ACP when it passes over the ACP.

The following conditions are required to satisfy the properties of the ADS.

(1) Uniformity   Each ACP must be self-contained and independent of other ACPs, so that it can continue to operate even if others fail. That is, every ACP is uniform.

(2) Equality   Any software subsystem could behave incorrectly because of its faults. Therefore, it is not permitted

for one ACP to direct any other ACPs. That is, all ACPs are
equal in function.

(3) Locality   Failure of one subsystem could mean a
breakdown in communication and a failure to collect global
information from other subsystems. Hence, every ACP must be
able to control itself and to coordinate with the other
subsystems on a local-information basis only.

The uniformity and equality conditions mean that every processor installs the same ACP and there is no master-slave relationship among the processors. The content code protocol in Fig.3 is
used. The content code indicates the meaning of the data. Every
item of data attaching its corresponding content code is broadcast into the DF and it is selected to be received by the ACP. No
data in the DF has priority. Each ACP judges autonomously how to
process the data without being dependent on its priority. A
software module is driven by the ACP when all the necessary input
data, for which content codes are previously specified within the
ACP, is received from the DF and arranged.

4.3. Fault Tolerant Technique

Fault   tolerance,   expandability   and   maintainability   are
attained by the following ACP structures and functions.

4.3.1. ACP Software Structure

In this structure every software subsystem is connected to the
DF. A software subsystem in a computing unit(CU) has the same
structure as the main software system. Several ACP modules are
connected to the atom data field(ADF), which acts as a data field
in the CU. In the ADF, an area is set, which shows the relationship
between the module and the content codes necessary to execute
the module.

The data necessary to drive a module may be complex, and the
same data may be used at different modules. Execution-result
data, with its content code, is sent out through the ADF to the DF.

In this ACP software structure, the ACP has two basic functions: data-field management and execution management. By
these two modules, the data-driven mechanism is achieved.

Software fault tolerance can be improved by this software
structure and by the following ACP functions.

The ACP achieves software fault tolerance by means of two
functions: data- consistency management and faulty-module
management. Even if the management modules of one ACP fail, the

other CU's ACP acts independently to prevent error propagation from the faulty processor.

4.3.2. Data-Consistency Management

According to the fault-tolerance level required, the same application software module is replicated in the different CUs.

It is assumed that the total software system structure is not previously fixed and varies by the expansion and the failures of the software subsystem. Moreover, the replicated modules in the different CUs run independently, and some of them may be faulty. Faulty modules send out incorrect data or no data at all; also the timing of this may differ from that of normal modules.

The first function of the data-consistency management module is to collect

The second function is to select the correct data among 'the same data'. A threshold-voting technique is proposed for this selection. The correct data is selected through the majority voting logic by the software. This logic has two types. In its first form, it is performed for 'the same data' collected within a threshold time interval since the first data is received. In its second, the voting logic is realized after a threshold number of 'the same data' is collected.

4.3.3. Faulty-Module Management

The faulty-module management module detects the rogue module in its own CU and prohibits the sending out of the faulty data into the DF and judges the modules to be faulty or not by checking the execution time and the content codes of the output data.

Even if the module in one CU should fail to detect a fault, this fault can be detected by the other CU's data-consistency management modules.

4.3.4. Fault Diagnosis

For fault diagnosis, The Built-In-Tester(BIT) and The External-Tester(EXT) have a fault-analysis function and a fault-synthesis function, respectively. Each BIT broadcasts the results of the fault analysis. When EXT receives the fault detection and the bypassing information broadcasted from BITs, it recognizes that the faults have occurred somewhere in the area.

EXT can recognize multiple faults at system level merely by intercepting the BIT information. It need not direct the fault diagnosis to the BITs.

5. Subsystems of ADS

Some of the subsystems which consist ADS are shown in this chapter.

5.1. Autonomous Decentralized Loop Network System

The autonomous decentralized loop(ADL) is a system constituting a subsystem that is positioned at the same level as other subsystems. As shown in Fig.4, it has a double-loop structure designed for optical transmission in opposite directions. The network control processor(NCP) is a controller that controls the transmission line. Two NCPs in each loop are fused and connected to a host processor. The length of communication can be selected arbitrarily. In addition, the NCP has a built-in tester and is identical for both hardware and software; the software(stored in the ROM) is used for transmission control. Each NCP broadcasts an information containing the content code instead of the receiver's address. An NCP decides whether or not to accept the information on the basis of content.

The originating NCP does not need to know which NCPs are receivers or where they are located in the loop. This communication protocol enables every NCP to have autonomy in sending and receiving informations.

The loop is not occupied by any NCP, since each NCP functions in the store- and-forward transmission. When any new information is generated, the host computer sends it to the NCP with the content code. Since information is sent to the transmission buffer of an NCP by the FIFO system, transmission lags do not occur and there is no need for priority processing.

Detection, removal, and recovery of faults in the transmission line are performed independently by each NCP. Each NCP checks the line to determine the possibility of transmitting to neighboring NCPs and selects a bypass if the transmission is not possible. The NCP that has detected the faults and restructured the transmission route, periodically originates the loop check signal. The NCP that receives its own check signal cancels the alternate route and takes the normal route.

5.2. Autonomous Decentralized Multi-Microprocessor System

The fault-tolerant multi-microprocessor system based on the autonomous decentralized system properties is designed as an aggregate of microprocessors whose homogeneous structure and autonomous functions suggest organic cell. The cells, which connected in a hexagonal shape(see Fig.5) by the fault-tolerant bus(FTB) have the same characteristics as the ADL. The FTB, however, provides bidirectional gates for each cell. Gates are controlled by the cell. When an FTB fault is detected by the adjoining cell, the gate of that cell is opened and no information is transmitted further to cells. Each cell is connected with the three- way FTB and information generated in the cell is immediately and consecutively broadcast to the three FTBs in the format shown in Fig.3.

A cell receiving an information relays it in the other directions of the FTB(where the same information has not yet been received). If any cell fails to relay an information, the information is relayed by another route. In this way, communication between nonfailed cells is maintained.

This system constitutes a fault-tolerant structure; its functional reliability is assured by task distributions. While each cell executes one or more tasks, several cells are instructed to execute the same tasks and the results are fetched for checking by other cells. By so doing, (n-r) out of n can be selected--according to the importance of the task--by majority voting or threshold-voting.

5.3. On-Line Maintenance System Tester

On-line maintenance is provided by two components: the Built-In Tester, or BIT, which is installed in every subsystem for subsystem-level maintenance support, and the External Tester, or EXT, which integrates the BIT's information for system-level maintenance support.

Each software module, including the management modules in the ACP, can be easily debugged and tested by attaching an EXT to the DF. The EXT generates test data and broadcasts it into the DF. Only the corresponding module to be tested is driven by the test data, and its module outputs the results into the DF.

The EXT monitors the output data in the DF, and it can detect the faulty modules. The EXT can isolate those modules to be investigated from the others by setting the execution prohibition flags; this then prohibits the modules from successively executing.

6. Application to Real Systems

This autonomous decentralized control system concept is still in the research stage, but has been applied in various systems to control trains, multistage dams, water supply, production, iron and steel making process and so on. The realization of this new concept is not so rapidly accepted because of compromise with the already-accepted technologies, however, some of idea, mentioned above, are step by step applied to the control systems.

6.1. Train Control

There is a great demand for developing the rapid transit system with higher performance reliability, safety and efficiency. The total computer system for the rapid transit system has the following six major functions, which are carried out through the combination of elements located on the train, along the truck, in the stations and at the remote control facilities;

(1) Train supervision; The direction of train movement in relation to schedule.

(2) Train operation; The control of train movement and stopping at station.

(3) Electric power supply control; The control and supervision of traction power substations and electric rooms.

(4) Station management and control; The management of fare collection, control of public address and destination indicator.

(5) Alarms and malfunction recording; Alerting to malfunctions, breakdowns or problems, and recording their times, locations and items.

(6) Supporting business management; The management of operational logs and records for business, maintenance and technical statistics.

Based on the ADS concept, the decentralized computer control system has been proposed as shown in Fig. 6. This system provides a systemwide control autonomously among central control room, vehicles, traction power substations, passenger stations and other building facilities equipments.

Fig.7 shows the control system of Kobe City Traffic Bureau's subway, which was commissioned in June 1983. It ensures the quick and adequate transit guidance information and automatic broadcasting service at suitable intervals.

The local control units installed at all stations and in railway divisions, together with the management unit, are linked by ADL. The maximum transmission rate is 1M bps. As for the system size, the optical fiber cables have a total length of 40,000 meters, and computers incorporated include one unit of minicomputer, three units of 16-bit microcomputer, and 64 units of the eight-bit microprocessors. The NCP is mounted on a 5.3-inch x 6.8-inch printed circuit board, together with the power supply and the optical fiber link modules. It consists of one single-chip microprocessor, one EPROM (8K bytes), two 1600 gate array CMOS chips, one CMOS RAM, and three data-link controllers. Optical couplings are used for external interfacings to provide electrical insulation. The Local Control Processor(LCP) at each station is composed of three 8-bit microprocessors. It performs process control and the Expander Unit (EXP) performs input and output device control. The two LCPs perform in dual operation by receiving input data such as train positions at regular intervals from interlockings. The External Tester is installed at the maintenance center to monitor the status of ADL and other equipments connected with LCPs.

The functions were divided between the management system and the host at each station using the principle of "control by a decentralized system and management by a centralized system." Train movement, route signaling, transit guidance, and a broadcasting service are tracked by the host, while functions such as the train diagram, man-machine interface, and operating data control are handled by the management system.

Kobe City Traffic Bureau extended the underground route farther east from Okurayama Station, and to the west from Naya Station. Then extension of the autonomous decentralized train control system was easily done in 1985 and will be in 1987 in commissioning the new routes.

Figure 8 is a schematic drawing of the automatic passenger information system of the Marunouchi Line of the Teito Rapid Transit Authority, Tokyo. This system, designed mainly for passenger guidance functions, was put in operation in April 1983 at six stations, including the two management stations of Shinjuku and Ikebukuro. It is also realized to operate at the remaining 12 stations in April 1984. The system design was based on a principle of uniform control by all hosts, without a master control station. The two management stations are quite far apart from each other, but this makes the entire route a double system; one management station can perform the functions of the other in case an accident occurs at either end. The expandability of the autonomous decentralized control system permitted the remaining 12 stations to be incorporated in the existing loop with great ease.

Other three systems have been in operation at Yurakuchyo Line of the Teito Rapid Transit Authority, mono-rail line of the Kitakyushyu municipal Transit Authority and Keihan line of Keihan

Railway Co. and another 3 systems are now under construction.

6.2. Autonomous Decentralized FA System

In factory automation(FA) control and planning applications, it is strongly desired to provide highly flexible system. The configurations of the systems controlled are frequently modified because of enhancements in systems or changes in the system objectives.

FA system requires (1) unified management and control in all areas from overall production scheduling to on-line control at the smallest unit in production lines; (2) a high degree of expandability and maintainability in system hardware and software; (3) a high level of system reliability and fault tolerance.

To meet these requirements, the total FA architecture is based on autonomous decentralization concept.

The production administration and manufacturing facilities control are performed by organically combining three types of computers;

(1)   High order computer: Determines the product specifications and delivery period, and designs the products(CAD), while interconnecting the Business Department and Enterprise Department.

(2)   Mid-order computer: Performs the production plan and production design according to the data from arrangements, drawings and delivery timings made up by the high order computer, and transmits the resultant data to the shop microcomputer.

(3)   Shop microcomputers: Not only control the manufacturing facilities within the relevant shops, but also have the process control terminal function with the data displayed on the CRT(Cathode Ray Tube) screen.

(4)   Network: Data transfer system between the mid-order computer and each microcomputer, and between each shop microcomputer and the manufacturing facilities.

The key subsystem of this architecture is the autonomous decentralized FMCs(flexible manufacturing cell controllers) connected to each other with an ADL in Fig.9.

The FMC, a controller based on a 16-bit microprocessor, has been developed as the work center and shop level controller. Even during scheduled or non- scheduled power outages at the upper level business/process computer, processes at the FMC level must continue. Should the FMC fail, the surviving FMC's need to continue cooperative control and monitor functions.

Control software developed through conventional methods, such as use of conventional languages or a ladder diagram, is incomprehensible and hard to maintain. To resolve such difficulties and to provide a high level of system flexibility and maintainability, FMC has the features of rule-based control software, that is, knowledge engineering based software. Control logics are described by such problem-oriented forms as IF-THEN rules. Control actions are automatically inferred from the system situations by using production system methodology.

To ensure a high degree of expandability and maintainability in the network structure, the content-coded broadcasting is incorporated into data transmission.

The control code transmission means that any FMC can transmit transactions with a certain code, not with the destination address, and therefore, any FMC can receive transaction or some FMCs can receive the same transaction simultaneously.

As a result, the control functions or data processing functions can be transferred to any alternative FMC if the corresponding FMC has the same control or data processing logic in itself.

Control systems are divided into multiple FMCs according to the location of each work station for the purpose of avoiding total system failure, and then FMCs are connected to each other via ADL.

7. Conclusion

As the computer system and the control system are getting huger and more complex in response to social requests, they are required not only to be dependable but also to be expandable and maintainable without system shutdown. The ideal system with those features is observed in the living things. The recent molecular biology gives many suggestions to the computer system and the control system.

By analogy of the living things, the autonomous decentralization concept and the key technical issues are briefly presented here with Hitachi's R/D history and our several applications to the industry.

It is my great pleasure to be able to contribute to Barden symposium in honor of Dr. W. C. Carter, one of my dear colleagues of IFIP WG 10 4. Moreover, I would like to express my gratitude to Prof. A Avizienis for his valuable comments.

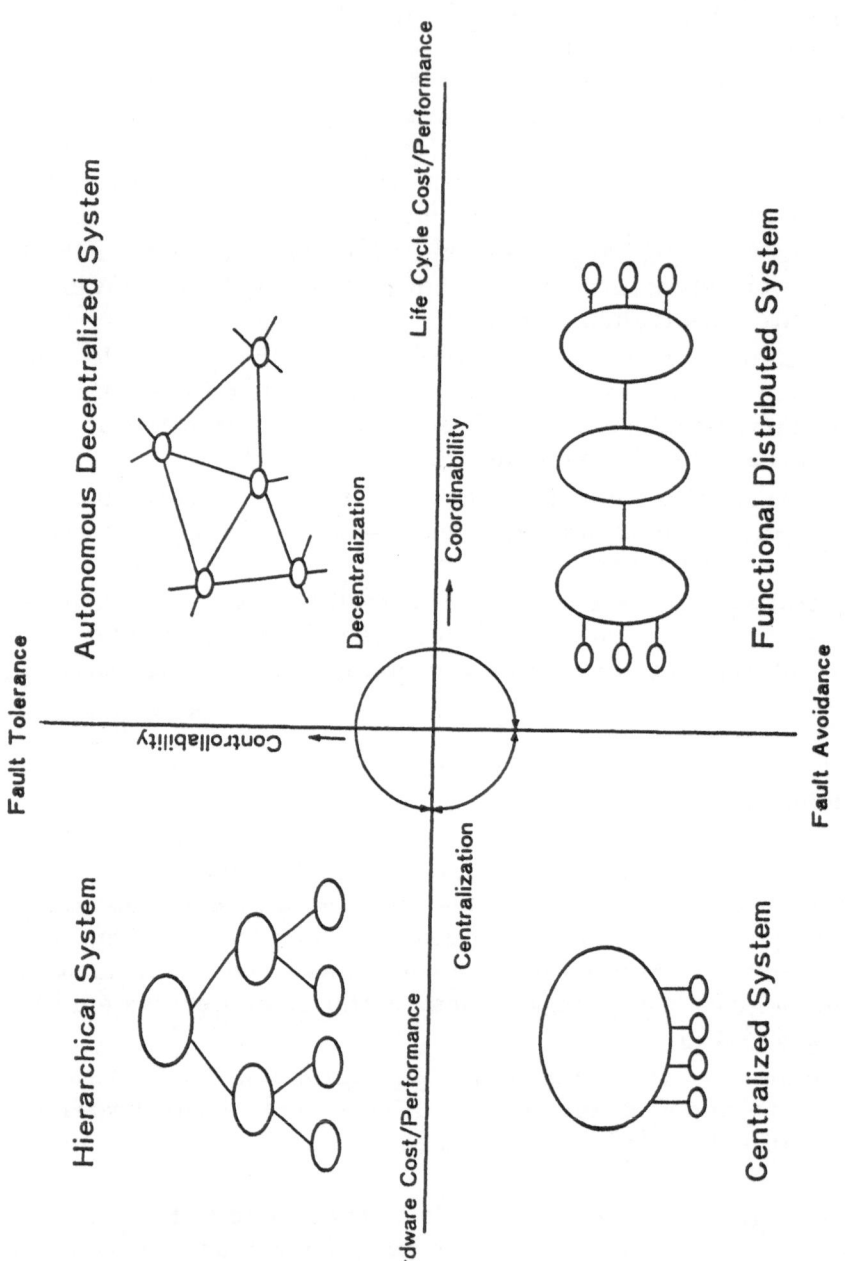

Fig. 1 System classification

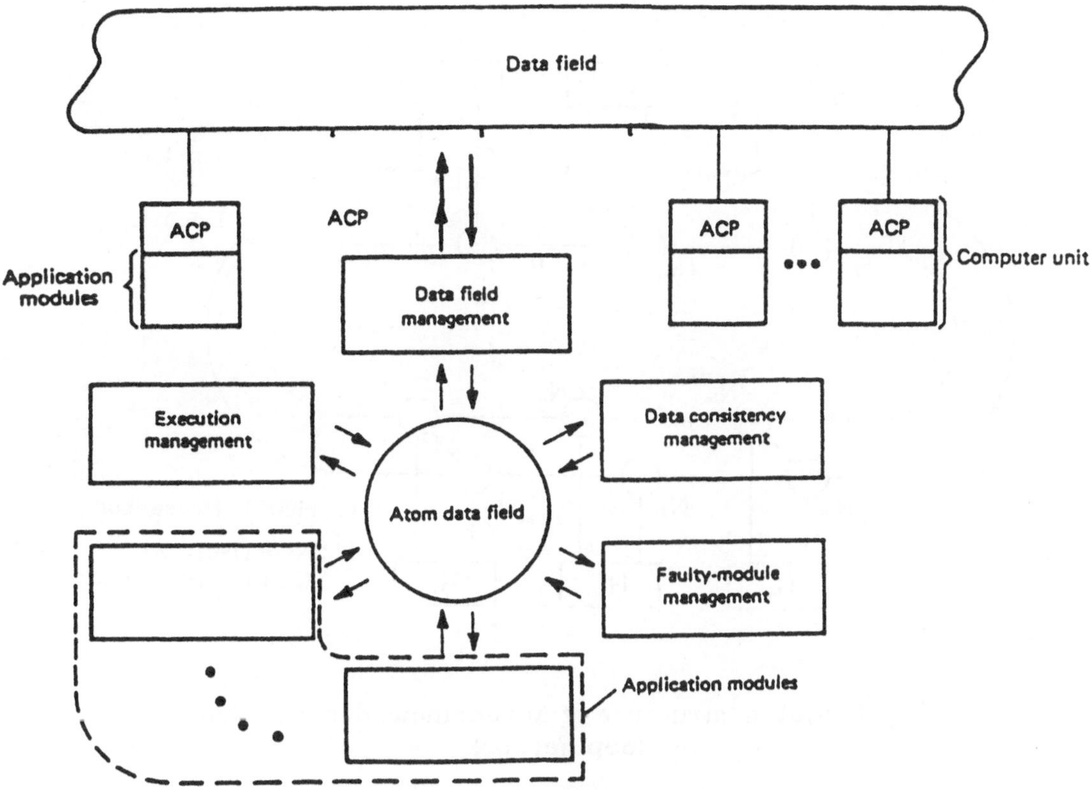

Fig. 2 System classification

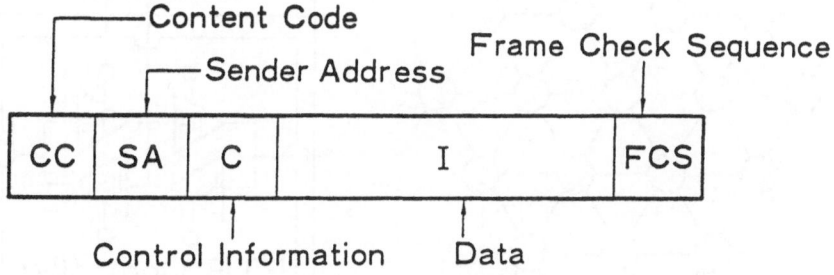

Fig. 3 Software structure

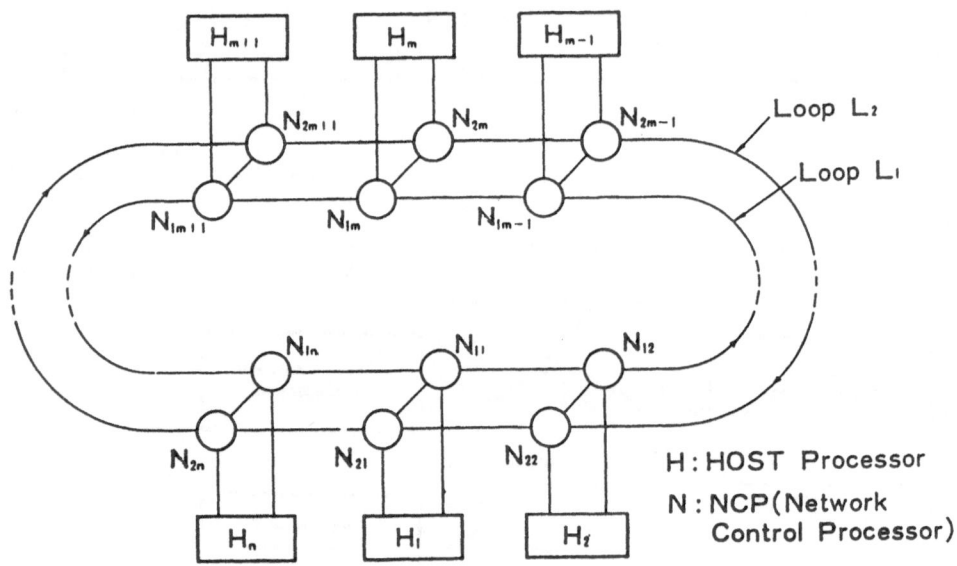

Fig. 4 System structure of autonomous decentralized
loop network

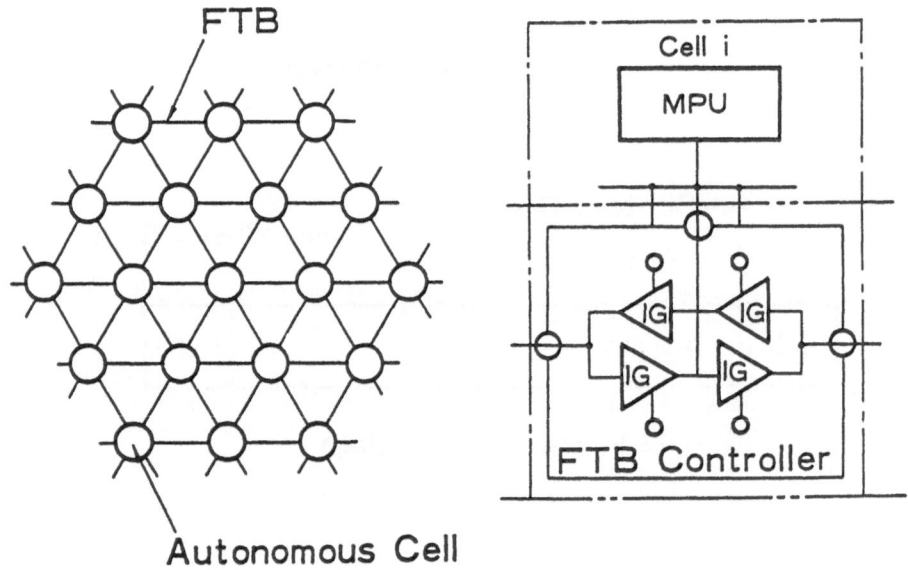

Fig. 5 System structure of autonomous decentralized
multi-micro processor

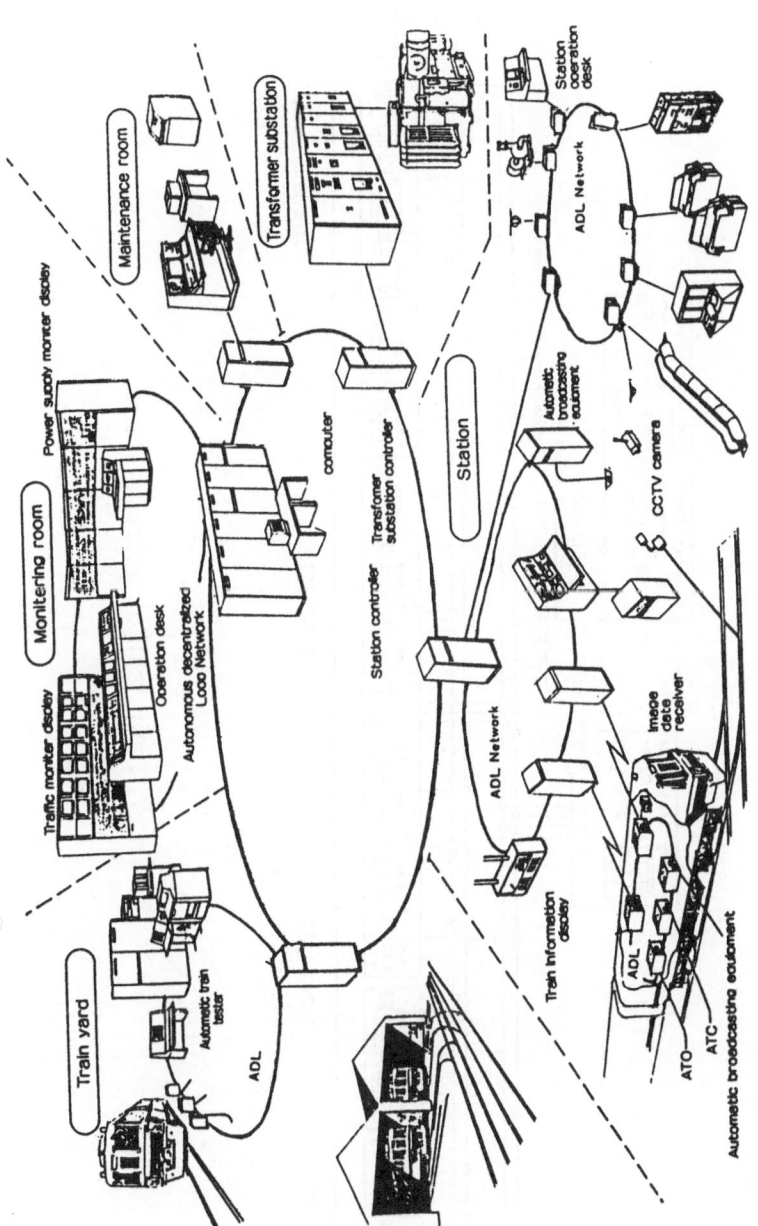

Fig. 6 Autonomous decentralized railway control system

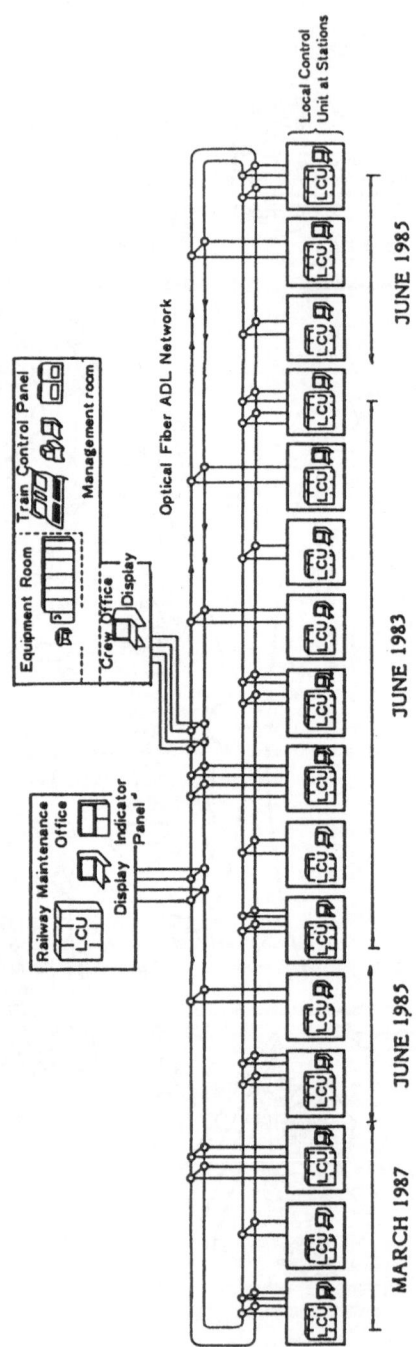

Fig. 7 Train traffic control system

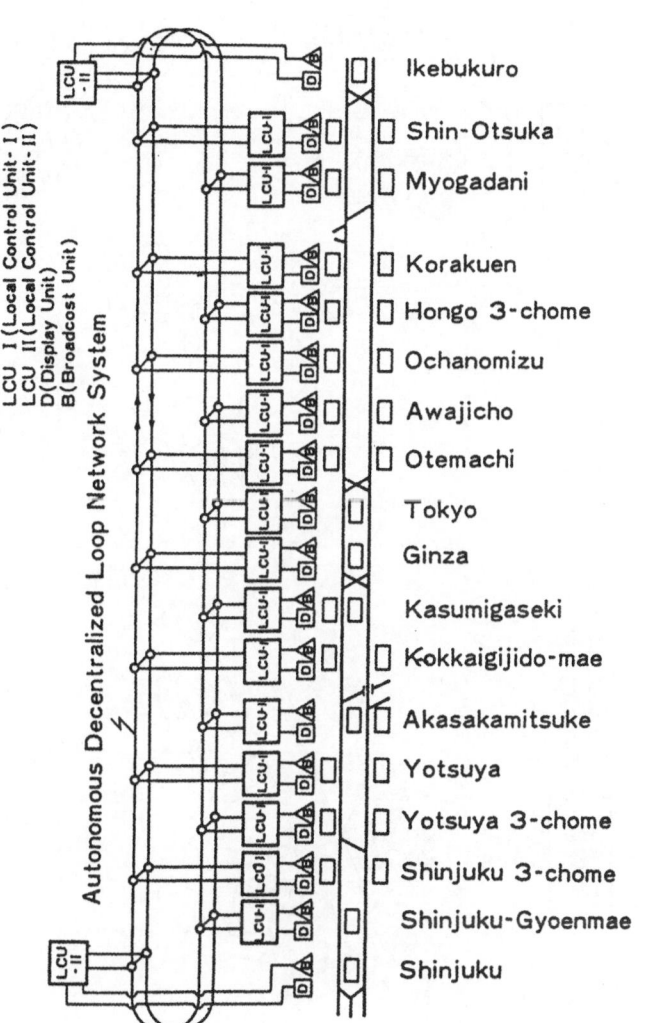

LCU I (Local Control Unit- I)
LCU II (Local Control Unit- II)
D (Display Unit)
B (Broadcast Unit)

Autonomous Decentralized Loop Network System

Ikebukuro
Shin-Otsuka
Myogadani
Korakuen
Hongo 3-chome
Ochanomizu
Awajicho
Otemachi
Tokyo
Ginza
Kasumigaseki
Kokkaigijido-mae
Akasakamitsuke
Yotsuya
Yotsuya 3-chome
Shinjuku 3-chome
Shinjuku-Gyoenmae
Shinjuku

Fig. 8 Passenger information system

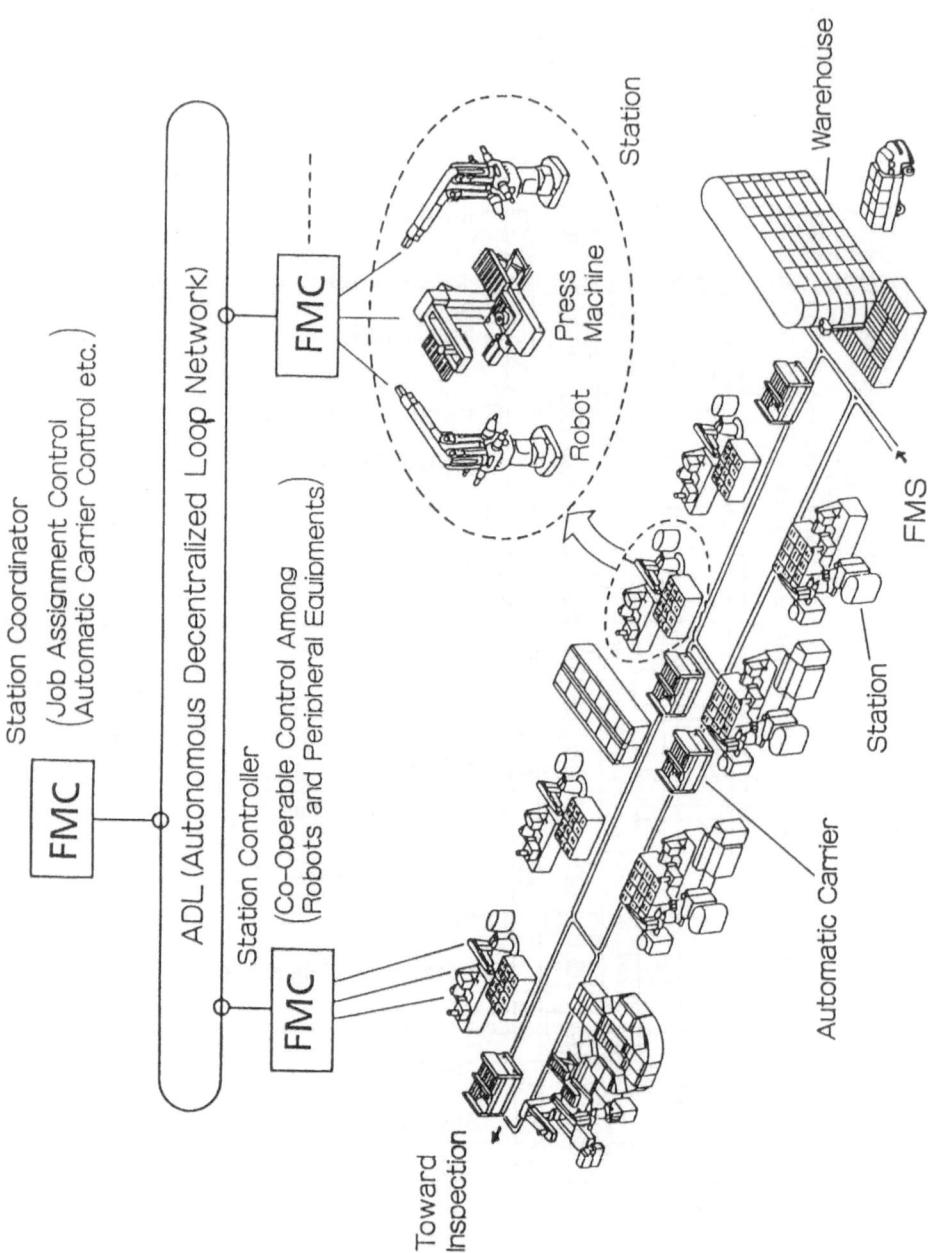

Fig. 9 Autonomous decentralized FA System

8. References

[IhShId 67] Ihara,H., Shiraishi,H., Ide,J., 1967: Control Computer "HICOM 2300" for Industry Use. HITACHI HYORON vol.49,No.4 pp.430-435 (In Japanese)

[FuTaMo 68] Fujiki,K., Takuma,U., Morita,K., 1968: Control Computer and its Application. HITACHI HYORON 50 year memorial issue pp.44-47 (In Japanese)

[MoSoIs 69] Morita,K., Soga,M., Ishikawa,T., 1969: Hitachi Control Computer System. HITACHI HYORON vol.51.No.2 pp.57-62 (In Japanese)

[Ka 78] Kamiuchi,T., et al 1978: H-80 - A Load Sharing, N:1 Back up Multisystem. COMPCON Spring '78 pp.261-264

[IhFuKuYo 78] Ihara,H., Fukuoka,K., Kubo,Y., Yokota,S., 1978: Fault-Tolerant Computer System with Three Symmetric Computers. Proc. IEEE vol.66,No.10 pp.1160-1177

[IhMo 82] Ihara,H., Mori,K., 1982: Highly Reliable Loop Computer Network System on Autonomous Decentralization Concept. Proc. FTCS-12, pp.187-194

[IhMo 84] Ihara,H., Mori,K., 1984: Autonomous Decentralized Computer Control Systems. IEEE Computer No.8, pp.57-66

[MoSaIh 81] Mori,K., Sano,K., Ihara,H., 1981: Autonomous Controllability of Decentralized System Aiming at Fault-Tolerance. IFAC World Congress(8th Triennial Congress) pp.1833-1839

[MoIh 82] Mori,K., Ihara,H., 1982: Autonomous Decentralized Loop Network. Proc. COMPCON SPRING 1982 pp.192-195

[MoMiNoIh 84] Mori,K., Miyamoto,S., Nohmi,M., Ihara,H., 1984: On-Line Maintenance in Autonomous Decentralized Loop Network: ADL, Proc. COMPCON FALL '84 pp.323-332

[MoMiIh 85] Mori,K., Miyamoto,S., Ihara,H., 1985: Autonomous Decentralized Computer System and Software Structure. computer systems vol.1, No.1,pp.17-22 Butterworths

[MiNoMo 83] Miyamoto,S., Nohmi,M., Mori,K., Ihara,H., 1983: FMPA: Fault Tolerant Multi- Micro processor System based on Autonomous Decentralization Concept. Proc. FTCS-13, pp.4-9

[MiMoIhMa 84] Miyamoto,S., Mori,K., Ihara,H., Matsumaru,H., 1984: Autonomous Decentralized Control and its Application to the Rapid Transit System. Computers in Industry vol.5, No.2 pp.115-124. Elsevier Science Publishers B.V.

A History of Research in Fault Tolerant Computing at SRI International

Jack Goldberg
SRI International
Menlo Park, California

1. Introduction

This paper offers a history of the research in fault-tolerant computing at the Computer Science Laboratory of SRI International. This research program, one of several in the lab, started in 1961 and from time to time has involved almost every lab member. The author did not initiate the program, but has had the good fortune of participating in it since its inception.

The paper starts with a brief picture of the SRI and CSL context and an overview of major themes and contributions in fault tolerance. It then reviews the history of the significant project work and related lab activities. It concludes with some remarks on future research directions.

2. The SRI and CSL Context

Not-for-profit innovation. SRI International, formerly known as Stanford Research Institute, is a not-for-profit institution dedicated to basic and applied research for industry and government. Shortly after its founding in 1948, SRI decided to add innovation to its charter of service, and encouraged its staff to build innovative programs in the various challenging technical areas of the day. Among these have been many pioneering activities in artificial intelligence, personal and organizational computing, and digital communication, as well as the laboratory's own program in computer science. Our association with creative researchers in other branches of computer technology has been tremendously stimulating and encouraging.

Innovation and relevance. Since SRI has no academic program and no endowment, its existence is based on contract research for clients. Some contract research organizations perform specific services for clients, such as testing and evaluation. SRI has chosen to be a leader in technology, and its clients look to it to lead them into new kinds of activities or new ways to realize their present goals. Many of our clients are not themselves the users of new technology, but sponsors of technical innovation, who hope that we will demonstrate the feasibility of new methods to manufacturers and users. This means that we must continually innovate, but our innovations cannot be so far into the future that our clients (or the communities they serve) will not be able to use the results. In other words, our survival requires our work to have the right combination of innovation and relevance. This reality is a continuing source of stimulus and frustration to us in seeking support for our work.

One of our responses to this need for relevant innovation has been to try to develop and present our results with the greatest feasible generality, often in the form of a new paradigm for how a system should be designed or analyzed. We will consider paradigm hunting later in the paper.

3. Origins

After ERMA. The Computer Science Laboratory had its origins in 1957, with the completion of the design and construction of the ERMA computer for the Bank of America (the first computer for commercial check transactions, and the origin of magnetic-ink check encoding). Several members of the design team had been frustrated by the ad hoc logic-design techniques of the time and, under the leadership of William Kautz, decided to build a program of research into more systematic techniques for computer design. The term Computer Science had only recently been invented. The first research program, a natural choice following the hardware-intensive ERMA project, was in Switching Theory.

Early fault intolerance and fault tolerance. At that time computers were being designed for critical applications such as telephone switching, train control and spacecraft, but there was great concern that the new semiconductor technology was too unreliable to allow such applications. SRI launched a major effort into an alternate technology, All-Magnetic Logic, that used only copper wire and multi-aperture ferrite cores. This technique allowed the building of arbitrary logic networks with prospects of extremely long life. (Commercial versions were built that indeed had remarkable ruggedness and reliability, but they were too slow to compete with semiconductor circuits.) The young Computer Science Group chose to pursue the complementary direction of fault tolerance. Its first effort in 1961, was a study of fault diagnosis and fault masking in logic networks, extremely-simple computer systems, and fault-tolerant magnetic-core memories, sponsored by the Jet Propulsion Laboratory.

An interesting, indirect interaction of the magnetics program and the fault tolerance program occurred when the JPL STAR fault-tolerant computer team, led by Al Avizienis, enlisted the talents of the magnetics researchers to develop a fault-tolerant (broken wires, shorted turns), all-magnetic switch for controlling subsystem power. It worked.

4. The Era of Technique Development

NASA ERC. Our early work in logic-level testing and redundancy encouraged us, both for its intrinsic technical interest and for its obviously growing importance for real systems. Our results helped us to win a competitive procurement for research into techniques for "Ultra-reliable Spaceborne Computers", conducted by the new (and since defunct) NASA Electronics Research Center. This contract gave us the opportunity to explore a wide range of issues in fault-tolerant computing. Included were
• Logic design of majority voters.
• Design of interconnection networks for fault-tolerant multiprocessors.
• Coding techniques for memories and interconnections systems.

Our work on majority voters and our reading of papers on renewal processes (Kruus) and Adaptive Logic (Tryon) led us to the notion of Hybrid Redundancy, a combination of voting (for error masking and fault diagnosis) and spare switching (for fault elimination). This scheme was subsequently studied in several theses (e.g., Mathur, Siewiorek), and became the basic algorithm of the SIFT computer.

Fault-tolerant interconnection networks. Our work on interconnection networks was quite extensive. It was stimulated by the publications of Clos and Benes on telephone switching networks built of elementary permutation cells. We adapted the approach for fault tolerant systems and also developed fault tolerant versions of the switches themselves. In retrospect, the work (presented as a prize-winning paper at FJCC 68) presaged the

explosive growth in fault tolerant multistage interconnection networks of recent years.

A fortuitous meeting in UCLA. This work earned Karl Levitt and me
several invitations to lecture at sessions of Al Avizienis's summer
course on fault-tolerant computing at UCLA, in the early 70s. A
Mr. Nick Murray, of NASA Langley Research Center, was a student
in one of these courses, and one day we got a question from Mr.
Murray: Would we be interested in putting the various techniques
we had been espousing into a real system? That question led to
the SIFT program, and was the start of a relationship with one of
the most supportive and technically active research monitors we
have encountered.

An attempt at charting a course for fault tolerance research. The
fifth symposium on fault tolerant computing, in Paris, 1975, came
at a time when the lab had some decent research results under its
belt, and thus it gave me the opportunity to take a broad view of
the research in which we had been engaged. Fault-tolerant computing had been served well by the classical notion of fault as a
fixed malfunction in a logic element, but reports from the field
were showing that this model was being stretched to the breaking
point. Therefore, I tried to come to grip with the question "what is
a fault?", and with possible new approaches to fault tolerance. I
made some effort to take note of recent results in other areas of
computer science, e.g., software methodology and artificial intelligence.

The paper that resulted, "New Problems in Fault-Tolerant
Computing"[7], presented two-dozen problems in the areas of Distributed Systems, Hierarchical Systems, Reliability Analysis, System Integration, Intelligent Fault Tolerance, and Optimization. In
the interim, many of the issues have been pursued within the Fault
Tolerance and other research communities. Several have not, for
example operator errors (which I labeled "Fool Tolerance", in a
whimsical mood), and goal-directed fault tolerance. For these two
items, at least, the problems and opportunities have not gone
away (see the section on New Directions). The question "what is a
fault" remains as fresh as ever.

5. The SIFT Program

An historic lab enterprise. The theoretical and technique development work conducted during the period 1961-76 reached its frui-
tion in the SIFT (Software Implemented Fault Tolerance) computer
development program [8, 9]. The SIFT program required us to
integrate previously independent techniques in a practical

working prototype. Through the foresightedness of the sponsor, NASA Langley Research Center, we were allowed to add yet another techniques to the list, the new and unexplored art of formal verification of fault-tolerant designs.

Should we do it? The laboratory was not at all in full agreement about undertaking such an ambitious effort. Some members were concerned that it would divert us from basic research, others that it was too risky, but there was sufficient agreement to proceed. Later we realized that our basic research interests were satisfied beyond our imagining in terms of intellectual content and new programs, and that our practical experience in the reality of fault tolerance gave us insights that could not be obtained from purely theoretical investigations. Added to these benefits must be reckoned the personal pleasure of having demonstrated the feasibility of some new technology that soon found its way to industry.

Getting started. Our work started with a study of requirements on the reliability and performance of computers that would be needed by the new generation of air transports. All-weather landing and the stabilization of new fuel-efficient airframes clearly would require a new level of reliability. We surveyed and recommended various architectural approaches that would allow such reliability. One was the concept of Albert Hopkins [14], which became the source of the FTMP computer design [15]. Another was SIFT, conceived during the study by John Wensley. The two differed in their mix of software and hardware in the implementation of fault tolerance functions.

Intuitions. Several notions were combined in our choice to emphasize software implementation. First, we felt that by maximizing the use of available hardware products, the equipment would tend to be intrinsically more reliable than if it made extensive use of specially designed parts (because of the lower production volumes of special designs). Second, we felt that reconfiguration below the processor level was likely to be decreasingly useful with the advance of device integration. Third, we were eager to apply the new technology of program verification, which at that time was oriented only to conventional (non-real time) software designs.

The intuitions in retrospect. We think the first two intuitions have been validated, except for performance. The overhead cost of software voting turned out to be a heavy damper on performance for the application (whose real-time and reliability requirements demanded a certain rate of voting) and technology at hand (a hardware voter would have been a profitable retreat from purity of concept!). Despite this shortcoming, the simplicity and portability of the SIFT scheme apparently has inspired its use by many other system designers. One unexpected application has been the use of the SIFT algorithm as a layer of operating system functionality in a distributed computing system [22]. SIFT is now seen more as a basic algorithm for fault tolerance than as a software-based implementation scheme.

With regard to formal verification, we succeeded in demonstrating the feasibility of mechanical proof for a small but central part of the software, but we found that the tools at hand were too crude and limited for the larger task. In the meantime, others have demonstrated good techniques for formal hardware verification. We will comment further on this matter in the Conclusions.

Unexpected science. Several problems arose during the design of SIFT that appeared first as engineering issues, but several of us recognized that they had general significance. These included: (1) synchronization of an arbitrary number of faulty clocks and (2) preservation of the consistency of replicated data in distributed systems in the presence of arbitrary and perhaps malicious faults (we found that assuming that signal values and timings were under the control of a malicious agent was a great way to visualize worst-case conditions!). The SIFT project was, therefore both a demonstration of the feasibility of existing fault tolerant technology for critical real-time applications and the seed bed for a new set of technical issues, generally referred to as the Byzantine Generals problem (a name coined by Leslie Lamport in a popular exposition of the concept).

An unintended model for research and development teams. Our perception of the scientific potential of the various design issues of SIFT was a happy consequence of the makeup of the research team. As a major laboratory undertaking, the project required help from both engineering and scientifically oriented lab members. The latter, who proved to be excellent engineers, were able to perceive the general implications of the specific problems they encountered. We believe that this combining of scientific and engineering talents in prototype system developments, with appropriate care for individual long-range professional needs, is an excellent model for conducting research.

A great sponsor. Another very significant factor in the success of the SIFT project was the strong support of the sponsor, NASA Langley Research Center, in several difficult situations. On one crucial occasion they were willing to fund a costly redesign of the interconnection system, which we proposed following a new worst-case analysis of combined fault and loading conditions. Also, in the final integration stage, they became directly involved in a heroic debugging effort that successfully exposed a particularly nasty hardware problem (multiple instances of time-and-usage-sensitive faults in memory chips). Their interest in SIFT has continued in an ongoing program of academic research conducted on SIFT and its companion computer, FTMP, in the AIRLAB facility at the LRC center.

A great competitor. Our interaction with the FTMP development team at C.S. Draper Laboratory had both technical and personal aspects. In the early stage of design, NASA wisely limited the communication between the two teams in order to ensure undiluted pursuit of their respective technical visions. When the barriers were dropped, the competition (essentially a struggle to succeed in our respective goals) was intense, fruitful, and friendly. This model for sponsorship and management of technical development has been noted with interest by several government research managers.

Leadership. John Wensley, who invented the SIFT concept and led the initial design effort, left SRI to form a company, August Systems, whose product is a computer for industrial process control based on the SIFT idea. At that time I was director of the Computer Science Laboratory, and a natural candidate for project leader by virtue of my past research and my experience with computer hardware. I worried that I could not do an adequate job in both roles. I received the assurances of enthusiastic support by CSL staff ("We're right behind you, Jack"), and agreed to take the leadership (those assurances were pretty well fulfilled). I learned a great deal about theoretical and practical fault tolerance, about project management (especially about what subcontractor delays mean to a development plan) and a bit about research management, but each role would have benefited so much more if it had been given exclusive attention!

6. Major Themes

6.1. Concern for the Extreme

Extreme requirements. CSL research in fault tolerance has been nourished by a wide variety of other laboratory research in logic design, architecture, software methodology and computer security. A frequent characteristic of those programs has been a concern with extreme conditions, arising either from advances in technology, e.g., problems and opportunities of ever-growing component densities, or from system requirements, such as extreme reliability in automatic aircraft control or extreme security for

sensitive data in a shared computer. This concern continues in
current CSL work, e.g., in studies of risks and safe design in computer controlled systems and in the design of highly parallel computers.

Extreme confidence. A concommitent concern in such applications is a need for extreme confidence in the correctness of the
design. Such confidence may extend beyond that provided by
simulations and experiments, and it has led us to the pursuit of
mathematical proof of correctness of critical properties, e.g.,
provably secure or provably fault-tolerant operating systems.

6.2. Searching for Paradigms

Why paradigms? Our response to the need for broadly relevant
innovation has been to formulate new methods for the design of
computing systems whose logic extends beyond the specifics of a
particular design or technique; the greater the generality, the
more paradigmatic. In this way we can test and explain the
significance of our work for other designers. Examples of some of
the paradigms we have developed include Cellular Logic networks
and machines, Propagation-limited Computing (these last two,
perhaps fifteen years before technology made them engineering
practice) Software-Implemented Fault Tolerance, Hierarchical
Development Methodology, and Provably-Dependable Systems.

Our general approach has been to

1. Examine current practice in computer system development for
    problems that are getting worse (e.g. the increasing need for
    dependable systems for critical applications, the increasing
    dominance of interconnection problems, the difficulty of syn-
    chronizing large, very-fast circuits), and

2. Observe techniques that are getting more powerful (e.g.,
    micro-electronics, formal specification and automated proof of
    program correctness).

At this point, a crucial input will often be a result from basic
research, often academic, that suggests a strong theoretical basis
for the new technique. For example, a 1963 thesis by Kruus at the
University of Illinois, on the use of a pool of spares to renew a
faulty system, led us to the notion of hybrid redundancy, and a
1967 paper by R. Floyd, of Stanford, on the use of loop invariances
to break a program into segments, encouraged us to believe that
program verification might become a practical art.

With these ingredients, we imagine models of some future
technology or development practice and express this as a new and
hopefully general development technique. A crucial step is to

project how this new technique may be useful in the real world for as broad a class of applications as we can find, so that the effort to develop the technique will be seen as a justifiable investment by a client. We have not had this model as a conscious paradigm, but that is what we really have been doing.

6.3. Themes and Concerns in Fault Tolerance

SRI's work in fault tolerance, both prior to and since the SIFT program, has encompassed most of the topics of concern in the field. In architecture: logic, functional subsystems, software, and systems; in analysis: fault modeling and model verification, and in requirements: reliability and safety. It has included theoretical studies, development of new design techniques, and in the case of SIFT, construction of a working prototype system.

In retrospect, the following themes and concerns appear among the diverse research efforts:

- A search for the appropriate level of abstraction
- A concern for the system context
- A desire to integrate fault tolerance with other computer technologies.

In the matter of **abstraction**, continuing questions for us have been "What are the important types of faults?" and "What is the most effective level of abstraction for dealing with a given fault type?" Our answers progressed in step with the continuing advances in device technology and system organization. For example, our first architectural studies, in 1961, were in fault diagnosis and fault masking in logic networks. We proceeded to investigate memory subsystems (1973), and then multiprocessor systems (i.e., SIFT, in 1976), in which the fault model was at the level of an entire processor. Our search also led us (as well as others) to a consideration of non-physical fault modes, e.g., in design and operation. (The path toward abstraction was not strictly monotonic inasmuch as we did return to the logic level in our 1982 study of on-chip fault tolerance for complex VLSI devices.

This drive to abstraction in the definition and treatment of faults was strongly nourished by the laboratory's work in software methodology, a field that has been dominated by a continuing advance of abstraction in programming. A direct impact of that work on the fault tolerance work was our use of techniques for program specification and verification of fault-tolerant designs. This question is re-visited in the section New Directions.

Our concern for **system context** has stemmed, in part, from SRI's status as a contract research organization. Relations with our clients frequently have required that we be aware of the system concerns that motivate their desire for new technology. It has also been encouraged by SRI's multidisplinary organization and ability to undertake substantial system development efforts. For example, in the studies that led to the SIFT development, members of an SRI laboratory working in the transportion area studied requirements for critical control in transport aircraft and helped to quantify computer reliability requirements. In the area of hardware, other SRI staff helped in studying the needs for electromagnetic shielding.

On the technical level, our pursuit of the system context was nourished by laboratory work on techniques for hierarchical system structure (a form of programming abstraction), which is deeply concerned with the relationship of functions and their context.

Our pursuit of the **integration of fault tolerance with other computer technology** has been expressed in numerous ways. Examples include the application of modern software methodology (specification and formal verification), new techniques for fault-tolerant distributed processing (problems of synchronization and consistency), and (to a limited extent) the application of techniques from the field of artificial intelligence.

We have also sought an integration of engineering and scientific viewpoints. In some instances, this has been deliberate, as in our undertaking of purely theoretical research alongside our technique-oriented work. In some cases, it has been fortuitous, as in the spinning off of the Byzantine Generals problem (dealing with consistency problems in distributed computing) from a seemingly routine problem in clock synchronization. That problem has taken on a life of its own; several workshops in the theory have been organized, and the number of papers is beyond easy enumeration.

We have considered these forms of integration to be vital to the health of the field in the face of (1) the natural trend of scientific disciplines toward specialization, (2) the inevitable discovery of fault tolerance by technologists who operate in different contexts, with the inevitable tendency to re-invention, and (3) the increasing demand for cost-effective ways to integrate fault tolerance with other performance objectives in systems, such as high computing power and programmability.

7. Summary of Fault Tolerance Research Projects

This section summarizes the significant project efforts in fault tolerance. It gives the subject, the sponsor, the date, the main topics of research, and the names of key participants. The listing of a single year may indicate the approximate midpoint of an effort; also, a span of years may have contained a dormant period. The titles listed are paraphrases of the official titles of the various projects. Individual contributors are designated by their initials. [1]

Reliable logic networks (Jet Propulsion Laboratories, 1961)

- A pioneering study of functional (non-structural) diagnosis of permanent faults in logic networks (WK [16])

- A study of fault masking of individual logic elements (WK, JG), soon to be outdated by integrated circuits.

Techniques for realization of ultra-reliable spaceborne computers (NASA Electronic Research Center, 1966-69)

- The concept (and name) of adaptive/hybrid redundancy, which combines voting (for fault masking and fault location), and sparing (to preserve the effectiveness of voting); a study of design approaches for large-order voting networks (JG [5]). The notion of hybrid redundancy was pursued in numerous academic theses and was the basis for the SIFT architecture.

- A set of interconnection switch designs for reconfigurable multiprocessors, exploiting the flexibility of the binary permutation element introduced by Benes and Clos (WK, KL, MG, JG, AW). A summary of the work was given in a prize-winning paper at the 1968 SJCC [19]

- Reliable computer architecture based on maximal use of fault-tolerant memories for processing functions (JG).

- A study of burst-error correcting codes for use in memories (KL, HS)

Survey of fault-tolerant architecture (Advanced Research Projects Agency, 1972)

---

[1]The individual contributors, cited by initials, are: Robert Boyer (RB), Bruce Clarke (BC), David Elliott (DE), Bernard Elspas (BE), Jack Goldberg (JG), Milton Green (MG), Dwight Hare (DH), William Kautz (WK), Leslie Lamport (LL), Karl Levitt (KL), Michael Melliar-Smith (MM-S), Robert C. Minnick (RCM), J Moore (JM), Peter Neumann (PN), Marshall Pease (MP), Robert Ratner (RR), T.R.N. Rao (TRNR), Richard Schwartz (RS), Robert Shostak (RES), Harold Stone (HS), Sven Wahlstrom (SW), Abraham Waksman (AW), Charles Weinstock (CW), John Wensley (JW), and Howard Zeidler (HZ). BC, RR and HZ were members of other SRI laboratories, and TRNR was a summer visitor. Incorrect and omitted citations are inevitable in such listings. We apologize to the victims of such errors.

- A survey of contemporary fault-tolerant architectures (PN, JG [33]).
- Novel byte-error correcting codes, oriented to byte-slice-organized memories and interconnections (PN, TRNR [25]).

Ultra-reliable air-transport computers (NASA Langley Research Center-NASA LRC) (1972-73)

- Survey of computing and reliability requirements for advanced commercial air transports; quantification of computer reliability requirements implied by existing FAA guidelines (RR, HZ).
- Survey of trends in device technology for the 1980s (SW, BC).
- Invention of the SIFT (Software Implemented Fault Tolerance) computer concept (JW) as part of a selection of candidate architectures (JW, KL, JG).
- Invention and analysis of schemes for highly reconfigurable memories (JG, JW, KL [6]).

Design of the SIFT computer (NASA-LRC, 1975-76)

- Design of an architecture based on software voting, reconfiguration of whole processor-memory pairs, and demand-based communication among processors via selected busses (JW, JG, MG, WK, KL).
- Proposal to use formal specification and proof to verify fault tolerance designs and support the definition of reliability models (KL, RB).
- Development of a Markov reliability model (MG,MM-S).
- Publication of a comprehensive paper on the architecture and proof concept [34]

Detailed design and integration of the SIFT computer (NASA-LRC, 1978-82 [10])

- Hardware design based on a standard avionic computer (The Bendix Corporation [4])
- Discovery of a serious performance threat while attempting to prove the correctness of the design for interprocessor communication. The result was a redesign, changing from demand-driven communication over redundant busses to broadcast communication in a fully connected network, over direct, intercomputer links (LL, MM-S [31]).
- Discovery of a fundamental problem while attempting to prove the correctness of schemes for clock synchronization and for consistency of data replications in the presence of faults. Engineering solutions were developed and general treatments were found for the problems for arbitrary numbers of faults (RS, MP, MM-S [31]) .

- Formal specification of the SIFT executive using the HDM-Special specification language (KL, MM-S).
- Markov models of reliability and availability (MG, MM-S).
- Software implementation in about 800 lines of Bendix-Pascal code (CW [32])
- A plan for the testing of fault latency and coverage in the physical prototype (WK).
- Design for a power supply capable of tolerating internal faults and loss of two out of four redundant primary power sources (August Systems).

Performance proving of SIFT (NASA-LRC, 1979-82 [21])

- Development of theories, techniques, and tools for proof of SIFT software and system properties (RB, DE, JM, MG, DH, KL, MM-S, RS, RES).
- Successful computer verification of a subset of the SIFT executive (RS, RES, MM-S [23]) .

Distributed fault-tolerant architecture (NASA-LRC, 1983-84)

- Concepts for a distributed architecture based on SIFT-type microprocessor clusters (KL, MM-S).

Reliable shipboard computer (Naval Oceans Systems Center 1983, 1984)

- Application of SIFT techniques at the operating system level to an existing Navy computer system (MG, JG).

Hardware support of fault-tolerant software (NASA-LRC, 1982, 1984)

- Special memory system design to support recovery-blocks operations in a Bendix avionic computer (MM-S, DE).
- General architectural support for a variety of fault-tolerant software schemes (JG, KL).

Fault-tolerant techniques for VLSI-VHSIC (Rome Air Development Center-RADC, 1982-83)

- On-chip testing (WK) and control of on-chip fault tolerance (JG).
- Study of asynchronous redundant logic (LL) and parallel processing (WK,DE).

Distributed fault-tolerant computing (RADC, 1981-83)

- Hierarchical function structure in distributed systems. (PN).
- The Byzantine Generals consistency problem in distributed systems (LL [18]).

Fault-tolerant multiprocessor arrays (SRI, 1984)

- A distributed-execution algorithm for load balancing in a distributed processing array (MP).

8. Related Research

The following research efforts in the Computer Science Laboratory had significant influence on our research in fault tolerance: [2]

- **Cellular logic**. Design of two-dimensional arrays for general logic realization (RCM), cellular logic-in-memory arrays, and testing of iterative arrays (1964) [17]
- **Propagation-limited logic**. Antiparallel asynchronous logic, self-timed cellular (now called systolic) logic, and the N(d,k) graph models of delay-bounded networks (1965) * [3].
- **Multiprocessor architecture**. The Binary N-cube array * [27] and a parallel architecture for the Discrete Fourier Transform (1975).
- **Hierarchical Development Methodology (HDM)**. A general approach to computing system development based on formal specification and verification of hierarchically-structured systems (1973-80).
- **Secure computing**. Design of a hierarchically structured, provably secure operating system (PSOS) * [24]; a tool for verification of the Multi-level Security property; data privacy; distributed secure systems (1974--).
- **Formal program verification**. Theories and tools for symbolic evaluation * and proof of program and property correctness (1972--) * [1, 30, 29].
- **Programming languages**. A candidate design for Ada; language and special architecture design for a functional programming language (Lucid) and an object-oriented language (OBJ).

9. New Directions

A researcher's view of the future is usually murky and tentative until he stumbles upon (or is overtaken by) a fertile idea. Stated another way, a statement of an Important Problem usually has a solution lurking in the vicinity. The following remarks are offered as exceptions to these truths.

---

[2]An asterisk indicates a paper that has received unusually a large and long-term citation record, and again, a single date may indicate the midpoint of an effort.

Ambiguity tolerance. We must continually revisit our basic assumption as to what is a fault. In examining problems of large, real-time computations, we have seen several sources of uncertainty or ambiguity that arise from conditions other than physical or conceptual malfunctions. For example, in decomposing a large problem into a set of small problems (to take advantage of multiple computing resources), a source of error results from the fact that a part of the context of a computation is unavailable until the sub-elements of a solution are assembled. Also, it is well known that for many problems, only heuristic methods are available, and that different heuristics may be more or less successful, depending on the data. Another source of ambiguity may be the need for estimating the value of data that is unavailable due to deficiencies in a computer's environment. None of these circumstances come from a fault in the subject system, in the classical sense. This suggests a need to extend the notion of fault tolerance, as a method of coping with *malfunctions*, into a methodology for coping with multiple sources of *ambiguity* in computations.

Very long lifetime. We need ways to extend unattended system life from the order of weeks, as at present, to years. This cannot be done merely by stretching existing techniques, but will demand bold measures.

Very-high-order fault tolerance. A related need is for tolerance of multiple faults in highly parallel systems. The number of processors in future systems will be 10 to some large power. Present fault tolerance doctrines, which aim to find and isolate single faults in an environment where faults are few and infrequent, are woefully inadequate. A new abstraction of fault definition is probably needed to deal with faults in systems of such complexity. The author once speculated that techniques of artificial intelligence may be useful in our field [7]. This was an early instance of what has turned out to be a standard speculation by people who do not know how to deal with, and even to describe their current problems ("What we need is an AI system for solving X"). Hope springs eternally.

Unification of fault tolerance with other system objectives. In current practice, system properties such as fault tolerance, security, safety, programmability, and high performance are treated as orthogonal design problems. When combined, the several objectives may become seriously compromised, or the cost of independent mechanisms for each concern may become prohibitive. Improved solutions may be obtained by good models and tools, but a deeper need is for theories of system design that unify multiple objectives [26,12].

Safety. Safety of systems that are controlled (in part) by computers (call them Plants) requires more than just a dependable program-execution engine. Real safety requires that the computer maintain an accurate model of both the plant and its environment (which may contain people and other plants), and that its programs be capable of guiding the plant through an intricate maze of multiple hazards, using incomplete and unreliable information. This view requires that we extend our concern from dependable program execution to dependable physical-information system operation.

Design. The goal of tolerating design faults remains elusive. We are coming to an understanding of the strengths and weaknesses of using redundancy to tolerate implementation faults [13] but the larger problems of tolerating faults in intent, requirement, specification, and design remain as refractory as ever.

Operator faults. Hardly anything fundamental has been done about operator faults (incuding maintenance and related operations), despite early recognition of this important problem, and despite the continuing string of tragedies whose source has some significant direct human component. Perhaps we engineers are not the right people to do it, but we should not be proud of the little attention we have given to the issue. Why can't we even include a black box on our system block diagrams labled "Operator fault monitoring and recovery", as a reminder of some designing--and some research to be done?

Verification. SRI's mechanical proof of a portion of the SIFT executive demonstrated the feasibility of formal verification for small systems. In the four years since that work was done, the tools have become stronger, but the systems have continued to grow more complex. The only hope seems to be more and more abstraction in our design descriptions, combined with rigorous adherence to simplicity in structure [11]. But then if we introduce heuristic methods to deal with uncertainty in very complex systems, what will it mean to verify that the system behaves as we intend it to?

10. Conclusion

The field of fault tolerance can support very special views of the world, or it can be a window for viewing the broad expanse of computing technology. The program of research at SRI has had its share of special topics, but we have tried to conduct our work as a part of computer science. We are optimistic about the vitality of the field.

11. Acknowledgements

This paper has described a community effort in an industrial research laboratory. It has taken place during a historic period in the growth of technology, where ideas have had to be shaped and tested by continuing collegial interaction. The author has many valued memories of his collaborations with colleagues and friends, both within the lab and in the fault tolerance community at large, from the earliest days to the most recent. It is a special pleasure to recognize the inspiration we gained from the work and personality of our friend William Carter, in whose honor this symposium is held.

12. References

[1] Boyer, R., Moore, J., "A Computational Logic", Academic Press,1979.

[2] Boyer, R.S., Elspas B., Levitt K.N., "SELECT--A System for testing and debugging programs by symbolic execution", In Porc. Intl. Conf. on Reliable Software, pages 234-245, 1975.

[3] Elspas, B., "Topological constraints on interconnecting limited logic", In Conf. on Switching Circuit Theory and Logical Design, pages 133-147, 1964.

[4] Forman, P., Moses, K., "SIFT: Multiprocess architecture for software implemented fault tolerance flight control and avionics computers", In In 3rd Digital Avionics Systems Conference, pages 325-329, 1979.

[5] Goldberg, J., "Logical design techniques for error control", In IEEE Wescon 66, 1966.

[6] Goldberg, J., Levitt, K.N., Wesley. J.H., "An organization for a highly survivable memory", IEEE Tr. on Computers C-23(7): 693-705, July 1974.

[7] Goldberg, J., "New Problems in fault-tolerant computing",In Dig. 5th Ann Intl. Symp. on Fault-Tolerant Computing, pages 29-34, 1975.

[8] Goldberg, J., "SIFT: A provable fault tolerant computer for aircraft control", In Proc. Info. Proc. 80, Tokyo, Japan, 1980.

[9] Goldberg, J., "the SIFT computer and its development", In Proc.4th Dig Avionics Conf. November 1981.

[10] Goldberg, J., Green, M.W., Kautz, W.H., Lamport, L.B., Levitt, K.N., Melliar-Smith, P.M., Schwarz, R.L. Weinstock, C.B. "Development and analysis of the software implemented fault-tolerance (SIFT) Computer", Technical Report, SRI International, Menlo Park, CA, February 1984. Nasa Contractor

Report 172146, Contract NAS1-15428.

[11] Goldberg, J., "The problem of confidence in fault-tolerant computer design", In Informatik-Fachberichte 78: Proc. GI/NTG conference: Architektur und Betrieb von Rechensytemen, pages 347-361. Springer Verlag, 1984.

[12] Goldberg, J., "A time for integration ", In Digest, 12th Ann. Intl. Symp. on Fault-Tolerant Computing, pages 42, 1984.

[13] Goldberg, J., "Perspectives in fault-tolerant software", In IEEE COMPCON 85, pages 264-269, 1985.

[14] Hopkins, A.L., "A fault-tolerant information processing concept for spaces vehicles", IEEE Tr, on Computers C-20(11): 1394-1403, November 1971.

[15] Hopkins, A.L., Smith, T.B., III, Lala J.H., "FTMP--A highly reliable fault-tolerant multiprocessor for aircraft", Proceedings of the IEEE 66(10): 1221-1239, October 1978.

[16] Kautz, W.H., "Automatic fault detection in combinational switching networks", In Proc. Second Ann. Symp. on Switching Circuit Theory and logical Design, pages 195-214, 1961.

[17] Kautz, W.K., "Testing for faults in combinational cellular logic arrays", In Conf. Record of 8th Ann. Symp. on Switching and Automata Theory, pages 161-174, 1967.

[18] Lamport, L., Shostak, R.E., Pease, M.C., "The Byzantine Generals problem", ACM TOPLAS 4(3): 382-401, July 1982.

[19] Levitt, K.N., Green, M.W., Goldberg, J., "A study of the data communication problems in a self-repairable multiprocessor", In Proc. Spring Joint Computer Conference, pages 515-527, 1968.

[20] Levitt, K.N., Stone, H., "The burst detecting capability of burst correcting codes", In Proc. Intl. Symp. on Information Theory, 1969.

[21] Levitt, K.N., Melliar-Smith, P.M., R. Schwartz, Shostak, R.E., Hare, D., Boyer, R., Moore, J.S., Green, M., Elliot, W.D. Integration, development, and evaluation of performance proving for fault-tolerance computers", Technical Report, SRI International, Menlo Park, CA, August, 1983, NASA Contractor Report 166008, Contract NAS1-15528.

[22] Lu, L.Y., "A virtual TMR node", In FTCS 15, pages 286-292, 1985.

[23] Melliar-Smith, P.M., Schwartz, R., "Formal specification and mechanical verification of SIFT: a fault-tolerant flight control system", IEEE TC C-31(7): 616-630, July, 1982.

[24] Neumann, P.G., Fabry, R.S., Levitt, K.N., Robinson, L., Wensley, J.H. "on the design of a provably secure operating system" In proc. of the Intl. Workshop on Protection in Operating Systems, pages 161-175, 1974.

[25] Neumann, P.G., Rao, T.R.N., "Error-correction codes for byte-organized arithmetic processors", IEEE Tr. on Computers C-24(3): 226-232, March, 1975.

[26] Neumann, P.G., "On Hierarchical designs of computer systems for critical applications", IEEE Tr. on Software Engineering, 1987. To appear.

[27] Pease, M.C., "The indirect binary n-cube multiprocessor array", IEEE Trans. on Computers C(26): 458-473, May, 1976.

[28] Pease, M., Shostak, R.E., Lamport, L., "Reaching agreements in the presence of faults", Jrnl. ACM 27(2): 228-234, April, 1980.

[29] Robinson, L., Levitt, K.N., "Proof techniques for Hierarchically structured programs", CACM, April, 1977.

[30] Shostak, R.E., Schwartz, R., Melliar-Smith, P.M., STP: A mechanized logic for specification and verification", In 6th Conf. on Automated Deduction, June, 1982.

[31] Weinstock, C.B., Goldberg, J., "SIFT: Software implemented fault-tolerance", In Dig. 9th Intl. Symp. on Fault-Tolerant Computing, pages 169, 1979.

[32] Weinstock, C.B., "SIFT: System design and implementation", In Dig. 10th Intl. Symp. on Fault-Tolerant Computing, pages 75-77, 1980

[33] Wensley, J., Levitt, K.N., Neumann, P.G., "A comparative study of architectures for fault tolerance", In Dig. Fourth Intl. Symp. on Fault-Tolerant Computing, pages 4/16-4/21, 1974.

[34] Wensley, J.H., Lamport, L., Goldberg, J., Green, M.W., Levitt, K.N., Melliar-Smith, P.M., Shostak, R.E., Weinstock, C.B.,"SIFT: The design and analysis of a fault-tolerant computer for aircraft control", Proceedings of the IEEE 66(10): 1255-1268, October, 1978.

The Evolution of Fault Tolerant Computing at the Charles Stark Draper Laboratory, 1955-85

Albert L. Hopkins, Jr.
ITP Boston, Inc.
Cambridge, MA 02138, USA

Jaynarayan H. Lala
C.S. Draper Laboratory, Inc.
Cambridge, MA 02139, USA

T. Basil Smith, III
Hamilton Standard Corp.
Carrollton, TX 75006, USA

ABSTRACT

Fault-tolerant computing became an issue of importance at the Draper Laboratory at the same time that digital computers began to be incorporated into guidance, navigation, and control systems. Early systems emphasized fault avoidance, with satisfactory results. More complex systems, which followed, incorporated redundancy.

Early redundancy architecture was constrained by size, weight, and cost penalties, and tended toward standby dual forms. As integrated circuits grew in complexity, more massive forms of redundancy evolved in Draper's architectures.

The challenge of full-time, full authority control of commercial aircraft motivated a number of research activities directed toward the realization of extremely low system failure rates. These activities revealed substantial problems to be encountered in the practical realization of redundant systems, even though such systems seem extremely simple in abstraction. One example of such problems is the synchronization of redundant clocks, where a fundamental rule was discovered that later emerged in a more general form as the "Byzantine Generals Problem". A hybrid-redundant multiprocessor with reconfigurable triads (FTMP) resulted from the research.

Recent research has capitalized on large scale integrated circuits, as well as fault-tolerant system architectures of the past, to yield a modular n-redundant, tightly synchronized computer, virtually transparent to software, thus able to capture software written for simplex systems, including certain n-version software forms. Computers of this type are being deployed in numerous applications.

1. Introduction

The Charles Stark Draper Laboratory, Inc., was formed in the early 1970's as a not-for-profit corporation, with a mission to serve the United States Government in system research and development areas. In this article, we refer to this corporation and its antecedent, the MIT Instrumentation Laboratory, as "Draper". The Instrumentation Laboratory was founded at MIT in the 1930's by Dr. Charles Stark Draper, who, with his coworkers, was responsible for several very important advances in gyroscopic instruments, including the development of inertial navigation systems. Real-time information processing was intrinsic to the operation of all of these systems; early implementations were analog. When transistors became available in sufficient number, performance, and reliability, Draper was one of the leaders in the design of miniaturized digital computers for guidance and control.

Today, Draper employs some 2,000 individuals in pursuing its charter, and remains one of the major centers in the design and implementation of fault-tolerant computers and systems.

2. Missile and Spacecraft Guidance, 1955-70

Draper's principal activity has been in guidance systems for missiles and spacecraft. Examples are Polaris, Poseidon, Trident, and Apollo.

2.1. Polaris

One of the earliest implementations of digital computers in inertial guidance was the Draper-designed Digital differential Analyzer used in guiding the Polaris missile. Reliability considerations raised redundancy issues even at this infant stage of digital system development. The decision in this case, as in most cases of the era, avoided redundancy and relied upon component engineering to enhance reliability.

2.2. Apollo

In the early 1960's the lack of redundancy became a volatile issue in the design of various on-board systems used for the Apollo project's lunar expeditions. The Saturn rocket's digital guidance computer, the LVDC, designed by the IBM Federal Systems Division, was a landmark triple modular redundancy design, in which a large number of redundancy problems were encountered and solved. Almost contemporaneously, the Apollo spacecraft's Draper-designed guidance, navigation, and control computer, the AGC, was chosen to be simplex. Both computers used first-generation integrated circuits. The LVDC had a shorter mission time than the AGC, but it had no backup. The AGC was backed up by alternative methods and systems in the Command Module and Lunar Module spacecraft. Nevertheless, the issue of redundancy for the AGC was raised time and again during the project. Consideration was given to substitution of the AGC by LVDCs, and to duplication of the AGC with either in-flight module replacement or a cold standby with manual switchover. Ultimately, the AGC remained simplex, and achieved an MTF of over 70,000 hours. No failures were ever observed in a mission.

2.3. SIRU-DCA

As the Apollo project neared its conclusion, Draper prepared a design study for a substitute "strapdown" system for the Apollo inertial guidance system. The name of this system was SIRU (strapdown inertial reference unit). The system contained a dedicated computer to perform continual coordinate frame conversions to allocate angle and velocity increments to the proper coordinate axes in a fixed frame of reference. As before, the avoidance vs. tolerance issue arose. In this case, the arguments led to a redundant computer architecture, which we called the SIRU-DCA, the SIRU digital computer assembly. The redundancy hypothesis in this case was primitive. The computers were dual. Two processor modules and two memory modules composed the DCA. Checking within each module was used to select the primary processor and the primary memory. The primary processor wrote results in both memories, so that the secondary memory was, in principle, "hot", i.e. it had equal contents to the primary memory. One important redundancy issue was solved, which was the issue of restarting after reconfiguration. The solution was called "single-instruction restart". It was rather like the two-phase commit protocols in use today, except that it was microprogrammed into each instruction. Any instruction could be restarted in either phase: the read/compute phase, or the store phase. Because the registers of the computer were in the memory modules, which were available to both processors, it was possible to stop and exchange processors within a single instruction under the single fault hypothesis.

Fault detection in the SIRU-DCA was by hardware reasonableness checks, such as parity, parity prediction, duplication with comparison, and complementary bus pairs. A simplex model of the DCA was built and tested. The coverage of these checks was assessed in an experiment and found to be substantially less than the 99 per cent that was originally sought. This was forewarning of the numerous problems to come in the realization of seemingly simple redundancy concepts.

3. Multiprocessors 1965-1980

Draper was intimately involved in integrated circuit technology, and in the latter 1960's was in a position to foresee with some certainty the coming of the computer on a single chip. Actually, at the time, the belief was that the "chip" would actually be an entire wafer. The direction of Draper's research in embedded computer architecture shifted to trying to capitalize on such computers through multiprocessing structures, an idea that sooner or later sprang up independently almost everywhere in those years (Alonso 67).

Beginning with the naive approximation that a multiprocessor is intrinsically fault-tolerant, a development activity was undertaken that soon became sidetracked by a series of proposed missions, which precipitated design concepts before the anticipated large scale integration became available. As these concepts were laid out, the notion of intrinsic fault tolerance in a multiprocessor quickly evaporated, as the myriad failure modes of a multiprocessor became apparent to the development group.

3.1. Manned Spacecraft Proposal

After the SIRU DCA design, in 1971, a redundant multiprocessor structure was proposed for manned spacecraft (Hopkins 71). Each processing complex had a triplicated memory module and dual processors. The dual processor concept was the single-instruction restart organization inherited from the SIRU-DCA. Memory modules were triplicated in order to mask single faults. This design represented a compromise position between the expense of triplication and the lower coverage of dual systems. Processors could be interchanged with minimal initialization, while memory contents were so valuable as to justify the expense of triplication.

The complexes were connected by serial buses, and voters selected valid transmissions in case of faults. This proposal was never implemented. NASA's Shuttle data management system was developed by IBM under different precepts, and consisted of a set of general purpose computers, redundant I/O buses, redundant inter-computer buses, and redundant interface units attached to redundant sensors and effectors. Four of the five computers receive identical inputs, execute identical instruction streams, and produce identical outputs. The remaining computer, meanwhile, is a concurrently operating backup whose software was developed by Draper independently of the software in the primary set. (This independence was intended as a defense against generic software errors, though ironically it compromised the launch readiness somewhat because of a launch requirement for certain independently-derived timing signals to be in agreement). Draper also contributed redundancy management strategies, I/O error handling, primary computer cluster synchronization, time management, and inter-computer communication to the Shuttle system design.

As fault detection and recovery coverage became increasingly important issues, and as hardware minimization became less important, the idea of dual processors gave way to triplicated processors as well as triplicated memories. It was clear that without massive redundancy, fault coverage would not be able to be predicted or measured with any accuracy. Consideration was given to a modification of the 1971 design where three processors and three memories were used, in order to cope with unsolved problems of fault detection in processors. What was really wanted was a means of flexibly allocating processors and memories to triads, but the methodology for doing so was elusive. Under National Science Foundation sponsorship, Smith proposed a Bus Guardian concept that provided a solution to the problem. The power of the concept was that it allowed reconfiguration to take place at any time, but only if it was commanded by a proper majority. No one misbehaving processor, memory, guardian, or bus could cause a catastrophic reconfiguration fault (Smith 73, Hopkins 75).

3.2. Cerberus

During this time, Draper commissioned a breadboard model of a single computer triad, called Cerberus. Cerberus could be configured as a redundant triad, or, alternatively, as a simplex multiprocessor. This permitted us to study tight synchronization on one hand, and multiprocessor performance on the other. Studies in this regard were sponsored by the National Science Foundation.

3.3. F-8 Digital Fly-by-Wire Aircraft

Draper supported the NASA Dryden Research Center's testing program of a so-called "fly-by-wire" reconfiguration of a Navy F-8 airplane. Fly-by-wire denotes a system in which mechanical linkages from the pilot to the airplane's control surfaces are removed and replaced by electronic control signals. Draper designed and constructed a triple computer system with triple I/O. The computers were the same kind as those used in the space shuttle, and the redundancy structure was a variation of the frame synchronized voting structure of the shuttle system.

A redundant I/O system was incorporated including front-end processing that gave each computer access to identical input data.

3.4. Research

Some research results from this period were useful to the eventual development of Draper's highly survivable computers. The concept of coverage by Carter, et al., made clear the sensitivity of success probability to the correct characterization of failure modes (Bouricius 71).

The Missionary work of Avizienis in fault-tolerant computing principles and nomenclature was an important underpinning of our work. Likewise, his early reliability models offered a useful basis for our later modeling efforts (Avizienis 75, Mathur 71, Ng 75).

At Draper, William Weinstein made a significant contribution to the modeling of correlated faults, discovering an analogy between correlation and non-coverage. (He also pointed out the ironic result that fault correlation "helps" reliability in a redundant system at the stage in life after a mean-time to failure has elapsed with no failures).

William Daly and John McKenna developed logic for implementing a fault-tolerant clocking system using delay elements and discrete circuits. They discovered the now-classical "3f+1" rule for the number of independent clocks required, where f is the number of faulty clocks to be tolerated. This rule allows for what have come to be called Byzantine faults as a result of the thorough examination of agreement phenomena by SRI, International (Daly 73).

(Later, John Howatt and Basil Smith developed a method for synchronizing variable frequency oscillators in a fault-tolerant manner (Smith 81). Their initial supposition was that this design could safely violate the 3f+1 rule, but Michael Melliar-Smith of SRI quickly proved that the rule holds in this case as well as all others.

Efrem Mallach analyzed the performance of a hypothetical multiprocessor, using actual Apollo guidance routines as models for the distribution of job step run times. Mallach's assumption was that run times and arrival times were random. His results indicated that a multiprocessor structure was viable as a real-time system control computer.

Robert Filene and Alan Green studied job dispatch strategies in the multiprocessing environment, and reported on a simple executive concept that was used later in the CARDS prototype discussed below (Filene 71).

Lala studied the reliability of partitioned systems, composed of some pooled resources and some dedicated resources. He also studied the performance of multiprocessors under the assumption that arrivals and run times were not wholly random. He discovered that the usual queuing curve does not apply to such systems when the near-worst case of dispatch delay is examined (Colson 75).

Christian Colson studied the impact of dedicating a processing stream to I/O management (1975).

Filene and Daly published a combinatorial analysis of the impact of mission abort strategies and coverage on mission safety and success (1974).

John Deyst and his colleagues did significant research on fault detection, identification, and recovery (FDIR) for redundant (analog) sensors and effectors using computational algorithms (Desai 79). Their work, together with the fault-tolerant multiprocessor and mesh network development, led to an integrated fault-tolerant system concept for avionics (Deyst 78).

3.5. CARDS

In 1974, Draper commissioned a prototype model of the multiprocessor architecture proposed by Smith (1973). It consisted of separate processors and memory modules, three serial buses, and bus guardians. Five processor triads and two memory triads were built, all fitting within two standard racks. The modules were all tightly synchronized, although the clock was not a fault-tolerant one. This system demonstrated the ability to run indefinitely in tight synchronism in the absence of faults and noise, and to re-associate and re-synchronize under executive control. Along with a fault-tolerant mesh network prototype, CARDS was integrated with a KC-135 aircraft simulation and a training cockpit to provide a demonstration of fault-tolerant system behavior. A program running in CARDS performed a digital autopilot function for the airplane, and simulated hard faults in the redundant system elements according to a fixed time schedule.

3.6. FTMP

In 1975, we began to address the problem of full-authority, full-time control of commercial aircraft, under sponsorship of the NASA Langley Research Center. This effort was sponsored "in parallel" with the SIFT program at SRI International (Murray 77, Wensley 78). The initial objectives for Draper were to identify a concept for a fault-tolerant computer, to model its reliability parameters, to provide a concept for software reliability, and to study means of validating the design.

The concept offered to NASA was derived from Smith's multiprocessor architecture, and was based on bus guardians. The logical structure was that of a homogeneous multiprocessor (hence FTMP for Fault-Tolerant Multi-Processor), where a shared memory made up of several memory module triads served several processing module triads. Each processing module contained its own "cache" memory, reducing main memory bus loading, and adding to the performance capability, while somewhat penalizing its reconfiguration agility (Hopkins 78a).

Numerous problems had to be solved in order to make this simple concept tractable. A particularly vexing problem was the degree of ambiguity in fault symptoms. Simple inductive logic simply could not pinpoint a fault source with one set of observations. Smith proposed a system of accumulating fault symptoms over a number of error events, and of adjusting the system configuration to give different perspectives on error events.

Another problem was that of faults that lasted such a short time that their error symptoms could not be traced through several reconfigurations to isolate the source of the fault. Lala proposed a probabilistic algorithm that assigned demerits to suspect units and isolated faults with a priori determined false alarm and missed alarm probabilities (Lala 83b). This technique allowed failure diagnosis to be based on fuzzy and confused observations. Particularly important was its allowance for the diagnosis of multiple failures in those cases where multiple but highly latent failures coexist in the system at the same time. Highly latent failure modes are particularly troublesome, in that they seldom manifest themselves, giving intermittent errors that appear to result from intermittent faults. Given the long detection and isolation times for such failures, it is, therefore, not impossible that multiple failures of this nature might coexist, considerably blurring the fault symptoms.

Clocking was another problem to be solved, which led to the solution by Howatt and Smith referred to earlier.

Still another problem was the need to design certain regions of the system in such a way that faults within one region were not able to propagate to other regions. Thus, physical fault containment regions were defined. Processors, memory modules, bus guardians, and bus isolation gates were each in separate fault containment regions.

Access to inputs and outputs presented a problem whose initial solution concept was to use special modules along with processors, memory modules, and guardians to service I/O buses.

Finally, the problem of cold start needed to be addressed. The FTMP could not be started from a cold, random configuration in the presence of an arbitrary number of faults. Automatic cold start was possible, but appeared to present a single point threat to the system while in normal operation. A manual cold load was therefore devised.

Reliability Modeling was accomplished with a Markov model, whose basic notion was the one earlier used by Avizienis, but whose structure was not constrained to any particular architecture (Lala 83b). Solutions were developed iteratively, which allowed parameters to be changed as functions of time as the solution proceeds. Intermittent faults were incorporated into the model following a notion used by Breuer (1973). Dispatch probability was also modeled (Lala 78).

Draper did not offer a proof-based verification scheme for FTMP as SRI did for SIFT. Rather Draper proposed that any flight versions of FTMP follow conventional critical system verification procedures as currently practiced by the aircraft industry, since this would have to be done in any case. Draper did offer, however, a sequential structured validation plan designed to produce analytical and physical models of increasing fidelity for analysis and test (Hopkins 78b).

A model of the FTMP was built by the Collins Division of Rockwell International, in Cedar Rapids, Iowa (Fig. 1). Packaging considerations led us to combine a memory module and a processor into a single line replaceable unit box along with bus guardians and isolation gates. I/O access was made part of each processor. Five sets of serial buses were used, each set containing processor, memory, and clock buses. Bus speed presented design problems. Transmission had to be made asynchronous because of unequal propagation delays in various circuits, and transceivers had to be specially located at the ends of the boxes in order to avoid creating serious reflections. Power transmission was a problem, as well.

From a software standpoint, the FTMP was able to be implemented within the architecture of the Collins processor, the CAPS-6, with the exception that a test and set instruction had to be added to the CAPS-6 instruction repertoire. All programming was in AED, a higher level language closely related to ALGOL.

Active and latent fault testing and system reconfiguration were extensively exercised using a gate pin fault injection facility (Lala 83b). Some twenty thousand faults were injected into the circuitry during this testing.

The FTMP development effort was highly successful. The prototype embodied solutions to numerous problems raised in the implementation of parallel hybrid redundancy with flexible assignment. The overall viability of an approach based upon tight synchronization, the high fault coverage of triplex computation, and the ease of failure recovery, were all confirmed by this project.

4. Triads and Quads, 1980-1984

In addition to the expected, and hoped for results, several unexpected lessons were learned from the FTMP design, as well as from the companion SIFT project. These lessons led directly to the FTP series of triplex and quad redundant monoprocessors.

Probably the most unexpected of these lessons dealt with machine performance and the overall tractability of the programming tasks associated with the FTMP and SIFT computers. Both teams overestimated the performance of their prototype hardware. The error source was essentially the same for both projects: the performance burden associated with "source congruency" or "interactive consistency" processing of each input data item was far greater than initially allowed for. In the FTMP, with a hardware assisted implementation of an appropriate algorithm, this burden cut overall performance to 20 - 30 per cent of projections. For SIFT the impact was substantially greater.

This bad news was ameliorated in the case of the FTMP by the ease with which the executive and demonstration software was assembled and tested. It proved to be no more difficult to program than conventional nonredundant hardware. Programmer productivity over the project averaged 40 to 50 lines of debugged code per day of higher level language statements, which is comparable to experience with nonredundant machines with similar software development tools. This was attributed to the moderate degree of software transparency afforded by the FTMP architecture.

It was also observed that neither multiprocessor performance nor hybrid redundancy was required for many of the potential fault-tolerant computer target applications other than commercial aircraft. This is due in large part to the astonishing performance increases which were occurring in microprocessor technology.

These factors led Draper to a new thrust toward a smaller monoprocessor architecture, called the Fault-Tolerant Processor (FTP) architecture. The principal components of the FTP design philosophy were:

1. Software transparency
2. Equivalent performance characteristics when compared with state-of-the-art nonredundant machines
3. Rigorous correctness of design

The fault-tolerant computational paradigm for this concept is to deliver redundant sensor data to all channels, perform a consistency interchange, execute the FDIR input algorithm, the control algorithm, and any output compensation algorithm in all channels, perform a consistency interchange on the outputs, and deliver the outputs redundantly to system effectors. All consistency interchanges are mechanized in the system as primitive hardware operations.

The objectives of software transparency and equivalent performance represented a significant break from the FTMP in one respect. The FTMP attempted to suggest new architectural features for real-time processing. Many of these suggestions were motivated by the need to accommodate fault tolerance, and proved to be counterproductive when measured against other metrics. The FTP architecture, in contrast, attempted to emulate known processor architectures. It was realized that a significant improvement in architectural merit would be difficult to achieve by consistently deviating from state of the art mainstream architectures, and that visible architectural accommodations for fault tolerance should be kept to a minimum.

A first generation triplex FTP was proposed as a dedicated aircraft engine controller, or flight control. A prototype design employing the Motorola MC68000 microprocessor was built for an

"Iron Bird" avionics simulator at the NASA Dryden Research Center. This design used relatively simple programmed I/O, with only internally sourced interval timer interrupts. While this design was representative of the software environment desired, it did not use either rigorously correct synchronization or input algorithms.

The second generation triplex design was the first FTP to use a rigorously correct I/O implementation. A second generation machine, based on the Zilog Z8000 microprocessor, was built for a client as a prototype industrial turbine controller. This machine was also the first fault-tolerant computer design that extended source congruency to the hardware processing of externally sourced interrupts. The exclusion of external interrupt sources had been a major accommodation to fault tolerance in the FTMP, SIFT, and first generation FTP designs, and represented a significant performance penalty in the conventional real-time environment. A close derivative of this prototype was built for Fairchild Republic as a prototype flight control system for the A-10 aircraft.

A third generation FTP design was initiated under internal R&D funding. This design returned to the MC68000 for its processor technology. The design could be implemented either as a triplex or quad redundant system. It was also the first FTP design to use a rigorously correct synchronization (clocking) algorithm. All succeeding versions of the FTP architecture have used rigorously correct synchronization, input, and interrupt processing algorithms.

5. Triads and Quads, 1984-Present

A number of significant lessons were learned from the third generation quad FTP. These lessons and several architectural innovations were incorporated in subsequent quadruplex FTP's designed and fabricated for NASA Langley Research Center and Argonne National Laboratory (Lala 86a, Lala 86b). These may be termed the fourth generation FTP's. First of all, the interstages, the additional fault containment regions necessary to tolerate Byzantine faults, were greatly simplified to eliminate voters, latches, and control and data paths, and instead perform just the principal function of replicating processor data to be distributed independently to other processors. Simplex source data selection was shifted from interstages to the communicators.

Another step was the incorporation of VME and VMX bus compatible I/O ports, which enables users to interface off-the-shelf cards to the FTP. Previously, only clock deterministic peripherals could be accommodated.

In 1984, NASA chose an FTP architecture as one of the building blocks for its Advanced Information Processing System, (AIPS). Each channel of the FTP was expanded to multiple CPU's that shared the additional fault containment regions as well as the paths linking the channels. This was a powerful multiprocessor system without the proportional increase in overheads of inter-connecting redundant channels. The AIPS version of the FTP has been built with two processors per channel. The concept is general enough to extend to multiple synchronized triads.

Another development added attached processors to the FTP that do not share the data exchange medium with the core processors. The attached processors operate asynchronously with respect to one another. They can enhance the throughput of the FTP considerably, for those noncritical tasks that do not need replication. Moreover, by delegating N versions of fault-tolerant applications software to single attached processors individually, and by allowing the core of the FTP to do the voting, a unified hardware-software fault-tolerant architecture emerges that has the overheads proportional to the sum of the hardware and software redundancy levels, rather than the product, as might be the case in a more brute-force approach. The concept is being tested in NASA's AIRLAB, mating the quad FTP with four VAX 11/750 computers, which will emulate attached processors.

Finally, some robust, simple, real-time operating systems have been designed for architectures of the FTP class (Alger 86). A timer interrupt-driven operating system is being validated by Argonne National Laboratory for application in the EBR-II nuclear plant.

6. Fault Tolerant Networks 1972-Present

In 1972, Smith proposed a mesh network topology as a high survivability alternative to I/O buses. This topology has been studied and implemented in various forms up to the present. The mesh network consists of point to point links between network nodes arrayed so as to form a mesh with the property that the loss of any n links does not isolate a node nor partition the network. Nodes must be able to receive commands from a master node (i.e. a fault-tolerant computer), and perform internal switching (Smith 75a, Smith 75b).

A prototype reconfigurable data acquisition unit based on this topology has been delivered to the NASA Dryden Center.

7. Current Philosophy for Fault-Tolerant System Design

Seven major precepts for fault-tolerant system design have evolved over the years at Draper through designing, building, testing, evaluating, and using fault-tolerant systems:

1. Redundancy: All fault-tolerant building blocks are based on the use of hardware redundancy to protect against random hardware faults.

2. Rigorously correct architecture: Redundancy by itself does not guarantee fault tolerance. It is necessary to meet certain requirements whose origin lies in the theory of distributed communication. These requirements in essence dictate that in order to tolerate f simultaneous faults it is necessary to have 3f+1 fault containment regions, that these regions be connected via 2f+1 disjoint paths, and that f+1 rounds of communication are required between the regions to achieve consensus.

3. Exact consensus: Redundant digital elements must be in exact agreement in the absence of faults, and all those that are correctly operating must be in exact agreement in the presence of f or fewer faults.

4. Process Synchrony: To achieve exact consensus, especially in the presence of Byzantine faults, it is necessary to meet the canonical requirements described in precept 3. It is further necessary to provide a level of synchronization between redundant processes executing on redundant hardware elements. Process synchrony is achieved in background using clock deterministic hardware transparent to the process, the operating system, and the applications programmer.

5. Containment of output errors: Processor interfaces to the outside world are designed so that a majority can terminate interfaces at will.

6. Hardware/software partitioning: To minimize overheads, fault detection and error masking functions are generally implemented in hardware, while fault isolation, error recovery, and hardware reconfiguration functions are implemented in software.

7. Temporal and diagnostic checks: Redundancy is augmented by low-overhead temporal and diagnostic checks for uncovering latent faults.

Adherence to these principles has resulted in architectures that have several attractive features. These include:

- User-transparent implementation of fault tolerance features and redundancy management
- High fidelity to simplex (nonredundant) architectures
- 100 per cent coverage for all single fault containment region failures including all malicious and Byzantine failures
- Very high useful throughput

8. Current Fault-Tolerant System Activities

Current fault-tolerant system architecture activities can be divided into two major areas, applications and advanced concepts.

8.1. Applications

The advanced research and development performed at Draper during the 1970's and early 1980's is starting to find its way into a number of real-time, critical systems. The field of applications is broad and far-reaching. Examples include advanced jet engine controllers, aircraft flight control computers, underwater vehicles, and so forth. A number of triplex and quad redundant Byzantine resilient fault-tolerant computers have been fabricated using various commercial microprocessors as well as the MIL-STD-1750A instruction set architecture. Current activities include design and implementation of theoretically sound fault-tolerant building blocks using state-of-the-art microelectronics technology, such as the 32-bit microprocessors, high-density gate arrays, and fiber optics, to provide increased throughput and I/O performance with reduced size, weight, volume, and power. The use and insertion of DoD's VHSIC line replaceable modules into such building blocks is under investigation.

8.2. Advanced Concepts

Since about 1983, research and development in fault-tolerant systems at Draper has been expanded to encompass many new areas of endeavor. The AIPS architecture addresses a number of issues important to distributed fault-tolerant systems, such as graded redundancy, function migration, and Byzantine failure protection in inter-computer communications (Lala 84, Lala 85). A proof of concept configuration of AIPS with five processing sites is now in the hardware-software integration phase, and will soon be undergoing extensive test and evaluation (Fig. 2) (Brock 86).

As the hardware fault tolerance technology has matured, the focus has shifted to errors in applications and operating system software. Two programs are under way in this area. One is addressing the operating system for an aircraft flight-critical computer using the hardened kernel approach, the other program is the one under way at AIRLAB to evaluate the N-version attached processor architecture, as well as to examine the many subtle issues in N-version schemes, such as correlated errors, and to provide protection against them with "confidence voters".

With the advent of small and powerful microprocessors, many schemes of connecting large numbers of processors together have been put forward in order to achieve powerful supercomputer systems. Although these parallel processors are currently being designed for non-real-time applications, there will eventually be a need for such large machines in real-time critical applications as well. For example, to implement some of the expert systems being proposed and designed now, such as the Pilot's Associate and the Electronic Flight Engineer, would require orders of magnitude more power than currently available in fault-tolerant computers. It is evident that the machines that implement such advanced expert systems will have to be dependable and reliable. Just as we discovered in the early seventies that a multiprocessor is not necessarily fault-tolerant, so are many people coming to the realization that parallel processors are not necessarily fault-tolerant just because they contain large numbers of microprocessors. A novel architecture, termed the Fault-Tolerant Parallel Processor (FTPP), has been designed at Draper to make large, parallel processors fault-tolerant, while minimizing the massive redundancy overheads, subject to having a correct architecture and connectivity to tolerate Byzantine faults. Another important feature of the FTPP is that the throughput and reliability can be dynamically traded depending on mission phase and other criteria. A hardware implementation of an FTPP prototype is in detailed design using Draper's internal R&D funding.

Other advanced areas of research at Draper currently include multipath distributed communication networks, wafer scale integration and its impact on fault tolerance and parallel architectures, fault-tolerant signal processors, and rule-based expert systems to aid architecture synthesis and evaluation. An expert system to help in the test, evaluation, and repair of fault-tolerant computers (TEARS) is also under development.

Fig. 1 FTMP

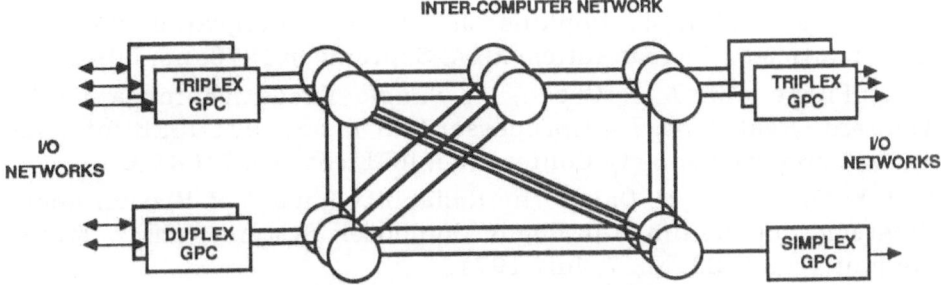

Fig. 2 AIPS proof-of-concept configuration

9. References

L. S. Alger and J. H. Lala, "A Real Time Operating System for a Nuclear Power Plant Computer", IEEE Computer Society Real Time Systems Symposium, New Orleans, LA, December 1986.

R. L. Alonso, A. L. Hopkins, Jr., and H. A. Thaler, "A Multiprocessing Structure," IEEE Computer Conf., Chicago, IL Sept. 1967, IEEE Cat. No. 16C51.

A. A. Avizienis, "Architecture of Fault-Tolerant Computing Systems," 1975 International Symposium on Fault-Tolerant Computing, Paris, France, June 1975, IEEE Computer Society, IEEE Cat. No. 75CH0974-6C.

W. G. Bouricius, W. C. Carter, D. C. Jessep, P. R. Scheider, and A. B. Wadia, "Reliability Modeling for Fault-Tolerant Computers," IEEE Trans. Comput., vol. C-20 No.11, pp. 1306-1311, Nov. 1971.

M. A. Breuer, "Testing for Intermittent Faults in Digital Circuits," IEEE Trans. comput., vol. c-22 no. 3, pp. 241-246, Mar. 1973.

L. D. Brock and J. H. Lala, "Advanced Information Processing System: Status Report," IEEE National Aerospace and Electronics Conf. (NAECON), Dayton, OH, May 1986.

C. F. Colson, A. L. Hopkins, Jr., and J. H. Lala, "Program and Input-Output Management for a Distributed Fault-Tolerant Digital System," 1975 International Symposium on Fault-Tolerant Computing, Paris, France, June 1975, IEEE Computer Society, IEEE Cat. no. 75CH0974-6C.

W. M. Daly, A. L. Hopkins, Jr., and J. F. McKenna, "A Fault-Tolerant Digital Clocking System," 1973 International Symposium on Fault-Tolerant Computing, Palo Alto, CA, June 1973, IEEE Computer Society, IEEE Cat. No. 73CH0772-4C.

M. N. Desai, J. C. Deckert, and J. J. Deyst, "Dual-Sensor Failure Identification Using Analytic Redundancy," AIAA Journal of Guidance and Control, Vol. 2, No. 3, May-June 1979, pp. 213-220.

J. J. Deyst and A. L. Hopkins, Jr., "Highly Integrated Avionics" Astronautics and Aeronautics, AIAA, September 1978, pp. 30-41.

R. J. Filene and A. I. Green, "A Simple Executive for a Fault-Tolerant, Real-Time, Multiprocessor," in Proc. 1971 IEEE International Computer Society Conference, IEEE cat. No. 71C41-C.

R. J. Filene and W. M. Daly, "The Reliability Impact of Mission Abort Strategies on Redundant Flight Computer Systems," IEEE Trans. comput., vol. C-23, No. 7, July 1974.

A. L. Hopkins, Jr., " A Fault-Tolerant Information Processing Concept for Space Vehicles," IEEE Trans. comput., vol. C-20, No. 11, pp. 1394-1403, Nov. 1971.

A. L. Hopkins, Jr., and T. B. Smith, III, "The Architectural Elements of a Symmetric Fault-Tolerant Multiprocessor," IEEE Trans. Comput., vol. C-24, no. 5, pp. 498-505, May 1975.

A. L. Hopkins, Jr., T. B. Smith , III, and J. H. Lala, "FTMP--A Highly Reliable Fault-Tolerant Multiprocessor for Aircraft," Proc. IEEE, vol. 66, No. 10, Oct. 1978 (a).

A. L. Hopkins, Jr., T. B. Smith, III, and J. H. Lala, "The Problem of Validation for a High Reliability, Fault Tolerant Computer," 1978 (b), not published.

J. H. Lala and A. L. Hopkins, Jr., " Survival and Dispatch Probability Models for the FTMP Computer," 1978 International Symposium on Fault-Tolerant Computing, Toulouse, France, June 1978, IEEE Computer Society, IEEE Cat. No. 81CH1600-6.

J. H. Lala, "Interactive Reductions in the Number of States in Markov Reliability Analysis," AIAA Guidance and Control Conference, Gatlinburg, TN, August 1983 (a).

J. H. Lala, "Fault Detection, Isolation, and Reconfiguration in FTMP: Methods and Experimental Results," 5th IEEE-AIAA Digital Avionics Systems Conference, Seattle, Oct. 1983 (b).

J. H. Lala, "An Advanced Information Processing System," 6th AIAA-IEEE Digital Avionics Systems Conference Baltimore, MD, Dec. 1984.

J. H. Lala, "Advanced Information Processing System: Fault Detection and Error Handling," AIAA Guidance, Navigation and Control Conf., Snowmass, CO, Aug. 1985.

J. H. Lala, "A Byzantine Resilient Fault-Tolerant Computer for Nuclear Power Plant Applications," 1986 International Symposium on Fault-Tolerant Computing, Vienna, July 1986 (a).

J. H. Lala, L. S. Alger, R. J. Gauthier, M. J. Dzwonczyk, "A Fault Tolerant Processor Architecture to Meet Rigorous Failure Requirements", 7th AIAA-IEEE Digital Avionics Systems Conference, Fort Worth, TX, October 1986 (b).

F. P. Mathur, "Reliability Modeling, Analysis and Prediction of Ultrareliable Fault-Tolerant Digital Systems," 1971 International Symposium on Fault-Tolerant Computing, Pasadena, CA, March 1971, IEEE Computer Society, IEEE Cat. No. 71C6-C.

N. D. Murray, A. L. Hopkins, Jr., and J. H. Wensley, "Highly Reliable Multiprocessors," in AGARDograph #224, Integrity in Electronic Flight Control Systems, P. Kurzhals, Ed., AGARD-NATO, Neuilly-Sur-Seine, France, Apr. 1977.

Y. W. Ng and A. A. Avizienis, "A Unifying Reliability Model for Closed Fault-Tolerant Systems," 1975 International Symposium on Fault-Tolerant Computing, Paris, France, June 1975, IEEE Computer

Society, IEEE Cat. No. 75CH0974-6C.

T. B. Smith, III, "A Highly Modular Fault-Tolerant Computing System," Ph.D Thesis, Mass. Inst. of Technology, Dept. of Aeronautics and Astronautics, Cambridge, MA, Nov. 1973.

T. B. Smith, III, "A Damage- and Fault-Tolerant Input/Output Network," IEEE Trans. Comput., vol. C-24, No. 5, pp. 505-512, May 1975.

T. B. Smith, III, "Test Algorithms for Active Input/Output Networks," 1975 International Symposium on Fault-Tolerant Computing, Paris, France, June 1975, IEEE Computer Society, IEEE Cat. No. 75CH0974-6C.

T. B. Smith, III, "Fault-Tolerant Clocking System," 1981 International Symposium on Fault-Tolerant Computing, Portland, ME, June 1981, IEEE Computer Society, IEEE Cat. No. 81CH1600-6.

J. H. Wensley, et al., "SIFT: The Design and Analysis of a Fault-Tolerant Computer for Aircraft Control," Proc. IEEE, vol. 66, pp. 1240-1255, Oct. 1978.

The Evolution of Fault Tolerant Computing at the Jet Propulsion Laboratory and at UCLA: 1955 - 1986

Algirdas Avižienis
David A. Rennels

UCLA Dependable Computing and
Fault-Tolerant Systems Laboratory
University of California,
Los Angeles, CA 90024, U.S.A.

1. Early Efforts at JPL

The Jet Propulsion Laboratory (JPL) is a research facility in Pasadena, California, that was founded by Professor Theodore von Karman of the California Institute of Technology as a test site in 1936 and was supported by the U.S. Army until October 1958, when it was transferred to the recently founded NASA, the U.S. National Aeronautics and Space Administration. The primary mission of JPL within the NASA structure is to develop unmanned interplanetary spacecraft and to conduct scientific investigations of the other planets of our solar system. Unmanned investigations of the Moon by Ranger spacecraft were the first step in the series of space exploration missions that have continued with the Mariner, Viking, and Voyager series of interplanetary spacecraft that thus far have reached Mercury, Venus, Mars, Jupiter, Saturn and Uranus.

Until 1958 the task of JPL was the development of guided rockets for the U.S. Army (the Corporal and Sergeant series) that offered interesting dependability problems of their own. Upon arriving at JPL in July, 1955 as a recent M.S. graduate from the University of Illinois, A. Avizienis was assigned to solve the problem of dependable guidance parameter insertion in the new Sergeant system. The previous Corporal system employed hand-set dials within the rocket's guidance compartment that did not provide any verification of settings. The design for the new Sergeant system employed a system that read a punched card in a remote command post, transmitted the readings to control a stepping motor in the guidance compartment, and then independently read back the settings to the command post, where they were matched against the card to verify that the proper setting had been accomplished. This custom-tailored error detection mechanism employed relay logic for its control and identified several dependability issues that reemerged a few years later in the context of spacecraft guidance and control computing.

Dependability issues for spacecraft computing emerged at JPL after its transfer to NASA in 1958. A. Avizienis encountered them soon after returning to JPL from a four-year educational leave with a Ph.D. earned in May, 1960 at the Digital Computer Laboratory of the University of Illinois, where he designed parts of the ILLIAC II arithmetic unit and did thesis research on high-speed signed-digit arithmetic that did not address dependability problems. The problem that was perceived at JPL was the need for longevity of the spacecraft computer: unmanned interplanetary missions of 1 to 10 years duration were being considered, while the mean-time-to-failure of contemporary guidance computers was measured in fractions of a year. The NASA-specified OAO satellite on-board processor employed component redundancy that was not suitable for integrated circuits, while the SATURN V guidance computer employed a TMR CPU and was designed for a mission length of 250 hours [Kueh 69]. Both designs from the IBM Federal Systems Division at Owego, N.Y., provided valuable insights, but did not offer a solution to the problem of unattended operation for several years, with the critical performance demands coming at the very end of a long mission that leads to the flyby or orbiting of a planet.

Late 1960 marked the beginning of a multi-year research effort at JPL. It was the search for an effective solution to the problem of building a long-life onboard information processing system for unmanned spacecraft. A. Avizienis was the only full-time researcher for the first three years, working with the support of research group supervisor John J. Wedel, Jr. and with expert advice on spacecraft design, guidance, control, and computing from members of JPL Section 341 ("Flight Computers and Sequencers") and other members of JPL technical staff.

Valuable information on the SATURN V computer was gained during visits to NASA Marshall Spaceflight Center in Huntsville, AL, and to IBM Federal Systems in Owego, N.Y. Supporting research on the application of error detecting and correcting codes in system design was done under a contract with the Stanford Research Institute, Menlo Park, CA., by Dr. William H. Kautz and others. Two meetings also provided new breadth of viewpoint: a small Conference on Diagnosis of Failures in Switching Circuits (17 talks, 54 participants) in May, 1961 at Michigan State University, and a well-attended (over 500 participants) Symposium on Redundancy Techniques in Computing Systems held in Washington, D.C., on February 6-7, 1962. The latter consisted of 23 presentations that ranged from solid results to sketchy suggestions and philosophical discourses [Wilc 1962].

2. The STAR Computer at JPL

Existing theoretical studies of the long-life problem indicated that large numbers of spares offered a promise of longevity, given that **all** spares could be successfully employed in sequence [Reed 62]. The JPL problem was to translate the idealized "spare replacement" system model into a flightworthy implementation of a spacecraft guidance and control computer. About one year after rejoining the JPL staff, A. Avizienis submitted on October 6, 1961 a ten-page JPL Interoffice Memo to Henry A. Curtis, the Manager of Section 341, outlining the design of "a Self-Testing-And-Repairing System for Spacecraft Guidance and Control", designated by the acronym "STAR". The proposal was fully supported by JPL and NASA research management, and the research effort continued for more than ten years, culminating with the construction and demonstration of the laboratory model of the JPL-STAR computer [Aviz 71a].

The above reference and many other publications have adequately documented the final design of the JPL-STAR computer, and it shall not be detailed here. However, an interesting view of the STAR system evolution may be gained from the October 6, 1961 JPL memo that is reproduced as Appendix A to this paper. The memo has been used as evidence for the patent application filed by JPL in 1967 that resulted in U.S. Patent No. 3, 517, 171, "Self Testing and Repairing Computer", granted on June 23, 1970 to A. Avizienis and assigned to NASA, but it has not been previously published.

The 1961-1965 interval of STAR research was dedicated to the evolution of system organization concepts and an in-depth study of error detection techniques that led to the evolution and adoption of low-cost arithmetic error codes in the STAR design. The AN, residue, and inverse residue arithmetic error codes were investigated and developed [Aviz 71b]. In 1963, Allen D. Weeks joined the STAR effort as a logic designer and John Buchok as a senior technician. In June of 1965 David A. Rennels, then a doctoral student at Caltech, accepted a summer position with the STAR project and worked on the design and construction of a byte-serial arithmetic unit for "AN"-coded 32-bit operands with the check constant A = 15 [Aviz 73]. D. A. Rennels rejoined the STAR project in 1966 to serve as the principal hardware designer, and later as the main evaluator of the STAR laboratory model, conducting numerous coverage evaluation experiments [Aviz 72], [Renn 73a].

The initial goal of the STAR design was to place the test and repair features into hardware; however, as the design evolved, it became apparent that a hardware-software interface had to be devised to enable the implementation of program rollbacks. To develop the software, the STAR team recruited John A. Rohr, then a Ph.D. student and ILLIAC III software designer at the University of Illinois. He joined JPL in September, 1967 and served as the principal software designer to the end of the STAR project. His work produced a programming system (assembler, loader, simulator, executive), a programming manual, test and demonstration programs, and culminated with the development of STAR rollback techniques and a system executive program that interfaced with the hardware features [Rohr 73a], [Rohr 73b]. The first program was successfully executed on the STAR laboratory "breadboard" model in 1969.

Publication of STAR papers was held back until the design was well defined; the first description was presented on request at a NASA-sponsored meeting in October, 1966 [Aviz 66]. The Central Control Unit described there and later renamed as the Test-And-Repair Processor TARP [Aviz 71a] was quite probably the first appearance of the Service Processor concept. The characterization of the computer as "self-repairing" appeared to be too specific and the term "fault-tolerant" was devised for all subsequent descriptions, beginning with a paper on "Design of Fault-Tolerant Computers" at the 1967 Fall Joint Computer Conference [Aviz 67]. This paper introduced the term "fault-tolerant" and the concept of fault tolerance into technical literature. Several technical papers dealing with various aspects of the STAR design followed during the next six years [Aviz 68], [Aviz 71a], [Gill 72], [Renn 73b], [Rohr 73b], [Aviz 73].

Additional research efforts were initiated in 1968, with Francis P. Mathur undertaking reliability modeling studies [Math 70a], [Math 70b], [Math 71] and George C. Gilley investigating the systematic extension of STAR techniques for the automatic maintenance of an entire autonomous interplanetary spacecraft [Gill 70], [Gill 72]. An adaptation of the STAR design to a specific application was carried out for the JPL Thermoelectric Outer Planet Spacecraft (TOPS) that was intended for the 15-year "Grand Tour" flyby of four outer planets of the solar system [A&A 70]. David K. Rubin led the effort, with support from the entire STAR team. Two elements of the STAR breadboard were designed outside of JPL. A highly reliable magnetic power switch was developed by the Stanford Research Institute, Menlo Park, Calif., and a fault-tolerant read-only memory was built by the M.I.T. Instrumentation Laboratory, Cambridge, Mass., under contracts from JPL.

Regrettably, deep cuts in NASA budgets for unmanned space exploration led to the termination of the TOPS project in 1972, and research on the STAR system breadboard itself was ended in 1973. The STAR system remained in the laboratory as a utility computer for subsequent research until July, 1977, when it was "mothballed" in a JPL storage facility. The California Museum of Science and Industry requested the STAR computer for an exhibit in 1983; however, it could not be located in storage, and its fate remains unknown.

The only apparent direct descendant of the JPL-STAR fault-tolerant architecture was the Fault-Tolerant Spaceborne Computer (FTSC) [Burc 76]. The architecture of FTSC is the joint result of two architectural studies [Conn 72], [Stif 73]. The STAR contribution came through the study done at Ultrasystems, Inc., Irvine, CA. [Conn 72]. The effort was directed by R. B. Conn, while STAR designers A. Avizienis, D. A. Rennels, and J. A. Rohr served as principal consultants in this study, sponsored by the U.S. Air Force. This study updated the STAR architecture by taking into account the increasing levels of circuit integration and combined all processing into a single replaceable CPU. The TARP was significantly refined and designated as the CCU (Configuration Control Unit). A second iteration of the design led to a duplication of the CPU for improved error detection. The complexity of the CCU was reduced by using the CCUs to monitor the pair of CPUs, and relegating to the CPUs the monitoring and recovery management of the rest of the system.

The study done at Raytheon [Stif 73] contributed a single-error correcting and burst-error detecting code in the memory and for bus transfers, as well as single bit-plane replacement within a memory module by means of a "rippler" switch. The STAR approach to pooled memory sparing and assignment was retained. Two "brassboard" models of FTSC were built by Raytheon and were evaluated by extensive fault injection tests [Burc 76]. However, the design needed about 20 custom-designed and radiation-hardened LSI chips. The rapid development of microprocessors made the FTSC single-processor custom design excessively costly to implement for space applications, and the project was terminated before any flight-qualified machines could be built.

D. A. Rennels took over the lead role in fault tolerance research at JPL in 1972. At that time, A. Avizienis initiated a major research project in fault-tolerant computing at UCLA, which is described in the second half of this paper. He also remained in a supporting role as an Academic Member of Technical Staff at JPL until 1981, collaborating with D. A. Rennels and others on some of the subsequent projects that are described below. Contributions of the STAR project were noted by the awarding of the biannual Information Systems Award of the American Institute of Aeronautics and Astronautics in 1979 and of the NASA Exceptional Service Medal in 1980. While both awards were given to A. Avizienis, they actually recognized more than a decade of dedicated effort by a diversely talented group of contributors, who demonstrated the feasibility of building fault-tolerant long-life systems for autonomous operation.

3. After STAR: Fault-Tolerant Distributed Systems at JPL

In the STAR computer hundreds of SSI/MSI chips were needed to make a single processor. Therefore the processor was subdivided into three simpler functional units (each with several hundred SSI/MSI chips), and the memory was subdivided into 4096-word modules. By 1970, major improvements were anticipated in component technology, and it was clear that single-chip processors would soon be available for flight computers. JPL spacecraft were already being designed with several independent digital controllers for command, telemetry and attitude control processing. It could be expected that small general purpose computers would take over these functions and also be embedded in various payload subsystems. It was clear that the next step in computing technology would lead to distributed systems for spacecraft onboard computing.

3.1. The Unified Data System (UDS)

The Unified Data System (UDS) project was begun in the early 1970s as an attempt to define and breadboard a distributed computer architecture to be used on the next generation of spacecraft. At that time the STAR investigation had been concluded, and A. Avizienis was directing a research effort at UCLA. The principal architects of the UDS system were D. Rennels, V. Tyree and B. Riis-Vestergaard. The architecture consisted of a set of computer modules connected by a redundant set of serial busses. Computer modules were of two types, High Level Modules (HLM) and Terminal Modules (TM). This approach made an important distinction between those (HLM) computers which supplied shared global functions (e.g. system executive, telemetry formatting, data analysis) and those (TM) computers which would be embedded in spacecraft subsystems and used for local control and data handling. HLMs were connected only to the buses, were non-dedicated and could be backed up by a common pool of spares. TMs had specific I/O lines to the subsystems in which they were embedded and had to be backed up by dedicated spares which had the same custom I/O connections [Renn 76].

The spacecraft for which this system was designed operated with a synchronous executive. All activities were time-driven. Each computing function was carried out in periodic intervals and all functions were synchronized much like gears on a clock. For example, a television picture was taken every 48 seconds, another instrument would go through eight 6-seconds cycles every picture cycle, etc.

A number of novel features were included in the design of UDS to enhance its reliability [Renn 78a]. A key element was to make its operation simple, predictable, and verifiable. We observed that although the system was required to satisfy hard real-time timing constraints, the minimum resolution on timing of inputs and outputs of various subsystems was a multiple of a basic period of several milliseconds. A real-time interrupt was supplied to all computer modules to define the minimum RTI interval. Inputs were sampled and held over specified intervals (of one or more RTIs) and all outputs were changed only at the end of the intervals. As a result, collections of computations could be treated as atomic events in the specified time intervals. They could be executed in any order with exactly the same results, and unused time could be inserted in each interval to allow an error recovery to occur without changing the input-output characteristics of the computations. Previous spacecraft computers were interrupt driven, making simulation expensive and the system response much less predictable because it was more dependent on the ordering of closely timed events. This approach made the system more predictable and simplified verification of its programs.

Another basic approach was to view the purpose of subsystem-embedded computers as a mechanism to create virtual subsystems which simplified system interfaces and reduced timing constraints on the buses interconnecting the computers. To guard against error propagation due to software errors, the subsystem-embedded Terminal Modules (which were expected to be supplied by subcontractors) were not allowed to initiate bus transmissions. Instead, the High Level Modules moved data between designated memory areas in the TMs on a periodic basis and checked on its validity. A software executive was developed by H. F. Lesh which provided scheduling of tasks in the various computer modules. A PDL-like specification language was used, augmented by timing constructs such as WAIT, WHEN, BACKSTART to suspend and reactivate programs in appropriate synchronization [Lesh 76].

A distributed microcomputer breadboard was constructed and programmed to simulate a Mariner-class spacecraft. There were two HLMs: one dedicated to spacecraft system executive and command, and another to telemetry and control of data movement between computers. TMs were implemented to control a flight television camera, a tape recorder, and the uplink-downlink functions. The breadboard was demonstrated taking a picture of an image across the lab, shipping it out as a digital telemetry stream, and displaying it on a monitor. This research breadboard was a precursor to a distributed computer system which will soon fly on the Galileo mission to Jupiter.

This research resulted in a better understanding of the system-level issues in a distributed real-time system. The approaches used for a fault-tolerant bus system, the techniques for fault containment, the hierarchic control strategies developed to simplify and reduce time-criticality of intercommunications, and special features of the system executive all apply to contemporary spacecraft systems. They were used later in the JPL Fault-Tolerant Building Block Computer (FTBBC). Due to limited resources, the UDS design assumed concurrent fault detection in processors but did not attempt to implement it in the breadboard. The subsequent FTBBC program addressed this issue.

3.2. The Fault-Tolerant Building Block Computer

In the mid 1970s, Reeve Peterson of the Naval Ocean Systems Center (NOSC) was managing a program in VLSI development, and was interested in developing circuits for fault-tolerant systems. He was interested in the possibility of producing fault-tolerant VLSI-based computers which could last throughout the operational life of their host systems and provide "maintenance-free missions." A joint program sponsored by NOSC and NASA was initiated. An architecture was developed by D. Rennels which resulted in a breadboard of the FTBBC [Renn 78b].

The JPL Fault-Tolerant Building-Block Computer (FTBBC) architecture was designed to use a small set of VLSI building-block circuits to interconnect existing microprocessor and memory chips to form Self-checking Computer Modules (SCCM). The SCCMs were designed to contain redundant communications interfaces which allowed them to be connected with other active and spare (SCCM) computers to form a fault-tolerant distributed system. Self-checking (morphic) logic design was used throughout the SCCM design to provide concurrent fault detection in each SCCM computer module. Four building-block circuits were designed: (1) a Memory Interface building block, (2) an I/O building block, (3) a Bus Interface building block which allowed the SCCMs to be connected with similar SCCMs into a network, and (4) a Core building block which compared the outputs of two (duplicate) processors, checked information on internal buses for proper coding, and collected fault messages from other building blocks. After detecting a fault the Core could initiate a program rollback to correct transient faults, and disable the SCCM if the fault persisted, indicating a permanent fault. A breadboard SCCM was constructed, and experimental fault insertion was carried out which verified the concurrent fault detection capabilities of the SCCM. Faults were inserted into both the operational logic and the check circuits by shorting randomly selected wires to ground [Renn 81].

The design used a redundant set of MIL-STD-1553A buses for fault-tolerant intercommunication, and a local executive similar to the UDS design was employed. I/O and software scheduling was synchronized by a real-time interrupt as in UDS. The majority of SCCMs were standby redundant, but the system executive function was duplicated in two SCCMs, so that if one failed, the dedicated backup could continue system control without excessive delays and loss of system state information. Only a single SCCM was constructed, therefore the distributed system has not been tested experimentally. An SCCM with a backup spare was used as a baseline fault-tolerant processor in an autonomous satellite study conducted by JPL for the US Air Force. Fault detection mechanisms and redundant elements were added to a USAF satellite design, and automatic recovery algorithms were written for the SCCM [Aren 83]. David Eisenman was responsible for much of the algorithm development and software architecture of this system.

3.3. Current Research Issues

The FTBBC design is characterized by the use of redundancy at several levels. Spare (memory and processor) chips can be employed within SCCMs to enhance their reliability. Similarly, redundant I/O and memory modules can be employed within each SCCM. Fault tolerance is achieved by also employing spare SCCMs within the network. The use of redundancy at several levels has been found to be necessary in order to achieve long unattended life with a moderate amount of spare hardware. This presents difficult reliability modeling problems, since subsystems with internal redundancy no longer have constant failure rates, and Markov models become very large. Modeling multi-level redundant systems has been shown to be an important new research issue. Similarly, the implementation of concurrent fault detection using self-checking logic raises new VLSI design issues. Fault Tolerance and Dependable Computing at UCLA: 1962-1986

In the early 1980s, a program was initiated at JPL to develop methodologies to design self-checking VLSI circuits which also are self-exercising. The goal was to develop a computer which in addition to having concurrent fault detection, also exercises its internal circuits in such a way as to flush out latent faults within milliseconds (concurrently with normal operation). The approach was to modify generic VLSI circuits used in self-checking computer design and add internal self-exercising features to expose both transient errors and permanent faults quickly. Existing circuits for concurrent fault detection were used to detect the faults which are exposed. A self exercising memory design was presented at FTCS-16 [Renn 86a]. Preliminary results indicate that, given that concurrent fault detection is implemented, the additional use of self-exercising design is both effective and relatively inexpensive.

In 1986, NASA support was shifted from fault-tolerant computing to the development of a dataflow machine, so at the current time JPL is assisting other government agencies in the development of fault-tolerant computers. This program involves assisting in program planning and conducting small technology development activities at JPL. Current activities involve evaluating the fault tolerance potential of several existing high-performance architectures, as well as developing and evaluating design approaches for implementing fault tolerance in them. An evaluation of fault-tolerance issues in Hypercube architectures was completed and alternative design approaches have been proposed [Renn 86b].

4. Fault Tolerance and Dependable Computing at UCLA: 1962–1986

4.1. The First Decade: 1962–1972

By 1960 Professor Gerald Estrin at the University of California, Los Angeles, (UCLA) had initiated research on the very stimulating and advanced concept of the "Fixed-plus-Variable" computer architecture. After a few exchanges of visits and presentations between JPL and UCLA, A. Avizienis joined the UCLA Department of Engineering faculty and Dr. Estrin's project in September of 1962 and started teaching undergraduate and graduate courses on computer system design and computer arithmetic, while also directing research at JPL. He presented the first formal course on fault-tolerant computer design at UCLA in 1966, and this course has been offered annually since then. A second, advanced graduate seminar course was established in 1975, and a seminar on fault-tolerant software was started in 1983. About 500 graduate students have taken at least one of these courses, and over 800 practicing designers and other computer professionals have taken a "short course" version offered annually through UCLA Extension, and also presented in other U.S. cities, in London, in Paris, and in Tokyo.

Research activities in fault tolerance began at UCLA in late 1962, with the first Master's thesis "A Study of Redundant Switching Circuits" by K.B. de Graaf being completed in June, 1964. This thesis was followed by 14 more M.S. and 18 Ph.D. theses on various aspects of fault tolerance, supervised by A. Avizienis, who also authored or co-authored over 100 publications in this area. Several more M.S. and Ph.D. theses were supervised and papers published by other UCLA faculty, as discussed later.

Fault tolerance research at UCLA during the 1963-72 decade was characterized by a very effective collaboration with the STAR project at JPL. The excellent laboratory facilities and expert technicians at JPL enabled the design, construction, and evaluation of the experimental STAR computer, while the academic environment at UCLA provided the opportunity to the researchers to present their results and insights through the rigorous form of Ph.D. dissertations. The STAR computer research led to the UCLA Ph.D. theses by F. P. Mathur [Math 70b], G. C. Gilley [Gill 70], and D. A. Rennels [Renn 73a], all directed by A. Avizienis, and the University of Illinois Ph.D. thesis by J. A. Rohr [Rohr 73a]. The immediate supervision of this research was delegated to A. Avizienis by the thesis committee chairman, Prof. J. A. Robertson of the University of Illinois.

4.2. Two Early Formative Meetings

The first organizational manifestation of UCLA activities in the fault tolerance field was initiated by A. Avizienis in 1965. It was the Workshop on the Organization of Reliable Automata, held in Pacific Palisades, California on February 2-4, 1966 and co-sponsored by the UCLA Department of Engineering and the Technical Committee on Switching Circuit Theory and Logic Design of the IEEE Computer Group. The organizing committee consisted of Dr. Raymond E. Miller (IBM Research, Yorktown Heights, N.Y.), Dr. Robert A. Short (Stanford Research Institute, Menlo Park, CA), and was chaired by Professor Algirdas Avizienis, UCLA. The event attracted 43 participants, many of whom later formed the nucleus of the IEEE CG Technical Committee on Fault-Tolerant Computing that was founded in 1969. Presentations were given by 30 speakers. Texts of the talks were not published as a volume, but the workshop speakers provided three sessions (12 papers) at the First Annual IEEE Computer Conference held on September 6-8, 1967 in Chicago [IEEE 67]. Since a published reference to this 1966 Workshop does not exist, the program is reproduced as Appendix B to this paper.

The success of the Workshop and the continued support and interest of several participants led A. Avizienis to propose to the IEEE Computer Group (IEEE-CG) in early 1969 that a Technical Committee on Fault-Tolerant Computing (TC-FTC) should be formed to promote further activities in this field. The approval of the IEEE-CG Administrative Committee was granted on November 18, 1969. A letter from Computer Group Chairman E. J. McCluskey, dated November 20, 1969, appointed A. Avizienis to serve as the first Chairman of the new TC-FTC and requested him to invite the founding members. The 18 initial members were: A. Avizienis, W. G. Bouricius, W. C. Carter, H. Y. Chang, J. Goldberg, A. L. Hopkins, E. C. Joseph, E. J. McCluskey, E. G. Manning, F. P. Mathur (TC Secretary), G. Metze, C. V. Ramamoorthy, J. P. Roth, R. A. Short, C. V. Srinivasan, S. A. Szygenda, C. Tung, and S. S. Yau. The new TC met for the first time on May 5, 1970 during the Spring Joint Computer Conference in Atlantic City, New Jersey.

The first objective of the new TC-FTC was the establishment of a technical conference, since an open conference dedicated to the theory and design of fault-tolerant computers had not been held since the 1962 Symposium on Redundancy Techniques for Computing Systems in Washington, D. C. [Wilc 62]. Co-sponsorship of the new meeting and strong organizational support was provided by JPL, and the initial International Symposium on Fault-Tolerant Computing took place on March 1-3, 1971 at the Huntington-Sheraton Hotel in Pasadena, California, with A. Avizienis serving as

Symposium Chairman, and W. C. Carter as Program Chairman. A total of 251 participants registered for the meeting, representing the following countries: USA 230, Canada 9, France 4, Japan 3, England 3, Federal Republic of Germany and Italy, 1 each.

The program consisted of 33 papers (including three from France, one from England, and one from Japan) arranged in six sessions, and a panel discussion on diagnosis and testing [Gill 71]. The session titles were: test generation and diagnosis, fault location and testing, reliability modeling and analysis, architecture and design, error protection and recovery, and software reliability. At the conference banquet, the distinguished space scientist and Director of JPL, Dr. William C. Pickering, addressed the participants, outlining plans for future exploration of the planets and noting the key role of fault-tolerant computing in this endeavour. Many participants of the Symposium subsequently visited JPL for a tour and a demonstration of the STAR computer that included fault injection tests during program execution.

The annual series of comprehensive symposia on fault-tolerant computing took off with an auspicious start, and the TC-FTC began building an international membership of fault tolerance experts. The Call for Papers of the second annual Symposium, to be held in the Boston, Massachusetts area on June 19-21, 1972 was distributed at the Pasadena meeting.

4.3. The Second Phase at UCLA: Scope of Activities, 1972-1986

A major new research effort in fault-tolerant computing began at UCLA in July of 1972, when A. Avizienis became the Principal Investigator for a five-year, $887,900 research grant "Fault-Tolerant Computing" from the U.S. National Science Foundation (NSF) and established the Reliable Computing and Fault Tolerance research group that has recently evolved into the Dependable Computing and Fault-Tolerant Systems (DC & FTS) Laboratory. Further research grants and contracts from NSF, the Office of Naval Research, the Federal Aviation Administration, NASA, the State of California, and industry have raised the total funding received for research support since 1972 to over $3.5 million.

Faculty participation in research related to fault tolerance also grew steadily: beginning with two co-investigators (Professors W. W. Chu and D. F. Martin) on the initial NSF grant in 1972, ten more regular faculty members and several visiting professors and research scientists have taken part in research projects during the 1972-1986 period. Graduate student participation has also been very strong. It is estimated that about 200 publications, 30

Ph.D. dissertations, and 20 M.S. theses have resulted from the research on dependable computing and fault-tolerant systems that has been carried out by faculty and students associated with the projects of the Reliable Computing and Fault-Tolerance research group and its successor, the DC & FTS Laboratory, established in July, 1985.

A broad range of research problems have been addressed, including fault-tolerant architectures for distributed systems, supercomputers, and real-time applications, modeling and evaluation of fault-tolerant systems, fault tolerance in associative processors and database machines, fault-tolerant VLSI design, arithmetic error detecting and correcting codes, design of self-checking PLA's, fault-tolerant computer communications, software reliability, and design methodologies for fault-tolerant systems. Research on the tolerance of design faults by design diversity was initiated in 1975, and has resulted in a series of N-version programming experiments, as well as the implementation of the DEDIX distributed supervisory system for N-version software, and the development of a design paradigm for diverse multichannel systems.

4.4. Methodology Research and a Design Paradigm

The specification and design of the STAR computer at JPL involved much improvisation and experimentation with design alternatives. It became apparent that the lessons learned during this process could serve as the foundation for a more orderly approach that would utilize a set of guidelines for the choice of fault masking, error detection, diagnosis, and system recovery techniques.

The first effort to present such guidelines appeared in the 1967 Fall Joint Computer Conference paper "Design of Fault-Tolerant Computers" [Aviz 67]. This paper introduced the concept of a "fault-tolerant system", presented a classification of faults, and outlined the alternate forms of masking, detection, diagnosis, and recovery techniques along with some criteria for choices between "massive" (i.e., masking) and "selective" application of redundancy. The design of the JPL STAR computer was used to illustrate the application of these criteria in choosing the fault tolerance techniques for a spacecraft computer that had long life and autonomy requirements with strict weight and power constraints. The 47 references covered the most relevant published work to mid-1967.

The earlier book by W. H. Pierce "Failure-Tolerant Computer Design" [Pier 65] served as an important reference; however, it must be noted that Pierce's definition of "failure tolerance" corresponded exactly to fault masking in logic circuits, including voting, adaptive, and interwoven logic, redundant relay contact networks, and application of error correcting codes as a masking technique. It is a definitive work on masking forms of redundancy that were known at that time. However, neither error detection, nor fault diagnosis, nor recovery techniques were included as elements of Pierce's "failure-tolerant" computers.

The 1967 paper was the first of a sequence of publications intended to formulate an evolving view of dependable computing as the consequence of a judicious introduction of fault tolerance and fault avoidance during system design. Two different classes of faults - those due to physical causes, and those due to human mistakes and oversights are considered. This evolving view has been presented in a series of papers on the techniques, scope, and aims of fault tolerance. The key contributions to this series are: [Aviz 71c], [Aviz 72b], [Aviz 75a], [Aviz 75b], [Aviz 76], [Aviz 77c], [Aviz 78a], [Aviz 79], [Aviz 82a], [Aviz 82b], [Aviz 84b], [Aviz 86a].

The unifying theme of these papers has been the evolution of a design paradigm for fault-tolerant systems that guides the designer to consider fault tolerance as a fundamental issue throughout the design process. The series shows a progressive refinement of concepts and an expansion of the scope to include the tolerance of "human-made" design and interaction faults. Other recent themes are the balancing of performance and fault tolerance objectives during system partitioning and the integration of subsystem recovery procedures into a multi-level recovery hierarchy. Strong emphasis is also placed on the application of design diversity in all parts of a multichannel system in order to attain tolerance of design faults. Very valuable support for this research effort has come from the author's participation in the activities of IFIP Working Group 10.4, and quite especially from the discussions of fundamental concepts of fault tolerance that have been taking place since the very first meeting of the WG 10.4 in 1981. Most specifically, the work of Dr. J.-C. Laprie has been of great value, especially through collaboration during his stay as a Visiting Professor at UCLA in 1985 [Aviz 86a].

A closely related current effort is the development of a paradigm for the qualitative evaluation of the fault tolerance attributes of complex system designs. This "inverse" of the design paradigm is being developed as part of the research related to the Advanced Automation System for air traffic control in the U. S. [Aviz 87].

4.5. Fault-Tolerant System Design and Analysis

A major research effort in the design of fault-tolerant systems has been a natural consequence of the design methodology research described above. Results in several areas that have been addressed at UCLA since 1972 are summarized below.

Fault-Tolerant High Speed Systems. The emphasis in this area has been on the introduction of low-cost error detection, fault diagnosis, reconfiguration, and recovery techniques into large multiprocessor and "supercomputer" architectures. The results consist of three Ph.D. dissertations [Vine 71], [Thom 77], [Bond 81], as well as several publications [Vine 73], [Sylv 74], [Aviz 74a], [Sylv 75], [Thom 75], [Baqa 76a], [Baqa 76b], [Thom 76], [Aviz 77a], [Aviz 77b], [Aviz 78b], [Aviz 83a], [Ragh 84]. Faculty collaborators in this effort were Profs. M. D. Ercegovac and T. Lang. Under direction of Prof. W. W. Chu, performance and fault tolerance of multiport memories was studied in the Ph.D. thesis of P. Korff [Korf 76]. More recently, D. Rennels and A. Avizienis have initiated a study of the issues involved in implementing fault-tolerance in highly parallel multicomputers. Recommendations for implementing fault-tolerance in hypercube connected systems (e.g., the JPL Hypercube) have been presented [Renn 86b].

Associative Processors and Database Machines. Here the emphasis has been on introducing fault tolerance in a systematic manner and assessing the cost and the effectiveness. The associative processor work includes the Ph.D. thesis by B. Parhami [Parh 73c] and related papers that considered fault tolerance issues in this class of machines [Parh 73b], [Parh 74]. The later database machine work, done in collaboration with Prof. A. F. Cardenas, consisted of one Ph.D. thesis [Alav 81] and two papers [Card 83], [Aviz 84a].

Error Detection Methods. Majority of the research in error detection has dealt with continuing investigation of arithmetic error detecting codes. Previous arithmetic code work had introduced the concepts of "low-cost" arithmetic codes [Aviz 64], inverse residue codes, and multiple residue and AN codes with "low-cost" and "hybrid-cost" variations [Aviz 65], [Aviz 67b], [Aviz 69], [Aviz 71b]. Later results were: algorithms for coded operands [Aviz 73], applications to storage errors [Parh 73a], [Parh 78], coding and algorithms for signed-digit representations [Aviz 81a], and two-dimensional residue codes [Aviz 83a], [Aviz 85a], [Aviz 86b]. Other studies considered external monitoring [Aviz 81b] and diagnosis [Ng 77c]. Further work on arithmetic error codes was contributed by Prof. A. Svoboda [Svob 78], and a Ph. D. dissertation on error-coded algorithms for on-line arithmetic was done by A. Gorji-

Sinaki [Gorj 81] under direction of Prof. M. Ercegovac.

Design of Distributed Systems. The "building block" approach to fault-tolerant distributed system design was pioneered by D. A. Rennels [Renn 78a], [Renn 78b], [Grey 84], [Renn 86a], [Renn 86b]. Much of the work in this area has focused on fault-tolerant real-time space systems. D. Rennels has supervised several research studies on the architectures required for the next generation of on-board computer systems [Renn 81a], [Renn 81c], [Depa 82], [Renn 84]. In the area of ground-based distributed systems a study was completed by C. Covey under the direction of D. Rennels which examined hardware augmentations to speed up functions for maintaining consistency and synchronization when data is replicated at several sites [Cove 82]. The Ph.D. thesis of B. Grey examined the potential use of highly fault-tolerant shared storage servers for large distributed systems. A preliminary architecture was completed, and highly secure capabilities-based storage management techniques were explored [Grey 85].

Under direction of A. Avizienis, Ph.D. dissertations were done on interconnection networks [CheH 81], on distributed architectures for N-version software execution [Maka 82a], [Maka 84], and on communication architectures [Ragh 82a], [Ragh 82b], [Ragh 85]. Professor D. S. Parker directed an investigation of distributed operating system and application algorithms, with emphasis on distributed concurrency control [Park 81]. The problem also was investigated in the Ph.D. thesis by R. A. Ramos [Ramo 82], [Park 82a]. A new type of network, called the Gamma network, which is a multi-processor interconnection network with redundant paths was introduced and analyzed using redundant number systems [Park 82b], and regular networks were investigated [Malo 82]. Distributed communication systems were investigated under the direction of Prof. M. Gerla. A new fault-tolerant ring architecture was developed which consists of two interleaved rings [Grna 80a]. Computationally efficient techniques for reliability evaluation of a network in which both nodes and links can fail with given probabilities were devised [Grna 79], [Grna 81b]. An extended model of distributed systems, Stochastic Petri Nets, was developed and its properties in both discrete and continuous time as well as some practical applications were studied in the Ph.D. dissertation of M. Molloy, which demonstrated the capabilities of the Stochastic Petri Net models to analyze systems for both correctness and performance [Moll 81]. Approximations and bounds on the performance of multibus interconnection schemes were derived [Mars 82]. Collaborating faculty included Profs. M. D. Ercegovac, M. Gerla, D. S. Parker, and B. Bussell.

Fault Tolerance Aspects of VLSI Design. This research included studies of self-checking design [OryC 73], [Sum 75], [Sum 76] and the Ph.D. dissertation by S. L. Wang on totally self-checking PLAs [Wang 79], [Wang 81]. The Ph.D. thesis of M. W. Sievers explored computer-aided design of totally self-checking logic [Siev 80], [Siev 81]. Yield-improving designs were investigated in Ph.D. research by T. E. Mangir [Mang 81], [Mang 82]. An investigation into the feasibility of a circuit-oriented approach in enhancing testability of VLSI chips by dynamically controlled partitioning was performed as a Ph.D. thesis by V. G. Oklobdzija, directed by Prof. M. Ercegovac [Oklo 82a], [Oklo 82b]. In 1984, D. A. Rennels initiated studies to develop VLSI circuits which are both self-checking and provide concurrent self-testing during normal operation. This work is being conducted with S. Chau who is nearing completion of a Ph.D. dissertation [Renn 86a]. Dr. Yuval Tamir joined the UCLA faculty in 1985 after receiving his Ph.D. at UC Berkeley [Tami 85]. His Ph.D. thesis addressed a number of problems in the implementation of fault-tolerant VLSI circuits and their application in fault-tolerant multicomputer architecture [Tami 83, 84a, 84b, 84c]. Recently, he has addressed recovery issues in large multicomputer systems [Tami 87]. A study led by Y. Tamir and D. Rennels is also under way to reduce error checking delays in high speed VLSI processors by pipelining the error checks and providing several cycle rollback capability to compensate for delayed error signals.

Modeling and Evaluation of Fault-Tolerant Systems. Directed by A. Avizienis, early work in this area was done by F. P. Mathur [Math 70a], [Math 70b], including the CARE reliability modeling program [Aviz 71a]. Further work, including experimental evaluation of the JPL-STAR computer and the RMS modeling system, was done by D. A. Rennels [Aviz 72a], [Renn 73a], [Renn 73b]. A major advance in Markov modeling was contributed through the Ph.D. dissertation of Y. W. Ng [Ng 76a], who devised an unified model [Ng 73], [Ng 75], [Ng 80], that introduced transient faults [Ng 76b], degradability, and repair [Ng 77a]. The ARIES 76 reliability modeling system (written in APL) contained all these features [Ng 77b], [Ng 78], [Ng 80], and found wide acceptance for education, research, and in industry. The sucessors to ARIES 76 were the ARIES 81 [Maka 82b] and ARIES 82 [Maka 82c] systems that were written in the language C and introduced the model of a "periodically renewed" fault-tolerant system [Maka 81]. ARIES 82 is still widely used in research and industry. Under the direction of D. Rennels, several reliability models were developed by A. DePaula to deal with the use of multi-level redundancy and systems with time-varying failure rates. These were based on recursive integral formulations, with closed form solutions in some cases and numerical integrations in more complex cases to evaluate systems in which Markov matrices become unwieldy [Depa 82]. A separate effort addressed the modeling of transient faults in TMR systems [Merr 75].

4.6. Tolerance of Design Faults by Design Diversity and N-Version Software

By early 1970s significant progress had been made in the tolerance of physical faults, and it became clear that design faults, especially as represented by software "bugs", presented the next challenge to the researchers in fault tolerance. A research effort to attain tolerance of design faults by means of multi-version software was started by A. Avizienis at UCLA in early 1975. The method was first described as "redundant programming" at the April 1975 International Conference on Reliable Software in Los Angeles [Aviz 75a], and was renamed as "N-version programming" in the course of the next two years [Aviz 77d]. The entire UCLA design diversity research effort through mid-1985 has been summarized in [Aviz 85b]. The name "Multi-Version Software" (MVS) is also used.

The N-version programming approach to fault tolerant software systems employs functionally equivalent, yet independently developed software components. These components are executed concurrently under a supervisory system that uses a decision algorithm based on consensus to determine final output values. >From its beginning in 1975, the fundamental conjecture of the MVS approach at UCLA has been that errors due to residual software faults are very likely to be masked by the correct results produced by the other versions in the system. This conjecture does not assume independence of errors, but rather a low probability of their concurrence and similarity. MVS systems achieve reliability improvements through the use of redundancy and diversity. A "dimension of diversity" is one of the independent variables in the development process of an MVS system. Diversity may be achieved along various dimensions, e.g., specification languages, specification writers, programming languages, programmers, algorithms, data structures, development environments, and testing methods.

The scarcity of previous results and an absence of formal theories on N-version programming in 1975 led to the choice of an experimental approach: to choose some conveniently accessible programming problems, to assess the applicability of N-version programming, and then to proceed to generate a set of programs.

Once generated, the programs were executed as N-version software units in a simulated multiple-hardware system, and the resulting observations were applied to refine the methodology and to build up the concepts on N-version programming. The first detailed assessment of the research approach and a discussion of two sets of experimental results, using 27 and 16 independently written programs, obtained from Prof. D. Berry's software engineering class, was published in 1978 [CheL 78b]. The detailed results appear in the Ph.D. thesis by Liming Chen [CheL 78a].

The preceding exploratory research demonstrated the practicality of experimental investigation and confirmed the need for high quality software specifications. As a consequence, the first aim of the next phase of UCLA research (1979-82) was the investigation of the relative applicability of various software specification techniques. Other aims were to investigate the types and causes of software design faults, to propose improvements to software specification techniques and their use, and to propose future experiments for the investigation of design fault tolerance in software and in hardware.

To examine the effect of specification techniques on multi-version software, an experiment was designed in which three different specifications were used. The first was written in the formal specification language OBJ [Gogu 79b]. The second specification language chosen was the non-formal PDL that was characteristic of current industry practice. English was employed as the third, or "control" specification language, since English had been used in the previous studies [CheL 78b]. The detailed description of the experiment has been reported in the Ph.D. dissertation by J. P. J. Kelly [Kell 82], and the main results have been presented in [Aviz 82c], [Kell 83] and [Aviz 84b].

In parallel with the experiment, a general model for unified interpretation of N-Version Programming and Recovery Block methods was developed. The same model allows modeling of sequential and parallel N-Version Programming (NVP) as well as of the Recovery Block scheme. Following this model, queueing models have been developed to analyze the performance of the fault tolerance techniques. The average segment processing time (average throughput) and reliability were the performance measures. The same queueing models were used for examination of both performance measures as functions of system parameters which include: average segment processing time, recovery rate, repair rate and segment failure probability. The obtained results and a comparison of the two fault tolerance techniques were published in [Grna 80b], [Grna 80c].

The NASA Langley Research Center is sponsoring the NASA Four-University experiment in fault tolerant software which has been underway since 1984. During the summer of 1985, the NASA experiment employed 40 graduate students at four universities to design, code and document 20 diverse software versions of a program to manage redundancy and to compute accelerations for a redundant inertial measurement unit. The analysis of this software currently engages researchers at six sites: UCLA, the University of Illinois at Urbana-Champaign, North Carolina State University, and the University of Virginia, as well as the Research Triangle Institute (RTI), and Charles River Analytics (CRA). Empirical results from this experiment will be jointly published by the cooperating institutions after the verification, certification, and final analysis phases are complete. While the joint results still await publication, some independent results from the UCLA effort led by John P. J. Kelly have been reported in [Kell 86].

In the course of the experiments at UCLA it became evident that the usual general-purpose campus computing services were poorly suited to support the systematic execution, instrumentation, and observation of N-version fault-tolerant software. In order to provide a long-term research facility for experimental investigations of design diversity as a means of achieving fault-tolerant systems, the UCLA Reliable Computing and Fault Tolerance research group designed and implemented the prototype DEDIX (DEsign DIversity eXperiment) system [Aviz 85c], a distributed supervisor and testbed for multiple-version software, at the UCLA Center for Experimental Computer Science. DEDIX is supported by the Center's Olympus Net local network, which utilizes the UNIX-based LOCUS distributed operating system to operate a set of VAX 11/750 computers. The purpose of DEDIX is to supervise and to observe the execution of N diverse versions of an application program functioning as as fault-tolerant N-version software unit. DEDIX also provides a transparent interface to the users, versions, and the input/output system, so that they need not be aware of the existence of multiple versions and recovery algorithms. The prototype DEDIX system has been operational since early 1985. Several modifications have been introduced since then, most of them intended to improve the speed of the execution of N-version software. The first major test of DEDIX that is currently taking place is the experimentation with the set of 20 programs produced by the NASA-sponsored four-university project discussed earlier. At the same time, a formal specification effort for the DEDIX is being initiated.

The past experience at UCLA has pinpointed an effective specification as the keystone of success for N-version software implementation [Aviz 84b]. Significant progress has occurred in the development of formal specification languages since our previous experiments. Our current goal is to compare and assess the ease of use by application programmers of several formal program specification methods. Presently the first choice is the Larch specification language family [Gutt 85]. The NASA Four-University experiment software that was originally specified in English has been specified in Larch [Tai 86], and work has been initiated on specifying parts of DEDIX in Larch as well. Valuable advice and support in the efforts have been received from the originators of Larch, Prof. J. V. Guttag of M.I.T., Dr. J. J. Horning of the DEC Systems Research Center, and Prof. J. M. Wing of Carnegie-Mellon University.

In an MVS system, several versions of a program are executed, usually in parallel, and their intermediate results are compared. In this way, faults in the individual versions are masked by a consensus. Without recovery the accumulation of failures is eventually large enough to saturate the fault-masking ability, and the entire system fails. It is therefore essential to recover these versions as they fail, and to transform the erroneous state of the failed versions to an error-free state from which normal execution can continue. The method of Community Error Recovery (CER) developed at UCLA in the Ph.D. dissertation of K. S. Tso [Tso 87a] makes use of the assumption that at any given time during execution a majority of good versions exists which can supply information to recover the failed versions. Experimental evaluation of the CER method has been performed, using the DEDIX supervisory system and the five diverse programs written at UCLA for the NASA experiment described previously [Kell 86]. A summary of the implementation and modeling of the CER method has been presented in [Tso 86], and a discussion of the evaluation appears in [Tso 87b].

Related research on the NASA experiment programs (in two completed M.S. theses) has considered statistical data on coincident and similar errors [Dora 86], and the branch coverage test has been applied to study various aspects of the programs [Swai 86]. In late 1986 a new experiment was initiated with support from the Sperry Commercial Flight Systems Division of Honeywell, Inc., Phoenix, AZ., in which six teams of two programmers each will use six different programming languages (Pascal, C, Modula-2, Ada, Lisp, and Prolog) to write a flight control program. The goal is to study the diversity that can be attained by the use of very different languages.

4.7. Reliable Software, Formal Specification, and Program Correctness

With the start of the 1972-78 NSF grant, Professor David F. Martin took charge of a study on various aspects of attaining reliable software. This research focused on semantic and pragmatic issues of the correct implementation of programming languages. The investigations carried out comprised a balanced combination of foundational theoretical studies and practical implementations. During the 1972-78 period, Ph.D. dissertations were completed and contributions were made in the areas of acyclic parallel program schemata [Hadj 75], compiler correctness [Chir 76], portable translator writing systems [Heis 76], high-level microprogramming languages and the synthesis of correct microprograms [Patt 77], and the design and proof of correct implementation of an expression-oriented, microcomputer-based high-level programming language [Clea 78].

Beginning in 1973, Professor Joseph A. Goguen conducted algebraic research on program semantics, specification and synthesis [Gogu 79a]. Results included the development of the basic mathematical definitions and results which underlie the algebraic approach to abstract data types [Gogu 78a], a method to introduce abstract error messages into abstract data types and programs [Gogu 77], and the new programming specification language OBJ [Gogu 78b]. An interactive implementation called OBJ-T was done on UCLA's PDP-10 [Gogu 79b]. Professor R. Burstall from the University of Edinburgh and J. Goguen developed an algebraic specification language named CLEAR [Burs 77].

In 1979, a three-year NSF grant "Improvement of the Reliability of Computing," was received that supported the N-Version fault-tolerant software research as well as the continuation of above discussed research concerned with the development of techniques for formal algebraic specification of semantics, and studies of techniques and tools to assure the correct implementation of programming languages. Two Ph.D. dissertations were completed under the guidance of Prof. D. F. Martin. The thesis research conducted by M. Zamfir, developed a mathematical model of concurrent computing agents, the *flow net*. Parallel programming languages can also be defined in this model in the usual syntax-directed fashion [Zamf 82]. The principal accomplishment toward correct implementation of programming languages was the Ph.D. dissertation by R. Bigonha which produced the design of a language and system for the modular specification of the denotational semantics of programming languages [Bigo 82].

Directed by Prof. J. Goguen, Ph.D. thesis research by K. Parsaye-Ghomi produced a theory of higher order data types, i.e., abstract data types with higher order operations and equations [Pars 82].

5. Acknowledgements

The evolution of fault-tolerant computing at JPL and at UCLA began late in 1960. During the past twenty six years, numerous individuals have made significant contributions to these efforts. Many of them are recognized by citations of publications; we also wish to thank those contributors whose names appear in the acknowledgments of the referenced papers, and also to those colleagues whose valuable contributions have remained less evident.

An especially important and pleasant aspect of our research has been the opportunity to welcome at UCLA and to work with visiting colleagues from abroad. We sincerely thank them all and look forward to many return visits: T. Anderson (U.K.), J. Arlat, J.-P. Blanquart, M. Buchwalter, J. P. Chinal, A. Costes, J.-C. Laprie, P. Traverse (France), W. Giloi, W. Goerke, U. Voges (Fed. Rep. Germany), H. Kopetz (Austria), M. Ajmone Marsan, L. Strigini (Italy), P. Gunningberg (Sweden), Y. Hatakeyama, H. Ihara, H. Mori, T. Sasada (Japan), R. Huslende (Norway), A. Grnarov (Yugoslavia), R. Jasinevicius, J. Mockus, V. Statulevicius (Lithuania), C.-L. Chen (P. R. China).

It has been a special pleasure to put together this overview of past efforts as part of the IFIP WG 10.4 Baden Symposium honoring our dear friend and colleague, Dr. William C. Carter. Ever since our first meeting in 1965, Bill has been a constant source of advice, support, and inspiration. Thank you, Bill, for your personal standard of integrity and excellence that set an admirable example for us to follow.

6. References

Note: The single asterisks at the references, e.g. [Alav 81]*, designate Ph.D. dissertations, and the double asterisks (**) designate M.S. theses completed at UCLA.

[A&A 70] "TOPS Outer Planet Spacecraft," Astronautics and Aeronautics (Special Issue), Vol. 8, No. 9, September 1970.

[Alav 81]* Alavian, F., "Database Recovery and Fault-Tolerance Analyses in Parallel Associative Database Processors," Ph.D. dissertation, UCLA Computer Science Department, University of California, Los Angeles, December 1981; also Technical Report No. CSD-820318, March 1982.

[Aren 83] Arens, W., Rennels, D. A., "A Fault-Tolerant Computer for Autonomous Spacecraft," Digest of FTCS-13, the 13th International Symposium on Fault-Tolerant Computing, Milano, Italy, June 1983, pp. 467-470.

[Aviz 64] Avizienis, A., "A Set of Algorithms for a Diagnosable Arithmetic Unit," Jet Propulsion Laboratory, Pasadena, California, Technical Report 32-546, March 1, 1964.

[Aviz 65] Avizienis, A., "A Study of the Effectiveness of Fault-Detecting Codes for Binary Arithmetic," Jet Propulsion Laboratory, Pasadena, California, Technical Report 32-711, September 1, 1965.

[Aviz 66] Avizienis, A., "System Organization of the JPL Self-Testing and Repairing Computer and Its Extension to a Multiprocessor Configuration," Proceedings of the NASA Seminar on Space-borne Multiprocessing, October 1966, Boston, pp. 61-66.

[Aviz 67a] Avizienis, A., "Design of Fault-Tolerant Computers," AFIPS Conference Proceedings, 1967 Fall Joint Computer Conference, Vol. 31, Washington, D. C.: Thompson, 1967, pp. 733-743.

[Aviz 67b] Avizienis, A., "Concurrent Diagnosis of Arithmetic Processors," Digest of the 1st Annual IEEE Computer Conference, Chicago, IL, September 1967, pp. 34-37.

[Aviz 68] Avizienis, A., "An Experimental Self-Repairing Computer," in Information Processing '68, Proceedings of the IFIP Congress 1968, Vol. 2, pp. 872-877.

[Aviz 69] Avizienis, A., "Digital Fault Diagnosis by Low-Cost Arithmetical Coding Techniques," Proceedings of the Purdue University Centennial Year Symposium on Information Processing, April 1969, pp. 81-92.

[Aviz 71a] Avizienis, A., Gilley, G. C., Mathur, F. P., Rennels, D. A., Rohr, J. A, Rubin, D. K., "The STAR (Self-Testing-and-Repairing) Computer: An Investigation of the Theory and Practice of Fault-Tolerant Computer Design," IEEE Trans. on Computers, Vol. C-20, No. 11, November 1971, pp. 1312-1321; also in Digest of the 1971 International Symposium on Fault-Tolerant Computing, Pasadena, CA, March 1971, pp. 92-96.

[Aviz 71b] Avizienis, A., "Arithmetic Error Codes: Cost and Effectiveness Studies for Application in Digital System Design," IEEE Trans. on Computers, Vol. C-20, No. 11, November 1971, pp. 1322-1330; also in Digest of the 1971 International Symposium on Fault-Tolerant Computing, Pasadena, CA, March 1971, pp. 118-121.

[Aviz 71c] Avizienis, A., "Fault-Tolerant Computing An Overview", IEEE Computer, Vol. 4, No. 1, February 1971, pp. 5-8.

[Aviz 72a] Avizienis, A., Rennels, D. A., "Fault-Tolerance Experiments With The JPL STAR Computer", in Digest of COMPCON '72 (Sixth Annual IEEE Computer Society Int. Conf.), San Francisco, California, 1972, pp. 321-324.

[Aviz 72b] Avizienis, A., "The Methodology of Fault-Tolerant Computing," Proceedings of the 1st USA-Japan Computer Conference, Tokyo, October 1972, pp. 405-413.

[Aviz 73] Avizienis, A., "Arithmetic Algorithms for Error-Coded Operands", IEEE Trans. on Computers, Vol. C-22, No. 6, June 1973, pp. 567-572; also in Digest of FTCS-2, the 2nd International Symposium on Fault-Tolerant Computing, Newton, MA, June 1972, pp. 25-29.

[Aviz 74a] Avizienis, A., Parhami, B., "A Fault-Tolerant Parallel Computer System for Signal Processing," Digest of FTCS-4, the 4th International Symposium on Fault-Tolerant Computing, Champaign, IL., June 1974, pp. 2-8 - 2-13.

[Aviz 75a] Avizienis, A., "Fault-Tolerance and Fault-Intolerance: Complementary Approaches to Reliable Computing," Proceedings of the 1975 International Conference on Reliable Software, Los Angeles, April 1975, pp. 458-464.

[Aviz 75b] Avizienis, A., "Architecture of Fault-Tolerant Computing Systems," Digest of FTCS-5, the 5th International Symposium on Fault-Tolerant Computing, Paris, June 1975, pp. 3-16.

[Aviz 76] Avizienis, A., "Fault-Tolerant Systems," IEEE Trans. on Computers, Vol. C-25, No. 12, December 1976, pp. 1304-1312.

[Aviz 77a] Avizienis, A., "Fault-Tolerance and Longevity: Goals for High-Speed Computers on the Future," Proceedings of the Symposium on High-Speed Computer & Algorithm Organization, University of Illinois at Urbana-Champaign, April 1977, Academic Press, pp. 173-178.

[Aviz 77b] Avizienis, A., Ercegovac, M., Lang, T., Sylvain, P., Thomasian, A., "An Investigation of Fault-Tolerant Architectures for Large-Scale Numerical Computing," Proceedings of the Symposium on High-Speed Computer & Algorithm Organization, University of Illinois at Urbana-Champaign, April 1977,

Academic Press, pp. 173-178.

[Aviz 77c] Avizienis, A., "Fault-Tolerant Computing: Progress, Problems, and Prospects," Information Processing 77, Proceedings of the IFIP Congress 1977, Toronto, August 1977, pp. 405-420.

[Aviz 77d] Avizienis, A., Chen, L., "On the Implementation of N-version Programming for Software Fault Tolerance During Execution," Proceedings COMPSAC 77, (First IEEE-CS International Computer Software and Applications Conference), Chicago, November 1977, pp. 149-155.

[Aviz 78a] Avizienis, A., "Fault-Tolerance: The Survival Attribute of Digital Systems," Proceedings of the IEEE, October 1978, 66-10, pp. 1109-1125.

[Aviz 78b] Avizienis, A., Bond, J. W. III, "Fault Tolerance in Large Computing Systems," Proceedings of the 3rd Jerusalem Conference on Information Technology, Jerusalem, August 1978, pp. 9-16.

[Aviz 79] Avizienis, A., "Toward a Discipline of Reliable Computing," Proceedings of the EUROIFIP 79, (European Conference on Applied Information Technology), London, September 1979, pp. 701-706.

[Aviz 81a] Avizienis, A., "Low Cost Residue and Inverse Residue Error-Detecting Codes for Signed-Digit Arithmetic," Proceedings of the 5th IEEE Symposium on Computer Arithmetic, Ann Arbor, MI, May 1981, pp. 165-168.

[Aviz 81b] Tolerance by Means of External Monitoring of Computer Systems," AFIPS Conference Proceedings, Vol. 50, May 1981, pp. 27-40.

[Aviz 82a] Avizienis, A., "The Four-Universe Information System Model for Fault-Tolerance," Digest of FTCS-12, the 12th International Symposium on Fault-Tolerant Computing, Santa Monica, California, June 1982, pp. 6-13.

[Aviz 82b] Avizienis, A., "Design Diversity - the Challenge of the Eighties," Digest of FTCS-12, the 12th International Symposium on Fault-Tolerant Computing, Santa Monica, California, June 1982, pp. 44-45.

[Aviz 82c] Avizienis, A., Kelly, J. P. J. "Fault-Tolerant Multi-Version Software: Experimental Studies of a Design Diversity Approach," Proceedings of 6th International Conference on Software Engineering (Poster Sessions), Tokyo, Japan, September 1982, pp. 101-102.

[Aviz 83a] Avizienis, A., Raghavendra, C. S., "Applications for Arithmetic Error Codes in Large, High-Performance Computers," Proceedings of the 6th IEEE Symposium on Computer Arithmetic, Aarhus, Denmark, June 1983, pp. 169-173.

[Aviz 84a] Avizienis, A., Cardenas, A. F., Alavian, F., "On the Effectiveness of Fault Tolerance Techniques in Parallel Associative Database Processors," Proceedings of the IEEE 1984 International Conference on Data Engineering, April 1984, pp. 50-59.

[Aviz 84b] Avizienis, A., Kelly, J. P. J., "Fault Tolerance by Design Diversity: Concepts and Experiments," Computer, Vol. 17, No. 8, August 1984, pp. 67-80.

[Aviz 85a] Avizienis, A., "Arithmetic Algorithms for Operands Encoded in Two-Dimensional Low-Cost Arithmetic Error Codes," Proceedings of the 7th IEEE Symposium on Computer Arithmetic, Urbana, Illinois, May 1985, pp. 285-292.

[Aviz 85b] Avizienis, A., "The N-Version Approach to Fault-Tolerant Software", IEEE Transactions on Software Engineering, Vol. SE-11, No. 12, December 1985, pp. 1491-1501.

[Aviz 85c] Avizienis, A., Gunningberg, P., Kelly, J. P. J., Strigini, L., Traverse, P. J., Tso, K. S., Voges, U., "The UCLA DEDIX system: a Distributed Testbed for Multiple-Version Software," Digest of FTCS-15, the 15th International Symposium on Fault-Tolerant Computing, Ann Arbor, Michigan, June 1985, pp. 126-134.

[Aviz 86a] Avizienis, A. Laprie, J. C., "Dependable Computing: From Concepts to Design Diversity," Proceedings of the IEEE, Vol. 74, No. 5, May 1986, pp. 629-638.

[Aviz 86b] Avizienis, A., "Two-Dimensional Low-Cost Arithmetic Residue Codes: Effectiveness and Arithmetic Algorithms," Digest of FTCS-16, the 16th International Symposium on Fault-Tolerant Computing, Vienna, Austria, July 1986, pp. 330-336.

[Aviz 87] Avizienis, A., Ball, D. E., "On the Achievement of a Highly Dependable and Fault-Tolerant Air Traffic Control System," Computer, Vol. 20, No. 2, February 1987, pp. 84-90.

[Baqa 76a]** "The Reliability Aspects and Interconnection Network Strategies for ILLIAC IV type Like Array Processors," M.S. thesis, UCLA Computer Science Department, University of California, Los Angeles, March 1976.

[Baqa 76b] Baqai, I., Lang, T., "Reliability Aspects of the ILLIAC IV Computer," Proceedings of the 1976 International Conference on Parallel Processing, August 1976, pp. 123-131.

[Bigo 82]* Bigonha, R. S., "A Denotational Semantics Implementation System," Ph.D. dissertation, UCLA Computer Science Department, University of California, Los Angeles, March 1982; also Technical Report No. CSD-820317, March 1982.

[Bond 81]* Bond, J. W., III, "A Comparison of Fault-Tolerance in Large Scale Scientific Computer Systems," Ph.D. dissertation, UCLA Computer Science Department, University of California, Los Angeles, September 1981; also Technical Report No. CSD-810601, June 1981.

[Burc 76] D. D. Burchby et al., "Specification of the Fault-Tolerant Space-Borne Computer (FTSC)," Digest of FTCS-6, the 6th International Symposium on Fault-Tolerant Computing, Pittsburgh, PA, June 1976, pp. 129-133.

[Burs 77] Burstall, R. M., Goguen, J. A., "Putting Theories Together to Make Specifications," Proceedings of the 5th International Joint Conference on Artificial Intelligence, (MIT, Cambridge, Mass.) 1977, pp. 1045-1058.

[Card 83] Cardenas, A. F., Alavian, F., Avizienis, A., "Performance of Recovery Architectures in Parallel Associative Database Processors," ACM Transactions on Database Systems, Vol. 8, No. 3, September 1983, pp. 291-323.

[CheH 81]* Chen, H. P. D., "The Analysis and Synthesis of Interconnection Networks for Distributed Computer Systems," Ph.D. dissertation, UCLA Computer Science Department, University of California, Los Angeles, June 1981; also Technical Report No. CSD-820203, February 1982.

[CheL 78a]* Chen, L., "Improving Software Reliability by N-version Programming," Ph.D. dissertation, UCLA Computer Science Department, University of California, Los Angeles, June 1978; also Technical Report No. UCLA-ENG-7843, June 1978.

[CheL 78b] Chen, L., Avizienis, A., "N-version Programming: A Fault Tolerance Approach to Reliability of Software Operation," Digest of FTCS-8, the 8th International Symposium on Fault-Tolerant Computing, Toulouse, France, June 1978, pp. 3-9.

[Chir 76]* Chirica, L. M., "Contributions to Compiler Correctness," Ph.D. dissertation, UCLA Computer Science Department, University of California, Los Angeles, September 1976; also Technical Report No. UCLA-ENG-7697, October 1976.

[Clea 78] Cleaveland, J. C., "Design, Implementation and Correctness of an Expression-Oriented Language for Microcomputers," UCLA Computer Science Department, Technical Report No. UCLA-ENG-7837, July 1978.

[Conn 72] Conn, R. B., Alexandridis, N. A., Avizienis, A., "Design of a Fault-Tolerant Modular Computer with Dynamic Redundancy," AFIPS Conference Proceedings, Vol. 41, Fall JCC 1972, pp. 1057-1067.

[Cove 82] Covey, C., Rennels, D. A., "Hardware Support Mechanisms for Concurrency Control in Local Computer Networks," Digest of International Workshop on High Level Language Architecture, Fort Lauderdale, Florida, December 1982.

[Depa 82]* DePaula, A., "Evaluation and Reliability Estimation of Distributed Architectures for On-Board Computers," Ph.D. dissertation, UCLA Computer Science Department, University of California, Los Angeles, September 1982; also Technical Report No. CSD-821205, December 1982.

[Dora 86]** Dorato, K., "Coincident Errors in N-Version Programming," M.S. thesis, UCLA Computer Science Department, University of California, Los Angeles, June 1986.

[Gill 70]* Gilley, G. C., "Automatic Maintenance of Spacecraft Systems for Long-Life, Deep-Space Missions", Ph.D. dissertation, UCLA Computer Science Department, University of California, Los Angeles, September 1970.

[Gill 71] Gilley, G. C., Editor, Digest of the 1971 International Symposium on Fault-Tolerant Computing, Pasadena, California, March 1971.

[Gill 72] Gilley, G. C., "A Fault-Tolerant Spacecraft", in Digest of FTCS-2, the 2nd International Symposium on Fault-Tolerant Computing, Newton, MA, June 1972, pp. 105-109.

[Gogu 77] Goguen, J. A., "Abstract Errors for Abstract Data Types," Proceedings IFIP Working Conference on Formal Description of Programming Concepts, (ed. J. Dennis), MIT, 1977, pp. 21.1-21.32; also in Formal Description of Programming Concepts, (ed. E. Neuhold), North Holland, 1978.

[Gogu 78a] Goguen, J. A., Thatcher, J. W., Wagner, E. G., "An Initial Algebra Approach to the Specification, Correctness, and Implementation of Abstract Data Types," Current Trends in Programming Methodology, Vol. 4, Data Structuring (ed. R. Yeh), Prentice Hall, 1978, pp. 80-149.

[Gogu 78b] Goguen, J., "Some Design Principles and Theory for OBJ-0, A Language for Expressing and Executing Algebraic Specifications of Programs," Proceedings, International Conference on Mathematical Studies of Information Processing, Kyoto, Japan, 1978, pp. 429-475.

[Gogu 79a] Goguen, J. A., "Algebraic Specification," Research Directions in Software Technology (ed. P. Wegner), MIT Press, 1979, pp. 370-376.

[Gogu 79b] Goguen, J. A., Tardo, J. J., "An Introduction to OBJ: A Language for Writing and Testing Formal Algebraic Program Specifications," Proceedings of the Conference on the Specification of Reliable Software, Cambridge, MA, April 1979, pp. 170-189.

[Gorj 81]* Gorji-Sinaki, A., "Error-coded Algorithms for On-line Arithmetic," Ph.D. dissertation, UCLA Computer Science Department, University of California, Los Angeles, February 1981; also Technical Report No. CSD-810303, March 1981.

[Grey 84] Grey, B. O., Avizienis, A., Rennels, D. A., "A Fault-Tolerant Architecture for Network Storage Systems," Digest of FTCS-14, the 14th International Symposium on Fault-Tolerant Computing, Kissimmee, Florida, June 1984, pp. 232-239.

[Grey 85]* Grey, B. O., "FTSS: A Fault-Tolerant Storage System Supporting High Availability and Security in a Distributed Processing Environment," Ph.D. dissertation, UCLA Computer Science Department, University of California, Los Angeles, March 1985.

[Grna 79] Grnarov, A., Kleinrock, L., Gerla, M., "A New Algorithm for Network Reliability Computation," Proceedings Computer Networking Symposium, Gaithersburg, Maryland, December 1979.

[Grna 80a] Grnarov, A., Kleinrock, L., Gerla, M., "A Highly Reliable Distributed Loop Architecture," Digest of FTCS-10, the 10th International Symposium on Fault-Tolerant Computing, Kyoto, Japan, October 1980, pp. 319-324.

[Grna 80b] Grnarov, A., Arlat, J., Avizienis, A., "Modeling of Software Fault-Tolerance Strategies," Proceedings of the 11th Annual Pittsburgh Modeling & Simulation Conference, University of Pittsburgh, Pennsylvania, Vol. 11, Part 2, May 1980, pp. 571-578.

[Grna 80c] Grnarov, A., Arlat, J., Avizienis, A., "On the Performance of Software Fault-Tolerance Strategies," Digest of FTCS-10, the 10th International Symposium on Fault-Tolerant Computing, Kyoto, Japan, October 1980, pp. 251-253.

[Grna 81b] Grnarov, A., Gerla, M., "Multiterminal Analysis of Distributed Processing Systems," Proceedings of the International Conference on Parallel Processing, August 1981.

[Gunn 85] Gunningberg, P., Pehrson, B., "Protocol and Verification of a Synchronization Protocol for Comparison of Results," Digest of FTCS-15, the 15th International Symposium on Fault-Tolerant Computing, Ann Arbor, Michigan, June 1985, pp. 172-177.

[Gutt 85] Guttag, J. V., Horning, J. J., Wing, J. M., "Larch in Five Easy Pieces," Report No. 5, Digital Equipment Corporation Systems Research Center, Palo Alto, California, July 24, 1985.

[Hadj 75]* Hadjioannou, M., "Acyclic Parallel Program Schemata," Ph.D. dissertation, UCLA Computer Science Department, University of California, Los Angeles, March 1975; also Technical Report No. UCLA-ENG-7521, April 1975.

[Heis 76]* Heiser, J. E., "METAFOR - A Verified, Portable Translator Writing System," Ph.D. dissertation, UCLA Computer Science Department, University of California, Los Angeles, 1976.

[*IEEE 67*] *Chicago, IL, September 1967.*

[Kell 82]* Kelly, J. P. J., "Specification of Fault-Tolerant Multi-Version Software: Experimental Studies of a Design Diversity Approach," Ph.D. dissertation, UCLA Computer Science Department, University of California, Los Angeles, June 1982; also Technical Report No. CSD-820927, September 1982.

[Kell 83] Kelly, J. P. J., Avizienis, A., "A Specification-oriented Multi-version Software Experiment," Digest of FTCS-13, the 13th International Symposium on Fault-Tolerant Computing, Milano, Italy, June 1983, pp. 120-126.

[Kell 86] Kelly, J. P. J., Avizienis, A., Ulery, B. T., Swain, B. J., Lyu, R. T., Tai, A., Tso, K. S., "Multi-Version Software Development," Proceedings IFAC Workshop SAFECOMP 86, Sarlat, France, October 1986, pp. 43-49.

[Korf 76]* Korff, P., "A Multiaccess Memory," Ph.D. dissertation, UCLA Computer Science Department, University of California, Los Angeles, June 1976; also Technical Report UCLA-ENG-7607, July 1976.

[Kueh 69] Kuehn, R. E., "Computer Redundancy: Design, Performance, and Future", IEEE Transactions on Reliability, Vol. R-18, Feb. 1969, pp. 3-11.

[Lesh 76] Lesh, H. F., et al., "Software Techniques for a Distributed Real-time Processing System," Proceedings of the IEEE National Aerospace and Electronics Conference (NAECON), Dayton, Ohio, pp. 290-295, May 1976.

[Maka 81] Makam, S., Avizienis, A., "Modeling and Analysis of Periodically Renewed Closed Fault-Tolerant Systems," Digest of FTCS-11, the 11th International Symposium on Fault-Tolerant Computing, Portland, Maine, June 1981, pp. 134-144.

[Maka 82a]* Makam, S. V., "Design Study of a Fault-Tolerant Computer System to Execute N-Version Software," Ph.D. dissertation, UCLA Computer Science Department, University of California, Los Angeles, December 1982; also Technical Report No. CSD-821222, December 1982.

[Maka 82b] Makam, S., Avizienis, A., "ARIES 81: A Reliability and Life-Cycle Evaluation Tool for Fault-Tolerant Systems," Digest of FTCS-12, the 12th International Symposium on Fault-Tolerant Computing, Santa Monica, California, June 1982, pp. 267-274.

[Maka 82c] Makam, S., Avizienis, A., Grusas, G., "ARIES 82 User's Guide," Technical Report No. 820830, UCLA Computer Science Department, University of California, Los Angeles, August, 1982.

[Maka 84] Makam, S. V., Avizienis, A., "An Event-Synchronized System Architecture for Integrated Hardware and Software Fault-Tolerance," Proceedings of the 4th International Conference on Distributed Computing Systems, San Francisco, California, May 1984.

[Malo 82]** Malony, A. D., "Regular Interconnection Networks," M.S. thesis, UCLA Computer Science Department, University of California, Los Angeles, September 1982; also Technical Report No. CSD-820825, August 1982.

[Mang 81]* Mangir, T. E., "Use of On-Chip Redundancy for Fault-Tolerant VLSI Design," Ph.D. dissertation, UCLA Computer Science Department, University of California, Los Angeles, June 1981; also Technical Report No. CSD-820201, February 1982.

[Mang 82] Mangir, T. E., Avizienis, A., "Fault-Tolerant Design for VLSI: Effect of Interconnect Requirements on Yield Improvement of VLSI Designs," IEEE Transactions on Computers, Vol. C-31, No. 7, July 1982, pp. 609-616.

[Mars 82] Marsan, A. M., Gerla, M., "Markov Models for Multibus Multiprocessor Systems," IEEE Transactions on Computers, Vol. C-31, No. 3, March 1982, pp. 239-248.

[Math 70a] Mathur, F. P., Avizienis, A., "Reliability Analysis and Architecture of a Hybrid-Redundant Digital System: Generalized Triple Modular Redundancy with Self-Repair", in Proceedings of the Spring Joint Computing Conference, AFIPS Conference Proceedings, Vol. 36. Montvale, N. J.: AFIPS Press, 1970, pp. 375-383.

[Math 70b]* Mathur, F. P., "Reliability Modeling and Estimation of Fault-Tolerant Digital Computers," Ph.D. dissertation, UCLA Computer Science Department, University of California, Los Angeles, June 1970.

[Math 71] Mathur, F. P., "On Reliability Modeling and Analysis of Ultra-Reliable Fault-Tolerant Digital Systems," IEEE Transactions on Computers, Vol. C-20, No. 11, November 1971, pp. 1376-1382.

[Merr 75] Merryman, P. M., Avizienis, A., "Modeling Transient Faults in TMR Computer Systems," Proceedings of the 1975 Reliability and Maintainability Symposium, Washington, D.C., January 1975, pp. 333-339.

[Moll 81]* Molloy, M., "On the Integration of Delay and Throughput Measures in Distributed Processing Models," Ph.D. dissertation, UCLA Computer Science Department, University of California, Los Angeles, June 1981; also Technical Report No. CSD-810921, September 1981.

[Ng 73]** Ng, Y. W., "Reliability Modeling for Fault-Tolerant Computers," M.S. thesis, UCLA Computer Science Department, University of California, Los Angeles, December 1973.

[Ng 75] Ng, Y. W., Avizienis, A., "A Unifying Reliability Model for Closed Fault-Tolerant Systems," Digest of FTCS-5, the 5th International Symposium on Fault-Tolerant Computing, Paris, June 1975, pp. 224.

[Ng 76a]* Ng, Y. W., "Modeling and Analysis of Fault-Tolerant Computers," Ph.D. dissertation, UCLA Computer Science Department, University of California, Los Angeles, September 1976; also Technical Report No. UCLA-ENG-7698, September 1976.

[Ng 76b] Ng, Y. W., Avizienis, A., "A Model for Transient and Permanent Fault Recovery in Closed Fault Tolerant Systems," Digest of FTCS-6, the 6th International Symposium on Fault-Tolerant Computing, Pittsburgh, June 1976, pp. 182-188.

[Ng 77a] Ng, Y. W., Avizienis, A., "A Reliability Model for Gracefully Degrading and Repairable Fault-Tolerant Systems," Digest of FTCS-7, the 7th International Symposium on Fault-Tolerant Computing, Los Angeles, June 1977, pp. 22-28.

[Ng 77b] Ng, Y. W., Avizienis, A., "ARIES - An Automated Reliability Estimation System for Redundant Digital Structures," Proceedings of the 1977 Annual Reliability and Maintainability Symposium, Philadelphia, January 1977, pp. 108-113.

[Ng 77c] Ng, Y. W., Avizienis, A., "Local Irredundancy in Combinational Circuits," Digest of FTCS-7, the 7th International Symposium of Fault-Tolerant Computing, Los Angeles, June 1977, pp. 109-113.

[Ng 78] Ng, Y. W., Avizienis, A., "ARIES 76 User's Guide," Technical Report No. UCLA-ENG-7894, UCLA Computer Science Department, University of California, Los Angeles, December 1978.

[Ng 80] Ng, Y. W., Avizienis, A., "A Unified Reliability Model for Fault-Tolerant Computers," IEEE Transactions on Computers, Vol. C-29, No. 11, pp. 1002-1011, November 1980.

[Oklo 82a]* Oklobdzija, V. G., "Design for Testability of VLSI Structures through the Use of Circuit Techniques," Ph.D. dissertation, UCLA Computer Science Department, University of California, Los Angeles, 1982; also Technical Report No. CSD-820820, August 1982.

[Oklo 82b] Oklobdzija, V. G., Ercegovac, M. D., "Testability Enhancement of VLSI Using Circuit Structures," Proceedings of IEEE 1982 International Conference on Circuits and Computers, New York, 1982.

[OryC 73]** Ory-Cristelly, R., "Design of a Dynamically Checked, Signed-Digit Arithmetic Unit," M.S. thesis, UCLA Computer Science Department, University of California, Los Angeles, November 1973; also Technical Report No. UCLA-ENG-7366, November 1973.

[Parh 73a] Parhami, B., Avizienis, A., "Application of Arithmetic Error Codes for Checking of Mass Memories," Digest of FTCS-3, the 3rd International Symposium on Fault-Tolerant Computing, June 1973, pp. 47-51.

[Parh 73b] Parhami, B., Avizienis, A., "Design of Fault-Tolerant Associative Processors," Proceedings of the 1st Annual Symposium on Computer Architecture, Gainesville, FL., December 1973, pp. 141-145.

[Parh 73c]* Parhami, B., "Design Techniques for Associative Memories and Processors," Ph.D. dissertation, UCLA Computer Science Department, University of California, Los Angeles, March 1973; also Technical Report No. UCLA-ENG-7321, March 1973.

[Parh 74] Parhami, B., Avizienis, A., "A Study of Fault-Tolerance Techniques for Associative Processors," AFIPS Conference Proceedings, Vol. 43, National Computer Conference, Chicago, May 1974, pp. 643-652.

[Parh 78] Parhami, B., Avizienis, A., "Detection of Storage Errors in Mass Memories Using Low-Cost Arithmetic Codes," IEEE Transactions on Computers, Vol. C-27, No. 4, April 1978, pp. 302-308.

[Park 81] Parker, D. S., Popek, G. J., et al., "Detection of Mutual Inconsistency in Distributed Systems," Proceedings of the 5th Berkeley Workshop on Computer Networks and Distributed Data Management, Emeryville, California, February 1981.

[Park 82a] Parker, D. S., Ramos, R., "A Distributed File System Architecture Supporting High Availability," Proceedings of the 6th Berkeley Workshop on Distributed Data Management & Computer Networks, Asilomar, California, February 1982, pp. 161-183.

[Park 82b] Parker, D. S., Raghavendra, C. S., "The Gamma Network: A Multiprocessor Interconnection Network with Redundant Paths," Proceedings of the 9th Annual Symposium on Computer Architecture, Austin, Texas, April 1982, pp. 73-80.

[Pars 82]* Parsaye-Ghomi, K., "Higher Order Data Types," Ph.D. dissertation, UCLA Computer Science Department, University of California, Los Angeles, January 1982; also Technical Report No. CSD-820112, January 1982.

[Patt 77] Patterson, D. A., "Verification of Microprograms," Technical Report No. UCLA-ENG-7707, UCLA Computer Science Department, January 1977.

[Pier 65] Pierce, W. H., "Failure-Tolerant Computer Design," Academic Press: New York and London, 1965.

[Ragh 82a]* Raghavendra, N., "Fault Tolerance in Computer Communication Architectures," Ph.D. dissertation, UCLA Computer Science Department, University of California, Los Angeles, June 1982; also Technical Report No. CSD-820928, September 1982.

[Ragh 82b] Raghavendra, C. S., Gerla, M., Avizienis, A., "Reliability Optimization in the Design of Distributed Systems," Proceedings of the 3rd International Conference on Distributed Computing Systems, Miami, Florida, October 1982, pp. 388-393.

[Ragh 84] Raghavendra, C. S., Avizienis, A., Ercegovac, M. D., "Fault Tolerance in Binary Tree Architectures," IEEE Transactions on Computers, Vol. C-33, No. 6, June 1984, pp. 568-572.

[Ragh 85] Raghavendra, C. S., Gerla, M., Avizienis, A., "Reliable Loop Topologies for Large Local Computer Networks," IEEE Transactions on Computers, Vol. C-34, No. 1, January 1985, pp. 46-55.

[Ramo 82]* Ramos, R. A., "High Reliability, Availability and Consistency in Distributed Systems," Ph.D. dissertation, UCLA Computer Science Department, University of California, Los Angeles, September 1982; also Technical Report No. CSD-821214, December 1982.

[Reed 62] Reed, I. S., Brimley, D. E., "On Increasing the Operating Life of Unattended Machines", RAND Corp., Memo. RM-3338-PR, November 1962.

[Renn 73a]* Rennels, D. A., "Fault Detection and Recovery in Redundant Computer Using Standby Spares", Ph.D. dissertation, UCLA Computer Science Department, University of California, Los Angeles, June 1973; also Technical Report No. UCLA-ENG-7355, July 1973.

[Renn 73b] Rennels, D. A., Avizienis, A., "RMS: A Reliability Modeling System for Self-Repairing Computers," Digest of FTCS-3, the 3rd International Symposium on Fault-Tolerant Computing, June 1973, pp. 131-135.

[Renn 76] Rennels, D.A., et al., "The Unified Data System: A Distributed Processing Network for Control and Data Handling on a Spacecraft," Proceedings of the IEEE National Aerospace and Electronics Conference (NAECON), Dayton, Ohio, May 1976, pp. 283-289.

[Renn 78a] Rennels, D. A., "Architectures for Fault-Tolerant Spacecraft Computers", Proceedings of the IEEE, October 1978, Vol. 66, No. 10, pp. 1255-1268.

[Renn 78b] Rennels, D. A., Avizienis, A., Ercegovac, M., "A Study of Standard Building Blocks for the Design of Fault-Tolerant Distributed Computer Systems", Digest of FTCS-8, the 8th International Symposium on Fault-Tolerant Computing, Toulouse, France, June 1978, pp. 144-149.

[Renn 81a] Rennels, D. A., et. al., Fault-Tolerant Computer Study Final Report, JPL Publication 80-73, Jet Propulsion Laboratory, California Institute of Technology, Pasadena, California, February 1981.

[Renn 81b] Rennels, D. A., "Some Past Experiments and Future Plans in the Experimental Evaluation of Fault-Tolerance", UCLA Computer Science Department Quarterly, vol. 9, no. 2, Spring 1981, University of California, Los Angeles, pp. 91-98.

[Renn 81c] Rennels, D. A., DePaula, A., Fremont, M., "Fault-Tolerant Design Considerations for Future Spacecraft Computer Systems," UCLA Report Prepared for the Aerospace Corporation, El Segundo, California, Aerospace Library Call Number A81-04858, October 1981.

[Renn 84] Rennels, D. A., "A Building Block Architecture for a High-Speed Distributed Processing System," Digest GOMAC Government Microcircuits Applications Conference, Las Vegas, Nevada, November 1984.

[Renn 86a] Rennels, D. A., Chau, S., "A Self-Exercising Self-Checking Memory Design", Digest of FTCS-16, the 16th International Symposium on Fault-Tolerant Computing, Vienna, Austria, July 1986, pp. 358-363.

[Renn 86b] Rennels, D. A., "On Implementing Fault Tolerance in Binary Hypercubes," Digest of FTCS-16, the 16th International Symposium on Fault-Tolerant Computing, Vienna, Austria, July 1986, pp. 344-349.

[Rohr 73a] Rohr, J. A., "System Software for a Fault-Tolerant Digital Computer," Ph.D. dissertation, Department of Computer Science, University of Illinois, Urbana, Illinois, February 1973.

[Rohr 73b] Rohr, J. A., "STAREX Self-Repair Routines: Software Recovery in The JPL-STAR Computer", Digest of FTCS-3, the 3rd International Symposium on Fault-Tolerant Computing, Palo Alto, California, June 1973, pp. 11-16.

[Siev 80]* Sievers, M. W., "Computer-Aided Design and Reliability of a General Logic Structure for Custom VLSI," Ph.D. dissertation, UCLA Computer Science Department, University of California, Los Angeles, June 1980; also Technical Report No. CSD-820111, January 1982.

[Siev 81] Sievers, M., Avizienis, A., "Analysis of a Class of Totally Self-Checking Functions Implemented in a MOS LSI General Logic Structure," Digest of FTCS-11, the 11th International Symposium on Fault-Tolerant Computing, Portland, Maine, June 1981, pp. 256-261.

[Stif 73] Stiffler, J. J., Parke IV, N. G., Barr, P. C., "The SERF Fault-Tolerant Computer," Parts I and II, Digest of FTCS-3, the 3rd International Symposium on Fault-Tolerant Computing, Palo Alto, California, June 1973, pp. 23-31.

[Sum 75]** Sum, E., "Evaluation Techniques for Self-Checking Logic Circuits," M.S. thesis, UCLA Computer Science Department, University of California, Los Angeles, June 1975.

[Sum 76] Sum, E. K. S., Avizienis, A., "A Probabilistic Model for the Evaluation of Signal Reliability of Self-Checking Logic Circuits," Digest of FTCS-6, the 6th International Symposium on Fault-Tolerant Computing, Pittsburgh, June 1976, pp. 83-87.

[Svob 78] Svoboda, A., "Arithmetic Circuit Fault Detection by Modular Encoding," Proceedings of the Fourth IEEE Symposium on Computer Arithmetic, Santa Monica, California, October 1978, pp. 208-219.

[Swai 86]** Swain, B., "Group Branch Coverage Testing of Multi-Version Software," M.S. thesis, UCLA Computer Science Department, University of California, Los Angeles, December 1986; also Technical Report No. CSD-860013, December 1986.

[Sylv 74]** Sylvain, P., "Evaluating the Array Machine," M.S. thesis, UCLA Computer Science Department, University of California, Los Angeles, June 1974.

[Sylv 75] Sylvain, P., Vineberg, M., "The Design and Evaluation of the Array Machine: A High-Level Language Processor," Proceedings of Second Annual Symposium on Computer Architecture, Houston, TX, January 1975, pp. 119-125.

[Tai 86]** Tai, A. T., "A Study of the Application of Formal Specification for Fault-Tolerant Software," M.S. thesis, UCLA Computer Science Department, Los Angeles, California, June 1986.

[Tami 83] Tamir, Y., Séquin, C. H., "Self-Checking VLSI Building Blocks for Fault-Tolerant Multicomputers," International Conference on Computer Design, Port Chester, New York, November 1983, pp. 561-564.

[Tami 84a] Tamir, Y., Séquin, C. H., "Design and Application of Self-Testing Comparators Implemented with MOSPLAs," IEEE Transactions on Computers, Vol. C-33, No. 6, June 1984, pp. 493-506.

[Tami 84b] Tamir, Y., Séquin, C. H., "Error Recovery in Multicomputers Using Global Checkpoints," 13th International Conference on Parallel Processing, Bellaire, Michigan, August 1984, pp. 32-41.

[Tami 84c] Tamir, Y., Séquin, C. H., "Reducing Common Mode Failures in Duplicate Modules," International Conference on Computer Design, Port Chester, New York, October 1984, pp. 302-307.

[Tami 85] Tamir, Y., "Fault Tolerance for VLSI Multicomputers," Ph.D. dissertation, also CS Division Report No. UCB/CSD 86/256, Department of Electrical Engineering and Computer Sciences, University of California, Berkeley, California, August 1985.

[Tami 87] Tamir, Y., Gafni, E., "A Software-Based Hardware Fault Tolerance Scheme for Multicomputers," Proceedings of the 16th Parallel Processing Conference, St. Charles, Illinois, August 1987.

[Thom 75] Thomasian, A., Avizienis, A., "Dynamic Scheduling of Tasks Requiring Multiple Processors," Proceedings of the 11th Annual IEEE Computer Society Conference, Washington, DC, September 1975, pp. 76-80.

[Thom 76] Thomasian, A., Avizienis, A., "A Design Study of a Shared-Resource Computing System," Proceedings of the 3rd Annual Symposium on Computer Architecture, Clearwater, FL., January 1976, pp. 105-112.

[Thom 77]* Thomasian, A., "A Design Study of a Shared Resource Array Processing System," Ph.D. dissertation, UCLA Computer Science Department, University of California, Los Angeles, June 1977; also Technical Report No. UCLA-ENG-7702, August 1977.

[Tso 86] Tso, K. S., Avizienis, A., Kelly, J. P. J., "Error Recovery in Multi-Version Software," in Proceedings IFAC Workshop SAFECOMP'86, Sarlat, France, October 1986, pp. 35-41.

[Tso 87a]* Tso, K. S., "Recovery and Reconfiguration in Multi-Version Software," Ph.D. dissertation, UCLA Computer Science Department, University of California, Los Angeles, March 1987; also Technical Report No. CSD-870013, March 1987.

[Tso 87b] Tso, K. S., Avizienis, A., "Community Error Recovery in N-Version Software: A Design Study with Experimentation," Digest of FTCS-17, the 17th International Symposium on Fault-Tolerant Computing, Pittsburgh, Pennsylvania, July 1987.

[Vine 71]* Vineberg, M. B., "Implementation of a Higher Level Language on an Array Machine," Ph. D. dissertation, UCLA Computer Science Department, University of California, Los Angeles, June 1971; also Technical Report No. UCLA-ENG-7157, 1971.

[Vine 72] Vineberg, M., Avizienis, A., "Implementation of a Higher-Level Language on an Array Machine," Proceedings of COMPCON '72, 6th Annual IEEE Computer Society International Conference, September 1972, pp. 37-39.

[Vine 73] Vineberg, M., Avizienis, A., "Implementation of a Higher-Level Language on an Array Machine," Proceedings of the International Workshop on Computer Architecture, Grenoble, France, June 1973.

[Wang 79] Wang, S. L., Avizienis, A., "The Design of Totally Self-Checking Circuits Using Programmable Logic Arrays," Digest of FTCS-9, the 9th International Symposium on Fault-Tolerant Computing, Madison, WI, June 1979, pp. 173-180.

[Wang 81]* Wang, S. L., "The Design of Totally Self-Checking Circuits by Using Programmable Logic Arrays," Ph.D. dissertation, UCLA Computer Science Department, University of California, Los Angeles, June 1981; also Technical Report No. CSD-810608, June 1981.

[Wilc 62] Wilcox, R. H., Mann, W. C., editors, "Redundancy Techniques for Computing Systems", Spartan Press, Washington, DC, 1962.

[Zamf 82]* Zamfir, M., "Syntax and Semantics of Concurrent Computing," Ph.D. dissertation, UCLA Computer Science Department, University of California, Los Angeles, June 1982; also Technical Report No. CSD-820819, August 1982.

7. Appendix A

The following text is an exact reproduction of the JPL Spacecraft Computers and Sequencers Section interoffice memorandum addressed to Section Manager Henry A. Curtis that initiated the JPL STAR computer research project in 1961. It is the earliest existing description of the STAR concept, and it was used as evidence to support the U.S. Patent application filed by JPL in 1967. Subsequently, U.S. Patent No. 3, 517, 671 "Self Testing and Repairing Computer" was granted to A. Avizienis (assigned to NASA) on June 23, 1970. Figures 1 and 2 are taken directly from the original.

JET PROPULSION LABORATORY   **INTEROFFICE MEMO**
TO: H. A. Curtis   **FROM:**A. A. Avizienis   **DATE:** 10-6-61

SUBJECT: Preliminary Discussion of the Logical Design of a Self-Testing and Repairing   System for Spacecraft Guidance and Control.

I. OBJECTIVE

The objective of this memo is to discuss the organization and logical design of a Self-Testing-And-Repairing (STAR) system which can perform the guidance computer and sequencer functions in a spacecraft. It is expected that the self-repair property will increase the probability of successful operation of the system on long-term missions. It may also be a contribution in advancing the state of the art in design of reliable computing systems.

II. CHARACTERISTICS

The following system characteristics are considered to be essential in the STAR system for spacecraft guidance computing and sequencing:

1   Self-repair (including input and output mechanisms).

2   Evolution from presently used hardware and techniques. Flexibility and growth potential.

3   Linkage with ground-based computers.

4   Gradual ("graceful") degradation upon accumulation of failures.

Because of the special purpose of the STAR system,it is possible to make certain assumptions about its operational requirements and conditions. Several significant features are:

1   Speed requirement is relatively low.

2   Sequencer function as well as computing must be performed.

3   Available power is limited.

4   There may be long periods of idleness (standby).

5   Inputs are from transducers and radio link; outputs to radio link and actuators.

1   Operation may be linked with ground-based computer or operator.

2   Program is generally fixed for one mission; missions are variable in duration and purpose.

3   Self-repair must extend to input and output devices.

4   New techniques and components (adaptation, cryogenics, etc.) may become available.

5   Length of missions and reliability requirements are going to increase.

The listed objectives and properties form the basis for the following discussion of a possible configuration of the STAR system.

III. SELF-REPAIR

In order to achieve self-repair in space environment, the STAR system must be capable of auto-diagnosis or fault-masking. Auto-diagnosis must be followed by the replacement of a permanently defective part (to be called *failure*) or by a repetition of the operation if the result is diagnosed as invalid because of a transient malfunction (to be called *error*). Thus, errors are corrected by means of time redundancy, and failures are corrected by

Fault-masking is an alternative approach: here failure or temporary malfunction of an element does not produce an erroneous output because other (redundant) elements mask the effect of the failure. Masking will not be effective if an error (transient malfunction) is caused by external noise.

When information is coded in an error-detecting code, failures and both types of errors (of internal and external origin) will be detectable (subject to limitations of the code). The diagnostic (error-detecting) equipment itself, however, should not malfunction during diagnosis. For this purpose fault-masking must be incorporated with the diagnostic equipment. Furthermore, it must be especially protected (shielded) against externally originated errors. Automatic time redundancy (repetition of all diagnoses with voting) may be applicable here.

A review of above discussed characteristics leads to the preliminary choice of the organization of the STAR system which is shown in Fig. 1.

The system consists of a central Diagnostic Control and of arrays of peripheral Function Units of several types. Each array of Function Units includes one or more reserve units; a reserve unit is chosen when the Diagnostic Control detects a failure in the (presently) operating unit. The failed unit is permanently disconnected and the next reserve unit is connected to Diagnostic Control.

The power consumption is least when the reserve units are stored "cold"; furthermore the system will be operative as long as at least one unit in an array remains operative. These reasons relegate "triplicated with voting" use of Function Units to second place. The number of identical Function Units in one array may vary according to the length of the mission, the relative importance of the unit in the system, weight limitations, and the reliability of the type of unit used. The internal design of the Function Units is relatively independent of the Diagnostic Control as long as the standard format of information is retained; this should facilitate the introduction of changes and improvements.

IV. THE DIAGNOSTIC CONTROL

The Diagnostic Control of the STAR system performs all functions of a control unit in a conventional computer. Furthermore, it evaluates the validity of all information which passes between the operating Function Units and performs the self-test and self-repair sequences when invalid information is detected.

Obviously, all information flow must be routed through the Diagnostic Control; this requirement limits the speed of the entire system. All information must be coded in an error-detecting code; either a uniform code must be used in all Function Units, or a code conversion must be performed by the Diagnostic Control (conversion in the Function Unit itself is an alternative). Other failure-indicating inputs from the operating Function Units may be useful, such as indication of power loss, etc.

The Diagnostic Control itself must be the most reliable part of the STAR system. Fault-masking and redundancy at component level offer the most attractive approach to make it reliable. Self-diagnosis during periods of idleness may be applicable; this, however, requires a spare control unit or complete transfer to ground control in case of a failure.

The Diagnostic Control receives an instruction from the Fixed Storage unit and evaluates its validity. If the validity is questionable, the instruction is obtained once more (time-redundant check for errors); if it is still invalid, a reserve Fixed Storage unit is consulted for the instruction.

If the instruction is valid, the proper Function Unit is instructed to execute it; the result is then brought into the Diagnostic Control and tested for validity. Again, in case of indicated invalidity, the operation is repeated (one or more times); if the result is still invalid, a failure of the Function Unit is assumed. The Diagnostic Control contains a switching arrangement which is now actuated and the next Function Unit in the array is activated and connected to the Diagnostic Control. The failed unit is permanently deactivated and disconnected.

A flow diagram of the procedure described above is shown in Fig. 2. A special "degradation procedure" is necessary when the reserve Function Units of one type are exhausted, or when no valid instructions are available.

The Diagnostic Control is also the most likely location for the sequence generator and the clock of the STAR system. Input, output, arithmetic, and storage functions are relegated to the Function Units. It is desirable to keep the Diagnostic Control unit as small as possible, since it is the most vulnerable part of the STAR system. An effort should be made to incorporate most functions into the Function Units. A single general-purpose Diagnostic Control unit then could be used as center of many STAR systems of varying size, capacity and purpose.

V. THE FUNCTION UNITS

The most obviously needed types of Function Units are (1) Fixed Store, (2) Arithmetic, (3) Memory, (4) Input and (5) Output. Others may be found necessary, for instance, Clock and Sequencer, or Scientific Data Reducer units.

A. *Fixed Store Function Units*

These units contain programs for guidance computations, and all emergency, diagnostic and other internal procedures. Scientific data reduction program may also be contained here. The program data (instructions) are coded for detection of errors and failures. The redundancy is in the form of reserve units; time redundancy (repeated readout) is also to be used. An independent indication of the origin of the instruction delivered to the Diagnostic Control may be necessary.

B. *Arithmetic Function Units*

The Arithmetic Function Units must have a provision to retain the error-detecting code in the results of arithmetical operations. Furthermore, an independent indication of which arithmetic operation has been performed is desirable with the result; in this manner improper interpretation of the instruction by the Arithmetic unit can be detected.

C. *Memory Function Units*

This type of unit is used for storage of intermediate results and other non-fixed information. Two units are likely to be used at once to avoid loss of information; an error-correcting code is an alternative. An independent indication (to the Diagnostic Control) of the address from which (or into which) information was delivered would avoid errors due to incorrect address decoding.

D. *Input Function Units*

These units are the various sensors and transducers on the spacecraft and the radio receiver. Input data must appear in digital form and be coded in an error-detecting code. Such code may appear on shaft-position digitizers (code wheels), etc. Validity check procedures must be available for each input, either in form of a preliminary and terminal checkout, or by repeated measurements (by the same or different instruments). Spare input devices should be available for self-repair.

The radio receiver is expected to deliver coded information which can be checked for validity; a spare receiver is desirable.

E. Output Function Units

These units are the various actuators and the radio transmitter. An independent feedback of the output information as delivered by the output units will provide a check of their performance. Voting-type redundancy of actuators should be considered. A spare radio transmitter is considered desirable.

VI. OTHER CONSIDERATIONS

The design of an initial breadboard Diagnostic Control and Function Units would utilize the hardware and techniques which are most readily available, and have been used in earlier flights. There is no conceptual difficulty in starting a design with magnetic and semiconductor elements; adaptive switching circuits and new components may be introduced at a suitable time. The logical design of the STAR system is relatively independent of any specific set of circuits or components.

The separation into Function Units allows most flexibility in assembling a complete STAR system; only the format of information must be retained. Thus, many different systems may be put together from the set of units.

The design problem is also subdivided into: (1) development of the STAR system concept, (2) development of the information format; (3) development of the Diagnostic Control unit, (4) development of the various Function Units. It is necessary to consider the division of computational requirements between Earth-based computers and the STAR system in the spacecraft. The relative reliability and accuracy must be evaluated; however, duplicate operations with an assigned priority and comparison offer the greatest flexibility.

The ultimate use of the spacecraft for long exploratory flights and orbiting of planets favors a complete STAR system in the computer; however, provisions should be made to utilize ground support and also to achieve "graceful" degradation by relinquishing functions to ground computing systems if a non-repairable failure occurs in the spacecraft STAR system.

The degradation of the STAR computer should occur in an orderly manner, according to a special program in the Fixed Store. Preferably, control and execution of lost functions is requested from the ground. The communication with ground may be continuous and used as a back-up check while the STAR system is functioning properly.

The redundancy of communication equipment is implied by the above requirement; the level of redundancy remains to be established as well as the procedure of switchover (if needed).

VII. CLOSING REMARK

The above presented concept of the STAR system has been put down on paper for the first time; inevitably it is uncertain and too general on many important problems. However, it appears to offer an interesting and potentially very reliable computing system for the 1965-70 period of space exploration.

8. Appendix B

This is the program of a Workshop held on February 2-4, 1966 that served as a major stimulus for the subsequent formation of the IEEE Computer Group Technical Committee on Fault-Tolerant Computing in 1969.

WORKSHOP ON THE ORGANIZATION OF RELIABLE AUTOMATA
Terrace Room, Santa Ynez Inn, 17310 Sunset Blvd., Pacific Palisades, Calif.
Sponsored by:
The Switching Circuit Theory and Logical Design Committee, IEEE Computer Group,
Department of Engineering, University of California, Los Angeles,
Engineering Extension, University of California Extension, Los Angeles

Wednesday, February 2, 1966

10:00 am	Registration and Coffee Hour	
12:00 noon	Opening Luncheon	
	Speaker: Prof. C.M. Duke	
	Chairman, Department of Engineering	
	University of California, Los Angeles	
1:30 pm	*Introduction:*	
	"On the Problem of Reliable Automata"	A. Avizienis
	"A Survey of Soviet Activities in Reliability	R.A. Short
		and W. H. Kautz
2:30 pm	*Redundancy Theory and Techniques*	S. Winograd, Chairman
	"Stability of Threshold Element Nets	
	Subject to Common Shifts of Threshold"	A.M. Andrew
	(Paper was not presented - author did not attend)	
	"The Need and Means for Fault Detection	J.B. Angell
	in Redundant Systems"	
	"Reliability Estimation for Redundant Systems"	C.G. Masters
	"Placement of Voters in Modularly Redundant	D. Rubin
	Digital Systems"	
	"Reliability, Redundancy, Capacity and	
	Universality in Polyfunctional Nets"	R.H. Urbano
6:00 pm	Workshop Dinner	
	Keynote Speaker: Prof. E.J. McCluskey, Jr.	
	Chairman, Switching Circuit Theory and	
	Logical Design Committee, IEEE Computer Group	
7:30 pm	*Theory of Diagnosis*	R.A. Short, Chairman
	"Methods for Finding Fault Detection	D.B. Armstrong
	and Diagnostic Tests"	

"Minimization of the Number of Fault Detection Tests"	H.Y. Chang
"Evaluation of Computer Self-Test Process by Software Simulation"	J.W. Hirsch
"Fault Diagnosis in Combinational Networks"	W.H. Kautz
"Algorithms for the Diagnosis of Automaton Failures	J.P. Roth

Thursday, February 3, 1966

8:00 am	Breakfast	
9:00 am	*Application of Coding and Automata Theory*	W.W. Peterson, Chairman
	"Reliability of Sequential Machines"	J.A. Brzozowski
	"Error Codes for Arithmetic Operations"	H.L. Garner
	"Memory Failures in Automata"	J.F. Meyer
	"Coded Redundancy in Logic Nets"	C.L. Sheng
	"I: On Active Self-Correcting Systems; II: On Error Correction in Memory Systems"	C.V. Srinivasan
	"Functional Coding in Redundancy Techniques"	S. Winograd
12:30 pm	Luncheon	
2:00 pm	*Redundant and Self-Diagnosing Systems*	R.E. Forbes, Chairman
	"A Diagnosable Arithmetic Processor"	A. Avizienis
	"Study of Aerospace Computer Concepts"	M. Ball & F.H. Hardie
	"A Self-Diagnosable Computer"	R.E. Forbes
	"On Self-Diagnosis of Large, Multi-Processor Computers"	E. Manning
	"An Algorithmic Approach to Self-Diagnosis"	R.A. Marlett
	"Self-Checking Microprograms"	R.W. Heckelman
5:30 pm	Social Hour	
6:30 pm	Dinner	
8:00 pm	Ad Hoc Discussion Groups	

Friday, February 4, 1966

8:00 am	Breakfast	
9:00 am	*Multiprocessor and Replacement Systems*	R.E. Miller, Chairman
	"Improving Reliability by the Practical Application of Selected Redundant Techniques"	W.A. England
	"Network Schemes for Combined Fault Masking and Replacement"	J. Goldberg
	"Some Aspects of Self-Repairing Automata"	E.C. Joseph
	"Evaluation of Logical and Organizational Methods for Improving the Reliability and Availability of a Computer"	D.E. Muller
	"Some Techniques in Designing Computer Subsystems for Automated Maintenance and Reliability"	C.V. Ramamoorthy
	"On a Study of Self-Repairing Digital Computers"	I. Terris
12:00 noon	*Closing Remarks:*	
	"Review and an Extrapolation"	R.E. Miller
12:30 pm	Adjournment	

Workshop Participants

Dr. R. Alonso, M.I.T. Instrumentation Laboratory, Cambridge, Massachusetts

Prof. J. B. Angell, Stanford University, Stanford, California

Dr. D. B. Armstrong, Bell Telephone Laboratories, Inc., Murray Hill, New Jersey

Mr. M. Ball, IBM Space Guidance Center, Owego, New York

Prof. J. A. Brzozowski, University of California, Berkeley, California

Dr. H. Y. Chang, Bell Telephone Laboratories, Inc., Holmdel, New Jersey

Mr. C. Disparte, Hughes Aircraft Company, Culver City, California

Mr. W. A. England, Honeywell, Inc., St. Petersburg, Florida

Prof. G. Estrin, University of California, Los Angeles, California

Mr. R. E. Forbes, IBM Space Guidance Center, Owego, New York

Prof. H. L. Garner, University of Michigan, Ann Arbor, Michigan

Mr. J. Goldberg, Stanford Research Institute, Menlo Park, California

Mr. F. H. Hardie, IBM Space Guidance Center, Owego, New York

Mr. R. W. Heckelman, G. E. Electronics Laboratory, Syracuse, New York

Mr. J. W. Hirsch, Autonetics, Anaheim, California

Dr. E. C. Joseph, Univac, St. Paul, Minnesota

Prof. T. Kasami, Osaka University, Osaka, Japan

Dr. W. H. Kautz, Stanford Research Institute, Menlo Park, California

Mr. C. M. Klingman, BELCOM, Inc., Washington, D.C.

Mr. L. S. Levy, Aerospace Corporation, Los Angeles, California

Prof. E. J. McCluskey, Jr., Princeton University, Princeton, New Jersey

Prof. E. Manning, Massachusetts Institute of Technology, Cambridge, Massachusetts

Mr. R. A. Marlett, University of Illinois, Urbana, Illinois

Mr. C. G. Masters, Jr., Westinghouse Electric Corporation, Baltimore, Maryland

Prof. G. Metze, University of Illinois, Urbana, Illinois

Mr. J. F. Meyer, University of Michigan, Ann Arbor, Michigan

Prof. H. Mine. Kyoto University, Kyoto, Japan

Prof. D. E. Muller, University of Illinois, Urbana, Illinois

Prof. W. W. Peterson, University of Hawaii, Honolulu, Hawaii

Dr. C. V. Ramamoorthy, Honeywell, Inc., Waltham, Massachusetts

Dr. J. P. Roth, IBM Research Center, Yorktown Heights, New York

Mr. D. K. Rubin, Jet Propulsion Laboratory, Pasadena, California

Prof. C. L. Sheng, University of Ottawa, Ottawa, Canada

Dr. C. V. Srinivasan, RCA Laboratories, Princeton, New Jersey

Prof. A. Svoboda, University of California, Los Angeles, California

Dr. I. Terris, Hughes Aircraft Company, Culver City, California

Dr. R. H. Urbano, AF Cambridge Research Laboratories, Bedford, Massachusetts

Mr. J. J. Wedel, Jr., Jet Propulsion Laboratory, Pasadena, California

Dr. S. Winograd, IBM Research Center, Yorktown Heights, New York

Mr. H. S. Zieper, RCA Defense Electronic Products, Camden, New Jersey

Workshop Committee

Prof. A. Avizienis, UCLA, Los Angeles, and JPL, Pasadena, California, Chairman

Dr. R. E. Miller, IBM Research Center, Yorktown Heights, New York

Dr. R. A. Short, Stanford Research Institute, Menlo Park, California

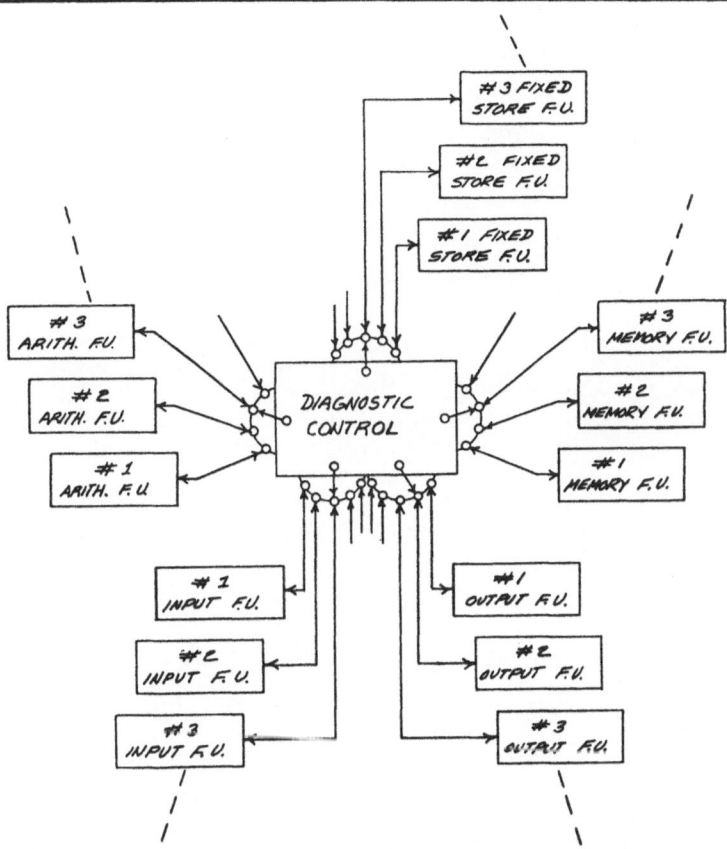

Fig. 1 Block diagram of "STAR" system

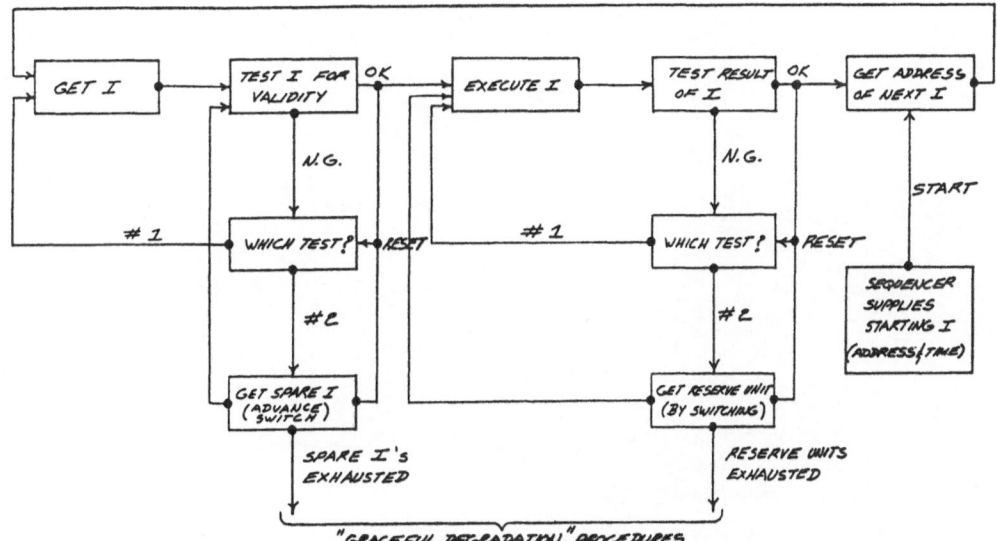

Fig. 2 Diagnostic control flow diagram for "STAR" system

Dependable Computing and Fault Tolerance at LAAS: a Summary

Jean-Claude Laprie and Alain Costes
LAAS-CNRS
7, Avenue du Colonel Roche - 31077 Toulouse CEDEX - France

1. Introduction

This paper reviews the work which has been performed at LAAS on dependable computing and fault tolerance for twelve years. From its very beginning, this work has had two main concerns: a) a system approach, and b) the need for quantification. The system approach has its source in complexity mastering, in the sense of dealing with a global problem by a global approach. The need for quantification is simply to acknowledge the fact that any scientific or technical discipline (even dealing largely with abstractions as does computer science) cannot mature without quantification.

Our work can be summarized as follows: an evaluation-based design methodology enables to motivate the choice of the specific techniques incorporated into a system. The building blocks of the methodology, i.e. the techniques for both fault tolerance and validation, are studied in conjunction with technology advances and users needs evolution. A global framework and the associated terminology contribute in users confidence.

In practice, all these points are, and have to be intimately intermixed. However, in the sake of clarity of the presentation, they will be treated separately. The paper is composed of five sections. The first four sections deal with the work performed on fault tolerance, on validation, on the evaluation-based methodology, and on the dependability concept, respectively. The fifth section gives a brief perspective of the on-going work. The annex 1 lists the dissertation theses which have been defended by the members of the group.

2. Fault Tolerance

The work carried out on fault tolerance techniques can be put into two categories:

- hardware self-checking,
- distributed fault tolerance.

2.1. Hardware Self-checking

2.1.1. Introduction

The rationale for hardware self-checking lies in the desire to process errors as close as possible from their generation. When dealing with hardware faults, this naturally leads to hardware mechanisms for error detection and processing. Our first realization was a microcomputer with built-in autodiagnostics; the microcomputer, called "Gordini", was intended for safety-related applications characterized by a naturally safe position. This initial realization led to two types of extensions: a) the design of a functionally diversified microcomputer, and b) the study of self-checking LSI circuits.

2.1.2. The Gordini Microcomputer [Lan 76, Mor 76]

As stated above, this microcomputer was intended for safety-related applications characterized by a naturally safe position; the aim was thus error detection and the freezing of the outputs upon detection of an error in the computation process, thus providing a fail-safe behavior. Functionally, the microcomputer was composed of an 8080 microprocessor-based CPU, of RAM and ROM memory banks, and of analog and digital inputs and outputs. The RAM, the memory banks and the I/O were communicating through a parallel bus. Error detection was based on the self-checking approach, together with totally self-checking checkers, in order to provide a close-to-100% detection coverage. The detection strategy was based mainly on duplexing and comparing (CPU, memory banks selection, I/O devices), with the exception of the memory blocks, which were organized in bit planes, and provided with simple parity; in addition, the outputs were read again in order to insure detection of the very output devices. In order to avoid error propagation, the bus was provided with isolating devices. A fault analysis module was aimed at localizing faults. Although the machine was not globally fault tolerant stricto sensu, a fault tolerant clock [Mor 75] was implemented in order to insure proper fail-safe operation. The comparators, the parity checkers and the fault analysis module were realized in self-checking logic, and the realization of these elements was performed in random, discrete logic in order that the realization be in conformity with the basic single-fault hypothesis of morphic boolean logic.

2.1.3. The Functionally Diversified Microcomputer [Arl 79]

This work was aimed at exploring measures against errors which are likely to have a common-mode manifestation in designs based on identical copy replication, i.e. a) hardware design faults and b) externally-induced (environmental) transient faults. This led us to design diversity, applied at the hardware level. The resulting microcomputer was based on two diverse microprocessors: a monolithic microprocessor (TMS 9900), and its emulation at the instruction set level by a bit-slice microprocessor (AMD 2900 series). Error detection was provided by comparison, and the microcomputer was providing fail-safe operation with respect to permanent faults, and tolerance to transient faults through checkpointing.

2.1.4. Self-Checking LSI Circuits

The main motivations for this work were twofold: a) facilitating the task of designers of highly dependable systems through the provision of self-checking building blocks, and b) reducing the considerable overhead in terms of IC package count involved by the realization of self-checking checkers in random logic. The work performed on self-checking LSI circuits has involved two steps: self-checking microprocessors, and self-checking microprocessor-based systems.

The work on self-checking LSI circuits was performed in cooperation with EFCIS, under the sponsorship of DRET, the agency for research of the French Department of Defense..

2.1.4.1. Self-Checking Microprocessors

A preliminary phase for this study was a) an analysis of the failure mechanisms in MOS LSI circuits [GAL 79], and b) a comparative study of the existing self-checking techniques in terms of their ability to be integrated.

A conclusion of the analysis of the failure modes was that some failures cannot be modeled as stuck-at-O's or -1's. As a consequence, a set of layout rules was produced aimed at preventing those failures modes to manifest. Applying these layout rules was also shown to improve the circuit's testability.

The comparative study of the self-checking techniques was focused on coding techniques: b-adjacent code made of b inter-leaved single bit parity checks, arithmetic low-cost residue code with check base A = 2b-1 obtained by adding the information b check bits which represent the residue modulo 2b-1 of the infor-mation, k-out-of-2k code, Berger code obtained by adding to the information nk check bits which represent the number of zeros contained in the data, two-rail logic on complementation code.

A four-bit microprocessor was selected as a target for per-forming a self-checking design; the choice of an already existing microprocessor (5000 transistor, P-MOS technology) was made in order to be able to easily quantify the overhead. An evaluation of the overhead brought about by self-check was performed, using three techniques selected from the preliminary phase: simple par-ity, k-out-of-n code, two-rail logic. The result was that the minimum overhead was equal to 73%, 29% being devoted to the checkers. This result has to be weighted by the fact that the con-sidered information width was low (4 bits).

2.1.4.2. Self-Checking Microprocessor-Based Systems

A logical conclusion of the previous study was that all the cir-cuits of a given family should be designed in a self-checking way in order to facilitate the design of self-checking systems. Although this approach is the one providing the best performance in terms of error detection with respect to latency and coverage, the need of (re-)designing all the circuits of a given microprocessor family has obvious drawbacks. This led us to explore another approach, consisting of developing a circuit dedicated to error detection which, through its association with a set of off-the-shelf com-ponents, would ease the realization of self-checking systems, and thus of fault tolerant systems. Such a detection processor should be self-checking, hence the name of the circuit which was designed: the self-checking detection processor, or PAD, which the corresponding initials in French.

The PAD [Cro 80, Cro 86], was intended for the 6800 family. It could handle or facilitate 1) the use of duplexed tightly or loosely synchronized CPUs, 2) the encoding, decoding and error correc-tion of memory words (simple parity, b-adjacent and Hamming SEC/DED), 3) the use of simplex or duplex I/O circuits and peri-pheral controllers, 4) the implementation of rollback and recovery strategies. More precisely, its functions were grouped into three classes:

- detection functions: comparison, watchdog checking, memory code generation and checking, detection of memory protection violation, invalide operation code detection,
- functions facilitating the setting up of a duplex structure: CPU synchronization, information exchange between CPUs, coupling of peripherals,
- error processing functions: processing of transient faults.

2.2. Distributed Fault Tolerance

2.2.1. Introduction

It is often told that distributed systems are more dependable than their centralized counterpart, due to the multiplicity of elements, thus offering a priori possibilities for redundancy and graceful degradation. These inherent qualities can only be fully exploited if the communication support system that interconnects these computing elements is itself dependable, hence the first theme of work: communication in local area networks. Distributed systems involve a multiplicity of communicating resources which constitute multiple access points to information, thus multiple intrusion possibilities, where the term intrusion designates the deliberate interaction human faults. Hence the second theme of work: fault and intrusion tolerance.

2.2.2. Communication in Local Area Networks

The keyword of the work carried out on this theme is decentralization: at no level in the communication hierarchy should there be a single hardware or software component that is essential for correct system operation.The work carried out was performed in the context of real-time applications, and was centered upon two issues: a) the interconnection structure, and b) the medium access control algorithms.

The interconnection structures we studied are buses, loops, and meshed networks. These structures were studied from the fault tolerance viewpoint [Pow 78]. Tolerance to mechanical aggressions was also devoted attention in the case of meshed networks.

Concerning the medium access control algorithms, the aim of decentralization led naturally to favor channel access techniques referred to as competition (CSMA-CD). The frequently encountered desire of guaranteeing bounded, deterministic, access times for some classes of messages (e.g. alarms) led us to study and propose several alternatives to conventional CSMA that enable channel access time to be bounded [Pow 81, Val 84], especially through the inclusion of a forcing header in the exchanged messages. The latter algorithm was implemented in the RHEA network, designed and realized in cooperation with CROUZET under the sponsorship of DRET; RHEA was a 3-connected meshed network for aggressive environments [Pow 78, Cau 82], intended for avionics applications.

The study of high performance communications led us to devote some attention to token-passing schemes. Original algorithms were proposed for the recovery from the simultaneous removal of several stations of a network (a situation frequently encountered in avionics applications on power-shedding), and an implementation under the form of a double bus was designed, the ANTINEA system, in cooperation with ESD under the sponsorship of DRET [PowJ85].

2.2.3. Fault and Intrusion Tolerance: the SATURNE Project

Security is of no lesser importance than reliability or availability for the users of a distributed computing system. In spite of some common underlying mechanisms, such as memory protection techniques, those attributes are traditionally thought of as being separate. In association with INRIA, a project has been launched, aimed at building a bridge between reliability and security, by defining and implementing a fault and intrusion tolerant network: SATURNE [Des 86, Fra 86].

In the SATURNE system, two original mechanisms are explored for fault and intrusion tolerance, which we term saturation and fragmentation, respectively.

The principle of saturation for fault tolerance (hence the name SATURNE: SATURation NEtwork) consists of generating multiple copies of all the active processes, which satisfy the following requirements:

- each site in the network runs a copy of a process;
- the most critical processes are executed with the highest number of copies, and the number of copies of an active process varies dynamicaly as a function of the creation or termination of the other processes;
- error processing is performed through voting on the exchanged data as well as on the remanent information.

This approach offers two major advantages: a) the redundancy level of each process is maximized, according to the available sites in the system, and b) fault latency is minimized since there is no idle site.

An obvious limitation of this approach lies in the high overhead in performance, which should however be bearable due to the utilization of a broadcast communication support.

The principle of fragmentation for intrusion tolerance consists of cutting the files into pieces - the fragments - in such a way that the information contained in each piece be non-significant for an intruder. The fragments are scattered throughout archive sites. Security sites are responsible for managing the access and exclusion rights: they memorize the fragmentation keys (necessary for re-assembling the archived files) and the authentication keys (enabling each user's rights to be acknowledged). A threshold scheme provides protection against the intrusion of the security files, as well as the tolerance to their failures.

3. Validation

3.1. Introduction

In our terminology, as it will be presented in section 4, the term *validation* refers to the means intended for reaching *confidence* in a system ability to deliver the specified service, i.e. both fault removal through verification, and fault forecasting through evaluation.

Most of the work we performed under this headline actually deals with the modeling and evaluation of the measures of dependability: reliability, availability, safety, etc. This work is currently being complemented by verification based on symbolic execution and by fault injection, in order to constitute a comprehensive validation framework for safety-related systems: the EVE project.

3.2. Modeling and Evaluation of the Measures of Dependability

When modeling and evaluating the failure behavior of a system, a distinction has to be made whether the successive times between failures are stochastically equal or not, or which is equivalent, whether design faults are being removed or not. The consequence of design fault removal is known as *reliability growth*, and we label the converse situation as *steady reliability*.

3.2.1. Steady Reliability

Our work in this domain [Lap 84a] can be classed into two topics: a) a unified formulation for the various measures of dependability, b) Markov modeling.

The unified formulation of the dependability measures has first focused on the usual measures: reliability, availability, maintainability, safety [Lap 75]. This formulation has then been extended to a) performance-related measures [Lap 82, Arl 83], to b) cost and profit measures through the utilization of the stochastic reward concept [Mor 80, Mor 81], and to c) distributed systems through the concept of cooperability which is an aggregated measure characterizing the interconnection possibilities of local area communication support systems [Pow 82, Pow 86].

The work devoted to Markov modeling has embodied:

- the study of a) the problems associated with the constancy of the hazard rates, and of b) the model stiffness;
- the construction of Markov models.

A (classical) criticism of the Markov approach is the limitation brought about by the consideration of constant hazard rates, or equivalently of exponentially distributed events. A comparison of the methods enabling to overcome this limitation, i.e. able to account for non constant hazard rates, led to the conclusion that a well-suited method is the device of stages, also known as phase expansion [Lap 81]; we especially shown that the theoretically important expansion of a Markov model brought about by this method can be practically reduced to manageable size.

Model stiffness is introduced by the large dynamics existing between the rates of occurrence of the various events governing the behavior of a computing system, especially when dealing with maintainable systems. We established a formulation enabling to simplify a Markov model subjected to high frequency events [Lap 76].

Model construction is of no lesser importance than model processing, especially with respect to model validation. We have been very early concerned with model construction, and especially with how to account for stochastic dependencies. We first approached this problem heuristically [Lan 78], and then through stochastic Petri nets [Beo 85].

An important milestone in our work on dependability evaluation is the design and realization of the SURF software package [Lan 78, Cos 81], which has been extensively utilized in the evaluation of several classes of computing systems. We especially investigated:

- safety-related systems for process control: active, control, systems [Arl 85], as well as dormant, monitoring, systems [Lap 80];
- supercomputer systems [Arl 83];
- software fault tolerance strategies [Lap 84c, Lap 86].

3.2.2. Reliability Growth

The work performed in this field has been mainly directed towards software reliability. We have adopted an original approach, departing from most studies in this field (characterized by proposing models based on assumptions which are often questioned). This approach consists of modeling the failure behavior under weak assumptions, and then proposing models for capturing the growth phenomena which are deliberately approximations of this behavior. In doing this, we concentrated our efforts on the operational phase of software systems, where availability is equally of importance [Cos 78, Lap 84c, Kan 85].

An aim in this domain is to provide a global framework for enabling the modeling of system dependability with respect to both hardware and software faults, which is actually of interest to the users [Lap 84b, Kan 85].

3.3. The EVE Project

When validating a system, evaluation plays (or should play) a central rle. An evaluation is based on a model of a system, and thus on an abstraction of the system; it has thus to be validated itself. Two points have to be paid a specific attention in such a validation: a) the assumption that some parts of the system are free from faults, especially design faults, and b) the effectiveness of error and fault processing mechanisms.The EVE project [Arl 84b] is precisely aimed at providing a comprehensive framework and a set of tools to explore diversified and complementary methods to address the problem of computer system dependability validation.

The EVE project tackles the problem both of an a priori basis (during the design) and on an a posteriori basis (when a prototype is available). The a priori validation is based on:
- verification by formal methods using symbolic execution;
- evaluation by Markov methods (implemented in the SURF program).

The a posteriori validation is based on fault injection for both verification   (mutation   testing)   and   evaluation   (physical simulation) [Cro 82].

A preliminary study, conducted in cooperation with IRISA, was performed on the Gordini microcomputer, which enabled to a) quantify the error detection mechanisms, and b) to uncover some implementation faults of the detection mechanisms.

A fault injection tool, named MESSALINE, has been realized, which enable two types of fault injections to be performed: fault insertion and fault forcing on the pins of the IC's of the target systems; synchronization between the target and the fault injection modules is provided in order to enable temporary faults to be injected.

The whole validation methodology - evaluation by Markov modeling, verification by symbolic execution, fault injection - has been applied to a prototype of computerized interlocking system under the sponsorship of SNCF, the French Railways.

4. Evaluation-Based Design Methodology

It is widely recognized that the choices made in the design of a system are all the more important as they are performed early in the design process. When dealing with dependability, reliance can all the more be placed on a computing system as the choice of the specific techniques it employs has been motivated by quantified evaluations accompanying the successive refinements which take place in the design process. From there stems the rationale for an evaluation-based design methodology, gradualy built and updated by designing and validating systems for various applications.

Among the system designs we have performed, two of them have been especially conducted according to this methodology:

- a fault tolerant computer for the full authority regulation of turbo-jet engines, ASMARA [Beo 76, Beo 78]; this study, conducted in cooperation with ELECMA under the sponsorship of DRET, involved:

    - the description of the functional specification by Petri nets and the evaluation of possible solutions through transforming the Petri nets into PERT-like nets,

    - the selection of the fault tolerance techniques through Markov modeling of reliability and safety;

- a fault tolerant double-loop distributed system for the monitoring of extra high voltage (EHV) substations, REBECCA [Bla 83]; this study, conducted under the sponsorship of EDF, the French Electricity Board, involved:

- the modeling of the control system embedded in its environment: switches, lines, transformers,

- the design of the monitoring system: an optical double-loop accessed by register insertion.

5. The Dependability Concept

As mentioned in the introduction, we feel the design and the realisation of trustworthy computer systems as being a global problem, which cannot be solved in a satisfactory way without a global framework a) enabling the various techniques involved to be situated, b) providing a means of communication between the experts of these various techniques, and c) helping the users to develop confidence in the computing systems. A continuous effort has been devoted to this task for more than ten years; this effort has found considerable encouragement and our work has been enriched through the extensive discussions which took place in the IFIP WG 10.4. Dependability is a global and structured concept [Lap 82, Lap 85, Avi 86] which encompasses reliability, safety and security. Dependability has three classes of attributes:

- the impairments to dependability: faults, errors, and failures;
- the means for dependability: dependability procurement by fault avoidance and fault tolerance, and dependability validation by fault removal and fault forecasting;
- the measures of dependability: reliability and availability.

The annex 2 gives a summary on the dependability concept and the associated terminology.

6. Perspective

The ever increasing deployment of more and more complex and integrated computing systems will certainly not lower the necessity of adopting a global approach to informatics dependability. Fortunately, an increasing number of voices tell that some barriers are arbitrary and have to be gradualy removed in order to make significant progress in providing the users with computer systems which are reliable, safe and secure, i.e. dependable. Examples are numerous, and we deliberately restrict ourselves in giving two of them on which we are currently working:

- a unified hardware-and-software reliability theory, emphasizing fault activation by input data, rather than fault occurrence as in the classical interpretation of the reliability theory;

- building a bridge between safety and security, from the viewpoints of both the techniques for providing them, and quantified measures for assessing the effectiveness of these techniques.

7. Conclusion

What has been presented in this paper is an attempt to restitute the work performed during more than twelve years by 15 researchers on the average. A number of studies performed as a response to queries originating from industrial partners have not been mentioned up to now; among these, we wish to mention the following ones:

- the determination of a b-adjacent error detecting and correcting code for the Omega interconnection network of the MARIANE supercomputer, performed for SINTRA [Arl 84a];
- the study of failure mode and criticity analysis techniques for software systems, performed for AEROSPATIALE;
- the validation of the SACEM system, a new automatic pilot for subways, performed for RATP, the Paris subway agency.

Fault tolerance is more than a scientific discipline: it is actually a model for thinking and behaving. Bill Carter, who devoted his whole professional life to fault tolerance, would certainly not deny this statement. It is a real pleasure to contribute in this symposium held in his honour, as a modest acknowledgement witness for his constant encouragement in our two leit-motiv: think global and quantify. Interacting with Bill has lasted for more than 11 years, and was especially appreciated by all the members of the group during his sabbatical stay at LAAS, in 1981.

8. Acknowledgements

The research group "Fault Tolerance and Dependable Computing" at LAAS has always shared our enthusiasm for struggling against faults of any kind. We especially wish to thank those members which have accompanied us for several years, and who are still with us in spite of (or because of) the common difficulties: Jean Arlat, Christian Beounes, Jean- Paul Blanquart, Yves Crouzet, Yves Deswarte, Karama Kanoun, and David Powell. Among those who left us for different activities or different countries, we especially think to Christian Landrault and Jorge Moreira de Souza. Other people are performing related work at LAAS, among which Michel Diaz deserves special attention.

We have largely appreciated the interaction with our colleagues of the French community; this interaction developed particularly during the SURF pilot project. Our Grenoble colleagues Bernard Courtois, René David and Pascale Thvenod-Fosse are especially acknowledged.

We have received a strong support from numerous colleagues abroad. Several of them are now long time friends with whom it is a real pleasure to interact and whose work has been a continuous source of inspiration. We are proud to count Jacob Abraham, Tom Anderson, Al Avizienis, Bill Carter, and Brian Randell among them.

9. References

[Arl 79] J. Arlat, "Design of a microcomputer tolerating faults through functional diversity", Dr. Engineer thesis, Toulouse National Polytechnic Institute, April 1979; in French.

[Arl 83] J. Arlat, J.C. Laprie, "Performance-related dependability evaluation of supercomputer systems", in Proc. 13th Int. Symp. on Fault Tolerant Computing, Milano, June 1983, pp. 276-283; extended version: Microelectronics and Reliability, vol. 24, no. 4, Aug. 1984, pp. 717-742.

[Arl 84a] J. Arlat, W.C. Carter, "Implementation and evaluation of a (b,k)- adjacent error-correcting/detecting scheme for supercomputer systems", IBM Journal of Research and Development, vol. 28, no. 2, March 1984, pp. 159-169.

[Arl 84b] J. Arlat, J.P. Blanquart, J.C. Laprie, "On the certification of computing systems: the EVE project", in Proc. 4th Int. Conf. on Reliability and Maintainability, Perros-Guirec, France, May 1984, pp. 650-656; in French.

[Arl 85] J. Arlat, J.C. Laprie, "On the dependability evaluation of high safety systems", in Proc. 15th Int. Symp. on Fault Tolerant Computing, Ann Arbor, Michigan, June 1985, pp. 318-323.

[Avi 86] A. Avizienis, J.C. Laprie, "Dependable computing: from concepts to design diversity", Proceedings of IEEE, vol. 74, no. 5, May 1986, pp. 629-638.

[Beo 76] C. Beounes, J.C. Laprie, "Design of a secure and modular micro computer for process control: ASMARA", in Proc. EUROMICRO Symposium, Venice, Italy, Oct. 1976.

[Beo 78] C. Beounes, F. Cereja, "Design methodology for secure micro computers: application to the implementation of the control of a turbo-jet engine",in Proc. 8th Int. Symp. on Fault Tolerant Computing, Toulouse, June 1978, pp. 10-15.

[Beo 79] C. Beounes, F. Cereja, J.C. Laprie, "Design of a secure and modular microcomputer for the control of a turbo-jet engine", in INFOTECH on Microprocessor Applications, 1979, pp. 155-177.

[Beo 85] C. Beounes, J.C. Laprie, "Dependability evaluation of complex computer systems: stochastic Petri net modeling", in Proc. 15th Int. Symp. on Fault Tolerant Computing, Ann Arbor, Michigan, June 1985, pp. 364-369.

[Bla 83] J.P. Blanquart, K. Kanoun, J.C. Laprie, M. Rodrigues dos Santos, "REBECCA: A dependable communication support system for a distributed monitoring and safety system", in Proc. 3rd Int. Workshop SAFECOMP'83, Cambridge, UK, Sept. 1983, pp. 261-268.

[Bou 80] J.L. Boussin, F. Cereja, J.C. Laprie, K. Medhaffer, "Reliability and safety evaluation by Markov processes of the control system of a very high voltage station", in Proc. EUROCON'80, Stuttgart, March 1980, pp. 459-463.

[Cau 82] G. Caumont, J.C. Laprie, D. Powell, "RHEA: A fault- and damage- tolerant hierarchical communication support system for local area computing in aggressive environments", in Proc. 3rd Int. Conf. on Distributed Computing Systems, Miami, Oct. 1982.

[Cha 82] J. Chavade, Y. Crouzet, "The PAD: a self-checking LSI circuit for fault detection in microcomputers", in Proc. 12th Int. Symp. on Fault Tolerant Computing, Santa Monica, California, June 1982, pp. 55-62.

[Cos 78] A. Costes, C. Landrault, J.C. Laprie, "Reliability and availability models for maintained systems featuring hardware failures and design faults", IEEE Trans. on Computers, vol. C-27, no. 6, June 1978, pp. 548-560.

[Cos 81] A. Costes, J.E. Doucet, C. Landrault, J.C. Laprie, "SURF: A program for dependability evaluation of complex fault tolerant computing systems", in Proc. 11th Int. Symp. on Fault Tolerant Computing, Portland, Maine, June 1981.

[Cro 79] Y. Crouzet, C. Landrault, "Design of self-checking LSI circuits; application to a 4 bit microprocessor", in Proc. 9th Int. Symp. on Fault Tolerant Computing, Madison, Wisconsin, June 1979, pp. 189- 192; also IEEE Trans. on Computers, vol. C-29, no. 6, June 1980, pp. 532-537.

[Cro 80] Y. Crouzet, C. Landrault, "Design specifications of a self-checking detection processor", in Proc. 10th Int. Symp. on Fault Tolerant Computing, Kyoto, Oct. 1980, pp. 275-277.

[Cro 82] Y. Crouzet, B. Decouty, "Measurement of fault detection mechanisms efficiency: results", in Proc. 12th Int. Symp. on Fault Tolerant Computing, Santa Monica, California, June 1982, pp. 373-376.

[Cro 86] Y. Crouzet, J. Chavade, "A 6800 coprocessor for error detection", Proceedings of the IEEE, vol. 74, no. 5, May 1986, pp. 723-731.

[Des 86] Y. Deswarte, J.C. Fabre, J.C. Laprie, D. Powell, "A saturation network to tolerate faults and intrusions", in Proc. 5th Symp. on Reliability in Distributed Software and Database Systems, Los Angeles, Jan. 1986, pp. 74-81.

[Dia 74] M. Diaz, "Design of totally self-checking and fail-safe sequential machines", in Proc. 4th Int. Symp. on Fault Tolerant Computing, Urbana, Illinois, June 1974.

[Fra 86] J.M. Fray, Y. Deswarte, D. Powell, "Intrusion tolerance using fine-grain fragmentation-scattering", in Proc. 1986 Symp. on Privacy and Security, Oakland, California, April 1986, pp. 194-201.

[Gal 79] J. Galiay, Y. Crouzet, M. Vergniault, "Physical versus logical faults in MOS LSI circuits; impact on their testability", in Proc. 9th Int. Symp. on Fault Tolerant Computing, Madison, Wisconsin, June 1979, pp. 195-202; also IEEE Trans. on Computers, vol. C-29, no. 6, June 1980, pp. 527-531.

[Kan 85] K. Kanoun, J.C. Laprie, "Modeling software reliability and availability from development-validation up to operation", LAAS Report no. 85.042, Aug. 1985.

[Lan 76] C. Landrault, J.C. Laprie, "Design, realization and performance evaluation of a microcomputer with built-in autodiagnostics", in Proc. Fault Diagnosis of Digital Networks and Fault Tolerant Computing Symposium, Katowice, Poland, May 1976.

[Lan 78] C. Landrault, J.C. Laprie, "the SURF program for modeling and reliability prediction for fault tolerant computing systems", in Proc. 3rd Jerusalem Conference on Information Technology, Jerusalem, Aug. 1978.

[Lap 75] J.C. Laprie, "Reliability and availability of repairable structures", in Proc. 5th Int. Symp. on Fault Tolerant Computing, Paris, June 1975.

[Lap 76] J.C. Laprie, "On reliability prediction of repairable redundant structures when neglecting repair times", IEEE Trans. on Reliability, vol; R-25, no. 4, pp. 256-258, Oct. 1976.

[Lap 80] J.C. Laprie, K. Medhaffer, "Dependability modeling of safety systems", in Proc. 10th Int. Symp. on Fault Tolerant Computing, Kyoto, Oct. 1980, pp. 245-250; extended version: Microelectronics and Reliability, vol. 22, no. 5, pp. 341-348, Oct. 1982.

[Lap 81] J.C. Laprie, A. Costes, C. Landrault, "Parametric analysis of 2- unit redundant computer systems with corrective and preventive maintenance", IEEE Trans. on Reliability, vol. R-30, no. 2, June 1981, pp. 139-144.

[Lap 82] J.C. Laprie, A. Costes, "Dependability: a unifying concept for reliable computing, in Proc. 12th Int. Symp. on Fault Tolerant Computing, Santa Monica, California, June 1982, pp. 18-21.

[Lap 84a] J.C. Laprie, "Trustable evaluation of computer systems dependability", in Mathematical Computer Performance and Reliability, G. Iazeolla, P.J. Courtois, A. Hordijk, Eds., North Holland, 1984, pp. 341-360.

[Lap 84b] J.C. Laprie, "Dependability modeling and evaluation of software- and-hardware systems", in Proc. 2nd GI Conf. on Fault Tolerant Computing, Bonn, Sept. 1984, pp. 202-215.

[Lap 84c] J.C. Laprie, "Dependability evaluation of software systems in operation", IEEE Trans. on Software Engineering, vol. 10, no.6, Nov. 1984, pp. 701-714.

[Lap 85] J.C. Laprie, "Dependable computing and fault tolerance: concepts and terminology", in Proc. 15th Int. Symp. on Fault Tolerant Computing, Ann Arbor, Michigan, June 1985, pp. 2-11.

[Lap 86] J.C. Laprie, J. Arlat, C. Beounes, C. Hourtolle, K. Kanoun, "Software fault tolerance", LAAS Report no. 86.044, April 1986, 250 p.; in French

[Mor 75] J. Moreira de Souza, E. Peixoto Paz, "Fault tolerant digital clocking systems", Electronics Letters, Sept. 1975, vol. 11, no. 18, pp. 433-434.

[Mor 76] J. Moreira de Souza, E. Peixoto Paz, C. Landrault, "A research oriented microcomputer with built-in auto-diagnostics", in Proc. 6th Int. Symp. on Fault Tolerant Computing, Pittsburgh, June 1976, pp. 3-8.

[Mor 80] J. Moreira de Souza, "A method for the cost benefit analysis of fault tolerance", in Proc. 10th Int. Symp. on Fault Tolerant Computing, Kyoto, Oct. 1980, pp. 201-203.

[Mor 81] J. Moreira de Souza, C. Landrault, "Benefit analysis of concurrent redundancy techniques", IEEE Trans. on Reliability, vol. R-30, no. 1, April 1981, pp. 67-70.

[Pow 78] D. Powell, J.C. Laprie, P. Romand, C. Aleonard, "RHEA: A system for reliable and survivable interconnection of real time processing elements", in Proc. 8th Int. Symp. on Fault Tolerant Computing, Toulouse, June 1978, pp. 117-122.

[Pow 81] D. Powell, "Performance evaluation and comparison of dependable channel access techniques for locally distributed computing systems", in Proc. 2nd Int. Conf. on Distributed Computing Systems, Paris, April 1981.

[Pow 82] D. Powell, "Dependability evaluation of communication support systems for local area distributed computing", in Proc. 12th Int. Symp. on Fault Tolerant Computing, Santa Monica, California, June 1982, pp. 259-266.

[Pow 85] D. Powell, J.C. Valadier, "Dependable avionic data transmission", in AGARD Lecture Series no. 143 "Fault Tolerant Hardware/Software Architecture for Flight Critical Function", 1985, pp. 5.1-5.19.

[Pow 86] D. Powell, "A hierarchical approach to distributed computer system dependability evaluation", The Journal of Systems and Software, vol. 1, no. 2, 1986, pp. 183-198.

[Val 84] J.C. Valadier, D. Powell, "On CSMA protocols allowing bounded access times", in Proc. 4th Int. Conf. on Distributed Computing Systems, San Francisco, May 1984, pp. 146-153.

10. Annex 1: Theses

This annex gives the list of the theses defended by members of the Research Group "Dependable Computing and Fault Tolerance" of LAAS in the framework of their research activity. They are listed in chronological order. The original French title is given inside brackets.

J.C. Laprie Dependability prediction and architecture of repairable real-time digital structures [Prévision de la sureté de fonctionnement et architecture de structures numériques temps réel réparables], Doctor ès-Sciences thesis, Paul Sabatier University, Toulouse, June 16, 1975.

C. Landrault Dependability prediction of repairable digital systems [Prévision de la sureté de fonctionnement des systèmes numériques réparables], Doctor ès-Sciences thesis, Paul Sabatier University, Toulouse, March 11, 1977.

A. Lestrade-Carbonnel Dependability prediction through stochastic processes - The SURF program - Modeling of non-continuously functioning structures [Prévision de la sureté de fonctionnement par les processus stochastiques - Le programme SURF -

Modélisation des structures à fonctionnement discontinu], 3rd Cycle thesis, Paul Sabatier University, Toulouse, June 7, 1977.

C. **Beounes** ASMARA: A dependable and modular computer for avionics applications - Design by successive refinements - Realization [Automate sur et modulaire adapté aux régulations avioniques ASMARA - Conception par raffinements successifs - Réalisation], Doctor-Engineer thesis, Paul Sabatier University, Toulouse, November 9, 1977.

G. **Juanole** Dependability prediction of inter-computer communications - Application to geographically distributed processing systems [Prévision de la sureté de fonctionnement des communications entre calculateurs - Application aux systèmes de traitement géographiquement distribués], Doctor ès-Sciences thesis, Paul Sabatier University, Toulouse, June 20, 1978.

Y. **Crouzet** Design of totally self-checking LSI circuits [Conception de circuits à large échelle d'intégration totalement autotestables], Doctor-Engineer thesis, Polytechnic National Institute, Toulouse, November 15, 1978.

J. **Arlat** Design of a microcomputer tolerating faults by functional diversification [Conception d'un microcalculateur tolérant les fautes par diversification fonctionnelle], Doctor-Engineer thesis, Polytechnic National Institute, Toulouse, April 5, 1979.

K. **Medhaffer-Kanoun** K. Medhaffer-Kanoun Dependability evaluation of safety systems - Application to the control of ultra high voltage stations [Evaluation de la sureté de fonctionnement des systèmes de sécurité - Application à la commande de postes à très haute tension], Doctor-Engineer thesis, Polytechnic National Institute, Toulouse, July 4, 1980.

J. **Moreira de Souza** Predictive evaluation of the behavior of computing systems according to economics and dependability criteria [Evaluation prévisionnelle du comportement de systèmes informatiques selon des critères économiques et de sureté de fonctionnement], Doctor ès-Sciences thesis, Polytechnic National Institute, Toulouse, February 26, 1981.

D. **Powell** Dependable local control networks [Réseaux locaux de commande-controle surs de fonctionnement], Doctor ès-Sciences thesis, Polytechnic National Institute, Toulouse, October 23, 1981.

A.M. **Legwinski** Influence of non solid faults upon computing systems dependability [Influence des fautes non solides sur la sureté de fonctionnement des systèmes informatiques], Doctor-Engineer thesis, Polytechnic National Institute, Toulouse, December 18, 1981.

J.P. Blanquart Design of a dependable communication support for monitoring and safety systems [Conception d'un support de communication sur de fonctionnement pour systèmes de surveillance et de sécurité], Doctor-Engineer thesis, Polytechnic National Institute, Toulouse, April 22, 1983.

P. Traverse On the validation of dependability by mutation - Design of a tool for error injection [Sur la validation de la sureté de fonctionnement par mutation - Conception d'un outil d'injection d'erreurs], Doctor-Engineer thesis, Polytechnic National Institute, Toulouse, December 2, 1983.

P. Narayanan Contribution to the study of broadcast protocols in dependable distributed computing systems [Contribution à l'étude de protocoles à diffusion dans les systèmes informatiques distribués surs de fonctionnement], Doctor-Engineer thesis, Polytechnic National Institute, Toulouse, July 11, 1984.

J.C. Valadier Local control networks: design of an on-board network - ANTINEA [Réseaux locaux de commande-controle : conception d'un réseau embarqué - ANTINEA], Doctor thesis, Polytechnic National Institute, Toulouse, July 12, 1985.

J. Da Silva Fraga Data security by intrusion tolerance [La sécurité des données par la tolérance aux intrusions], Doctor thesis, Polytechnic National Institute, Toulouse, July 12, 1985.

M. Rodrigues dos Santos Error compensation by majority voting: performance evaluation [Compensation d'erreur par vote majoritaire : évaluation des performances temporelles], Doctor thesis, Polytechnic National Institute, Toulouse, November 15, 1985.

11. Annex 2: The Dependability Concept and the Associated Terminology

Dependability is that property of a computing system which allows *reliance to be justifiably placed on the service it delivers*. The **service** delivered by a system is its behavior as *it is perceived* by its user(s); a **user** is another system (human or physical) which *interacts* with the former.

A system **failure** occurs when the delivered service deviates from conditions stated in the service **specification**, the latter being an *agreed* description of the expected service. The failure occurred because the system was erroneous: an **error** is that part of the system state -with respect to the computation process-which is liable to lead to failure. The *adjudged or hypothesized* cause of an error is a **fault**. An error is thus the manifestation of a fault *in the system*, and a failure is the effect of an error *on the* *service*.

Achieving a dependable computing system calls for the *combined* utilization of a set of methods which can be classed into:

- **fault avoidance**: how to prevent, *by construction*, fault occurrence or introduction;
- **fault tolerance**: how to provide, *by redundancy*, a service complying with the specification in spite of faults;
- **fault removal**: how to minimize, *by verification*, the presence of faults;
- **fault forecasting**: how to estimate, *by evaluation*, the presence, the creation, and the consequences of faults.

Fault avoidance and fault tolerance may be seen as constituting dependability **procurement**: how to *provide* the system with the ability to deliver the specified service; fault removal and fault forecasting may be seen as constituting dependability **validation**: how to *reach confidence* in the system's ability to deliver the specified service.

The life of a system is perceived by its users as an alternation between two states of the delivered service with respect to the specified service:

- **proper service**, where the service is delivered *according* to specified conditions;
- **improper service**, where the delivered service *differs from* specified conditions.

A failure is thus a transition from proper to improper service. Quantifying the alternation of proper-improper service delivery leads to the two main measures of dependability:

- **reliability**: a measure of the *continuous* delivery of proper service -or, equivalently, of the *time to* failure;
- **availability**: a measure of the delivery of proper service *with respect to the alternation* of proper and improper service.

The notions introduced up to now constitute the *descriptive attributes* of dependability, which can be grouped into three classes:

- the **impairments** to dependability, which are undesired Qbut not unexpected-circumstances causing or resulting from undependability (whose definition is very simply derived from the definition of dependability: reliance cannot, or will not any longer, be placed on the service): faults, errors, failures;

- the **means** for dependability, which are the methods, tools, and solutions enabling a) to provide with the ability to deliver a service on which reliance can be placed, and b) to reach confidence in this ability: procurement by fault avoidance and fault tolerance, validation by fault removal and fault forecasting;
- the **measures** of dependability, which enable the service quality resulting from the impairments and the means opposing to them to be appraised: reliability and availability.

A more thorough description of dependability is brought about when viewing it according to different, but complementary, *viewpoints*:

- with respect to the *continuity of service*, dependable means **reliable**;
- with respect to the *non-occurrence of catastrophic failures*, dependable means **safe**;
- with respect to the *avoidance, or tolerance, of intentional faults*, dependable means **secure**.

These viewpoints in fact enable the *perceptive attributes* of dependability to be defined: reliability, safety, security. All or some of them are part of the service specification, according to the application considered for a computing system.

The help received thanks to previous work performed at LAAS on self-checking circuits [Dia 74] is acknowledged.

Reliable Digital Systems and Related Stanford University Research

E. J. McCluskey
Center For Reliable Computing
Computer Systems Laboratory
Departments of Computer Science
and Electrical Engineering
Stanford University

ABSTRACT

The various types of digital system applications as they relate to the required reliability characteristics are surveyed. High quality, cost-effective repair is identified as the most pressing current technical challenge to the design of systems having the required reliability attributes. A new approach that relies on system level error detection using schemes such as watchdog processors and built-in-self-test features for diagnosis of faulty units is described. The contributions of the Center for Reliable
Computing to the field of fault-tolerant computing are briefly summarized.

1. Introduction

The term "reliable" is used here in its non-technical sense to mean a system that is available for use according to its user's expectations. These expectations will vary according to the type of system and past experience with similar systems. For example, one washing machine is said to be "more reliable" than another washing machine if the first machine requires repair less often than the second machine. An automobile is reliable if it does not require any repair in addition to the standard scheduled prev entative maintenance. A reliable banking system should never present incorrect information and, in addition, should require unscheduled maintenance very infrequently. A digital control system for machine tools or aircraft should only present correct outputs and should never require unscheduled maintenance. On the other hand, a digital watch should operate without repair for several years and repair need not be possible.

The point of this discussion is that the criteria for deciding whether a system is "reliable" are not absolute, but rather they depend on the system application. The possibility of designing a system that is both reliable and cost-effective rests on several closely related but separate technical disciplines.

2. Fault Avoidance

Digital watches that operate for years without any failures can now be manufactured so inexpensively that no provision for repair or error control is required. The present rate of design innovation for digital watch features is such that a particular watch is very likely to become functionally obsolete before any failure occurs. The only important reliability attribute of such a system is the Mean Time to Failure (MTTF), the mean time that the system operates before the first failure occurs. This is an exa mple of a product in which the best approach to reliability is fault avoidance: It is economically feasible to manufacture systems with acceptable values of MTTF.

The technical disciplines upon which this depends are: semiconductor processing and explicit testing. It is not at present possible to manufacture quantities of Integrated Circuits (ICs) that are all free of defects. Defective chips are eliminated by testing all chips during production. The cost of IC testing is a significant portion of the manufacturing cost of an integrated circuit. There exists a considerable body of testing theory which is the result of many years of research and development aimed at both reducing the cost of testing and improving test quality. The Stanford contributions to testing are listed in Table 1.

Table 1. Stanford Testing Contributions   217

Table 1. Stanford Testing Contributions

TEST PATTERN GENERATION

SURVEYS
Path Sensitization

Module-level test generation using composite justification	[Sziray 79A,B,TN 124,129]
Formalization of critical path technique	[Wang 75A,B]
Multiple Fault	[Xu 83]

Algebraic

Unate function networks	[Betancourt 71] [Clegg 73,][Reese 73]

Sequential Circuits

Checking Experiments	[Chesarek 72]
Output fault checking experiments	[Boute 74A]
State identification in checking experiments	[Boute 74B]

Pseudo-exhaustive

Segment verification	[Bozorgui-Nesbat 80] [McCluskey 80A, 81B]
Fault coverage	[Archambeau 84]

Pseudo-random

Probabilistic Analysis techniques	[Parker TN 18, 75A,B, 78] [McCluskey 74, 78A] [Shedletsky 75A,B, 76, 77]
Adaptive weighted pattern generation	[Parker 76A]
Weighted pattern generation	[Chin TR 84-7]
Estimating test length and fault coverage	[Chin 85][Wagner 86]
Delay fault testing	[Wagner 85A]

PLA

Output function verification	[Bozorgui-Nesbat TR 85-19]
Complete test generation	[Min TR 83-4]
Unified fault model	[Min TR 83-5]

Iterative Logic Arrays

Truth table verification techniques	[Dias 76]

Intermittent faults

Combinational circuits	[Losq 78B] [Savir 77,78A,BC,80B]

FAULT MODELS

Algebraic Properties of Combinational Circuit Faults

Single and multiple stuck fault equivalence	[Clegg 71][McCluskey 71B]
Fault dominance	[Mei TN 2][Mei 74]
Fault masking	[Dias 74, 75]

Algebraic Properties of Sequential Circuit Faults

Fault equivalence in sequential machines	[Boute 71, TR 38]
Testing and diagnosing sequences	[Boute 75]

Bridging Faults

Formulation of model, stuck test detection properties	[Mei 73,74]
Electrical properties in CMOS	[Freeman 86B]

Multiple Faults

Fault coverage of single-stuck fault test set	[Hughes 84,85]
Extending single-stuck test to improve multiple-fault coverage	[Hughes 86]
Parity tree	[Mourad 86A,B,C,D]

Temporary Failures

A circuit for collecting temporary failure data	[McCluskey 81A]
Power supply disturbance effects	[Cortes 86A,B]
Intermittent failure effects	[Cortes 86C,D]
Testability sensor design	[Freeman 86A]

OUTPUT RESPONSE COMPACTION

Pseudo-random inputs	[Parker 76B]
	[Losq 76B,77B, 78A]

DELAY TESTING

Supply voltage control	[Wagner 85B]

SOFTWARE TESTING

Assertion techniques

Flight-control programs	[Andrews TR 85-15]
	[Mahmood 84A,B]
Fault-tolerant programs	[Andrews TR 85-22]
Grid and adaptive automation methods	[Andrews 85]

DESIGN FOR TESTABILITY (DFT)

Survey	[McCluskey 83 84C,D,E,F,G]
	[McCluskey 85B,C,D,E, 86A,C]
Amdahl 580 structures	[Wagner 83]
Scan path structure	[Williams 73]
Testability Analysis	[Wang 84B,85]
CMOS circuit design for testability	[Liu 86]

PLA DFT structures

Lower-overhead structure	[Khakbaz 83B, 84A, 85B]
	[Bozorgui-Nesbat 84A,TR 85-9]
	[Bozorgui-Nesbat 86]
Delay test structure	[Bozorgui-Nesbat 84B]
Redundancy elimination technique	[Dong TR 81-20]

Table 1. Stanford Testing Contributions   219

Sequential machines
Extra input design   [Pradhan TN 173]

BUILT-IN SELF TEST (BIST)

Survey   [Wang 85A]
Pseudo-exhaustive
Survey   [McCluskey 84A]
Output cone verification   [McCluskey 82B,C, 84B]
                                                    [Hirose TR 81-13]
Constant-weight pattern generator   [Ichikawa TR 82-7]
Segment verification   [Bozorgui-Nesbat 80]
                                                    [McCluskey 80A, 81B]
Segmentation technique   [Archambeau TR 85-10]
Adder test using checking circuits   [Lu 83]
and recurrent patterns
Checked binary addition using   [Wakerly 76B]
checksums
Syndrome response compaction   [Savir 80B]
design
Signature Analysis
Parallel analyzer properties   [Hassan TR 82-5,83A]
Parallel analyzer improvements   [Hassan TR 84-3,84]
Multiple signatures   [Hassan 84A]
Use for testing sequential machines   [Hassan 84B,C]
Circuit structures
PLA multiple signature analyzer   [Hassan 83B]
structure
Embedded RAMs   [Sun 84]
Test pattern generators
LFSR with on-line fault detection   [Wang 82]
Condensed LFSR design   [Wang 82A]
Concurrent built-in logic block   [Wang 86A]
observer
Efficient pseudo-exhaustive   [Wang 86B,C]
pattern generators

3. Error Masking

For digital watches the probability of a failure causing an incorrect, but plausible, output display is sufficiently small that output error is not an important design issue. Other systems such as the Space Shuttle avionics system have operating modes during which it is required that erroneous outputs be present for less than one second, [Sklaroff 76]. This is an example of a system for which the critical reliability requirement is error masking, the ability to prevent errors from occurring at the system outputs. For such a system, the appropriate reliability parameter is the failure tolerance, the total number of failed elements that can be present without causing output errors. For some designs it is important to consider both the total number of failed elements and the number of simultaneously failing elements that can be tolerated.

Error masking is achieved with massive redundancy: outputs are typically determined by some form of voting with signals that are identical when no failures are present. The usual forms of massive redundancy are triple-modular redundancy, quad components, and quadded logic.

If the mission time is not more than a few percent of the (irredundant) system MTTF, massive redundancy is sufficient for error masking. However, the ability of a redundant system to mask errors decreases as failures occur. To maintain the error masking attribute of a system for longer than a few percent of the MTTF, removal and perhaps replacement of failed components is necessary. Self-purging redundancy, [Losq 76] is a structure that combines error masking with automatic removal of failed modules. Such a technique is best for mission times ranging up to the irredundant MTTF. For longer missions, the best strategy depends on the ratio between the failure rates for powered and unpowered systems. If the failure rate for an unpowered system is substantially less than that of a powered system, the best design for long missions is probably a standby-spare structure. Voting is used to mask errors and failed modules are replaced by spare modules that are not powered until they are switched on line, [Losq 75]. If powered and unpowered failure rates don't differ, some form of self-purging redundancy is probably the best choice. The Stanford contributions to error masking are listed in Table 2.

Table 2. Stanford Contributions to Error Masking

Redundancy scheme for multiple-fault tolerance	[Losq TN 33]
Time redundancy	[Butner 81, TR 81-2,9]
Adaptive vote-takers	[Pierce 61]
Reliability evaluation	
TMR	[Abraham 74]
NMR	[Siewiorek TR 24]
Interwoven redundant logic	[Abraham 75]
Compensating failures in voted logic	[Siewiorek 74]
Microcomputer systems with TMR	[Wakerly 76A,C]
Signal reliability	[Ogus 74B, 75]
Markov model for reconfigurable computer systems	[Fregni TN 43]
Influence of fault detection and switching mechanisms	[Losq 75]
Transient failures in sequential TMR	[Wakerly 75A]
Hybrid redundancy	
Iterative Cell Switch design	[Siewiorek 73A,TR 20]
Switch complexity comparisons	[Siewiorek 73B]
Fault tolerance of the Iterative Cell Switch	[Ogus 74A]
Reliability analysis for nonperfect switches	[Ogus TR 65]
Self-purging redundancy	[Losq 76C]
Multiprocessors	
Quadruple computer fault-tolerant system	[Kiryukhin 78]
Consistency Unit for fault-tolerance	[Fu 80, TR 81-10]

4. Standby Redundancy for Continuous Operation

There are many systems that do not require error masking since some small number of output errors are tolerable. Examples of such systems are telephone switching systems, bank systems, and reservation systems. Such systems, called transaction processing systems, require continuous operation. They are required to be available "all the time" and thus a system cannot be taken out of service for maintenance.

As an example, the Bell System ESS systems are designed to be out of service for no more than a few minutes each year, [Kraft 81]. Although continuous operation is required, some very small number of errors are usually acceptable. The ESS systems permit no more than 0.01% of the telephone calls to be processed incorrectly. Bank systems have similar requirements, but any errors should be detected so that they can be corrected before they propagate.

Continuous system operation requires that there be at least two (not necessarily identical) components capable of implementing each system function. Any failure must be quickly detected and isolated. Reconfiguration with the failed component replaced by its alternate must occur rapidly. In order for this to be possible the system must include, in addition to the redundant functionality, elements to detect and localize failed components. One major reliability parameter for such systems is the fault coverage , the percentage of all possible faults that are detected by the detection circuits. Successful failure detection does not guarantee continued correct operation since the reconfiguration process can fail or a second failure can occur in the standby unit during reconfiguration. A more general coverage parameter is C, the conditional probability of system recovery given that a failure has occurred. Typical fault detection techniques are duplication and error detecting codes. Another important reliability par ameter for such systems is the mean time to repair, MTTR, since it is important that a failed component be repaired before a subsequent failure can occur in the duplicate component.

Continuous system operation requires good fault detection and localization, reliable reconfiguration circuits, and fast replacement of failed modules with the system still operational. Such systems cannot be turned off for repair and typically cannot be taken out of service for preventative maintenance. This class of system is sometimes called a gracefully degrading system . Immediate repair is not required since there are more than two copies of system functions: the system can continue to operate with re duced capability, but with redundancy still present, until repair is possible. Tandem and Stratus are two companies that build general purpose systems for continuous operation.

5. High Availability Systems

The type of system just described as achieving continuous operation through standby redundancy are sometimes called "high availability systems." It is preferable to reserve the term "high availability system" for that class of system which require that the system be operational almost full time, but which permit the system to be taken out of service for preventative maintenance or repair. Large mainframe computers such as the IBM 3081 are examples of such systems. They do not duplicate all system functions

Table 3. Stanford Cont. to High Avail. and Standby Red. Syst.   223

Table 3. Stanford Contributions to High Availability
and Standby Redundancy Systems
RELIABILITY MODELING

**Data collection and modeling of computer system
activity and reliability**

Performance-related system reliability measures	[Beaudry 77, 78A,B, 79 TR 141, TN 172]
Measurement and modeling of system activity and reliability	[Butner 80], [Andrews 85-18]
Failure/load relationship	[Iyer 82B]
CPU errors and system activity	[Iyer 82A, 83, 86, TR 83-6]
Hardware-related software errors	[TR 84-2, Iyer 85]
Software-related failures on the IBM 3081	[Rosetti 82] [Velardi 84]
Operating system reliability effects of workload	[Iyer 85B]
IBM MVS/XA operating system reliability	[Mourad 85]
Thermal effects on device reliability	[Cortes 84]

Sensitivity of reliability to failure rate characteristics

Variance of failure rate	[Iyer 79]
Uncertainty of failure rate and system reliability	Iyer 80]
Uncertainty of failure rate and memory system reliability	[Iyer TR 83-9]

HIGH-AVAILABILITY SYSTEMS

Survey	[McCluskey 75, 80B, 82C, 85A]
Comparative architecture	[McCluskey 77]
Time redundancy	[Butner 81, TR 81-2,9]
Coverage parameter calculation	[Amer 86]
Rollback interval	[Shedletsky 76A]
Alternate-data retry	[Shedletsky 76B]

FAILURE DIAGNOSIS

Probabilistic analysis

Model	[Blount 77, TR 144, TN 139]
Fail-soft computer systems	[Blount 78, 80]

Watchdog processors

Survey	[Mahmood TR 85-7]
Architecture	[Namjoo 83]
Control flow checking	[Lu 80A,B, 85]
Path signature analysis	[Namjoo TR 82-16]
Microprogrammed control units	[Namjoo 82A]
Assertion methods	[Mahmood TR 83-10, 85] [Ersoz TR 85-8]
Error coverage and overhead	[Mahmood TR 85-7]

A long MTTF is obtained by conservative, careful manufacturing, good error recovery routines, and very thorough testing. The cost of test is increasing very rapidly so that it is necessary to anticipate test requirements during design in order to obtain thorough tests at reasonable cost. Design-for-testability is now standard at large main frame computer manufacturers, and Built-in Self Test techniques [McCluskey 85] are becoming more common, [Daniels 85].

Short repair times require quick diagnosis of the failing element, spare part availability and ease of replacement. For large mainframe computers the standard method for guaranteeing fast diagnosis is the inclusion of checking circuits in each unit so that a failure is quickly recognized and reported. Parity check codes are the most common technique although residue codes are also used for arithmetic operations. The check circuits often can not localize the failure site to a single unit so that additional analysis may be needed to speed repair. Diagnostic programs are used to help identify failed units. They are also often run periodically in order to predict failures before they cause errors as well as to identify failed units.

Many systems require high availability, but do not include embedded checkers. These systems rely on diagnostic programs and human diagnosis to achieve low repair times. This methodology is becoming increasingly unsatisfactory and expert system techniques are now being explored for improving this situation.

Efficient, cost effective techniques for obtaining very good quality maintenance and repair are currently the most pressing issues in the field of reliable computing. Fault diagnosis and localization are major issues for both systems that require continuous operation and those that require high availability. The various alternatives and most promising approaches will be discussed next.

6. High Quality Failure Diagnosis and Localization

Embedded checkers provide the most thorough failure diagnosis and localization. In spite of this, their current usage is restricted to high availability systems such as telephone offices and to large main frame computers. There are two major reasons for this situation: the absence of a design tradition for checking circuits, and the high hardware overhead associated with them. The standard texts in logic design include almost no material on design with embedded checkers. Almost all of the design techniques for embedded checkers have been developed in the context of a general purpose instruction processor and the associated data paths. There are many systems that do not have this structure, but which require good repair. Since there is no general tradition for such design, the design cost associated with including such circuits can be very high. The hardware overhead approaches 100% of the cost of the unchecked system.

when the design and hardware costs are acceptable, using embedded checkers is an adequate method to guarantee high quality failure diagnosis and localization. The motivation for requiring high quality failure diagnosis was to ensure accurate and fast repair of a failed unit. Stanford contributions to checking and check circuit designs are listed in Table 4.

Table 4. Stanford Contributions to Concurrent Checking

Embedded Checkers

Fail-safe circuits for I/O subsystems	[Usas 75A]
Self-diagnosing Computers	[Wakerly 74B]
Detection of unidirectional multiple errors	[Wakerly 75B]
PLA structure for concurrent checking	[Dong TR 81-11, 82-11]
	[Khabaz 82A,85A]
Modified Berger codes for unidirectional errors	[Dong 82, 84]
Parity prediction for general combinational circuits, break faults	[Khodadad 79, TN 183]

Self-checking Checkers

Self-checking periodic-signal checker	[Usas 74,75B]
Partially self-checking circuits and logic operations	[Wakerly 74A]
Totally self-checking comparators with many inputs	[Hughes 83,84]
Totally self-checking checker for 1-out-of-n codes	[Khabaz 82C]
Self-testing embedded code checkers	[Khabaz 82B, 83A, 84B]
Cascade structure in self-checking networks	[Kolupaev 77]
Quantative comparison of self-checking designs	[Lu 78, 84]
Self-checking LFSRs	[Lu TN 177]
Self-checking microprogrammed processor	[Wakerly 76D]

There are two other approaches to good repair that are currently being explored as possibilities for avoiding the high cost of embedded checking: Expert system maintenance techniques and use of explicit testing BIST circuitry for maintenance.

7. Expert System Maintenance

This approach aims at constructing an Expert System facility that includes either the knowledge that expert maintenance technicians use to repair the system, or knowledge of the system structure along with the reasoning techniques used by maintenance experts, or both capabilities. To evaluate the promise of such an approach, the limitations of maintenance of a system with minimal built-in check circuitry by experts must be considered. In particular the difficult repair situations should be evaluated.

A typical first step for repair is to attempt identification of the failed unit by running a diagnostic program. If such an identification succeeds, the unit is replaced and the system restarted. The failed unit is returned for repair. This is the easy case of system repair. The more troublesome cases are when replacement of the unit identified as faulty does not correct the system-level problem and the case when the diagnostic program does not identify any unit as having failed. In fact, it is often not p ossible to demonstrate that any system-level failure is present even though a failure event occurred during normal operation. In this case, the repair action depends on the type of system. For a system used in non-critical applications, it may just be returned to service and the failure identified as being due to software or to an unexplained event. For critical applications the system will have to be taken out of service and probably be disassembled to locate the failure source.

When a system-level failure can be demonstrated, but the failing unit cannot be identified the standard approach is to replace suspect units one-by-one until the system failure is removed. A disturbing feature of this situation is that it is often not possible to verify by test that the removed units are faulty and thus not possible to repair them so that they can be returned to service.

It is possible that use of an expert system can provide better repair than repair by an actual maintenance person. The system can include the knowledge and reasoning abilities of many experts rather than just one. However, it does not appear that the expert system can provide large improvements over the best manual repair. The quality of repair will continue to be limited by the possibilities of reproducing failure symptoms and diagnosing failed components.

High quality maintenance of a system that is designed without adequate maintenance features is very unlikely. Either the traditional approach of including embedded checkers in the system must be adopted or a new technique for identifying causes of system failure must be developed. A very promising approach for obtaining high quality repair without extensive use of embedded checkers is described next.

8. System Level Concurrent Checking and Bist Facilities

The method described here is based on the use of thorough system-level checking techniques to provide error detection and approximate localization. Precise identification of failed components is obtained by using the built-in-self-test, BIST, features included for production testing.

Use of a small coprocessor, called a Watchdog Processor, has been demonstrated to provide very good error detection capability with reasonable overhead both in terms of required hardware resources and design complexity, [Mahmood 85A,B]. Inclusion of such a feature in a system provides error detection at the system level and approximate diagnosis of the failed unit. This should eliminate the problem that occurs when it is not possible to reproduce the system failure so that there is no indication of which u nit to test. Precise verification of the failed unit may not be provided by the system-level checking, but this can be obtained by use of the built-in self-test, BIST, facilities incorporated in chips and on boards for production test.

There is increasing recognition that cost-effective testing of modern integrated circuits will require the inclusion of on-chip circuitry to provide a self-test capability, [Daniels 85]. The possibility of using this capability for system repair has not been adequately explored, but it does seem feasible that these features could be made available for activation by system diagnostics and maintenance processors. This would then provide very precise localization of failed units.

One possible objection to this strategy relates to the common phenomenon of a replaced unit testing as fault-free in a production test even though the system failure was eliminated by its replacement. There is a belief that this is caused by intermittent failures and the inability to reproduce the same environment as the unit has in the system. Recent research, [Cortes 86], has demonstrated that there exist simple intermittent failure mechanisms that cause failures that cannot be modeled as single-stuck faults. This shows that there can be field failures that cannot be detected by single-stuck fault test sets even though a more complete combinational test would detect the fault. The inadequacy of a test based on the single-stuck fault model can be overcome by using a more thorough test technique such as pseudo-exhaustive testing, [McCluskey 81], [McCluskey 84].

9. Stanford Contributions

The previous sections have been an attempt to assess the current state-of-the-art of fault tolerant computing and summarize the major Stanford contributions. The major contributions can be grouped as the development of fault models and associated algebraic properties, the experimental characterization of temporary failures, the scan path structure for testable design, probabilistic methods for testability and test pattern generation analysis, pseudo-exhaustive test methods, hybrid and self-purging redundan cy structures and evaluation, the reliability - performance relation, the watchdog processor concept and implementations. Almost thirty Ph.D.s have been earned in the areas of fault tolerance, testing and reliable computing. These are listed in Table 5.

Table 5. List of Stanford Ph.D.s in Reliable Computing.

F.W. Clegg, Algebraic Properties of Faults in Logic Networks, 1970.

D.J. Chesarek, Fault Detecting Experiments for Sequential Machines, 1972.

D.P. Siewiorek, Fault-Tolerant Computers Using Self-Diagnosis and Hybrid Redundancy, 1972.

R.T. Boute, Faults in Sequential Machines: Algebraic Properties and Detection Methods, 1973.

J.A. Abraham, Reliability Analysis of Digital Systems Protected by Massive Redundancy, 1974.

J.F. Wakerly, Low-Cost Error Detection Techniques for Small Computers, 1974.

D.T. Wang, An Algorithm for the Generation of Test Sets for Combinational Logic Networks, 1974.

J. Losq, Modeling and Reliability of Redundant Digital Systems, 1975.

K.C.Y. Mei, Dominance Relations of Stuck-At and Bridging Faults in Logic Networks, 1975.

R.C. Ogus, Design and Evaluation of Ultra-Reliable Hybrid Redundant Digital Systems, 1975.

F.J. O.-Dias, Multiple Fault Analysis in Combinational Logic Circuits, 1975.

S.G. Kolupaev, Cutting Planes and Self-Checking Systems, 1975.

K.P. Parker, Probabilistic Test Generation, 1976.

J.J. Shedletsky, Error Latency in Digital Circuits, 1976.

A.M. Usas, Error/Management in Digital Computer Input/Output Systems, 1976.

R. Betancourt, Analysis and Synthesis of Sequential Circuits Using Clocked Flip-Flops, 1977.

J. Savir, Detection of Intermittent Failures in Combinational Circuits, 1977.

M.D. Beaudry, Performance Considerations for the Reliability Analysis of Computing Systems, 1978.

M.L. Blount, Probabilistic Fault Diagnosis Models for Digital Systems, 1978.

D. Lu, Concurrent Testing and Checking in Computer Systems, 1981.

S. Butner, Failures in Computers: A Study of Their Characteristics and a Tolerance Technique, 1981.

J. Khakbaz, Testing and Concurrent Checking for PLA's and Related Checker Design Issues, 1983.

M. Namjoo, Concurrent Testing at the Computer System Level, 1983.

S. Hassan, Design for Testability Techniques Using Signature Analysis, 1984.

S. Bozorgui-Nesbat, Design for Testability: Random Logic and Programmable Logic Arrays, 1985.

J.L.A. Hughes, Reliable Digital Systems: Multiple Fault Detection and Totally Self-Checking Comparators, 1986.

A. Mahmood, Concurrent Checking Using Watchdog Processors, 1986.

10. Conclusions

High quality, cost-effective maintenance is the most pressing current technical issue for digital system design. Just as design-for-testability is becoming accepted as a necessity for economic production testing, economical maintenance will not be possible without the inclusion of system facilities for on-line error detection and failure diagnosis. The use of watchdog processor techniques coupled with built-in self-test facilities are a very promising approach for obtaining good maintenance without the exp ense of embedded checkers. Expert systems are another promising approach, but will not eliminate the need for system aids to error detection and diagnosis

11. Acknowledgements

This work was supported in part by the National Science Foundation under Grant No. MCS-8200129, and in part by the Innovative Science and Technology Office of the Strategic Defense Initiative Organization and Administered through the Office of Naval Research under Contract No. N00014-85-K-0600. The author would like to thank Monroe Edwards and Ramaswami Dandapani for their helpful comments and Joseph and David McCluskey for their help with text preparation.

12. References

[Daniels 85] Daniels, R.G., and W.C. Bruce, "Built-In Self-Test Trends in Motorola Microprocessors," IEEE Design and Test , April 1985, pp. 64-71.

[Kraft 81] Kraft, G.D., and W.N. Toy, Microprogrammed Control and Reliable Design of Small Computers, Prentice-Hall, Inc, Englewood Cliffs, NJ, 1981.

[Sklaroff 76] Sklaroff, J.R., "Redundancy Management Technique for Space Shuttle Computers," IBM Journal, Jan. 1976, pp. 20-28.

13. Bibliography of Stanford Publications

[Abraham 74] Abraham, J.A., and D.P. Siewiorek, "An Algorithm for the Accurate Reliability Evaluation of Triple Modular Redundancy Networks," IEEE Trans. Comput., Vol. C-23, No. 7, Jul. 1974.(Also Dig. 1973 Int'l Symp on FTC)

[Abraham 75] Abraham, J.A., "A Combinatorial Solution to the Reliability of Interwoven Redundant Logic Networks," IEEE Trans. Comput., Vol. C-24, No. 5, pp. 578-584, May 1975.

[Amer 86A] Amer, H.H., and E.J. McCluskey, "Calculation of the Coverage Parameter for the Reliability Modeling of Fault-Tolerant Computer Systems," IEEE Int'l Conf. on Circuits and Systems, San Jose, CA, May 5-7, 1986. (See TR. 86-1)

[Amer 86B] Amer, H.H., and E.J. McCluskey, "Weighted Coverage in Fault-Tolerant Systems," to be presented at Reliability and Maintainability Symposium, Philadelphia, PA, Jan. 1987.
Andrews, D.M., A. Mahmood and E.J. McCluskey, "Dynamic

Assertion Testing of Flight Control Software," CRC TR 85-15.

Andrews, D.M., and E.J. McCluskey, "The Measurement and Statistical Modeling of Computer Reliability as Affected by System Activity," CRC TR 85-18.

Andrews, D.M., A. Mahmood, and E.J. McCluskey, "A Methodology for Testing Fault-Tolerant Software," CRC TR 85-22.

[Andrews 85] Andrews, D.M., "Automation of Assertion Testing: Grid and Adaptive Techniques," HICSS-19, Vol. 2, pp. 692-699.(CRC TR 84-12)

[Archambeau 84] Archambeau, E.C., and E.J. McCluskey, "Fault Coverage of Pseudo-Exhaustive Testing," FTCS-14 , pp. 141-145.(CRC TR 84-2) (CRC TR 83-20)

Archambeau, E.C., "Network Segmentation for Pseudo-Exhaustive Testing," CRC TR 85-10.

[Beaudry 77] Beaudry, M.D., "Performance Related Reliability Measures for Computing Systems," FTCS-7, pp. 16-21.(DSL TN 101)

Beaudry, M.D., "Dual Redundancy - a Survey," DSL TN 93 (1977).

Beaudry, M.D., "A Statistical Study of Service Interruptions at the SLAC Triplex Multiprocessor," CSL TR 141 (1978).

[Beaudry 78A] Beaudry, M.D., "Performance-related Reliability Measures for Computing Systems," IEEE Trans. Comput., pp. 540-547, June 1978. (DSL TN 101)

[Beaudry 78B] Beaudry, M.D., "Performance Considerations for Reliability Analysis - a Statistical Case Study," FTCS-8, p. 198.(DSL TR 126)

[Beaudry 79] Beaudry, M.D., "A Statistical Analysis of Failures in the SLAC Computing Center," Dig., Spring COMPCON'79, pp. 49-52, San Francisco, CA, Feb. 26 - Mar. 1, 1979.

Beaudry, M.D., "Stochastic Behavior of Failures in Computing Systems," CSL TN 172 (1980).

[Betancourt 73] Betancourt, R., "Derivation of Minimum Test Sets for Unate Logic Circuits," IEEE Trans. Comput., Vol. C-20, No. 11, pp. 1264-1269, Nov. 1973.

Betancourt, R., "Computer Programs for 'Reliability Evaluation Programs' - A Survey," CSL TN 119 (1979).

[Blount 77] Blount, M.L., "Probabilistic Treatment of Diagnosis in Digital Systems," FTCS-7, pp. 72-77.(DSL TR 102)

Blount, M.L., "A Probabilistic Model for Diagnosis in Digital Systems CSL TR 144 (1978).

Blount, M.L., "On the Calculation of the Parameter Set for the Probabilistic Diagnosis Model," CSL TN 139 (1978).

[Blount 78] M.L., "Modeling of Diagnosis in Fail-Softly Computer Systems," FTCS-8, pp. 53-58.(DSL TR 123)

[Blount 80] Blount, M.L., "Modeling of Diagnosis in Fail-Softly Computer Systems Design Automation & Fault-Tolerant Computing, Vol. III, Issue 3/4, pp. 171-189, 1980.(DSL TR 123)

[Boute 71] Boute, R.T., and E.J. McCluskey,"Fault Equivalence in Sequential Machines," Symp. on Comp.and Automata, pp. 483-507, Polytechnic Institute of Brooklyn,S Apr. 13-15 1971.

[Boute 72] Boute, R.T., "Equivalence and Dominance Relations Between Output Faults in Sequential Machines," DSL. TR. No. 38, Nov. 1972.

[Boute 74A] Boute, R.T., and E.J., McCluskey, "Optimal and Near-Optimal Checking Experiments for Output Faults in Sequential Machines," IEEE Trans. Comput., Vol. C-23, No. 11, pp. 1207-1213, Nov. 1974.

[Boute 74B] Boute, R.T., "Distinguishing Sets for Optimal State Identification in Checking Experiments," IEEE Trans. Comput., Vol. C-23, No. 8, pp. 874-878, Aug. 1974.

[Boute 75] Boute, R.T., "Algebraic Properties of Testing and Diagnosing Sequences," FTC-5, p. 242, Paris, June 18-20, 1975.

[Bozorgui-Nesbat 80] Bozorgui-Nesbat, S., and E.J. McCluskey, "Structured Design for Testability to Eliminate Test Pattern Generation," FTCS-10, pp. 158-163.(DSL TR 177)

[Bozorgui-Nesbat 84A]Bozorgui-Nesbat, S., and E.J. McCluskey, "Lower Overhead Design for Testability of Programmable Logic Arrays," ITC84 , pp. 856-865. (CRC TR 84-8)

[Bozorgui-Nesbat 84B]Bozorgui-Nesbat, S., and E.J. McCluskey, "Design for Delay Testing of Programmable Logic Arrays," ICCAD84 , pp. 146-148.(CRC TR 84-10)
Bozorgui-Nesbat, S., "LIST and Documentation of the PLA Testability Program," CRC TR 85-9.
Bozorgui-Nesbat, S., and E.J. McCluskey, "Verification Testing of Programmable Logic Arrays," CRC TR 85-19.

[Bozorgui-Nesbat 86] Bozorgui-Nesbat, S., and E.J. McCluskey, "Lower Overhead Design for Testability of Programmable Logic Arrays," IEEE Trans. on Comp., Vol. c-35, No. 4, pp. 379-383, April, 1986.

[Butner 80] Butner, S.E. and R.K. Iyer, "A Statistical Study of Reliability and System Load at SLAC," FTCS-10, pp. 207-209. (DSL TR 188) (DSL TN 177)
Butner, S.E., "A Universal Slice Element for Triple Time Redundant Systems," CRC TR 81-9.
Butner, S.E., "Triple Time Redundancy, Fault-masking in Byte-

Sliced Systems," CRC TR 81-2.

[Butner 81] Butner, S.E., "A Constructive Approach to Fault Tolerance in VLSI-Based Systems," Proc., 1981 International Conf. on Parallel Processing, pp. 264-265, Bellaire, MI, Aug. 25-28, 1981.

[Chen 84] Chen, Harry, H., R. Mathews, and J. Newkirk, "Test Generation for MOS Circuits," 1984 Int'l Test Conference.

[Chen 85] Chen, Harry, H., R. Mathews, and J. Newkirk, "An Algorithm to Generate Tests for MOS Circuits at the Switch Level," 1985 Int'l Test Conference.

[Chesarek 72] Chesarek, D.J., "Fault Detecting Experiments for Sequential Machines," Ph.D. Dissertation, DSL Stanford Ca. 1972. Chin, C.K., and E.J. McCluskey, "Weighted Pattern Generation for Built-in Self-Test," CRC TR 84-7.

[Chin 85] Chin, C.K., and E.J. McCluskey, "Test Length for Pseudo-Random Testing," ITC85, pp. 94-99.(CRC TR 85-14)

[Clegg 71] Clegg, F.W., and E.J. McCluskey, "The Algebraic Approach to Faulty Logic Networks," Dig. 1971 Int'l. Symp. on Fault Tolerant Computing, pp. 44-46, Pasadena, CA, Mar. 1-3, 1971.

[Clegg 73] Clegg, F.W., "Use of SPOOFS for Faulty Logic Network Analysis," IEEE Trans. Comput., Vol. C-22, No. 3, pp. 229-234, Mar. 1973.(Also Dig. 1972 Int'l. Symp. FTC)
CRC Faculty and Staff, "Center for Reliable Computing," DSL TN 112 (1977).

[Cortes 84] Cortes, M.L., and R.K. Iyer, "Device Failures and System Activity: A Thermal Effects Model," FTCS-14 , pp. 71-76. (CRC TR 84-2)

[Cortes 86A] Cortes, M., and E.J. McCluskey, "Modeling Power-Supply Disturbances in Digital Circuits, " IEEE Int'l Solid-State Circuits Conf., Anaheim, CA, Feb. 19-21, 1986. (See TR. 86-1)

[Cortes 86B] Cortes, M., E.J. McCluskey, K.D. Wagner, and D.J. Lu, "Properties of Transient Errors Due to Power Supply Disturbances," IEEE Int'l Conf on Circuits and Systems, San Jose, CA, May 5-7, 1986. (See TR 86-1)

[Cortes 86C] Cortes, M., and E.J. McCluskey, "An Experiment on Intermittent-Failure Mechanisms," ITC 86.

[Cortes 86D] Cortes, M., and E.J. McCluskey, "An Experiment on Intermittent-Failure Mechanisms," Submitted to IEEE Trans. Reliability, 9/86.

[Davies 78] Davies, D., and J.F. Wakerly, "Synchronization and Matching in Redundant Systems," IEEE Trans. Comput., pp. 531-539, June 1978.
Davies, D., "Reliable Synchronization and Matching in

Redundant Systems," CSL TR 169 (1979).

[Dias 75] Dias, F.J.O., "Fault Masking in Combinational Logic Circuits," IEEE Trans. on Comput., Vol. C-24, No. 5, May 1975.(Also FTCS-74)

[Dias 76] Dias, F.J.O., "Truth-table Verification of an Iterative Logic Array," IEEE Trans. Comput., C-25, No. 6, pp. 605-613, June 1976. DSL TN No. 94.

[Dong] Dong, H., and E.J. McCluskey, "Design of Fully Testable Programmable Logic Arrays," CRC TR 81-20.
Dong, H., and E.J. McCluskey, "Matrix Representation of PLA's and an Application to Characterizing Errors," CRC TR 81-11.
Dong, H., and E.J. McCluskey, "Concurrent Testing of Programmable Logic Arrays," CRC TR 82-11.

[Dong 82] Dong, H., "Modified Berger Codes for Detection of Unidirectional Errors," FTCS-12 , pp. 317-320.(CRC TR 82-3) (CRC TR 81-16)

[Dong 84] Dong, H., "Modified Berger Codes for Detection of Unidirectional Errors," IEEE Trans. Comput., C-33, No. 6, pp. 572-575, June 1984.(CRC TR 82-3) (CRC TR 81-16)

[Erzos] Ersoz, A., D.M. Andrews, and E.J. McCluskey, "The Watchdog Task: Concurrent Error Detection Using Assertions," CRC TR 85-8.

[Freeman 86A] Freeman, G.G., "Development of Logic Level CMOS Bridging Fault Models," CRC TR 86-10. (DSL N No. 298)

[Freeman 86B] Freeman, G.G., D. Liu, B. Wooley, and E.J. McCluskey, "Two CMOS Sensors," (CRC TR 86-4)

'[Fregni]Fregni, E. and R.C. Ogus, "Error Recovery Techniques in Computer Systems: A Survey," DSL TN 42, 1974.
Fregni, E., M.D. Beaudry, and R.C. Ogus, "A Markov Model of a Reconfigurable System," DSL TN No. 43, 1974.

[Fu 80] Fu, P.L., "Consistency Unit for Fault-Tolerant Multiprocessor," FTCS-10, pp. 363-368.(DSL TR 177)
Fu, P.L., "Consistency in Interprocessor Communications for Fault-tolerant Multiprocessors," CRC TR 81-10. ,

[Hassan] Hassan, S.Z., "Algebraic Analysis of Parallel Signature Analyzers," CRC TR 82-5.

[Hassan 83A] Hassan, S.Z., D.J. Lu and E.J. McCluskey, "Parallel Signature Analyzers Detection Capability and Extensions," COMPCON83, pp. 440-445.(CRC TR 82-20)

[Hassan 83B] Hassan, S.Z., and E.J. McCluskey, "Testing PLAs Using Multiple Parallel Signature Analyzers," FTCS-13, pp. 422-425. (CRC TR 83-13)(CRC TR 83-3)(CRC TR 82-9)

[Hassan 83C] Hassan, S.Z., "Signature Testing of Sequential Machines," ITC83, pp. 714-718.(CRC TR 83-10)(CRC TR 82-18) Hassan, S.Z., and E.J. McCluskey, "Increasing Effective Fault Coverage of Parallel Signature Analyzers," CRC TR 84-3.

[Hassan 84A] Hassan, S.Z., and E.J. McCluskey, "Increased Fault Coverage through Multiple Signatures," FTCS-14 , pp. 354-359.(CRC TR 84-2) (CRC TR 83-17)

[Hassan 84B] Hassan, S.Z., "Signature Testing of Sequential Machines," IEEE Trans. Comput., C-33, No. 8, pp. 762-764, Aug. 1984. (CRC TR 83-10)(CRC TR 82-18)

[Hassan 84C] Hassan, S.Z., and E.J. McCluskey, "Pseudo-Exhaustive Testing of Sequential Machines Using Signature Analysis," ITC84, pp. 320-326 (CRC TR 84-8)

[Hassan 84D] Hassan, S.Z., and E.J. McCluskey, "Enhancing the Effectiveness of Parallel Signature Analyzers," ICCAD84, pp. 102-104. (CRC TR 84-10)

[Hayes 80] Hayes, J.P., and E.J. McCluskey, "Testability Considerations in Microprocessor-Based Design, Computer, pp. 7-26, Mar. 1980. (CSL TR 179)

'[Hirose]Hirose, F., and V. Singh, "McDDP, A Program for Partitioning Verification Testing Matrices," CRC TR 81-13.
Hughes, J.L.A., "A High-level Representation for Implementing Control-Flow Structures in Dataflow Programs," CRC TR 82-4.

[Hughes 82] Hughes, J.L.A., "Implementing Control-flow Structures in Dataflow Programs," COMPCON82 , pp. 87-90.

[Hughes 83] Hughes, J.L.A., E.J. McCluskey, and D.J. Lu, "Design of Totally Self-Checking Comparators with an Arbitrary Number of Inputs," FTCS-13, pp. 169-172.(CRC TR 83-18)(CRC TR 83-3)

[Hughes 83] Hughes, J.L.A., "Error Detection and Correction Techniques for Dataflow Systems," FTCS-13, pp. 318-321.(CRC TR 83-3) (CRC TR 83-1)

[Hughes 84A] Hughes, J.L.A., E.J. McCluskey, and D.J. Lu, "Design of Totally Self-Checking Comparators with an Arbitrary Number of Inputs," IEEE Trans. Comput., C-33, no. 6, pp. 546-550, June 1984. (CRC TR 83-1)(CRC TR 83-3)

[Hughes 84B] Hughes, J.L.A., and E.J. McCluskey, "An Analysis of the Multiple Fault Detection Capabilities of Single Stuck-At Fault Test Sets," ITC84 , pp. 52-58.(CRC TR 84-8)

[Hughes 85] Hughes, J.L.A., S. Mourad, and E.J. McCluskey, "An Experimental Study Comparing 74LS181 Test Sets," COMPCON85 , pp. 384-387.(CRC TR 84-13)

[Hughes 86] Hughes, J.L.A., and E.J. McCluskey, "Multiple Stuck-At Fault Coverage of Single Stuck-At Fault Test Sets," to be presented at ITC'86.

[Ichizuka] Ishizuka, O., "Application of Multi-valued Multi-threshold Network for Realizing Unary Functions," CRC TR 81-4.

[Ichikawa] Ichikawa, M., "Constant Weight Code Generators," CRC TR 82-7.

[Iyer 79] Iyer, R.K., "On the Employment of Variance for Reliability Modeling of Fault Tolerant Systems," FTCS-9, pp. 63-66.

[Iyer 80] Iyer, R.K., "A Study of the Effect of Uncertainty in Failure Rate Prediction on System Reliability," FTCS-10, pp. 219-224. (CSL TR 177)
Iyer, R.K., S.E. Butner and E.J. McCluskey, "An Exponential Failure/Load Relationship: Results of a Multi-computer Statistical Study," CRC TR 81-6.

[Iyer 82A] Iyer, R.K., and D.J. Rossetti, "A Statistical Load Dependency Model for CPU Errors at SLAC," FTCS-12, pp. 363-372.(CRC TR 81-19) (CRC TR 82-3)

[Iyer 82B] Iyer, R.K., S.E. Butner, and E.J. McCluskey, "A Statistical Failure/Load Relationship: Results of a Multicomputer Study," IEEE Trans. Comput., pp. 697-706, July 1982.
Iyer, R.K., and D.J. Rossetti, "Hard CPU Related Failures and System Activity: Measurement and Modeling," CRC TR 83-6.
Iyer, R.K., and H.H. Amer, "Effect of Uncertainty in Failure Rate on Memory System Reliability," CRC TR 83-9.

[Iyer 83] Iyer, R.K., and D.J. Rossetti, "Permanent CPU Errors and System Activity: Measurement and Modeling," Proc., Real-time Systems Symposium , Arlington, VA, pp. 61-72, Dec. 6-8, 1983.(CRC TR 83-11) Iyer, R.K., and P. Velardi, "A Statistical Study of Hardware-Related Software Errors in MVS," CRC TR 84-2.(CRC TR 83-12)
Iyer, R.K., and D.J. Rossetti, "Measurement and Modeling of Computer Reliability as Affected by System Activity," CRC TR 85-21.

[Iyer 85A] Iyer, R.K., and P. Velardi, "Hardware-Related Software Errors: Measurement and Analysis," IEEE Trans. Software Engineering ," Vol. SE-11, No. 2, pp. 223-230, Feb. 1985.

[Iyer 85B] Iyer, R.K., and D.J. Rossetti, "Effect of System Workload on Operating System Reliability: A Study on IBM 3081," IEEE Trans. Software Engineering ," Vol. SE-11, No. 12, pp. 1438-1448, Dec. 1985.

[Iyer 86] Iyer, R.K.,and Rossetti, D.J., "A Measurement-Based Model for Workload Dependence of CPU Errors," IEEE Transactions on Computers, Vol. C-35, No. 6, June 1986. Khakbaz, J., "A Novel Totally-self-checking 1-out-of-n Checker," CRC TR 81-12. Khakbaz, J., and E.J. McCluskey, "Self-testing Embedded Parity Checkers -- Exhaustive XOR Gate Testing," CRC TR 82-10.

[Khakbaz 82A] Khakbaz, J., and E.J. McCluskey, "Concurrent Error Detection and Testing for Large PLA's," Joint Special Issue on VLSI, IEEE Trans. on Electron Devices , pp. 756-764 and IEEE J. of Solid-State Circuits, pp. 386-394, April 1982. (CRC TR 81-14)

[Khakbaz 82B] Khakbaz, J., "Self-Testing Embedded Parity Trees," FTCS-12, pp. 109-116. (CRC TR 82-3)

[Khakbaz 82C] Khakbaz, J., "Totally Self-Checking Checker for 1-out-of-n Code Using Two-Rail Codes," IEEE Trans. Comput., pp. 677-681, July 1982.

[Khakbaz 83A] Khakbaz, J. and E.J. McCluskey, "Self-Testing Embedded Code Checkers," COMPCON83, pp. 452-457.(CRC TR 83-19) (CRC TR 82-20)

[Khakbaz 83B] Khakbaz, J., "A Testable PLA Design with Low Overhead and High Fault Coverage," FTCS-13 , pp. 426-429.(CRC TR82-1) (CRC TR 83-3)

[Khakbaz 84A] Khakbaz, J., "A Testable PLA Design with Low Overhead and High Fault Coverage," IEEE Trans. Comput., C-33, No. 8, pp. 743-745, Aug 1984. (CRC TR 82-1)(CRC TR 83-3)

[Khakbaz 84B] Khakbaz, J., and E.J. McCluskey, "Self-testing Embedded Parity Checkers," IEEE Trans. Comput., C-33, No. 8, pp. 753-756, Aug. 1984.

[Khakbaz 85A] Khakbaz, J., and E.J. McCluskey, "Concurrent Error Detection and Testing for Large PLA's," DIGITAL VLSI SYSTEMS, M.I. Elmasry, ed., pp. 494-502, IEEE Press, New York, 1985. (Reprinted from IEEE Trans. Electron Devices, Vol. ED-29, April 1982, pp. 756-764.) (CRC TR 81-14)

[Khakbaz 85B] Khakbaz, J., and S. Bozorgui-Nesbat, "Minimizing Extra Hardware for Fully Testable PLA Design," Proc., IEEE Int'l Conf. on Computer-Aided Design, Santa Clara, CA, pp. 102-104, Nov. 18-21, 1985.

[Kiryukhin 78] Kiryukhin, V.V., and A.M. Chernykh, "A Quadruple-Computer Redundant Type Fault-Tolerant System," USA-Japan , pp. 374-377.

[Khodadad-Mostashiry] Khodadad-Mostashiry, B., "Break Fault in Circuits with Parity Prediction," CSL TN 183 (1980).

[Khodadad-Mostashiry 79] Khodadad-Mostashiry, B., "Parity Prediction in Combinational Circuits," (FTCS-9), pp. 185-188, Madison, WI, June 20-22, 1979.(CSL TR 151)

[Kolupaev 76] Kolupaev, S., "Cascade Structures in Self-Checking Networks," DSL TN No. 108, Apr. 1976.

[Kolupaev 77] Kolupaev, S., "Cascade Structure in Self-checking Networks," FTCS-7, pp. 150-154.

[Liu 86] Liu, D., and E.J. McCluskey, "Design of CMOS VLSI Circuits for Testability," Proc. of the IEEE 1986 Custom Integrated Circuits Conf., May 12-15, Rochester, NY, pp. 421-424, 1986. (See TR 86-1)

[Losq 74] Losq, J., "Redundant Scheme for Optimum Multiple Fault Tolerance," DSL TN No. 33, Jan. 1974.

[Losq 75] Losq, J., "Influence of Fault-Detection and Switching Mechanisms on the Reliability of Stand-By Systems," FTCS-5, pp. 81-86, June 1975.

[Losq 76A] Losq, J., "Multiple Failures and Redundant Systems," Digest of 1976 Johns Hopkins Conf. on Information Sciences and Systems, pp. 52-57, Baltimore, MD, April 1976.

[Losq 76B] Losq, J., "Referenceless random testing," FTCS-6, pp. 108-113.

[Losq 76C] Losq, J.,"A Highly Efficient Redundancy Scheme: Self-purging Redundancy," IEEE Trans. Comput., C-25, No. 6, pp. 269-278, June 1976.
Losq, J., "Effects of Failures on Performance of Gracefully Degradable Systems," DSL TN 103 (1976).

[Losq 77A] Losq, J., "Effects of Failures on Gracefully Degradable Systems,"FTCS-7, pp. 29-34.

[Losq 77B] Losq, J., "Efficiency of Compact Testing for Sequential Circuits,"FTCS-7, pp. 168-174.(DSL TN 104)

[Losq 78] Losq, J., "Enumeration of the Critical Fault Patterns in Fault-Tolerant Computer Systems," FTCS-8, pp. 31-36.(CSL TN 128)

[Losq 78] Losq, J., "Fault-Tolerant Communication Networks for Computer Networks," FTCS-8, p. 204.(CSL TN 127)

[Losq 78] Losq, J., "Efficiency of Random Compact Testing," IEEE Trans. Comput., pp. 516-525, June 1978.

[Losq 78B] Losq, J., "Testing for Intermittent Failures in Combinational Circuits,"USA-Japan , pp. 165-170.

[Lu78] Lu, D.J., "Quantitative Comparison of Self-Checking Circuit Designs," DSL TN 130 (1977).
Lu, D.J., "Structural Integrity Checking," CSL TN 149 (1978).

[Lu 78] Lu, D.J., "Quantitative Comparison of Self-checking Circuit Designs: Definitions and an Example for Linear Feedback Shift Registers," FTCS-8, p. 221.

[Lu 80] Lu, D.J., Self-Checking Linear Feedback Shift Registers," (CSL TN 177).

[Lu 80] Lu, D.J., "Watchdog Processors and VLSI," Proc., 1980 National Electronics Conf., pp. 240-245, Chicago, IL, Oct. 27-28, 1980. (CSL TN 179)

[Lu 80] Lu, D.J., E.J. McCluskey, and M. Namjoo, "Summary of Structural Integrity Checking," Proc., Distributed Data Acquisition, Computing, and Control Symposium, pp. 107-109, Miami Beach, FL, Dec. 3. (CSL TN 181)
Lu, D.J., "Quantitative Measures and Figures of Merit for Self-checking Circuits," CRC TR 81-8.
Lu, D.J., "Testing VHSIC Devices," CRC TR 82-15.

[Lu 83] Lu, D.J., and E.J. McCluskey, "Recurrent Test Patterns," ITC83, pp. 76-82.(CRC TR 83-10)

[Lu 84] Lu, D.J., and E.J. McCluskey, "Quantitative Evaluation of Self-Checking Circuits," IEEE Trans. Computer-Aided Design, CAD-3, No. 2, pp. 150-155, Apr. 1984.

[Lu 85] Lu, D.J., "Watchdog Processors and Structural Integrity Checking," Reliable Distributed System Software , J.A. Stankovic, ed., pp. 208-212, IEEE Computer Society Press, Silver Spring, Maryland, 1985. (Reprinted from IEEE Trans. Comput., Vol. C-31, No. 7, pp. 681-685, 1982.) (CRC TR 81-5)
Mahmood, A., E.J. McCluskey and D.J. Lu "Concurrent Fault Detection Using a Watchdog Processor and Assertions," CRC TR 83-10.(CRC TR 83-16)
Mahmood, A., and E.J. McCluskey, "Concurrent Error Detection Using Watchdog Processors - A Survey," CRC TR 85-7.

[Mahmood 84] Mahmood, A., D.M. Andrews, and E.J. McCluskey "Writing Executable Assertions to Test Flight Software," Eighteenth Annual Asilomar Conference on Circuits, Systems, and Computers , Pacific Grove, CA, Nov. 5-7, 1984.(CRC TR 84-14)

[Mahmood 84] Mahmood, A., D.M. Andrews, and E.J. McCluskey "Executable Assertions and Flight Software," DASC, pp. 346-351. (CRC TR 84-11)(CRC TR 84-16)

[Mahmood 85A] Mahmood, A., and E.J. McCluskey, "Watchdog Processors: Error Coverage and Overhead," FTCS-15 , pp. 214-219.(CRC TR 84-15)

[Mahmood 85B] Mahmood, A., A. Ersoz, and E.J. McCluskey, "Concurrent System-Level Error Detection Using a Watchdog Processor," ITC85 , pp. 145-152.(CRC TR 85-11)

[McCluskey 71A] McCluskey, E.J., "Test and Diagnosis Procedures for Digital Networks," Computer, Vol. 4, No. 1, pp. 17-20, Jan./Feb, 1971.

[McCluskey 71B] McCluskey, E.J., and F.W. Clegg, "Fault Equivalence in Combinational Logic Networks," IEEE Trans. Comput., Vol. C-20, No. 11, pp. 1286-1293, 1971.

[McCluskey 74] McCluskey, E.J., "Probability Models for Logic Networks," Proc. of the Fourth Manitoba Conf. on Numerical Mathematics, pp. 21-28, Winnipeg, Canada, Oct. 2-5, 1974.

[McCluskey 75] McCluskey, E.J., and R.C. Ogus, "Survey of Computer Reliability Studies," Electro-Technology, pp. 82-95, Dec. 1975.

[McCluskey 76] McCluskey, E.J., "A Survey of Research at the Center for Reliable Computing, Stanford University," J. of Design Automation and Fault-Tolerant Computing, Vol. 1, No. 1, pp. 85-90, Oct. 1976. (DSL TN 96)

[McCluskey 77] McCluskey, E.J., and R.C. Ogus, "Comparative Architecture of High Availability Computer Systems," Dig., Fourteenth IEEE Comp. Society Int'l Conf. (COMPCON'77 Spring), pp. 289-293, San Francisco, CA, Feb. 28 - March 3, 1977.(DSL TN 107) McCluskey, E.J., "Reliability and Computer Architecture," DSL TN 122 (1976).

[McCluskey 78A] McCluskey, E.J., K.P. Parker, and J. Shedletsky, "Boolean Network Probabilities and Network Design," IEEE Trans. Comput., pp. 187-189, Feb. 1978.

[McCluskey 78B] McCluskey, E.J., "Design for Maintainability and Testability," Proc., Government Microcircuit Applications Conference, pp. 44-47, Monterey, CA, Nov. 14-16, 1978.(CSL TN 145)

[McCluskey 79] McCluskey, E.J., "Testing and Diagnosis of Logic," Proc., Euro/IFIP 79, pp. 735-738, London, England, Sep. 25-28, 1979.

[McCluskey 80A] McCluskey, E.J., and S. Bozorgui-Nesbat, "Design for Autonomous Test," Proc., 1980 Test Conf., Philadelphia, PA, pp. 11-13, Nov. 11-13, 1980.(CRC TR 81-1)

[McCluskey 80B] McCluskey, E.J., "Reliable Computing Systems" Proc., International Computer Symposium 1980, pp. 714-723, Taipei, Republic of China, Dec. 16-18, 1980.(CSL TN 182)
McCluskey, E.J., "Testing Digital Circuits and Systems," CSL TN 166 (1979).
McCluskey, E.J., "Fault-tolerant Computing Systems," CSL TN 170 (1979).
McCluskey, E.J., "Testing VHSIC Devices," CRC TR 81-3.

[McCluskey 81A] McCluskey, E.J., and J.F. Wakerly, "A Circuit For Detecting and Analyzing Temporary Failures," Proc., COMPCON Spring 1981, pp. 317-321, San Francisco, CA, Feb. 24-26, 1981.(CSL TN 178)

[McCluskey 81B] McCluskey, E.J., and S. Bozorgui-Nesbat, "Design for Autonomous Test," IEEE Trans. Comput., pp. 866-875, Nov. 1981. (CRC TR 81-1)

[McCluskey 82A] McCluskey, E.J., "Fault Tolerant Systems," Journal, Information Processing Society in Japan, Vol. 23, No. 4, pp. 378-385, April 1982.(CRC TR 82-1)

[McCluskey 82B] McCluskey, E.J., "Verification Testing," Proc., 19th Design Automation Conf., Las Vegas, NV, pp. 495-500, June 14-16, 1982.(CRC TR 81-7)

[McCluskey 82C] McCluskey, E.J., "Built-in Verification Test," ITC82, pp. 183-190.

[McCluskey 83] McCluskey, E.J., "Design for Testability Survey," Proc., Bias Microelettronica, Sec. 4, Milan Italy, Feb. 23-25, 1983.
McCluskey, E.J., D.J. Lu, S. Bozorgui-Nesbat, and A. Mahmood, "Testing VHSIC Devices," CRC TR 84-1.

[McCluskey 84A] McCluskey, E.J., "Pseudo-Exhaustive Testing for VLSI Devices" ATE Silicon Valley Conf. , San Mateo, CA, pp. IV-5 - IV-21, Apr. 10-12, 1984.(CRC TR 84-6)

[McCluskey 84B] McCluskey, E.J., "Verification Testing-A Pseudoexhaustive Test Technique," IEEE Trans. mput., C-33, No. 6, pp. 541-546, June 1984.(CRC TR 83-8)

[McCluskey 84C] McCluskey, E.J., "VLSI Design for Testability," 1984 Symposium on VLSI Technology , San Diego, CA, Sep. 10-12, 1984. (CRC TR 84-4)(CRC TR 84-11)

[McCluskey 84D] McCluskey, E.J., "Built-In Self Test Architectures," Academic Curriculum Forum, ITC84 , pp. 4-6.(CRC TR 84-8)

[McCluskey 84E] McCluskey, E.J., "Testing Semi-Custom Logic"Wescon/84 , Anaheim, CA, paper 31/4, Oct. 30 - Nov. 2, 1984. (CRC TR 84-9)

[McCluskey 84F] McCluskey, E.J., "VLSI Design for Testability,"DASC pp. 523 530.(CRC TR 84-4)(CRC TR 84-11) ,

[McCluskey 84G] McCluskey, E.J., "A Survey of Design for Testability Scan Techniques," VLSI Design , vol. V, No. 12, pp. 38-61, Dec. 1984.

[McCluskey 85A] McCluskey, E.J., "Hardware Fault Tolerance," COMPCON 85, pp. 260-263.(CRC TR 84-13)

[McCluskey 85B] McCluskey, E.J., "Testable IC Design," Proc., Automated Design and Engineering for Electronics (ADEE) Conf., pp. 252-260, Anaheim, CA, Feb. 26-28, 1985. (CRC TR 85-2)

[McCluskey 85C] McCluskey, E.J., "Built-In Self-Test Techniques," IEEE Design & Test of Computers, pp. 21-28, April 1985.

[McCluskey 85D] McCluskey, E.J., "Built-In Self-Test Structures," IEEE Design & Test of Computers, pp. 29-36, April 1985.

[McCluskey 85E] McCluskey, E.J., "Testing Semi-Custom Logic, Semiconductor International, pp. 118-123, Sept. 1985.

[McCluskey 86A] McCluskey, E.J., Logic Design Principles, Prentice-Hall Inc., Englewood Cliffs, N.J., 1986.

[McCluskey 86B] McCluskey, E.J., "Comparing Causes of IC Failure," New Directions for IC Testing, March 18-20, 1986, Victoria, B.C. Canada.(See TR 86-2)

[McCluskey 86C] McCluskey, E.J., "Design for Testability," in Fault-Tolerant Computing, Vol.1, Chap. 2,D.K. Pradhan ed., Prentice-Hall Inc., Englewood Cliffs, N.J., 1986.

[Mei 70] Mei, K.C.Y., "Fault Dominance in Combinational Circuits," DSL TN No. 2, Aug. 1970.

[Mei 73] Mei, K.C.Y., "Bridging and Stuck-At Faults," 1973 Intl. Symp. on Fault Tolerant Computing, IEEE Publication No. 73CHO772-4C, pp. 91-94, 1973.

[Mei 74] Mei, K.C.Y., "Bridging and Stuck-At Faults," IEEE Trans. Comput., Vol. C-23, No. 7, pp. 720-727, July 1974.
Min, Y., "Generating a Complete Test for Programmable Logic Arrays (PLAs)," CRC TR 83-4.
Min, Y., "A Unified Fault Model for Programmable Logic Arrays," CRC TR 83-5.

[Mitarai 72] Mitarai, H., "Design of a Parallel Encoder/Decoder for the Hamming Code, Using ROM," First USA-Japan Computer Conf., Tokyo, Oct. 1972.

[Mitarai 75] Mitarai, H., "ROM Micro-Reduction Techniques," Dig. Second USA-Japan Computer Conf., Tokyo, Aug. 1975.

[Mourad 86A] Mourad, S., "Multiple Fault Detection in Parity Trees," Digest of Papers, COMPCON'86, San Francisco, March 1986.

[Mourad 86B] Mourad, S., J.L.A. Hughes, and E.J. McCluskey, "Stuck at Fault Detection in Parity Trees," Proc. of Fault-Tolerant Systems and Diagnostics, p. 142-147, Brno, Czechoslovakia, June 1986.

[Mourad 86C] Mourad, S., J.L.A. Hughes, and E.J. McCluskey, "Effectiveness of Single Stuck-At Fault Tests in Detecting Multiple Faults," IJCM 86.

[Mourad 86D] Mourad, S.,J.L.A. Hughes, and E.J. McCluskey, "Stuck-At Faults in Detecting Multiple Faults," IEEE Trans. Comput., July, 1986. (FJCC 86)
Mourad, S., and D. Andrews, "On the Reliability of the IBM/MVS/XA," CRC TR 85-1.
Mourad, S., J.L.A. Hughes, and E.J. McCluskey, "Stuck-At Fault Detection in Parity Trees," CRC TR 85-23.

[Mourad 85] Mourad, S., and D.M. Andrews, "The Reliability of the IBM MVS/XA Operating System," FTCS-15 , pp. 93-98.(CRC TR 85-3)
Namjoo, M., and E.J. McCluskey, "Watchdog Processors and Detection of Malfunctions at the System Level," CRC TR 81-17.
Namjoo, M., "Concurrent Testing Using Path Signature Analysis," CRC TR 82-16.

[Namjoo 82A] Namjoo, M., "Design of Concurrently Testable Microprogrammed Control Units," Proc., Micro-15 Workshop, Palo Alto, CA, pp. 173-180, Oct. 4-7, 1982.(CRC TR 82-6)(CRC TR 82-14)

[Namjoo 82B] Namjoo, M., "Techniques for Concurrent Testing of VLSI Processor Operation," ITC82, pp. 461-468. (CRC TR 82-13)

[Namjoo 83] Namjoo, M., "Cerberus-16: An Architecture for a General Purpose Watchdog Processor," FTCS-13 , pp. 216-219. (CRC TR 83-3)(CRC TR 82-19) Nassar, F.A., and D.M. Andrews, "A Methodology for Analysis of Failure Prediction Data," CRC TR 85-4, CRC TR 85-20.

[Ogus 73] Ogus, R.C., and J.F. Wakerly, "Fault-Tolerant Design of Minicomputers," Proc., Symp. on Minicomputers, South African Council for Automation and Computation, Pretoria, South Africa, Sept. 1973.

[Ogus 74A] Ogus, R.C., "Fault Tolerance of the Iterative Cell Array Switch For Hybrid Redundancy," IEEE Trans. Comput., Vol. C-23, No. 7., pp. 667-681, July, 1974.DSL TR No. 65.

[Ogus 74B] Ogus, R.C., "The Probability of a Correct Output from a Combinational Circuit," FTC-4.

[Ogus 75] Ogus, R.C., "The Probability of a Correct Output from a Combinational Circuit," IEEE Trans. Comput., Vol. C-24, pp. 534-544, May 1975.
Owicki, S.S., "Specifications and Proofs for Abstract Data Types in Concurrent Programs," DSL TR 133 (1977).
Owicki, S.S., "Verifying Concurrent Programs with Shared Data Classes," DSL TR 147 (1977).

[Parker 72] Parker, K.P., "Off Line Diagnostics for ILLIAC IV," Vol. 1, IAC Document UG-I4300-0000-a, NASA/Ames Institute for Advanced Computation, Moffett Field, CA Nov. 1972.

[Parker 73] Parker, K.P., "Probabilistic Test Generation," DSL TN No. 18, June 1973.

[Parker 74] Parker, K.P., and E.J. McCluskey, "Analysis of Logic Circuits with Faults Using Input Signal Probabilities," FTC-4, pp. 1-8 to 1-13, June 1974.

[Parker 75A] Parker, K.P., and E.J. McCluskey, "Analysis of Logic Circuits with Faults Using Input Signal Probabilities," IEEE Trans. Comput., pp. 573-578, May 1975.

[Parker 75B] Parker, K.P., and E.J. McCluskey, "Probabilistic Treatment of General Combinational Networks," IEEE Trans. Comput., pp. 668-670, June 1975.

[Parker 75] Parker, K.P., and E.J. McCluskey, "Sequential Circuit Output Probabilities from Regular Expressions," DSL TN No. 93, June 1975.

[Parker 76A] Parker, K.P., "Adaptive Random Test Generation," J. of Design Automation and Fault-Tolerant Computing, Vol. 1, No. 1, pp. 62-83 Oct. 1976.(DSL TN 109)

[Parker 76B] Parker, K.P., "Compact Testing: Testing with Compressed Data," FTCS-6, pp. 93-98.

[Parker 78] Parker, K.P., and E.J. McCluskey, "Sequential Circuit Output Probabilities from Regular Expressions," IEEE Trans. Comput., pp. 222-231, Mar. 1978.

[Pierce 61] Pierce, W.H., "Improving the Reliability of Digital Systems by Redundancy and Adaption," SEL TR 1552-3, July 17, 1961.

[Pradhan] Pradhan, D.K., "Design of Easily Testable Sequential Machines Using Extra Inputs," CSL TN 173 (1980).

[Reese 73] Reese, R.D., and E.J. McCluskey, "A Gate Equivalent Model for Combinational Logic Network Analysis," FTCS-3, pp. 79-84, 1973.
Rossetti, D.J. and T.H. Bredt, "The Design and Implementation of an Operating System Tracer," DSL TN 97 (1977).
Rossetti, D.J., and R.K. Iyer, "A Software System for Reliability and Workload Analysis," CRC TR 81-18.
Rossetti, D.J., and R.K. Iyer, "Analysis of Software Related Failures on the IBM 3081: Relationship with System Utilization," CRC TR 82-8.

[Rossetti 82] Rossetti, D.J., and R.K. Iyer, "Software Related Failures on the IBM 3081: A Relationship with System Utilization," Proc., COMPSAC82, pp. 45-54, Chicago, IL, Nov. 10-12, 1982.

[Savir 74] Savir, J., "Fault Detection in Modular Combinational Networks," Dec. 1974.

[Savir 77] Savir, J., "Optimal Random Testing of Single Intermittent Failures in Combinational Circuits," FTCS-7, pp. 180-185. (DSL TN 105)
Savir, J., "Detection of Single Faults in Modular Combinational Networks," DSL TN 136 (1977).
Savir, J., "Detection of Intermittent Faults in Sequential Circuits," CSL TR 120 (1978).

[Savir 78A] Savir, J., "Testing For Multiple Intermittent Failures in Combinational Circuits by Maximizing the Probability of Fault Detection," FTCS-8, p. 212.(DSL TR 146)

[Savir 78B] Savir, J., "Testing for Intermittent Failures in Combinational Circuits by Minimizing the Mean Testing Time for a Given Test Quality," USA-JAPAN, pp. 155-161.(DSL TR 148)

[Savir 78C] Savir, J., "Model and Random-Testing Properties of Intermittent Faults in Combinational Circuits," Design Automation & Fault-Tolerant Computing, pp. 215-230, 1978.(DSL TN 118)

[Savir 80A] Savir, J., "Testing for Single Intermittent Failures in Combinational Circuits by Maximizing the Probability of Fault Detection," IEEE Trans. Comput., pp. 410-416, May 1980.(DSL TR 146)

[Savir 80B] Savir, J., "Syndrome-Testable Design of Combinational Circuits," IEEE Trans. Comput., pp. 442-451, June 1980.(CSL TR 157)

[Shedletsky 75A] Shedletsky, J.J., "A Rationale for the Random Testing of Combinational Digital Circuits, COMPCON-East, Washington D.C., Sept. 9-11, 1975.

[Shedletsky 75B] Shedletsky, J.J., and E.J. McCluskey, "The Error Latency of a Fault in a Sequential Digital Circuit," FTCS-5.

[Shedletsky 76A] Shedletsky, J.J., "A Rollback Interval for Networks with an Imperfect Self-checking Property," FTCS-6, pp. 163-168.

[Shedletsky 76B] Shedletsky, J.J., and E.J. McCluskey, "The Error Latency of a Fault in a Sequential Digital Circuit,"IEEE Trans. Comput., C-25, No. 6, pp. 655-659, June 1976.

[Shedletsky 77] Shedletsky, J.J., "Comment on the Sequential and Indeterminate Behavior of an End-Around-Carry Adder," IEEE Trans. Comput., pp. 271-272, March 1977.

[Shedletsky 77] Shedletsky, J.J., "Random Testing: Practicality vs. Verified Effectiveness,"FTCS-7, pp. 175-179.

[Shedletsky 78] Shedletsky, J.J., "Error Correction by Alternate-Data Retry," IEEE Trans. Comput., pp. 106-112, Feb. 1978. (DSL TN 113) Siewiorek, D.P., "An Improved Reliability Model for NMR," DSL TR No. 24, 1971.

[Siewiorek 71] Siewiorek, D.P., "A Unifying Perspective of Fault Tolerant Computer Techniques," DSL TN No. 14, Dec. 1971.

[Siewiorek] Siewiorek, D.P., "Optimum Design of Self-Diagnosable Systems, DSL.

[Siewiorek 73A] Siewiorek, D.P., and E.J. McCluskey, "An Iterative Cell Switch Design for Hybrid Redundancy," IEEE Trans. Comput., Vol. C-22, No. 3, pp. 290-297, Mar. 1973.(Also DSL TR No. 20, 1971)

[Siewiorek 73B] Siewiorek, D.P., and E.J. McCluskey, "Switch Complexity in Systems with Hybrid Redundancy," IEEE Trans. Comput., Vol. C-22, No. 3, pp. 276-282, Mar. 1973.

[Siewiorek 74] Siewiorek, D.P., "Reliability Modeling of Compensating Module Failures in Majority Voted Redundancy, IEEE Trans. Comput., Vol. C-24, No. 5, pp. 525-534, May 1975.(Also FTC4)

[Sun 84] Sun, Z., and L.-T. Wang, "Self-Testing of Embedded RAMs," ITC84 , pp. 148-156.(CRC TR 84-8)

[Svobodova 73] Svobodova, L., "Measuring Computer System Utilization with a Hardware and a Hybrid Monitor," ACM SICME Performance Evaluation Review, No. 4, pp. 20-34, 1973.

[Svobodova 73] Svobodova, L., "Online System Performance Measurements with Software and Hybrid Monitors," Proc. ACM SIGOPS Fourth Symposium on Operating System Principles, pp. 45-53, Oct. 1973.

[Sziray 79A] Sziray, J. "A Test Calculation Algorithm for Module-level Combinational Networks," Digital Processes, Vol. 5, No. 1-2, pp. 17-26, Spring-Summer 1979.(DSL TN 124)

[Sziray 79B] Sziray, J., "Test Calculation for Logic Network by Composite Justification," Digital Processes, Vol. 5, No. 1-2, pp. 3-16, Spring-Summer 1979.(DSL TN 129)
Thompson, P.A., "A Simulator for the Evaluation of Reliability," DSL TN 106 (1976).
Thompson, P.A., "Critique of the SIRU Dual Computer System," DSL TN 111 (1977).
Thompson, P.A., "A Simulator for the Evaluation of Digital System Reliability," DSL TR 119 (1977). Thompson, P.A., "Using Simulation to Evaluate the Reliability of a Dual Computer System," DSL TR 121 (1977).
Thompson, P.A. "Manual for a General-Purpose Simulator Used to Evaluate Reliability of Digital Systems," DSL TR 132 (1977).

[Turcat 76] Turcat, C., and A. Verdillon, "Recursion and Testing of Combinational Circuits," IEEE Trans. Comput., pp. 652-654, June 1976.

[Usas 74] Usas, A.M., and E.J. McCl;uskey, "Design and Application of a Self-Checking Periodic Signal Checker," Dig. Fall 1974 COMPCON, Wash. D.C., Sept 10-12, 1974.

[Usas 75A] Usas, A.M., "Fail-Safe Circuits: A Means to Improve Reliability and Maintainability of I/O Subsystems," Dig. IEEE Comp. Society Int'l Conf., pp. 83-91, Wash. D.C., Sept. 11-12, 1975.

[Usas 75B] Usas, A.M., "A Totally Self-Checking Checker Design for the Detection of Errors in Periodic Signals, IEEE Trans. Comput., Vol. C-24, No. 5, pp. 483-489, May 1975
Usas, A.M., "Error Management in Digital Computer Input/output Systems," DSL TR 122 (1976).

[Velardi 84] Velardi, P., and R.K. Iyer, "A Study of Software Failures and Recovery in the MVS Operating System," IEEE Trans. Comput., C-33, No. 6, pp. 564-568, June 1984.(CRC TR 83-7)

[Verdillon 76] Verdillon A., "Procedures to Obtain Optimal Test Sequences," FTCS-6, p. 200, 1976.
Verdillon, A., "Symmetry, Automorphism and Test," DSL TN 87 (1976). IRIA,

[Wagner 83] Wagner, K.D., "Design for Testability in the Amdahl 580," COMPCON83 , pp. 384-388.(CRC TR 82-20)
Wagner, K.D., and E.J. McCluskey, "Tuning, Clock Distribution and Communication in VLSI High-Speed Chips," CRC TR 84-5. not published
Wagner, K.D., "Delay Testing of Digital Circuits Using Pseudorandom Input Sequences," CRC TR 85-12.

[Wagner 85A] Wagner, K.D., "The Error Latency of Delay Faults in Combinational and Sequential Circuits,"ITC85 , pp. 334-341. (CRC TR 85-11)

[Wagner 85B] Wagner, K.D., and E.J. McCluskey, "Effect of Supply Voltage on Circuit Propagation Delay and Test Applications," Proc., IEEE Int'l Conf. on womputer-Aided Design, Santa Clara, CA, pp. 42-44, Nov. 18-21, 1985.(CRC TR 85-17)

[Wagner 86] Wagner, K.D., "Fault Coverage of Pseudorandom Testing," ICCAD 86.

[Wakerly 73] Wakerly, J.F., "Low-Cost Error Detection Techniques for Small Computers," DSL TN No. 51, Dec. 1973.

[Wakerly 74A] Wakerly, J.F., "Partially Self-Checking Circuits and their use in Performing Logical Operations," IEEE Trans. Comput., Vol. C-23, pp. 658-666, July 1974.(Also FTC3)

[Wakerly 74B] Wakerly, J.F., and E.J. McCluskey, "Design of Low-Cost General-Purpose Self-Diagnosing Computers," Proc. of IFIP Congress 74, North-Holland Publishing Co., Amsterdam, 1974.

[Wakerly 74C] Wakerly, J.F., " Checked Binary Addition Using Parity Prediction and Checksum Codes," DSL TN No. 39, Jan. 1974.

[Wakerly 75A] Wakerly, J.F., "Transient Failures in Triple Modular Redundancy Systems with Sequential Modules," IEEE Trans. Comput., Vol. C-24, pp. 570-573, May 1975.

[Wakerly 75B] Wakerly, J.F., "Detection of Unidirectional Multiple Errors Using Low-Cost Arithmetic Codes," IEEE Trans. Comput., Vol. C-24, pp. 210-212, Feb. 1975.

[Wakerly 76A] Wakerly, J.F., "Eliminating the Unwanted Zero in Ones' Complement Addition,"Electronics , Vol. 49, No. 3, pp. 103-105, Feb. 5, 1976.

[Wakerly 76A] Wakerly, J.F., "Reliability of Microcomputer Systems Using Triple Modular Redundancy, "COMPCON 76, San Francisco, CA, pp. 23-26, Feb. 24-26, 1976.

[Wakerly 76B] Wakerly, J.F., "Checked Binary Addition with Checksum," J. of Design Automation & Fault-Tolerant Computing, Vol. 1, No. 1, pp. 18-27, Oct. 1976.

[Wakerly 76] Wakerly, J.F., "Microcomputer Reliability Improvement Using Triple Modular Redundancy, "Proc., IEEE, Vol. 64, No. 6, pp. 889-895, June 1976.

[Wakerly 76] Wakerly, J.F., "Design of a Self-Checking Microprogrammed Processor," FTCS-6, p. 191.
Wakerly, J.F., "Principles of Self-Checking Processor Design and an Example," DSL TR 115.

[Wakerly 77] Wakerly, J.F., and E.J. McCluskey, "Microcomputers in the Computer Engineering Curriculum," Computer, Vol. 10, No. 1, pp. 32-38, Jan. 1977.

[Wakerly 77] Wakerly, J.F., "Microprocessor Input/Output Architecture," Computer, Vol. 10, No. 2, pp. 26-33, Feb. 1977.

[Wang 75A] Wang, D.T., "An Algorithm for the Generation of Test Sets for Combinational Networks," IEEE Trans. Comput., Vol. C-24, No. 7, pp. 742-746, July 1975.

[Wang 75B] Wang, D.T., "Properties of Faults and Criticalities of Values Under Tests for Combinational Networks," IEEE Trans. Comput, Vol. C-24, No. 7, pp. 746-750, July 1975.

[Wang 82] Wang, LT., "Autonomous Linear Feedback Shift Register with On-Line Fault-Detection Capability," FTCS-12 , pp. 311-314. (CRC TR 82-3)

[Wang 84A] Wang, L.T., and E.J. McCluskey, "A New Condensed Linear Feedback Shift Register Design for VLSI/System Testing," FTCS-14 , pp. 360-365.(CRC TR 84-2)

[Wang 84B] Wang, L.T., and E. Law, "DTA: Daisy Testability Analyzer," ICCAD84 , pp. 143-145.(CRC TR 84-10)

[Wang 85A] Wang, L.T., and E.J. McCluskey, "Built-In Self Test for Random Logic," Proc., 1985 Int'l Symposium on Circuits and Systems, Vol. 3, Kyoto, Japan, pp. 1305-1308, June 5-7, 1985.(CRC TR 85-5)

[Wang 85B] Wang, L.T., and E. Law, "An Enhanced Daisy Testability Analyzer (DTA)," Proc., 1985 IEEE AUTOTESTCON Conf., Long Island, New York, pp. 223-229, Oct. 21-24, 1985.(CRC TR 85-13)
Wang, L.-T. and E.J. McCluskey, "Condensed Linear Feedback Shift Register (LFSR) Testing -- A Pseudo-Exhaustive Test Technique," CRC TR 85-24.

[Wang 86A] Wang, L.T.and E.J. McCluskey, "Concurrent Built-In Logic Block Observer (CBILBO)," IEEE Int'l Conf. on Circuits and Systems, San Jose, CA, May 5-7, 1986(See TR 86-1)

[Wang 86B] Wang, L.T., and E.J. McCluskey, "Circuits for Pseudo-Exhaustive Test Pattern Generation," ITC 86.

[Wang 86C] Wang, L.T., and E.J. McCluskey, "A Hybrid Design of Maximum-Length Sequence Generators," ITC 86.

[Williams 73] Williams, M.J.Y., and J.B. Angel, "Enhancing Testability of Large Scale Integrated Circuits via Test Points and Additional Logic," IEEE Trans. Comput., Vol. C-22, No. 1, pp. 46-60, Jan. 1973.

[Xu 83] Xu, X., and E.J. McCluskey, "Test Generation and Fault Diagnosis for Multiple Fault Combinational Circuits," FTCS-13 , pp. 110-113. (CRC TR 83-2)
Xu, X., "A Modularized Test Generation Method Using Matrices" (CRC TR 81-15)

Design Fault Tolerance

Brian Randell
Computing Laboratory,
University of Newcastle upon Tyne

ABSTRACT

The aim of this paper is to provide a personal perspective on the subject of design fault tolerance, and in
particular software fault tolerance, as it has developed
at Newcastle and elsewhere, and to speculate briefly on
how the subject might advance in the future. The principal topics covered are the search for an appropriate
set of basic concepts and definitions, the differing
styles of fault masking provided by recovery blocks and
N-version programs, the growing sophistication of error
recovery techniques, particularly in distributed systems, and the problems of assessing the
cost/effectiveness of design fault tolerance.

1. Introduction

The subject of fault-tolerant computer design was already well
established, through the efforts of hardware designers such as Bill
Carter, when in 1970, I and my colleagues first took an active
interest in the subject. Indeed we were aware that the subject
went back at least to the work of von Neumann in the mid-1950s.
Where our work differed from much of what had gone before (or so
we thought) was that we chose to concentrate on the topic which

has since become known as design fault tolerance and, in particular, on the problems of tolerating residual software design faults. However, within a year or so of starting the project my hobby of digging into the origins of digital computing led me to find out that in 1837 Charles Babbage had written: [1]

"When the formula to be computed is very complicated, it may be algebraically arranged for computation in two or more totally distinct ways, and two or more sets of cards may be made. If the same constants are now employed with each set, and if under these circumstances the results agree, we may then be quite secure of the accuracy of them all."

This quotation comes from a paper, unpublished during his lifetime, which Babbage wrote within three years of starting work on what later became known as the Analytical Engine. (The idea of so organizing the work of clerical staff ("computers") engaged in producing mathematical tables was in fact mentioned in an earlier published paper - one by Lardner describing Babbage's Difference Engine [2].) The Analytical Engine was to be a completely automatic mechanical computer, programmed (as we would now say) by means of Jacquard cards. Babbage's designs for this machine exhibited a very creative concern for mechanical reliability, and his paper makes it clear that he thought that in operation the principal reliability problems would arise from what we would now term software, rather than hardware errors, and from mistakes in input data.

Returning to the present century, as I have explained in the Introduction to the recently published compendium of Newcastle Reliability Project papers [3] one of the influences on my thinking, at the time we started the project, was the discussions I had taken part in at the 1968 NATO Software Engineering Conference:

"One major theme of the conference was the great disparity between the level of reliance that organizations were willing to place on complex real time systems and the very modest levels of reliability that were often being achieved - for example, it was also at about this time that there was considerable public debate over the proposed Anti-Ballistic Missile System, which we understood was to involve relying completely on a massively complicated computer system to position and detonate a nuclear device in the upper atmosphere in the path of each incoming missile!

At the NATO Conference there was thus much discussion about improved methods of software design, though there was a mainly implicit assumption that high reliability was best achieved by making a system fault-free, rather than fault-tolerant. Another much-debated topic concerned the practicality of attempting to provide rigorous correctness proofs for software systems of significant size and complexity. Such discussions, I am sure, played a large part in ensuring that, by the time I reached Newcastle, I was seeking to do something constructive abut the problems of achieving high reliability from complex computing systems, and yet was feeling rather pessimistic about the practicality of proving the correctness of other than relatively small and simple programs.

The plan for a major research project at Newcastle on system reliability in fact was developed very quickly in discussion with my colleague Jim Eve.... >From the start, our aim was to study the general problems of achieving high reliability from complex computing systems, rather than concentrate on problems specific to a particular application area or make of computer. Quoting from the original project proposal: "The intent is to investigate problems concerned with the provision of reliable service by a computing system, notwithstanding the presence of software and hardware errors. The approach will be based on the development of computer architecture and programming techniques which facilitate the structuring of complex computing systems so that the existence of errors can be detected and the extent of their ramifications be determined automatically, and so that uninterrupted service (albeit probably of degraded quality until the faulty hardware or software is repaired) can be provided ... [The proposed project] is thus parallel and complementary to work on achieving high reliability from individual hardware components, and on program validation. Both of these topics are of importance, but it is clear that for the foreseeable future the designers of large-scale computing systems will not be able to achieve adequate system reliability by depending entirely on the reliability of the hardware and software components which make up their system"."

Such concentration on system structuring issues has been a continued characteristic of much of our work. Another characteristic, and one that was not originally intended, was the extent of the efforts that we felt it appropriate to devote to issues of terminology. In what follows, I will briefly discuss these issues, before addressing various system structuring topics, and the problems of evaluating the cost/effectiveness of design fault tolerance. In so doing, my aim will be to provide a personal perspective on the subject of design fault tolerance as it has developed over the years, at Newcastle and elsewhere, before indulging myself briefly in some speculations as to how the subject might develop in the future.

2. Terminology Issues

After I and my colleagues at Newcastle had for some time been investigating techniques for designing software so as to include the redundancy necessary to tolerate residual design faults, we became aware of the inadequacies, for our purposes, of the standard terms and definitions then in use by the hardware fault tolerance community. These terms took the concept of a fault as their starting point, and defined it by enumerating the various classes of regrettable but unavoidable component behaviour which were to be classed as faults: for example stuck-at-one faults, bridging faults, etc. The notion of fault was thus synonymous with that of a component failing to meet its specification in some way, and there seemed to be an assumption that the cause of any system failure could in principle be identified unambiguously with one or more such component failures.

The definitions therefore made no allowance for such explicit design faults as the accidental use of a wrong component, or wrong inter-component connections. However the only software faults are design faults, of just such a character. Moreover, it is important to note that identification of the actual fault which has caused a complex software system to fail can be a somewhat subjective affair - depending on how it is thought the software should have been designed in the first place, then various different pieces of code will be identified as being at fault, and differing amounts of processing up to the point of system failure as having been erroneous.

It was Michael Melliar-Smith who first became actively concerned with these terminological (and conceptual) problems - I remember him even paying a special visit to the University's Department of Philosophy to find out whether anyone there had thought at all deeply about the notion of an "error". He got very little help though he reported that they seemed to know a lot about the notion of "truth". The solution that he eventually arrived at involved using a recursive definition of the term "system", and taking the concept of system failure (with respect to some specification) as the starting point, in terms of which fault and error could then be defined.

The first published account of these ideas is contained in a paper [4] which Michael and I wrote on recovery blocks and exception handling. Quoting from this paper:

> "A *failure* of a system occurs when that system does not perform its service in the manner specified, whether because it is unable to perform the service at all, or because the results and the external state are not in accordance with the

specifications. A failure is thus an event....

We term an internal state of a system an *erroneous state* when that state is such that there exist circumstances (within the specification of the use of the system) in which further processing, by the normal algorithms of the system, will lead to a failure which we do not attribute to a subsequent fault....

The term error is used to designate that part of the state which is "incorrect". An error is thus an item of information, and the terms *error, error detection* and *error recovery* are used as casual equivalents for erroneous state, erroneous state detection and erroneous state recovery.

A *fault* is the mechanical or algorithmic cause of an error, while a potential fault is a mechanical or algorithmic construction within a system such that (under some circumstances within the specification of the use of the system) that construction will cause the system to assume an erroneous state. It is evident that the failure of a component of a system is (or rather, may be) a mechanical fault from the point of view of the system as a whole."

This set of concepts and definitions served as a common basis for the sets of lectures making up an advanced course on computing system reliability which was first given in Newcastle in 1978, and repeated in California the following year. This course, incidentally, provided us with our first opportunity for extended interaction with Bill Carter, (though I personally had known Bill from my years at the IBM Research Center, Yorktown Heights), who provided a splendid series of lectures on hardware fault tolerance for the course [5].

Perhaps the most gratifying early response to our work on concepts and terminology came from some of the staff of International Computers Ltd. Although they were not involved in the design of fault-tolerant computing systems, they found that use of the terminology helped to clarify the varied responsibilities involved in designing, manufacturing, installing and maintaining computer systems - in other words they applied the terminology to ICL itself, viewing the whole enterprise as a fault-tolerant system!

In subsequent years improved versions of these definitions were produced, in particular by Tom Anderson and Pete Lee for their book "Fault Tolerance: Principles and Practice" [6]. Their work was one of the inputs to the very extensive discussions that took place within the IEEE Technical Committee on Fault Tolerant Computing and IFIP Working Group 10.4, starting in 1981/82. These discussions have, I hope, now culminated in the broadly similar, though significantly developed and extended, definitions documented in the paper by Jean-Claude Laprie [7] to whom is also due the introduction of the term "dependability" for the generic concept subsuming such system characteristics as reliability, availability, safety and security. Our original formulation had led us to speak of "reliability with respect to a particular specification", and so to think of safety and security, for example, merely as special cases of reliability. This attitude tended to provoke fruitless arguments with the safety and security communities, whereas the term dependability is somewhat more neutral.

The power of terminology to clarify (or confuse) continually impresses me. My most recent personal experience in this line in fact concerns the topic of security. With a colleague, John Dobson, I have lately been involved in discussions on the topic of how to design and structure highly secure computing systems. These discussions have their origins almost entirely in our realization that there are useful analogies to be discovered by considering security and reliability to be different special cases of dependability. In particular, this has led us to question a number of current practices with respect to the design of multi-level secure systems (such as the use of a so-called "Trusted Computing Base") and to feel that we now have a much better conceptual grasp on how to build computing systems intended to exhibit both high security and high reliability. The approach we have started to develop is outlined in papers [8, 9] which we suspect the security community will view as provocative but possibly interesting, whereas the reliability community may well regard them as belatedly obvious.

In essence, what we have done is realize that two research areas, which have developed largely independently of each other, each with its own jargon, its own conferences and its own fashions, can be usefully coalesced into a single subject. After all, in computing science we have more than enough unsolved problems, without having to create spurious ones simply through problems of terminology.

3. System Structuring

The provision of design fault tolerance requires the incorporation of useful redundant information into the design, for purposes of detecting and recovering from, or directly masking, the effects of residual design faults. This additional information will be useful only to the extent that it does not itself suffer from faults which are equivalent to those which it is intended to help tolerate - something which is facilitated (but unfortunately not guaranteed) by having as independent as possible a design process, i.e. by achieving a high degree of "design diversity" [10].

Since the principal cause of residual design faults is complexity, the use of appropriate structuring techniques is crucial if the addition of means of design fault tolerance to a system is not to increase its complexity to the point of being counter-productive. Thus issues of system structuring have been a principal concern of the Newcastle Reliability Project from the outset.

The first structuring technique which we developed was the recovery block scheme. Part of the thinking behind this scheme was that although good use could be made of a variety of different error detection mechanisms in a system, it was highly advantageous to have a single coherent error recovery strategy. I remember similar ideas being put forward by Roger Needham, who once suggested to me that the best way to implement a time-sharing system was to concentrate first on producing a dependable "checkpoint and restart" facility, before gradually adding in the various other features that users expected!

One source of the recovery block concept was, if my memory serves me correctly, a survey that a founder-member of the project, Tony Mascall, made of a number of then-current large real-time systems and, in particular, of their facilities for restarting after a failure. I remember feeling dissatisfied with the schemes he described, which seemed unduly ad hoc and limited. However it took Jim Horning, who was visiting from Toronto during the Summer of 1973, and Mike Melliar-Smith to find a simple linguistic formulation for structuring error detection and recovery in sequential programs which, being recursive in form, allowed nested recovery regions and so removed one of my principal objections to the earlier checkpoint and restart schemes. Their recovery block structure required a suitable mechanism for providing automatic backward error recovery, something that was central to the idea of having primary blocks and alternates be independent of each other. I produced the first such "recovery cache" scheme, a description of which was included in the first paper on recovery blocks [11] (although it was later superseded [12]), together with a discussion of "recoverable procedures" - a mechanism that Hugh Lauer and I had proposed as a means of extending the recovery block scheme to deal with programmer-defined data types.

By 1975 we had moved on to consider the problems of providing structuring for error recovery among sets of cooperating processes and, having identified the dangers of what we came to term the "domino effect", had come up with the notion of a "conversation" - something which we later realized was a special case of a nested atomic action, or transaction. These ideas were presented that year at the Los Angeles Conference on Reliable Software [13] a conference at which Al Avizienis, following in

Babbage's footsteps, discussed [14] the possibility of carrying out the same computation concurrently or sequentially by three or more independently-written programs and using either hardware or programmed comparisons to mask errors, i.e. what later became known as N-version programming [15, 16].

The recovery block scheme can be viewed as a software equivalent of the well-known hardware technique of standby sparing - however one in which (i) standby spares (the alternates) are switched in automatically and temporarily, as a result of a programmed check (the acceptance test), rather than until the module they were replacing had been repaired, and (ii) the spare is not just a replica of the primary component, so that the provision of graceful functional, as well as performance, degradation is permitted. N-version programming is of course an even more direct analogue to a hardware scheme, that of N-Modular Redundancy, though it uses design diversity, rather than simple replication, as a means of providing multiple modules. Also it can allow more complex schemes of voting, because of such difficulties as that of obtaining absolutely identical results from differently-designed numerical algorithms.

In the years that followed, much further work was done on both schemes. Comparing them, their principal difference is that though both attempt to achieve fault masking, recovery blocks also provide a hierarchical error recovery strategy, which can be invoked when fault masking is known to have been unsuccessful. The fault masking strategies provided by the two schemes differ in various ways. One is that N-version programs are obviously well-suited to take advantage of multiple processors. However the alternates within a recovery block could be executed in parallel with the primary block, even though the acceptance test is to be applied to each in turn. (Indeed schemes have been produced for continuing with the tentative execution of the code following a recovery block, in parallel with the evaluation of its acceptance test [17].)

The other obvious difference between the ways in which the two schemes attempt to mask faults concerns the method by which results are checked for errors - in the one case by checking the answers produced by rival algorithms for exact (or possibly near) identicality, in the other case principally via the use of a separate programmed acceptance test. (For a more comprehensive discussion of this point, see Chapter 9 of [4].) In fact, as Tom Anderson has recently shown [18] the use of a general adjudication mechanism, which first filters then arbitrates between the results produced by the redundant modules, can provide a general fault masking scheme within which those of recovery blocks and

N-version programming appear as special cases - moreover, one could embed this scheme within the sort of hierarchical error recovery scheme provided by recovery blocks, if one does not wish to assume that faults are invariably successfully masked.

Since the early work on recovery blocks, the Newcastle project has gone on to consider error recovery in more generality, and to develop an overall approach to exception handling in multi-level systems. We now regard recovery blocks as just a convenient notation for a stylized form of exception handling, in which backward error recovery is the only form of error recovery used. However, forward error recovery is more appropriate for predictable and well-defined errors (e.g. simple hardware component faults and input errors), leaving backward error recovery to be used just for faults whose consequences have not been, or cannot be, accurately specified (such as unmasked residual design faults).

Based on this approach of providing both forward and backward error recovery via exception handling, work has been undertaken by Flaviu Cristian at Newcastle, and subsequently elsewhere, on formal means of specifying and of designing programs incorporating exception handling [19] and in extending these ideas to the provision of robust abstract types [20]. The exception handling scheme which we have used is based on the "termination model". Operations on an abstract type are expected to provide a suitable exception report and to terminate, unless of course they can terminate normally. The user of an operation is expected to be able to assume that, in the absence of such a report, the operation has indeed been successful, and that no further checking of its results is needed. This, of course, is the software analogue of the well-known hardware scheme of self-checking circuits introduced by Bill Carter [21]. (Incidentally, another interesting link between the worlds of hardware and software fault tolerance is provided by the work, at the University of Waterloo, on extending both the theory and the practice of error detecting and correcting codes to various types of data structure, such as linked lists and binary trees [22, 23, 24]. Redundancy is added to such data structures so that it would require a given minimum number of elementary changes to modify a valid instance of a structure into another valid instance. If less than this number are produced, as a result of a fault, the error can be detected. Error correction consists in transforming the erroneous instance into a valid instance, using a minimum number of elementary changes.)

The main thrust of the work at Newcastle in recent years has been to extend these ideas on exception handling to situations involving asynchronous activity. We first considered problems relating to competition for shared resources [25], and then of cooperation among time-shared processes [26] within a single computing system, before concentrating particularly on distributed systems - not just distributed computing systems, but systems which could, for example, include people and machines, interacting with, and perhaps through, one or more computing systems. In common with other groups, we have made much use of the concept of an atomic action - the crucial notion of providing atomic actions as an explicit linguistic construct, independent of any particular means of guaranteeing atomicity, had been introduced to us by David Lomet when he spent the academic year 1975-76 at Newcastle on leave from the IBM Research Center, Yorktown Heights. Lomet's work, like similar ideas then being developed in the database world, can be seen as a way of making explicit some of the ideas behind the notion of "spheres of control" - pioneering work by Charlie Davies [27, 28] which has had a continuing influence on our own thinking (see, for example the paper by Santosh Shrivastava [29]) particularly since we had the pleasure of his participation in the 1978 and 1979 lecture courses referred to earlier.

As mentioned above, our own work on reliability in distributed systems has concentrated on the problems of coping with erroneous data flow rather than design faults per se. In fact comparatively few of the many groups working on distributed computing systems or distributed database systems have had an explicit interest in design fault tolerance. Rather, their recovery techniques are mainly intended to deal with occurrences such as processor crashes, disk failures, deadlocks, faulty input data, etc. Nevertheless the backward recovery facilities they provide are of potential relevance to errors due to software design faults. (For a recent survey of this work, see [30].) In our own treatment, as indicated earlier, we have not stopped at the provision just of backward error recovery, but have gone further, and investigated the provision of atomic actions for which both forward and backward recovery are permitted, so producing an overall framework suitable for tolerating both anticipated and unanticipated faults in asynchronous systems [31] - our belief is that such facilities, which approach the generality inherent in the spheres of control concept, will often be required in general distributed systems, even if it is possible to manage without them in distributed database systems.

In addition to work on recovery techniques, the world of distributed computing systems has also been the source of a quite separate thread of research of relevance to design fault tolerance. This is work on various synchronization and consistency algorithms which are expected to cope with arbitrary behaviour (including that due to possible design faults) by the processors and communications devices involved. Perhaps the best known such work is that on so-called Byzantine agreement protocols [32]. Note that the actual protocol design is assumed to be correct - direct attempts at designing distributed algorithms which are in some sense inherently fault-tolerant are very rare, though one most impressive example has been presented by Dijkstra [33]. Were such heroic efforts necessary for all forms of design fault tolerance, the future of the field would be bleak indeed. As it is, the sorts of approach discussed earlier, which are based on the assumption that reliable structuring facilities are first provided to aid fault masking and perhaps error recovery, seem more widely applicable, since they allow users to employ conventional programming techniques yet still gain a measure of design fault tolerance.

4. The Effectiveness of Design Fault Tolerance

In 1981 Tom Anderson and Pete Lee concluded the chapter on Software Fault Tolerance in their book [4] with the statement:

"Unfortunately, it may take some kind of computer-controlled disaster to bring about recognition that fault prevention techniques are not sufficient for high software reliability, and that software fault tolerance can and should be provided in application areas which have high reliability requirements. There are few theoretical reasons for not adopting fault tolerance in software systems, although practical justification must await the results of on-going research efforts."

In fact during 1981-84 a project at Newcastle led by Tom Anderson undertook a large scale investigation of the cost-effectiveness of software fault tolerance based on recovery blocks and recoverable "dialogues" between multiple processes. (A dialogue provides a restricted form of the concept of a conversation [34].) This project involved the implementation of a model Naval Command and Control System, and the use of the PDP11/45 hardware recovery cache which had been built earlier [35]. The model, though only partial, was as realistic as possible, being designed and implemented by people who were already experienced in this application area, using approved software design practices and languages, and with the whole exercise being closely monitored by Navy personnel. The actual evaluation was based mainly on comparing the reliability of the system with its fault tolerance provisions either enabled or disabled. Quoting from the final report of the project: [36]

"Over the entire program of experiments, the event counts show that 222 failures could have occurred due to "bugs" in the software of the command and control system. But of these 222 potential failures only 52 actually happened - the other 165 were masked by the use of software fault tolerance. This represents an overall success rate of 74 percent... Projections suggest that with further improvements to the recovery software a coverage factor of over 90% could have been achieved... The supplementary cost of incorporating fault tolerance in the command and control system was approximately 60 percent... Overheads in system operation were measured as: 33 percent extra code memory, 35 percent extra data memory, and 40 percent extra run time (though the system still had to meet its real-time constraints).... Our overall conclusion is that these experiments have shown that by means of software fault tolerance a significant and worthwhile improvement in reliability can be achieved at acceptable cost."

Ideally of course one would perform an experiment involving a large number of carefully controlled trials - this has been the approach to evaluating the effectiveness of N-version programs which has been taken by the UCLA group (who have recently developed a software test-bed for facilitating the assessment of N-version programs, and their parallel execution on a set of processors [37]). Of necessity these evaluation exercises, of which there have by now been several, have used much smaller, and hence somewhat less realistic, examples than the model command and control system.

In some cases, the reliability improvements observed have been somewhat modest. For example, Al Avizienis and John Kelly have described [38] an experiment involving the programming of an "airport scheduler" exercise independently by thirty Computer Science students. Eighteen acceptable programs were produced, and used to make up 816 different 3-version programs. Running independently, the programs produced in total a correct answer for 73.1% of the transactions, reported an error for 5.8%, and failed to detect an error in 21.1% of the transactions. Running in 3-version programs, the percentage of correct transactions went up to 80.1%, and the percentage in which there were failures to detect an error fell to 3.6%. (The percentage of transactions that reported an error increased to 16.3%, mainly because the voting procedure required strict equality.)

Much higher reliability gains are implied by the figures reported for a subsequent experiment at the University of Virginia and the University of California at [39], which was based on a small, but nevertheless reasonably realistic aerospace example. Each of twenty-seven experienced programmers, working independently, implemented and carefully tested one program. These programs were then each subjected to a total of a million tests, of which just 18,962 failed. (Thus even running independently, the programs achieved a success ratio in excess of 99.9%.) Although no actual N-version program trials are reported, it is clear from the data given in the paper that if these programs had been used to construct 3-version programs the vast majority of these potential failures would have been masked. Indeed I estimate that an average failure coverage factor of at least 93% would have been achieved, though of course at the cost of a threefold increase in resources. Unfortunately such facts are not immediately apparent from the paper, since the authors have chosen to concentrate their entire discussion on another (admittedly important) issue. This is that their results confirm that the reliability of an N-version system may not be as high as theory predicts under the assumption that independently written programs will fail independently - in practice people occasionally make the same mistakes even when they are working completely independently. (Similar cautions will of course also apply to predictions concerning recovery block programs.)

Despite their limitations, such assessment efforts are to be applauded, particularly when one remembers how few software (or hardware) design tools and methodologies have been adopted (or rejected) on the basis of an adequate quantitative evaluation exercise. In fact another important reason for pursuing the difficult task of producing cost/effectiveness assessments of the different software fault tolerance schemes is to provide constructive guidelines as to how and when such schemes should best be used. For although software fault tolerance is best thought of as complementary to, rather than competitive with, software fault prevention schemes such as testing and formal verification, it is not obvious how a given system development project should subdivide its limited time and resources between these different activities. There have nevertheless been some attempts to provide such guidelines, such as that by Hecht [40] and work on software reliability modelling is often aimed at assessing the amount of further testing which would be worthwhile.

Currently, the use of software fault tolerance in anger, so to speak, is largely limited to systems calling for ultra high reliability [41] - and few systems, even those in which system failures would endanger human life, aim to provide completely automatic means of tolerating software design faults. Instead, in most cases just duplicate programs are used [42, 43, 44], so as to provide error detection and reporting, i.e "fail-stop" operation [45], rather than fault masking. (Incidentally, such duplication has also been used to assist the testing process [46].)

In the present circumstances of comparatively little industrial experience, or experimental data, perhaps the best argument that can be deployed in favour of the use of software fault tolerance is one due to Michael Melliar-Smith. Formal verification, testing and fault tolerance each depend on a set of assumptions. For example, verification depends, inter alia, on the adequacy of the theorem proving tools and techniques, testing on the choice of tests and the care with which their results are inspected, and fault tolerance on the completeness of the error detection scheme and the degree of actual design diversity achieved. In addition, the three schemes all depend on having an adequate system specification. By using formal verification *and* testing *and* fault tolerance the number of assumptions on which belief in the reliability of a system rests can be reduced to the absolute minimum, namely that the system specification is satisfactory, for this is the single assumption that is shared by all three approaches.

5. The Future

Continued improvements in hardware cost/performance and in memory capacities are providing the world with a seemingly irresistible opportunity to design, implement and (try to) rely on ever larger and more complex software systems. There might of course be breakthroughs in formal verification, or in test case generation and analysis - however in the interim the future will surely bring increased acceptance and use, and continued development, of various software fault tolerance schemes.

However, I suggest that what is really needed is a broader perspective on the whole subject. Formal verification, testing and fault tolerance are all essentially just schemes for checking the consistency of a redundant body of information, namely a system's specification, design and implementation. They merely differ as to when, and therefore how, such checking takes place - either prior to the provision of any input data, or after some sample data is supplied but before the system is put into service, or while the system is in service and operating on real input data. Should such a consistency check fail, this implies that the implementation *and/or* the specification is at fault. (Ideally the specification is so much simpler than the implementation that the latter possibility can be ignored - in practice, all too often this is not the case.) When the three techniques are compared in this way, it seems clear that there ought to be a more coherent way of discussing their relative merits, and some more methodical way of deploying each to its best advantage - indeed of performing mean-ingful (and perhaps computer-assisted) tradeoffs between them.

Some of the work we have carried out can be seen in this light - for example that on formal methodologies for the automatic placement of certain kinds of acceptance test [4], and on "safe" programming, a scheme which makes use both of formal verification and of run-time evaluation of assertions [48]. How-ever, much more work could be done along these, and similar, lines.

A second issue is that, just as it is important to regard fault tolerance, when applied to design faults, as a part of a subject which also includes formal verification and testing, so is it neces-sary to view the problems of tolerating design faults within a per-spective which encompasses all types of fault. The problems of tolerating different kinds of fault have much in common. For example, they share a common dependence on mechanisms for limiting the spread of errors. In many cases, quite general fault tolerance mechanisms can be devised, which are capable of tolerating a variety of faults. This is just as well, since it is often difficult, if not impossible, to determine the exact cause of a failure in a complex computing system. However if design fault tolerance is to have its full impact on the reliability of large and sophisticated hardware/software systems, rather than just on relatively modest safety-critical software modules, say, then further research is needed towards making design fault tolerance a well-integrated part of an overall reliability strategy.

The third and final issue I wish to mention is that, as VLSI integration levels are increasing, improved hardware and software design methodologies and tools aimed at fault prevention are appearing. Unfortunately, it is by no means obvious that such improvements are doing more than keep up with the increases in complexity, if that. It therefore seems likely that design fault tolerance will be needed for VLSI, as well as software, particularly if wafer-scale integration succeeds in allowing even more complex designs to be attempted.

All this provides, I would argue, yet another reason to seek to minimize differences between hardware and software design methodologies, tools, languages and support environments. There seems to be no inherent reason why one should not use the same specification and high level design languages (and hence design fault tolerance schemes) regardless of whether the ultimate aim is an implementation stored in memory, or laid out as intricate geometrical patterns on silicon. This would facilitate the explora-tion of differing hardware/software tradeoffs, and also the testing and assessment of designs prior to their being committed to silicon.

Some investigations of these issues are being made at Newcastle, as elsewhere. For example, a prototype system for converting programs written in the OCCAM language directly to (schematic versions of) VLSI layouts has been constructed by a Ph.D. student, Mike Lynch. Secondly, Martin McLauchlan and Albert Koelmans, who are involved in the development of a successor to the VLSI design language STRICT ("Strongly Typed Recursive Integrated CircuiT" [49], are starting to consider what set of facilities it should contain related to the provision of design fault tolerance. These are, however, but initial explorations of what I feel sure will be a very interesting and fruitful area.

6. Concluding Remarks

Despite my comments above, to date the topic of design fault tolerance has largely been the province of software designers, who have tended to have little in common with hardware designers working on conventional fault tolerance. Few people have bridged this gap at all successfully - one of the most notable exceptions being Bill Carter, both through the wide scope of his achievements (e.g from self-checking circuits, to formal verification of microprograms) and through the "systems thinking" which characterizes his approach to the whole subject of reliability. It has therefore been both a pleasure and a privilege to provide this brief contribution on the topic of design fault tolerance to this symposium held in his honour.

7. Acknowledgements

I am indebted to Tom Anderson for his helpful comments on a draft of this paper. Research at Newcastle on system reliability is sponsored by the UK Science and Engineering Research Council, and the Ministry of Defence.

8. References

[1] C. Babbage, "On The Mathematical Powers of the Calculating Engine", (Unpublished Manuscript) Buxton MS7, Museum of the History of Science, Oxford, December 1837, (Printed in The Origins of Digital Computers: Selected Papers (ed. B. Randell) pp.17-52, Springer, 1974.)

[2] D. Lardner, "Babbage's Calculating Engine", Edinburgh Review, vol. 120, July 1834, (Reprinted in Charles Babbage and his Calculating Engines (eds. P. and E. Morrison) Dover, New York, 1961.)

[3] S. K. Shrivastava (ed.), "Reliable Computing Systems: Collected papers of the Newcastle Reliability Project", Springer 1985

[4] P. M. Melliar-Smith and B. Randell, "Software Reliability: The role of programmed exception handling", Proc. Conf. on Language Design For Reliable Software, pp. 95-100 Raleigh March 1977, (ACM SIGPLAN Notices, vol. 12, no. 3, March 1977.)

[5] W. C. Carter, "Hardware Fault Tolerance", pp. 211-263 Computing System Reliability, ed. T. Anderson and B. Randell, Cambridge Univ. Press 1979

[6] T. Anderson and P.A. Lee, "Fault Tolerance: Principles and practice", Prentice-Hall 1981

[7] J.-C. Laprie, "Dependable Computing and Fault-Tolerance", Digest of Papers FTCS-15: Fifteenth IEEE Int. Conf. on Fault-Tolerant Computing, pp. 2-11, Ann Arbor, June 1985

[8] B. Randell and J. E. Dobson, "Reliability and Security Issues in Distributed Computing Systems", Proc. 5th Symp. on Reliability in Distributed Software and Database Systems, pp. 113-118, IEEE, Los Angeles, January 1986

[9] J. E. Dobson and B. Randell, "Building Reliable Secure Systems Out of Unreliable Insecure Components", Proc. Conf. on Security and Privacy, Oakland April 1986

[10] A. Avizienis, "Design Diversity - The challenge of the eighties", Digest of Papers, FTCS-12: Twelfth Annual Int. Conf. on Fault-Tolerant Computing, pp. 44-45, IEEE, Santa Monica, 22-24 June 1982

[11] J. J. Horning, H. C. Lauer, P. M. Melliar-Smith and B. Randell, "A Program Structure for Error Detection and Recovery", Proc. Conf. on Operating Systems, Theoretical and Practical Aspects, IRIA, Rocquencourt, 23-25 April 1974, (Reprinted in Operating Systems (ed. E. Gelenbe and C. Kaiser), Lecture Notes in Computer Science, Vol. 16, Springer, pp. 171-187, 1974.)

[12] T. Anderson and R. Kerr, "Recovery Blocks in Action: A system supporting high reliability", Proc. 2nd Int. Conf. on Software Engineering, pp. 447-457, San Francisco, October 1976,

[13] B. Randell, "System structuring for software fault tolerance", Proc. Int. Conf. on Reliable Software, pp. 437-449, Los Angeles, 21-23 April 1975, (ACM SIGPLAN Notices, Vol. 10, No.6, June 1975)

[14] A. Avizienis, "Fault-Tolerance and Fault-Intolerance: Complementary approaches to reliable computing", Proc. Int. Conf. on Reliable Software, pp. 458-464, Los Angeles 21-23 April 1975, (ACM SIGPLAN Notices, Vol. 10, No. 6, June 1975)

[15] A. Avizienis and L. Chen, "On the Implementation of N-Version Programming for Software Fault-Tolerance During Program Execution", Proc. COMPSAC 77, pp. 149-155 (1st IEEE-CS Int. Computer Software and Applications Conference) Chicago, November 1977

[16] L. Chen and A. Avizienis, "N-Version Programming: A Fault-Tolerance Approach to Reliability of Software Operation", Digest of Papers FTCS-8: Eighth Annual Conf. on Fault-Tolerant Computing, pp. 3-9, IEEE, June 1978, Toulouse

[17] K. H. Kim and C. V. Ramamoorthy, "Failure Tolerant Parallel Programming and its Supporting System Architecture", pp. 413-423, Proc. 1976 NCC, AFIPS, New York June 1976

[18] T. Anderson, "A Structured Decision Mechanism for Diverse Software", Proc. 5th Symp. on Reliability in Distributed Software and Database Systems, pp. 125-129, IEEE, Los Angeles, 13-15 January 1986

[19] F. Cristian, "Exception Handling and Software Fault Tolerance", IEEE Transactions on Computers, vol. C-31, nr. 6, pp. 531-540, June 1982

[20] F. Cristian, "Robust Data Types", Acta Informatica, vol. 17, 1982, pp. 365-397,

[21] W. C. Carter and P. R. Schneider, "Design of Dynamically Checked Computers", Proc. IFIP 68, Edinburgh, 5-10 August 1968, pp. 878-883

[22] D. J. Taylor, D. E. Morgan and J. P. Black, "Redundancy in Data Structures: Improving software fault tolerance" IEEE Trans. on Software Engineering, vol. SE-6, nr. 6, November 1980, pp.585-594

[23] D. J. Taylor, D. E. Morgan and J. P. Black, "Redundancy in Data Structures: Some theoretical results", IEEE Trans. on Software Engineering, vol. SE-6, nr. 6, November 1980, pp. 595-602

[24] J. P. Black and D. J. Taylor, "Local Correctability in Robust Storage Structures", December 1984, Dept. of Computer Science, University of Waterloo, CS-84-44, (To appear in IEEE Trans. on Software Engineering)

[25] J.-P. Banatre and S. K. Shrivastava, "Reliable Resource Allocation Between Unreliable Processes", IEEE Trans. on Software Engineering, vol. SE-4, nr. 3, pp. 230-241, May 1978

[26] S. K. Shrivastava, "Concurrent Pascal with Backward Error Recovery", Software: Practice and Experience, vol. 9, nr. 12, 1979, pp. 1001-1020

[27] C. T. Davies, "Recovery Semantics for a DB/DC System", Proc. ACM National Conference, pp. 136-141, Atlanta, August 1973

[28] C. T. Davies, "Data Processing", Computing Systems Reliability, Cambridge Univ. Press 1979, ed. T. Anderson and B. Randell, pp. 288-354

[29] S. K. Shrivastava, "A Dependency, Commitment and Recovery Model for Atomic Actions", Proc. 2nd Symp. on Reliability in Distributed Software and Database Systems, IEEE, Pittsburgh, 19-21 July 1982, pp. 112-119

[30] T. Haerder and A. Reuter, "Principles of Transaction-Oriented Database Recovery", Computing Surveys, vol. 15, nr. 4, pp. 287-317

[31] R. H. Campbell and B. Randell "Error Recovery in Asynchronous Systems", Technical Report TR186, Computing Laboratory, University of Newcastle upon Tyne, July, 1983, (To appear in IEEE Trans. on Software Engineering)

[32] L. Lamport, R. Shostak and M. Pease, "The Byzantine Generals Problem", ACM Trans. on Prog. Lang. and Systems, July 1982, vol. 4, nr. 3, pp. 382-401

[33] E. W. Dijkstra, "Self-Stabilization in Spite of Distributed Control", Comm. ACM, vol. 17, nr. 11, November 1974, pp. 643-644

[34] T. Anderson and M. R. Moulding, "Dialogues for Recovery Coordination in Concurrent Systems", (In preparation)

[35] P. A. Lee, N. Ghani and K. Heron, "A Recovery Cache for the PDP-11", IEEE Trans. Computers, vol. C-29, nr. 6, pp. 546-549, June 1980

[36] T. Anderson, P. A. Barrett, D. N. Halliwell and M. R. Moulding, "Software Fault Tolerance: An evaluation", IEEE Trans. Software Engineering, vol. SE-11, nr. 12, pp. 1502-1510, December 1985

[37] A. Avizienis, P. Gunnenberg, J. P. J. Kelly, L. Strigini, P. J. Traverse, K. S. Tso and U. Voges, "The UCLA DEDIX System: A distributed testbed for multiple-version software", Digest of Papers, FTCS-15: Fifteenth Annual Int. Conf. on Fault-Tolerant Computing, IEEE, Ann Arbor, 19-21 June 1985, pp. 126-134

[38] A. Avizienis and J. P. J. Kelly, "Fault Tolerance by Design Diversity: Concepts and experiments", IEEE Computer, August 1984, pp. 67-80

[39] J. C. Knight, N. G. Leveson and L. D. St.Jean, "A Large Scale Experiment in N-Version Programming", Digest of Papers, FTCS-15: Fifteenth Annual Int. Conf. on Fault-Tolerant Computing IEEE, 19-21 June 1985, Ann Arbor MI

[40] H. Hecht, "Fault Tolerant Software for Real-Time Applications", ACM Computing Surveys, vol. 8, nr. 4, December 1976, pp. 391-407

[41] H. D. Welch, "Distributed Recovery Block Performance in a Real-Time Control Loop", Proc. Real Time Systems Symp., pp. 268-276, Arlington 1983

[42] J. R. Garman, "The "Bug" Heard Round the World", ACM Software Engineering Notes, vol. 6, nr. 5, pp. 3-10, October 1981

[43] D. J. Martin, "Dissimilar Software in High Integrity Applications in Flight Control", Software Avionics, AGARD Conf. Proc. No 300, pp. 36.1-36.9, January 1983

[44] O. B. Von Linde, "Computers Can Now Perform Vital Functions Safely", Railway Gazette International, pp. 1004-1006, November 1979

[45] R. D. Schlichting and F. B. Schneider, "Fail-Stop Processors: An approach to designing fault-tolerant computing systems", ACM Trans. Computer Systems, vol. 1, nr. 3, pp. 222-238, August 1983

[46] T. Gilb, "Parallel Programming", Datamation, vol. 20, nr. 10, pp. 160-161, October 1974

[47] E. Best and F. Cristian, "Systematic Detection of Exception Occurrences", Science of Computer Programming, vol. 1, nr. 1, pp. 115-144, North-Holland, 1981

[48] T. Anderson and R. W. Witty, "Safe Programming", BIT, vol. 18, pp. 1-8, 1978

[49] R. H. Campbell, A. Koelmans and M. R. McLauchlan, "STRICT - A Design Language for Strongly Typed Recursive Integrated Circuits", Proc. IEE, March/April 1985, vol. 132, Pts E and I, nr. 2, pp. 108-115

The Evolution of Fault Tolerant Computing at the University of Illinois

J. A. Abraham, G. Metze,
R. K. Iyer, and J. H. Patel

Department of Electrical and Computer Engineering
and the Coordinated Science Laboratory
University of Illinois
Urbana, Illinois 61801
U.S.A.

ABSTRACT

The University of Illinois has been active in research in
the fault-tolerant computing field for over 25 years.
Fundamental ideas have been proposed and major contributions made by researchers at the University of Illinois in the areas of testing and diagnosis, concurrent
error detection, and fault tolerance. This paper traces
the origins of these ideas and their development within
the University of Illinois, as well as their influence upon
research at other institutions, and outlines current
directions of research.

1. Introduction

The University of Illinois, though nestled in cornfields far from
any center of industry, has been surprisingly productive in the
field of computers. The first electronic digital computer at the
University was ORDVAC (Meagher and Nash, 1952), built for the
Ordnance Department and patterned after the machine developed
at the Institute for Advanced Study, Princeton. One of the

pioneers in the field of fault-tolerant computing was Professor S. Seshu whose fundamental contributions to fault diagnosis and fault simulation laid the groundwork for continued research in the field. From those beginnings in the late 50s and early 60s, the research has continued at a strong pace at the University where, at present, around 50 faculty and graduate students are active in the area.

Researchers at the University of Illinois have consistently contributed to the International Symposium on Fault-Tolerant Computing (FTCS), both by presentation of papers and by serving as program and general chairmen. Program and general chairmen who were at the University, or who have come from the University, include Professor Algirdas Avizienis (FTCS 1, 1971), Professor Gernot Metze (FTCS 2, 1972 and FTCS 4, 1974), Professor John Hayes (FTCS 7, 1977), and Professor Jacob Abraham (FTCS 11, 1981).

We are delighted with this opportunity to participate in a volume honoring Dr. William C. Carter. Bill has been extremely supportive of many of us in our professional careers. Some of the key work at Illinois in the area of Totally Self-Checking circuits was based on his fundamental work.

2. Testing and Diagnosis

2.1. Early Computers

When ILLIAC I (essentially a duplicate of ORDVAC) and ILLIAC II were built at the University of Illinois in the 1950s, fault diagnosis consisted of running a battery of programs that exercised different sections of the machine. These test programs typically compared answers computed two different ways (essentially emulating hardware multiplication in software) or tended to stress what was suspected to be a vulnerable part (e.g., punch and subsequently read a continuous stream of characters on paper tape). In ILLIAC I, a vacuum tube computer (about 2500 tubes, consuming 35 KW), the maintenance engineers found it useful to vary supply and heater voltages by some margins and to tap tubes and chassis with a small plastic mallet while the test programs were running, and to use only replacement tubes that had been aged at least 100 hours. Special tests were used for the electrostatic *Williams-tube* memory to determine the *Read-Around Ratio* (RAR) for the day, i.e., the number of times a cell's neighbors could be bombarded between refreshes without altering the cell's contents. An RAR of 300 was considered pretty good (Wheeler and Robertson, 1953).

By present-day standards, this approach was very primitive; no attempt was made to model faults systematically or to evaluate precisely which segments of the machine were *covered* by the tests. Yet the routine, preventive, marginal testing maintenance approach and the *clinical experience* of the maintenance engineers, coupled with the healthy skepticism of the users who didn't completely trust either their numerical methods or the computer, resulted in a highly reliable operation. Of course, the equivalent of the entire ILLIAC I, including its 1024-word memory, could now be put on one IC chip.

The approach to testing in ILLIAC II, a discrete-component transistor machine put in service in 1961, was quite similar. However, to simplify fault diagnosis, the arithmetic unit's control (involving the equivalent of about 100 flipflops) had been designed to operate asynchronously, using essentially a double handshake for each control signal and its acknowledgement. The basic idea came from the theory of speed-independent circuits developed at the University of Illinois (Muller and Bartky, 1959). A large percentage of failures would, therefore, simply cause the control to wait for the next step of the handshake sequence; the missing step could easily be identified from the indicator lights on the flipflops. By contrast, the logic for the lookahead control did not use handshaking and exhibited some failures that were extremely difficult to trace. (Incidentally, a subtle design bug in the arithmetic unit, (-2) * (-2) giving (-4), escaped detection by the tests using pseudo-random operands but was caught after about nine months by a numerical double check built into a user's program.) Note again that no attempt was made to model faults systematically, although the handshake mechanism used in the ALU control exhibited the basic idea of what is now called self-checking operation.

2.2. Fault Simulation and Automatic Test Generation

In the meantime, the *Sequential Analyzer* was being developed in another part of the University by S. Seshu (1962, 1964, and 1965). The Sequential Analyzer is a set of programs that can generate fault simulation data (for single, logical, stuck-line faults) for a given logic circuit and a given test sequence and also has the ability to generate test sequences for combinational as well as sequential circuits. Although these test sequences usually were not minimal, they were generated automatically. The Sequential Analyzer was applied directly, but on a limited scale, at Bell Telephone Laboratories to check for design errors in IC designs prior to production, to generate test sequences that could be incorporated into factory test equipment, and to improve diagnosis procedures for the No. 1 Electronic Switching System. It was also used extensively at the University of Illinois to study computer self-diagnosis where an unduplicated processor would perform checkout and diagnosis of itself (Manning, 1966; Marlett, 1966). Again, this self-diagnosis procedure relied on the idea that a processor fault could cause the processor to stop prematurely. Fault simulators were soon available commercially. Chang, Manning, and Metze produced, as a tribute to Seshu, what is probably the first book devoted entirely to digital fault diagnosis (Chang, Manning, and Metze, 1970).

Recent research in this area has been directed toward new techniques for improving the performance of fault simulation and automatic test generation. This is motivated by the fact that advances in technology are making possible the design and manufacture of extremely large circuits. Approaches which consider a flat, one-level view of the circuit are doomed to failure because of the sheer complexity involved. Exciting new results have been obtained in fault simulation through the use of techniques which simulate directly from a hierarchical circuit description without flattening to the level of primitives (Rogers and Abraham, 1985a). The approach also decouples the fault model from the simulator programs through the use of a fault library. This allows the user to mix both functional and technology-dependent fault models, allowing fault simulation for realistic failures, and also simulation early in the design, with refinements in the fault model and test coverage as the design progresses. This work resulted in the development of CHIEFS, a Concurrent, Hierarchical, and Extensible Fault Simulator (Rogers and Abraham, 1985b). The use of innovative partitioning techniques and exploitation of the hierarchy has allowed CHIEFS to obtain, in some cases, orders of magnitude improvement in simulator performance. Ongoing research includes the investigation of new optimization techniques, use of multiple processors, and automatic test generation techniques which can exploit the hierarchy in a circuit.

Along with the need to handle large circuits, fault simulation and test generation should address realistic failures such as shorts and opens at the transistor level. Shih, Rahmeh, and Abraham (1985) have developed FAUST, an MOS fault simulator which produces output waveforms for circuits under realistic physical failures. This simulator uses a table lookup of the transistor I-V characteristics for accurate fault simulation under shorts and opens. Such a simulator can be used as a powerful tool for characterizing the behavior of circuits, and the results are intended for use by CHIEFS when simulating a large circuit. Use of

FAUST also showed that tests generated for MOS VLSI circuits will not detect some physical failures if the tests are derived using only logic-level considerations (Abraham and Shih, 1985). Current research in this area includes automatic test generation at the transistor level.

2.3. Fault Models

Another area in which the research done at the University of Illinois proved to be seminal is fault representation (Schertz and Metze, 1968; Schertz, 1969; Schertz and Metze, 1972). Indistinguishable or dominated faults can easily be identified, *a priori*, from the network structure and be eliminated from further consideration. This approach not only reduces the number of faults to be analyzed, but also makes it possible to replace the 3-valued nature of a possibly faulty line (normal, stuck-at-1, stuck-at-0) with only two possible conditions (normal, faulty), where the faulty condition depends on the gate type (e.g., only stuck-at-1 input faults need be considered for NAND gates since any stuck-at-0 input is indistinguishable from a stuck-at-1 output.) Other research in fault representation was carried out, primarily at Stanford University (McCluskey and Clegg, 1971) and at Western Electric Company (To, 1973). Further work at the University of Illinois concentrated on the analysis of multiple faults, including masking relationships (Hayes, 1971; Cha, 1974), and some surprising results concerning the undetectability of certain multiple faults, i.e., multiple redundancies which have no sub-redundancies (Smith and Metze, 1975) and extensions (Smith, 1979).

Detailed studies at the transistor level have indicated that the conventional stuck-at fault model is inadequate for modeling the effects of physical failures on MOS circuits (Banerjee and Abraham, 1984a). These studies were used to develop accurate, higher level fault models for modules such as decoders and multiplexers, which include the effects of realistic physical failures. A new logical model, in the form of a multivalued algebra, has also been developed (Banerjee and Abraham, 1985). This can be used to model the effects of physical failures at the transistor level, since the model allows for strong interactions between all three terminals of a transistor. (There has been a long-term interest in multivalued logic at the University.) Ongoing work in this area includes the development of accurate fault models for other modules, fault collapsing at the transistor level, and the compact representation of fault models for use by hierarchical fault simulation and test generation programs.

2.4. Functional-Level Test Generation

As complex chips such as memories and microprocessors began to be used widely in systems because of their increasing density and decreasing cost, the problem of testing these chips without the availability of information about their internal structure became acute. An interesting solution to this problem was initially obtained in the case of memories, where a higher, functional-level fault model was developed, and this was used as the basis for deriving tests. Thus, the initial fault model for memories included stuck bits in the memory as well as coupling between cells in a memory. An $O(n \log_2 n)$ algorithm, which will detect all the faults in the fault model was developed by Thatte and Abraham (1977). This test generation algorithm was improved by Nair, Thatte, and Abraham (1978) to one of complexity $O(n)$. This work was extended by others, including Suk and Reddy (1981) at Iowa.

An extrapolation of the approach to testing memories, using only functional-level information, was used by Thatte and Abraham (1980) to develop test generation procedures for microprocessors in a user environment. A general graph-theoretic model was developed at the register-transfer level to model any microprocessor using only information about its instruction set and the functions performed. A fault model was developed on a functional level, quite independent of the implementation details. These were used to generate test patterns for microprocessors. A fault simulation study on a real microprocessor showed extremely good fault coverage for tests developed using these procedures. This work was extended by Brahme and Abraham (1984) where a simpler graph model was developed for very complex microprocessors and more general fault models were used as the basis of test generation procedures. The problem of having the microprocessor test itself was also addressed in this paper, and a methodology for self-test of complex microprocessor chips, which include integrated peripheral control modules, was developed by Fujii and Abraham (1985). This functional-level fault modeling and test generation approach was applied to other modules, including PLAs (Bose and Abraham, 1982). Ongoing work in these areas include the development of accurate functional fault models for arithmetic and other functions.

3. Testable Design of Regular Structures

Techniques for deriving testable structures from high-level descriptions were studied by Abraham and Gajski (1981). The generated structures in this case are cellular and interconnected in a tree structure, and a general algorithm to test these tree structures which grows only linearly with the size of tree was developed.

In 1985, Cheng and Patel (1985a, 1985b, and 1985c) developed a comprehensive theory of testing for multiple failures in iterative logic arrays. The theory provided the necessary and sufficient conditions for deriving small test sets and showed that testing for multiple faults required only slightly more effort than testing for single faults.

Techniques for testing VLSI bit-serial processors and designing these for testability were also studied by Davis, Kunda, and Fuchs (1985). The problem of testable CMOS logic circuits under arbitrary delays was studied by Jha and Abraham (1985b). Necessary and sufficient conditions for existence of a test set which cannot be invalidated under arbitrary delays were found, and a new hybrid CMOS realization, which is guaranteed to have a valid test set under arbitrary delays, was also proposed.

The testing of arbitrary sequential circuits is a very difficult problem. A solution to this problem, which was developed by Hua, Jou, and Abraham (1984), implements finite-state machines using the regular structure of PLAs with feedback. This was an extension of the work on testable PLAs by Fujiwara and Kinoshita (1981) and Hong and Ostapko (1980). Built-in tests were designed to test the finite-state machine with small additional hardware cost. This work was extended by Treuer, Fujiwara, and Agarwal (1985) at McGill University, where a lower overhead design was developed.

4. System Diagnosis

The basic idea of computer self-diagnosis, posed in simplified form as a problem (posed by Metze) on the Electrical Engineering Ph.D. qualifying examination given in December, 1965, led to abstract questions of mutual diagnosis of several computers, called the *Connection Assignment Problem* (Preparata, Metze, and Chien, 1967). This paper created an enormous amount of interest and systems using different fault models, more general test outcomes, other measures of diagnosability, probabilistic fault diagnosis, and diagnosis of intermittent faults, are still being investigated at several different institutions. A survey paper (Friedman and Simoncini, 1980) lists 26 derived papers.

The idea of not having a global supervisor which detects failures and removes failed units was investigated by Abraham and Metze (1978), where a new technique for distributed systems, called roving diagnosis, was presented. This work was extended by Breuer and Ismaeel (1983) in their concept of roving emulation. New research, aimed at using low-level error and recovery information to develop an intelligent failure diagnosis and repair system is now in progress. Preliminary results show that this technique is equally applicable for both hardware and software problems.

5. Concurrent Error Detection

5.1. Self-Checking Circuits

Self-diagnosis concepts, coupled with the earlier, fundamental results on "dynamically checked computers" by Carter and Schneider (1968), led to the formulation of Totally Self-Checking (TSC) circuits (Anderson, 1971; Anderson and Metze, 1973). A TSC circuit uses inputs and outputs that are encoded in a suitable code, together with a TSC checker that indicates whether the output is a code word or a noncode word. TSC circuits satisfy the following properties: (1) only codeword inputs are needed to completely diagram the circuit (*self-checking* property), and (2) no fault causes the circuit to output an incorrect code word, i.e., the output is either the correct codeword or is an incorrect, noncode word (*fault-secure* property). Actually, these requirements can be relaxed somewhat to *strongly fault-secure* networks which are a larger class of networks achieving the totally self-checking goal (Smith, 1976; Smith and Metze, 1978). The main advantages of TSC circuits are that transient errors are either caught or have no effect, that the outputs can be trusted as long as the checkers indicate no error, i.e., that erroneous information is not propagated, and that the circuit diagnoses itself with normally-occurring inputs. However, since the normally-occurring inputs do not necessarily cycle through the inputs required for a complete test, the circuit nevertheless has to be taken out of service periodically for testing. It should also be mentioned that the problem of finding a code whose error protection capabilities match the error generation capabilities of the logic is non-trivial (e.g., Dussault, 1977). TSC research has also led to numerous extensions at other institutions, e.g., Bell Telephone Laboratories, Stanford University, USC, University of Iowa, etc. The strongly fault-secure concept has also been adapted and extended, for example, by Jansch and

Courtois (1985).

5.2. Time Redundancy

The use of time redundancy for checking errors in hardware gained renewed attention in a series of papers from Illinois starting in the late seventies. The papers dealt with a variety of techniques and circuits. The first in a series of these results was the report on fault detection capabilities of alternating logic in circuits (Reynolds and Metze, 1978). The alternating logic used circuits which were arranged to be functionally self-dual. Conditions were presented which, if satisfied by a circuit, guaranteed to detect errors due to single stuck-at fault. The paper also discussed the application of alternating logic to sequential logic.

A method of error detection called Recomputing with Shifted Operands (RESO) was proposed and analyzed for arithmetic and logic units (ALU) by Patel and Fung (1982). This was the first time that a unified method was used for both arithmetic and logic operations. This paper was also a deviation from the earlier papers on self-checking logic in that it assumed a far more general fault model, which was suitable for the emerging VLSI circuits. Depending on the number of shifts used for the recomputed step, a variable amount of fault coverage was provided. For example, if k shifts were used in an adder, then any $(k-1)$ consecutive failed cells would be covered, although the cells may fail in any arbitrary way. The method of RESO was then applied to more complex circuits of multiply and divide arrays (Patel and Fung, 1983). The method was extended to arbitrary one-dimensional iterative logic arrays (Cheng and Patel, 1984). Variants of RESO were also used for error correction in arithmetic operations (Laha and Patel, 1983) and data transmission (Pollard and Patel, 1983).

5.3. Highly Structured Arrays

Mak, Abraham, and Davidson (1982) developed techniques for the design of PLAs which were strongly fault secure under stuck-at, shorts, and contact faults. These faults were shown to cause unidirectional errors at the outputs. Fuchs, Abraham, and Huang (1983) proposed comprehensive fault models for three broad classes of interconnection networks between processors and memories. System-level algorithms were given for concurrent error detection. Fuchs and Abraham (1984) developed a new uniform scheme of encoding the outputs of highly structured logic arrays (such as PLAs and ROMs). Comprehensive fault models were introduced which included faults on array input and output lines as well as faults within the arrays themselves. Jha and Abraham (1984) presented a new coding technique for a functional circuit so that the embedded checker is made totally self checking. Jha and Abraham (1985a) also studied techniques to reduce the transistor count of MOS implementations of totally self-checking checkers, as well as realizations for totally self-checking circuits in CMOS technology which are guaranteed to be self-testing, even when arbitrary delays and timing skews are present. Many of these ideas were incorporated in the design of microprogram control units with concurrent error detection (Wong, Fuchs, Abraham, and Davidson, 1983). Current research involves investigation of efficient and low-cost techniques for large circuits which also incorporate the effects of realistic failures.

6. Fault Tolerance

6.1. Design, Modeling, and Evaluation

Abraham, Davidson, and Patel (1983) developed a new memory system design for tolerating errors due to single-event radiation upsets. The proposed design uses coding, control duplication, and scrubbing for tolerating soft errors from single-event upsets, and has much lower cost than a straightforward application of redundancy. Abraham (1979) developed an improved algorithm for network reliability which involves the generation of disjoint Boolean products; this work has been subsequently extended by many researchers in the reliability area. Chou and Abraham (1980) developed models to analyze the performance and availability of shared resource multiprocessors. Also, Chou and Abraham (1983) developed a general model to analyze the behavior of algorithms which redistribute the workload of a failed processor to the remaining good processors in a distributed system. The redistribution may drive some of the good processors into overload (because of the increased workload directed toward them), resulting in serious degradation of system performance; criteria have been defined which, if adhered to, will guarantee that this will not happen in the event of failures.

6.2. Measurement and Experiment-Based Analysis for Reliable System Design

In computer science, more so than in physical sciences, the experimenter must make a decision on what to consider and what to ignore in the data gathering and in the analysis, sometimes without the benefit of prior information or easily available intuition. How to obtain general models from experiments or measurements made in a particular environment is by no means clear. The use of measured data to study failures in a real usage environment was published by Iyer and Rossetti (1986). In particular, the use of measured data to study the effect of increasing workload on hardware and software fault tolerance was discussed. Analysis shows that the probability of a CPU-related error increases non-linearly with increasing workload. The resulting increase in the error probability can be 50 to 100 times more than that at a low workload. These results show that current reliability models cannot be considered representative unless the system workload environment is taken into account since the gain in performance is more than offset by degradation in reliability. Similar results relating to operating system reliability appeared in Iyer and Rossetti (1985). Current research is investigating the causes of the observed phenomena. A novel experiment to obtain, for the first time, distributions of error latency was performed by Chillarege and Iyer (1985). The extension of this work to study various fault models appears in Chillarege and Iyer (1986). New research aimed at using the above-measured information for intelligent error diagnosis and circumvention, for application in a space station environment, is in progress.

6.3. Algorithm-Based Fault Tolerance

An exciting new direction in the design of fault-tolerant systems was started when Huang and Abraham (1982) developed matrix encoding schemes for detecting and correcting errors when matrix operations are performed using processor arrays. This was generalized to the new system-level method of achieving high reliability, called *algorithm-based fault tolerance*. The technique encodes data at a high level, and algorithms are designed to operate on the encoded data and produce encoded output data. The computation tasks within the algorithm are appropriately distributed among multiple computation units so that failure of one of the units affects only a portion of the output data, enabling the correct data to be recovered from the encoding (Huang and Abraham, 1984a). This result was applied to matrix operations using multiple processor arrays. This work was generalized to linear arrays by Jou and Abraham (1984), and also extended to Laplace equation solvers (Huang and Abraham, 1984b), as well as FFT networks (Jou and Abraham, 1985). Banerjee and Abraham (1984b) developed fault tolerance techniques for three powerful paradigms, the multiplex, the recursive combination, and the multiplex/demultiplex paradigms. Here, processors which are idle during normal computation are used to check the results of other processors. Recently, a general theory of algorithm-based fault tolerance has been developed which gives bounds on the processor and time overhead in this scheme (Banerjee and Abraham, 1986). This approach seems to be ideal for low-cost fault tolerance for special-purpose computations, including a wide class of signal processing applications. The work has been extended by Luk (1985), as well as Choi and Malek (1985). Ongoing work involves the design of encoding schemes for other classes of applications, including general systolic arrays, QR decomposition, and singular value decomposition.

7. Concluding Remarks

The last 25 years have witnessed the introduction of several new ideas in fault-tolerant computing and their development at the University of Illinois. With a strong commitment to this area of research by a large staff of researchers, we expect to see many more exciting results in the future. New research in testing, fault tolerance for signal processing and artificial intelligence architectures, etc., continue to maintain Illinois' role as a leading center in fault-tolerant computing research.

8. References

[1] Abraham, J. A., Metze, G., 1978: Roving Diagnosis for High-Performance Digital Systems. Proc. Conf. on Information Sciences and Systems, pp. 221-226.

[2] Abraham, J. A., 1979: " An Improved Algorithm for Network Reliability", IEEE Trans. on Network Reliability R-28, pp 58-61

[3] Abraham, J. A., Gajski, D. D., 1981: "Design of Testable Structures Defined by Simple Loops", IEEE Trans. on Computers C-30, pp. 875-884

[4] Abraham, J. A., Davidson, E. S., Patel, J. H., 1983: "Memory System Design for Tolerating Single-Event Upsets", IEEE Trans. on Nuclear Science NS-30, No. 6, pp. 4339-4344

[5] Abraham, J. A., Shih, H.-C., 1985: "Testing of MOS VLSI Circuits", Proc. Int. Symp. on Circuits and Systems, pp. 1297-1300.

[6] Anderson, D. A., 1971: "Design of Self-Checking Digital Networks", Coordinated Science Laboratory Technical Report R-527, University of Illinois, Urbana, Illinois.

[7] Anderson, D. A., Metze, G., 1973: "Design of Totally Self-Checking Circuits for m-out-of-n Codes", IEEE Trans. on Computers C-22, No. 3, pp. 263-269

[8] Banerjee, P., Abraham, J. A., 1984a: "Characterization and Testing of Physical Failures in MOS Logic Circuits", IEEE Design and Test 1, pp. 76-86

[9] Banerjee, P., Abraham, J. A., 1984b: "Fault-Secure Algorithms for Multiple Processor Systems", Proc. 11th Int. Symp. on Computer Architecture, pp. 279-287.

[10] Banerjee, P., Abraham, J. A., 1985: "A Multivalued Algebra for Modeling Physical Failures in MOS VLSI Circuits", IEEE Trans. on Computer-Aided Design, CAD-4, No. 3, pp. 312-321

[11] Banerjee, P., Abraham, J. A., 1986: "Bounds on Algorithm-Based Fault Tolerance in Multiple Processor Systems", IEEE Trans. on Computers C-35, No. 4,pp. 296-306

[12] Bose, P., Abraham, J. A., 1982: "Test Generation for Programmable Logic Arrays", Proc. ACM/IEEE 19th Design Automation Conf., pp. 574-580.

[13] Brahme, D., Abraham, J. A., 1984: "Functional Testing of Microprocessors", IEEE Trans. on Computers C-33, No. 6, pp. 475-485

[14] Breuer, M. A., Ismaeel, A. A., 1983: "Roving Emulation as a Fault Detection Mechanism", Proc. 13th Int. Symp. on Fault-Tolerant Computing, pp. 206-215.

[15] Carter, W. C., Schneider, P. R., 1968: "Design of Dynamically Checked Computers", Proc. IFIP Congress 2, pp. 878-883

[16] Cha, C. W., 1974: "Multiple Fault Diagnosis in Combinational Networks", Coordinated Science Laboratory Technical Report R-650, University of Illinois, Urbana, Illinois.

[17] Chang, H. Y., Manning, E., Metze, G, 1970: "Fault Diagnosis of Digital Systems", Huntington, NY: R"obert E", Krieger Publishing Company.

[18] Cheng, W.-T., Patel, J. H., 1984: "Concurrent Error Detection in Iterative Logic Arrays", Proc. 14th Int. Symp. on Fault-Tolerant Computing, pp. 10-15.

[19] Cheng, W.-T., Patel, J. H., 1985a: "A Minimum Test Set for Multiple-Fault Detection in Ripple-Carry Adders",

[20] Proc. Int. Conf. on Computer Design, pp. 435-438.

[21] Cheng, W.-T., Patel, J. H., 1985b: "Multiple-Fault Detection in Iterative Logic Arrays", Proc. Int. Test Conf., pp. 493-499.

[22] Cheng, W.-T. Patel, J. H., 1985c: "A Shortest Length Test Sequence for Sequential-Fault Detection in Ripple Carry Adders", Proc. Int. Conf. on Computer-Aided Design, pp. 71-73.

[23] Chillarege, R., Iyer, R. K., 1985: "The Effect of System Workload on Error Latency: An Experimental Study", Proc. ACM SIGMETRICS Conf. on Measurement and Modeling of Computer Systems, pp. 69-77.

[24] Chillarege, R., Iyer, R. K., 1986: "Fault Latency in the Memory--An Experimental Study on VAX 11/780", Proc. 16th Int. Symp. on Fault-Tolerant Computing.

[25] Choi, Y.-H., Malek, M., 1985: "A Fault-Tolerant FFT Processor", Proc. 15th Int. Symp. on Fault-Tolerant Computing, pp. 266-271.

[26] Chou, T. C.-K., Abraham, J. A., 1980: "Performance/Availability Modeling of Shared Resource Multiprocessors", IEEE Trans. on Reliability R-29, pp.70-74

[27] Chou, T. C.-K., Abraham, J. A., 1983: "Load Redistribution under Failure in Distributed Systems", IEEE Trans. on Computers C-32, pp. 799-808

[28] Dahbura, A. T., Masson, G. M., 1984: "An Order $O(n^{2.5})$ Fault Identification Algorithm for Diagnosable Systems", IEEE Trans. on Computers C-33, pp. 486-492

[29] Davis, T. A., Kunda, R. P., Fuchs, W. K., 1985: "Testing of Bit-Serial Multipliers", Proc. Int. Conf. on Computer Design, pp. 430-434.

[30] Dussault, J., 1977: "On the Design of Self-Checking Systems under Various Fault Models", Coordinated Science Laboratory Technical Report R-781, University of Illinois, Urbana, Illinois.

[31] Friedman, A. D., Simoncini, L., 1980: "System-Level Fault Diagnosis", Computer (Special Issue on Fault-Tolerant Computing) 13, No. 3, pp. 47-53

[32] Fuchs, W. K., Abraham, J. A., Huang, K.-H., 1983: "Concurrent Error Detection in VLSI Interconnection Networks", Proc. 10th Int. Symp. on Computer Architecture, pp. 309-315. Also reprinted in: Interconnection Networks for Parallel and Distributed Processing (Wu, C.-H., Fung, T.-Y., eds.), pp. 380-386. IEEE Press.

[33] Fuchs, W. K., Abraham, J. A., 1984: "A Unified Approach to Concurrent Error Detection in Highly Structured Logic Arrays", Proc. 14th Int. Symp. on Fault-Tolerant Computing, pp. 4-9

[34] Fujii, R., Abraham, J. A., 1985: "Self-Test for Microprocessors", Proc. Int. Test Conf., pp. 356-361.

[35] Fujiwara, H., Kinoshita, K., 1981: "A Design of Programmable Logic Arrays with Universal Tests", IEEE Trans. on Computers CD-30, No. 11, pp. 823-828

[36] Hayes, J. P., 1971: "A NAND Model for Fault Diagnosis in Combinational Logic Networks", IEEE Trans. on Computers C-20, pp. 1496-1506

[37] Hong, S. J., Ostapko, D. L., 1980: "FITPLA: A Programmable Logic Array for Function-Independent Testing", Proc. 10th Int. Conf. on Fault-Tolerant Computing, pp. 131-136.

[38] Hua, K. A., Jou, J.-Y., Abraham, J. A., 1984: "Built-In Tests for VLSI Finite-State Machines", Proc. 14th Int. Conf. on Fault-Tolerant Computing, pp. 292-297.

[39] Huang, K.-H., Abraham, J. A., 1982: "Low-Cost Schemes for Fault Tolerance in Matrix Operations with Array Processors", Proc. 12th Int. Symp. on Fault-Tolerant Computing, pp. 330-337.

[40] Huang, K.-H., Abraham, J. A., 1984a: "Algorithm-Based Fault Tolerance for Matrix Operations", IEEE Trans. on Computers (Special Issue on Reliable and Fault-Tolerant Computing) C-33, pp. 518-528

[41] Huang, K.-H., Abraham, J. A., 1984b: "Fault-Tolerant Algorithms and their Applications to Solving Laplace Equations", Proc. Int. Conf. on Parallel Processing, pp. 117-122.

[42] Iyer, R. K., Rossetti, D. J., 1985: "Effect of System Workload on Operating System Reliability: A Study on the IBM 3081", IEEE Trans. on Software Engineering (Special Issue on Software Reliability, Part 1) SE-11, No. : 2, pp. 1438-1448.

[43] Iyer, R. K., Rossetti, D. J., 1986: "A Measurement-Based Model for Workload Dependency of CPU Errors", IEEE Trans. on Computers C-35, No. 6 (to appear).

[44] Jansch, I., Courtois, B., 1985: "Strongly Language Disjoint Checkers", Proc. 15th Int. Symp. on Fault-Tolerant Computing, pp. 390-395.

[45] Jha, N. K., Abraham, J. A., 1984: "The Design of Totally Self-Checking Embedded Checkers", Proc. 14th Int. Symp. on Fault-Tolerant Computing, pp. 265-270.

[46] Jha, N. K., Abraham, J. A. 1985a: "Techniques for Efficient MOS Implementation of Totally Self-Checking Checkers", Proc. 15th Int. Symp. on Fault-Tolerant Computing, pp. 430-435.

[47] Jha, N. K., Abraham, J. A., 1985b: "Design of Testable CMOS Logic Circuits under Arbitrary Delays", IEEE Trans. on Computer-Aided Design, CAD-4, No. 3, pp. 312-321

[48] Jou, J.-Y., Abraham, J. A., 1984: "Fault-Tolerant Matrix Operations on Multiple Processor Systems using Weighted Checksums", Proc. SPIE Conf., pp. 94-101.

[49] Jou, J.-Y., Abraham, J. A., 1985: "Fault-Tolerant FFT Networks", Proc. Int. Symp. on Fault-Tolerant Computing, pp. 338-343.

[50] Laha, S., Patel, J. H., 1983: "Error Correction in Arithmetic Operations using Time Redundancy", Proc. 13th Int. Symp. on Fault-Tolerant Computing, pp. 298-305.

[51] Luk, F. T., 1985: "Algorithm-Based Fault Tolerance for Parallel Matrix Equation Solvers", Proc. SPIE Conf. (Real-Time Signal Processing VIII) 564.

[52] Mak, G.-P., Davidson, E. S., Abraham, J. A., 1982: "The Design of PLAs with Concurrent Error Detection", Proc. 12th Int. Symp. on Fault-Tolerant Computing, pp. 303-310.

[53] Manning, E., 1966: "On Computer Self-Diagnosis: Part I and II", IEEE Trans. Electronic Computers EC-15, pp. 873-890

[54] Marlett, R. A., 1966: "On the Design and Testing of Self-Diagnosable Computers", Coordinated Science Laboratory Technical Report R-293, University of Illinois, Urbana, Illinois.

[55] McCluskey, E. J., Clegg, F. W., 1971: "Fault Equivalence in Combinational Logic Networks", IEEE Trans. on Computers C-20, pp. 1286-1293.

[56] Meagher, R. E., Nash, J. P., 1952: "The ORDVAC", Review of Electronic Digital Computers, pp. 37-43.

[57] Muller, D. E., Bartky, J. S., 1959: "A Theory of Asynchronous Circuits", Proc. Int. Symp. on Theory of Switching, pp. 204-243.

[58] Nair, R., Thatte, S. M., Abraham, J. A., 1978: "Efficient Algorithms for Testing Semiconductor Random-Access Memories", IEEE Trans. on Computers C-27, No. 6, pp. 572-576

[59] Patel, J. H., Fung, L. Y., 1982: "Concurrent Error Detection in ALUs by Recomputing with Shifted Operands", IEEE Trans. on Computers, vol. C-31, pp. 589-595.

[60] Patel, J. H., Fung, L. Y., 1983: "Concurrent Error Detection in Multiply and Divide Arrays", IEEE Trans. on Computers, vol. C-32, pp. 417-422.

[61] Pollard, L. H., Patel, J. H., 1983: "Correction of Errors in Data Transmission using Time Redundancy", Proc. 13th Int. Symp. on Fault-Tolerant Computing, pp. 314-317.

[62] Preparata, F. P., Metze, G., Chien, R. T., 1967: "On the Connection Assignment Problem of Diagnosable Systems", IEEE Trans. on Electronic Computers EC-16, No. 6, pp. 848-854

[63] Reynolds, D. A., Metze, G., 1978: "Fault Detection Capabilities of Alternating Logic", IEEE Trans. on Computers, vol. C-27, pp. 1093-1098.

[64] Rogers, W. A., Abraham, J. A., 1985a: "High-Level Hierarchical Fault Simulation Techniques", Proc. ACM Computer Science Conference, pp. 89-97.

[65] Rogers, W. A., Abraham, J. A., 1985b: "CHIEFS: A Concurrent, Hierarchical, and Extensible Fault Simulator", Proc. Int. Test Conf., pp. 710-716.

[66] Schertz, D. R., Metze, G., 1968: "On the Indistinguishability of Faults in Digital Systems", Proc. 6th Ann. Allerton Conf. on Circuit and System Theory, pp. 752-760.

[67] Schertz, D. R., 1969: "On the Representation of Digital Faults", Coordinated Science Laboratory Technical Report R-418, University of Illinois, Urbana, Illinois.

[68] Schertz, D. R. and Metze, G., 1972: "A New Representation for Faults in Combinational Digital Circuits", IEEE Trans. on Computers, C-21, No. 8, pp. 858-866

[69] Seshu, S., Freeman, D. N., 1962: "The Diagnosis of Asynchronous Sequential Switching Systems", IRE Trans. on Electronic Computers EC-11, No. 4, pp. 459-465

[70] Seshu, S., 1964: "The Logic Organizer and Diagnosis Programs", Coordinated Science Laboratory Technical Report R-226, University of Illinois, Urbana, Illinois.

[71] Seshu, S., 1965: "On an Improved Diagnosis Program", IEEE Trans. on Electronic Computers EC-14, No. 1, pp. 76-79

[72] Shih, H.-C., Rahmeh, J. T., Abraham, J. A., 1985: "An MOS Fault Simulator with Timing Information", Proc. Int. Conf. on Computer-Aided Design, pp. 45-47.

[73] Smith, J. E., Metze, G., 1975: "On the Existence of Combinational Networks with Arbitrary Multiple Redundancies", Coordinated Science Laboratory Technical Report R-692, University of Illinois, Urbana, Illinois.

[74] Smith, J. E., 1976: "The Design of Totally Self-Checking Combinational Circuits", Coordinated Science Laboratory Technical Report R-737, University of Illinois, Urbana, Illinois.

[75] Smith, J. E., Metze, G., 1978: "Strongly Fault-Secure Logic Networks", IEEE Trans. on Computers C-27, No. 6, pp. 491-499.

[76] Smith, J. E., 1979: "On Necessary and Sufficient Conditions for Multiple Fault Undetectability", IEEE Trans. on Computers C-28, pp. 801-802

[77] Suk, D. S., Reddy, S. M., 1981: "A March Test for Functional Faults in Semiconductor Random Access Memories", IEEE Trans. on Computers C-30, pp. 982-984

[78] Thatte, S. M., Abraham, J. A., 1977: "Testing of Semiconductor Random Access Memories", Proc. 7th Int. Symp. on Fault-Tolerant Computing, pp. 81-87.

[79] Thatte, S. M., Abraham, J. A., 1980: "Test Generation for Microprocessors", IEEE Trans. on Computers C-29, No. 6, pp. 429-441.

[80] To, K., 1973: "Fault Folding for Irredundant and Redundant Combinational Circuits", IEEE Trans. on Computers C-22, No. 11, pp. 1008-1015.

[81] Treuer, R., Fujiwara, H., Agarwal, V. K., 1985: "A Low-Overhead, High Coverage, Built-In Self-Test PLA Design", Proc. 15th Int. Symp. on Fault-Tolerant Computing, pp. 112-117.

[82] Wheeler, D. J., Robertson, J. E., 1953: "Diagnostic Programs for the ILLIAC", Proc. IRE 41, pp. 1320-1325.

[83] Wong, C.-Y., Fuchs, W. K., Abraham, J. A., Davidson, E. S., 1983: " The Design of a Microprogram Control Unit with Concurrent Error Detection", Proc. 13th Int. Symp. on Fault-Tolerant Computing, pp. 476-483.

[84] Yen, M. M., 1984: "Design of a Microprogram Control Unit with Concurrent Error Detection", Computer Systems Group Technical Report CSG-30, Coordinated Science Laboratory, University of Illinois, Urbana, Illinois.

The Evolution of Fault Tolerant Computing at the University of Michigan

John F. Meyer
Department of Electrical Engineering and Computer Science
The University of Michigan
Ann Arbor, MI,USA

ABSTRACT

This paper reviews the history of research in fault-tolerant computing, as it has evolved at The University of Michigan over the past 20 years.

1. Introduction

The words that follow describe a succession of research activities at The University of Michigan which have shared a common goal: reliable computing. Although the evolution we discuss has been "housed" at the University throughout a 20 year period, little of this history would have happened without substantial extramural interactions. These interactions have involved both persons and organizations and, without restricting their nature, they are too numerous to list. To simplify matters, let me mention just one person, Bill Carter, who, by means of this symposium, is being recognized by all of us for his contributions to our field. For now and for me, he is also representative of all the people on that "too numerous to mention" list who are friends as well as professional colleagues.

2. Early Years

Generally, interest in computing at The University of Michigan has a long, rich history which dates back to the early 1950s. The beginning of this period included the development of MIDAC (Project Michigan), and the introduction of computer courses in both the Department of Electrical Engineering and the Department of Mathematics. In 1957, a graduate degree program in computer science was formally established by the university's Rackham School of Graduate Studies. This program, referred to then as *Communication Sciences*, involved faculty from several departments and colleges, and viewed this emerging science as a broad intersection of disciplines deriving from mathematics, electrical engineering, linguistics, philosophy (logic foundations), and psychology. One of the founders of the program was Arthur Burks who, before joining the Michigan faculty in 1946, worked with John von Neumann on the development of ENIAC at Princeton's Institute for Advanced Studies.

The seeds of Michigan work on fault-tolerant computing date back to the author's prior affiliation with Caltech's Jet Propulsion Laboratory (JPL). This association, which began in 1958 and continued on a part-time basis from 1962 to 1967, had considerable influence on the nature and direction of subsequent research at the University. It was at the beginning of this period that the National Aeronautics and Space Administration (NASA) was established by the US Space Act. When this act was signed in December 1958, the government contract with Caltech for JPL's operation was transferred from the US Army to NASA. Although concern for reliability was already an integral part of JPL's R&D culture (the laboratory was previously engaged in surface-to-surface missile development for the Army), specific problems associated with long-duration space missions posed a new set of challenges.

One particularly influential aspect of the JPL experience was an intensive exposure to "real-time" computing systems. As a consequence, much of the research on fault-tolerant computing at Michigan has been motivated by real-time considerations. In many cases, the results of such work have been meaningful in a more general context; in other cases, the results have been truly specific to real-time applications.

Another legacy of this early JPL association was an interest in "autonomous" systems, autonomous in the sense that there is little opportunity for direct human intervention in processes of error detection, fault location, system reconfiguration and, particularly, system maintenance. In certain instances, such intervention is precluded throughout the mission of the system (e.g., a computer aboard an unmanned spacecraft); in other situations, it is precluded periodically for shorter periods of time (e.g., an aircraft computer during flights of the aircraft, a factory cell controller during periods of fully automated operation). In either case, an important issue is the system's ability to perform (without human assisted repair or replacement) over a bounded period of use. This is in contrast with more conventional applications where, in the absence of such constraints, the basic reliability concerns are time-to-failure and availability.

As it influenced later work, one of the most important benefits of the JPL experience was an initial perspective of fault-tolerant computing that encompassed problems of specification, design, validation (particularly testing), and evaluation. This was due, in part, to a lack of specialists and specialization in the early days of the US space program. Consequently, a single group of individuals was often charged with carrying a system through several stages of its development, sometimes spanning the gamut from initial conception through pre-launch testing.

A particular example of this was the development of a time-multiplexing system for use in the telemetry and control systems of solar-powered, unmanned spacecraft (initially used on Ranger spacecraft which explored the moon in the early 1960s). An important reliability concern, in this instance, was failures caused by temporary losses of electrical power. The latter were possible because the power source depended on proper orientation of the solar panels with respect to the sun; on loss of correct orientation, stored energy could be consumed prior to restabilization of the spacecraft. Hence, one requirement was a non-volatile memory that could maintain knowledge of the multiplexer's state after loss of power. A second concern was recovery from transient faults, with the requirement that, after any perturbation of system state, the system would automatically recover to a normal (error-free) operating state within a short period of time. Moreover, all states encountered during recovery had to be "safe" in the sense that no two inputs could be switched simultaneously (causing an input to input short circuit). An implementation satisfying these requirements was eventually obtained [1] and subsequently incorporated in the hardware of both Ranger and Mariner spacecraft. The design itself became the subject of the first patent issued to NASA (US Patent No. 3,100,294).

Collectively, these aspects of the JPL/NASA indoctrination had an immediate impact on early research in fault-tolerant computing at The University of Michigan. Moreover, they have continued to exert their influence, at least indirectly, throughout the 20 year evolution of such work at the University. It began in 1966 when, under JPL sponsorship (until accepting a full-time position at Michigan the following year, the author was officially on a leave of absence from JPL), an effort was made to formulate a general, mathematical definition of system reliability that could account for varying degrees of "partial success"[2]. The definition was component-based and, in keeping with usual assumptions, took a binary view of a component's operational status at a given instant of time (either "operational" or "not operational"). On the other hand, the overall operation of a system was defined in terms of a finite set of "system functions," each function being characterized by a state set and a time interval associated with its realization. Accordingly, system "performance" was taken to be a vector-valued random variable that described, for each system function, whether or not it was successfully realized. Via a utility function defined on performance outcomes, a system's reliability was then identified with its "expected utility." In retrospect, use of the term "reliability" for this measure belied its general meaning and, for other reasons, this view was destined to lie dormant until the middle 1970s (see Section 3).

Further JPL sponsored work was initiated in 1969 under a project (JPL Contract No. 952492) concerned with theory and techniques for the design, analysis, and fault diagnosis of reliable spacecraft data systems. This research focused on foundations of hardware implementations at the logic level and, more specifically, concerned 1) the design and analysis of fault-tolerant combinational and sequential switching networks, and 2) fault detection and diagnosis at both logic and machine levels of abstraction. In 1971, continued work in these directions was supported directly by NASA Headquarters (NASA Grant NGR 23-005-463). During the four-year period from 1969 to 1973, this effort produced a number of contributions, particularly with respect to fundamental aspects of fault tolerance and fault diagnosis.

Regarding 1), emphasis was placed on sequential networks since much of the previous work in this area had dealt with the combinational case. Moreover, we found that many questions concerning fault tolerance in sequential networks could be answered at the (sequential) machine level and then translated back down to the network level. Use of this approach in dealing with permanent memory faults was first reported in 1970 [3] and further details were published the following year [4]. Among these results was an algorithm for fault-tolerant machine design (including assignment of states) that generalized a logic level technique used by Russo [5] in the design of "error-tolerant" counters. Another more fundamental outcome of this work was formal recognition of the role played by synchronization in modularly redundant systems, obtained by proving the impossibility of realizing a certain strong form of fault tolerance.

In area 2), detection and diagnosis were studied for both combinational and sequential networks. In the combinational case, a graphical/algebraic model was developed and used to determine network properties conducive to fault location. The type of fault location considered was quite general (relative to previous studies) and permitted nodes of a network to be classified as fault-free, faulty, or indeterminate. Likewise, the types of faults permitted were essentially unrestricted. Results of this work were initially presented at the first (1971) International Symposium on Fault-Tolerant Computing [6] and, later that year, appeared in a corresponding special issue of the *IEEE Transactions on Computers*[7]. Further research within this framework involved questions of fault tolerance as well as fault diagnosis, culminating in Gail Gray's doctoral thesis [8] and the subsequent publication of work concerning optimum fault-tolerant realizations [9].

In the case of sequential networks, detection and diagnosis problems were investigated at both logic and machine levels, with initial emphasis on what could be done at the machine level of abstraction. Based on an early paper by Moore [10], a number of people had investigated fault detection/diagnosis in a machine-theoretic framework, with one of the more interesting problems (from a practical point of view) being the design of machines with good diagnostic properties. One such property, considered earlier in this context by Kohavi and Lavalle [11], was the possession of a "distinguishing sequence," where machines with this property were referred to as *diagnosable*. Generalizing the approach taken in [11], machine behaviors were compared via the concept of one machine "realizing" another, using a formal definition of *realizes* that precluded slowdown (i.e., the realization was faithful in real-time). In terms of these concepts, the associated (machine level) design problem was stated as follows:

Given some machine M' (or, equivalently, a set of functions that constitute the behavior of some machine M'), design a diagnosable machine M that realizes M'. (With no loss of generality, M' can be taken to be a reduced machine.)

Various types of realizations were considered in this context, and initial results of this work were likewise presented at the 1971 International Symposium on Fault-Tolerant Computing [12]. Extensions of this research, including problems of analysis as well as design, were the subject of Ken Yeh's doctoral thesis [13], completed in 1972. These results established a solid foundation for subsequent work in this area during the next two years.

One aspect of this follow-on work was a more detailed investigation of off-line fault detection in sequential machines. Research here was based the definitions of a "checking sequence" and a "detecting sequence" that captured, at the machine level, the notions of logic level "test sequences" that could detect any (detectable) fault. Contributions of this work included conditions for the existence of such sequences in a given machine, the design of "checkable" machine realizations, and the formulation/study of a generalized class of distinguishing sequences. An abstract of some of these results was presented at FTCS-3 [14] and a detailed description of this effort appeared in Lo Hsieh's doctoral thesis [15].

A second important derivative of earlier work was a an examination of on-line fault detection, again at the machine level of abstraction. Faults, as interpreted at the logic level of some network that realizes the machine, were unrestricted, i.e., they could represent multiple faults that occur at the same time or multiple occurrences of such multiple faults. It was also possible for a second logic level fault to occur while the system was still trying to detect an earlier fault. The machine models employed in this study permitted a time-varying structure (needed because of on-line assumptions) and the definition used for on-line detection (referred to generically as "on-line diagnosis") precluded "false alarms" and allowed a bound on latency to be specified as part of the detection criterion.

Within this framework, a number of basic questions were addressed and answered. Among these, perhaps the most fundamental was the following. Let S be some specified sequential system and let D be a detector for S, where there are no restrictions on the type of on-line detection technique employed by D. Then how complex must D be, as compared to S, if D is to successfully detect any (detectable) fault of S? Using the size of the state set as the measure of complexity (in the case of S, its complexity was taken to be that of any minimum-state system equivalent to S), it was shown that D must always be at least as complex as S. In other words, when faults are unrestricted, the detection scheme can never be simpler than one involving duplication (i.e., let D be a copy of S) and comparison. Moreover, this remains the case for a detection criterion that permits errors to be latent (go undetected) for a bounded period of time, no matter how large the bound. These results, and others of a similar nature, were products of a doctoral thesis completed by Bob Sundstrom in 1974 [16]. Part of this work, including the results cited above, was subsequently published in [17].

A third effort that emerged from previous work was due to the fact that we had employed several different models to study a number of different questions. By examining this collection of models and looking for things they might have in common, we indeed found some striking similarities, e.g., the way faults were being represented in terms their resulting faulty systems (more precisely, the model representations thereof). This suggested the possibility of a general, formal model that could provide a uniform way of viewing faults, whether they occur before the system is put into operation (design faults) or after (operational faults). This, in turn, would permit us to formalize basic notions that are common to both (e.g. fault tolerance) and examine distinctions in fault-related procedures (e.g., testing) when systems are restricted to having one fault type vs. the other. A formalism with these features was subsequently developed, the central concept being a relatively general, notion of a "system with faults." These ideas were first presented in 1973[18] and subsequently published in a paper [19,20] which used this formalism to identify problem areas associated with the reliable design of software. (It has also served quite nicely in the classroom as a means for presenting fundamental concepts of reliable computing.)

During 1974, this move in the direction of more system-oriented questions continued. It was motivated, in part, by advances in technology which permitted relatively complex systems to appear (physically) as components previously appeared. Of greater influence, however, was a growing recognition of the following fact: computing systems were being used more and more frequently in application environments where the nature of the application had a lot to say about a system's ability to perform. On the other hand, most reliability models that existed at that time represented only the resources (structural components) of a system and ignored such things as workload and the internal states of the resources. A third factor, with an obvious connection to the second, was the emergence of NASA's Langley Research Center as a sponsor (NASA Grant NGR 23-005-622) of our work.

Our initial attempt to develop a more performance-oriented view of reliability took the position that success vs. failure was still the issue. However, to account for workload and internal state, success was defined in terms of computations that the system actually performs in response to workload demands, not simply the integrity of resources that support the computations. Accordingly, we referred to this view of reliability as being "computation-based". The results of this effort were first presented at FTCS-5 [21], where it was shown, via a small example, that a failure probability predicted via a computation-based analysis was less pessimistic (by two orders of magnitude) than that determined by a traditional structure-based analysis. This work was subsequently expanded on the following year [22].

3. Middle Years

In 1976, research in fault-tolerant computing at Michigan began to focus more sharply on problems of system evaluation and, particularly, the possibility of developing a more unified view of performance and reliability evaluation. The desire to do this grew from thoughts on the subject 10 years earlier [2], together with the recent look at computation-based reliability analysis [22] which, as discussed at the end of the previous section, accounted for performance (computations) in the evaluation process. This focus was further motivated by NASA-Langley's interest in evaluating the type of ultrareliable aircraft control computers being developed for them by both Stanford Research Institute Int'l (SIFT; [23]) and the C.S. Draper Laboratory (FTMP; [24]). One intended feature of these systems was an ability to shed workload (beginning with the least critical tasks) if a loss of computing resources, due to faults, demanded it. Accordingly, these systems could exhibit "degradable" performance and, hence, provide varying degrees of benefit over a specified period of use (e.g., the duration of a flight of the aircraft). It was this property of *degradable performance* that called for performance-reliability unification (we'll briefly review the reasons in a moment), thereby providing a principal incentive for further pursuit of this work. Indeed, this effort benefited from NASA-Langley's interest and support (NASA Grant NSG 1306) for a period of six years (1976-1982), permitting the continuity needed to develop and test a number of new ideas.

In usual interpretations of performance and reliability (particularly in the context of computing systems), the two have been distinguished by regarding "performance" as "how well the system performs, provided it is correct" and regarding "reliability" as "the probability of performing successfully." However, if system performance is degradable (in which case the system itself is said to be degradable) then a performance evaluation (of the correct or fault-free system) will generally not suffice since structural changes, due to faults, may be the cause of degraded performance. By the same token, an evaluation of reliability (or other dependability [25,26] measures such as availability and maintainability) will generally not suffice since "success" can take on various meanings and, in particular, it need not be identified with "absence of system failure."

What is called for instead are evaluations with respect to unified performance-reliability measures which, at the outset of this project, were identified with measures of system "effectiveness "[27,28]. (Note that the definition formulated in the 1966 JPL Report [2] is consistent with this point of view.) However, as work progressed during the first year of this investigation, we decided that performance-reliability aspects of effectiveness should be decoupled from the assignment of "worth" (utility, benefit) to performance outcomes. This permitted a more refined concept of combined performance-reliability which, if desired, could be used in higher level evaluations of system effectiveness. This concept was given the name "performability" (late 1976) and became the object of our subsequent work on model-based evaluation methods.

During the following year, the framework introduced in [27,28] was given a more precise formulation, where the basic ingredients can be summarized as follows (these were first described in [29] and subsequently published in [30]). Let S denote the system in question where, generally, S is interpreted as including not only a system, per se, but also relevant aspects of its environment (e.g., workload, sources of faults). Then the *performance* of S over a specified *utilization period* T is a random variable Y taking values in a set A. Elements of A are the *accomplishment levels* (performance outcomes) to be distinguished in the evaluation process. The *performability* of S is the probability measure *Perf* (denoted p_S in [29,30]) induced by Y where, for any measurable set B of accomplishment levels ($B \subseteq A$), *Perf* (B) is the probability that S performs at a level in B. Solution of performability is based on an underlying stochastic process X, called a *base model* of S, which represents the dynamics of the system's structure, internal state, and environment during utilization. A base model X together with a performance variable Y is a *performability model* of S. Performability model *construction* is the process of identifying a performance variable Y and determining a base model stochastic process X that permits a solution of performability. (If solutions are obtained via simulation, X is a conceptual reference to model behavior and need not be characterized analytically.) Performability model *solution* is the process of obtaining performability values *Perf* (B) for accomplishment sets B that are of interest to the user. Generally, knowledge of the probability distribution function (PDF) of Y suffices to determine such values. Accordingly, we regard an performability model as (fully) "solved" once the PDF of Y is obtained. Solution of a PDF can be either a closed-form solution (expressed as a function of base model and performance variable parameters) or a numerical solution (approximated for a finite number of values via analysis or simulation).

The concept of performability is thus quite general and, depending on the choice of base model X and performance variable Y, can be specialized to usual notions of (strict) performance, reliability, and other dependability concepts such as availability and maintainability. In the development of methods and tools for performability evaluation, we recognized the importance of these various special cases but, at the same time, sought techniques which would apply as well to the type of truly unified measures that are captured by this concept. As such techniques evolved, they were basically distinguished by the nature of the performance variable and, more specifically, according to whether Y was discrete (its range was finite or denumerable) or continuous. In the case of a *discrete performance variable* (DPV) and, particularly, when Y is finite-valued, the model construction and solution methods that evolved can be viewed, for the most part, as generalizations of reliability modeling techniques. In the case of a *continuous performance variable* (CPV), on the other hand, most of the methods that were developed derive from an appropriate blend of both reliability modeling and (strict) performance modeling techniques. In reviewing this evolution, we'll use a simple "discrete" vs. "continuous" distinction in referring to these two methodologies.

3.1. Discrete Methods

During the period of NASA-Langley sponsorship, most of our effort concerned evaluation methods and tools suited to discrete performance variables. As mentioned at the outset of this section, Langley was interested in user-oriented evaluations of fault-tolerant digital control computers for (next generation) commercial aircraft. The user in this case was assumed to be an airline that owns the aircraft and performance (as modeled by Y) was taken to be the quality of an aircraft flight controlled by the computer. With this view of performance, a relatively small number of accomplishment levels (possible values of Y) suffice, resulting in a DPV model of the system. More generally, user-oriented (sometimes referred to as "mission-oriented") evaluation problems of this type are naturally suited to DPVs and, indeed, to finite-valued performance variables where the number of accomplishment levels is at least 3 but typically no more than 10. (In the case of only 2 accomplishment levels, interpreted as "success" and "failure", performance is no longer degradable and performability reduces to reliability.) Our observations and results concerning DPV models, methods, and tools can be summarized as follows.

Generally, the base model part (the stochastic process X) of a DPV model should represent a sufficiently detailed probabilistic description of changes in a system's structure (due to faults and fault recovery), internal state, and environment to permit solution of performability for single levels of accomplishment (these are measurable since the performance variable is discrete). At the outset, such a model is usually a continuous-time, finite-state stochastic process which is constructed by first decomposing the utilization period $[0,t]$ into a finite number of consecutive time periods called *phases*. For each phase, a system's intraphase behavior is represented by a (continuous-time, finite-state) stochastic process which is typically a time-homogeneous Markov process. Different phases, however, may be modeled by different processes, subject to constraints which permit the determination of (conditional) interphase transition probabilities. Combination of these processes results in a *phased model* [31] which serves as the base model X. Relative to a specified performance variable Y, X is required to "support" Y in the sense that the end-of-phase samples of X uniquely determine the value of Y.

DPV performability evaluation can thus be viewed as a generalization of "phased mission" reliability evaluation (see [32,33,34], for example). Techniques used to construct and solve DPV models are likewise more general and complex, due in part to the less restricted nature of phased base models. A more challenging property of DPV models, however, is due to the general manner in which the base model X relates to the performance variable Y, via a function referred to as the *capability function* [29,30]. Relative to a given level of accomplishment, the end-of-phase samples of X can be *functionally dependent* [35], e.g., knowing that $Y = a$, knowledge of the state of X at the end of phase i can contribute to knowledge of the state of X at the end of some other phase j. In contrast, assumptions made in the construction of phased mission reliability models (see [34], for example) are such that, with respect to the accomplishment level "success," the phases must be functionally independent, as first established in [35].

Given a DPV model (X,Y) and an accomplishment level a, solution of the performability value $Perf(a)$ (the probability that $Y = a$), is, conceptually, a two-step procedure:

1) Determine the set of all base model state trajectories (as characterized by their end-of-phase samples) that correspond, via the capability function, to $Y = a$.

2) Using knowledge of X, determine the probability of the trajec-
tory set determined in 1); this is the value of $Perf(a)$.

Although easily stated, this procedure required considerable
additional research in order to achieve an effective implementation. This was accomplished over a period of several years, culminating in doctoral theses by Liang Wu in 1982 [36] and David
Furchtgott in 1984 [37]. Furchtgott's work also included an investigation of CPV techniques (see the following subsection) and the
development of software tools to aid the construction and solution
phases of the evaluation process. These tools (along with others
developed later) reside in a software package called **METAPHOR**
(**M**ichigan **E**valua**T**ion **A**id for Perp**HOR**mability) which is written in
C and runs under UNIX. The portion devoted to DPV methods,
called "meta_discrete", contains approximately 8,000 lines of
source code and has approximately 256 Kbytes of executable
code.

During the course of this research, there were also a number
of specific evaluation studies [36,37,38,39,40,41] which, aside from
their intrinsic usefulness, served to test the capabilities of the
discrete methodology and, specifically, the "meta_discrete" portion of METAPHOR. These included a relatively comprehensive performability evaluation of the SIFT computer [39,40] where SIFT's
computational environment was taken to be a transoceanic flight
of an advanced commercial aircraft. Performability, in this case,
was quantified in terms of 5 accomplishment levels, ranging from a
"perfect" flight to loss of the aircraft. Details concerning the use
of METAPHOR in this and other applications appear in [37].

Generally, DPV models are best suited to performability
evaluations where the user (of the evaluation results) is interested
in whether a system satisfies certain "bottom line" performability
requirements. In many cases, however, DPVs are not refined
enough to measure more detailed aspects of a system's ability to
perform, e.g., its productivity, responsiveness, etc. Typically, the
latter are more naturally represented by continuous performance
variables (CPVs), motivating the work reviewed in the subsection
that follows.

3.2. Continuous Methods

When system performance ranges over a continuum of accomplishment levels, the construction and solution of performability
models is complicated by the need to deal with a much greater
amount of information. In constructing the base model, a more
detailed representation of the system's internal state and environment is typically required so that the base model can support the

performance variable. On the solution side, performability is determined by the probability distribution function (PDF) of the performance variable (conceptually an uncountable set) as opposed to the kind of discrete distributions associated with DPVs.

Work on CPV models began in 1979 and, as indicated earlier, our subsequent effort involved an integration of concepts and constructs used in both performance modeling and reliability modeling. Accordingly, a typical base model can represent activities relating to performance (e.g., job arrivals, job processing) as well as activities relating to reliability (e.g., fault arrivals). However, a fundamental difficulty encountered in solving CPV performability models is due to the fact that some activities are repeated much more frequently than others (e.g., arrivals of jobs as compared with arrivals of permanent faults). Hence, in the case of a Markovian base model, the ratio between the highest and lowest state transition-rate can be many orders of magnitude. In other words, the differential equations describing the model's state behavior (i.e., those determined by the generator matrix of the Markov model) are "stiff" (see [42], for example) and, when solved numerically, require special treatment to avoid excessive errors.

Various approaches can be used to deal with this stiffness property and, as we noted later in a 1984 survey paper [43], all of them deserve more extensive investigation. The option we followed [44,45], was to lump states with high transition rates such that the lumped model is no longer stiff. Performance rates in the lumped states can then be determined via steady-state solution techniques, under the assumption that the consequences of high rate activities approach equilibrium conditions between the completions of low rate activities. (As a result of this assumption, the solution obtained is approximate; our experience, however, has shown it to be a good approximation, particularly in the case of very stiff base models). Once these performance rates are determined, performability is solved in terms of the lumped model. The latter step is far from trivial but is capable of producing closed-form solutions as well as numerical solutions.

Since the lumped model referred to above represents changes in the system's structure (due to faults), an equivalent approach is to regard the lumped model as the base model X. States of X are interpreted as "structure states" of S and hence X is a finite-state stochastic process. With this approach, however, we do not require that X be Markovian or even semi-Markovian. Performance aspects are then accounted for by associating a performance rate with each structure state. The stochastic process X together with the performance rates can thus be viewed as a *reward model* (see [46], for example) where the performance rates become reward rates. Accordingly, the performance variable Y is taken to be the total reward accrued during a specified utilization period $[0,t]$.

CPV models of this type constitute a broad class of performability models with widespread applicability. Of particular interest to us was their use in modeling systems which, during $[0,t]$, are "nonrepairable" (e.g., there is no human intervention during $[0,t]$ for the purpose of maintenance; cf. our remarks in the previous section regarding autonomous systems). In this case the base model process X is *acyclic*, i.e., the probability of entering the same (structure) state more than once is 0. If, further, one assumes that the reward rates are such that the reward model is *nonrecoverable* [36], i.e., reward rates experienced cannot increase with time, such models admit to a general method of solution that was first described in Furchtgott's thesis [37] and subsequently published in [47]. Specifically, if (X,Y) is a performability model satisfying the above conditions, this method determines the PDF $F_Y(y)$ of Y and, hence, the performability of the modeled system. The method involves expression of $F_Y(y)$ as a sum of definite integrals which, if solved symbolically, yields a closed-form solution. Alternatively, for a given assignment of model parameter values, this integral expression can be solved numerically for various values of y, resulting in a numerical solution of $F_Y(y)$. Since then, others (e.g. [48,49,50]) have developed solution methods that apply in Markovian cases.

Due to the inherent complexity of most CPV models, implementation of solution techniques for either closed-form or numerical solutions requires the support of programmed evaluation tools. This is particularly so in the case of numerical solutions, since these are sought when the model is too complex to admit a meaningful closed-form solution. Development of a computer program for this purpose, referred to as "meta_continuous", was completed in 1983 and incorporated in the CPV portion of META-PHOR [37]. Meta_continuous contains approximately 4,000 lines of C code, including menu and project management functions.

Applications of CPV methods and tools have been demonstrated for various types of degradable, nonrepairable systems, beginning with the dual-processor example considered in [44,45]. In this example, performance was taken to be the system's (normalized) average throughput rate; degradable performance resulted from the system's ability to recover (with a specified "coverage") from a processor fault. Using the lumping technique outlined above, the base model was simple enough to permit manual derivation of a closed-form solution of performability.

More complex systems involving multiple (more than 2) processors were evaluated [37,51] using the methods and tools described above.

4. Recent Years

On completion of the Langley-sponsored research in 1982, it became clear that model construction, as well as model solution, was an important issue in the context of both CPV and DPV evaluations. Indeed, what was needed was a systematic means of model construction that could support both types of variables. In addition, because of the emerging importance of distributed real-time systems, there was need to insure that, whatever the means of construction, it would be capable of accounting for properties of such systems. In particular, as noted in[43], distributed real-time systems have typical properties which impose special conditions on system structure and behavior. Such requirements typically call for high performance when the system is fault-free. This, coupled with the fact that resources are distributed, results in systems which exploit concurrent (parallel) processing. Secondly, real-time aspects of such requirements often impose conditions on the "timeliness" of the processing of activities, e.g., requirements for maximum allowable (input-output) response times which impose deadlines on the times that certain processes can be initiated or completed. Thirdly, real-time applications are typified by requirements for high reliability as well as high performance, resulting in fault-tolerant systems which employ added resources and processes for the purpose of tolerating specified types of faults. Finally, due to a balance of demands for both performance and reliability, such requirements typically call for systems which exhibit degradable performance in the presence of faults. These properties, namely 1) concurrency, 2) timeliness, 3) fault tolerance, and 4) degradable performance distinguish a class of systems which deserves increased attention with respect to the development of effective modeling methods. By their definitions, each affects a systems ability to perform and, hence, each property needs to be appropriately represented in models for performability evaluation.

These needs motivated the definition of a general class of probabilistic network models [52] which are well suited to the representation of concurrency and timeliness as well as fault tolerance and degradable performance. The models are referred to as and, informally, they can be viewed as models which generalize stochastic Petri nets [54,55] and incorporate certain features of queueing models. Moreover, our experience to date indicates that they are well-suited to the modeling of systems having the properties cited above.

Structurally, SANs have primitives consisting of *activities*, *places*, *input gates and output gates*. Activities ("transitions" in Petri net terminology) are of two types, *timed* and *instantaneous*. Timed activities represent activities of the modeled system whose durations impact the system's ability to perform. Instantaneous activities, on the other hand, represent system activities which, relative to the performance variable in question, are completed in a negligible amount of time. Cases associated with activities permit the realization of two types of spatial uncertainty. Uncertainty about which activities are enabled in a certain state is realized by cases associated with intervening instantaneous activities. Uncertainty about the next state assumed upon completion of a timed activity is realized by cases associated with that activity. Places are as in Petri nets. Gates were introduced to permit greater flexibility in defining enabling and completion rules.

The stochastic nature of the nets is realized by associating an activity time distribution function with each timed activity and a probability distribution with each set of cases. A *reactivation function* [53] is also associated with each timed activity. This function specifies, for each marking, a set of *reactivation markings*. Informally, given that an activity is activated in a specific marking, the activity is *reactivated* whenever any marking in the set of reactivation markings is reached. This provides a mechanism for restarting activities that have been activated, either with the same or different distribution. This decision is made on a per activity basis (based on the reactivation function), and is not a net-wide execution policy.

To assist the process of describing SAN behavior, a second class of models was defined. These models, referred to as *stochastic activity systems (SASs)* [53], provide a natural state-level representation of stochastic activity networks. This representation is achieved by constructing the SAS *realized* by a SAN. The *state behavior* [53] of the SAS is a stochastic process which serves as the base model of a performability model. Precise definitions of these model classes and their associated concepts were the work of Ali Movaghar and are included in his doctoral thesis[56]. The thesis also established conditions on a SAN under which the state behavior of the corresponding SAS is a Markov process; a second set of conditions was obtained for the semi-Markov case.

As stochastic activity network models grew in size and complexity, analysis by hand quickly became intractable. Both the growth in possible markings and the complexity of activity time distributions contributed to the difficulty. Considerations such as these led to the development of METASAN [57] at the Industrial Technology Institute (ITI) in Ann Arbor. METASAN is a software package that assists in the construction and solution of performability models based on stochastic activity networks. Development of the package, along with further investigation of SAN-based performability methods, is currently being done by William Sanders. His research assistantship at The University of Michigan is supported directly by ITI. METASAN is written using UNIX tools (C, Yacc, Lex, and Csh) and currently contains some 30,000 lines of source code. Models consist of two parts: a description of the structure of the net, and a description of the desired performance variables and solution method to be used in the evaluation process. Solution options include analytical techniques (applicable under certain well defined conditions) as well as both terminating and steady-state simulation.

A variety of analytic solvers are implemented in the package. Steady-state state occupancy probabilities are obtained either by Gaussian elimination or by Gauss-Seidel iteration, depending on the size of the state-space. Reward model solution techniques are also implemented. In the case of Markov reward models, a variation on a technique proposed by Goyal and Tantawi [48] is used. When the reward model is not Markov, the technique developed by Furchtgott and Meyer [47] described earlier is used. Solution for the state occupancy probabilities at a specific time for Markov stochastic activity systems is accomplished using a randomization technique proposed by Gross and Miller [58,59].

Conditions exist when solution of the base model via analytic means becomes intractable. This can occur, for example, when complex reactivation functions are specified, activity time distributions are general, the desired performance variables are sufficiently complex, or the state space is extremely large. In this case a simulation solver may be used. Both the terminating and steady-state simulation solvers are based on a discrete-event next-event time advance simulator core.

METASAN also provides for versatile definition of performance variables. Unlike many modeling packages, which restrict the analyst to a few pre-defined variables (e.g. queue length, server utilization), METASAN permits the specification of complex user-defined performance variables via the notion of a *path*. Informally, a path is a sequence of marking, activity, case triples which define a possible behavior on the net. Specific performance variables can then be constructed in terms of a set of paths and set of general variables which are parameterized in terms of path sets. Events such as initiations of paths, completions of paths, and traversals of paths are then naturally defined. Definition of these events make if possible to estimate a variety of time related characteristics of path sets. All conventional performance variables plus a wide class of un-conventional variables can be represented in this framework.

In reference to the title of this section, the recent years brought something else to Michigan that few other universities have had the pleasure of experiencing. In the very same year that marked the beginning of this period (1982), our fault-tolerant computing faculty tripled in size! This was due to the arrivals of John Hayes from the University of Southern California and Kang Shin from the Rensselaer Polytechnic Institute. Moreover, this was not simply a matter of an increase in head-count among faculty with serious interests in fault-tolerant computing. In coming to Michigan, John brought with him 10 years of USC experience in the field, during which he had already established an enviable reputation. Kang, although arriving with less experience, was fully underway the day he arrived with supported (NASA-Langley) research in fault-tolerant computing.

Among other activities, the three of us are currently working on a project (ONR Contract N00014 85 K 0531) concerning the analysis, design, and validation of very high performance, high reliability multiprocessor systems. Particularly relevant to aims of the project are Hayes' recent contributions to fault modeling and simulation in MOS circuits [60,61] and the results that Shin recently obtained with Lee [62] concerning the impact of error detection on computer performance. The author's effort is tied most closely to the validation aim, where the approach we're taking is referred to as "validation via evaluation." With additional interests and energy provided by six Graduate Research Assistants, it appears that the next 20 years of this evolution are off to a good start.

5. References

[1] J. F. Meyer, "Low-speed time-multiplexing with magnetic latching relays", IRE Trans. on Space Electronics and Telemetry, vol. 7, no. 2, pp. 34-41, June 1961.

[2] J. F. Meyer, "A definition of system reliability", Tech. Summary No. 3341-66-1, Jet Propulsion Laboratory, February 1966.

[3] J. F. Meyer, "On the structure of fault tolerant sequential machines", in Proc. of the Third Hawaii Int. Conf. on System Sciences, Honolulu, HI, Jan 1970, pp. 443-447.

[4] J. F. Meyer, "Fault-tolerant sequential machines", IEEE Trans. on Computers, vol. C-20, no. 10, pp. 1167-1177, Oct. 1971

[5] R. L. Russo, "Synthesis of error-tolerant counters using minimum distance three state assignments", IEEE Trans. Electron. Comput., vol. EC-14 pp. 359-366, June 1965

[6] F. G. Gray and J. F. Meyer, "Locatability of faults in abstract networks", in Digest 1971 Int. Symp. on Fault-Tolerant Computing, March 1971, pp. 30-33.

[7] F. G. Gray and J. F. Meyer, "Locatability of faults in combinational networks", IEEE Trans. on Comput., vol. C-20, pp. 1407-1412, Nov. 1971

[8] F. G. Gray, "Fault tolerance, detection, and location in abstract combinational networks", Ph.D Thesis, University of Michigan, 1971.

[9] F. G. Gray and J. F. Meyer, "Algebraic properties of functions affecting optimum fault-tolerant realizations", IEEE Trans. on Comput., vol. C-25, no. 11, pp. 1078-1088, Nov. 1976.

[10] E. F. Moore, "Gedanken experiments on sequential machines", Automata Studies 34, pp. 129-153, 1956.

[11] Z. Kohavi and P. Lavalle, "Design of sequential machines with fault-detection capabilities", IEEE Trans. on Electr. Comput., pp. 473-484, Aug. 1967.

[12] J. F. Meyer and K. Yeh, "Diagnosable machine realizations of sequential behavior", Digest 1971 Int. Symp. on Fault-Tolerant Computing, March 1971, pp. 22-25.

[13] K. Yeh, "A theoretic study of fault detection problems in sequential systems", Ph.D Thesis, University of Michigan, 1972.

[14] L. Hsieh and J. F. Meyer, "Diagnosis of unrestricted faults in sequential machines", in Digest 1973 Int. Symposium on Fault-Tolerant Computing, Palo Alto, CA, June 1973, p. 175.

[15] L. Hsieh, "Detection of unrestricted faults in sequential systems", Ph.D Thesis, University of Michigan, 1973.

[16] R. J. Sundstrom, "On-line diagnosis of sequential systems", Ph.D Thesis, University of Michigan, 1974.

[17] J. F. Meyer and R. J. Sundstrom, "On-line diagnosis of unrestricted faults", IEEE Trans. on Comput., vol. C-24, no. 5, pp. 468-475, May 1975.

[18] J. F. Meyer, "A general model for the study of fault tolerance and diagnosis", in Proceedings of the Sixth Hawaii Int. Conf. on System Sciences, Jan. 1973, pp. 163-165.

[19] J. F. Meyer, "Reliable design of software", in Proc. of the Symp. on Rational Fault Analysis, Lubbock, TX, Aug. 1974, pp. 163-165.

[20] J. F. Meyer, "Reliable design of software" in Rational Rault Analysis, edited by R. Saeks and S.R. Liberty, Marcel Dekker, NY, 1977, pp. 112-113.

[21] J. F. Meyer, "Computation-based reliability analysis", in Proc. 1975 Int. Symp. on Fault-Tolerant Computing, Paris, June 1975, p. 223.

[22] J. F. Meyer, "Computation-based reliability analysis", IEEE Trans. on Comput., vol. 25, no. 6, pp., June 1976.

[23] J. H. Wensley and et al., "SIFT: Design and analysis of a fault-tolerant computer for aircraft control", Proc. of the IEEE, vol. 66, pp. 1240-1255, Oct. 1978.

[24] A. L. Hopkins and et al., "FTMP--A highly reliable fault-tolerant multiprocess for aircraft", vol. 66, pp. 1221-1239, Oct. 1978.

[25] J. C. Laprie and A. Costes "Dependability: A unifying concept for reliable computing", in Proc. 1982 Int. Conf. on Fault-Tolerant Computing, 1982, pp. 18-21.

[26] J. C. Laprie, "Dependable computing and fault tolerance: Concepts and terminology", in Proc. 1985 Int. Conf. on Fault-Tolerant Computing, Ann Arbor, MI, June 1985, pp. 2-11.

[27] J. F. Meyer, "An approach to evaluating the effectiveness of computing systems", in Proc. 1976 Conf. on Information Sciences and Systems, The Johns Hopkins Univ., Baltimore, MD, April 1976, pp. 376-383.

[28] J. F. Meyer, "A model hierarchy for evaluating the effectiveness of computing systems", in Proc. 3rd National Reliability Symp., Perros-Guirec, France, Sept. 1976, pp. 539-555.

[29] J. F. Meyer, "On evaluating the performability of degradable computing systems", in Proc. 1978 Int. Symp. on Fault-Tolerant Computing, Toulouse, France, June 1978, pp. 44-49.

[30] J. F. Meyer, "On evaluating the performability of degradable computing systems", IEEE Trans. Comput., vol C-22, pp. 720-731, Aug. 1980.

[31] L. T. Wu and J. F. Meyer, "Phased models for evaluating the performability of computing systems", in Proc. of the 1979 Johns Hopkins Conf. on Information Sciences and Systems, Baltimore, MD, March 1979, pp. 426-431.

[32] H. S. Winokur, Jr. and L. J. Goldstein, "Analysis of mission-oriented systems", IEEE Trans. Reliability, vol. R-18, no. 4, pp. 144-148, Nov. 1969.

[33] J. L. Bricker, "A unified method for analyzing mission reliability for fault tolerant computer systems", IEEE Trans. Reliability, vol. R-22, no. 2, pp. 72-77, June 1973.

[34] J. D. Esary and H. Ziehms, "Reliability analysis of phased missions", in Reliability and Fault Tree Analysis, Philadelphia, PA, SIAM, 1975, pp. 213-236

[35] R. A. Ballance and J. F. Meyer, "Functional dependence and its application to system evaluation", in Proc. 1978 Johns Hopkins Conf. on Info. Sci. and Syst., Baltimore, MD, March 1978, pp. 280-285.

[36] L. T. Wu, "Models for evaluating the performability of degradable computing systems", Ph.D Thesis, Univ. of Michigan, 1982.

[37] D. G. Furchtgott, "Performability models and solutions", Ph.D Thesis, Univ. of Michigan, 1984.

[38] D. G. Furchtgott and J. F. Meyer, "Performability evaluation of fault-tolerant multiprocessors", Government Micro-circuit Applications Conf. Digest of Papers, Monterey, CA, Nov. 1978, pp. 362-365.

[39] J. F. Meyer, D. G. Furchtgott and L. T. Wu, "Performability evaluation of the SIFT computer", in Proc. 1979 Int. Symp. on Fault-Tolerant Computing, Madison, WI, June 1979, pp 43-50.

[40] J. F. Meyer, D. G. Furchtgott and L. T. Wu, "Performability evaluation of the SIFT computer" IEEE Trans. Comput., vol. C-22, pp. 501-509, June 1980

[41] J. F. Meyer and L. T. Wu, "Evaluation of computing systems using functionals of a Markov Process", in Proc. 14th Annu. Hawaii Int. Conf. on Syst. Sci., Honolulu, HI, Jan. 1981, pp. 74-83.

[42] C. W. Gear, "Numerical Initial Value Problems in Ordinary Differential Equations", Englewood Cliffs, NJ, Prentice-Hall, 1971.

[43] J. F. Meyer, "Performability modeling of distributed real-time systems", Mathematical Computer Performance and Reliability, G. Iazeolla, P. J. Courtois and A. Hordijk, Amsterdam: North-Holland, 1984.

[44] J. F. Meyer, "Closed-form solutions of performability", Proc. 1981 Int. Symp. on Fault-Tolerant Computing, Portland, ME, June 1981, pp. 66-71.

[45] J. F. Meyer, "Closed-form solutions of performability", IEEE Trans. Comput., vol. C-31, pp. 648-657, July 1982.

[46] R. A. Howard, "Dynamic Probabilistic Systems, Vol II: Semi-Markov and Decision Processes", New York, NY: Wiley, 1971.

[47] D. G. Furchtgott and J. F. Meyer, "A performability solution method for degradable, nonrepairable systems", IEEE Trans. Comput., vol. C-33, June 1984.

[48] A. Goyal and A. N. Tantawi, "Evaluation of performability for degradable computer systems", IBM Res. Report RC10529 (Revised), Dec. 1984

[49] L. Donatiello and B. R. Iyer, "Analysis of a composite performance reliability measure for fault tolerant systems", IBM Res. Report RC10325, January 1984

[50] V. G. Kulkarni, V. F. Nicola, K. S. Trivedi and R. M. Smith, "A unified model for the analysis of job completion time and performability measures in fault-tolerant systems", CS-1985-13, Dept. of Computer Science, Duke University, 1985.

[51] D. G. Furchtgott and J. F. Meyer, "Performability evaluation of computing systems using reward models", Tech. Report CRL-TR-27-83, Univ. of Michigan, Ann Arbor, MI, Aug. 1983.

[52] A. Movaghar and J. F. Meyer, "Performability modeling with stochastic activity networks", Proc. 1984 Real-Time Systems Symp., Austin, TX, Dec. 1984.

[53] J.F. Meyer, A. Movaghar and W.H. Sanders. "Stochastic activity networks: Structure, behavior, and application", in International Workshop on Timed Petri Nets, Torino, Italy, July 1-3, 1985, pp. 106-115.

[54] S. Natkin, "Reseaux de Petri Stochastiques", Thése de Docteur-Inge'nieur, CNAM-PARIS, June 1980.

[55] M. K. Molloy "Performance analysis using stochastic Petri nets", IEEE Trans. Comput., vol. C-31, pp. 913-917, Sept. 1982.

[56] A. Movaghar, "Performability modeling with stochastic activity networks", Ph.D Thesis, University of Michigan, 1985.

[57] W. H. Sanders and J. F. Meyer, "METASAN: A performability evaluation tool based on stochastic activity networks", in Proc. of the ACM-IEEE Comp. Soc. 1986 Fall Joint Comp. Conf. (To Appear), Dallas, TX, Nov. 1986.

[58] D. Gross and D. R. Miller, "The randomization technique as a modeling tool and solution procedure for transient Markov processes", Operations Research, vol. 32, no. 2, pp. 343-361, March-April 1984.

[59] D. R. Miller, "Reliability calculation using randomization for Markovian fault-tolerant computing systems", in Proc. 1983 Int. Symp. Fault-Tolerant Computing, Milano, Italy, June 1983, pp. 284-289.

[60] J. P. Hayes, "Fault modeling for digital MOS intergrated circuits", IEEE Trans. Computer-Aided Design, vol. CAD-3, pp. 200-207, July 1984.

[61] M. Kawai and J. P. Hayes, "An experimental MOS fault simulation program CSASIM", in Proc. 21st Design Automation Conf., Albuquerque, June 1984, pp. 2-9.

[62] K. G. Shin and Y. H. Lee, "Error detection process: model, design, and its impact on computer performance", IEEE Trans. on Computers, vol. C-33, no. 6, pp. 529-540, June 1984.

Experimental Research in Reliable Computing
at Carnegie Mellon University

Daniel P. Siewiorek
Department of Computer Science
Department of Electrical and Computer Engineering

John P. Shen
Department of Electrical and Computer Engineering

Roy A. Maxion
Department of Computer Science

Carnegie Mellon University
Pittsburgh, Pennsylvania 15213
USA

1. Introduction

In 1945 the Carnegie Plan for higher education was evolved. The basic philosophy of the plan is "learning by doing". The strong emphasis on experimental research at Carnegie Mellon University (CMU) is an example of the Carnegie plan in operation. Research in reliable computing at Carnegie Mellon University has spanned three decades. In the early 1960's, Westinghouse Corporation in Pittsburgh had an active research program in the use of redundancy to enhance system reliability. William Mann, who had been associated with Carnegie Mellon University, was one of those researchers. In 1962, a symposium on redundancy techniques was held in Washington, DC.; it lead to the first comprehensive book on the topic of redundancy and reliability. Bill Mann was one of the coauthors of that book [73]. One of the papers in that volume, on adaptive voting, was written by CMU's Professor William H. Pierce [41]. Later Professor Pierce published one of the first text books on redundancy [42].

During the next two decades a large number of experimental computer systems were designed, implemented, and made operational at CMU. These systems covered a range of computer architecture, from uniprocessors, to multiprocessors, to networks. Each system represented a unique opportunity to include reliability features in the design, and to measure the results. This paper surveys the theoretical results leading up to the designs as well as their empirical measurements.

2. Multiprocessor Architectures

In 1966, Gordon Bell joined the CMU faculty after successfully heading up the engineering design team for the PDP-6 (the forerunner to the popular PDP-10 series) at Digital Equipment Corporation. Over the next six years Gordon initiated a number of computer architecture projects that were leaders in their time and even today are still influencing computer architecture. Gordon's desire to understand and to formalize the design process lead to a rich set of taxonomies culminating in the concept of "computer space" and in the ISP (Instruction Set Processor) and PMS (Processor, Memory, Switch) notations popularized in the classical text book written with Allen Newell [4]. In 1969, Gordon headed up a research seminar whose goal was to design an architecture especially suited for artificial intelligence applications. The result of the seminar was a paper study outlining C.ai. One subunit of the C.ai architecture was a multiprocessor employing a crossbar switch. Ultimately the multiprocessor portion of C.ai was built as C.mmp (Computer.multi-mini-processor). The DARPA-funded C.mmp project, started in 1971, became operational in mid-1975, and was decommissioned in March 1980. C.mmp (see Fig. 1) was comprised of sixteen PDP-11 processors communicating with 16 memories through a crossbar switch [74] C.mmp added a minimal amount of error detection in its hardware. The natural redundancy in the replicated processors and memory provided opportunities for substantial software error detection and reconfiguration techniques [30].

In 1972 Professors Samuel Fuller and Daniel Siewiorek joined CMU as new faculty members upon completion of their Ph.D.s at Stanford University. Sam Fuller's interests were in the areas of performance evaluation and modelling, while Dan Siewiorek's interests were in the design and modelling of reliable systems. During that time, hardware design for C.mmp was in full swing. It was a fruitful period for analytical models of both performance [5] and reliability [60]. The description of major results in the C.mmp project can be found in [75].

Fig. 1 The "H" shaped configuration of C.mmp with crossbar switch and memory in the center, surrounded by banks of four processors.

Fig. 2 Two of the five clusters of Cm*. The open cluster has four computer modules on the top backplane; K.map is on the bottom.

With the C.mmp hardware development under way, Gordon Bell returned to DEC during the summer of 1972 to become Vice President for Engineering. During the fall of 1972, a seminar was started at CMU to explore the architectural possibilities of using microprocessors in a large-scale multiprocessor whose cost grew linearly in the number of processors employed. Architectural specifications for the computer module project were developed and reported [61]. Architectural studies continued on the computer module project under National Science Foundation sponsorship through 1974. In the late fall of 1974 DEC was well into the design of the LSI-11, a single board PDP-11. The LSI-11 had sufficient computational power to provide a basis for a large-scale multiprocessor. Detailed architectural design was undertaken culminating in the Cm* architecture (see Fig. 2) [66].

Cm* was extensively studied with performance and reliability models during the design process. A 10-processor system became operational in 1977. As a result, Cm* had incorporated many more performance and reliability features than C.mmp [62]. Equipment donations from Digital Equipment Corporation, and funding from DARPA, facilitated the production of a 50-processor experimental system complete with two independent operating systems. The system became operational in 1979. Further details on the Cm* project can be found in [21].

Dan Siewiorek spent the summer of 1975 with the Research and Development group at Digital Equipment Corporation. The summer's goal was to study issues of testing and reliability in computer structures. The work culminated in an architectural specification for C.vmp (Computer, voted multiprocessor) as shown in Fig. 3. C.vmp employed off-the-shelf components with little or no modification to achieve hard and transient fault survivability [63]. C.vmp executed an unmodified operating system. In addition to a voting mode, the bus-level voter also allowed a nonreplicated device (such as a console terminal) to broadcast results to all three processors, or it allowed the system to divide into three independent computers intercommunicating through parallel interfaces. C.vmp could switch between independent-mode and voting-mode operation, thus permitting the user to dynamically trade performance for reliability.

Fig. 3 C.vmp with processor "C" removed. Note diagnostic panel on the upper left indicating that processors "A" and "B" are running, processor "C" is halted, and bus "C" is disagreeing.

C.vmp became operational in the fall of 1976. Experience indicates that C.vmp is about six times more reliable for transient faults than the single LSI-11 systems employed in Cm* [62]. C.vmp was operational for five years. Performance degradation due to the voter has been theoretically predicted as well as experimentally measured [58]. The voter reduced the system level performance by about 15 per cent. The voter design has been generalized to include both asynchronous and synchronous bus protocols [36].

At the time of C.vmp's inception, engineers and designers were becoming aware of the predominance of transient errors over hard failures. A major goal of the C.vmp project was to use C.vmp as a transient meter whereby the sources of transients could be measured in much the same way that a volt meter can measure sources and magnitudes of voltages. A statistics board was added to the C.vmp design [53]. The statistics board compared the three buses for disagreements and stored the contents of all three buses (including a unique time stamp) into a shift register when a disagreement was noted. Subsequently, the generalized voter design was implemented in a VLSI chip by Sandia Laboratory (see Fig. 4) [35]. Each chip had two data and two control voters so that approximately ten chips were required to replace the more than 120 chips used in the C.vmp design.

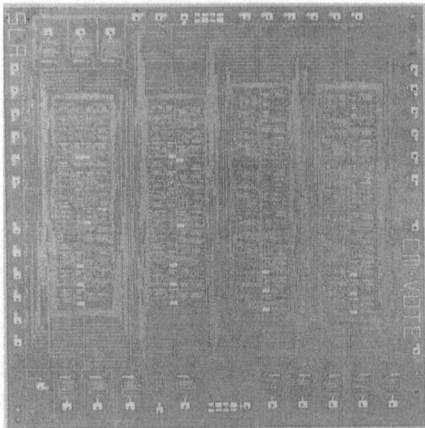

Fig. 4 Photomicrograph of the CMU voter chip with two data-line voters at the top, and two control-line voters at the bottom.

In the spring of 1981 a group of Dan Siewiorek's students were taking a VLSI design course, and were in search of a class project. Thus was born C.fast (Computer, fault-tolerant and self-testing) whose goal was to incorporate fault-tolerance and self-testing design concepts into a VLSI implementation of a microprocessor. The Fairchild F8 instruction set was selected as a test vehicle. The fault-tolerant and self-testing techniques were designed to be transparent to the F8 instruction set. Thus all existing F8 software could be executed on C.fast. C.fast incorporated parity on internal data buses, registers, and PLA's. Three major machine registers had redundant copies so that internally detected errors could be recovered from by employing macro-instruction retry. Duplication and retry were used at the chip level to recover from external faults or from internal faults that were not detected by other error detection mechanisms. C.fast employed a central bus that was externally controllable and observable. This control bus was a major means for effective testing of the system (see Fig. 5) [69, 71]. These and other architectures were summarized in [55, 56].

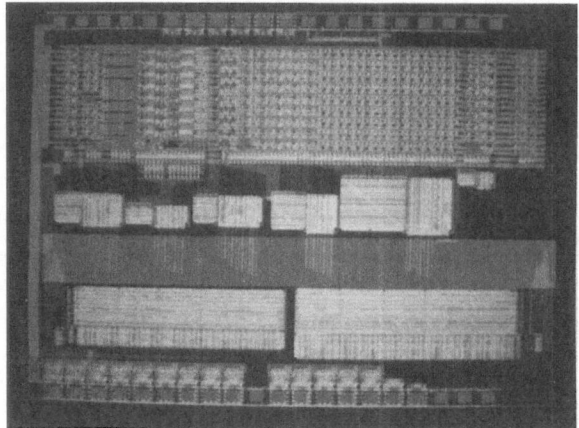

Fig. 5 Photograph of the layout of the C.fast chip.

In the fall of 1981 Alfred Spector joined the Computer Science Department at Carnegie Mellon University after completing his Ph.D. thesis at Stanford University by analyzing performance in a distributed network of workstations. He initiated the TABS [64, 65] project which provides the facility to support distributed applications requiring high reliability and availability. Unlike C.vmp and C.fast, the TABS Prototype runs on a networked collection of processors, each of which is fail-fast. Storage is assumed to fail in a detectable way. The fundamental hypothesis is that a general purpose, distributed transaction facility is useful in simplifying the construction of distributed applications, and that such a facility can be implemented efficiently. Unlike a data-base system's transaction facility that has been specialized to support only a particular data-base model, a general purpose transaction facility is integrated into an operating system, and it supports a collection of data types in a uniform way. The TABS prototype was implemented in Pascal on a group of networked Perq workstations [40] running a modified version of the Accent operating system kernel [43]. At each node, there is one instance of the TABS system facility as well as one or more user-program data servers and/or applications that access the facilities of TABS. Data servers use a write-ahead log-based recovery mechanism [46] which is implemented with the cooperation of the Recovery Manager in the Accent Kernel. TABS began operation in the fall of 1984. A variety of demonstration applications providing high data integrity and high availability have been constructed. An example is a replicated directory package based on weighted voting [13, 6]. It permits lookup, update, insert, and delete operations to proceed despite the failure of one of three storage nodes. Because TABS uses nearly the minimum number of expensive operations such as disk I/O's, log writes, and internode messages and datagrams, TABS performance is sufficient for many applications in the CMU interactive workstation environment [65]. Though use of TABS is continuing as of the summer of 1986, a new system called CAMELOT (Carnegie Mellon Low Overhead Transaction System) is now being designed for a UNIX-compatible operating system called MACH [1]. CAMELOT will have much higher performance than TABS; it is intended for use by nonimplementors in a geographically distributed environment.

3. Data Collection

Often designers must make tradeoffs between alternative reliability techniques with inadequate knowledge about how systems fail during operation. In 1977, Dan Siewiorek took a one-semester leave of absence from CMU and spent eight months working with the VAX-11/750 design team on the issues of reliability, availability, and maintainability. To answer questions about modelling hard failures, data was collected from Cm*. Several different module types were utilized in Cm*. A chip count for each module was tabulated followed by the modules of that type in the system, followed by the total number of hours these modules were utilized, followed by the total number of failures. Data was found to follow an exponential distribution with the failure rate predicted by the Military Handbook 217 [72] suitably modified to take into account the time rate of change of technology [62].

While substantial progress has been made in the area of understanding hard failures, transient faults pose a much harder problem. Once a hard failure has occurred, it is possible to isolate uniquely the faulty component. On the other hand, by the time a transient fault manifests itself (perhaps by a system software crash) all traces of its nature and location are long gone. Hence, work was started on data collection and modelling of transient faults.

Data was collected from four time-sharing systems, from an experimental multiprocessor, and from an experimental fault-tolerant system. These systems ranged in size from microprocessors to large ECL mainframes. The method of detecting transient-induced errors varied widely. For the PDP-10 time-sharing systems, internally detected errors were reported in a system event log file. For the experimental multiprocessor, Cm*, a program was written under the guidance of Sam Fuller that automatically loaded diagnostics into idle processors, initiated the diagnostics, and periodically polled diagnostics as to their state. For the triply redundant C.vmp, a manually-generated crash log was kept. Transient faults were seen to be approximately 20 times more prevalent than hard failures [37]. Gross attributes of observed transients were recorded [62]. Data from C.mmp illustrated that the manifestation of transient faults was much different than the traditional permanent fault models of stuck-at-1 and stuck-at-0 [1].

In early 1978, Sam Fuller left CMU to work at DEC where he is currently Vice President for Research and Development. During the summer of 1978, Dan Siewiorek worked at DEC on a project whose goals were to improve the reliability, availability, and maintainability of DEC systems. The VAX cluster concept was evolving and one offshoot of the summer's activity was a diagnosis and maintenance plan for VAX clusters. Some of the concepts advocated were increased number of user-mode diagnostics (up until that time the majority of DEC diagnostics executed in either stand-alone mode or under a separate diagnostic supervisor), and on-line analysis of system event logs to determine trends and advise the operating system of desirable reconfigurations prior to catastrophic failure. Subsequently, three separate internal DEC groups started projects in off-line analysis of system event logs. The extra user-mode diagnostics were used to exercise suspected system components in order to gather more evidence in the system event log.

Back at CMU, research continued in understanding system event logs. The first step was to analyze the interarrival times of transient errors. Studies of these times indicated that the probability of crash decreased with time. That is, a decreasing failure

---

1.: Examples included incorrect time-out indications, incorrect number of arguments pushed or popped onto a stack, loss of interrupts, and incorrect selection of a register from a register file.

rate Weibull function (and not an exponential) is the best fit to the data. Since experimental data supported the decreasing failure rate model, a natural question was "How far can you stray if you assume an exponential function with constant failure rate, instead of a decreasing failure rate?". The difference in reliability -- as a function of time between an exponential and a Weibull function of the same parameters -- was examined. Reliability differences of up to 0.25 were found. Since the reliability function can range only between 0 and 1, this error is indeed substantial [34, 9]. Another area of modelling involved the relationship between system load and system error rate. Software was developed to analyze system event log entries and to statistically sample load [7, 8]. From those data a model of system reliability was developed which predicted failures involving hardware and software errors. Starting with first principles[2] a model called cyclostationary was derived. The cyclostationary model was an excellent match to the measured data. It also exhibited the property of a decreasing failure rate. A physical test demonstrated that for the cost of some modelling accuracy, the Weibull function was a reasonable approximation to the cyclostationary model with the advantage of less mathematical complexity.

A natural extension of our work with system event logs was to analyze log entries to discover trends [70]. From a theoretical perspective, trend analysis of event logs is based on the common observation that a hardware module exhibits a period of (potentially) increasing unreliability before final failure. Trend analysis develops a model of normal system behavior and watches for a shift that signifies abnormal behavior. Trend analysis techniques based on data from normal system workloads are better suited for pointing up failure mechanisms than specification-based diagnostics are. This is because normal system workloads tend to stress systems in ways different than specification-based diagnostic programs do. Moreover, trend analysis can learn the normal behavior of individual computer installations. By discovering these behaviors and trends, it is possible to predict certain hard failures (and even discern hardware/software design errors) prior to the occurrence of catastrophic failure. One trend analysis method employs a data-grouping or clustering technique called tupling. Tuples are clusters, or groups, of event log entries exhibiting

---

2.: It is assumed the system has two modes of operation: user and kernel. The probability of being in kernel mode is a random event with measurable statistics. A second random event is the occurrence of a system fault. It is assumed that the system is much more susceptible to crashing if a fault occurs while in kernel mode than if a fault occurs in user mode. Thus a doubly stochastic process is set up between the probability of being in kernel mode and the probability of the occurrence of a system fault.

temporal or spatial patterns of features. The tuple approach is based on the observation that because computers have mechanisms for both hardware and software detection of faults, single-error events can propagate through a system, causing multiple entries in an event log. Tupling forms clusters of machine events whose logical grouping is based primarily on proximity and time in hardware space. A single tuple may contain from one to several hundred event log entries.

During 1978-1979, an exchange of researchers occurred between the CMU group and Professor Gabriele Saucier's group in Grenoble, France. Steve McConnel and Mickey Tsao visited Grenoble.

4. Automated Monitoring and Diagnosis

The research at CMU was slowly progressing toward the online diagnosis of trends in systems. The work gained critical mass with the addition of Roy Maxion in the summer of 1984. Roy had built a system at Xerox [33] wherein a network of host workstations was automatically monitored and diagnosed by a diagnostic server that employed system event logs in making diagnostic decisions.

There are three basic **parts** to the monitoring and diagnostic process, and correspondingly, three basic *requirements* for building a system to implement the process.

- **Gathering data/*sensors*.** Sensors must be provided to detect, store, and forward performance and error information (e.g., event log data) to a diagnostic server whose task it is to interpret the information.

- *Interpreting data/analyzers*. Once the system performance and error data have been accumulated, they must be interpreted or analyzed. This interpretation is done under the auspices of expert problem-solving modules embedded in the diagnostic server. The diagnostic server provides profiles of normal system behavior as well as hypotheses about behavior exceptions.

- **Confirming interpretation/*effectors*.** After the diagnostic server interprets the system performance and error information, an hypothesis must be confirmed (or denied) before issuing warning messages to users or operators. For this purpose there must be effectors for stimulating the hypothesized condition in the system. Effectors can take the form of diagnostics or exercisers that are down-line loaded to the suspected portion of the system, then run under special conditions to confirm the fault hypothesis or to narrow its range.

Roy has been leading a group to study system diagnosis from both the theoretical and practical perspectives, employing techniques from artificial intelligence where appropriate. The group, comprised of students, staff, and faculty, is involved in several projects that are being merged into a single system for on-line diagnosis and maintenance-aiding of distributed systems. Three of these projects are described below.

The first involves the Perq/Spice project, a distributed personal computing environment based upon a message-oriented operating system called Accent. The monitoring and diagnostic system for the Perq/Spice project is a passive one, since it does not actively communicate with network devices for the purposes of hypothesis confirmation or loading and running test suites. Data collection is done with an Auto-Logging tool embedded in the operating system kernel. When a fault is exercised, error events propagate from the lowest hardware error detectors, through the microcode level to the highest level of the operating system. Event log analysis in a distributed computing environment has some fundamental differences from the uniprocessor environment. The workstations, and indeed the diagnostic server, go through cycles of power-on and power-off. Yet it is still possible to piece together a consistent view of system activity through a coordinated analysis of the individual workstations' view of the entire system. In addition, the utilization of workstation resources is highly individualized. Thus the law of large numbers does not apply, and there is no "average" behavior as on a large, multiuser mainframe. The error dispersion index -- the occurrence count of related error events -- was developed to identify the presence of clustered error events which might cause permanent failure in a short period of time [28]. Work on the Perq/Spice monitoring and diagnostic project is in progress. At this writing, the network and host monitoring functions are implemented and fully operational, and event logs are being collected daily. Programs whose purpose is to characterize event logs have already isolated similarities among user/system profiles.

A second project now in progress at CMU involves the active, on-line diagnostic monitoring of Andrew, the CMU campus computing network. The system is termed active because it has the ability to initiate tests to confirm or deny its own hypotheses of failing network nodes or devices. The CMU/Andrew network currently supports about 600 workstations, servers, and gateway/routers. The number of nodes on the network is expected to grow to about 1000 by the fall of 1986 and to about 5000 by the end of 1987. The system as a whole currently monitors eight network routers, as well as the Computer Science Department's entire Ethernet network, for traffic and diagnostic information. Example of traffic parameters monitored are packets transmitted and received, network load, and network collisions. Examples of diagnostic parameters monitored are CRC errors, packet alignment errors, router resource errors due to buffer limitations, and router overrun errors due to throughput limitations [31]. At this writing the monitoring and analysis programs have discovered signatures for a particular network interface failure and for a design error in a network router.

A third project concerns fault-tolerance at the user-system interface. Roughly 30% of all system failures are due to human error [68]. Any diagnostic system eventually involves people, either to perform certain tests, or to make physical repairs or system adjustments. Rather than considering the human as a mere peripheral element, we consider the human to be a component of the overall system. This requires that care be taken to ensure fault-tolerance or fault-avoidance for human-related activities. A study was done to identify the cognitive sources of human error at the user-system interface [32]. A new interface architecture was developed to account for cognitive limitations of users. An interface based on that architecture was built and user-tested against a pre-existing program that performed the same task, but with a traditional interface design. The interface based on the new architecture was effective in reducing user error to almost zero, and in facilitating a task speedup by a factor of four. Error reduction and task speedup are of particular importance in critical applications such as air traffic control and nuclear plant monitors.

5. Tools and Techniques for Reliability Analysis

Even with the current interest in reliability, designers have had to use intuition and ad hoc techniques to evaluate design trade-offs, since there have been few, if any, reliability-oriented, computer-aided design tools. If such a tool existed, it usually would stand alone (that is, not be integrated in the CAD database) and would require a reliability expert to operate it. Starting with the VAX-11/750 in 1977, through the design of the VAX 8600 and 8800, Dan Siewiorek was involved in the design and evaluation of the reliability, availability, and maintainability features of VAX CPU design and other major DEC projects. During that time, a design methodology with supporting CAD tools for reliable design was developed. The experiences gained have been documented in a textbook [59].

Design for reliability starts at the highest level (task description), and it pervades the entire design process. A unique aspect of design for reliability is the number of factors that affect the design, including: hardware error detectors, software error handlers, mechanical design, and environmental parameters. Reliability analysis tools must have access to a wide variety of data bases. Design for reliability is an integrating activity which pervades the entire design process.

It is easy to envision a reliability design cycle. The cycle begins with an architecture and a space of reliability techniques. The current state of the architecture is modelled and evaluated. Weak points in the design are identified, and suitable reliability techniques are selected and applied to the architecture. The design evaluation cycle is repeated until the overall design goals are met. It is our contention that enough fault-tolerant techniques have been discovered that there exists a spectrum from which the designer can choose. For example, we have developed a taxonomy that divides techniques into on-line/off-line detection/correction. The designer determines whether off-line detection/off-line correction, on-line detection/off-line correction, or on-line detection/on-line correction is desired and what can be paid in cost and performance. The designer then enters the catalog according to detection/correction cost, and picks out techniques in a region which applies to the design at hand (e.g., memory, random logic, etc.). The catalog is organized according to the taxonomy, providing reliability formulas and cost evaluations for each technique [16].

A program called LAMBDA [15] helps to automate the evaluation process. A companion program, called SEC [17], calculates the mean time to failure of a fault-tolerant memory given the memory organization and failure rate per bit. LAMBDA evolved under actual usage conditions while Steve Elkind applied his research to DEC projects over the two-year period of his residency in the field service organization at DEC.

Another program, ADVISER [23, 24] calculates reliability and availability of systems composed of processor, memory, and switch components. ADVISER takes as input a description of a computer system at the PMS level as well as other user constraints and produces a symbolic reliability equation for the system. A user requirement might consist of "require one processor, one primary memory, and one secondary memory". ADVISER would then use graph techniques to derive the symbolic reliability equation. ADVISER would also fill in missing information. Thus ADVISER can be used to design a global structure of a redundant system while LAMBDA can be used to design a structure of individual processor, memory, and switch components.

A number of simulators have also been developed. ISP was extended to describe arbitrary digital systems from a functional level down to and including the gate level [3, 2]. ISP compiler and companion simulator are in use by over eighty government, university, and industrial organizations. The simulator has the ability to insert faults into memories, registers, and control logic. These faults can be permanent, intermittent, or transient. The ISP simulator and fault inserter has been used by Bendix to explore, at the gate level, the fault-tolerant properties of the SIFT computer.

There are also two simulators for architecture definition. STARS is a recursive, hierarchically-structured, event-driven simulator. Component failures and repairs are scheduled in an event list according to their probability distributions. When a component changes state (i.e., from working to failed, or vice versa) the simulator tests all subsystems employing the component to determine whether or not the subsystem state has changed (i.e., from working to idle, or vice versa). STARS provides reliability, availability, mean time to failure, mean up-time, and mean down-time evaluations. Mark I simulates a Markov model of a system given as a transition matrix. Mark I provides availability, mean time to failure, and state occupancy information [16].

The use of redundancy to enhance the yield of large semiconductor chips is a common practice. One of the oldest forms of redundancy is triplication with majority voting. With triplication no external repair procedure, such as laser cutting of fuses, is required. Faults, if they exist, are masked. Furthermore, redundancy that is not used in the manufacturing process can be used to tolerate additional failures during operational life. The classical model of triplicated systems, which assumes that a system fails when two or more copies fail, is pessimistic. Indeed, there are many cases in which all three copies can have faults, though the majority vote remains correct. The theoretical model has been extended to account for these compensating failures [76]. This analytical model has been coupled with a fault simulator to predict yield and reliability of actual designs. A prototype system, which reads design data directly from a CAD database, was developed for the Trilogy wafer-scale integration process; it gave designers early feedback on yield. The yield prediction simulator was installed at Trilogy by Gary York in the summer of 1984.

Work in the catalog of reliability techniques and CAD tools takes us toward our ultimate goal of a reliability designer's workbench. As an experiment in a reliability designer's workbench, LAMBDA and ADVISER were integrated into a unified environment called D0 [22]. This experimental system emulates a portion of a typical design scenario: a designer wants to evaluate quickly the reliability of a system at the PMS level before further expanding the design. DO provides a system that invokes appropriate tools, and displays results in an easily understood form. The final result of each iteration is an automatically generated diagram depicting the estimated system reliability at various times.

Another topic of interest is generation of tests [57]. A program has been written which generates functional diagnostics automatically from an ISP-like description of a digital system [25, 26]. To calibrate the quality of the automatically generated functional diagnostics, a comparison was made between the manufacturer's diagnostics and automatically generated diagnostics for a PDP-8. Using the ISP fault inserter, almost 1500 faults were inserted into the PDP-8 description after which the respective diagnostics were simulated. The results showed that the automatically generated diagnostics had a higher detection percentage (95.5% versus 85.5%) and required a factor of 20 fewer instruction executions.

Once a fault-tolerant architecture has been designed, modelled, and built there remains the question of whether the system meets its original specifications. Two fault-tolerant multiprocessors, FTMP and SIFT, were developed and delivered to the Air-Lab facility at the NASA Langley Research Center. In 1979 a weekend workshop was held at the Research Triangle Institute to develop a suite of experiments for these fault-tolerant systems [38, 39]. Starting in 1981, CMU performed a series of experiments to validate the fault-free and faulty performance of FTMP and SIFT. The methodology was developed initially from Cm*, and later transferred to FTMP. The same experiments were then conducted on SIFT to demonstrate that the methodology was robust and that it transcended individual architectures [10][12][18][11][19]. Subsequently, the methodology has been used to assist the Federal Aviation Administration in the design of the next-generation air traffic control system. The methodology consists of a set of baseline measurements meant to characterize the performance of the system. A synthetic workload generator (SWG) was developed which allowed experimental parameters to vary at run-time. The synthetic workload generator drastically reduced the turnaround time for experimentation by eliminating the edit/compile/downline-load portion of the experimental cycle. The avionic workload was developed and the results of the baseline experiments were reproduced through appropriate settings of the synthetic workload generator's runtime parameters. The synthetic workload generator has been modified to include software fault insertion. The next step in this research is to study the differences in manifestation and statistics between software and hardware fault injection.

6. Testing-Related Research

In the fall of 1981, John Shen joined the CMU faculty upon completion of his Ph.D. at the University of Southern California and following a stint as an aerospace engineer at Hughes Aircraft Company. John started a research program in the area of testing and error-detection in real-time systems. Array multipliers were studied [48, 20, 47]. Simple modifications to the basic array multiplier cell made it C-testable (i.e., all cells are exhaustively tested in a constant number of test patterns). The testability of other array-structured circuits and systems have also been investigated [27, 54]. These circuits include array signal processors, systolic arrays, and multicomputer interconnection networks.

Motivated by the IBM Federal Systems Division's concern about error detection in real-time signal processors, John developed Signatured Instruction Streams (SIS), an innovative approach to the on-line detection of control-flow errors caused by transient and intermittent faults [50, 49]. At compile time an application program is analyzed; "signatures" characterizing the control flow of the program are generated and embedded in the object code. At run time, special built-in hardware regenerates these signatures using run-time information, and compares them with the precomputed signatures. A mismatch indicates the detection of an error.

A demonstration system has been designed and built based on an MC68000 processor, incorporating the SIS approach. In order to validate the effectiveness of the SIS, as well as the effectiveness of other techniques, a General Purpose Fault Inserter (GPFI) has been designed and built. The fault inserter can be programmed to inject faults of varying duration to various bit lines of the system bus, simulating the occurrence of transient errors. Extensive fault-insertion experiments have been performed to determine the transient error coverage and error detection latency of the SIS and voting schemes [45]. The applicability of the SIS approach in a multiple processor environment has also been studied and demonstrated [51, 67, 14]. An extension of the SIS scheme, called roving monitoring, has been developed; this permits a single monitoring processor to concurrently monitor multiple applications processors.

A new research effort was started in 1984 to develop a methodology and associated software tools for the testing of MOS VLSI circuits. Inductive Fault Analysis (IFA) is a systematic procedure to predict all the faults that are likely to occur in an MOS integrated circuit during manufacturing [52, 29]. The three major steps of the IFA procedure are:

- Generation of physical defects using statistical data from the fabrication process;
- Extraction of circuit-level faults caused by these defects; and
- Classification of fault types, and ranking of faults, based on the likelihood of occurrence.

The entire IFA procedure has been automated. A difficult step in this procedure is the extraction of circuit-level faulty behavior from physical defects. The function of the fault extractor resembles that of a standard circuit extractor. The fault extractor makes use of the layout description of a fault-free circuit. It extracts the faulty circuit diagram from the modified layout, incorporating the defect.

The results of IFA analysis of actual circuits indicate that many fault types, including non-classical faults, are likely to occur, and at best only 64% of the faults can be modelled by the classical stuck-at fault model. Multiple faults and unusual faults such as creation of new transistors can occur.

Most existing test-generation algorithms use logic level modules, but modern MOS VLSI circuits are predominately represented and implemented as networks of transistors. Frequently, a gate level representation must be generated artificially in order to make use of the available test-pattern generation programs. An alternative is to generate test patterns directly from a transistor-level or switch-level description of the circuit. A switch-level automatic test-pattern generation algorithm has been developed; it is targeted for static CMOS circuits [44]. The algorithm employs a combination of cubic algebra and circuit topology techniques.

7. Conclusions

Fault-tolerant computing research at CMU spans both the Computer Science Department and the Department of Electrical and Computer Engineering. In addition to the authors, Zary Segall and Alfred Spector are also currently involved.

Three axes of integration characterize the CMU research philosophy.

- **Integration of Theory and Practice.** CMU research has had a strong and balanced emphasis on both the development of theoretical concepts and the application of these concepts to practical systems. Experimental approaches have been a key element in our fault-tolerance research. Currently, there is a plan to establish a laboratory for the study of machine and human diagnosis of complex systems from both theoretical and experimental perspectives. The main objective of the laboratory is the exploration, definition, and implementation of advanced systems for intelligent diagnostic problem solving. This work is now in progress.

- **Integration of Hardware and Software.** Traditional fault-tolerant techniques have been directed primarily at hardware systems. As systems become more complex and software engineering costs increase, an approach involving synergistic integration of hardware and software techniques will be essential. Most traditional techniques can be labeled as system/structure based. One direction of our future research is *algorithm-based/behavior-based* fault-tolerance.

- **Integration of Space/Defense and Commercial.** While most early research in reliable systems was geared for space and defense applications, in recent years we have seen fault-tolerance concepts being applied in many commercial applications. We believe that research in both sectors can -- and should be -- mutually benefiting.

There has been substantial research effort in fault-tolerant computing at CMU, and there is strong indication that this research area will continue to grow in both scope and visibility at Carnegie Mellon University.

8. Acknowledgements

The authors would like to acknowledge the multiple funding sources who, through the years, have made this research possible. These funding sources include BMD, DARPA, DEC, IBM, NASA, NSF, ONR, and Xerox. We also thank Laura Forsyth for her help in preparing this paper.

9. References

[1] Accetta, M., R. Baron, W. Bolosky, D. Golub, R. Rashid, A. Tevanian, and M. Young, *Mach: A New Kernel Foundation for UNIX Development*, In Proceedings of Summer Usenix, Atlanta, July, 1986.

[2] Barbacci, M., *Instruction Set Processor Specifications (ISPS): The Notation and Its Application*, In IEEE Transactions on Computers, C-30, nr 1, pp. 24-40, January, 1981.

[3] Barbacci, M., G. Barnes, R. Cattell, and D.P. Siewiorek, *The ISPS Computer Description Language*, Carnegie Mellon University, Department of Computer Science Technical Report, 1977.

[4] Bell, C.G. and A. Newell, *Computer Structures: Readings and Examples*, McGraw-Hill, New York, 1971.

[5] Bhandarkar, D.P., *Analytic Models for Memory Interference in Multiprocess Computer Systems*, PhD thesis, Carnegie Mellon University, Pittsburgh, Pennsylvania, September, 1972.

[6] Bloch, J.J., D. S. Daniels, and A. Z. Spector, *Weighted Voting for Directories: A Comprehensive Study*, Technical Report CMU-CS-84-114, April, 1984.

[7] Castillo, X., *A Compatible Hardware/Software Reliability Prediction Model*, PhD thesis, Carnegie Mellon University, July 1981, Also Department of Computer Science Technical Report.

[8] Castillo, X. and D.P. Siewiorek, *A Workload Dependent Software Reliability Prediction Model*, In 12th International Fault Tolerant Computing Symposium, June, 1982.

[9] Castillo, X., S.R. McConnel, and D.P. Siewiorek, *Derivation and Calibration of a Transient Error Reliability Model*, IEEE Transactions on Computers, C-31, nr. 7, pp. 658-671, July 1982

[10] Clune, E., Z. Segall and D. P. Siewiorek, *Validation of Fault-Free Behavior of a Reliable Multiprocessor System, FTMP: A Case Study*, In International Conference on Automation and Computer Control, San Diego, CA, June 6-8, 1984,

[11] Clune, E., Z. Segall, and D. Siewiorek, FIFault-Free Behavior of Reliable Multiprocessor Systems: FTMP Experiments in AIR-LAB, NASA Contractor Report 177967, Grant NAG1-190, Carnegie Mellon University, August 1985.

[12] Czeck, E. W., F. E. Feather, A. M. Grizzaffi, G. B. Finelli, Z. Z. Segall, and D. P. Siewiorek, *Fault-Free Performance Validation of Avionic Multiprocessors*, In 7th Digital Avionic Systems Conference, October 1986, Dallas, Texas

[13] Daniels, D.S. and A.Z. Spector, *An Algorithm for Replicated Directories*, In Proceedings of the Second Annual Symposium on Principles of Distributed Computing, pp. 104-113, August 1983, Montreal, Canada.

[14] Eifert, J. and J.P. Shen, *Processor Monitoring Using Asynchronous Signatured Instruction Streams*, In Proceedings of 14th International Fault-Tolerant Computing Symposium, June 1984.

[15] Elkind, S.A., *LAMBDA User Manual*, Carnegie Mellon University, 1983.

[16] Elkind, S.A., *Approaches to Reliable Systems Design*, PhD thesis, Carnegie Mellon University, May 1985

[17] Elkind, S. and D.P. Siewiorek, *Reliability and Performance of Error-Correcting Memory and Register Arrays*, In IEEE Transactions on Computers, vol. 29, nr. 10, pp. 920-927, October 1980.

[18] Feather, F., D. Siewiorek, and Z. Segall, *Validation of a Fault-Tolerant Multiprocessor: Baseline Experiments and Workload Implementation*, Technical Report CMU-CS-85-145, Carnegie Mellon University, July 1985.

[19] Feather, Frank, Daniel P. Siewiorek, and Zary Segall, *Validation of a Fault-Tolerant Multiprocessor: Baseline Experiments and Workload Implementation*, Technical Report CMU-CS-8 5-127, Carnegie Mellon University, July 1985.

[20] Ferguson, F.J. and J.P. Shen, *The Design of Two Easily-Testable Array Multipliers*, In Proceedings of the 6th Computer Arithmetic Conference, June 1983.

[21] Gehringer, E. F., D. P. Siewiorek, and Z. Segall, *Parallel Processing: The Cm* Experience*, Digital Press, Bedford MA, 1987.

[22] Guise, D., D.P. Siewiorek, and W.P. Birmingham, *DEMETER: A Design Methodology and Environment*, In Proceedings of the IEEE International Conference on Computer Design/VLSI in Computers, 1983.

[23] Kini, V., *Automatic Generation of Reliability Functions for Processor-Memory-Switch Structures*, PhD thesis, Carnegie Mellon University, Department of Electrical Engineering, February 1981.

[24] Kini, V. and D.P. Siewiorek, Automatic Generation of Symbolic Reliability Functions for Processor-Memory-Switch Structures, IEEE Transactions on Computers, vol. C-31, nr. 8, pp. 752-771, August 1982.

[25] Lai, K.W., *Functional Testing of Digital Systems*, PhD thesis, Carnegie Mellon University, Department of Computer Science, 1981]

[26] Lai, K.W. and D.P. Siewiorek, *Functional Testing of Digital Systems*, In 20th Design Automation Conference Proceedings, Miami Beach, FL, June 27-29 1983.

[27] Lee, D.C.H. and J.P. Shen, *Easily-Testable (N,K) Shuffle-Exchange Networks*, In Proceedings of International Conference on Parallel Processing, August 1983.

[28] Lin, T-T.Y. and D.P. Siewiorek, *Architectural Issues for On-Line Diagnostics in a Distributed Environment, In IEEE International Conference on Computer Design, Port Chester NY, October 1986.*

[29] Maly, W., F.J. Ferguson, and J.P. Shen, *Systematic Characterization of Physical Defects for Fault Analysis of MOS IC Cells*, In Proceedings of International Test Conference, October 1984.

[30] Mashburn, H. H., *The C.mmp/Hydra Project: An Architectural Overview*, In Siewiorek, D. P., C. G. Bell, and A. Newell, Computer Structures: Principles and Examples, pp. 350-370, McGraw-Hill, New York 1982.

[31] Maxion, R. A., *Distributed Diagnostic Performance Reporting and Analysis*, In IEEE International Conference on Computer Design, Port Chester NY, October 1986.

[32] Maxion, R. A., *Toward Fault-Tolerant User Interfaces*, In Proceedings of the 5th IFAC International Conference on Achieving Safe Real-Time Computing Systems (SAFECOMP-86), Sarlat, France, October 1986.

[33] Maxion, R.A., *Human and Machine Diagnosis of Computer Hardware Faults*, IEEE Computer Society Workshop on Reliability of Local Area Networks, South Padre Island, Texas, February 1982.

[34] McConnel, S.R., *Analysis and Modeling of Transient Errors in Digital Computers*, PhD thesis, Carnegie Mellon University, Department of Electrical Engineering, June 1981, Also Department of Computer Science Technical Report.

[35] McConnel S.R. and D.P. Siewiorek, *The CMU Voter Chip*, Technical Report Carnegie Mellon University, Department of Computer Science, 1980

[36] McConnel, S.R. and D.P. Siewiorek, *Synchronization and Voting*, In IEEE Transactions on Computers, vol. C-30, nr. 2, pp. 161-164, February 1981.

[37] McConnel, S.R., D.P. Siewiorek and M.M. Tsao, *Transient Error Data Analysis*, Technical Report, Carnegie Mellon University, Department of Computer Science, May 1979]

[38] NASA-Langley Research Center, *Validation Methods for Fault-Tolerant Avionics and Control Systems - Working Group Meeting I*, NASA Conference Publication 2114, Research Triangle Institute, 1979.

[39] NASA-Langley Research Center, *Validation Methods for Fault-Tolerant Avionics and Control Systems - Working Group Meeting II*, NASA Conference Publication 2130, Research Triangle Institute, 1979.

[40] *Perq System Overview*, March Edition, Perq Systems Corporation, Pittsburgh, Pennsylvania, 1984.

[41] Pierce, W.H., *Adaptive Vote-Takers Improve the Use of Redundancy*, In Wilcox R.H. and W.C. Mann, Redundancy Techniques for Computing Systems, pp. 229-250, Spartan Books, Washington, D.C. 1962.

[42] Pierce, W.H., *Failure Tolerant Design*, Academic Press, New York 1965.

[43] Rashid, R. and G.G. Robertson, *Accent: A Communication-Oriented Network Operating System Kernel*, Computer Science Department Technical Report, Carnegie Mellon University, 1981.

[44] Robinson, S.H. and J.P. Shen, *Switch-Level Automatic Test Generation for CMOS Circuits*, In Proceedings of International Conference on Computer-Aided Design, November 1985.

[45] Schuette, M.A., J.P. Shen, D.P. Siewiorek and Y.X. Zhu, *An Experimental Evaluation of Two Concurrent Error Detection Approaches*, In Proceedings of 16th International Fault-Tolerant Computing Symposium, July 1986.

[46] Schwarz, P.M., *Transactions on Typed Objects*, PhD thesis, Computer Science Department, Carnegie Mellon University, December 1984, Available as Technical Report CMU-CS-84-166, Carnegie Mellon University,

[47] Shen, J.P. and F.J. Ferguson, *Easily-Testable Array Multipliers*, In Proceedings of 13th International Fault-Tolerant Computing Symposium, June 1983.

[48] Shen, J.P. and F.J. Ferguson, The Design of Easily-Testable VLSI Array Multipliers, In IEEE Transactions on Computers, June 1984.

[49] Shen, J.P. and M.A. Schuette, *On-Line Self-Monitoring Using Signatured Instruction Streams, In Proceedings of International Test Conference, October 1983*.

[50] Shen, J.P. and M.A. Schuette, *Processor Control Flow Monitoring Using Signatured Instruction Streams*, IEEE Transactions on Computers, 1986.

[51] Shen, J.P. and S.P. Tomas, *A Roving Monitoring Processor for Detection of Control Flow Errors in Multiple Processor Systems*, In Microprocessing and Microprogramming: The Euromicro Journal, 1986.

[52] Shen, J.P., W. Maly, and F.J. Ferguson, *Inductive Fault Analysis of MOS Integrated Circuits*, In IEEE Design and Test of Computers, December 1985.

[53] Shombert, L., *The C.vmp Statistics Board Experiment*, Master's thesis, Carnegie Mellon University, Department of Electrical Engineering, 1981.

[54] Shombert, L. A., *Using Redundancy for Testable and Repairable Systolic Arrays*, PhD thesis, Carnegie Mellon University, Pittsburgh, Pennsylvania, 1985.

[55] Siewiorek, D.P., *Architecture of Fault-Tolerant Computers*, In Computer, vol. 17, nr. 8, pp. 9-18, August 1984.

[56] Siewiorek, D. P., *Architecture of Fault-Tolerant Computers*, In D.K. Pradhan, Fault-Tolerant Computing: Theory and Techniques, Vol. II, pp. 417-466, Prentice-Hall, Englewood Cliffs, N.J., 1986.

[57] Siewiorek, D.P. and K.W. Lai, *Testing of Digital Systems*, In Proceedings of the IEEE, pp. 1321-1333, October 1981.

[58] Siewiorek, D.P. and S.R. McConnel, *C.vmp: The Implementation, Performance, and Reliability of a Fault-Tolerant Multiprocessor*, In Proceedings of the Third US-Japan Computer Conference, October 1978.

[59] Siewiorek, D.P. and R. S. Swarz, *The Theory and Practice of Reliable System Design*, Digital Press, Bedford MA, 1982.

[60] Siewiorek, D., V. Kini, R. Joobbani, and H. Bellis, *A Case Study of C.mmp, Cm*, and C.vmp: Part II. Predicting and Calibrating Reliability of Multiprocessor Systems*, In Proceedings of the IEEE, vol. 66, nr. 10, pp. 1200-1220, October 1978.

[61] Siewiorek, D.P., C.G. Bell, R.C. Chen, S.H. Fuller, J. Grason, and S. Rege, *The Architecture and Applications of Computer Modules: A Set of Components for Digital Systems Design*, In Proceedings of the 1973 COMPCON Conference, pp. 177-180, San Francisco, CA, February 1973.

[62] Siewiorek, D.P., V. Kini, H. Mashburn, S. McConnel and M. Tsao, *A Case Study of C.mmp, Cm*, C.vmp: Part I - Experiences with Fault Tolerance in Multiprocessor Systems*, In Proceedings of the IEEE, vol. 66, pp. 1178-1199, October 1978,

[63] Siewiorek, D. P., M. Canepa, and S. Clark, *C.vmp: The Architecture and Implementation of a Fault-Tolerant Multiprocessor*, In 7th International Symposium on Fault-Tolerant Computing, Los Angeles CA, June 1977.

[64] Spector, A.Z., J. Butcher, D.S. Daniels, D.J. Duchamp, J.L. Eppinger, C.E. Fineman, A. Heddaya, P.M. Schwarz, *Support for Distributed Transactions in the TABS Prototype*, In IEEE Transactions on Software Engineering, vol. SE-11, nr. 6, pp. 520-530, June 1985.

[65] Spector, A.Z., D.S. Daniels, D.J. Duchamp, J.L. Eppinger, R. Pausch, *Distributed Transactions for Reliable Systems*, Proceedings of the Tenth Symposium on Operating System Principles, December 1985.

[66] Swan, R.J., S.H. Fuller, D.P. Siewiorek, *Cm*: A Modular, Multi-Microprocessor*, In AFIPS: Proceedings of the National Computer Conference, June 1977.

[67] Tomas, S.P. and J.P. Shen, *A Roving Monitoring Processor for Detection of Control Flow Errors in Multiple Processor Systems*, In Proceedings of the International Conference on Computer Design, October 1985.

[68] W.N. Toy, *Fault-Tolerant Design of Local ESS Processors*, In Proceedings of the IEEE, vol. 66, nr. 10, pp. 1126-1145, October 1978.

[69] Tsao, M.M., *Transient Error and Fault Prediction*, PhD thesis, Carnegie Mellon University, Department of Electrical Engineering, January 1981.

[70] Tsao, M.M. and D.P. Siewiorek, *Trend Analysis on System Error FilesFP*, In *13th International Fault Tolerant Computing Symposium, June 1983, Milan, Italy*.

[71] Tsao, M.M., A.W. Wilson, R.C. McGarity, C-J. Tseng and D.P. Siewiorek, *The Design of C.Fast: A Single Chip Fault-Tolerant Microprocessor*, In 12th International Fault-Tolerant Computing Symposium, June 1982, Santa Monica, CA.

[72] U.S. Department of Defense, *Military Standardization Handbook: Reliability Prediction of Electronic Equipment*, MIL-STD-HDBK-217B, Notice 1, 1976.

[73] Wilcox, R.C. and W.C. Mann, *Redundancy Techniques for Computer Systems*, Spartan Books, Washington, D.C., 1962,

[74] Wulf, W.A. and C.G. Bell, *C.mmp: A Multi-Mini-Processor*, In AFIPS Conference Proceedings, vol. 41, pp. 765-777, Montvale, NJ., 1972.

[75] Wulf, W.A., R. Levin, and S. Harbison, *Hydra/C.mmp: An Experimental Computer System*, McGraw-Hill, New York, New York, 1980.

[76] York, G., D.P. Siewiorek, Y.X. Zhu, *Compensating Faults in Triple Modular Redundancy*, In Proceedings of the Fifteenth International Symposium on Fault-Tolerant Computing, June 19-21 1985.

A History of Research in Fault Tolerant Computing at the Grenoble University

René David
LAG/INPG, B.P. 46 - 38402 St Martin d'Heres, France

Bernard Courtois
TIM3-IMAG/INPG, 46 Avenue Félix Viallet - 38031
Grenoble CEDEX, France

Gabriéle Saucier
LCS-IMAG/INPG, 46 Avenue Félix Viallet - 38031 Grenoble
CEDEX, France

ABSTRACT

This paper presents the research in Fault-Tolerant Computing at the Grenoble University for over fifteen years. The main topics are random testing of digital circuits, testing VLSI, self-checking circuits, and validation of high dependability systems.

1. Introduction

About 1960 J. Kuntzmann started research and teaching about Computer Science and R. Perret started research and teaching about Automatic Control at the Grenoble University. Research about Computer Science was developed at the "Institut de Mathémathiques Appliquées de Grenoble" (IMAG). During several

LAG,TIM3/IMAG, LCS/IMAG are within Institut National Polytechnique de Grenoble.
They are associated with the Centre National de la Recherche Scientifique.

years Boolean Algebra was an important topic at IMAG. The work of Gabriéle Saucier was firstly on sequential machines. Then she started research on Fault-Tolerant Computing. The growth of IMAG leaded to split it into several laboratories. Gabriéle Saucier is now head of one of them: "Laboratoire Circuits et Systémes" (LCS). Bernard Courtois is responsible of the Architecture Group in another one : "Techniques de l'Informatique, des Mathémathiques, de la Microélectronique et de la Microscopie Quantitative" (TIM3) which is widely involved in design and test of VLSI. Research about Automatic Control was developed in the "Laboratoire d'Automatique de Grenoble" (LAG). René David is responsible of the team Logic and Discrete Systems which was first concerned by digital circuits for logic control, then by testing of digital circuits.

In the following, three main topics are addressed : random testing of digital circuits, testing VLSI and self-checking circuits, and validation of high dependability systems.

2. Random Testing of Digital Circuits

This research has been leaded in the Laboratoire d'Automatique de Grenoble for a long time. The first work on this subject was a student project by AGUILHON and D'ISSERNIO, during the academic year 1969-70. This project was proposed and directed by P. Deschizeaux. By interconnection of NOR gates on a logic simulator, the students built a little random tester and did some trials of testing. Then a Ph.D. by R. Tellez-Giron started in 1970. During several years this research was considered by some people as an academic amusement. However R. David decided to continue on this way. Approximately at the same time, and independently, J-C. Rault at Thomson/CSF, Paris, E.J. McCluskey at Stanford University, and P. and VD. Agrawal at Automation Technology Company, Champaign, started some work on similar subjects. These teams stopped this activity ten years ago. The LAG team was alone to tackle random testing analysis for circuits as complex as microprocessors. During several years studies about random testing seemed to be more or less left by other researchers. About 1980 this research took up again, at IBM company, in particular P.H. Bardell in Poughkeepsie, at Stanford University and in some other places.

2.1. Theoretical Studies

All these studies seek to answer the following question : given a digital circuit wich is randomly tested, *what is the length of the input sequence* which corresponds to some quality level ? The input probabilities and a prescribed set of faults, are generally assumed to be given.

First the considered "quality level" was the probability to apply a random input sequence testing all the possible faults in the prescribed set [Te 74], [TeDa 74]. In other words it is the probability to have a 100 percent coverage. This has been applied to both combinational and sequential circuits (approximative method). Let PD(f) the average detection probability by a random pattern for the fault f and PDmin the value corresponding to the hardest to detect. It has been shown that all the faults with PD at least twice PDmin could be neglected for determining L [TeDa 74].

Then it has been shown that the preceding "quality level" was rather pessimistic. It can be replaced by the probability to apply a random input sequence testing the hardest fault [DaBl 76]. The random test length L which is obtained now is shorter than the preceding one, an easier to calculate, since L=logQD/log(1-PDmin), where QD is the detection uncertainty. That means "quality level"=1-QD. This has been applied to combinational circuits [DaBl 76] then to other kinds of circuits. The problem consists in evaluating PDmin.

The memories : at first the stuck-at model has been considered [ThDa 78] ; more recently the faults models which were introduced by various authors between 1977 and 1985 have been considered. Random pattern testing taking into account these models have been studied according to a contract between LAG and IBM company (Bordeaux). This work involved TIM3 [FuDa 86].

A method has been developed to analyse random testing of small and medium scale integrated sequential circuits. It is based on cutting the circuit to obtain blocks. Each block is studied thanks to the new concept of Minimal Detection Transition Sequence [DaTh 80]. The method has been applied to obtain random testing lengths for some flip-flop, register and counter packages [DaTh 81].

In 1978 it was decided to tackle analysis of random testing for microprocessors. No existing method could be used or extended for a circuit of this complexity. A completely new method was necessary. P. Thevenod-Fosse took this subject in hand for her "Doctorat d'Etat". The faults in the data processing section were first analyzed using a new graphical model, a bipartite graph made of actual registers and functional operators [ThDa 81]. Then the faults in the control section have been studied and the application to a real life microprocessor has been done [ThDa 83].

Now random testing of a board containing a microprocessor and a ROM is analyzed, considering faults in the ROM [AbTh 86].

2.2. Experimental Studies

The first testing machine was built in 1973 [Te 74]. It was able to perform both asynchronous and synchronous testing of combinational and sequential circuits. A new one performing only synchronous testing, but with some improved features was built in 1978. Some experimental results obtained with these machines appear in [DaTh 81].

A random tester for microprocessor, with a software generation of the random patterns was built in 1981. Then, in 1983, a new random tester for MC6800 microprocessors was realized by X. Fedi. The generator of random pattern (which has been patented) is an hardware one. Hence the random test sequence can be fast, and as long as one wants since it is real time generated. Some experiments performed with this machine were very surprising [FeDa 86]. Our random tester detected more faulty circuits than deterministic testers, because unexpected faults (not covered by deterministic testing) were found thanks to randomness.

Another kind of experiments was performed to compare deterministic and random testing. The same common industrial tester was used for both. Deterministic test input sequences were provided by the designers of the circuits. Random input sequences, off-line software generated were stored in the tester. Most of the results are favourable to random testing [DeTh 84]. This study was done in collaboration with the French Centre National d'Etudes des Télécommunications (CNET), which is now designing a microprocessor with built-in-test. This project, based on random testing and signature analysis is done with the collaborations of the LAG team.
Other random tester were built with industrial collaborations (for a microprocessor, for a board).

2.3. Signature Analysis

Can signature analysis be included into a section on random testing ? Obviously not in a general case. However it is justified here since this problem has been considered from a probabilistic point of view by LAG researchers.

When an input sequence has some statistical properties, an output has a given probability (i.e., average probability to have the logical value 1), and a set of test points can be characterized by a vector of expected average includes. This has been exploited for diagnosis by comparison between the expected vector and the vector obtained during an experiment [DeSi 76].

Signature analysis by Linear Feedback Shift Registers considers usually one the two following assumptions :

1) all the responses have the same probability, i.e., each bit has a probability 0.5 to be faulty ;
2) the possible errors belong to some class, for example the maximum number of faulty bits is known. A new assumption has been introduced by LAG : each bit has a probability p (p may be different of 0.5) to be faulty [Da 80]. This idea has been extended for studying multi-output circuits, with introduction of the new notion of correlated errors [Da 86]. A similar approach is used by T.W. Williams, at IBM Boulder, for studying the rapidity of convergence of various polynomials.

3. Testing VLSI and Self-Checking Circuits

The research on VLSI testing began to be a major theme within the Computer Architecture Group of IMAG in 1977, when very complex circuits appeared. Physical failure mechanisms were studied, and fault hypotheses for the test of NMOS-LSI circuits were described. Such fault hypotheses took in consideration a transistor layout level of description of a digital circuit, rather than a logical level for which the classical logical stuck-at fault model was used. Those fault hypotheses have been named analytical fault hypotheses [Co 81-1]. Together with functional fault hypotheses [Co 81-2], those were used as a part in a methodology for on line (concurrent) testing of microprocessors [Co 81-3]. Initially applied to the M6800 this methodology has been further applied to the MC68000 [MaCo 82] and general results have been made available [Ma 85]. This methodology was aimed at the detection of failures occurring in microprocessors that were not specifically designed for that. On the contrary, partially specifically designed systems were next taken into account [Co 82].

Those fault modeling problems and their use in on-line detection of faults had several extensions :
- use in large distributed systems,
- consideration of specific behaviour in CMOS technology,
- basis for the design of self-checking integrated circuits.

The methodology has been used in large distributed systems for basic fault tolerance [Co 81-4]. Further, data recovery has been studied [BeCo 82] and finally process recovery [Al 86]. This extension took advantage of former studies on the evaluation of reliability, availability, etc... [Co 81-5]. The two other extensions are briefly reported below.

3.1. Self-checking Systems

The basic idea who lead to the development of this topic is as follows : if we consider that the classical logical stuck-at fault model is not representative of real failures for test pattern generation, then this model can no longer be considered for the design of self-checking integrated circuits. This is why realistic fault hypotheses have been considered for the design of NMOS self-checking circuits [NiCo 85] [NiCo 86]. The largest class of checkers, i.e. the Strongly Code Disjoint checkers (SCD) to be associated to Strongly Fault Secure systems, has been defined [NiJa 84]. This definition allows to consider checkers having very interesting properties needed for the application in the real word. NMOS SCD checkers have been designed [JaCo 84] and next Strongly Language Disjoint Checkers have been defined for sequential systems [JaCo85]. These results are now being considered altogether with the definition of sequentially self-checking circuits given in 1980 [ViDa 80]. A complete set of definitions and guidelines for real applications will be given in 1987. Those guidelines will be based on already studied applications : an evaluation of what could be a self-checking version of the MC 68000 [Ni 85-2], the design of a self-checking real-time controller [OsNi 86], and the application to a very large circuit designed by an industrial firm.

3.2. Testing CMOS Circuits

This extension of the study of MOS failure mechanisms was aimed at considering specific behaviours that occur when CMOS technology is considered. First results appeared in 1984 [BaCo 84] for the test of transistors s-on and shorts. For the test of s-open faults, a *one input test* has been used, based on the application of the triplet (1,0,1) or (0,1,0) to the tested input and sensitizing a path until an output. Static and dynamic gates have been considered, and general theorems have been derived. Those theorems extend to CMOS s-open testing the results that had been formulated in 1973 by TO following ideas given by Armstrong in 1966 and Kohavi in 1970, for the test of *logical (single)* stuck-at faults in networks.

Multiple s-opens have also been addressed, and theorems have been derived extending to CMOS multiple s-open faults the results of Bossen and Hong derived in 1971 for the test of multiple stuck-at faults.

S-on faults have been detailed. Two faulty behaviors have been considered for s-on testing : modification of the output voltage level and modification of the gate transfer time. It has been shown that s-on testing requires design for s-on testability (DFT) in order to test networks.

If DFT is considered then single s-on faults and multiple s-on/s-open faults may be tested easily, using basic theorems.
The 20 theorems which have been derived [BaCo 86] extend to CMOS a lot of work that had been given in the past for stuck-at faults testing.

3.3. Self-Checking and Built-in Test

The development of this topic may be summarized as follows. Self-checking circuits cannot be used as they stand for off-line testing i.e. for the test after manufacturing. A major way for off-line testing being built-in test (e.g. [Ni 85-1]), a new concept has been identified, in which a design for built-in test and for self-check are merged. This concept has been named *Unified Built-in Self Test* : UBIST [Ni 86].

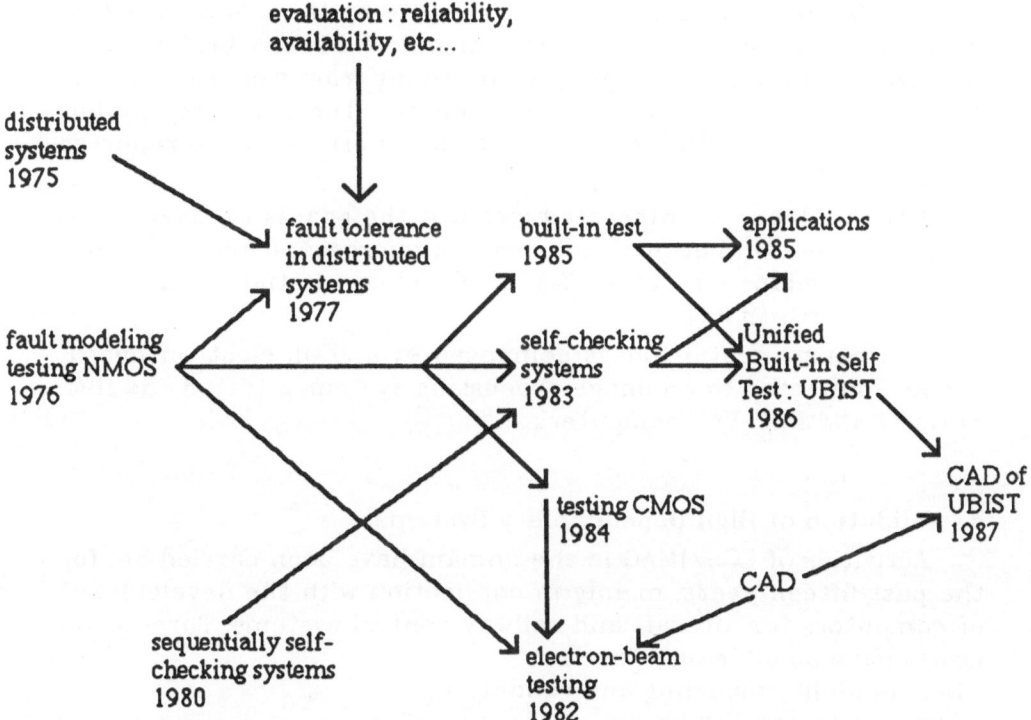

Fig. 1 Evolution of the topic

Another development consists in taking into account the test problems inside the CAD tools. This is exemplified by the compilation of "testable" circuits by the SYCO silicon compiler [JeVa 86]. The figure 1 is a scheme of the evolution of the topic. More details are given in [Co 85].

3.4. Electron-Beam-Testing

Another important topic which is in progress concerns the test of integrated circuits using an electron beam.

This type of test makes use of an electron microscope with a voltage contrast The interest is to be able to visualize the electrical state of the connections in an integrated circuit in course of activity. That is to say that is eliminated one of the components of the test problems which is observability. The applications are principally :
- debug
- failure analysis.

The failure analysis project of circuits by the electron microscope has begun since 1982. The objective of this project is to localize the faults on an integrated circuit from which the structure (in gates, transistors, ...) is unknown. The methodology has been presented in [BaBe 83], and first experiments are reported in [BeLa 86].

For the debug of integrated circuits, the goal is to make available a connection between the electron microscope and CAD tools, and to develop strategies for the debug. Initial results are reported in [GuMi 86].

The experimental tool is composed of a JEOL electron microscope, connected to an image processing system, a tester and IBM. Series 1 and DEC-VAX computers

4. Validation of High Dependability Systems

Activities of LCS/IMAG in the domain have been carried on, for the past fifteen years, mainly in connection with the development of computers for aircraft and railway control systems. Three main issues have been dealt with :
- Dependability modeling and validation,
- Test and testability issues
- Software reliability.

4.1. Dependability Modeling and Validation

An important feature of these systems is their very high dependability requirements controlled by certification authorities : the system manifacturers have to demonstrate that their systems meet the requirements ; these are so high that it will not be possible to demonstrate their fulfillment by direct experiments. The solution widely adopted to cope with this problem, and in the development of which W.C. Carter has played so great a part, consists in using models on which the demonstration will be achieved. Those models which are often built up from Markov Chains, represent the probabilistic behavior of the systems with respect to external fault events and internal fault tolerance decisions. Models are abstract representation of systems and their construction is a quite difficult task, based upon modeling choices : whenever an uncertainty appears, two kinds of answers can be used : either a worst case analysis will allow to solve the problem in a pessimistic sense, or

hypotheses must be stated which can be either of structural or numerical type. When the system is designed, and the model results fulfill the requirements, the validation task consists in verifying that the hypotheses the model is built on, hold, either because they are admitted as state-of-the-art facts (for instance fault independency of carefully isolated units) or by means of experimental measurements, that is to say, in a statistical sense.

Thus the activity of designing fault tolerant architectures and strategies cannot be isolated from their dependability modeling [CaPu 81] and any result that allows to avoid making hypotheses while preserving models results from being too pessimistic, will prove to be valuable. In this sense we have shown how to avoid stating hypotheses on the distribution of the error latency of faults in majority redundant systems [Pi 82]. This methodology is currently under application to a railway control system of the French National Railway Company.

The dependability evaluation raises two important and well known issues which introduce the next sections of this paper. One is the high sensitivity of models to test coverage factors both on-line and off-line (at the beginning and at renewal points of the operational life cycle). The other one is the hypothesis of correct design, which is often a basic one in fault tolerance strategy modeling.

4.2. Test and Testability Issues

Certification efforts of highly dependable systems have shown that parameters such as error latency and test coverage are of prime importance. The research in the LCS/IMAG laboratory has mainly focused on the use of high level architectural and functional models in the test area both for off-line test of VLSI [RoSa 75, RoSa 78] and on-line test [Be 80]. Three recent results which have led to important industrial developments will be outpointed.

4.2.1. Qualification of Components for Severe Environments

The objectives are to qualify components either because they are new products or because of a very severe environment. The efforts have mainly concerned microprocessors [RoSa 79] and led to the design of the GAPT system.

The GAPT system [Be82] [BeVe 84b] is based upon a functional test method ; but unlike other approaches (Thatte and Abraham's one, for example), neither error nor fault model is used : instead of this, a set of representative functionings are tested (identification test method).

The main characteristics of GAPT consist in considering the circuit behavior in the aggregate (instruction set and response to asynchronous input signals [BeVe 84a]), and the test problem as a whole : test generation and tester.

The GAPT system is thus composed of a software and a tester. From a description of the microprocessor in a high-level language, the GAPT software generates the test program in assembly language. The dedicated tester allows the execution of these programs and the test results are either go/no-go or a functional diagnosis which indicates the first erroneous instruction.

Early experiences of microprocessor functional testing have concerned 8-bits microprocessors (6800, Z80) and more recent experiments have led to validate 68000 and 80C86 second source microprocessors, a dedicated signal processor of CNET and a floating point arithmetic coprocessor (IBM).

The present experiments aim at qualifying components submitted to space radiations, and at functional localization of failures [VeKo 85]. A diagnosis expert system is under development.

4.2.2. Design of a Microprocessor Dedicated for Highly Dependable Control Systems [JaSa 84]

A CMOS 16 bits microprocessor "HSURF" dedicated for highly dependable control systems is developed at LCS/IMAG under various sponsorships (EEC project for instance). The approach is a RISC machine approach as the set of instructions is a dedicated set for the control process area. On-line test is completely integrated in the microprocessor. It consists in compacting the sequences of instruction codes in the application programs. The method uses a strategy based upon the well-known "justifying signature principles". The implementation of a special test instruction : AJST in HSURF microprocessor eases the use of this strategy without any extra hardware ; it consists in modifying the application program in order to obtain a constant signature for each program segment whatever the path followed in the execution program is. In addition, the use of AJST instruction allows the signature verification to be transparent for the user.

Off-line test is guaranteed by an access to all internal elements with programmable compaction devices. Test programs are stored in the microprocessor with the compacted results. A dedicated test automaton is integrated.

This microprocessor is designed in a CMOS technology ; it contains approximately 25000 transistors for a silicon area of 17.2 mm2 (36% for the Data Processing Part, 38% for the controller, 6% for the dedicated testing devices : automaton, compaction registers, and 20% for the pads). Its typical cycle time is 500 ns.

4.2.3. Test Strategy and Testability Analysis for Logic Systems

Following an early experiment of system testing [RoSa 76] we tried to formalize the concepts leading to a methodology for testing large systems in various contexts (manufacturing, production, field maintenance). Some attention has been particularly given to the particular case of microprocessor-based systems [RoSa 79] [RoSa 80]. The research work has led to an automatic computer-aided test analysis tool CATA [RoMa 84] which guides the hardware engineer in designing a system that can be easily tested by manufacturing or field operation procedures. This tool is based upon behavioral/functional descriptions of the considered systems, a partition into basic modules which are test entities and the "data flow" paths through the system. The CATA tool defines a top-down organization of test procedures, suggests design modifications and appraises the expected performance of the test strategy in terms of diagnosis resolution. Moreover CATA integrates the testability criteria : three testability measures were defined [CaMi 78], based on information theory, which give indications for design modifications and orientate the test strategy.

4.3. Software Reliability

The question investigated here deals with the feasibility of statistically testing the hypothesis of correct design (from both hardware and software points of view), within a reasonable amount of debugging and test time. We attempted to answer the question by applying software reliability models. An exact test, which can be seen as a debugging stopping rule at a given statistical risk, was derived from the Jelinsky-Moranda model [CaKo 84]. This rule is a very simple one, and it may provide positive answers to the correctness question within reasonable amount of debugging time. However its application to highly dependable systems is questionable since the Jelinsky-Moranda model is known to be an optimistic model. Moreover more sensible models such as Lillewood-Verral's were shown not to be able to cope with the problem when a very low failure rate is required ; the debugging time necessary to assert this rate may have the same order of magnitude as the inverse of this rate. Thus the stated question remains unsolved. However we feel that our stopping rule may prove to be of interest, first in the field of ordinary systems, and also in the field of highly dependable systems in that it can provide quite soon negative answers such as : the remaining test time for this system is so large that it cannot be expected to meet the requirements for a highly dependable application.

5. Conclusion

The Grenoble University has been involved in research on Fault-Tolerant Computing for over fifteen years. Several topics studied in Grenoble are indebted to W.C. Carter for starting research in this domain, and Grenoble researchers are pleased to contribute to the book in the honor of their friend Bill.

6. References

[Te 74] R. Tellez-Giron "Contribution à l'Etude du test aléatoire des systèmes logiques" Docteur-Ingénieur Thesis, Grenoble University, March 1974.

[TeDa 74] R. Tellez-Giron, David R., "Random fault detection in logical networks" in IFAC Int. Symp. on Discrete Systems Dig., Zinatne, Riga, USSR, vol. 2, Oct 1974, pp.232-241

[RoSa 75] C. Robach, G. Saucier, "Diversified test methods for local control units" IEEE Trans. on Computers, Vol. C-24, N.5, May 1975, pp.562-567.

[DaBl 76] R. David, G. Blanchet, "About random fault detection in combinational networks" IEEE Trans. on Computers Vol. C-25, pp. 659-664, June 1976.

[RoSa 76] C. Robach, G. Saucier, J. Lebrun, "Processor testability and design consequences", IEEE Trans. on Computers, Vol. C-25, N.6, June 1976, pp.645-652.

[DeSi 76] P. Deschizeaux, M. Silva-Suarez, G. Nicoud, F. Martin "Statistical Fault-location in Logical Circuits", 6th Fault-Tolerant Computing Symposium, Pittsburg, June 1976, pp.88.92

[CaMi 78] P. Caspi, A. Mili, C. Robach, "An information measure on nets - Application to testability of digital systems", Information and Systems, ed. by B. Dubuisson, New York, Pergamon, 1978, pp.35-39.

[ThDa 78] P. Thevenod-Fosse, R. David, "Test aléatoire des mémoires", Rev. Française d'Automatisme, d'informatique, de Recherche. Op., Vol.12, N.J1,   pp.43-61., 1978

[RoSa 78] C. Robach, G. Saucier,"Dynamic testing of control units", IEEE Trans. on Computers, Vol. C-27, N.7 July 1978, pp.617-623.

[RoSa 79] C. Robach, G. Saucier, C. Aleonard, "Microprocessor systems testing : a review and future prospects" EUROMICRO Journal, Vol.5, N.1, January 1979, pp.31-37.

[RoSa 80] C. Robach, G. Saucier, "Application oriented microprocessor test method", 10th Fault-Tolerant Computing Symposium, Kyoto (Japan), October 1980, pp. 121-125.

[DaTh 80] R. David, P. Thevenod-Fosse, "Minimal detection sequences : application to random testing", IEEE Trans. on computers, Vol. C-29, June 1980, pp.514-518.

[Da 80] R. David, "Testing by Feedback Shift Registers", IEEE Trans. on Computers, Vol. C-29, July 1980, pp. 668-673.

[ViDa 80] J. Viaud, R. David "Sequentially self-checking Circuits", 10th Fault Tolerant Computing Symposium. Kyoto, JAPAN - October 1980, pp.263-268

[CaPu 81] P. Caspi, J. Pulou, "A method for improving the reliability of functionally distributed networks", Journal of Digital Systems, Vol.4, 1981.

[DaTh 81] R. David, P. Thevenod-Fosse, "Random Testing of Integrated Circuits", IEEE Trans. on Instrumentation and Measurement, Vol. IM-30, March 1981, pp. 20-25

[ThDa 81] P. Thevenod-Fosse, R. David, "Random Testing of the Data Processing Section of a Microprocessor", 11th Fault-Tolerant Computing Symposium", Portland, June 1981, pp.275-280.

[Co 81-1] B. Courtois, "Failure mechanisms, fault-hypotheses and analytical testing of LSI-NMOS (HMOS) circuits" VLSI 81, University of Edinburgh, 18.21.8.81, Academic Press

[Co 81-2] B. Courtois, "On-line oriented functional testing of control sections of integrated CPU", EUROMICRO Symposium, Paris, September 1981, France

[Co 81-3] B. Courtois, "A methodology for on-line testing of microprocessors" 11th Fault Tolerant Computing Symposium, Portland, June 81, USA

[Co 81-4] B. Courtois, "SKALP :Skeleton Architecture for fault tolerant distributed processing" EUROMICRO Journal, Vol. 7, N.5, May 1981

[Co 81-5] B. Courtois, "Safety Availability and Maintenance Evaluation of Redundant Systems" Digital Processes - 1981

[Co 82] B. Courtois "Performance modeling of partially self-checking systems", 12th Fault Tolerant Computing Symposium, Santa Monica, June 1982, USA

[MaCo 82] P. Marchal, B. Courtois, "On detecting the hardware failures disrupting programs in microprocessors" 12th Fault Tolerant Computing Symposium, Santa Monica, June 1982, USA

[BeCo 82] M. Ben Romdhane, B. Courtois, "Error confinement/data recovery in distributed systems", 2nd Symposium on reliability in distributed software and data base systems. Pittsburg, July 1982, USA.

[BeSa 82] C. Bellon, G. Saucier, "Protection against external errors in a dedicated system", IEEE trans. on Computers, Vol.C-31, N.4, April 82.

[Be 82] C. Bellon et alt., "Automatic generation of microprocessor test programs", 19th Design Automation Conference Proc. pp.566-573, Las Vegas Nevada, June 1982.

[Pi 82] E. Pilaud, "Design and validation of high dependability computer systems", Ph.D. Thesis, INPG, Grenoble, November 1982.

[BaBe 83] G. Baille, L. Bergher, B. Courtois, J. Laurent, C. Rubat Du Merac "Testing for failure analysis : new tools and new test methods", 13th Fault Tolerant Computing Symposium. Milano, June 1983, Italy

[ThDa 83] P. Thevenod-Fosse, R. David, "Random Testing of the Control Section of a Microprocessor", 13th Fault-Tolerant Computing Symposium, Milan (I), June 1983, pp. 366-373.

[DeTh 84] H. Deneux, P. Thevenod-Fosse, L. Beghin, "Test aléatoire de circuits développés par le CNET/CNS", 4th Conference on Reliability and Maintainability, Perros-Guirec (F), May 1984.

[NiJa 84] M. Nicolaidis, I. Jansch, B. Courtois, "Strongly code disjoint checkers", 14th Fault-Tolerant Computing Symposium Orlando, June 1984, USA

[JaCo 84] I. Jansch, B. Courtois, "On the design of checkers based on analytical fault hypotheses", ESSIRC 1984. Edinburgh. August 1984, United Kingdom

[BaCo 84] D. Bashiera, B. Courtois, "Testing CMOS : A challenge ?", VLSI Design, October 1984

[RoMa 84] C. Robach, P. Malecha, G. Michel, "CATA : a Computer Aided Test Analysis System" IEEE Design and Test of Computers, Vol.1, N.2 , May 1984, pp.68-79.

[CaKo 84] P. Caspi, E.F. Kouka, "Stopping rules for a debugging process based on different software reliability models", 14th Fault-Tolerant Computing Symposium, Orlando, June 1984.

[BeVe 84] C. Bellon, R. Velazco, "Taking into account asynchronous signals in functional test of complex circuits", 21st Design Automation Conference Proc., pp.490-496, Albuquerque, New Mexico, june 1984.

[BeVe 84b] C. Bellon, R. Velazco, "Hardware and software tools for microprocessor functional test" International Test Conference 1984, pp.804-810, Philadelphia, October 1984.

[JaSa 84] C. Jay, G. Saucier,"A testable microprocessor for process control", ICCD 84, pp.284-289, New York, October 1984.

[VeKo 85] R. Velazco, E. Kolokithas, H. Ziade, "A microprocessor approach allowing fault localization" International Test Conference 1985, pp.737-743, Philadelphia, November 1985.

[Co 85] B. Courtois, "Computer Architecture Group. Activity Report 1985" IMAG/TIM3 Report 1985

[Ma 85] P. Marchal, "Functional fault hypotheses for the test of microprocessors internal bus malfunctions". 15th Fault Tolerant Computing Symposium, Ann Arbor, Michigan, June 1985 USA.

[JaCo 85] I. Jansch, B. Courtois, "Strongly Language Disjoint checkers", 15th Fault Tolerant Computing Symposium, Ann Arbor, Michigan, June 1985, USA

[Ni 85-1] M. Nicolaidis, "An efficient built-in self test scheme for functional test of embedded RAMs." 15th Fault Tolerant Computing Symposium, Ann Arbor, Michigan, June 1985, USA

[Ni 85-2] M. Nicolaidis, "Evaluation of a self-checking version of the MC68000 microprocessor", 15th Fault Tolerant Computing Symposium, Ann Arbor, Michigan, June 1985, USA

[NiCo 85] M. Nicolaidis, B. Courtois, "Layout rules for the design of self-checking circuits" VLSI 85, Tokyo, Japan, August 1985

[Al 86] M. Aliouat, "Reprise de processus dans un environnement distribué après pannes matérielles transitoires ou permanentes", Thesis INPG, April 1986

[JeVa 86] A. Jerraya, P. Varinot, R. Jamier, B. Courtois, "Principles of the SYCO compiler", Design Automation Conference, Las Vegas, June 1986, USA

[NiCo 86] M. Nicolaidis, B. Courtois, "Design of NMOS Strongly Fault Secure Circuits using unidirectional errors detecting codes" 16th Fault Tolerant Computing Symposium, Vienna, July 1986. Austria

[OsNi 86] A. Osseiran, M. Nicolaidis, J.P. Schoellkopf, B. Courtois, B. Le Trunc, D. Bied Charreton "Design of a self-checking microprocessor for real-time application in transportation systems", 5th IFAC/IFIP/IFORS, Vienna, July 1986. Austria

[Ni 86] M. Nicolaidis, "An unified built-in self-test scheme : UBIST", ESSIRC Conference Deft, Septembre 1986, Netherlands

[BeLa 86] L. Bergher, J. Laurent, J.P. Collin, B. Courtois "Towards automatic failure analysis of complex ICs through e-beam testing", International Test Conference, Washington, September 1986, USA

[GuMi 86] I. Guiguet, D. Micollet, J. Laurent, B. Courtois "Electron beam observability and controlability for the debugging of integrated circuits", ESSIRC Conference, Delft, September 1986. Netherlands

[BaCo 86] D. Bachiera, B. Courtois, "Advances in fault modeling and test pattern generation ", International Conference on Computer Design, New York, October 1986.

[FeDa 86] X. Fedi, R. David, "Some Experimental Results from Random Testing of Microprocessors", IEEE Trans. on Instrumentation and Measurement, Vol. IM-35, March 1986, pp. 78-86.

[AbTh 86] Z. Abazi, P. Thevenod-Fosse, "Markov Models for the Random Testing Analysis of Cards", 16th Fault-Tolerant Computing Symposium, Vienna (A), July 1986, pp. 272-277.

[FuDa 86] A. Fuentes, R.David, B. Courtois, "Random Testing versus Deterministic Testing for RAMs", 16th 16th Fault-Tolerant Computing Symposium, Vienna (A), July 1986, pp.266-271.

[Da 86] R. David, "Signature Analysis for Multiple output Circuits", IEEE Trans. on Computers, Vol.C-35, September 1986, pp.830-837.

Research Activities on FTC in Japan

Yoshihiro Tohma
Department of Computer Science
Tokyo Institute of Technology
Tokyo, Japan

ABSTRACT

A brief survey of research activities on fault-tolerant computing in Japan is presented with an emphasis on basic researches. Industrial developments and applications in Japan will be presented elsewhere [Ihara1986].

1. Introduction

At the first International Symposium on Fault-Tolerant Computing (which will be abbreviated as FTCS in the sequel) in 1971, the number of participants from Japan was only one. However, in 1985 it has grown up to 24 and the cumulative number of presented papers from Japan since 1971 accounts for 51. This shows the rapid growth of research activities on fault-tolerant computing in Japan. In 1980, FTCS-10 was held in Kyoto, Japan. Since then, Japan FTC Committee was organized under the frame of the Institute of Electronics and Communication Engineers (IECE) of Japan. A survey committee on fault-tolerant computing was organized by the Ministry of International Trade and Industry (MITI) of Japan in 1982 and is still continuing its effort toward technology standardization. Most recently, Technical Committee on Fault-Tolerant Systems has begun its activities in 1985 to host technical meetings 4 times a year, workshop, and other stimulation. FTCS-18 is scheduled to be held in Tokyo in 1988.

In addition to these rather formal organizations, we are enjoying informal meeting twice a year, which originates from a group of several members of universities formed just before FTCS-10.

Thanks to these local as well as international activities, many unique and interesting contributions have emerged in Japan. They include (in chronological order):

Theory of Fail-Safe Circuits Adjacent Error Detection and Correction Testability Design and Fast Test Generation Algorithm Self-Checking Design Methods Evaluation of Software Reliability System Architectures

Each of them will be briefly presented in the following sections

2. Theory of Fail-Safe Circuits

A circuit is defined to be fail-safe, if and only if it produces either the correct or the safe-side output even under the presence of fault(s) of the prescribed set. This definition is very close to that of the fault-secureness, and accordingly has close connection to that of totally self- checking circuits.

Depending on the actual implementation of applications, the safe-side outputs may be elements of a subset of the output code space normally generated from the circuit, or those out of the output code space. For example, the safe- side output may be 0 of output code space $\{0, 1\}$. Otherwise, they may be $\{00, 11\}$, while the output code space is $\{01, 10\}$. If we choose the latter, the fail-safeness turns out to be just the fault-secureness. The essential distinction between fail-safe and TSC circuits is the requirement for the existence of tests by elements of the input code space, which is normally applied to the circuit.

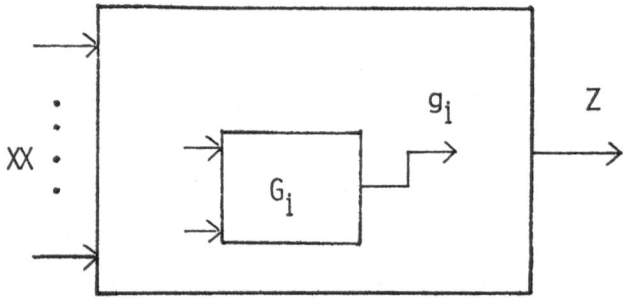

Fig. 1 Circuit structure.

The concept of fail-safe circuits itself can be traced back to the early 1960's [Hill1962]. However, the first theoretical treatment of combinational fail-safe circuits was given by Mine and Koga [Mine1967] in 1967, assuming that value 0 is the safe-side output. They showed that the monotonic contribution of the output of a component subcircuit (gate) to the primary output in Fig. 1 is the sufficient condition for the circuit to be fail-safe against a stuck-at-0 fault developed at the output of this subcircuit. Yamamoto refined this condition as the necessary and sufficient condition in 1972 [Yamamoto1972].

Consider, for example, the circuit of Fig. 2 (a), of which primary output realizes the majority-decision function of variables $x1$, $x2$, and $x3$. Note, however, that none of $g1$, $g2$, and $g3$ is positive in z, because

$$z = g1 + g2 + g3 \tag{1}$$

In this circuit, if $(g1\ g2\ g3)=(110)$ will change to (010) due to the stuck-at-0 fault at $g1$, z will take erroneously value 1 as shown in Fig. 2 (b) and therefore, this circuit does not look fail-safe. However, under the application of normal inputs, $(g1\ g2\ g3)=(110)$ and $(g1\ g2\ g3)=(101)$ never occur, nor $(g1\ g2\ g3)=(011)$. Hence, this circuit is actually fail- safe, even though the monotonicity in $g1$ (as well as $g2$ and $g3$) is violated.

Taking such situations into ·consideration, Yamamoto's theorem says: Let the primary output z be a function $Z(gg)$ of vector $gg=(g1g2...gm)$ of intermediate variables $g1$, $g2$,.., gm, where gi, $i=1$, 2,..., m is a function $Gi(xx)$ of vector $xx =(x1x2...xn)$ of primary input variables $x1$, $x2$,..., xn. Sets of all n-tuples and all m-tuples of binary values 0 and 1 are denoted by L and L , respectively. Further, M, Mc, N, and Nc are defined as follows.

$$M = \{ gg \mid xx \quad L \} \tag{2}$$

$$Mc = L - M \tag{3}$$

$$N = \{ gg \quad Mc \mid gg' \quad M, gg'>=gg,\ Z(gg')=0 \} \tag{4}$$

$$Nc = Mc - N \tag{5}$$

where >= means 'greater than or equal to'. Then, the circuit is fail-safe against a stuck-at-0 fault developed at gi, if and only if

$$gg',\ gg'' \quad M,\ gg'>=gg'',\ Z(gg')>=Z(gg'') \text{ and} \tag{6}$$

$$gg \quad N, \; Z(gg)=0 \qquad\qquad (7)$$

as shown in Fig. 3.

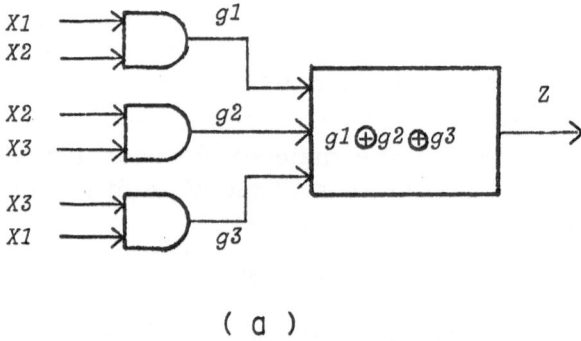

(a)

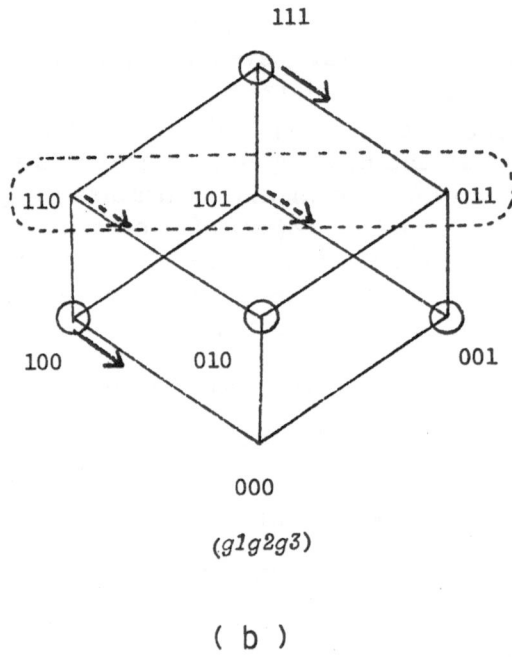

(b)

Fig. 2. Majority-decision circuit.

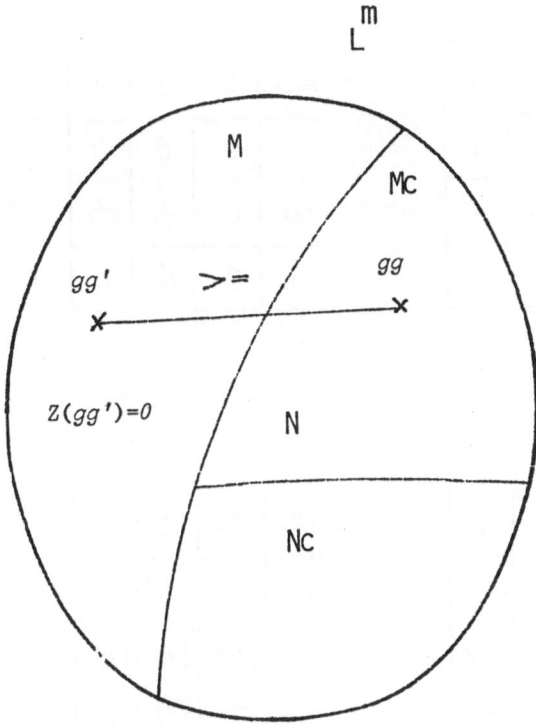

Fig. 3. Domain.

In terms of 3-value logic, various fail-safe logic systems such as shown in Fig. 4 have been argued [Hirayama1969], [Mukaidono1969],[Takaoka1971].

When a unidirectional error/fault such as stuck-at-0 fault is assumed, fail-safe sequential circuits can easily be realized by using a constant-weight code for the state as signment [Tokura1966]. However, the assumption of such unidirectional nature of error/fault looks unrealistic in circuits made of electronic components. Relaxing such restriction, Tohma et al have shown two methods to realize fail-safe sequential circuits even in the case where a faulty component subcircuit may take erroneously value 0 or 1. The first one is to use the constant-weight code state assignment as well as the combination of the AND-OR and the OR-AND types of the realization of state variable functions [Tohma1971]. Diaz et

Type- ϕ(N)

OR	0	ϕ	1
0	0	ϕ	1
ϕ	ϕ	ϕ	1
1	1	1	1

AND	0	ϕ	1
0	0	0	0
ϕ	0	ϕ	ϕ
1	0	ϕ	1

NOT	
0	1
ϕ	ϕ
1	0

Type-C

OR	0	1/2	1
0	0	1/2	1
1/2	1/2	1/2	1/2
1	1	1/2	1

AND	0	1/2	1
0	0	1/2	0
1/2	1/2	1/2	1/2
1	0	1/2	1

NOT	
0	1
1/2	1/2
1	0

Fig. 4. Fail-Safe logic.

al showed later that only one type of the realization of state variable functions was enough, claiming that the realization of one type was simpler than that of two types [Diaz1974]. However, which of AND-OR and OR-AND realizations is simpler looks to remain unsolved . The second method is to employ flip-flops for representing state variables with the parity check code [Tohma1974].

3. Adjacent Error Detection and Correction

With the advent of IC technologies for memory chips, byte-error(adjacent-error)-detecting/correcting code have become of practical significance. In 1981, Fujitsu employed for the first time in the world the byte(4-bit width)-error- correcting code in the global buffer storage of its commercial computer system M380/382.

The fundamental coding theory says that a single-byte- error-correcting (which will be denoted by SbEC in the sequel) code is simply generated by a parity check matrix of elements of

GF(2**b), of which any two column vectors are linearly independent of each other. However, the direct implementation of
mathematical operations on GF(2**b) is imperatively complicated,
requiring much hardware penalty.

In 1970 Bossen gave us the way of transforming a matrix of
elements of GF(2**b) into a binary matrix of elements of GF(2) by
using the companion matrix for the primitive generator polynomial of GF(2**b) [Bossen1970]. Following this way of interpretation, E. Fujiwara uncovered the interesting property of a matrix of
GF(2**b) where the sum of elements of any column vector reduces
to I (T**0 in terms of the companion matrix T)[Fujiwara1977]. Any
two different column vectors of such a matrix are linearly
independent of each other, and further a double error of the same
pattern at different two bytes is not confused with a single-byte
error. Thus, this type of matrices not only correct single-byte
errors but also detect a class of double-byte errors.

In order to achieve full detection of double-byte errors and
the correction of all single-byte errors, a linear code of elements
of GF(2**b) with the minimum Hamming distance 4 like Reed-
Solomon code may be employed. In this case, how ever, the choice
of numbers of rows and columns of the parity check matrix is
rather restricted. Kaneda and Fujiwara also showed the way of
merging two parity check matrices for SbEC as well as DbED
(double-byte-error-detecting) codes to relax the above restriction
[Kaneda1980].

Majority decodable codes have the advantage of fast correction of random multiple errors in spite of the necessity of larger
extent of redundancy in code words. An extension of a majority
decodable code to a SbEC code has been investigated by
Matsuzawa and Tohma [Matsuzawa1978].

4. Testability Design and Fast Test Generation Algorithm

It is well recognized that LSSD (Level Sensitive Scan Design)
was first publicized by IBM at 1977 DA Conference [Eichel-
berger1977] and has been widely employed in real applications.
Since the test for sequential circuits is difficult, the essential idea
of this design is to cut feedback loops to reduce a sequential circuit to a combinational one and to provide the circuit with a way
of shifting in and out test patterns/responses to and from latches.
However, NEC people is a little unhappy, because they presented
the similar paper earlier in 1968 [Kobayashi1968]. See Fig. 5.
Instead of serial scan-in/scan-out, Ando proposed a way to put
in/out test patterns/responses to/from latches selected by means
of addressing mechanism [Ando1980].

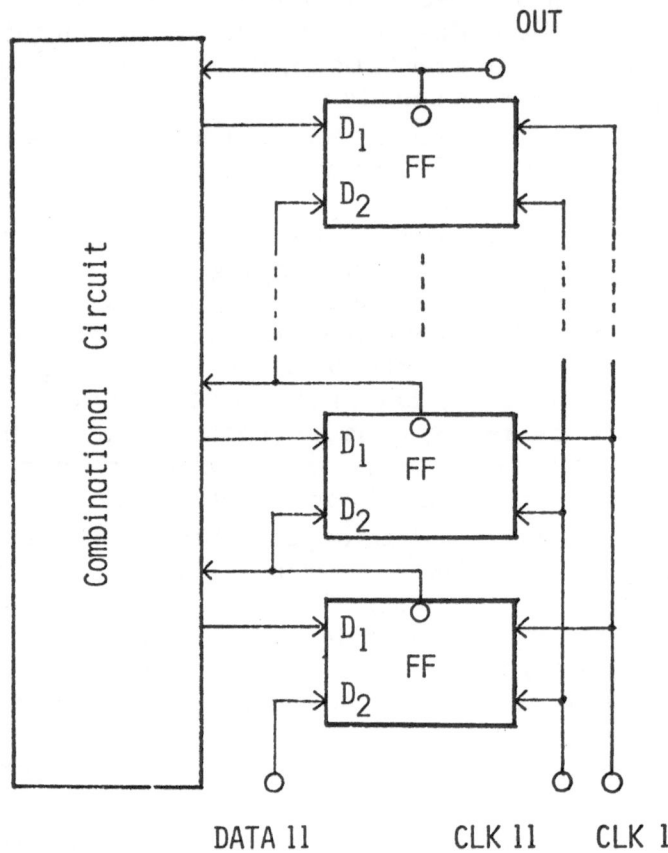

Fig. 5. NEC's proposal.

Because of the structural regularity and the ease of production, PLA is one of major constructional components of digital systems in these days of LSI/VLSI and therefore, much attention has
been focused on the test of PLAs. At FTCS-10 in 1980, two methods
concerning the test of PLAs were proposed by S. J. Hong and D. L.
Ostapko [Hong1980] and H. Fujiwara et al [Fujiwara1980], which
were surprisingly very similar to each other but found independently. The essential feature of their methods is to add extra
gates, lines, and shift registers to activate input lines and product
lines individually and to observe the parity check implemented by
the extra lines. Thus, the test patterns and the expected outputs
can be determined independently of the function which the PLA
realizes. In this configuration, however, the structural homo-
geneity is violated by the use of shift registers and EXOR gates

(which use inverters), and accordingly a considerable amount of extra area for implementing these hardware is needed. To remove the shift registers, the implementation of a PLA structure for addressing mechanism was proposed by Sato and Tohma [Sato1982]. An idea which needs no EX-OR gates for the error detection was presented by Saluja et al [Saluja1981].

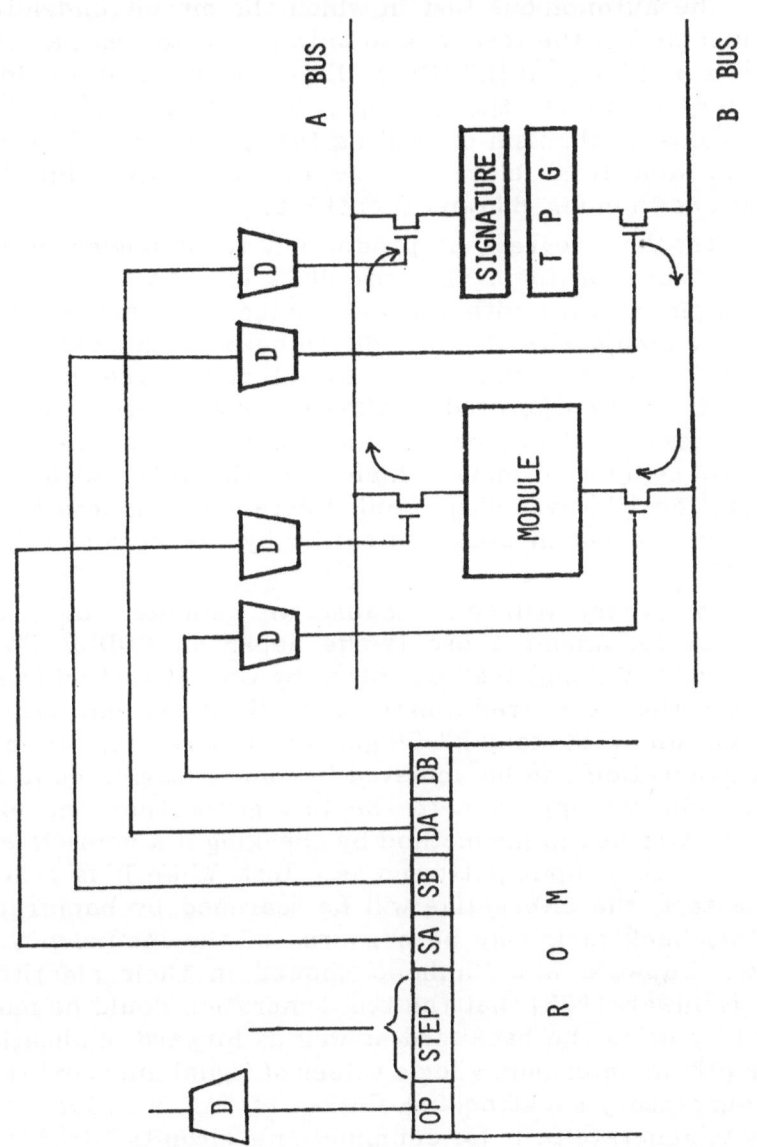

Fig. 6. Multiple use of built-in test hardware.

Another approach to cope with the difficulty in testing LSI/VLSI circuits is to use the random test. The idea of the random test itself is found in the early 1970's [Rault1971]. Since the proposal of BILBO [Koenemann1979], however, it is attracting much interest from industries, because the generation of random test patterns and the analysis of the responses (signature analysis) can be done easily by built-in linear feedback shift registers (LFSRs) and thus the necessity of an external test equipment is eliminated. The autonomous test in which the circuit under test itself was included in the feedback loop to generate test patterns was proposed by Eiki et al [Eiki1980]. Hitachi developed a chip of disccontroller, in which the multiple use of a built-in test hardware with a mechanism of routing test patterns and output responses to and from blocks to be tested in the chip was exploited as shown in Fig. 6 [Yamaguchi1984].

Along with the progress of production technologies, it will become more common for a VLSI circuit to take the form of an array of functional units with various connection schemes. However, the more complexity of a circuit increases, it is more prone to be faulty. Therefore, some means to detect and recover from errors should be incorporated. Following Shedletsky [Shedletsky1978], Furuya et al argued the implementation of the error recovery into cellular dividers, which uses the retry with data complementation [Furuya1983]. Fault-tolerant multipliers based on the similar idea was investigated earlier by Takeda and Tohma [Takeda1980].

FTCS-10 was very fruitful, because we benefited by many impressive papers. Among those is the paper on PODEM (Path Oriented Decision Making) test algorithm by Goel [Goel1980]. His paper claims that the traditional DALG (D-Algorithm) is not efficient in circuits with many EX-OR gates and more than 30 times faster test generation can be achieved in some cases. In contrast to the deterministic approach to the test generation, the high efficiency was attained in his method by checking if a heuristically determined (partial) input pattern was a test. When it is proved not to be a test, the alternative will be searched by backtrack. However, this backtrack may be a source of the inefficiency in some cases. Fujiwara and Shimono showed in their algorithm called FAN [Fujiwara1983] that the test generation could be more accelerated by using the backward as well as forward implication more efficiently in determining logic values of signal lines and thus avoiding unnecessary backtracking. Currently, FAN is de facto the fastest way to generate tests for combinational circuits.

4.1. Self-Checking Design Methods

Since the concept of totally self-checking (TSC) circuits was first introduced by Carter and Schneider in 1968 [Carter1968], this technical area has grown up to be one of major disciplines of fault-tolerant computing. Many papers on TSC checkers as well as functional circuits are still flooding at sessions of recent FTCS's.

1-out-of-n codes (one-hot codes) are used in various applications and the way of constructing TSC checkers for these codes was first given by Anderson and Metze [Anderson 1973]. Their method is to convert first the 1-out-of-n code into a k-out-of-2k code by, say, an array of OR gates and then check the latter code by a TSC k-out-of-2k code check er. In this implementation, however, 5 logic levels are required.

Quite differently, Izawa showed an interesting method which needs only 3 logic levels [Izawa1981]. In his implementation, the 1-ou-of-n code is first converted to the (n-1)- out-of-n code. Then n signal lines of the (n-1)-out-of-n code are divided into two groups in which the signal lines are ANDed with each other to convert the (n-1)-out-of-n code to the two-rail code. As shown in Fig. 7 (a), the conversion from the 1-out-of-n code to the (n-1)-out-of-n code can be performed simply by an array of n gates of OR function of all primary input lines except xi, i=1,2,...,n, respectively. However, this method cannot be employed, because the self- testing condition for the stuck-at-0 (s-t-0) fault at an input line of an OR gate is not met. Instead of feeding all (n-1) primary input lines directly to an OR gate G1 in Fig. 7 (b), an appropriate subset of primary input lines are connected to an additional OR gate (which will be called shared gate) G2 and the output of G2 together with the remaining primary input is fed to G1. The output of G2 is also connect ed to an OR gate G3, of which output is a signal line of the (n-1)-out-of-n code, belonging to a different group from that of G2. This is the reason why G2 is called the shared gate.

The idea of the shared gate was extended to the construction of TSC checkers for more general m-out-of-n codes by Nanya and Tohma [Nanya1983]. The advantage of this implementation over previous methods is obviously the minimum requirement of logic levels. However, it needs disadvantageously more gates.

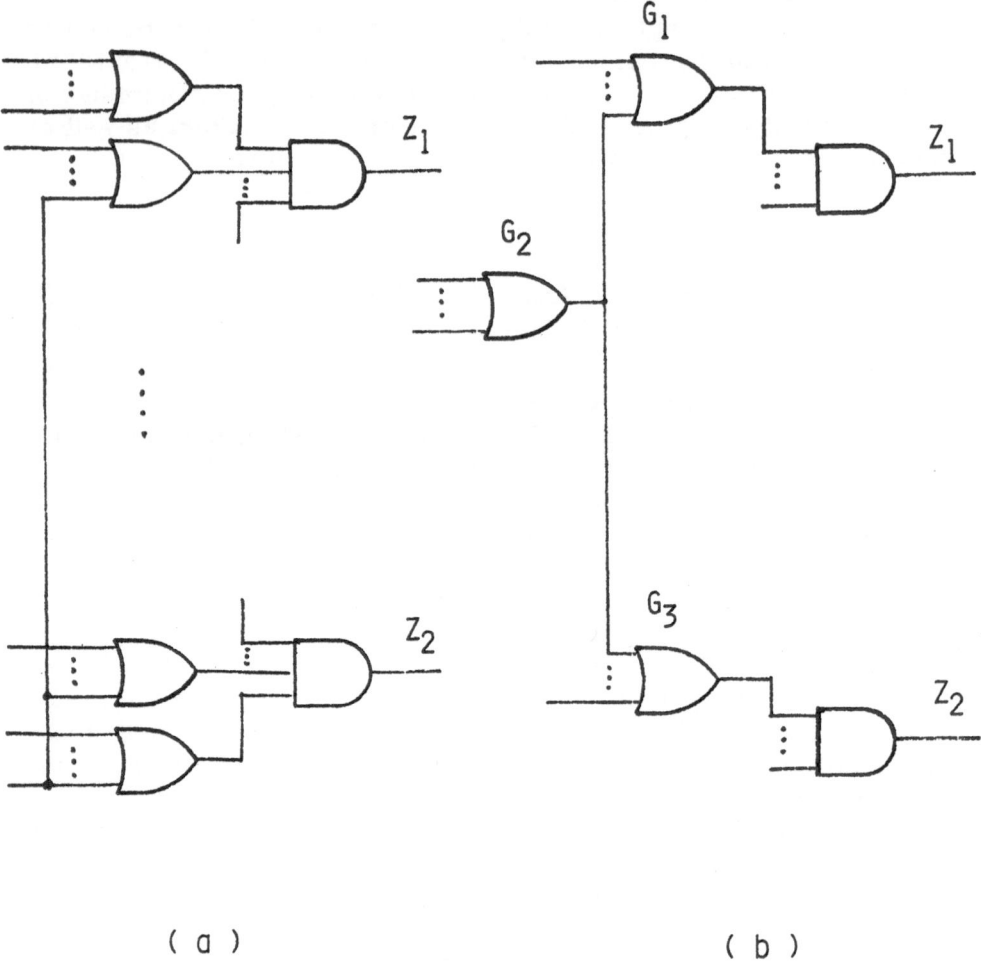

(a)   (b)

Fig. 7. TSC 1-out-of-n code checker.

In order to reduce the hardware penalty in the construction of TSC circuits, TSC checkers should be placed in a circuit as less as possible. The error secure/propagating concept was proposed for this purpose by Nanya and Kawamura [Nanya1985]. They exploited this idea in the implementation of self-checking microprocessors.

The idea of the signal reliability was first introduced by Ogus [Ogus1975]. The signal reliability of self-checking circuits was evaluated by Kwek and Tohma [Kwek1980].

5. Software Reliability Evaluation Model

It is observed recently that a considerable percentage of system failures is caused by software faults and there fore, the attainment of high reliability and fault tolerance in software has become one of key issues to reliable computing.

However, what is meant by the software reliability? We still see much controversy on the definition of software reliability. Someone is proposing as a metric the coverage of tested paths of a program, while the estimates of the number of remaining faults, error rate, and etc. are other possible candidates.

Many papers have been published on the estimate of the number of remaining faults and Yamada and Osaki's paper is among those [Yamada1985]. They argued a model of the growth of the cumulative number of detected faults in the test phase of a program, regarding the process to be a nonhomogeneous Poisson process. The model based on the hyper-geometric distribution was proposed by Tohma and Tokunaga [Tohma1986].

6. System Architectures

Beside real applications, experimental fault tolerant systems have been developed at Tohoku University and Tokyo Institute of Technology, which are all based on the triple modular redundancy. Together with a hardware mechanism of synchronization at clock level, the former employed the timeskew in order to tolerate a simultaneous disturbance to all component units of TMR [Kameyama1979]. The interrupt handler was developed for the latter called SAFE (Software Assisted Fault-tolerant Experimental) system [Yoneda1984], which is synchronized at task level by a software aid [Yoneda1985].

A fault-tolerant as well as fail-safe system was constructed at Railway Technical Research Institute, Japan National Railways and is now under the evaluation for the real application to railway interlocking systems [Kawakubo1980]. In this system, specially designed fail-safe logic IC circuits which originates from Komamiya's idea [Komamiya1966] are used partially.

A data communication technique not only recoverable from errors but also secure against intentional violation and/or wiretapping in computer networks was proposed by Koga et al [Koga1982]. Their basic idea is to divide a block of information into segments and the duplicate of each segment will be transmitted through disjoint paths to the destination. In order to make this transmission efficient, a member of each duplication is concatenated with members of other duplications to form a string in a hashed way.

A faulty link/node may prevent the normal flow of packets on such a path in a computer network that does not include the faulty link/node. A mechanism called the container concept, where a packet is conveyed from a node to the next by a container assigned to the source of the packet and ready at the node, was investigated to cope with this problem by Yoneda and Tohma [Yoneda1986].

7. Concluding Remarks

This paper has reviewed Japanese (rather academic) research activities in the context of the evolution of Fault- Tolerant Computing. Some papers which were published rather locally or might be not familiar to international FTC people were explained by using illustrations. This way of presentation is not intended to stress their relative significance.

Studies on the software reliability are currently encouraged by many forces in Japan and we expect the related papers to appear shortly.

8. References

Anderson, D. A., Metze, G., 1973: Design of Totally Self- Checking Check Circuits for m-out-of-n Codes, IEEE Trans. Comput., C-22, No.3, pp. 263-269.

Ando, H., 1980: Testing VLSI with Random Access Scan, Proc. COMPCON SPRING, pp. 50-52.

Bossen, D. C., 1970: b-Adjacent Error Correction, IBM J. Res. Develop., pp. 402-404.

Carter, W. C., Schneider, P. R., 1968: Design of Dynamically Checked Computers, Proc. IFIP-68, pp. 878-883.

Diaz, M., Geffroy, J. C., Courvoisier 1974: On-Set Realization of Fail-Safe Sequential Machines, IEEE Trans. Comput., C-23, No.2, pp. 133-138.

Eichelberger, E. B., Williams, T. W., 1977: A Logic Design Structure for LSI Testability, Proc 14th DA Conference, pp. 462 - 468.

Eiki, H., Inagaki, K., Yajima, S., 1980: Autonomous Testing and its Application to Testable Design of Logic Circuits, Digest of Papers, FTCS-10, pp. 173-178.

Fujiwara, E., 1978: Odd-Weight-Column b-Adjacent Error Correcting Codes, Trans. IECE, E-61, No.10, pp.781-787, and Fujiwara, E., Kawakami, T., 1977: Modularized b-Adjacent Error Correction, Digest of Papers, FTCS-7, pp. 199.

Fujiwara, H., Kinoshita, K., Ozaki, H., 1980: Universal Test Sets for Programmable Logic Arrays, Digest of Papers, FTCS-10, pp. 137-142.

Fujiwara, H., Shimono, T., 1983: On the Acceleration of Test Generation Algorithms, IEEE Trans. Comput., C-32, No.12, pp. 1137-1144.

Furuya, K., Akita, Y., Tohma, Y., 1983: Logic Design of Fault-Tolerant Dividers based on Data Complementation Strategy, Digest of Papers, FTCS-13, pp. 306-313.

Goel, P., 1980: An Implicit Enumeration Algorithm to Generate Tests for Combinational Logic Circuits, Digest of Papers, FTCS-10, pp. 145-151.

Hill, J., 1962 : Failsafe Circuits, Report No. 120, Digital Computer Laboratory, University of Illinois, June.

Hirayama, H., Watanabe, S., Urano, Y., 1969: Synthesis of Fail-Safe Logical Systems, Trans. IECE, 52-C, No.1, pp. 33- 40 (in Japanese).

Hong, S. J., Ostapko, D. L., 1980: FITPLA: A Programmable Logic Array for Function Independent Testing, Digest of Papers, FTCS-10, pp. 131-135.

Ihara, H., 1986 : in this Volume.

Izawa, N., 1981: 3-Level Realization of Self-Checking 1-out- of-n Code Checkers, Proc. 1981 IECE National Convention on Information and Systems, No. 504 (in Japanese).

Kameyama, M., Higuchi, T., 1979: A Method of Construction of Fault Tolerant Microcomputer Systems with TMR, IECE Technical Report, EMCJ78-57, pp. 11-16.

Kaneda, S., Fujiwara, E., 1980: Single Byte Error Correcting- Double Byte Error Detecting Codes for Memory Systems, Digest of Papers, FTCS-10, pp. 41-46.

Kawakubo, K., Nakamura, H., Okumura, I., 1980: The Architecture of a Fail-Safe and Fault-Tolerant Computer for Railway Signalling Device, Digest of Papers, TmCS, mpp37m2-4.m

Kobayashi, T., Matsue, S., Shiba, H., 1968: Flip-Flop Circuit Suitable for FLT, Proc. National Convention, IECE, No.892 (in Japanese).

Koenemann, B., Mucha, J., Zwiehoff, G., 1979: Built-In Logic Block Observation Techniques, Digest of Papers, 1979 Test Conference, pp. 37-41.

Koga, Y., Fukushima, E., Yoshihara, K., 1982: Error Recoverable and Securable Data Communication for Computer Network, Digest of Papers, FTCS-12, pp. 183-186.

Komamiya, Y., Morisawa, k., Tsuchiya, S., 1966: A Fail-Safe Logic Component Circuit, Proc. Joint Convention of Four Institutes of Electrical Engineers, No.1987 (in Japanese).

Kwek, K. H., Tohma, Y., 1980: Signal Reliability Evaluation of Self-Checking Networks, Digest of Papers, FTCS-10, pp.257-262.

Matsuzawa, K., Tohma, Y., 1977: A Way of Multiple Error Correction for Computer Main Memory, Trans. IECE, 60-D, No.10, pp.869-876 (in Japanese), and Matsuzawa, K., Tohma, Y., 1978: An Adjacent-Error-Correcting Code Based on the Threshold Decoding, Digest of Papers, FTCS-8, pp.225.

Mine, H., Koga, Y., 1967: Basic Properties and a Construction Method for Fail-Safe Logical Systems, IEEE Trans. Electron. Comput., EC-10, No.6, 282-289.

Mukaidono, M., 1969: On the Mathematical Structure of the C- type Fail Safe Logic, Trans. IECE, 52-C, No.12, pp. 812-819 (in Japanese).

Nanya, T., Tohma, Y., 1983: A 3-Level Realization of Totally Self-Checking Checkers for m-out-of-n Codes, Digest of Papers, FTCS-13, pp. 173-176.

Nanya, T., Kawamura, T., 1985: Error Secure/Propagating Concept and its Application to the Design of Strongly Fault Secure Processors, Digest of Papers, FTCS-15, pp. 396-401.

Ogus, R., 1975: Probability of a Correct Output from a Combinational Circuit, IEEE Trans. Comput., C-24, No.5, pp.573- 578.

Rault, J. C., 1971: A Graph Theoretical and Probabilistic Approach to the Fault Detection of Digital Circuits, Digest of Papers, FTCS-1, pp. 26-29.

Saluja, K. K., Kinoshita, K., Fujiwara, H., 1981: A Multiple Fault Testable Design of Programmable Logic Arrays, Digest of Papers, FTCS-11, pp. 44-46.

Sato, T., Tohma, Y., 1982: A New Configuration of PLA with Function-Independent Test, Trans. IECE, J65-D, No. 8, pp. 1073-1079 (in Japanese).

Shedletsky, J. J., 1978: Error Correction by Alternate Data Retry, IEEE Trans. Comput., C-25, No.2, pp. 106-112.

Takaoka, T., Mine, H., 1971: N-Fail-Safe Logical System, IEEE Trans. Comput., C-20, No.5, pp. 536-542.

Takeda, K., Tohma, Y., 1978: Logic Design of Fault-Tolerant Arithmetic Units based on the Data Complementation Strategy, Digest of Papers, FTCS-10, pp. 348-350.

Tohma, Y., Ohyama, Y., Sakai, R., 1971: Realization of Fail- Safe Sequential Machines using K-Out-Of-n Codes, IEEE Trans. Comput., C-20, No.11, pp.1270-1275.

Tohma, Y., 1974: Design Technique of Fail-Safe Sequential Circuits using Flip-Flops for Internal Memory, IEEE Trans. Comput., C-23, No.11, pp. 1149-1154.

Tohma, Y., Tokunaga, K., 1986: A Model for Estimating the Number of Software Faults, IECE Technical Report, FTS86-6.

Tokura, N., Kasami, T, Ozaki, H., 1966: On failsafe sequential machines, IECE Technical Report on Automata and Automatic Control, June 24 (in Japanese).

Yamada, S., Osaki, S., 1985: Software Reliability Growth Modeling: Models and Applications, IEEE Trans. Software Eng., SE-11, No. 12, pp. 1431-1437.

Yamaguchi, N., Funabashi, T., Iwasaki, K., Shimura, T., Hagiwara, Y., Minorikawa, K., 1984: A Self-Testing Method for Modular Structured Logic VLSIs, Proc. ICAD84, pp. 99-101.

Yamamoto, Y., 1972: On the Necessary Conditions for Elements of a Fail-safe Logical Circuit, Trans. IECE, 55-D, No.1, pp.68-69 (in Japanese).

Yoneda, T., Kawamura, T., Furuya, K., Tohma, Y., 1984: Fault Diagnosis and System Reconfiguration of the Fault-Tolerant System with Majority Voting, Trans. IECE, J67-D, No.7, pp. 737-744 (in Japanese).

Yoneda, T., Tohma, Y., 1985: Implementation of Interrupt Handler for Loosely-Synchronized TMR Systems, Digest of Papers, FTCS-15, pp. 246-251. The Container Concept for Relaying Packets in Fault-Tolerant Computer Networks, Digest of Papers, FTCS-16, pp. 190-195.

The Evolution of Dependable Computing in Italy

P. Ciompi
F. Grandoni
L. Strigini
Istituto di Elaborazione dell'Informazione, Pisa

L. Simoncini
Universita' di Reggio Calabria, Reggio Calabria

1. Introduction

This brief history of the evolution of dependable computing in Italy begins at the end of the sixties with the need to produce test sequences and testing tools to verify hardware implemented using discrete components. At the same time, as the relevance of a system approach to the problem of dependability had already been perceived, research work was being started in the academic world in the error detecting and correcting codes fields, and in complex system diagnosis. These studies greatly benefitted from the strong mathematical background of the researchers initially involved. This work was considerably developed during the seventies, following the technological evolution. The difficulties involved in generating tests with high coverage determined the need to embed features for easy testability and diagnosability into system design. The architectural evolution from uniprocessor to multiple processor systems, either in tightly coupled or in loosely coupled configurations, together with the medium term industrial interest in promoting prototyping efforts, particularly in the industrial process control and on-line transaction processing fields, have produced a wide range of studies covering all system aspects (physical configuration, operating systems, programming languages and environments). This interest has steadily grown up until the present days, with increased emphasis being placed on dependability attributes.

The growing interest of the Italian computer science and engineering community in dependability issues has produced several joint studies and development ventures between industrial and academic partners. A first coordinated effort, the Progetto Finalizzato Informatica, (National Computer Science Program of the Italian National Research Council CNR), involved the largest Italian electronic industries together with almost all the research and university institutions working in this area, from 1979 to 1984. Two of the three main projects, namely Project P1 "National Computer Industry" and Project P3 "Industrial Automation and Process Control", placed strong emphasis on dependability issues. Interest in joint research efforts on these issues, has recently been shown at European level, with the participation in some projects of the ESPRIT Program, recently approved by EEC.

Italian groups and individuals have been and are active in all international forums which deal with dependability. For example, Italian participation in the Annual International Symposiums on Fault Tolerant Computing and contributions to their organization, in the SAFECOMP Workshops, organized by IFAC, in the 10.4 Working Group of TC10 of IFIP, and in industrial and standardization organizations such as ECMA, EWICS, CCITT etc. has been steadily increasing.

It is worthwhile observing that the 13th Annual International Symposium on Fault Tolerant Computing was held in Milan, Italy, and the main responsibilities for the General Program Committee, and Steering Committee Chairing were assigned to Italian scientists by the IEEE Computer Society.

This paper will survey the main scientific and technical results obtained during this period. In the following Section, we describe contributions to the theory of dependability, in Section 3 the main prototyping projects of the National Computer Science Program are mentioned, Section 4 details the main industrial products which embed dependability features, and in Section 5 future trends are discussed. We hope that the information reported in this paper covers most Italian activities in this field and apologize for any unintentional omission. We have omitted work performed by Italian scientists abroad since this would overlap with other papers in this volume.

2. Theoretical Studies

2.1. Residue Codes

The importance of these codes, which have a closure property under the sum and product operations, is that they are also able to deal with errors in arithmetic units besides treating errors in data transmission. This particular feature is a result of the fact that the digits of a residue code are independent, thus eliminating the possibility of errors due to carry, and also of the absence of a natural ordering of these digits.

The necessary and sufficient conditions have been derived, so that code redundancy can be related to error detection and correction abilities, and in order to permit fault tolerant features to be obtained easily by reconfiguring and degrading the number representation field and/or the code diagnostic ability. These conditions have been obtained both for systematic codes and product (AN) codes, whereas several interesting properties have been shown for other classes of codes: codes using a magnitude index and codes using a set of non pairwise-prime moduli.

2.1.1. Systematic Codes

The necessary and sufficient conditions of residue digits up to a given error multiplicity for error detection and correction have been determined [Barsi72, 73, 74c, 78b]. Furthermore the necessary and sufficient conditions for detection and correction of subclasses of errors on single residue digits and for the concurrent detection of errors and sum overflow have been studied [Barsi74a]. New algorithms for error syndrome decoding have been proposed [Barsi78c], and these codes, together with the product codes, have been shown to be optimal in that the redundancy they use for diagnosis is minimal [Barsi77, 78b]. Fault tolerant architectures based on the use of these codes have been proposed [Barsi74c].

2.1.2. Product (AN) Codes

With reference to the redundancy needed, identical results have been obtained for AN codes [Barsi74b, 78a, 78b, 78c]. In this respect, this class of codes is equivalent to that for systematic codes and both are optimal classes.

2.1.3. Residue Codes with Magnitude Index

In this case, the representation range of the residue number system is divided into equal intervals. The magnitude index of a number is defined as an integer which locates that number in a given interval. It has been shown that the redundancy needed for diagnosis is the same as for the two previous classes of codes. These codes allow the detection of any error in the residue representation, and preserve the exact number within a given approximation [Barsi74d, 78c, 78d].

2.1.4. Residue Codes with Non-Pairwise-Prime Moduli

In this class of codes, the constraint that the moduli must be pairwise- prime is eliminated. These codes, which are considered to be very inefficient, have the peculiarity of covering a very high percentage of "random" errors. A subclass of these codes has been identified which corrects all errors in a single residue digit, most double errors and a large percentage of higher multiplicity errors [Barsi79, 80].

2.2. System Level Diagnosis

A new diagnostic model, known as BGM, has been introduced. This model differs from the well known PMC model with regard to the test invalidation hypothesis. The assumption is that a faulty unit is always detected as such whether tested by a non-faulty or by a faulty unit. The BGM model has been completely solved for both one-step diagnosability and diagnosability with repair [Barsi75, 76].

System diagnosability has also been studied on a probabilistic basis, assuming that the units composing the system have different probabilities of being faulty and that the test results are not deterministic. An algorithm, with $O(n)$ complexity, which identifies the most likely fault pattern has been proposed. This algorithm is applicable to graphs which have at least one Eulerian cycle [Barsi81].

[Ciompi75] obtained sufficient conditions for diagnosability with repair in the PMC model, which are the most stringent known, and identified design classes of quasi-optimal diagnosable with repair systems. In these classes, the number of diagnostic connections has been shown to grow linearly with diagnosability [Ciompi74, 79]. These results have been applied to the design of a bit-sliced self diagnostic mini-computer in which the self-diagnosis procedure is managed by a fail-safe control unit [Ciompi77].

The original PMC model has been generalized by assuming incomplete fault coverage for diagnostic tests in complex systems. By associating a detection probability to the tests, the relationship between the topological structure of the diagnostic connections and the system fault detection ability has been obtained [Friedman78]. Interesting invariant properties for undirected graphs with equal girth have been identified based on this topology [Simoncini80a].

Concurrent fault diagnosis has been studied with the aim of making diagnosis transparent to the user, and the feasibility of this approach has been evaluated for a meaningful subclass of systems [Friedman79], [Simoncini79a, 80b].

The extension and generalization of diagnostic models, with respect to the original PMC model, have been arranged in a unitary frame [Friedman80]. Finally, constraints in the application of theoretical models deriving from different system organizations have been studied, and the mutual relationship between organization and diagnosability parameters (diagnosis time, parallelism of execution and diagnosability level) has been derived [Simoncini79b, 80c].

The problem of syndrome decoding for diagnosability with repair in the PMC model has been investigated. Structural properties of the diagnostic graph which determine the existence of simple decoding algorithms with O(n) complexity have been identified. [Maestrini79a, 79b] refer to graphs which contain as subgraphs an optimal structure such as that introduced in [Ciompi79] and a k-rosace, respectively. In these graphs, a linear syndrome decoding algorithm is applicable if the cardinality of faults is tg<ts, where ts is the diagnosability with repair of the graph.

[Liu81] applies the previous results to the existence, in the graph, of a subgraph belonging to a class named 2-star, and analyzes some families of graphs which present this property and their decoding algorithms.

2.3. Interconnection Networks

Rerouting techniques for connection requests in interconnection networks, used in MIMD systems, have been studied. Such networks guarantee connection in spite of a given number of faults. These techniques were applied to both packed switched and circuit switched networks [Ciminiera81].

In a study of single stage recirculating-networks, the relationship between performance and fault-tolerance was modeled, and a class of networks with good performability was identified [Ciminiera82].

The diagnosability of rectangular Banyan networks has been studied, and simple diagnostic procedures have been shown to locate faults in data lines. Faults on the routing lines are much harder to locate; therefore the network design was modified with respect to its routing mechanism, and diagnostic procedures were given for the modified networks [Ciminiera84].

2.4. Testing and Verification

We only report the most recent research work. One major challenge has been the development of the technology towards VLSI, and several studies have been directed towards this topic.

In [Somenzi83, 85] a program was proposed, named PART, which produces a very compact test set for all detectable cross point defects of a programmable logic array (PLA). This program requires a low amount of CPU time and storage: this was achieved by an efficient partitioning algorithm, together with powerful heuristics. Experimental results and a comparison with competing strategies were provided.

Functional testing of VLSI has been considered [Distante85], and results toward automatic functional test pattern generation have been presented. The relationship between the operators involved in test sequences is modeled by Petri nets.

Transient and intermittent faults in VLSI devices have been considered [Antola85]. In particular, the problem of implementing a microprogrammed control unit, capable of coping with this class of errors, has been studied. Error identification is by signature analysis, and a backward error recovery scheme is implemented at microprogram level.

Work has been also done in the field of verification. [Cabodi85b] presented a methodology, based on CONLAN (which is a formal construction method for HDLs), for the formal verification of HDLs syntax and semantics. Beginning with the problem of verifying the correctness of formal languages, general approaches to language specification and verification have been investigated. The CONLAN approach has been proposed as a structured solution to the problem.

In the field of description languages, a general purpose language, named TPDL (Extended Temporal Profile Description Language), has been proposed [Cabodi85a], to express logical and temporal conditions. The use of TPDL in a hierarchical environment involving descriptions at different abstraction levels has been described. In a very recent paper [Cabodi86], an experience in using Prolog for executable specification and verification of easily testable design has been proposed.

2.5. Design Methodology

In [Ciuffoletti81a, 81b, 81c], a general methodology for fault tolerant systems has been studied for the integration of the different design aspects of dependability features. Fault treatment in the different functional levels of a design has been unified, providing a method for obtaining systems which are robust at all levels. Particular attention has been focused on attaining a high degree of fault confinement and on being able to reconfigure the system.

In parallel with more basic research, several designs for fault tolerant components and subsystems have been produced, both as a result of research work [Annaratone83], [Lamponi84a], [Stefanelli84], and as parts of research prototypes [Ravasi81].

The fault tolerant component design has received new interest with the advent of VSI and, later, WSI technology. A survey of recent activity in the field is given in [Negrini86]. [Sami83] proposed a number of reconfigurable structures for VLSI arrays, with varying degrees of complexity and fault tolerance; trade-offs between these two features were discussed. [Sami84b] discussed fault tolerance through time redundancy in similar structures.

A general formal definition of reconfiguration algorithms for VLSI/WSI arrays was published in [Negrini85a], and a new algorithm, called "fault stealing" was introduced [Sami85].

WSI components require fault tolerance strategies which allow for the possibility of clustered faults. Extensions of previous work to tolerate this class of faults are given in [Negrini85b] for the area-redundancy approach and in [Negrini85c] for the time-redundancy approach.

A relevant topic in the field of fault tolerant architectures is data protection. We mention two studies on capability-based protection. [Ancilotti83b] discussed how capability-based protection mechanisms can be incorporated into concurrent programming languages, implementing abstract data types. [Lopriore82], [Corsini84c, 84d] discuss how capabilities can be used to create user-defined protection subsystems. A full description of a capability-based, tagged memory architecture supporting user-defined abstract data types is given in [Lopriore84]. These ideas were implemented in a research prototype [Corsini82b, 83].

2.6. Distributed Systems

As multiprocessor and distributed systems became an important research topic during the seventies, several research activities were begun in Italy, dealing with different aspects of dependability potentials and problems of distributed systems.

These studies have dealt with many inter-related aspects of distributed computing and, as the main focus of research has shifted, the different problems which have gradually emerged during the development of experimental projects have been tackled.

2.6.1. Design Issues

A first class of studies have dealt with systems built of many similar, low-cost computing elements. The fault-tolerance requirement was to achieve either continuous operation or very high availability through a limited number of spare modules with on-line repair; software-based error recovery was the typical policy.

The problem here lies in the complexity of treating distributed information. Diagnosis is necessary to identify faulty modules; processes must be re-located after the failure or repair of a computer element (reconfiguration), back-up information for restarting relocated processes must be maintained during normal operation and then retrieved when needed. When a process is relocated and restarted, its state must be consistent with the states of the other processes with which it interacts. All the information used in these activities is produced at different points within the distributed system, and maintaining a global, consistent, up-to-date view of the system is not simple.

This problem may be addressed by either a centralized or a distributed management approach. The former, concentrating both information and decisions in a single locus of control, such as a supervisory computer, was simpler and sufficiently well understood, but had two important shortcomings: it created a single point of failure, and the centralized supervisor limited the expandability of the distributed system. Therefore, most research has been directed toward schemes in which all actions related to fault-tolerance are performed without any centralized supervision. This causes new problems to arise in data consistency and synchronization.

Distributed diagnosis was treated in [Negrini81, 84]. Emphasis was put on separating the different "abstraction levels" of test activity (from memory-error detection up to testing of full computer elements). System-level diagnosis, i.e. recognition of computer-element faults, is performed through local test actions:

for each computer element that must be tested, a small "jury" of other, physically close elements is created, such that it is able to perform the test, provided that at most one "juror" is faulty. The results are then propagated throughout the entire system, to guide reconfiguration.

After diagnosis, reconfiguration is usually achieved by reassigning processes to processors. This problem has been studied in [Barigazzi82a], again with the constraint that purely distributed algorithms, in which global actions must be the result of concurrent actions autonomously performed by every unit involved, should be used. [Barigazzi82b] proposed a distributed algorithm for assigning processes to processors, which is suitable for systems that are too large to compute and store static reconfiguration tables. Proofs of termination and consistency have been provided.

The most difficult problem for the class of fault-tolerance policies that have been considered is the checkpointing and rollbacking (or backward recovery) of distributed, communicating processes.

A completely process-transparent approach, investigated in [Barigazzi83], has been intended to allow easy implementation of fault tolerance without changes to existing application software. A single consistent recovery line is maintained. Recovery points for each process are periodically updated, with frequencies that are system configuration parameters. Whenever periodic updates take place, additional updates are automatically performed for other processes, to preserve the consistency of the recovery line.

Several studies focus on how checkpointing can be driven by the activity of application processes (especially interprocess communication), in order to minimize the amount of stored back-up information, or the amount of computation to be rolled-back, or any combination of the two. [Adorni81] proposed improvements to the "occurrence graph" technique for the selection of recovery points. [Corsini82] described a way of saving certifiably correct recovery points in coincidence with inter-process communication; the amount of checkpointing activity is limited by grouping processes into "process families", based on locality of communication. [Antola84a] described an implementation of conversation-like distributed recovery blocks in an iAPX432-based architecture.

A more general approach to distributed updating of recovery lines has been documented in [Ciuffoletti83, 84], [Briatico85]. Here, the main concern has been to avoid all unnecessary synchronization among distributed processes, as this is likely to become exceedingly expensive with the growth in system size. Recovery points are autonomously established and updated by each process. With every inter-process message, additional information is included on the history (checkpoints, communications, roll-backs) of the sending process. Each process uses local algorithms which permit it to establish when it needs to roll-back, and to which recovery point, and when it is convenient to save a new recovery point.

An approach to the development of fault tolerant distributed software, using a high level concurrent language, has been discussed in [Baiardi84, 86]. Language constructs were proposed which support mutual control and consensus for decisions on the distributed system state. Emphasis was placed on process structuring, parallel activation and termination control. It has been shown that both forward and backward recovery (based upon nested atomic actions) can be expressed in the proposed language. In this paper, systems with a large number of processing elements have been discussed. It has been argued that the best policies for such systems are based on forward recovery since such policies do not constrain the degree of parallelism of a computation. A methodology to increase the degree of concurrency of a computation has been proposed and its integration with recovery policies has been considered.

All the studies described so far assume message-based inter-process communication. A scheme for an environment based on remote procedure calls has been given in [Corradi83a]. This schema routes all communications pertinent to checkpointing and recovery along a "virtual ring" (a subgraph of the interconnection network), which is preserved across failures by a reconfiguration algorithm. An arbitrary number of faults can be tolerated, subject to constraints on network topology. In [Natali84], a structure for exception handling in distributed systems with remote procedure call mechanisms has been described.

2.6.2. Evaluation Issues

In parallel with the development of new design concepts for dependable distributed computing, new evaluation techniques were developed to measure dependability relevant parameters.

A new field of research is performability evaluation, i.e. a composite measure both for performance and reliability of a system, observed over a finite mission time. [Donatiello84a] has computed the probability distribution of such a measure for non- repairable systems, exploiting the acyclic property of the Markov process used in the model. A recursive formula to compute all the moments of the performability measure has been proposed by

[Iyer84]. The recursive formula is useful for both repairable and non-repairable systems.

In the data base field, work on availability and reliability in distributed data bases with data replication has been presented in [Martella80, 81, 82, 85], [Schreiber84a]. Here too, there is a very close relationship between availability and performance. This interrelationship, and directions for future research, have been discussed in [Schreiber84b].

2.7. Reliable and Robust Software

The introduction of Ada has stimulated work on language extensions aimed at improving reliability. In particular, two new syntactic constructs have been presented and their semantics and implementation issues have been discussed [Liotta85]. A comparison between these two techniques with the scope of providing a suitable evaluation method for each particular application environment has also been proposed. Starting from an analysis of the limitations of the exception handling mechanisms of Ada, [DiSanto83] has proposed an Ada dialect to facilitate the writing of reliable and robust software. In the field of program verification, an attempt has been made [Negrini83] to deduce particular properties which indicate possible sources of errors or faulty behaviour from the structure of the control flow and of relationships among program variable. In particular, it has been found that information on the termination of loops and the relevance of acceptance tests in recovery blocks can be extracted from such a structural analysis. Criteria which can be used to apply this analysis to programs with arbitrary structures have also been presented.

3. The National Computer Science Program of CNR

From 1979 to 1984, CNR promoted the National Computer Science Program. This Program was organized in three main sectors. Two of these sectors, the Project P1 "National Computer Industry" and the Project P3 "Industrial Automation and Process Control", put strong emphasis on dependability issues. In particular these issues have been present in Project P1, in the research area dedicated to "Distributed systems based on microcomputer and minicomputer systems", whereas in Project P3 dependability issues have been present in the research area dedicated to "Systems for industrial automation based on microcomputer and minicomputer systems". Several prototyping activities have been also developed. Here we shall briefly describe the MuTEAM and Cnet systems, developed in Project P1, and the MODIAC System, developed in Project P3.

3.1. MuTEAM

MuTEAM has been an experimental prototype, designed to be used for the evaluation of hardware and software design concepts.

Main features:

- Z-8001 based multiprocessor;
- high bandwidth parallel buses;
- specialized interprocessor communication units;
- control-access-list based protection of shared memory segments;
- interprocess communication through message passing only;
- type checking on interprocess communications;
- strong fault confinement;
- decentralized fault treatment.

Fig. 1 shows a block diagram of the system.

The fault hypothesis assumed in MuTEAM is that each node in the system is either completely available or faulty. Error detection and fault treatment consist of the following phases:

Error Detection. A violation of access rights or limits on a memory segment causes interrupts to the violating processor and to the processor of the node where the addressed segment resides: in both nodes, a diagnostic process is notified. Similarly, the kernel treats a set of error conditions detected during execution of the communication primitives. Periodic scheduling of the diag nostic processes provides supplementary error detection.

Error Confinement. Confinement consists of: i) deleting the access rights of the nodes diagnosed as faulty frm the memory protection tables, and ii) modifying the communication data structures to disable the pertinent logical channels.

Diagnosis. This is performed by a set of diagnostic processes (one in each node), which run tests and compare the results using a distributed algorithm. Each diagnostic process requires other diagnostic processes to run test routines on their nodes (and to report the results); the process also runs test routines on its own node on behalf of other diagnostic processes.

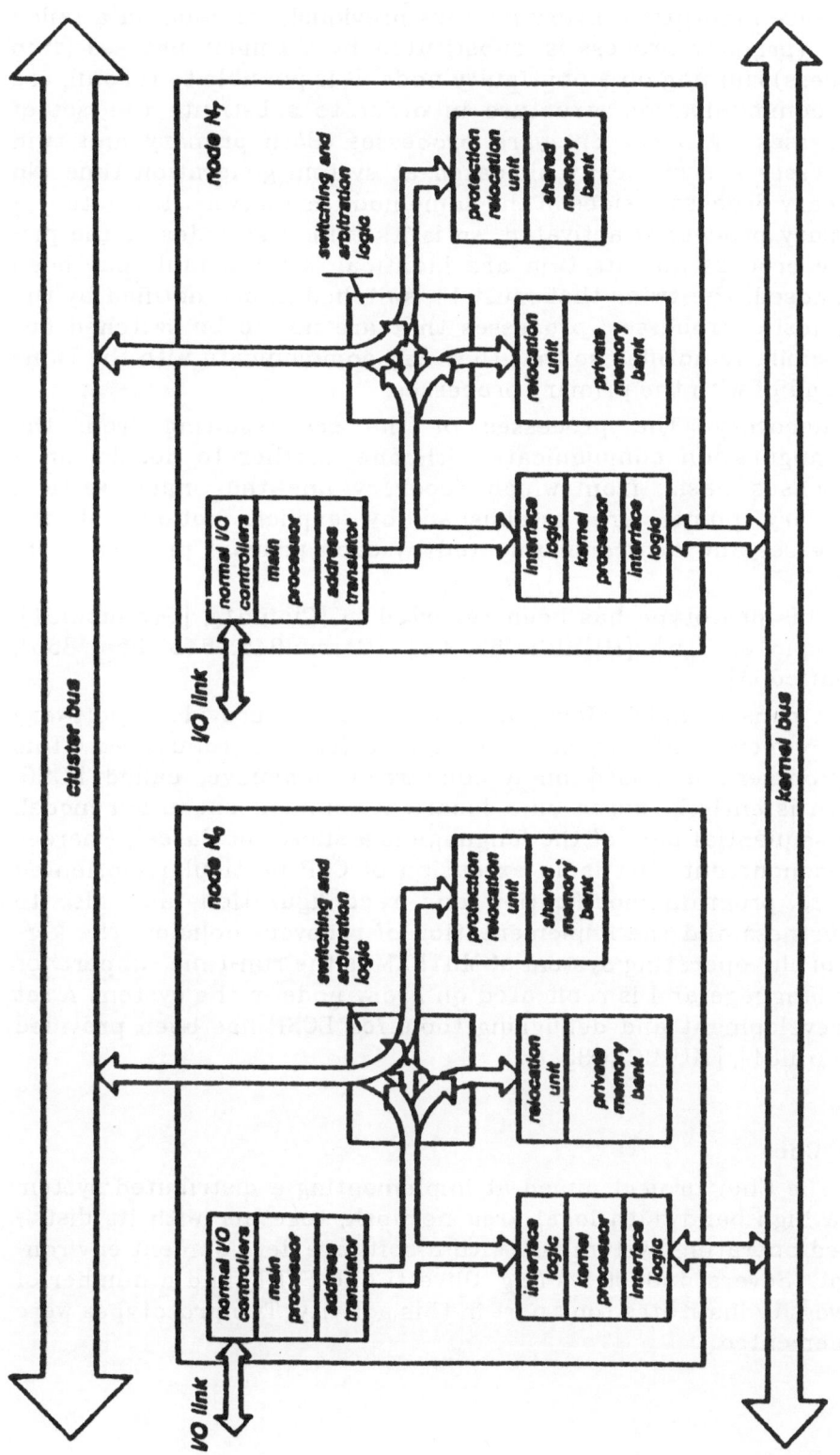

Fig. 1

Reconfiguration. Every process previously running on a failed node (primary process is substituted by a similar process (twin process) running on a non-faulty node. It is possible to reconfigure the communication structure in order to substitute this set of processes by a set of spare processes. Both primary and twin processes are statically allocated at system generation time. No primary process resides in the same node as its twin. Every time a primary process is activated, so is its twin. The codes of the primary process and its twin are identical. After a fault has been diagnosed, the twins that must be switched in are notified by the diagnostic processes; processes that are not to be switched out are similarly notified so that they can communicate with the twins instead of with the primary processes.

Recovery. The processes of the set resulting from the reconfiguration communicate with one another to decide, on a consensus basis, from which recovery line they must restart. Recovery points are established by explicit actions of the processes and are communicated by each primary process to its twin.

This prototype has been reported in [Cioffi81], [Grandoni81], [Ciompi81a, 81b], [MUMICRO83, 84], [Corsini84a, 84b, 85a, 85b], [Briatico85].

A considerable effort has been made to provide a software environment with features of modularity and robustness. This environment is based on a concurrent language, called ECSP, which is entirely based on a local environment execution model. The sequential part of the language is a subset of Pascal, whereas the concurrent part is an extension of CSP particularly oriented toward program modification and reconfiguration, and also to robustness and the implementation of recovery policies. The kernel of the operating system of MuTEAM is the run-time support for this language and is replicated on every node in the system. A set of development and debugging tools for ECSP has been provided [Baiardi81], [MUMICRO83, 84].

3.2. Cnet

The Cnet project aimed at implementing a distributed system on a high-bandwidth local area network, together with its distributed operating system and with a software development environment. Several industries (e.g. Olivetti and STET) and a number of university institutes took part in this activity. Two prototypes were implemented.

Ada has been chosen both as the system and the application language. The abstraction facilities of Ada have been extensively used in defining the communication and fault tolerance packages that are part of the run-time system resident on each node.

One of the goals of Cnet has been to provide a crash recovery mechanism for those applications that need a high degree of fault tolerance. This mechanism must be integrated in the system language. For this reason it is conceived as a set of packages which export those features needed to program reliable distributed applications in terms of atomic actions.

Properties of atomic actions have been analyzed with specific reference to crash recovery problems, and implementation schemes have been developed [Ancilotti83]. Atomicity is obtained by implementing a stable memory which provides the two primitive atomic actions, stable-read (SR) and stable-write (SW). A particular SW, called SET, is provided for saving the control state of a process.

The recovery mechanisms of Cnet have been intended to support transactional applications. Three different kinds of transactions can exist: 1) single-site transactions performed by a single process; 2) single-site transactions performed by a set of cooperating processes; 3) distributed transactions. The recovery mechanisms developed are suitable for all three kinds of transactions.

A brief description follows for the more complex cases 2) and 3). The second kind of transaction corresponds to a set of operations on stable objects, local to a site, performed by a set of local processes. These processes are created by a coordinator process, which starts the transaction as shown in Figure 2.

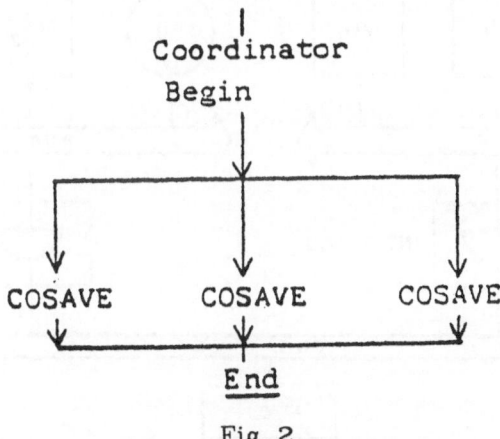

Fig. 2

This kind of transaction is similar to the concept of conversation introduced by Randell. Each participant process uses a two-phase- lock protocol to access stable objects. Each participant terminates by executing a COSAVE operation which implements a two- phase commit protocol [Ancilotti83, 84].

In the third transaction type, both the participant processes and the objects are distributed. The scheme for this transaction is an extension of the previous scheme, using both the Cnet intranode and internode communication mechanisms.

A very well organized set of documentation has been produced by the Cnet management and can be obtained on request.

3.3. MODIAC

MODIAC was a distributed computer system for industrial automation and process control structured on a local area network of multiprocessor nodes with a distributed operating system.

Main features: - the node is a Z-8001 or Z-8002 based multiprocessor;
- building-blocks approach to system configuration;
- high bandwidth parallel buses;
- fully distributed and parallel arbitration scheme;
- hardware relocation and protection mechanisms for memory management and error confinement.

One of the main characteristics of the MODIAC architecture was that flexible configurations, tailored to particular applications, can be produced. Two possible configurations are shown in Figure 3a and 3b.

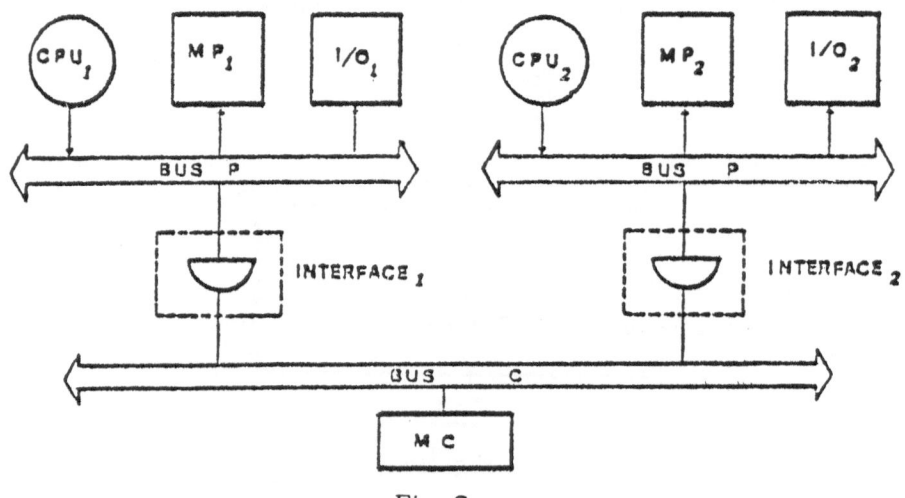

Fig. 3a

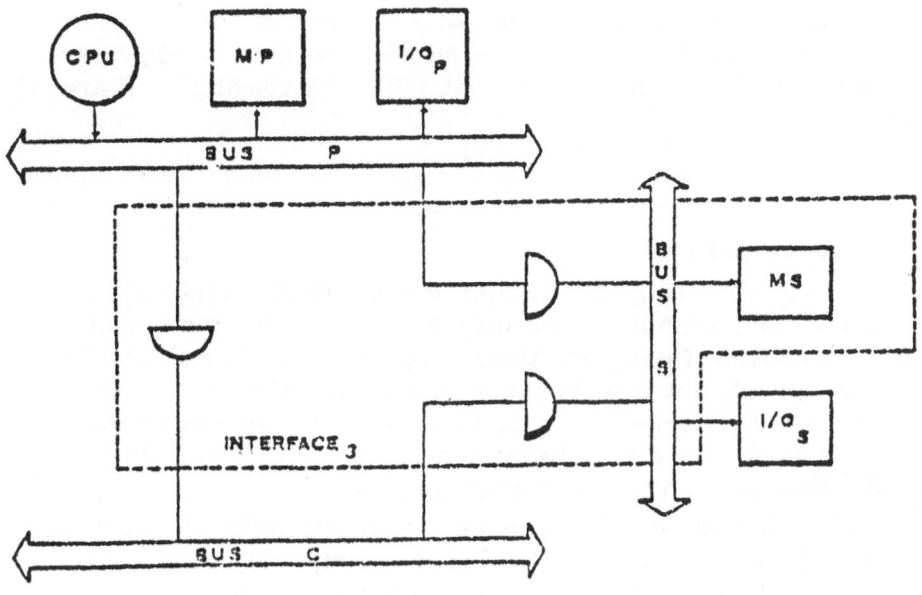

Fig. 3b

In Figure 3a, all the shared resources are connected to the
common bus, and the devices connected to the local bus are
private. In Figure 3b, the resource connected to the S bus can be
accessed by all processors connected to the C bus. This is an
example of a more efficient architecture, which reduces the
congestion on the common bus for accessing shared data. This
high flexibility is also maintained for fault tolerance, which may be
scaled according to the criticality of the application.

Control signals which allow a refinement of the basic memory
protection strategy are present in the bus. This basic strategy is
the responsibility of the MMU (Memory Management Unit), which is
on the CPU board. Protection is based on segment-limit violation
detection and control of access rights on the accessed segment.
This protection scheme is active for all memory accesses and
works in parallel with them without slowing down system operation. Basically, it is a simplified "capability" scheme. Error detection and correction codes are provided for memory. Time-outs are
provided to avoid hanging up the bus. A "processor down" signal is
provided to allow the "suicide" of a processor in a multiple
configuration.

The MODIAC architecture provided a set of mechanisms for error detection and notification, whereas fault tolerant configuration could be implemented by a suitable arrangement of multiple MODIAC nodes [Garetti82], [Rivoira82], [Faro84], [Bruno85].

4. Industrial Activity

It is not easy to give a complete account of industrial activity in dependable computing, not only because of the number of companies involved (many of them are not traditional electronic manufactures), but also because of the fact that much information is either proprietary or defense-related. The aim of this section is thus to give a handful of examples, highlighting the variety of advanced applications currently produced.

Italian industries that are active in the field of dependable computing can be classified into three groups: 1) general purpose computing; 2) telecommunications; 3) industrial controls.

In the first group, the prominent company is Olivetti, which holds a leading position among the European manufacturers of data processing equipment, from terminals to minicomputers. In its products, mainly aimed at the large office automation market, the company's goal is to achieve the best availability and maintainability figures, without using redundant architectures. Therefore R&D activities are oriented towards: a) improving diagnostic techniques: increasing fault coverage, on-line (concurrent) diagnostics, error logging and analysis, remote diagnosis; b) applying Artificial Intelligence techniques to circuit board testing; c) developing simulators for VLSI circuits in the presence of faults [Gai84], [Morpurgo85].

In the telecommunications group, the activities of Italtel, Telettra, and CSELT should be mentioned.

Italtel is the main telecommunications equipment manufacturer in Italy; its products range from home telephones to large telephone exchanges. Due to the high availability requirements of such equipment, the company has long been involved in the design and production of fault tolerant switching systems. The current family of digital exchanges for public switching networks, named Proteo 2, is a modular architecture, planned to handle from 1,000 to 100,000 subscribers. The high-end product of the Proteo 2 line is the UT 100/60 exchange, which can handle over 100,000 subscribers or 60,000 trunks. The goals of reliability and maintainability are pursued by careful managing of redundancy in the highly modular structure [Bovo84], [Bellman86].

Telettra mainly produced microwave links and frequency-division multiplexers for telephone networks up until the early seventies. From that time, it has been involved in the design of digital telephone exchanges. The first products were: DST1, a 2,000- subscriber End Office, featuring a distributed set of small processors controlling the exchange; DTN1, a 15,000-termination Toll Office for PCM switching, with duplicated stored-programs control; AFDT1, a 8,000-termination Toll Office for PCM switching, handling data as well as voice traffic. In 1983 Telettra started a project for a new system, called MIC30, which should offer a wide performance range. The basic configurations in the MIC30 family are: MIN30/S, a self-checking unit to be used as a building-block for more complex architectures, and as a work station for software development; MIC30/D, a reliable system composed by two MIC30/S processors interconnected in an active/stand-by redundant structure; MIC30M, a distributed system whose structure includes a MIC30/D and up to four MIC30/S [Bellman76], [Morganti78].

CSELT is a research firm belonging to the STET group, a government-owned holding which controls some major telecommunication companies in Italy, e.g. Italtel, Selenia, SIP (the main telephone operating company). CSELT is in charge of carrying out basic and applied research as support to the industrial activities of the STET group.

In the field of industrial control systems, several companies have developed computer (sub)systems, exhibiting various degrees of dependability, to be used in embedded applications.

Selenia has produced duplex systems, used in auxiliary functions in large telephone exchanges (e.g. in the local-call billing system TUT). For more demanding real-time applications, such as radar data processing, command and control systems, etc., Selenia has developed MARA, a multiprocessor based on 8086/80286 16-bit microprocessors. The architecture features extensive on-line checking (ECC, watch-dog timers, etc.) and a five-level, hardware supported, protection scheme. Duplex MARA configurations are also provided. A Stable Storage subsystem to support atomic transactions has been developed on MARA; a distributed redundant architecture, based on replicated copies of critical data, is currently being investigated [MARA83], [Ciompi83b, 83d] [LaManna85b].

Selenia Spazio, formerly a division of Selenia S.p.A., produces on-board satellite computers and electronics. The firm is currently involved in several ESA (European Space Agency) programs, and is the prime contractor for the Italian Communications Satellite ITALSAT project. In this activity, Selenia Spazio is designing the computer-controlled on-board switching matrix, in close cooperation with CSELT.

Nuclear activity in Italy is under the authority of a national regulatory agency called ENEA (Comitato Nazionale per la Ricerca e per lo Sviluppo dell'Energia Nucleare e delle Energie Alternative). In the specific field of dependable computing, ENEA sets certification standards for plant control systems and, in particular, is active in software certification.

Ansaldo S.p.A. is the main Italian supplier for nuclear power plants; in this field, reliability and safety are key design issues. The company is now developing a computer-based Integrated Projection and Control System (IPCS). The reliability and availability requirements will be satisfied by a distributed, modular and flexible architecture, designed to be fault tolerant, self-diagnosable and gracefully degradable. To achieve the required high safety standards, several levels of protection will be provided in the design, so that equipment failures and humans errors will be both covered. Concepts such as independency, redundancy and diversity will be applied in each design phase. The development program is now at the end of the requirements phase [Bagnasco85].

ESACONTROL S.p.A. is a company of the STET group, producing process-control systems, in particular for public transportation systems and power plants. The firm is now designing a fault-tolerant system for real-time process control, based on a TMR architecture, triplicated data acquisition devices, and majority-voted fail-safe output devices. The first application of the system will be as a traffic controller in a railway station.

Finally, we should mention that several other companies have products embedding digital subsystems with high dependability requirements. We can cite here ELSAG, STET-owned, producing multiprocessors for real-time pattern recognition; FIAT, the major car manufacturer in Italy, which produces systems for hard-real-time process control, for in-house use; COMAU, one of the world major manufacturers of industrial robots, which embeds control systems in its production.

5. Future Trends

In our opinion, the most relevant current trends in dependability- related activities in Italy can be outlined as follows:

-   in the field of business-oriented and scientific computing, the main concern of both industry and the academic world is software dependability. A considerable effort is being made towards acquiring and developing software engineering techniques and tools. Research is underway on Ada tools and specification, verification and validation methods and tools;

-   in the business machine market, there is growing customer awareness of availability problems. So far, most improvements have been made by the vendors, offering better assistance and maintenance procedures, rather than by introducing novel architectures. Generally speaking, vendor-provided hardware and software maintenance seems to be the most important dependability factor for business customers; many vendors are trying to apply AI techniques to hardware maintenance;

-   a rapidly growing subsector all over the world is on-line transaction processing. In this field, there is certainly a growing market for fault tolerant architectures and operating systems; but it is not clear how many vendors can be supported by this market. Security is another important concern, which at the moment seems to be studied in-house by specific customers (banks), rather than offered by vendors on the general marketplace;

-   the field of distributed processing is expanding slowly, due in part to the strict regulation of long-distance networks. Again, a strong concern for security is exhibited by customers (banks and the military);

-   in the field of embedded systems, a division can be made between those industries which have a long-established experience and those which are only now entering the field. The former (e.g. manufacturers of telecommunications, defense and avionic systems) have been using dependability techniques for a long time. The main work of these companies is currently in software dependability, and can profitably exploit similar research efforts mentioned above. Many companies are newcomers to the field of embedded computer systems because sophisticated control systems are now being added to formerly simpler products. Most of these companies are not electronic manufacturers. In this sector, there is a strong new demand for all aspects of dependability, both in hardware and software. Some examples are: safety and reliability in microprocessor-controlled appliances; safety of medical monitoring equipment; reliability and security in automatic teller machines. These industries are not, as a general rule, customers for advanced research, but can benefit from interaction with academia to speed up the period needed to learn dependable computing technologies.

Apart from the trends currently observable in the marketplace and in the scientific community, it may be interesting to mention some dependability-related issues with a more general social scope. We will briefly describe some plausible cause-and-effect mechanisms, which may be useful in forecasting future trends and needs:

-   customers are becoming more aware of the economic risks associated with computer unreliability. If vendors could put more effort into competing with regard to the dependability characteristics of their products, greater confidence on the users' side would ensue. Furthermore, marketing emphasis on dependability would help educate customers, with a feed-back effect on the vendors' attitude;

-   certification procedures are still being produced, mainly as a result of concern by large (especially government) customers with an interest in critical applications. Adaptation of such procedures to the needs of a less limited marketplace, so that they can be used by vendors to state a guaranteed dependability level, and (for test procedures) by customers as an acceptance test for products they purchase, would have a great impact on the process described in the previous point;

-   within the computer industry itself, the main problems are organizational and educational. In most system and software companies there is ample space for improvement of dependability standards by means of organizational changes: creation of internal reliability/safety programs; managerial emphasis on software quality, e.g. by explicitly including it in productivity indexes. A relevant improvement can also come from more systematic acquisition and analysis of data regarding problems in the field. Of course, all these developments are bound to interact with changes in the customers' attitude, as stated above;

- the recent rapid growth of component and subsystem reliability has generated overconfidence in some sectors of the industry that dependability problems were going to disappear. Instead, requirements for new systems have been upgraded until these problems reappear at the system level. If the techonology keeps growing at such a fast pace, it is possible that such cycles could occur again;

- fast computerization of many critical tasks (i.e. tasks where, however small the probability of failures, the cost of a failure is very high) implies that awareness of dependability problems is going to be required not only from technical decision-makers, but from politicians (and voters) as well. As in all complex technologies, there is danger both in lack of information and in an abundance of uncomprehensible information (i.e. people may blindly refuse computers or blindly accept them: both attitudes may be dangerous);

- in order to improve computer literacy, basic programming courses are being introduced in primary and secondary school. This is likely to produce a marked increase in familiarity with computers in the coming generations. For all courses above a very basic level, some attention should be devoted to dependability problems in order to avoid creating overconfidence, with possible ensuing disappointment and backlash. Another possible (though not very probable) risk is that the marketplace be flooded with low-cost, low-quality programmers. This might interfere with the previously mentioned vendor-customer relationship and with organizational evolution, possibly perturbing the action of economic factors favouring quality improvement and market clarification.

Due to the relative youth and fast growth of computer technology, there is a visible gap between the state of the art and the quality of what is available on the marketplace. Dependability is one of the aspects in which this gap is most evident. The user community is not yet sufficiently knowledgeable to impose quality standards and the manufacturers cannot put newer techniques into use fast enough to close the gap. In this respect, significant improvement in the dependability of computers, which is essential if the advantages of computerization are to be spread over a larger part of the community, can be expected as a result of the technical advancement in industry and the growing competence of customers and of the general public. In a word, it is a matter of education, rather than of new research.

However, another phenomenon can be observed. With the powerful growth of the component technology and a history of successes in computer applications, requirements on computer systems are constantly being increased, in terms of both power and complexity: supercomputers, networks of embedded computers controlling fully automated plants or defense machinery, human organizations in which the computer is fully integrated and a crucial assistant in communication and decision-making. All of these systems, now in various stages of development from conception and deployment, have strong dependability requirements, which it will only be possible to satisfy by research into the new problems they create.

6. References

[Adorni81] Adorni, A., Boccalatte, A., Di Manzo, M., "Modello di Recovery per Sistemi Concorrenti", Proc. AICA 81, Pavia, Sept. 1981, pp. 493-499

[Ancilotti83a] Ancilotti, P., Fusani, M., "Implementation Schemes "Implementation Schemes for a Crash Recovery Mechanism", CNET Internal Report No. 79, Proc. International Computing Symposium, Nurnberg, Mar. 1983 .

[Ancilotti83b] Ancilotti, P., Boari, M., Lijtmaer, N., "Language Features for Access Control", IEEE Trans. on Software Engineering, Vol. SE-9, No. 1, Jan. 1983, pp. 16-24.

[Ancilotti84] Ancilotti, P., Fusani, M., "Distributed Algorithm "Distributed Algorithm for Deadlock Detection in Distributed Systems", Proc. First International Symposium on Applied Informatics, Innsbruck, Feb. 1984.

[Ancilotti85] Ancilotti, P., Fusani, M., "Support for Transaction and Recovery in CNET Applications", IEEE Computer Architecture TC, Newsletter, June 1985.

[Annaratone82] Annaratone, M., Sami, M. G., "An Approach to Functional Testing of Microprocessors", Proc. FTCS-12, Santa Monica, June 1982.

[Annaratone83] Annaratone, M., Stefanelli, R., "A Multiplier with Multiple Error Correction Capabilities", Proc. 6th Symposium on Computer Arithmetic, IEEE, Aarhus, 1983. Computer Arithmetic, IEEE, Aarhus, 1983.

[Antola84a] Antola, A., Scarabottolo, N., "Backward Error Recovery in Concurrent Environment", Proc. EUROMICRO, Copenhagen, Aug. 1984, pp. 45-52.

[Antola84b] Antola. A., Scarabottolo, N., "Concurrent Programming Robustness", Proc. COMPSAC, , Chicago, Nov. 1984, pp. 333-339.

[Antola85] Antola, A., Negrini, R., Sami, M. G., Scarabottolo, N., "Transient Fault Management in Microprogrammed Units: A Software Recovery Approach", Proc. EUROMICRO, Brussels, Sept. 1985, pp.453-461.

[Bagnasco85] Bagnasco, S., Manzo, F., Piazza, F., "Requirements and Design for a Distributed Computerized System for Safety and Control Applications", Proc. SAFECOMP 85, Como, Oct. 1985, pp. 85-94.

[Baiardi81] Baiardi, F., Fantechi, A., Tomasi, A., Vanneschi, M, "Mechanisms for a Robust Multiprocessing Environment in the MuTEAM Kernel", Proc. FTCS-11, Portland, June 1981, pp. 20-24.

[Barigazzi82a] [Barigazzi82a]. Barigazzi, G., Ciuffoletti, A., Strigini, L., "Reconfiguration Procedure in a Distributed Multiprocessor Systems", Proc. FTCS-12, Santa Monica, June 1982, pp. 71-76.

[Barigazzi82b] Barigazzi, G., Ciuffoletti, A., Strigini, L., "A Distributed Algorithm for Post-Failure Load Redistribution", Proc. 3rd International Conference on Distributed Computing Systems, Miami, Oct. 1982, pp. 73-80.

[Barigazzi83] Barigazzi, G., Strigini, L., "Application- Transparent Setting of Recovery Points", Proc. FTCS-13, Milano, June 1983, pp. 48-55.

[Barsi72] Barsi, F., Maestrini, P., "Arithmetic Error Correction in Redundant Residue Number Systems", Proc. of Colloque International sur la Conception et Maintenance des Automatismes Logiques", Toulouse, Sept. 1972.

[Barsi73] Barsi, F., Maestrini, P., "Error Correcting Properties of Redundant Residue Number Systems", IEEE Trans. on Comp., Vol.C- 22, No. 3, Mar. 1973, pp. 307-315.

[Barsi74a] Barsi, F., Maestrini, P., "Concurrent Detection of Additive Overflow and Arithmetic Errors in Residue Codes", Calcolo, Vol. 11, No. 2, June 1974, pp. 1-24.

[Barsi 74b] Barsi. F., Maestrini, P., "Error Detection and Correction by Product Codes in Residue Number Systems", IEEE Trans. on Comp., Vol.C-23, No. 9, Sept. 1974, pp. 915-924.

[Barsi74c] Barsi, F., Maestrini, P., "Fault-Tolerant Computing by Using Residue Number Systems", Proc. International Computing Symposium, 1973, edited by Gunther, Levrat, Lipps, North Holland Publishing Company, 1974, pp. 225-230.

[Barsi74d] Barsi, F., Maestrini, P., "Error Detection in Residue Number Systems with Magnitude Index", Proc. International Symposium on Discrete Systems, Riga, Oct. 1974.

[Barsi75] Barsi, F., Grandoni, F., Maestrini, P., "Diagnosability of Systems Partitioned into Complex Units", Proc. FTCS-5, Paris, June 1975.

[Barsi76] Barsi, F., Grandoni, F., Maestrini, P., "A Theory of Diagnosability of Digital Systems", IEEE Trans. on Comp., Vol.C- 25, No. 6, June 1976, pp. 585-593.

[Barsi77] Barsi, F., Maestrini, P., "Arithmetic Codes in Residue Number Systems", Abstracts of papers of the 1977 International Symposium on Information Theory, Ithaca, Oct. 1977, p.131.

[Barsi78a] Barsi, F., Maestrini, P., "A Class of Multiple-Error Correcting Arithmetic Residue Codes", Information and Control, Vol. 36, No. 1, Jan. 1978, pp. 28-41.

[Barsi78b] Barsi, F., Maestrini P., "Arithmetic Codes in Residue Number Systems", Digital Processes, Vol. 4, No. 2, pp. 121-135, Summer 1978.

[Barsi78c] Barsi, F., Maestrini, P., "Improved Decoding Algorithms for Arithmetic Residue Codes", IEEE Trans. on Inform. Theory, Vol. IT-24, No. 5, Sept. 1978, pp. 640-643.

[Barsi78d] Barsi, F., Maestrini, P., "Error Codes in Residue Number Systems with Magnitude Index", Calcolo, Vol. 15, No. 3, Sept. 1978, pp. 299-316.

[Barsi78e] Barsi, F., Maestrini, P., "Arithmetic Codes in Residue Number Systems with Magnitude Index", IEEE Trans. on Comp., Vol. C-27, No. 12, , Dec. 1978, pp.1185-1188.

[Barsi79] Barsi, F., Maestrini, P., "A Class of Error Correcting Codes Constructed in Residue Number Systems with Non-Prime Moduli", Abstracts of Papers of the 1979 International Symposium on Information Theory, Grignano, June 1979.

[Barsi80] Barsi, F., Maestrini, P., "Error Codes Constructed in Residue Number Systems with Non-Pairwise-Prime Moduli", Information and Control, Vol. 46, No. 1, July 1980, pp. 16-25.

[Barsi 81] Barsi, F., "Probabilistic Syndrome Decoding in Self-Diagnosable Digital Systems", Digital Processes, Vol. 7, No. 1, , Jan. 1981, pp. 33-46.

[Bellman76] Bellman, A., "Redundancy Design Approach Applied to Electronic Telephone Exchange Realizations", Proc. FTCS-6, Pittsburgh, June 1976, pp. 9-15.

[Bellman86] Bellman, A., "Switching Architectures Towards the Nineties", Proc. 1986 International Zurich Seminar on Digital Communications, Zurich, Mar. 1986.

[Bovo84] Bovo, A., Bellman, A., "UT100/60. An Electronic Digital Family of Exchanges for Large Capacity Applications", Proc. ISS'84, Florence, May 1984.

[Briatico84] Briatico, D., Ciuffoletti, A., Simoncini, L., "A Distributed Domino-Effect Free Recovery Algorithm". Proc. 4th Symposium on Reliability in Distributed Software and Database Systems, Silver Spring, Oct. 1984.

[Briatico85] Briatico, D., Ciuffoletti, A., Simoncini, L., Strigini. L., "An Implementation of Error Detection and Fault Treatment for the MuTEAM Prototype", IEEE Distributed Processing TC Newsletter, Oct. 1985.

[Bruno85] Bruno, G., Ciminiera, L., "MODIAC: A Distributed System for Industrial Automation", IEEE Computer Architecture TC Newsletter, June 1985.

[Cabodi85a] Cabodi, G., Camurati, P., Prinetto, P., "TPDL: A Language to Describe Temporal Conditions from Behaviour to Electric Level", Proc. EUROMICRO, Brussels, Sept. 1985, pp.487-495.

[Cabodi85b] Cabodi, G., Camurati, P., Prinetto, P., "The Use of CONLAN in Formal Syntactic and Semantic Verification of Hardware Description Languages", Proc. EUROMICRO, Brussels, Sept. 1985, pp. 497-606.

[Cabodi86] Cabodi, G., Camurati, P., Prinetto, P., "The Use of Prolog for Executable Specification and Verification of Easily Testable Designs", Proc. FTCS-16, Vienna, July 1986.

[Capizzi83] Capizzi, G., Cianci, C., Melgara, M., "An Easily Testable Speech Synthesizer", Proc. EUROMICRO, Madrid, Sept. 1983.

[Ciaramella79] Ciaramella, A., "Testing of Microprogrammed Units", Proc. FTCS-9, Madison, June 1979.

[Ciminiera81] Ciminiera, L., Serra, A. "Tolleranza ai Guasti e Tecniche di Reinstradamento nelle Reti di Interconnessione", Proc. AICA 81, Pavia, Sept. 1981, pp. 601-606.

[Ciminiera82] Ciminiera, L., Serra, A. "Performance-Fault Tolerance Tradeoffs in Single Stage Connecting Networks", Proc.
FTCS-12, Santa Monica, June 1982, pp. 209-212.

[Ciminiera84] Ciminiera, L., "Design for Diagnosability Issues in
Rectangular Banyan Networks", Proc. FTCS-14, Kissimee,
Florida, June 1984, pp. 178-183.

[Cioffi81] Cioffi, G., Corsini, P., Frosini, G., Lopriore, L., "MuTEAM:
Architectural Insights of a Distributed Multimicroprocessor
System", Proc. FTCS-11, Portland, June 1981, pp. 17-19.

[Ciompi74] Ciompi, P., Simoncini, L., "The Boundary Graphs: An
Approach to the Diagnosability with Repair of Digital Systems",
Proc. 3rd Texas Conference on Computing Systems, Austin,
Nov. 1974.

[Ciompi75] Ciompi, P., Simoncini, L., "Fault Detection and Diag-
nosis of Digital Systems: A Review", Proc. 3rd International
Seminar on "Applied Aspects of the Automata Theory", Varna,
June 1975.

[Ciompi77] Ciompi, P., Simoncini, L., "Design of Self-Diagnosable
Minicomputers Using Bit Sliced Microprocessors", Journal of
Design Automation and Fault Tolerant Computing, Vol. I, No. 4,
Oct. 1977, pp. 363-375.

[Ciompi79] Ciompi, P., Simoncini, L., "Analysis and Optimal Design
of Self Diagnosable Systems with Repair", IEEE Trans. on
Comp., Vol. C-28, May 1979, pp. 362-365.

[Ciompi81a] Ciompi, P., Grandoni, F., Simoncini, L., "Distributed
Diagnosis in Multiprocessor Systems: The MuTEAM Approach",
Proc. FTCS-11, Portland, June 1981, pp. 25-29.

[Ciompi81b] Ciompi, P., Grandoni, F., Simoncini, L., "Self- Diagnosis
in Multiprocessor Systems: The MuTEAM Approach", Proc.
FTSD, Brno, Sept. 1981, pp. 193-199.

[Ciompi83a] Ciompi, P., La Manna, M., Lissoni, C., Martin, I. R.,
Simoncini, L., "A Proposal for Highly Available Multiprocessor
System", Proc. 5th International Conference on Control Sys-
tem and Computer Science, Bucharest, June 1983.

[Ciompi83b] Ciompi, P., La Manna, M., Lissoni, C., Martin, I. R.,
Simoncini, L., "A Highly Available Multiprocessor System for
Real- Time Applications", Proc. SAFECOMP 83, Cambridge, Sept.
1983.

[Ciompi83c] Ciompi, P., La Manna, M., Lissoni, C., Simoncini, L.,
"Proposta per un Sistema Distribuito Fault-Tolerant per Appli-
cazioni Real-Time", Proc. AICA 83, Napoli, Sept. 1983.

[Ciompi 83d] Ciompi, P., La Manna, M., Lissoni, C., Simoncini, L., "A Redundant Distributed System Supporting Atomic Transactions for Real-Time Control", Proc. 1983 Real-Time Systems Symposium, Arlington, Virginia, Dec. 1983 and in Actes Journees Europeennes d'Etude sur les Systemes Informatiques Distribues, Le Mont Saint Michel, Sept. 1983, pp. 45-50.

[Ciuffoletti81a] Ciuffoletti, A., Simoncini, L. "Design of Multilevel Fault Tolerant Systems", Workshop on Self-Diagnosis and Fault Tolerance, Tubingen, July 1981 e in Self Diagnosis and Fault Tolerance, ATTEMPTO Verlag, Tubingen GmbH, pp. 65-83.

[Ciuffoletti81b] Ciuffoletti, A., Simoncini, L., "Integrated Design Methodology of Failure Tolerant Systems", Proc. FTDS, Brno, Sept. 1981, pp. 49-53.

[Ciuffoletti81c] Ciuffoletti, A., Simoncini, L., "Structured Design of Failure Tolerant Systems", Proc. AICA 81, Pavia, Sept. 1981, pp. 587-593.

[Ciuffoletti83] Ciuffoletti, A., "Specifiche per un Algoritmo di Error Recovery Distribuito", Proc. AICA 83, Napoli, Sept. 1983, pp. 325-341.

[Ciuffoletti84] Ciuffoletti, A., "Error Recovery in Systems of Communicating Processes", Proc. 7th Int. Conference on Software Engineering, Orlando, Mar. 1984, pp. 6-17.

[Corradi83a] Corradi, A., Natali, A., "Towards Fault Tolerance in Distributed Systems Via Replication of Data: An Implementation", Proc. FTCS-13, Milano, 1983, pp. 14-23.

[Corradi83b] Corradi, A., Natali, A., "A Fault Tolerant Implementation of Rendez-vous in a Distributed Environment". Communication in Distributed Systems. Informatik-Fachberichte, Springer Verlag 1983.

[Corsini82a] Corsini, P., Lopriore, L., Strigini, L., "A Proposal for Fault-Tolerance in a Multiprocessor System", Proc. 20th Annual Allerton Conference, Monticello, Oct. 1982, pp. 996-1007.

[Corsini82b] Corsini, P., "Z8001-Based Central Processing Unit with Capability Addressing", Electronics Letters, Vol. 18, No. 18, Sept. 1982, pp.780-782.

[Corsini83] Corsini, P., "Intelligent Memory Subsystem Supporting Memory Virtualisation", Electronics Letters, Vol. 19, No. 7, March 1983, pp.265-266.

[Corsini84a] Corsini. P., Simoncini, L., Strigini, L., "MuTEAM: A Multimicroprocessor Architecture with Decentralized Fault Treatment" Proc. 17th Annual Hawaii, Intern. Conf. on System Sciences, Jan. 1984, and in Actes de Journees Europeennes d'Etude sur les Systemes Informatiques Distribues, Le Mont Saint Michel, Sept. 1983.

[Corsini84b] Corsini, P., Simoncini, L., Strigini, L., "The Architecture and the Fault Treatment of MuTEAM", Proc. 2nd GI/NTG/GMR Conference on Fault Tolerant Computing Systems, Bonn, Sept. 1984.

[Corsini84c] Corsini, P., Frosini, G., Lopriore, L., "The Implementation of Abstract Objects in a Capability Based Addressing Architecture", The Computer Journal, Vol. 27, No. 2, 1984, pp. 127-134.

[Corsini84d] Corsini, P., Frosini, G., Lopriore, L., "Distributing and Revoking Access Authorizations on Abstract Objects: A Capability Approach", Software-Practice and Experience, Vol. 14(10), Oct. 1984, pp. 931-943,.

[Corsini85a] Corsini, P., Simoncini, L., Strigini, L., "The MuTEAM Distributed Multiprocessor Architecture", IEEE Computer Architecture TC Newsletter, June 1985.

[Corsini85b] Corsini, P., Prete, C. A., Simoncini, L., "MuTEAM: An Experience in the Design of Robust Multimicroprocessor Systems", Journal of Computer Systems Science and Engineering, Butterworths, Vol. 1, No. 1, Oct. 1985.

[Crespi83] Crespi Reghizzi, S., Natali, A., "Software Tools for Adding Fault-Tolerance to Concurrent, Distributed Programs", Actes de Journees Europeennes d'Etude sur les Systemes Informatiques Distribues, Le Mont Saint Michel, Sept. 1983.

[DiSanto83] Di Santo, M., Nigro, L., Russo, W., "Programming Reliable and Robust Software in ADA", Proc. FTCS-13, Milano, June 1983, pp. 196-203.

[Distante85] Distante, F., "A Petri Net Matrix Approach in VLSI Functional Testing", Proc. EUROMICRO, Brussels, Sept. 1985, pp. 347-355.

[Donatiello] Donatiello, L., Iyer, B. R., "Analysis of a Composite Performance Reliability Measure for Fault Tolerant Systems', IBM RC 10325, NY., to appear in ACM.

[Faro84] Faro, A., et al., "The MODIAC Local Communication Network for Process Control", Proc. 1st. Int. Conf. on Computers and Applications, Beijing, June 1984, pp.669-676.

[Friedman78] Friedman, A. D., Simoncini, L., "Incomplete Fault Coverage in Modular Multiprocessor Systems", Proc. ACM Annual Conference 1978, Washington, D. C., Dec. 1978, pp. 210-216.

[Friedman79] Friedman, A. D., Simoncini, L., "Concurrent Diagnosis in Parallel Systems", Proc. 1979 International Conference on Parallel Processing, Bellaire, Aug. 1979, pp. 270- 286.

[Friedman80] Friedman, A. D., Simoncini, L., "System Level Fault Diagnosis", Computer, Vol. 13, No. 3, Mar. 1980, pp. 47-53.

[Gai84]Gai, S., Mezzalama, M., Olla F., "Optimal Algorithms for PLA Testing", Olivetti Res. & Tech. Review No. 1/1984.

[Garetti82]Garetti, P., Laface, P., Rivoira, S., "MODIAC: A Modular Distributed Operating System Kernel for Real-Time Process Control", the EUROMICRO Journal, Vol. 9, No. 4, Apr. 1982, pp. 201-213.

[Giovannetti81] Giovannetti, G., Tucci, S., "Valutazione di uno Schema di Recovery per una Base di Dati Distribuita", Proc. AICA 81, Pavia, Sept. 1981, pp. 741-750.

[Grandoni81] Grandoni, F., Baiardi, F., Cioffi, G., Ciompi, P., Corsini, P., Fantechi, A., Frosini, G., Lopriore, L., Simoncini, L., Tomasi, A., Vanneschi, M., "The MuTEAM System: General Guidelines", Proc. FTCS-11, Portland, June 1981, pp. 15-16.

[Iyer] Iyer, B.R., Donatiello, L., Heidelberger, P., "Analysis of Performability for Stochastic Models of Fault-Tolerant Systems", IBM RC 10719, M. Y., to appear on IEEE Trans. on Comp.

[LaManna85a] La Manna, M., Simoncini, L., "An Implementation of Optimistic Policy for Concurrency Control on a Computer Network for Real-Time Applications", Microprocessing & Microprogramming, North Holland Pub. Co. 1985.

[LaManna85b] La Manna, M., "Real Time Systems with Highly Reliable Storage Media: A Case Study", Proc. SAFECOMP 85, Como, Oct. 1985, pp. 79-84.

[Lamponi84] Lamponi, P., Maggioni, V., "A Fault-Tolerant Interface for a Fiber-Optics Lan", Proc. EUROMICRO, Copenhagen, Aug. 1984, pp. 79-86.

[Liotta85] Liotta, L., Sciuto, D., "Static and Dynamic Redundancy: Proposal and Evaluation of Two Constructs of Software Fault Tolerance", Proc. EUROMICRO, Brussels, Sept. 1985, pp. 463-473.

[Liu81] Liu, C. L., Maestrini, P., "On the Sequential Diagnosability of Digital Systems", Proc. FTCS 11, Portland, June 1981, pp. 112-115.

[Lopriore82] Lopriore, L., "User-Defined Protection Subsystems in Capability Architectures", Proc. AICA 82, Padova, Oct. 1982, pp. 613-621.

[Lopriore84] Lopriore, L., "Capability Based Tagged Architectures", IEEE Trans. on Comp., Vol. C-33, No. 9, Sept. 1984, pp. 786-803.

[Maestrini79a] Maestrini, P., "A Connection Assignment Yielding Easily Diagnosable Systems", Proc. FTSD, Brno, 1979.

[Maestrini79b] Maestrini, P., "Complexity Aspects of a Class of Digital Systems", Proc. 17th Annual Allerton Conference, Allerton House, 1979, pp. 329-338.

[MARA83] Several Authors, "Tecniche di Tolleranza ai Guasti per MARA", Volume Collana Sottoprogetto P1, Obiettivo MUMICRO, PFI, Dec. 1983.

[Martella80a] Martella, G., Ronchetti, B., Schreiber, F., "Una Proposta per un Metodo di Analisi della Disponibilita' nelle Basi di Dati Distribuite", Proc. AICA 80, Bologna, Oct. 1980, pp. 1515-1530.

[Martella80b] Martella, G., Schreiber, F., "Improving Access Interference in Distributed Databases", Proc. 18th Allerton Conference on Communication, Control and Computing, Monticello, Oct. 1980.

[Martella81] Martella, G., Ronchetti, B., Schreiber, F., "On Evaluating Availability in Distributed Database Systems', in Performance Evaluation, Vol. 1, Nov. 1981, pp. 201-211; also in Proc. 5th Berkeley Workshop on Distributed Data Management Comput. Networks, Feb. 1981.

[Martella82] Martella G., Pernici. B., Schreiber, F., "Distributed Data Base Reliability Analysis and Evaluation", in Proc. 2nd Symposium on Reliability in Distributed Software and Database Systems, Pittsburgh, July 1982, pp. 94-102.

[Martella85] Martella, G., Pernici, B., Schreiber, F. "An Availability Model for Distributed Transaction Systems", IEEE Trans. on Software Engineering, Vol. SE-11, No. 5, May 1985, pp. 483-491.

[Morganti78] Morganti, M., Coppadoro, G., Ceru, S., "UDET 7116 - Common Control for PCM Telephone Exchange: Diagnostic Software Design and Availability Evaluation", Proc. FTCS-8, Toulouse, June 1978, pp. 16-23.

[Morpurgo85] Morpurgo, S., Segre, C., "Fault Simulation, at Register Transfer Level of VLSI", Olivetti Res. & Tech. Review No. 3/1985.

[MUMICRO83] Several Authors, "The MuTEAM Experience in Designing Distributed Systems for Microprocessors", Volume Collana Sottoprogetto P1, Obiettivo MUMICRO, PFI, Dec. 1983.

[MUMICRO84] Several Authors, "MuTEAM: Distributed Multiprocessor Architecture and ECSP Concurrent Language", Volume Collana Sottoprogetto P1, Obiettivo MUMICRO, PFI, Nov. 1984.

[Natali84] Natali, A., Mello, P., "Strumenti per la Gestione di Errori in Programmi Distribuiti", Proc. AICA 84, Roma, Oct. 1984, Vol. 2, pp. 109-128.

[Negrini81] Negrini, R., Sami. M. G., Scarabottolo N. "System- Level Fault Diagnosis in a Distributed System", Proc. EUROMICRO, Paris, Sept. 1981, pp. 55-62.

[Negrini82a] Negrini, R., Sami. M. G., Stefanelli, R., "Verification of Complex Programs and Microprograms", in Designing and Programming Modern Computer Systems, S. L. Kartashev and S. P. Kartashev, Eds. Vol. 1, LSI Modular Computer Systems, Englewood Cliffs, NJ, Prentice Hall, 1982, Chap. 4.

[Negrini82b] Negrini, R., Scarabottolo, N., "Multimicro Processor Debugging based on Fault-Tolerance Techniques: A Case Study", Proc. EUROMICRO, Antwerp, Dec. 1982, pp. 323-330.

[Negrini83] Negrini, R., Sami, M. G., "Some Properties Derived from Structural Analysis of Program Graph Models", IEEE Trans. on Software Engineering, Vol. SE-9, No. 2, Mar. 1983.

[Negrini84] Negrini, R., Sami, M. G., Scarabottolo, N., "Policies for System-Level Diagnosis in a Nonhierarchical Distributed System", IEEE Trans. on Reliability, Vol. R-33, No. 4, Oct. 1984. pp. 333-342.

[Negrini85a] Negrini, R., Sami, M. G., Stefanelli, R., "Fault- Tolerance Approaches for VLSI/WSI Arrays", Proc. Conference on Computers and Communication, IEEE, Phoenix, 1985.

[Negrini85b] Negrini, R., Stefanelli, R., "Algorithms for Self-Reconfiguration of Wafer-Scale Regular Arrays", Proc. ICCAS, IEEE, Beijing, 1985.

[Negrini85c] Negrini, R., Stefanelli, R., "Time Redundancy in WSI Array of Processing Elements", Proc. 1 Conf. Supercomputing Systems (SCS-85), Dec. 1985, pp. 429-438.

[Negrini86] Negrini, R., Sami. M. G., Stefanelli, R., "Fault Tolerance Techniques for Array Structures used in Supercomputing", Computer, Vol. 19, No. 2, Feb. 1986, pp. 78-87.

[Ravasi81] Ravasi, G., Rizzi, G., "Memoria a Doppia Porta Fault Tolerant", Proc. AICA 81, Pavia, Sept. 1981, pp. 613-618.

[Rivoira82] Rivoira, S., Serra, A., "A Multimicro Architecture and its Distributed Operating System for Real-Time Control", Proc. Int. Conf. on Distributed Computing Systems, Ft. Lauderdale, Oct. 1982, pp. 238-246.

[Sami83] Sami, M. G., Stefanelli, R. "Reconfigurable Architectures for VLSI Implementation", Proc. NCC 83, AFIPS, Los Angeles, May 1983, pp. 565-578.

[Sami84a] Sami, M. G., Bedina, M., Distante, F., "A Formal Approach to Computer-Assisted Generation of Functional Test Patterns for VLSI devices", Proc. ISCAS 84, Vol. 1, Montreal, May 1984, pp. 19-23.

[Sami84b] Sami, M. G., Stefanelli, R. "Fault Tolerance of VLSI Processing Arrays: the Time-Redundancy Approach", Proc. 1984 Real- Time Systems Symp., Dec. 1984, pp. 200-207.

[Sami85] Sami, M. G., Stefanelli, R., "Fault-Stealing: An Approach to Fault-Tolerance of VLSI Array Structures", Proc. Int. Conf. Circuits and Systems (ICCAS-85), June 1985, pp. 205-210.

[Schreiber81] Schreiber, F., "Quantitative Evaluation of Availability in Distributed Systems", Proc. AICA 81, Pavia, Sept. 1981, pp. 729-732.

[Schreiber84a] Schreiber, F., "A Framework for Research in Performance-Availability of Automated Information Systems", in Proc. 4th Symposium on Reliability in Distributed Software and Database Systems, Silver Spring, Oct. 1984.

[Schreiber84b] Schreiber, F., "State Dependency Issues in Evaluating Distributed Database Availability", Computer Networks, Vol. 8, Sept. 1984.

[Simoncini79a] Simoncini, L., Saheban, F., Friedman, A. D., "Concurrent Computation and Diagnosis in Multiprocessor Systems", Proc. FTCS 9, Madison, June 1979, pp. 149-155.

[Simoncini79b] [Simoncini79b]. Simoncini, L., "Recent Developments in Self- Diagnostic Models", Proc. FTSD, Brno, Sept. 1979, pp. 79-92.

[Simoncini80a] Simoncini, L., Taylor, H., "Subgraphs Smaller than the Girth in a Regular Graph", Journal of Graph Theory, Wiley Interscience, Vol. 4, 1980, pp. 101-105.

[Simoncini80b] Simoncini, L., Saheban, F., Friedman, A. D., "Design of Self-Diagnosable Multiprocessor Systems with Concurrent Computation and Diagnosis", IEEE Trans. on Comp., Vol. C-29, No. 6, June 1980, pp. 540-546.

[Simoncini80c] Simoncini, L., "Recent Developments in System Level Fault Diagnosis and their Relation to the General Organization of Multiprocessor Systems", IFIP Working Conference on "Reliable Computing and Fault Tolerance in the 1980's", London, Sept. 1979.

[Somenzi83] Somenzi, F., Gai, S., Mezzalama, M., Prinetto, P., "PART: Programmable Array Testing based on a PARTitioning algorithm", Proc. FTCS-13, Milano, June 1983, pp. 430-433.

[Somenzi85] Somenzi, F., Gai, S., Mezzalama, M., Prinetto, P., "Testing Strategy and Technique for Macro-Based Circuits", IEEE Trans. on Comp., Vol. C-34, No. 1, Jan. 1985, pp. 85-89.

[Stefanelli84] Stefanelli R., "Multiple Error Correction in Arithmetic Units with Triple Redundancy", Proc. EUROMICRO, Copenhagen, Aug. 1984, pp. 205-216.

Fault Tolerant Computing Systems in Germany

Winfried Görke
Institut für Informatik IV
Universität Karlsruhe

ABSTRACT

The paper consists of a survey of recent activities in the field of fault-tolerant computing in Germany. Three different sections of the paper emphasize industrial applications designed to tolerate hardware failures, designs intended to make use of software diversity against software faults, and research oriented projects having the goal of designing a complete system or investigating only partial aspects of fault tolerance. Since publications were scattered in literature and several projects are documented in German language only, an extented list of references has been added to the paper which also indicates current activities of the German professional societies with respect to fault tolerance.

1. Introduction

When discussing the activities in the field of fault tolerance it should be well remembered that fault tolerance is just one possibility to achieve a high level of dependability of any system in contrast to increasing inherent component reliability. Hence the series of biannual conferences on Technical Reliability being organized since 1961 in Nürnberg may be mentioned as early documented sources to look up also projects related to fault tolerance. Singular workshops were devoted completely to the subject, but they are generally not documented except in more recent years [Görk 79, DCin 81], such that the latter ones may be considered as forerunners of the series of conferences on fault-tolerant computing systems starting in 1982 [IFB 82, IFB 84b]. Of course there are also more recent workshops to be mentioned [IFB 84c], whereas several conferences devoted the one or other of their sessions to that subject [NTG 82, IFB 84a, IFB 84d].

Nobody will expect a separate evolution of work in Germany, since there was always a strong interest to follow international developments. Single contributions to almost all of the international symposia on fault tolerant computing (FTCS) since 1975 underline this remark, although other European nations may have been engaged more deeply in this cooperation. However, there is no complete record of the activities in the FTCS series, in particular since some authors submitted their first basic publication even to other conferences [Kope 74, KoMu 79]. It is hoped that this paper will be able to compensate a little the lack of concentrated documentation. Since space is limited it will not be possible to achieve completeness in this respect. Therefore, the particular selection of projects to be described is a choice based on a personal judgment of the author of what should be considered to be mentioned as an essential contribution toward the implementation or operation of fault tolerant computers in Germany. Naturally it must be incomplete in the one or other sense. This is also true for the references referred to in the paper. Some more related papers can be found in the conference proceedings referenced.

Emphasis has been put on well documented studies, investigations, or design proposals achieving practical application or leading to results just short of a real implementation. They are grouped into three more or less related areas:

1. Industrial applications designed to tolerate hardware faults
2. Systems including software diversity
3. Research oriented projects on fault tolerance

The survey of the next three sections of the paper tries to outline the main characteristics of some of these proposals. Many related areas at the same time are being neglected, namely fault diagnosis, self-testing methods, reliability analysis, design for testability, distributed systems, system simulation, performance analysis, interface implementation, VLSI design, to name just a few. In order to limit the extend to be covered the following survey will be restricted to redundant computing systems announcing in some sense the feature of fault tolerance. Intended applications will range from industrial process control via general computer applications and fault-tolerant storage up to operating system extensions.

2. Industrial Applications Designed to Tolerate Hardware Faults

2.1. RDC *Really Distributed Control* Computer

The first system to be described originated already in the late seventies and was intended to interconnect a large number of process control computers using fiber optics. It was designed by the Fraunhofer Institute of Information and Data Processing at Karlsruhe cooperating with a steel company [Bonn 79,Syrb 81].

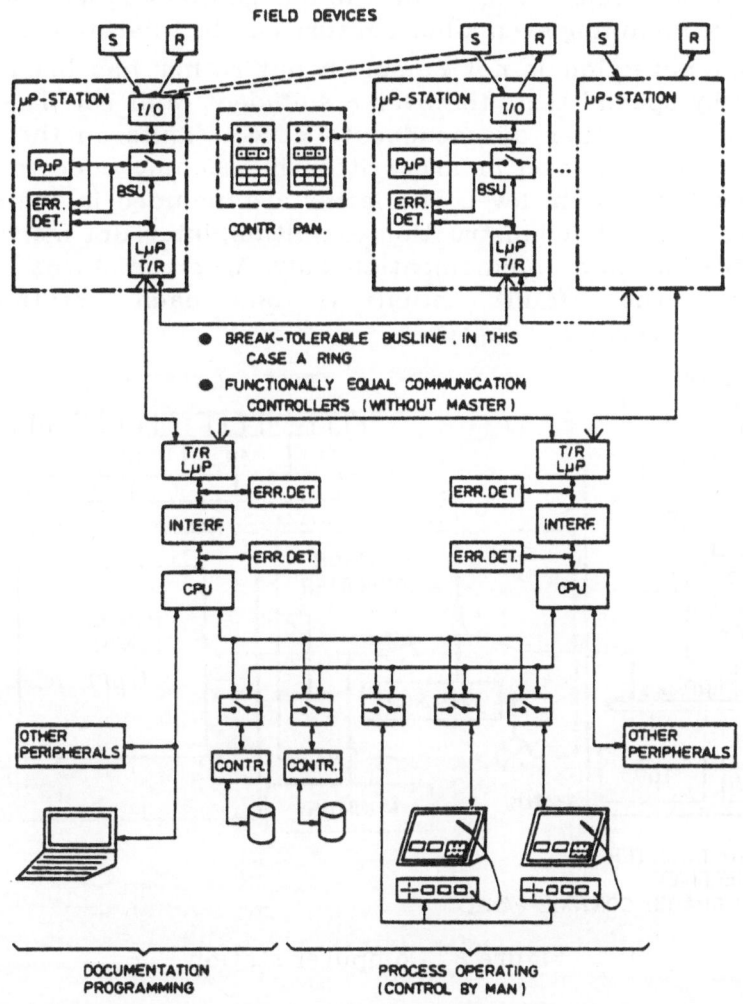

Figure 1.: RDC system concept

The system consists of distributed microcomputer stations being attached to partial control processes. They are connected to each other and also to the central control room via an optical global ring bus. Fig. 1 outlines the system concept, making use of dynamic redundancy. Important sensors and actuators are connected to e.g. two stations such that after occurrence of a failure a second computer can take over the task of the failed one. Fig. 2 shows the computer station in more detail. It consists of a line microcomputer being connected via a transmitter/receiver adapter TRA to the bus interface, the bus switch and converter, the process control computer, and the interface to the process sensors and actuators. The operation is completely decentralized. Since the transmission mode on the bus can be changed, any single failure including even a bus rupture can be tolerated.

Fault detection is not complete but rather has been implemented by special tests to cover a sufficient fault set. These test programs are either microcoded to detect faults on the circuit board or subunit level or are written in machine code to detect faults on the system level. The latter are included in the system software and test for instruction execution, interrupt mechanism, i/o operation, and communication only. An error status register indicates the fault situation on each station or transmitter/receiver adapter.

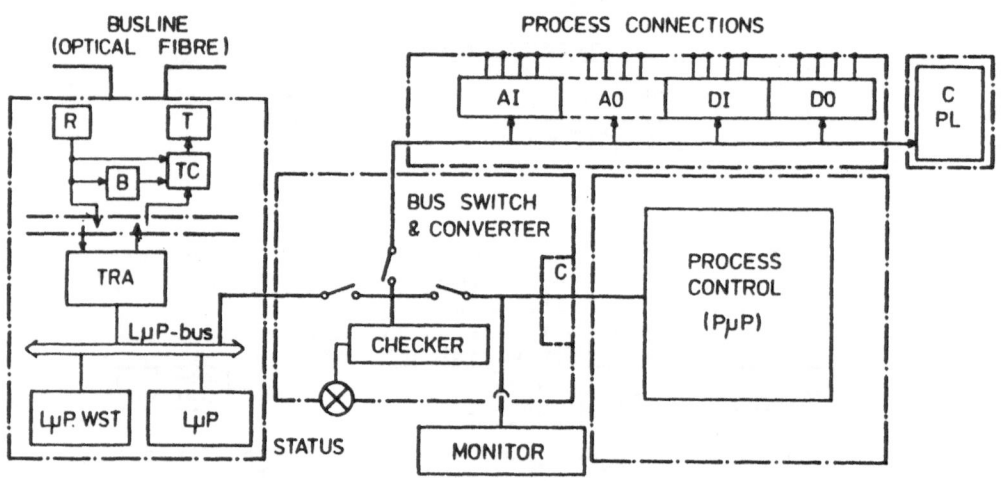

T   = TRANSMITTER
R   = RECEIVER
CPL = OPERATOR CONTROL PANEL

Figure 2.: Computer station

Fault recovery consists of a reconfiguration including a redistribution of tasks after a fault has been isolated. An application in steel production used simplified backward recovery. Since the application programs consist of small tasks, they can be restarted at task entry. Data validity represents no problem and cooperating tasks are considered as being a unit to prevent deadlock situations. By this concept a minimal additional system load can be achieved. Experience so far demonstrated a success of the system concept for real time applications [Syrb 84].

2.2. Telephone Switching and Communication Control

In the area of communication control the system SSP 103D (*Siemens Switching Processor*) has been introduced in 1981 [Bern 82]. It is designed to perform the switching in the new digital communication net EWSD, after electronic switching was incorporated into the German communication system in 1972 for telex and in 1974 for telephone circuits carrying conventional analog signals. Rather than dealing with the older system, the more recent generation is to be described here. During the same time the goal has shifted from primarily hardware oriented fault tolerance to an inclusion of software problems which however are limited to a mere system software. Requirements call for very high levels of availability, only a few accumulated hours of down time for the whole system life can be accepted.

Hardware duplication and software stand-by operations are the approaches to achieve this goal [Jung 82]. Both processors represent equivalent system partitions, one being responsible for the current activity, the other operating in a clock synchronous idling mode, ready to take over immediately if an error is going to be detected. Although this can easily be achieved by a comparator microprogrammed test routines are required to determine which of the processors is the faulty one thus avoiding a wrong decision for switch over. For the memory a (39,32) error correcting Hamming code is used which permits a correction of single bit memory errors. To achieve a maximum accumulated down time of 30 min. within 30 years of operation, a maximum repair time of two hours must be met. More details concerning the communication aspects of these systems are described in [Suck 82].

More recent developments - sometimes called second generation digital communication switching systems which are characterized by distributed control - are the systems SSP 112D and SSP 113D designed for medium size and large size exchange offices respectively. Some remarks on the control processor of ther latter system, the CP 113, are to be included here [Bern 84, Schr 86], since this modern processing system meets the requirements of high modularity and contains essential attributes with respect to fault tolerance to achieve the high level of availability required.

The CP 113 is structured as a multiprocessor system based on 32 bit microprocessors. Fig. 3 shows that fault tolerance is a basic characteristic of this system. Duplication is used as in other parts of the EWSD system, namely switching or operation and maintenance (O&M) peripherals.

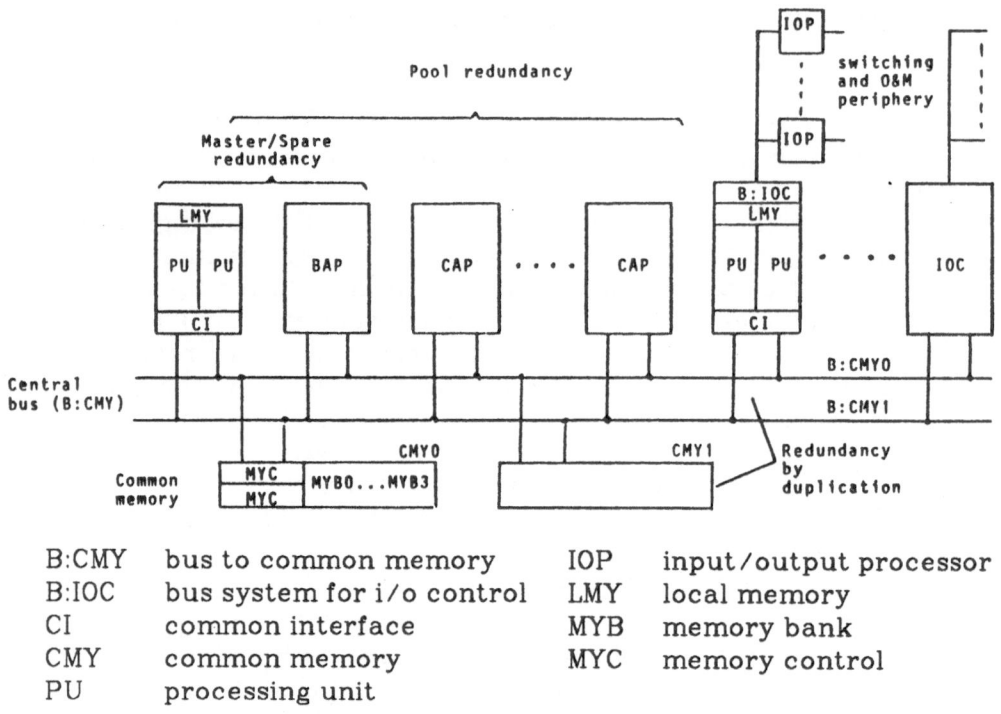

B:CMY	bus to common memory	IOP	input/output processor
B:IOC	bus system for i/o control	LMY	local memory
CI	common interface	MYB	memory bank
CMY	common memory	MYC	memory control
PU	processing unit		

Figure 3.: Structure of the coordination processor CP 113D

To achieve the benefits of function sharing administration, safeguarding, and maintenance are implemented on a base processor (BAP), whereas call processing is run on one or more call processors (CAP). There is an additional type of processor named I/O controller (IOC) to which the switching periphery as well as O&M peripherals are connected. All processor types BAP, CAP, and IOC are identical with respect to their hardware. They are internally duplicated in order to ease error location. Each processor contains a large local memory holding all resident code and process specific data, e.g. (stack of) dynamically critical tasks (namely operating system, call processing). Thus access collisions to common memory are reduced. This enables an enhanced system performance. Additionally a high percentage of software faults can be limited to one processor at a time.

Because of security reasons both the central bus system (B:CMY) and common memory (CMY) are duplicated. These duplicated units are operating cycle synchronously in parallel and they are processing identical information in case of the standard operational mode. Some of the processors may operate in a master/spare configuration, others may be pooled or work in a combination of both depending upon the size of the system. All CP 113 units contain self-checking mechanisms to detect hardware failures. The data paths and the storage medium of the local and common memories are supervised by a (39,32) error correcting code and are checked by duplicated circuitry. All other hardware logic is duplicated internal to the unit and is permanently monitored concerning synchronism. Latent failures of the safeguarding mechanism (e.g. comparators) are detected periodically by means of checking routines.

In order to detect software faults checking circuitry in the hardware and additional monitoring features in the operating system are provided:

- Each processor contains a watch dog timer to interrupt endless loops.
- Microprocessor internal checks are supervising plausibility.
- The access control which is provided in each processor (BAP, CAP or IOC) is operating as a memory management unit (MMU) and checks access permission to all addressable hardware units and memories.
- The system status analysis checks the plausibility of the central processor configuration periodically.
- A system monitor checks the real time conditions of the system periodically.
- Audits are run in preset time intervals to check semipermanent and transient data consistency.

The modularity of the control processor CP 113 guarantees that a suspicious unit will be determined as soon as a checking mechanism triggers an alarm signal. In case of a detected hardware failure (e.g. comparator alarm) a lock circuit is activated. These lock circuits are provided for every B:CMY interface and they are able to isolate the suspicious unit before a faulty operation can effect the entire system. Diagnosis programs are started automatically in order to verify the fault and to localize the defective module.

If the software error supervision rises an alarm flag a software error handling program is being started. Besides a very extensive collection of fault symptoms an analysis is being performed to determine the measure necessary to obtain service recovery. For support different recovery levels are defined. Hardware failures in

B:CMY and CMY do not require any recovery measure. Operation can proceed without interruption by using the duplicated unit which is operating cycle synchronously. Hardware failures in one of the processors as well as most of the software faults effect the currently operating process only. In general, only this process has to be restarted (lowest recovery level). In case of more severe faults which however are less probable more extensive recovery measures may be required. They range from a restart of all processes in all processors up to a complete system restart including the reload of program code and semipermanent data from backup memory.

2.3. Switching in Railway Engineering

In contrast to the preceding section where continuous operation is the main concern of process control, public transport systems require very high safety considerations resulting in shutdown of operation if a dangerous situation can arise due to any system malfunction. Since it is rather easy to stop any train or vehicle in order to escape the danger of collision or derailing, the fail-safe principle can be used efficiently: if an error is detected all signals and semaphores at set to cause a general system stop. Fault-tolerance is used to identify these error situations which includes a signal check on the lowest level and makes use of low energy states wherever possible. A special self-checking type of circuitry has been developed long time ago in order to provide electronics with a similar feature of fail-safe operation as was inherent in mechanical implementations.

Microprocessors, however, are not very suitable for self-checking circuitry due to the overwhelming number of possible internal failure situations which prevent a detailed investigation of all possible responses under realistic failure assumptions. Therefore, a family of microprocessor based components for railway signal control applications has been developed [StUe 78, Lohm 80]. Named SIMIS (a German abbreviation for safe microcomputer system) its design is based on two microcomputer components in lock step operation including duplicated clock generators and comparators for the output data, which block further operation if a deviation between the duplicated channels is detected. By a transformer coupled analog signal translator all output signals are forced to a zero state if the microcomputers enter their state of blocked operation. Hence the well-known fail-safe techniques for railway signaling can be controlled by a SIMIS based electronic interlocking unit.

It is worth mentioning that this approach has successfully completed the prototype application phase in a Berlin subway station and the Duisburg harbor railway extension [Suwe 83]. A first installation by the German federal railway was opened for experimental operation in 1986 in Murnau. Competitive installations are scheduled for the near future, namely in Köln, Dortmund, Hilversum(NL), and Chiasso(CH), where the largest application conceived so far will consist of 30 compact components (SIMIS-C), an advanced version of the original concept.

2.4. Other Fault-tolerant Computer Proposals

Also some other announced computer systems propagate the idea of fault tolerance against consequences of hardware failures. The Synchron-Duplex-Rechner SDR 1300/1500 by Krupp Atlas Elektronik makes use of parallel processors in lock step operation running identical software and achieving a very small failure latency [SchZ 84]. Intended for all process control applications its main goals are high availability, real-time operation and smooth program continuation after failure at reasonable additional costs.

The system 8832 proposed by Nixdorf Computer AG (more recently also named TARGON 32) addresses the area of transaction processing where loosely coupled components and software implementation of fault tolerance features are of main concern [Herr 84]. It has been developed on the principles published earlier in connection with the Auragen 4000 fault-tolerant computer system [BoBa 83]. In case of failure a back-up process can take over program operation since it receives copies of all interprocess messages. Although the concept offers the possibility for a more efficient use of computing power since the stand-by processor can perform tasks of its own, the interprocess messages have to be triplicated (receiver process, receiver process backup, and sender process backup) which is likely to compensate to a certain degree the gain achieved.

For general process control applications currently microprocessor based computer systems have been made available by different companies (e.g. Siemens Teleperm/M or MMC 201, BBC Procontrol). These systems offer fault-tolerant configurations according to their intended applications, but a description is beyond the scope of this paper.

3. Systems Including Software Diversity

Most of the systems addressing fault tolerance are an application of the replication principle: the parts containing possible faults are simply replicated making use of the (2-out-of-3) configuration including majority voting. This is perfectly legal as long as independent physical faults are assumed to occur most likely. Hence under careful observation of design guidelines this seems to be a good approach for hardware fault tolerance, in particular if the environment of operation guarantees the prevention of common mode failures, e.g. by use of independent power supplies for the replicated units.

Software on the other hand has basically different characteristics. Although a program can very easily be copied after having been completed and thoroughly tested, it does not make sense to use replicated programs in a computer system to safeguard against software faults. As can easily be shown any error contained still in the copied program will show up in all copies under the same input conditions in an identical manner. Of course, using replicated hardware computer components will also require a replication of the software, but still only hardware failures of the system can be tolerated. Any software error will jeopardize even a fault-tolerant system.

Unfortunately it has turned out that software errors are also of major concern, because it is extremely difficult to supply software which can be guaranteed to be free of errors. Of course, this also holds for fault-tolerant systems. Many proposals therefore simply require the software to be correct and leave it to the programmer to achieve this goal. For safety related digital computer applications it is a condition to demonstrate also the design correctness of the software, at least to the same degree as is generally required for the hardware parts. Therefore, software diversity is one of the main research issues intended to enhance fault tolerance.

Among the early approaches toward software diversity the experimental investigations aiming at nuclear reactor safety control have to be mentioned [GmVo 79]. As was noticed in this paper software diversity can be achieved by different means: independent programmers create different programs using the same language and tools, using different programming languages and different tools, or programming even different computers by different languages thus achieving the utmost extent of diversity.

In the experiment reported three different languages were used for the same computer (IFTRAN, PASCAL, PHI2 for Siemens 330). A common formal specification was formulated from the user requirements, the software was implemented using project oriented programming guidelines. Testing was performed by the programmers in the first stage, then by other persons and by automated tools. Since also internal check points had been specified the different results could be compared to each other, thus discovering about 14% of the errors still contained in the programs. Unfortunately there are no detailed discussions of the test methods used, only a total of about 130 program errors are reported. A considerable portion of them could be attributed to incomplete or ambiguous specification.

It can be concluded that independently developed programs are likely not to demonstrate common mode errors, in particular if the programming languages and compilers used are also diverse. Very important is the specification since it is not covered by the fault tolerance. A too detailed specification may compensate for the achievements in fault tolerance as it facilitates common design errors. The most important result consists of a reduction of the test and validation expense generally required for safety related applications.

3.1. MIRA

Based on the principle outlined above a microcomputer controlled reactor shut down system (named MIRA according to its German abbrevation) is under current development [VoFe 82]. Its design makes use of 4 groups of 3 microcomputers each to perform the 4 tasks intended:

- determine the input data from triplicated thermocouplers at each of about 30 nuclear fuel elements,
- calculate the temperature and check for overflow of limiting values, evaluate the temperature by filtering and reference to former readings, also check for overflow conditions,
- evaluate the results of the two preceding steps and discriminate any condition requiring reactor shut down.

Each group receives 3 independent inputs from the computers in other groups and provides internal communication to decide about the value to be considered as an output. Therefore identical microcomputers can be used, which process diverse programs written in different languages (IFTRAN, PASCAL, and PL/M), thus resulting in an application example of diverse redundancy on the software level to achieve fault tolerance also of certain design faults.

3.2. DIRMU

It may be interesting to note that with respect to the DIRMU system discussed in detail in section 4 a single paper on the possibilities of multiversion programming to achieve fault tolerance has been published [MaMo 84]. The approach taken consists of the development and implementation of 4 different algorithms to solve the well-known Traveling Salesman Problem where the number of places to be visited is small. One of these programs did not meet specifications and was excluded from the experiment. The others were run on different DIRMU units with an ideal voter/evaluator running on a fourth unit. The results reported state that

- the feasibility of this approach could be demonstrated,
- parallel operation of the versions keep time overhead low,
- the time out limit turned out to be very critical in particular for slow implementations of the problem,
- transient and permanent hardware failures are also tolerated due to the multicomputer configuration.

Disadvantages observed are

- the high effort necessary for software development,
- difficulties to achieve a complete and unique specification,
- problems of voting on real numbers which are not identical, and
- the existence of coincident program errors.

4. Research Oriented Projects on Fault Tolerance

The most complete documentation is available on projects carried on in the academic environment. About one half of them were even presented at different FTC symposia, but they will be included here again because they may be considered important. Since it is not easy to provide a distinct scheme of discussion they will be grouped according to the proposed field of application, starting again with process control, then general applications, fault-tolerant storage, and finally operating systems organization.

4.1. FUTURE

This system has been designed at the TU München to be particular suitable for process control problems in which the user can decide whether it is necessary for any task to be performed in a fault-tolerant manner. Since redundancy means additional expense mostly in form of costly hardware a user determined selection will indeed be fairly economical. Hence the name FUTURE is to be interpreted as *f*ault-tolerant and *u*ser friendly system with *t*ask specific *u*tilization of *re*dundancy. Several references describe the concept as well as single aspects of implementation [Färb 81, Endl 82, Demm 82, Demm 84].

Task dependent degrees of fault tolerance seem appropriate if in a multicomputer system several tasks of different importance are available to the scheduler. Four different classes of importance are easily to be discriminated:

class 0: ordinary task behavior, operator initiates repetition,

class 1: faults are acceptable if detected, no time critical operation, recovery from check point possible,

class 2: no faulty output permitted, duplication necessary, comparison for error detection, fault diagnosis required or system restart,

class 3: neither faulty output nor service interrupt permitted, data must be available even after failure.

As will be noted from this class description the user is responsible for the degree of redundancy to be introduced for the different tasks of a control program. However, he is asked only to indicate the class type required, the system will allocate all the resources, one, two, or three copies of the program section as well as the distribution to one or several processors of the computer system or for class 1 programs the determination of the necessary check point information.

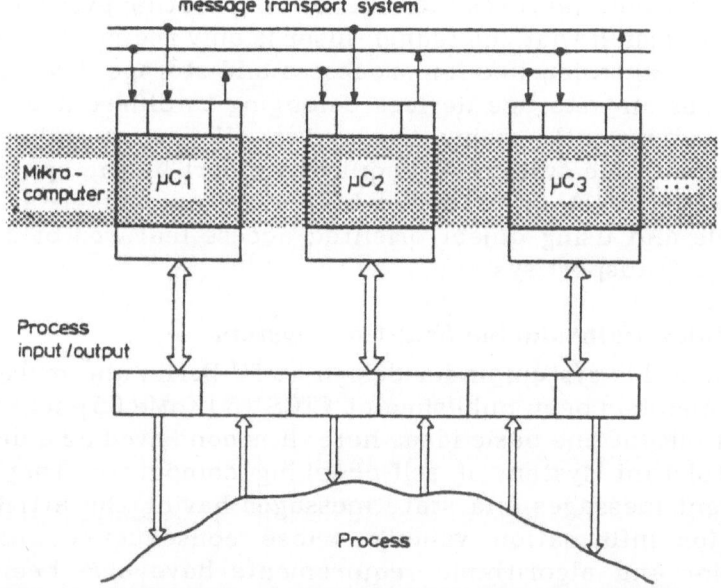

Figure 4.: Hardware structure of the FUTURE system

A particular feature of the hardware computer system which was designed to use commercially available modules as far as possible is the write-only bus used. As is indicated in Fig. 4 each computer module broadcasts its output to all other modules whereas it receives its input from any other unit via the particular dedicated bus. Since voting is supported by the controller of the hardware communication system a masking of faulty messages will be achieved. Although the amount of memory required by this scheme is rather large all information is available at any time to all system components, hence no more than a hardware supported system synchronization is necessary.

Since it is not easy to implement user specific fault tolerance for industrial control systems a big problem consisted in the real time operating system providing for multitasking as well as real time response behavior and also scheduling of user implemented tasks at various reliability classes. It was realized in MODULA2 using a real time operating system core to which a couple of language constructs were added to permit correct interaction, namely task(), send(), receive(), wait for event(), etc. As an example the parts storage management of an automated fabrication facility has been implemented.

It may be mentioned that in cooperation with the University of Dortmund and since 1985 with the University of Erlangen-Nürnberg a project similar to FUTURE has the goal to integrate fault tolerance features into the UNIX operating system [Bran 84, Demm 86] such that the (super-)user is only required to indicate a class of fault tolerance for processes and storage devices. Several processes and storage devices belonging to different classes may exist concurrently within the system. Hence an unhomogenous process and file system set requires support by the operating system, which must be extended by leaving unchanged as much as possible and using object oriented access features of a complex message transport system.

4.2. MARS *Ma*intainable *R*eal-time *S*ystem

Since this system under design at TU Berlin and more recently at TU Wien has been published at FTCS 15 [KoMe 85], it is sufficient to just outline the basic ideas here. It is conceived as a distributed fault-tolerant system of self-checking computers. They interact via event messages and state messages having the attribute of a time for information validity whose consequences on system behavior and algorithmic requirements have also been investigated [Kope 86]. The main concepts with respect to fault tolerance are also discussed in [Kope 82].

A very important general aspect of real time systems with applications for industrial process control consists in the observation of time dependent information validity. Messages in these systems may become obsolete if not processed within due time intervals. Hence care must be taken to avoid the possibility that outdated messages start system activities which are no longer of any physical relevance. To handle these effects correctly is even more important for fault-tolerant systems, in which messages can be influenced by faults in various manners. In order to overcome these problems event messages are a result of sudden situations, they are queued and will be removed after being read. State messages on the contrary can be read more than once as long as they are valid, hence no queuing is needed but they are rather overwritten at the next validity interval. Their contents are undetermined after validity has expired.

The fault tolerance features require static redundancy to mask hardware faults of a system component. Input information is to be distributed to redundant components which can be achieved via group addresses (m to n communication). A basic assumption was made for message generation: all modules fail in a self-checking manner, that is they produce a correct output or no output at all. Hence components can select any redundant event message, if it is the same as one already received it is simply discarded. Real time synchronization and reintegration of repaired components without system halt are further characteristics of this system. Software diversity is possible but restricted to synchronization constraints.

A prototype implementation made use of six DEC LSI 11 components with a communication link based on Ethernet. It could be demonstrated that addition of redundant components or reintegration of passive components is possible without modification of application software and 10 to 100 messages per second can be processed by the processor cluster.

More recently some closely related areas are under investigation, namely fault-tolerant clock synchronization, fault-tolerant operating systems, and the development of communication protocols for distributed real-time systems [Damm 86].

4.3. DIRMU

Designed at the University of Erlangen-Nürnberg the acronym abbreviates *di*stributed *r*econfigurable *mu*ltiprocessor kit. Thus it consists of building blocks suitable to be tailored to any arbitrary application, in particular by being used as array, cube, tree or ring arrangements to achieve high computational performance [HäMa 85a, HäMa 85b, Maeh 85]. About 25 components have been implemented in order to permit experiments on different DIRMU applications. Originally designed to be used as a tool for investigations of distributed diagnosis in loosely coupled microcomputer systems their inherent features of fault tolerance are a highly appreciated byproduct useful even for general applications. First ideas on this project were published in [HäSc 79] and [HäRo 80], the implementation of an earlier prototype is also discussed in [MaHu 81].

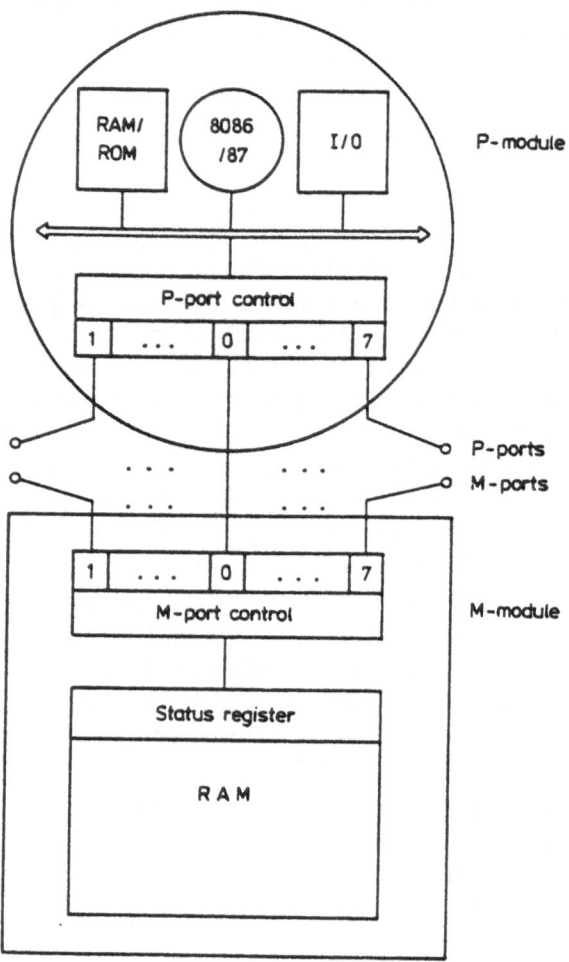

Figure 5.: DIRMU building block.

The basic building block is shown in Fig. 5. It consists of a processing and a memory module offering both multiport communication. Hence each module can be connected to several other modules by simply connecting a P- with a M-port of a different module. There are seven of such ports available, the eighth being used for the internal P-M connection. Apparently modules of this type can be easily connected to form the above mentioned arrangements and fault-tolerant structures are also straight forward. E.g. a double ring connection to be discussed later in relation with the BFS system can easily be formed by DIRMU components.

Of course operation of DIRMU configurations depends also on the software available. A multiprocessor operating kernel and a library containing system support routines (synchronization primitives, memory management for the multiport memories, message handling, etc.) can be called by the user to perform functions required for his particular application. It may be interesting to note that the possibility of software diversity is explicitly mentioned as one of several applications with respect to fault tolerance. Some more recent results of this project have been reported in [MaMo 86].

4.4. FIPS - *F*ault-tolerance *I*mplementation in *P*rocess Automation *S*ystems

Goals of this system which was proposed at the TH Darmstadt were primarily [Mänc 84]:

- to extend the structure of the distributed microcomputer automation system given to include fault tolerance,

- to achieve fault tolerance at minimal additional expense by making use of standard modules and task specific redundancy,

- to preserve extensibility of the automation system,

- to permit parallel processing to meet real time requirements if this does not decrease reliability.

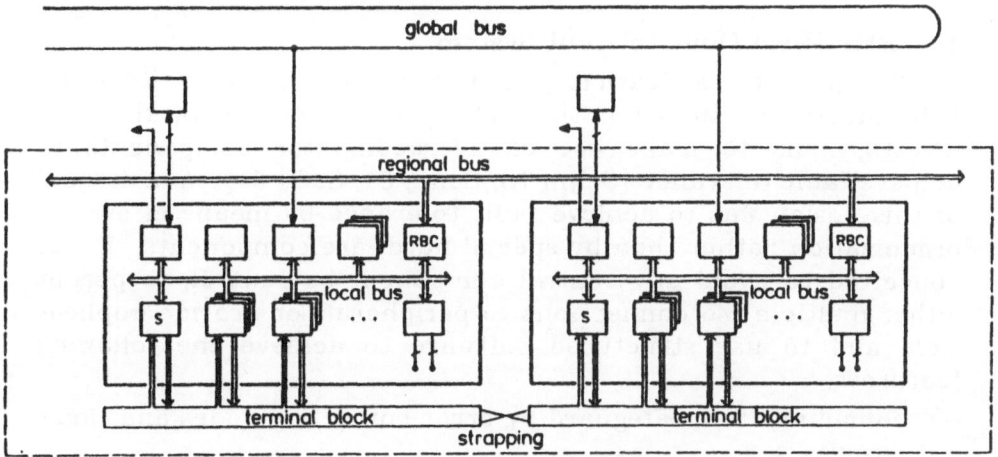

Figure 6.: FIPS configuration showing regional bus and
i/o interconnections.

As is demonstrated in Fig. 6 there are additional elements provided to implement fault tolerance, namely a regional bus connecting several local computing units via regional bus couplers (RBC), switching units (S), and also additional connections to the process environment to facilitate comparisons and majority voting on process input and output signals. Automation functions are available in form of configurable software modules meeting different requirements [Mänc 86]:

— high availability based on (2-out-of-3) majority voting,
— fail-safe behavior achieved by requiring identity of intermediate computing results and i/o signals of two units,
— economical fault tolerance realized by task reconfiguration,
— unchanged properties of nonredundant modules.

A special application combines parallel processing of an adaptive control algorithm with fault tolerance resulting in graceful degradation of the control function in case of microcomputer failures. This however requires extensive communication and a narrow synchronization between local units in particular in the presence of failures. Therefore the time drift of cooperating jobs has to be carefully controlled.

Again the operating system has to provide for local, regional, and global types of communication and job control. Very important are the synchronization tools to support comparisons and voting. Task execution, message handling as well as clock trimming on a local scale had to be implemented. It is mentioned that a resolution in the microsecond range is sufficient to achieve local time differences below one or 0.1 msec. [Mänc 84].

4.5. BFS *B*asic *F*ault Tolerant *S*ystem

Designed as a feasibility study at the Siemens Research Laboratories at München the BFS system was one of the first investigations to make use of microcomputer components to achieve fault tolerance [Schm 78, Schm 81, SaSc 81]. A main goal of this design was to achieve fault tolerance by means of system organization rather than by special hardware components. It was conceived to avoid any central component or control, to permit either multiple i/o connections to peripherals or provide duplication, and to use structured software to achieve the following features:

— communication safeguard by error correcting codes and timer circuits,
— status reports on neighbors by messages,
— preserve ring structure even in case of computer component failure,

- execute task of faulty unit on other unit,
- self-tests of computer components,
- neighbor test at scheduled intervals using acknowledge,
- restart computer component by user set breakpoints,
- reconfiguration based on graceful degradation and fail-safe principle.

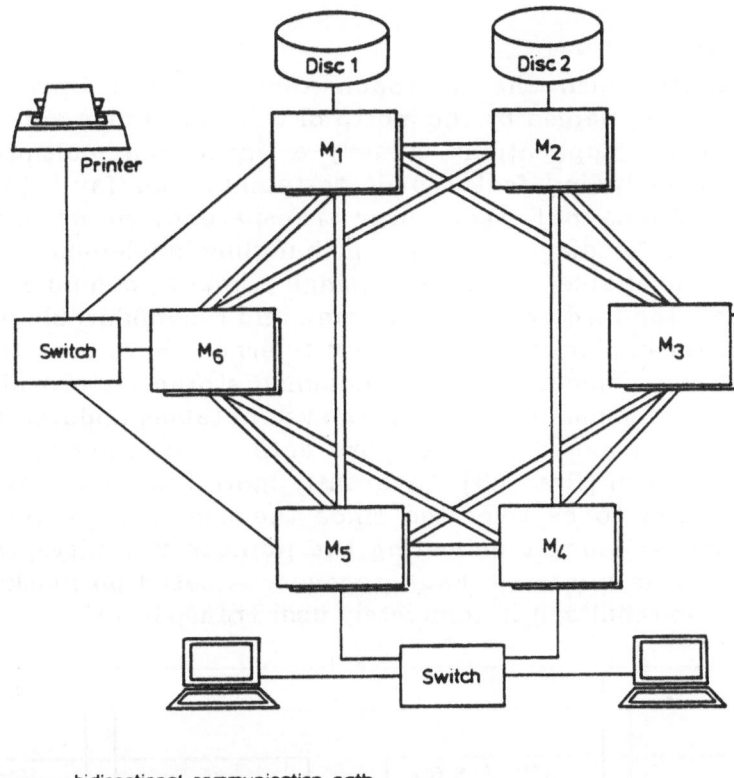

Figure 7.: BFS system structure.

    The basic system structure is outlined in Fig. 7, showing a characteristic double ring connection between all the computer components available. Each microcomputer is connected to the next two components via bidirectional communication links, such that any unit is controlled by the one having the next higher index (here mod 6). Up to two arbitrary failures can thus be tolerated since the next unit in sequence can take over control. After a failed unit has been identified by diagnostic routines reconfiguration can be initialized. As a disadvantage it was observed that throughput may be reduced to 35 % as compared to nonredundant performance. Therefore a hardware support for testing would be very suitable (e.g. self-checking circuitry). Also software support for checkpointing will be required. The availability could be increased considerably, especially if reintegration after repair is implemented [BeKl 82]. Although the system has not been made available to the market a fault-tolerant file management system has been implemented [BeKl 84].

4.6. Attempto

Like BFS also the approach taken at the University of Tübingen (and named by the motto of this university) aims toward more general applications, namely a workbench multiprocessor computer including features of testability and fault tolerance [Riss 84, Amma 83]. Again user transparency of decentralized mechanisms for diagnosis and fault handling, implementation with common available hardware (single board computers) and software (standard operating system), and reconfigurable program modules for implementation of fault tolerance have been the main goals of this project. Hence no common storage is provided, but each processor maintains separate system tables updated according to system messages. Therefore data consistency has been a special concern [Brau 83]. Apparently more than one major fault is considered to be tolerated since the user can provide a job name and an index t indicating the number of faulty processor modules to be tolerated. Fault recovery is based on masking and comparison results, it is completely user transparent.

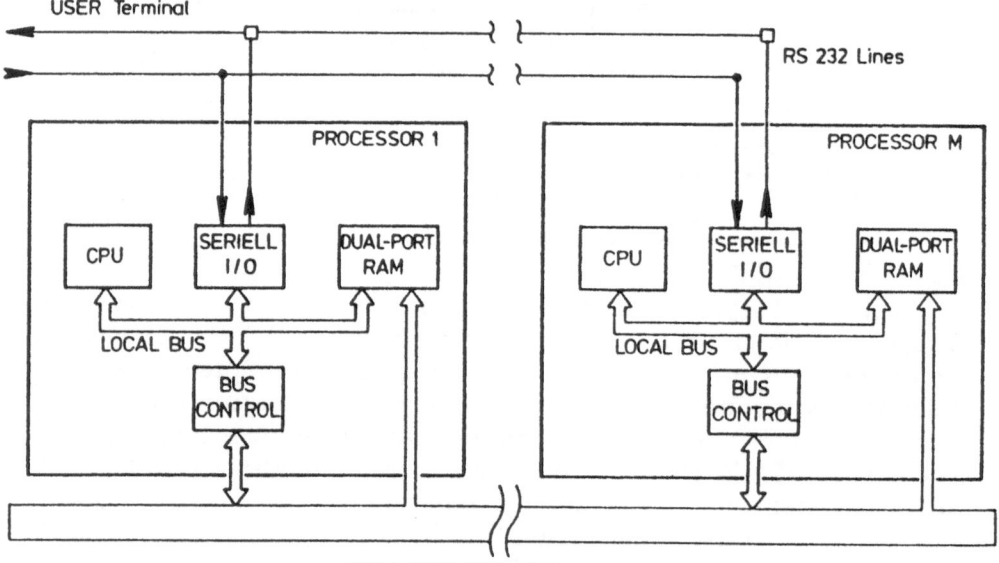

Figure 8.: Attempto hardware configuration.

The hardware structure of the system is outlined in Fig. 8. Apparently it is designed as a conventional multi-microcomputer configuration, hence the single bus is a weak element since certain bus errors can only be detected. At the time when the project started no single board computers with multiple multi-master buses were available. Presently *Attempto* is being redesigned and implemented as a multiprocessor system with VME bus and UNIX kernels.

4.7. M3R *Modular Multi-Microprocessor* System

Without going too much into details a few other projects shall be mentioned. At the University of Karlsruhe the M3R system has been investigated making use of single board computer modules connected via a global bus system [Nils 81]. Since the bus control unit represents a centralized element critical to fault tolerance a substitution of function has been provided. In case of a failure of either one of the two global busses or one of the bus control units any other processor module can take over. In order to achieve this all computer elements keep parallel system status tables, switch over is being done by software. Main concern were the possibilities of self-diagnosis of the computer elements. By an appropriate data exchange system state information is provided for all active computer units. A failed unit is isolated from further cooperation within the system.

More recently fault-tolerant communication has been under investigation, in particular simulation and modeling of message exchange protocols [Echt 84a],[Echt 84b],[Echt 86a]. Emphasis is being placed on the possibilities to reduce redundancy by use of reconfiguration. Only in case of some fault e.g. full (2-out-of3) software voting is required, whereas in a fault-free environment the third input of the voter can be neglected. First results demonstrate the feasibility of this approach [Echt 86b].

4.8. R+DS *Redundant Restorable Reconfigurable Distributed* System

A further project which has been investigated at the University of Karlsruhe was named R+DS [Seif 82a], [Seif 82b]. The goal of this project was an investigation of the software structure of a fault-tolerant process control system, how to create recovery points and what has to be added to the task management in order to achieve fault recovery and reconfiguration in a user defined multicomputer environment. The system has been implemented using a net configuration of several PDP 11 computers under operating system RSX-11M and DECnet-11M for communication. Excluding errors in the data base and the communication system it was found that 30% of the system software was required for fault tolerance functions. Also larger memories and higher communication data rates are recommended.

4.9. UPPER Distributed Multicomputer System

Designed at the GMD Research Group for Innovative Computer Systems and also at the Technical University of Berlin the UPPER system originally was aimed at high speed processing, modular design for extension, and simplified system and application software. More recently fault tolerance is to be included into the project goals [BeGi 84], which requires a duplication of the high speed bus including bypass arrangements in case of a processor node failure. Since fault tolerance must not decrease processing speed the concept provides for the addition of processing power by more computer components or a trade-off of processing speed versus fault tolerance possibilities.

4.10. Reconfiguration of Memory Chips

Many of the techniques available to prevent possible faults of memory storage locations make use of error correcting codes which simply mask single bit errors. An alternative proposal developed at the GMD Research Center in Bonn provides additional memory chips to be switched in as a substitute of a chip having demonstrated a failure [GrKa 81], [GrKa 82]. Since in bitwise organized memories each bit position in a memory word is assigned to a separate chip, a spare chip can substitute the failed one if spares are provided, the fault has been located, and switching is made possible. Additional elements required to implement such a reconfigurable memory are a failure status table providing for each memory word an indication which bit has failed and a reconfigurator net decoding this information and connecting the bit position of the memory data register to either the original chip or one of the spares. The failure status table is read out at any memory access. If it contains an error entry it reroutes the data bit from/to the spare chip. More entries can correct more bit failures per word. Two spare chips permit up to two permanently failing bits in any memory word. The entire reconfiguration hardware has been implemented on a single VLSI chip [GrMu 85].

More recently a content-addressable memory featuring fault tolerance has been developed. It was implemented by use of standard VLSI cell design techniques [GrHu 86].

5. Summary

The paper intended to give a survey on the more or less scattered projects related to fault tolerance which were initiated in Germany. Not all of them could be mentioned explicitly. The reader will find further hints in the conference proceedings referenced and in the various FTC symposium digests. Most of those included have not been described in detail because of limited space. Therefore, it will be difficult to assess their range of fault coverage without studying the references in detail. However, it may be stated that most of the projects make use of a masking of hardware failures, they do not address the area of design errors which is so important if software faults are to be included into fault tolerance.

Several projects mention different classes of redundancy or fault tolerance which means that the user can run tasks of different degree of fault tolerance at the same time. Indeed it also means that the higher class levels only are truly fault-tolerant since the lower level tasks cannot be recovered if a fault situation occurs. It is claimed that in this way a better use of computing power can be achieved thus enhancing overall efficiency. Although this is certainly true there are so far no quantitative hints on where or to which degree such a system operation is acceptable. Since computing resources are costly it would be interesting to investigate the possibilities of a reduction of redundancy in favor of better system efficiency in more detail. For most of the projects an evaluation of gain in reliability or service versus cost of fault tolerance is missing. Indeed it seems difficult to justify the requirement of fault tolerance in some cases considering the high margins of reliability performance of nonredundant equipment achieved today.

Nevertheless, fault tolerance must be considered as a future alternative to improve reliability for any case of application. No wonder that during the past few years activity and concern about fault tolerance has increased considerably. The remarkable number of contributions from German speaking countries having been accepted for the 1986 FTC symposium can be taken as an indicator for this trend which is supported concurrently by efforts of the professional society for communication engineers to reorient its membership to include and represent also engineers exclusively engaged in software development. Hence a special interest group on fault tolerance in computing systems has been created under participation of GI (Gesellschaft für Informatik), NTG/VDE (Nachrichtentechnische Gesellschaft im Verband Deutscher Elektrotechniker), and VDI (Verein Deutscher Ingenieure). Its purpose is to coordinate activities and organize working group meetings and conferences in the field, as has been successfully started in 1982 and 1984. It is hoped that these activities will lead to an improved cooperation also on the international level during the oncoming years and that FTCS 1986 will turn out to be a cornerstone in this direction, addressing in particular a possible closer cooperation within the scientific community of the European nations.

6. Acknowledgement

The author gratefully acknowledges the discussions with A. Avizienis and J.P.J. Kelly, Los Angeles, and Udo Voges and K. Echtle, Karlsruhe. He is indebted to the investigators of the projects mentioned for the many hints he has received in order to prepare the updated version of this paper and also to the German Research Foundation (DFG) for supporting a sabbatical term at UCLA by grant Go 347/5-1.

7. References

7.1. Conference Proceedings

[DCin 81] Self-diagnosis and Fault-tolerance, M. DalCin, E. Dilger (eds.), Werkhefte Nr. 4, Attempto Tübingen 1981

[Görk 79] Zuverlässigkeit elektronischer Systeme, W. Görke (ed.), Band 7 Reihe 9, Oldenbourg München 1979

[IFB 82] Fehlertolerierende Rechensysteme, E. Nett, H. Schwärtzel (eds.), Informatikfachberichte 54, Springer Berlin 1982

[IFB 84a] Architektur und Betrieb von Rechensystemen, H. Wettstein (ed.), Informatikfachberichte 78, Springer Berlin 1984

[IFB 84b] Fehlertolerierende Rechensysteme, K.-E. Grosspietsch, M. DalCin (eds.), Informatikfachberichte 84, Springer Berlin 1984

[IFB 84c] Software-Fehlertoleranz und -Zuverlässigkeit, F. Belli, S. Pfleger, M. Seifert (eds.), Informatikfachberichte 83, Springer Berlin 1984

[IFB 84d] Prozessrechner 1984, H. Trauboth, A. Jaeschke (eds.), Informatikfachberichte 86, Springer Berlin 1984

[NTG 82] Struktur und Betrieb von Rechensystemen, J. Swoboda (ed.), NTG-Fachberichte 80, VDE Berlin 1982

7.2. Publications

[Amma 83] Ammann, E. et al., Attempto: A fault-tolerant multiprocessor working station; design and concepts, Dig. of papers FTCS 13, 1983, p. 10...13

[BeGi 84] Behr, P., Giloi, W.K., Mechanismen zur Realisierung von Fehlertoleranz im UPPER-System, GMD-Spiegel Nr. 2, 1984, p. 21...30

[BeKl 82] Bernhardt, D., Klein, A., Das fehlertolerierende Mehrrechnersystem BFS, p. 289...314 in [IFB 82]

[BeKl 84] Bernhardt, D., Klein, A., Implementation of a fault-tolerant file management system, p. 252...264 in [IFB 84b]

[Bern 82] Berndt, H., Fehlertolerante Computersysteme in der Nachrichtenvermittlungs- und Prozessautomatisierungstechnik, p. 315...322 in [IFB 82]

[Bern 84] Berndt, H., A multimicroprocessor approach to communication switching system control, Eurocon 84: computers in communication and control, P. Peregrinus, London 1984, p. 51...53

[Bonn 79] Bonn, G. et al., Selbsttest und Selbstrekonfiguration von Prozessrechnersystemen am Beispiel des RDC-Systems, FhG-Berichte, München 1979, no. 1/2, p. 47...54

[BoBa 83] Borg, A., Baumbach, J., Glazer, S., A message system supporting fault tolerance, Proc. 9th Symp. Oper. Syst. Princ., ACM Oper. System Review 17, No. 5, 1983, p. 90...99

[Bran 84] Brand, T. et al., Ein fehlertolerantes UNIX-Prozess-System auf der Basis von Zuverlässigkeitsklassen, p.52...65 in [IFB 84b]

[Brau 83] Brause, R. et al., Softwarekonzepte des fehlertoleranten Arbeitsplatzrechners Attempto, in Microcomputing II, (W. Remmele, H. Schecher (eds.)), Teubner Stuttgart 1983, p. 328...341

[Damm 86] Damm, A., The effectiveness of software error detection mechanisms in real-time operating systems, Dig. of papers FTCS 16, 1986, p. 171...176

[Demm 82] Demmelmeier, F., Ries, W., Implementierung von anwendungsspezifischer Fehlertoleranz für Prozessautomatisierungssysteme, p. 299...314 in [IFB 82]

[Demm 84] Demmelmeier, F., Anwenderwerkzeuge für das fehlertolerante Multimikrocomputersystem FUTURE, p. 14...26 in [IFB 84b]

[Demm 86] Demmelmeier, F., Fischbacher, P., Koller, G., Communication in a configurable fault-tolerant and distributed UNIX system, Dig. of papers FTCS 16, 1986, p. 2...7

[Echt 84a] Echtle, K., Fehlermaskierende verteilte Systeme zur Erfüllung hoher Zuverlässigkeitsanforderungen in Prozessrechnernetzen, p. 315...328 in [IFB 84a]

[Echt 84b] Echtle, K., Bestimmung der Protokollmenge für verteilte Fehlermaskierungssysteme, p. 337...352 in [IFB 84b]

[Echt 86a] Echtle, K., Fehlermaskierung durch verteilte Systeme, Informatikfachberichte 121, Springer Berlin 1986, (Ph.D. thesis)

[Echt 86b] Echtle, K., Fault masking with reduced redundant communication, Dig. of papers FTCS 16, 1986, p. 178...183

[Endl 82] Endl, H., Prozess-Ein-/Ausgabe für ein fehlertolerantes Multimikrorechnersystem, p. 250...264 in [IFB 82]

[Färb 81] Färber, G., Task-specific implementation of fault tolerance in process automation systems, p. 84...102 in [DCin 81]

[GrHu 86] Grosspietsch, K.-E., Huber, H., Müller, A., The concept of a fault-tolerant and easily testable associative memory, Dig. of papers FTCS 16, 1986, p. 34...39

[GrKa 81] Grosspietsch, K.-E., Kaiser, J., Nett, E., A dynamic standby system for random access memories, Dig. of papers FTCS 11, 1981, p. 268...270

[GrKa 82] Grosspietsch, K.-E., Kaiser, J., Nett, E., Eine dynamische Standby-Organisation für Fehlertoleranz in Speichersystemen, p. 32...44 in [IFB 84b]

[GrMu 85] Grosspietsch, K.-E. et al., The VLSI implementation of a fault-tolerant memory interface - a status report, Proc. Int. Conf. VLSI '85, Tokyo 1985, p. 149...158

[GmVo 79] Gmeiner, L., Voges, U., Software diversity in reactor protection systems: an experiment, Proc. IFAC Workshop on Safety of Computer Control Systems, 1979, p. 75...79

[HäSc 79] Händler, W., Schreiber, H., Sigmund, V., Computation structures reflected in general purpose and special purpose multi-microprocessor systems, Proc. 1979 Int. Conf. on Parallel Processing, p. 95...102

[HäRo 80] Händler, W., Rohrer, H., Gedanken zu einem Rechner-Baukasten-System, Elektron. Rechenanl. 22, 1980, p. 3...13

[HäMa 85a] Händler, W., Maehle, E., Wirl, K., DIRMU multiprocessor configurations, Proc. 1985 Int. Conf. on Parallel Processing, p. 652...656

[HäMa 85b] Händler, W., Maehle, E., Wirl, K., The DIRMU testbed for high performance multiprocessor configurations, Proc. 1985 Int. Conf. on Supercomputing Systems, p. 468...475

[Herr 84] Herrmann, F., Das fehlertolerante Informationssystem 8832 - Das Fehlertoleranzkonzept, p. 180...188 in [IFB 84c]

[Jung 82] Jung, K., Verfügbarkeit und Fehlertoleranz von Rechnern zur Steuerung elektronischer Vermittlungsanlagen, p. 392...403 in [NTG 82]

[KoMe 85] Kopetz, H., Merker, W., The architecture of MARS, Dig. of papers FTCS 15, 1985, p. 274...279

[KoMu 79] Könemann, B., Mucha, J., Zwiehoff, G., Built-in logic block observation techniques, Dig. of papers 1979 Int. Test Conf., Cherry Hill, N.J. p. 37...41

[Kope 74] Kopetz, H., Software redundancy in real-time systems, Proc. IFIP Congress 1974, p. 182...186

[Kope 82] Kopetz, H. et al., Fehlertoleranz in MARS, p. 205...219 in [IFB 82]

[Kope 86] Kopetz, H., Accuracy of time measurement in distributed real-time systems, Proc. 5th Symp. on Reliability in Distr. Software and Database Systems, 1986, p. 35...41

[Lohm 80] Lohmann, H.-J., Sicherheit von Mikrocomputern für die Eisenbahnsignaltechnik, Elektron. Rechenanl. 22, 1980, p. 229...236

[Maeh 85] Maehle, E., Fault-tolerant DIRMU multiprocessor configurations, Computer Architecture Techn. Comm. Newsletter, IEEE CS 51-56, June 1985

[MaHu 81] Maehle, E., Hu, S.C., Ein Baukastensystem für fehler-tolerante Multi-Mikroprozessorsysteme, Informatikfachber-ichte 50, Springer Berlin 1981, p.307...317

[MaJo 82] Maehle, E., Joseph, H., Selbstdiagnose in fehlertoleranten DIRMU Multimikroprozessor-Konfigurationen, p. 59...73 in [IFB 82]

[MaMo 84] Maehle, E., Moritzen, K., Wirl, K., Experimente mit n-version Programmierung auf dem DIRMU Multiprozessorsys-tem, p. 133...154 in [IFB 84c]

[MaMo 86] Maehle, E., Moritzen, K., Wirl, K., A graph model for diag-nosis and reconfiguration and its application to a fault-tolerant multiprocessor system, Dig. of papers FTCS 16, 1986, p. 292...297

[Mänc 84] Mäncher, H., Synchronization tools and a restart method in the fault-tolerant distributed automation system FIPS, p. 280...291 in [IFB 84b]

[Mänc 86] Mäncher, H., Synchronization tools and a restart method in an experimental fault-tolerant automation system, Computers in Industry 7, 1986, p. 351...359

[Nils 81] Nilsson, S.-A., Konzept und Architektur eines fehlertoleranten Mehrmikrorechnersystems, Reihe Informatik Bd. 9, Hochschulverlag Freiburg 1981, (Ph.D. thesis)

[Riss 84] Risse, Th. et al., Entwurf und Struktur einer Betriebssystemschicht zur Implementierung von Fehlertoleranz, p. 66...76 in [IFB 84b]

[SaSc 81] Sauer, A., Schmitter, E.J., The fault-tolerant microcomputer system BFS, Dig. of papers FTCS 11, 1981, p. 252

[Schm 78] Schmitter, E.J., Structure principles for fault-tolerant multimicroprocessor systems, Siemens Forsch. u. Entw.Berichte 7, 1978, p. 326...331

[Schm 81] Schmitter, E.J., Development of the fault-tolerant multi-microcomputer system BFS, p. 186...200 in [DCin 81]

[SchZ 84] Schmees-van Zadelhoff, C., Synchron-Duplex-Rechner, p. 329...346 in [IFB 84a]

[Schr 86] Schreier, K., High throughput processing scheme in digital communication, Proc. 1986 Intern. Zürich Seminar in Digital Communication, p.213...218

[Seif 82a] Seifert, M., Verwaltung fehlertoleranter Multi-Prozess-Systeme in lokalen Multi-Rechnersystemen, p. 358...370 in [NTG 82]

[Seif 82b] Seifert, M., Experimente mit fehlertoleranten Prozess-Systemen im lokalen Mehrrechnersystem R+DS, p. 189...204 in [IFB 82]

[StUe 78] Strelow, H., Uebel, H., Das sichere Mikrocomputersystem SIMIS, Signal+Draht 70, 1978, p. 82...86

[Suck 82] Suckfüll, H., Architecture of a New Line of Digital Switches, Electronic Switching, A. M. Joel (ed.), IEEE New York 1982, p. 180...186

[Suwe 83] Suwe, K.-H., Das elektronische Stellwerk der Bauform Siemens, Signal + Draht 75, 1983, p. 210...215

[Syrb 81] Syrbe, M., The description of fault-tolerant systems - a necessity of the practice, p. 260...273 in [DCin 81]

[Syrb 84] Syrbe, M., Zuverlässigkeit von Realzeitsystemen: Fehlermanagement, Informatik-Spektrum 7, 1984, p. 94...101

[VoFe 82] Voges, U., Fetsch, F., Gmeiner, L., Use of microprocessors in a safety-oriented reactor shut-down system, Reliability in Electr. and Electronic Compon. and Systems, (E. Lauger, J. Moltoft, eds.), North Holland, Amsterdam 1982, p. 493...496

The Technical Committee
on
Fault Tolerant Computing
of
The IEEE Computer Society

* * *

Tom Anderson
Computing Laboratory
University of Newcastle upon Tyne
Newcastle upon Tyne, NE1 7RU
England

Algirdas Avižienis
Computer Science Department
UCLA
Los Angeles, CA 90024
USA

Jean-Claude Laprie
LAAS-CNRS
7, Avenue Colonel Roche
31400 Toulouse
France

* * *

The origins of this Technical Committee go back to early 1969, when Professor Algirdas Avizienis of the UCLA Computer Science Department proposed to the IEEE Computer Group (IEEE-CG) that a Technical Committee on Fault-Tolerant Computing (TC-FTC) should be formed to promote further activities in this field. The approval of the IEEE-CG Administrative Committee was granted on November 18, 1969. A letter from Computer Group Chairman E. J.

McCluskey, dated November 20, 1969, appointed A. Avizienis to serve as the first Chairman of the new TC-FTC and requested him to invite the founding members. The 18 initial members were: A. Avizienis, W. G. Bouricius, W. C. Carter, H. Y. Chang, J. Goldberg, A. L. Hopkins, E. C. Joseph, E. J. McCluskey, E. G. Manning, F. P. Mathur (TC Secretary), G. Metze, C. V. Ramamoorthy, J. P. Roth, R. A. Short, C. V. Srinivasan, S. A. Szygenda, C. Tung, and S. S. Yau. The new TC met for the first time on May 5, 1970 during the Spring Joint Computer Conference in Atlantic City, New Jersey. It was decided at this initial meeting that the first objective of the new TC-FTC was the establishment of a technical conference, since an open conference dedicated to the theory and design of fault-tolerant computers had not been held since the 1962 Symposium on Redundancy Techniques for Computing Systems in Washington, D. C. Co-sponsorship of the proposed conference and strong organizational support was provided by Caltech's Jet Propulsion Laboratory, and the initial International Symposium on Fault-Tolerant Computing took place on March 1-3, 1971 at the Huntington-Sheraton Hotel in Pasadena, California, with Al Avizienis serving as Symposium Chairman, and Bill Carter as Program Chairman. A total of 251 participants registered for the meeting, representing the following countries: USA 230, Canada 9, France 4, Japan 3, England 3, Federal Republic of Germany and Italy, 1 each. The program consisted of 33 papers (including three from France, one from England, and one from Japan) arranged in six sessions, and a panel discussion on diagnosis and testing. Since its first meeting, the history of the Technical Committee on Fault-Tolerant Computing (FTC-TC) can hardly be separated from the series of the annual International Symposia on Fault Tolerant Computing (FTCS) that started in 1971. The successive TC chairs were:

- Prof. Algirdas Avizienis, from the University of California at Los Angeles, who was then with the Jet Propulsion Laboratory (Pasadena, USA),
- Dr. William Carter, consultant, who was then with the IBM T.J. Watson Research Center (Yorktown Heights, USA),
- Prof. John F. Meyer, from the University of Michigan (Ann Arbor, USA),
- Dr. Albert L. Hopkins Jr., from ITP Boston who was then with the C.S. Draper Laboratory (Cambridge, USA),
- Prof. Daniel Siewiorek, from Carnegie-Mellon University (Pittsburgh, USA),

- Dr. Jean-Claude Laprie, from LAAS-CNRS (Toulouse France),
- Prof. Tom Anderson, from the University of Newcastle-upon-Tyne (England).

Prof. Gerald M. Masson (The John Hopkins University, Baltimore, USA) has served as the secretary and the newsletter editor of the TC for many years.

In addition to its main activity, the FTCS's, the FTC-TC has also organized a number of workshops, often held in conjunction with other TC's of the IEEE Computer Society. The TC is editing a newsletter which is distributed to its 1200 members, originating from both the academic and the industrial world. The TC is sponsoring the special issues on Fault Tolerant Computing which are published generally once a year by the IEEE Transactions on Computers.

The impact and the trends of the TC are best illustrated by the evolution of the FTCS's, which is analyzed in the sequel through statistical data.

Figure 1 displays global Data concerning the attendance, the submission and presentation of papers. The growing success of the Symposium is clearly apparent, from both the number of attendees (from 172 to 376) and the number of submitted papers (from 75 to 292). In contrast, the number of accepted papers is more stable, which indicates that the selection process is becoming more and more strict as the field matures. Moreover, these data show that the additional capacity for attracting papers when the symposium was held in Europe or Asia -as compared to the situation when being held in the USA- becomes progressively attenuated.

Figure 2 gives the distribution of the accepted papers according to four broad domains: a) design and architecture of fault tolerant systems, b) methods, algorithms and techniques for fault tolerance, c) testing and verification, and d) the evaluation of dependability. A statistical processing of these data enables the following trends to be identified:

- after a significant growth, the proportion of the papers devoted to the description of fault tolerant systems tends to be stabilized,
- the contributions dealing with the methods, algorithms and techniques for fault tolerance exhibit a significant growth in the last five years,

- The proportion of papers dealing with testing and verification (the majority of them being hardware oriented) is continuously decreasing,
- after a significant growth, the proportion of the papers devoted to the evaluation of dependability tends to be stabilized.

Figures 3 and 4 give the distribution of the accepted papers and of the attendees respectively, with respect to their origin in terms of academis type institutions or industrial organizations. If the papers are dominated by academic type institutions, the situation more balanced as far as attendance is concerned, with a slight

Figures 5 to 8 give data relative to geographic distribution: continent-wise in figures 5 and 6, details according to the countries in figures 7 and 8. In addition to the expected dominance of the country where the symposium is being held, the growth over the years of the number of US attendants when FTCS is held outside of the USA is noteworthy. These figures confirm the strong international character of FTCS. This is an opportunity to acknowledge the constant action of the founders of the TC in support of this international aspect.

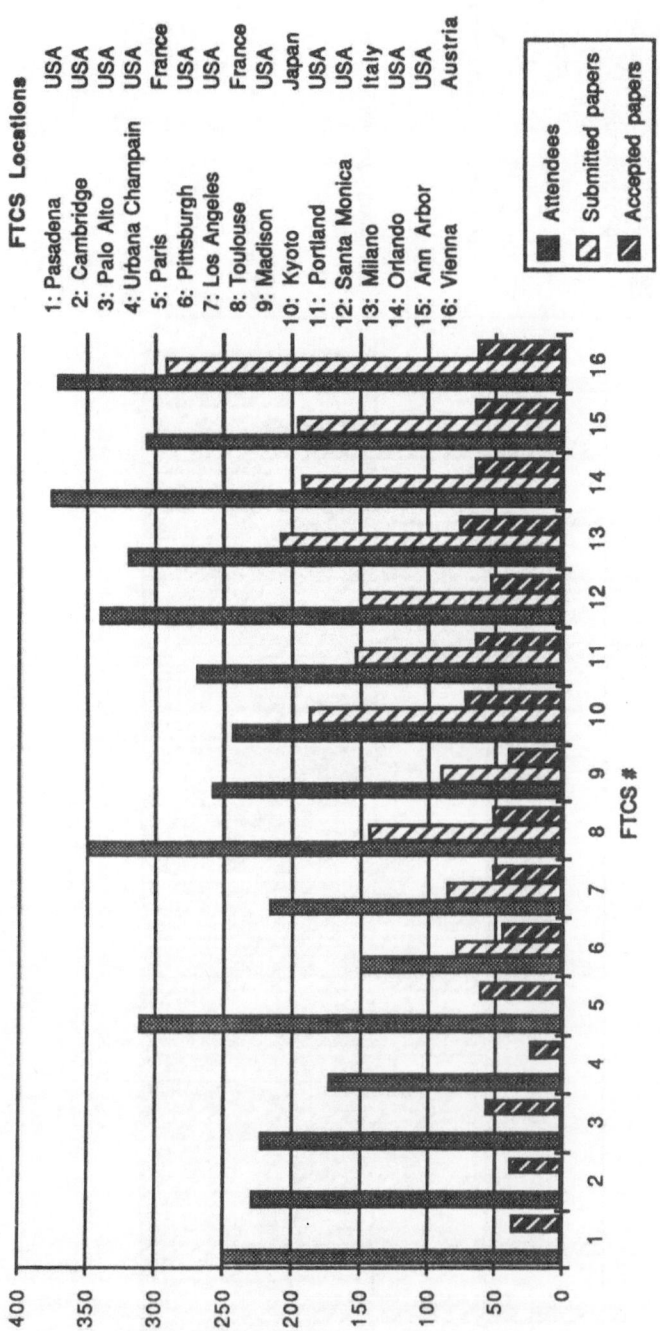

Fig. 1 FTCS global statistics

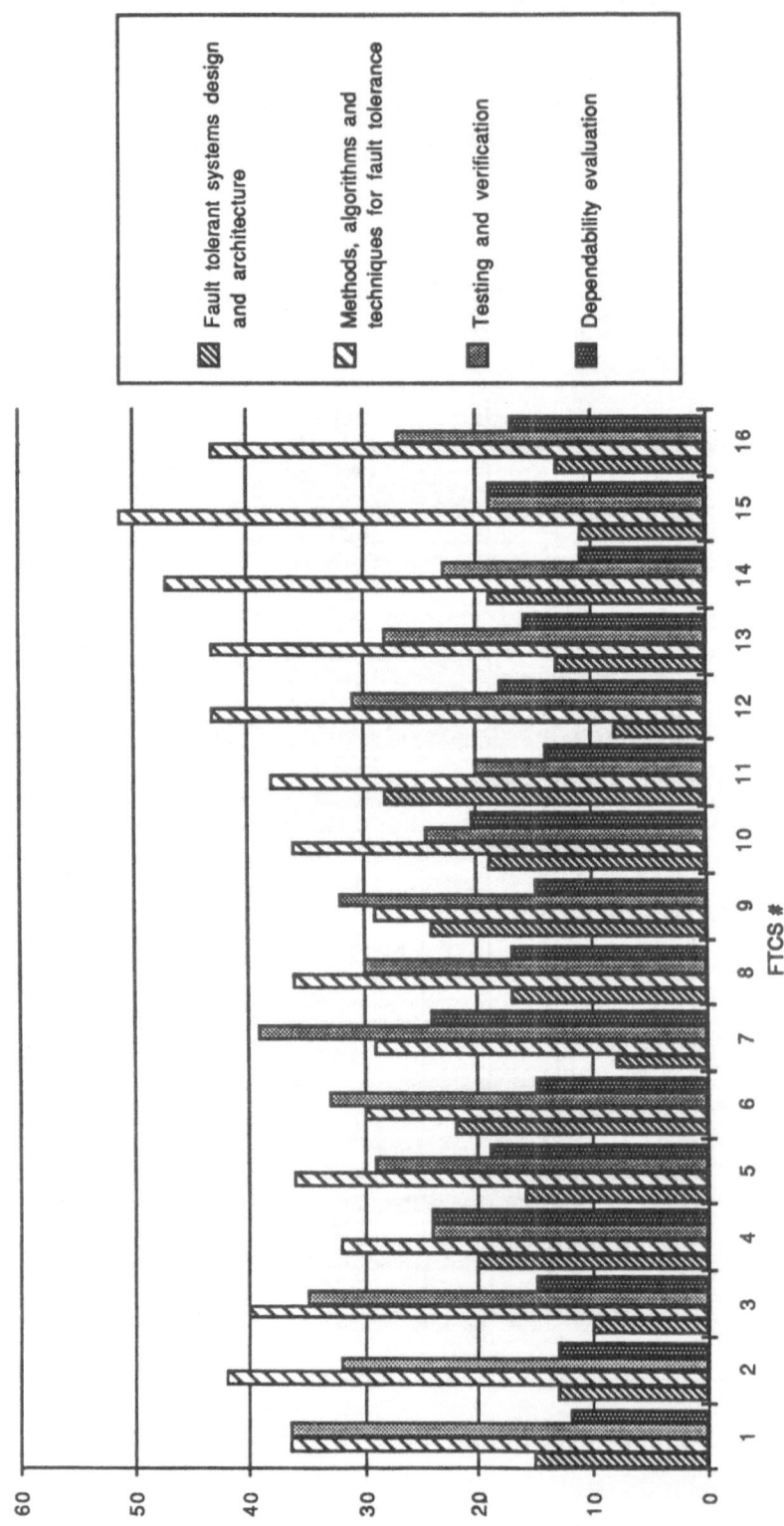

Fig. 2 Distribution of scientific and technical domains

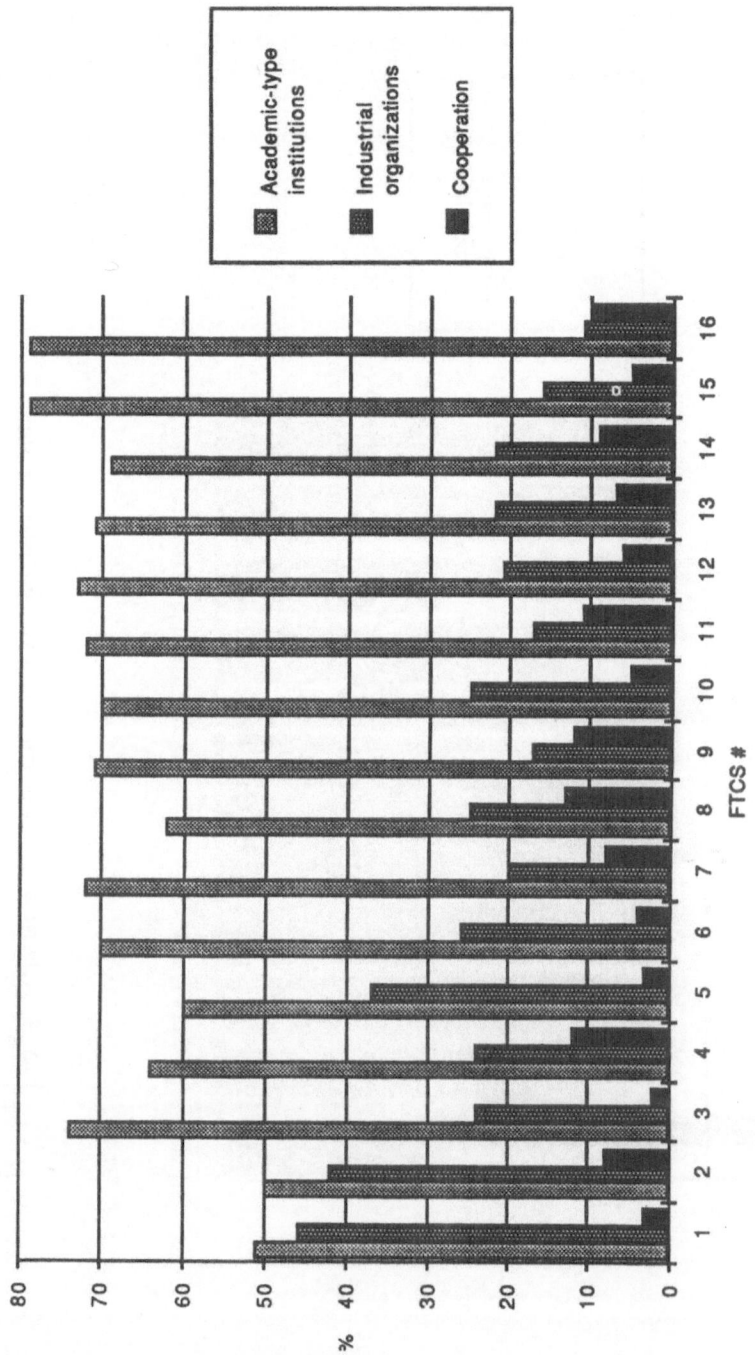

Fig. 3 Accepted papers academia/industry distribution

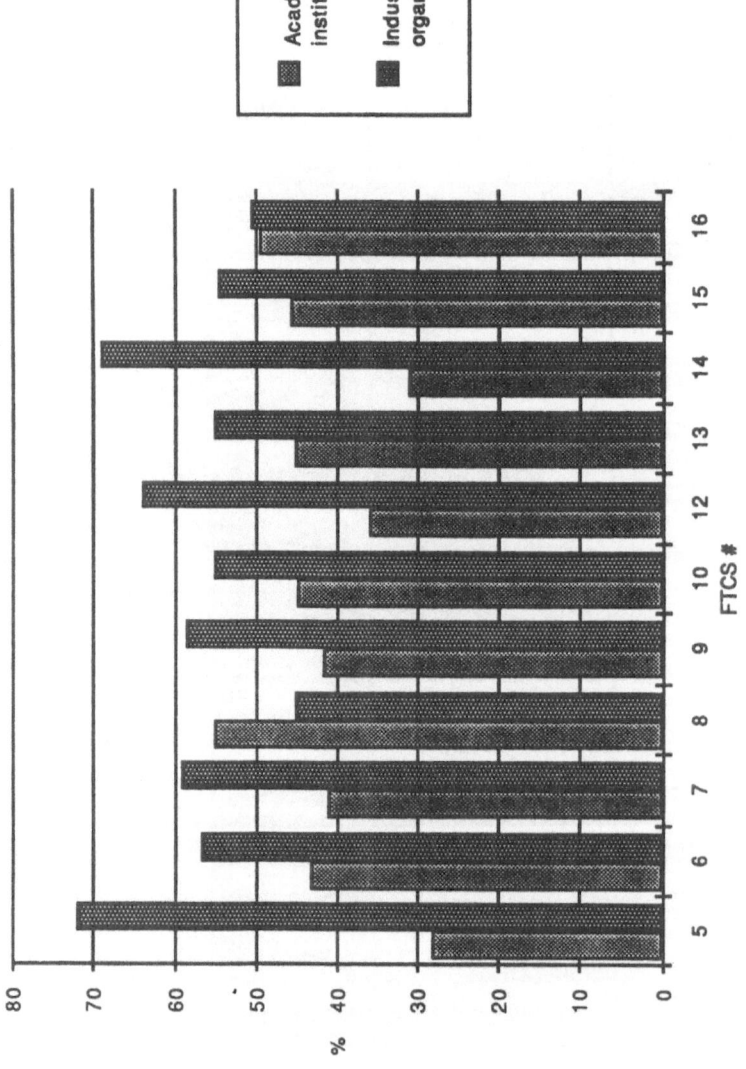

Fig. 4 Attendees academia/industry distribution

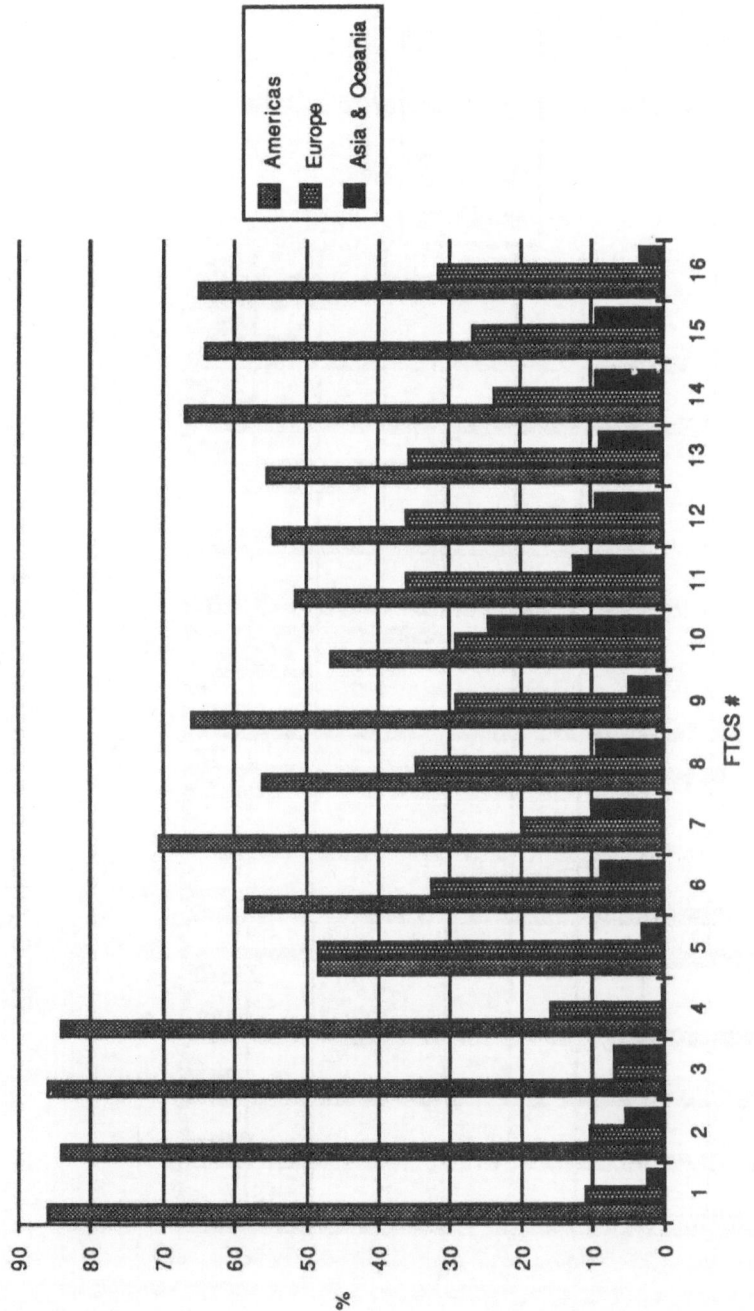

Fig. 5 Accepted papers geographical distribution

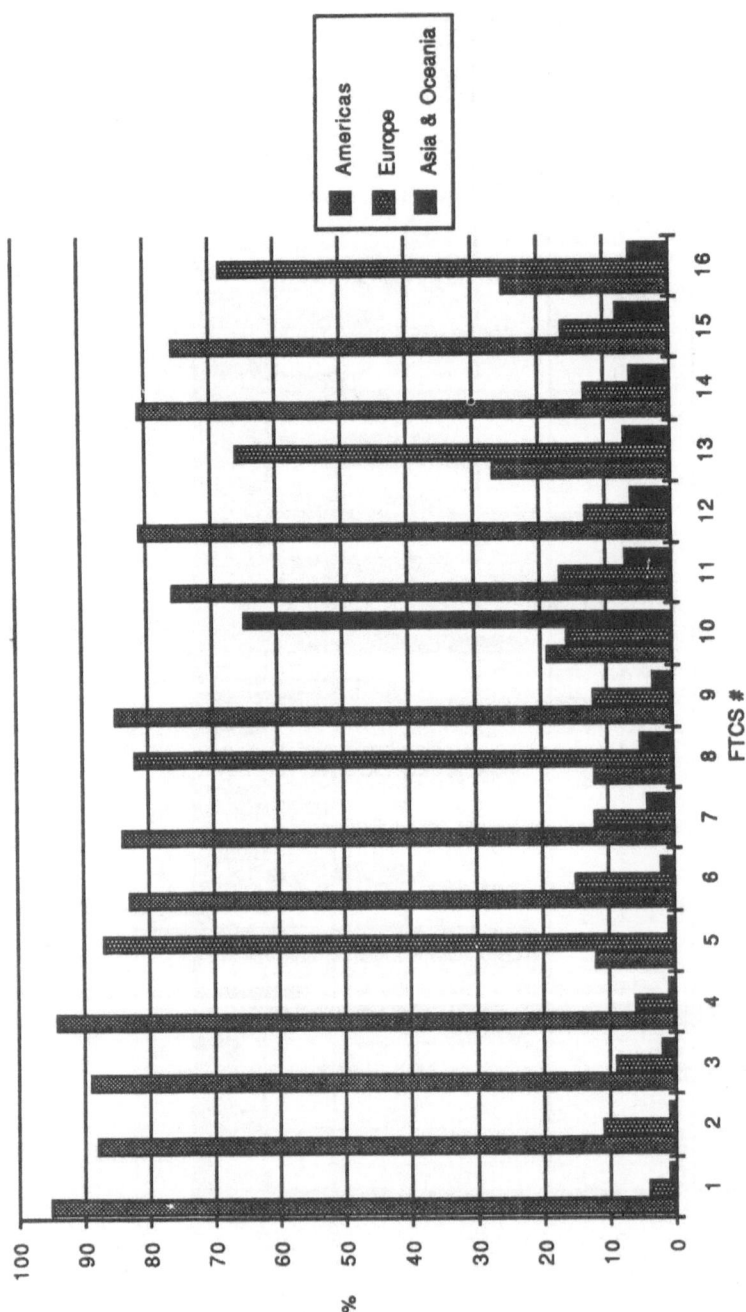

Fig. 6 Attendees geographical distribution

	FTCS 1	FTCS 2	FTCS 3	FTCS 4	FTCS 5	FTCS 6	FTCS 7	FTCS 8	FTCS 9	FTCS 10	FTCS 11	FTCS 12	FTCS 13	FTCS 14	FTCS 15	FTCS 16	TOTAL
Number of Countries	4	5	5	3	13	10	10	11	8	13	11	13	16	11	14	12	29
USA	32	32	47	21	29	27	35	29	25	32	31	27	40	42	36	36	521
FRANCE	3	2	4	3	17	9	6	7	7	13	12	9	5	4	10	4	115
JAPAN	1	2	2		1	2	2	3	2	16	6	4	6		3	2	54
FEDERAL GERMANY					3	1	1	4	1	1	3	1	2	2	1	6	25
ITALY					2	2	1	2	1	2	4	3	4	2	1	1	24
CANADA			1		1	1	1		2	2	2	2	2	1	4	5	23
UNITED KINGDOM	1	1		1	1	1		2		1	2	1	3	1	1	1	23
POLAND					2	1	2	2	2	1	2	1	3	2	1	2	13
CHINA						1		1		1	1		4	2	1		8
AUSTRALIA								1		1	1	1	1	2	2		7
USSR					2	1		1		1	1		2	2	1		7
ISRAEL			2		1	1	1			1		1	2				6
CZECHOSLOVAKIA		2						1					1		1	1	6
SWEDEN		1							1		1	1	1				5
GREECE									1			1	1	2	1		5
NORWAY								1	1	1		1	1				4
AUSTRIA								1								2	4
IRAN					1		1								1		3
BULGARIA												1	1				3
NETHERLANDS												1			1		2
ROMANIA												1	1				2
SWITZERLAND												1	1				2
BELGIUM					1											2	2
BRAZIL																	1
HUNGARY											1						1
MALAYSIA										1							1
SPAIN										1							1
TURKEY							1									1	1
YUGOSLAVIA							1								1		1
TOTAL	37	38	56	25	62	46	51	52	41	73	64	53	76	64	64	63	865

Fig. 7 Detailed geographical distribution of the accepted papers

	FTGS 1	FTGS 2	FTGS 3	FTGS 4	FTGS 5	FTGS 6	FTGS 7	FTGS 8	FTGS 9	FTGS 10	FTGS 11	FTGS 12	FTGS 13	FTGS 14	FTGS 15	FTGS 16	TOTAL
Number of Countries	7	8	10	7	19	12	13	26	11	18	16	14	22	17	22	24	42
USA	230	200	192	159	36	121	177	38	215	42	195	264	80	298	214	82	2543
FRANCE	4	11	13	5	204	11	12	164	18	19	21	19	28	15	17	34	593
JAPAN	3	3	3	1	2	2	7	5	7	148	14	16	13	15	12	14	264
Federal GERMANY	1	2		1	18	1		24		6	5	2	48	5	5	93	211
ITALY	1				11		3	30	4	3	9	10	88	8	7	17	191
CANADA	9	3	5	2	2	4	5	4	8	3	9	8	4	8	16	7	97
UK	3	8	3	1	12	2	5	24	1	1	3	4	8	7	2	7	91
SWEDEN		1	2	3			1	1	3	2	2	5	8	5	4	17	54
AUSTRIA													3		2	44	49
CHINA								9		7	2		8	3	6	4	39
NETHERLANDS			1		5		1	5		1		2	2	3	3	12	35
CZECHOSLOVAKIA					1			12					11	1		3	28
USSR			1		2	2	2	6	2	3	1	5	2			4	25
POLAND					1	2		2		1	1		3	2	1	4	22
ISRAEL			1	1	1	1		3	1	1	3	2	4	2	1		18
BRAZIL								1					2		2	5	16
YUGOSLAVIA					3			5					1			7	16
HUNGARY					4			7								3	13
NORWAY							1	2	1		1		1	3	2		12
AUSTRALIA										2		1	1		2	3	10
SWITZERLAND			1		1	1		1		1	1		2	1	1	4	10
BELGIUM					5			2									9
SPAIN					2			1				1	2			3	9
INDIA														1	1	4	6
FINLAND															4		4
KOREA															3	1	4
IRAN							1	1									3
DENMARK		1			1												2
GREECE							1					1				1	2
KUWAIT												1		1	1		2
BULGARIA										1							1
Democratic GERMANY								1									1
EGYPT								1									1
ICELAND							1										1
INDONESIA										1							1
IRELAND														1			1
IVORY COAST					1												1
LIBYA																1	1
MALAYSIA											1						1
NIGERIA										1							1
SINGAPORE								1									1
TURKEY							1										1
TOTAL	251	229	222	172	312	150	217	351	259	243	269	340	320	376	307	372	4390

Fig. 8 Detailed geographical distribution of the attendees

Biographies

Jacob A. Abraham received his B.Sc. degree in Electrical Engineering from the University of Kerala, India, in 1970. His M.S. degree, also in Electrical Engineering and Computer Science, were received from Stanford University, Stanford, California, in 1971 and 1974, respectively. Dr. Abraham is a Professor in the Departments of Electrical and Computer Engineering, Computer Science and the Coordinated Science Laboratory at the University of Illinois Urbana-Champaign. His research interests include fault-tolerant computing, VLSI systems, computer-aided design, and computer architecture. He is the Principal Investigator of several contracts and grants in these areas of interest. He is the Director of a major research program in Reliable VLSI Architectures, funded by the Semiconductor Research Corporation. He is also a consultant to industry in the areas of VLSI, testability, and fault-tolerant computing. Dr. Abraham is a fellow of the IEEE and a member of ACM and Sigma Xi.

Dr. Algirdas Avižienis: Algirdas Avižienis was born in Kaunas, Lithuania in 1932 and has resided in the United States since 1950. He received the B.S., M.S., and Ph.D. degrees, all in electrical engineering, from the University of Illinois, Urbana-Champaign, in 1954, 1955, and 1960, respectively. From 1956 to 1960 he was associated with the Digital Computer Laboratory at the University of Illinois as a Research Assistant and Fellow, participating in the design of the ILLIAC II computer In 1960 he joined the Jet Propulsion Laboratory, California Institute of Technology, and initiated research on reliability of computing systems that originated the concept of fault tolerance. He organized and directed the JPL STAR research project from 1961 to 1972. Dr. Avižienis joined the faculty of the University of California, Los Angeles (UCLA) in 1962. Currently he is Professor and Director of the Dependable Computing and Fault-Tolerant Systems Laboratory in the Computer

Science Department of UCLA, where he served as Chairman from 1982 to 1985. His present research at UCLA focuses on software fault tolerance, fault-tolerant distributed system architectures, and design methodology for fault-tolerant systems. He also has served as a consultant for studies of computer systems design and fault tolerance sponsored by the U.S. Air Force, U.S. Navy, NASA, and the Federal Aviation Administration, as well as for industrial research in the U.S. and abroad. For his pioneering efforts in the field of fault-tolerant computing, Dr. Avižienis has received numerous honors and awards, among them the Honor Roll of the IEEE Computer Society in 1968; the NASA Apollo Achievement Award in 1969; election to Fellow of IEEE "for fundamental contributions in fault-tolerant computing" in 1973; the biannual AIAA Information System Award in 1979 with the citation, "for the original conception and development of fault-tolerant computing and leadership in the theoretical and practical application of highly reliable aerospace computers"; the NASA Exceptional Service Medal in 1980 "in recognition of outstanding achievements and widely recognized leadership in the field of fault-tolerant computing"; and the second annual IEEE Computer Society Technical Achievement Award "for sustained contributions to fault-tolerant computing" in 1985. In recognition of his scientific accomplishments, Dr. Avižienis was awarded the honorary degree "Docteur Honoris Causa" by the Institut National Polytechnique of Toulouse, France in November, 1985. He was advanced to the rank of Faculty of Highest Distinction at UCLA in 1986, which is the top professorial rank in the University of California system. In international activities, Dr. Avižienis served as the founding Chairman of the Working Group 10.4 on "Reliable Computing and Fault Tolerance" of IFIP from 1980 to 1986. The General Assembly of IFIP presented the Silver Core award to him in 1986. Dr. Avižienis has lectured and conducted joint research at the National Polytechnic Institute of Mexico, the University of Sao Paulo, Brazil, the Laboratoire d'Automatique et d'Analyse des Systemes (LAAS) in Toulouse, France, Keio University in Tokyo, Japan, the Innovative Computer Systems Center of the Technical University of Berlin, FRG, and the Microelectronics Research Institute in Lintong, Peoples' Republic of China. In 1974 he spent a five-month research visit, sponsored by the U.S. National Academy of Science, at the Institute of Mathematics and Cybernetics, Lithuanian Academy of Sciences, Vilnius, Lithuania, USSR.

Joel F. Bartlett received his masters degree in 1972 from Stanford University. He then joined Hewlett Packard Computers where he worked on the HP3000 II operating system. He was a founding member of Tandem Computers where he made contributions to the machine architecture, operating system, fault tolerance methods, and the implementation and use of Lisp implementation. He recently joined the Digital Equipment Corporation's Western Research Laboratory.

Dr. Carter received the B.A. (magna cum laude) from Colby College in 1938 and the Ph. D. in Mathematics from Harvard University in 1947. From 1947 to 1952 he was at the Ballistic Research Laboratories at Aberdeen Proving Ground and was an adjunct instructor at the University of Maryland and Johns Hopkins University. From 1952 to 1955 he was head of the Systems Section, Raytheon Computer Department, and was adjunct professor at Boston University until 1956. From 1955 to 1959 he was Manager of the Systems Analysis Department, EDP Division, of Minneapolis Honeywell. From 1959 to 1961 was a technical staff member in the IBM Research Division in Poughkeepsie, NY. From 1961 to 1966 he was in the Systems Development Division in charge of systems automation for IBM System/360. In 1966 he rejoined the Research Division in Yorktown Heights, NY and continued work on fault tolerant computing. He remained there until he retired from IBM on March 1, 1986. Since then he has done some consulting. He has an IBM 6th Level Patent Award. Dr. Carter is a Fellow of the IEEE, and a member of American Men and Women of Science, Who's Who in America, American Association of Rhodes Scholars, Phi Beta Kappa, Sigma Xi, Association for Computing Machinery, and Society for Industrial and Applied Mathematics. He helped found the Computer Society Technical Committee in 1970, and was Vice Chairman from 1971 to 1973 and Chairman from 1973 to 1976. He has been a member of IFIP Working Group 10.4 since its founding. He has been an IEEE Computer Society Distinguished Visitor and ACM National Lecturer. He was named to the Computer Society Honor Roll in 1974.

Paolo Ciompi was born in Udine, on August 8, 1943. He received the Doctoral degree in Electrical Engineering from the University of Pisa in 1969. From 1969 he joined the Istituto di Elaborazione dell'Informazione (I.E.I.) of Pisa of the Italian National Research Council (C.N.R.) where he is currently carrying out his research activity. His past research interests were in microprogramming and microprogrammed systems, test and diagnosis, self-diagnosis and self-diagnosable systems, computer aided design, fault simulation and functional simulation of digital systems. His current research interests are in distributed systems and algorithms, local area networks, system reliability, fault-tolerant real time systems, self-diagnosis theory.

G.F. Clement - BSEE, 1940, New York University; M.A. (Physics), 1947, Columbia University; Bell Laboratories 1934 - Mr Clement has worked on electronic field studies and solid solutions. During World War II he worked on the Manhatten Project and the application of analog computers to military systems. He has worked on UNICOM system maintenance and No. 1ESS AUTOVON. In 1968, he became head of a department responsible for No. 1ESS maintenance and 1A Processor recovery. He has also worked on design and support of SXS and No. 1 crossbarswitching systems. Currently, he is head of a department responsible for design and development of support systems for digital toll applications. He is a senior member of IEEE, a member of IFIPS W.G.10.4 on dependability and a member of Eta Kappa Nu.

Alain Costes received the Certified Engineer degree from the Higher National Engineering School in "E.N.S.E.E.I.H.T.", Toulouse, France, in 1963, and the degree of Doctor in Engineering and Doctor ès-Sciences from the University of Toulouse, in 1966 and 1972, respectively. He is currently a professor at the Polytechnic National Institute of Toulouse. He joined the Laboratory of Automation and Systems Analysis (LAAS) of CRNS, Toulouse, in 1963, where he is currently Director. He has been involved with research in fault-tolerant computing in the team "Dependable Computing and Fault Tolerance" managed by Dr. Laprie since it was created. From 1977 to 1983, he has participated in the Directorate team of the French National Action for Systems Dependability as a scientific Advisor of the Agency for Informatics. From 1980 to 1985 he was Vice-chairman of the Working Group 10.4 on "Reliable Computing and Fault Tolerance" of the International Federation for Information Processing.

Bernard Courtois got the Engineer degree in 1973 from the Ecole Nationale Supérieure d'Informatique et Mathematiques Appliquées de Grenoble, France, and next the "Docteur-Ingénieur" and "Docteur ès-Science" degrees from the Institut National Polytechnique de Grenoble, France. Since 1973, he has been doing research in fault tolerance, fault modeling and VLSI testing. He is currently responsible of the Computer Architecture Group of the IMAG/TIM3 Laboratory, where researches include CAD, architecture and testing of VLSI. VLSI testing researches include fault modeling, test pattern generation, self-checking circuits, built-in test and electron-beam testing.

René David is Director of Research at CNRS (Centre National de la Recherche Scientifique). He is responsible of the team Logic and Discrete Systems in the Laboratoire d'Automatique de Grenoble (INPG). His research is about testing of digital circuits (mainly random testing and signature analysis) and performance evaluation of Flexible Manufacturing Systems.

Paul K. Giloth - BSEE and MSEE Northwestern University. During service with U.S 9th Air Force in Europe, he was involved with bombing and navigation systems. He has been employed by the Bell System for 39 years and up to 1961, he had a broad variety of design work on mobile radio, analog computers, and digital computers for bombing, navigation, and anti-missile defense. In 1961, he was promoted to Department Head and has had responsibilities for the design of digital global communication systems, store and forward systems, and digital toll switching systems. He is presently Head of the Toll Digital Project Management and Applications Department responsible for 4ESS TM and 5ESS TM Toll program management, testing, deployment, and support. Mr Giloth is a Senior Member of the IEEE, Sigma XI, and is a registered professional engineer in the State of Illinois.

Jack Goldberg is a Senior Staff Scientist in the Computer Science Laboratory of SRI International, Menlo Park, California. He has been employed at SRI since 1951, arriving shortly after his graduation with the BSEE degree from the University of California. He obtained a MSEE from Stanford while working at SRI, and from 1957-1959 was a Weizmann Fellow at the Weizmann Institute of Science. His major research activity has been in fault-tolerant computing, but in recent years he has also done work in computer architecture, software methodology and computer-aided design. His early work at SRI included contribution to the logic design and programming of the ERMA computer, and research on associative memories and on cellular and propagation-limited logic networks. For twenty years he was director of the Computer Science Laboratory. He is a Fellow of the IEEE, an editor of the IEEE Transactions on Software Engineering, and co-program chairman of the 17th Annual Symposium on Fault-Tolerant Computing.

Winfried Görke was born in Berlin, Germany, and received his degree as a Diplom-Ingenieur from the Technical University of Darmstadt, Germany, in 1959. After completing his studies with a master's degree in electrical engineering from Purdue University, Lafayette, Ind., also in 1959 he joined the Institute of Information Processing at the University of Karlsruhe, Germany, to complete the Ph.D. degree in 1965. His major research interests then covered reliability engineering and fault diagnosis of digital systems. At the same university he became a professor of computer science after this department was created. More recently his interests were in the area of self-testing of microcomputers, design for testability, and fault tolerance of digital systems. His list of publications contains about 35 contributions to journals and conferences, among them three books.

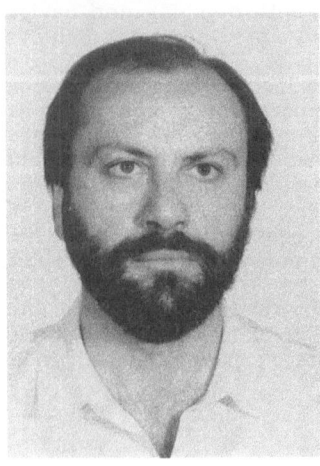

Fabrizio Grandoni was born in Falerone, Italy, on July 12, 1944. He received the Doctoral degree in Electronic Engineering (cum laude) from the University of Pisa, in 1971. He was with Telettra S.p.A., Ente Nazionale Idrocarburi (ENI), and Selenia S.p.A.; then, in 1980, he joined the Istituto di Elaborazione dell'Informazione (I.E.I) of the Italian National Research Council (C.N.R.). He worked in the fields of self-diagnostic systems, parallel computer architecture, signal processing, distributed systems. His current research interests are in dependable distributed systems, distributed algorithm theory, high speed computer networks.

Jim Gray is in the Software Development Department of Tandem Computers where he is working on enhancements to the Encompass data management system. He has worked on the design and implementation of a system dictionary, parallel sort, and a distributed SQL. Prior to joining Tandem, he worked at IBM Research on projects including System R, SQL/DS, and DB2. Previously he worked on Telsim at Bell Labs, managed the development of Cal TSS at Berkeley, and wrote his doctoral dissertation there.

Albert L. Hopkins, Jr., (Ph.D. Harvard, 1957), was member of the MIT community for some 21 years as a member of the Instrumentation Laboratory staff, as Associate Professor of Aeronautics and Astronautics, and as a member of the Draper Laboratory staff. He was a co-designer of the Apollo Guidance Computer, and subsequently undertook a number of fault-tolerant computer design responsibilities at Draper. He has been active in the IEEE Computer Society in a number of positions, including a term as Chairman of the Technical committee on Fault-Tolerant Computing. He is presently a member of IFIP Working Group 10.4 on Reliable Computing. Since 1981, he has been associated with ITP Boston, Inc., a new company formed to engage in the design and implementation of computer-integrated manufacturing systems for discrete parts.

Robert W. Horst is a senior systems architect at Tandem Computers Inc. where he developed the hardware architecture for the NonStop TXP and NonStop VLX processors. Prior to joining Tandem, he was at Hewlett-Packard Co. where was a designer of the high-end HP3000 Series 64 processor. He received the B.S.E.E. from Bradley University in 1975 and the M.S.E.E. degree from the University of Illinois in 1977. He holds seven patents for the design of Tandem processors.

Hirokazu Ihara is senior chief engineer of Space Division at Hitachi, Ltd., where he has been since 1959. Prior to his present position, he was deputy general manager of Systems Development Laboratory. His R/D interests include multi-micro computer systems, fault-tolerant computing systems, artificial intelligence and computer control systems with autonomy. Ihara is a member of the Institute of Electrical Engineers of Japan, Information Processing Society of Japan, the Institute of Electronics Communication Engineers of Japan, the Society of Instrument and Control Engineers of Japan, the IEEE Computer Society, ACM and IFIP WG 10.4. He graduated from Shinsyu University, Japan in 1959 and majored in electronics and telecommunication technology.

Ravishankar K. Iyer received the B.E. and the Ph.D degrees from the University of Queensland, Brisbane, Australia, in 1973 and 1977, respectively. Between 1978 and 1979 he was with the Norwegian Institute of Technology, Trondheim, Norway on a research fellowship from the Royal Norwegian Council for Scientific and Industrial Research. From 1979 to 1983 he was with the Computer Systems Laboratory, Departments of Electrical Engineering and Computer Science, Stanford University, first as a visiting Scolar and then as a Research Associate and Acting Assistant Professor. Since the fall of 1983 he has been on the faculty of the Department of Electrical and Computer Engineering and the Coordinated Science Laboratory at the University of Illinois at Urbana-Champaign, where he is now an Associate Professor. His research interests are in the areas of reliable and fault-tolerant computing, experimental evaluation, statistical modeling, and intelligent real-time diagnosis. He served on the program committee for the 16th International Symposium on Fault-Tolerant Computing and is the co-program director of the Illinois Computer Laboratory for Aerospace Systems and Software (ICLASS) a NASA-sponsored Center for Excellence at the University of Illinois. He is also a consultant to industry in the area of reliable computing. Dr. Iyer is a member of ACM, Sigma Xi, and the IFIP Technical Committee on Fault-Tolerant Computing (Working Group 10.4).

Jaynarayan H. Lala is the leader of the Systems Architecture Division at the Charles Stark Draper Laboratory. He is responsible for providing the technical leadership in the areas of fault tolerant, distributed and parallel processing at Draper. He was the chief architect of the Advanced Information Processing System and was very closely involved with the FTP and the FTMP developments. He received his M.S. and Ph.D. from MIT in 1973 and 1976, respectively. He graduated from the Indian Institute of Technology, Bombay in 1971 with Bachelor of Technology in Aeronautical Eng.

Jean-Claude Laprie was born in Paris, France, in 1944. He received the Certified Engineer degree from the Higher National School for Aeronautical Constructions, Toulouse, France, in 1968; he received the Doctor in Engineering degree in Automatic Control and the Doctor ès-Sciences degree in Computer Science from the University of Toulouse, in 1971 and 1975, respectively. Dr. Laprie is currently "Directeur der Recherche" of CNRS, the National Organization of Scientific Research. He joined the Laboratory of Automation and Systems Analysis (LAAS) of CNRS in 1968, where he has directed the research group on Fault Tolerance and Dependable Computing since 1975. His research has focussed on dependable computing since 1973, and especially on fault tolerance and on dependability evaluation, subjects on which he has authored and coauthored more than 40 papers; he is the Principal Investigator of several contracts in these areas of interest. From 1977 to 1983, as a scientific advisor to the Agency for Informatics, he participated in the Directorate Board of the French National Action for Computing Systems Dependability. From January to August 1985, he was an Invited Visiting Professor at the UCLA Department of Computer Science, Los Angeles, USA. He is also a consultant in the area of fault tolerant computing in France and abroad. Dr. Laprie served in 1978 as the General Chairman of the 8th International Symposium on Fault Tolerant Computing, and on program committees for numerous conferences and workshops. He was the Chairman of the IEEE Computer Society's Technical Committee on Fault Tolerant Computing in 1984 and 1985. He is a founding member of the IFIP working Group on Reliable Computing and Fault Tolerance, which he is presently chairing. He is the founding Chairman of the AFCET (French Association for Economics and Techniques of Cybernetics) Group on Systems Dependability. He is on the editorial board of the AFCET journal *Technique et Science Informatiques* (Technology and Science of Informatics), and is co-editor of the Springer Verlag series on *Dependable Computing and Fault Tolerant Systems*. Dr. Laprie is a member of ACM, AFCET, and IEEE.

E.J McCluskey (S'51-M'55-SM'59-f'65) received the A.B. degree (summa cum laude, 1953) in Mathematics and Physics from Bowdoin College; and the B.S. (1953), M.S. (1953), and Sc.D (1956) degrees in Electrical Engineering from M.I.T. He worked on electronic switching systems at the Bell Telephone Laboratories from 1955 to 1959. In 1959 he moved to Princeton University where he was Professor of Electrical Engineering and Director of the University Computer Center. in 1966 he joined Stanford University where he is Professor of Electrical Engineering and Computer Science as well as Director of the Center for Reliable Computing. Dr. Mccluskey

served as the first President of the IEEE Computer
Society and as a member of the AFIPS Executive
Committee. He has been general chairman of the
Computer Architecture Symposium, the Fault-
Tolerant Computing Symposium and the Operating
Systems Symposium. He was Associate Editor of the
IEEE Transactions on Computers and the Journal of
the ACM. He is a member of the Editorial Board of
the IEEE Design and Test Magazine. In 1984 he
received the IEEE Centennial medal and the IEEE
Computer Society Technical Achievement Award in
Testing. He has published several books and book
chapters. Dr. McCluskey is President of Stanford
Logical Systems Institute which provides consulting
services on Fault-Tolerant Computing, Testing, and
Design for Testability.

Roy A. Maxion received the B.S. degree in
Mathematics from the University of Nevada (Reno)
in 1975 and the M.S. in Computer Science in 1982.
His Cognitive Science Ph.D. from the University of
Colorado (Boulder) was completed in 1985. Dr. Maxion is a Research Scientist in the Department of
Computer Science at Carnegie Mellon University
where he directs the CMU automated system monitoring, diagnosis, and fault prediction project; this
includes studies of human and machine diagnosis of
complex systems. His current research interests are
focused on symptom-based diagnosis and uses of
artificial intelligence in fault-tolerant and reliable
computing, including: human and machine mechanisms for diagnostic reasoning; automatic rule formation for expert diagnostic problem-solving systems
based on monitored data, design data, and cognitive
task analysis; and fault-tolerant human-machine
interfaces to complex systems. Dr. Maxion has
served as a consultant to commercial and government organizations including TRW, the industrial
Technology Institute of the University of Michigan
and the U.S. Air Force. He has performed work on
major contracts with Digital Equipment Corporation
and the Federal Aviation Agency. Dr. Maxion has
several published papers and book chapters, and he
is a member of AAAI, ACM, Cognitive Science Society,
IEEE, Pi Mu Epsilon, Psi Chi, and Sigma Xi.

John F. Meyer received the B.S. degree from the
University of Michigan, Ann Arbor, the M.S. degree
from Stanford University, Stanford, CA, and the
Ph.D. degree in communications sciences, also from
the University of Michigan , in 1957, 1958, and 1967.
respectively. He is currently a Professor in the
Department of Electrical Engineering and Computer
Science,at the University of Michigan. He is also
director of the Department's Computing Research
Laboratory. During the past 25 years, he has been
active in computer research and has published
widely in the areas of system modeling and reliable
computing. In addition to his university affiliation,
he is a consultant for several government and industrial firms, and has held visiting research positions

at laboratories in the US, France and Japan. Prior to joining the Michigan faculty in 1967, he was a Research Engineer at the California Institute of Technology Jet Propulsion Laboratory where his contributions included the first patent issued to the National Aeronautics and Space Administration. Dr. Meyer is a Fellow of the IEEE and a member of the Association for Computing Machinery, the American Association for the Advancement of Science, Sigma Xi, Tau Beta Pi, and Eta Kappa Nu. In the IEEE Computer Society, he served as Chairman of the Technical Committee on Fault-Tolerant Computing from 1976 to 1979 and has been a Guest Editor of the IEEE Transactions on Computers. He was a member of the Computer Society Governing Board from 1982 to 1986, was chairman of the Society's International Symposium on Fault-Tolerant Computing in 1985, and has received several awards from the Society including a Certificate of Appreciation in 1981 and a Meritorious Service Award in 1985. He is currently a member of the IEEE Aerospace R&D Committee and a vice-chairman of IFIP Working Group 10.4 on reliable Computing and Fault Tolerance.

Shoji Miyamoto was born in Tokyo, Japan, 1945. He received BS in Mechanical Engineering from Waseda University, Tokyo, in 1967. Since then he has been with Hitachi Ltd, From 1972 to 1985, he worked at Systems Development Laboratory, Hitachi Ltd.. He was engaged in research for computer control system in production system, transportation system and defense system. His research interests include fault-tolerant computing system artificial intelligent system and fuzzy control system. He is currently project manager at Research and Development Promotion Center, Corporate Research and Development Coordination Department of Hitachi Ltd. He is a member of the Institute of Electrical Engineers of Japan, the Society of Instrument and Control Engineers of Japan and the International Fuzzy Systems Association.

Kinji Mori has been with Systems Development Laboratory at Hitachi, Ltd. since 1974. He is now a senior researcher. He has engaged in research of decentralized control and computer systems, fault-tolerant computing, computer network and man-machine systems. His current research interests include decentralized control and information systems; multi-microcomputer systems; and fault-tolerant system architecture,software, and evaluation. Mori is a member of IEEE, the Institute of Electrical Engineers of Japan, and the Society of Instrument and Control Engineers of Japan. He received a BS, MS, and PhD in electrical engineering from Waseda University, Tokyo, in 1969, 1971, and 1974, respectively.

Janak H. Patel received the B.Sc. degree in physics from Gujurat University, India, the B. Tech. degree in Electrical Engineering from the Indian Institute of Technology at Madras and the M.S. and Ph.D. degrees, also in Electrical Engineering, from Stanford University in Stanford, California. Dr. Patel has been with the University of Illinois at Urbana-Champaign since 1980, where he is currently an Associate Professor at the Department of Electrical and Computer Engineering, Computer Science, and the Coordinated Science Laboratory. He is presently engaged in research and teaching of computer architecture, VLSI, and fault-tolerant systems. Dr. Patel is a member of the IEEE and the ACM.

Brian Randell graduated in Mathematics from Imperial College in 1957 and joined the English Electric Company where he held a team which implemented a number of compilers, including the Whetstone KDF9 Algol compiler. From 1964 to 1969 he was with IBM, mainly at IBM Research Center in the United States, working on operating systems, the design of ultra-high-speed computers and System design methodology. He then became Professor of Computing Science at the University of Newcastle upon Tyne, where in 1971 he initiated a programme which now encompasses several major research projects sponsored by the Science and Engeneering Research Council and the Ministry of Defense.

David A. Rennels was born in Terre Haute, Indiana in 1942. He received the BSEE degree from Rose Hulman Institute of Technology, Terre Haute, Indiana, in 1964, the MSEE from Caltech in 1965, and the PhD in Computer Science from UCLA in 1973. In 1966 he joined the Spacecraft Computers Section of the Jet Propulsion Laboratory (JPL) of the California Institute of Technology and participated in the design and experimental validation of the JPL-STAR (Self-Testing and Repairing) Computer. In 1976 he initiated the Fault-Tolerant Building Block Computer project at JPL. This program developed an architecture which uses a small number of standard LSI-implementable building block circuits along with existing microprocessors and RAMS to construct fault-tolerant distributed computer systems for spacecraft. The architecture has been implemented as a breadboard, and it was used as the control computer for an autonomous satellite design conducted by JPL for the U.S. Air Force. In 1978 Dr.

Rennels joined the faculty of the University of California, Los Angeles (UCLA), where he is currently an associate professor. At UCLA he has been a co-principal investigator in the "Distributed Processing" research project sponsored by the Office of Naval Research, and was principal investigator of a program titled "Fault-Tolerant Local Networks using VLSI Building Blocks", sponsored by the National Science Foundation. He is currently carrying out research sponsored by Hughes Aircraft, TRW, and Rockwell International. He has served as a consultant to a number of private companies in the areas of fault-tolerant computer architecture. He remains a part-time academic member of the technical staff at JPL. Dr. Rennels was the general chairman of the 12th International Symposium on Fault-Tolerant Computing in 1982, and is a member of the IFIP Working Group 10.4 on "Reliable Computing and Fault-Tolerance."

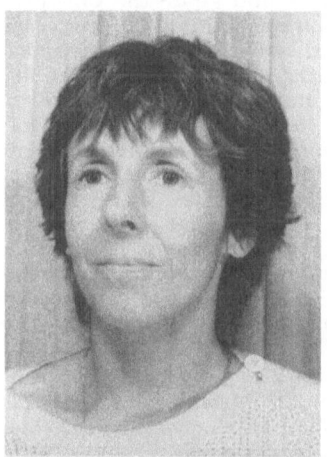

Gabrièle Saucier is Professor at the University of Grenoble (INPG) since 1971. She is responsible of a research laboratory : "Laboratoire Circuits et Systèmes" (LCS/IMAG). This laboratory has about 45 researchers involved in the design of fault tolerant systems, the design and test of VLSI and WSI.

John P. Shen received the B.S. degree from the University of Michigan, Ann Arbor, in 1973, and the M.S. and Ph.D. degrees from the University of Southern California, Los Angeles, in 1975 and 1981, respectively, all in electrical engineering. From 1973 to 1975 he was with the Hughes Aircraft Company where he participated in the design of fault detection/isolation and built-in-test circuits for avionic systems. In 1977 he was with the Systems Group of TRW Inc. where he was involved in the study and preliminary design of a local computer network. From 1977 to 1981 he performed research on multicomputer interconnection networks in the Department of Electrical Engineering (Systems), University of Southern California. In 1981 he joined the Electrical and Computer Engineering Department of Carnegie Mellon University, Pittsburgh Pennsylvania, U.S.A., where he is currently an Associate Professor. He has consulted for the IBM Federal Systems Division, the General Electric

Microelectronics Center, and the Aerospace Corporation. His research interests include computer-aided testing of VLSI circuits, application specific processor design, and fault-tolerant, mission-oriented systems. Dr. Shen is a member of IEEE, ACM, Tau Beta Pi, Eta Kappa Nu, and Sigma Xi. He is a recent recipient of an NSF Presidential Young Investigator Award.

Daniel P. Siewiorek was born in Cleveland, Ohio on June 2, 1946. He received the B.S. degree in Electrical Engineering (summa cum laude) from the University of Michigan, Ann Arbor, in 1968, and the M.S. and Ph.D. degrees in Electrical Engineering (minor in Computer Science) from Stanford University, Stanford, California, in 1969 and 1972, respectively. Dr. Siewiorek is a professor in the Departments of Computer Science and Electrical and Computer Engineering at Carnegie Mellon University where he helped to initiate and guide the Cm* project that culminated in an operational 50-processor multi-processor system. His current research interests include computer architecture, reliability modeling, fault-tolerant computing, modular design, and design automation. He has served as a consultant to several commercial and government organizations including DEC, Jet Propulsion Laboratory, the Naval Research Laboratory, Research Triangle Institute, and United Technologies Corporation. Elected an IEEE fellow in 1981 for contributions to the design of modular computing systems, he served as chairman of the IEEE Technical Committee of Fault-Tolerant Computing. He is a member of the IEEE, ACM, Tau Beta Pi, Eta Kappa Nu, and Sigma Xi.

Luca Simoncini was born in Florence, on April 22, 1946. He received the Doctoral degree in Electrical Engineering (cum laude) from the University of Pisa, in 1970. From 197-0 he joined the Istituto di Elaborazione dell'Informazione (I.E.I.) of Pisa of the Italian National Research Council (C.N.R.) where he is carrying out his research activity. In 1986 he has been appointed a full professorship position at the University of Reggio Calabria where he is carrying out his teaching activity. His research interests are in computer architecture, distributed systems, reliable and fault-tolerant computing, distributed algorithm theory.

T. Basil Smith received the S.B. and S.M. degrees in Aeronautical Engineering in 1969 and 1970 respectively, and a Ph.D. degree in Computer Systems, all from the Massachusetts Institute of Technology. He is currently a Research Staff Member at IBM T.J. Watson Research Center, Yorktown Heights, New York. His current research is directed toward solutions to availability and reliability problems in large commercial systems. From 1974 through 1983 he was at the C.S. Draper Laboratory, Inc. where he concentrated on the design of fault tolerant computers for avionics applications. Dr. Smith is a member of the IEEE, the IEEE Technical Committee on Fault Tolerant Computing, and a program committee member for FTSC-17.

Lorenzo Strigini was born in Florence, Italy, on August 5, 1956. He received the Doctoral degree in Electronic Engineering from the University of Pisa in 1980. From 1980 to 1983 he had a fellowship of the Italian National Council of Researches (C.N.R.) and in 1984 he joined the Istituto di Elaborazione dell'Informazione (I.E.I) of the C.N.R. in Pisa. He has been visiting scholar at the Computer Science Department of UCLA for a period of 14 months. His research interests are in distributed system architecture, reliable and fault-tolerant computing, software fault-tolerance, multiple version software. "Error Detection in Residue Number Systems with Magnitude Index", Proc. Ie.

Yoshihiro Tohma was born in Kawasaki, Japan on August 22, 1933. He received B.S., M.S., and Dr. Eng. degrees in Electrical Engineering from the Tokyo Institute of Technology, Tokyo, Japan in 1956, 1958, and 1961, respectively. In 1961 he joined the staff of the Tokyo Institute of Technology, where he is currently a Professor in the Department of Computer Science. He has been engaged in research on switching circuit theory, fault- tolerant systems, and computer architectures. Dr. Tohma is IEEE Fellow and a member of Information Processing Society of Japan, Institute of Electronics and Communication Engineers of Japan, and Institute of Electrical Engineers of Japan. He is cur- rently serving as Vicechairman, IFIP WG10.4, a member of the Advisory Board, Technical Committee on Fault-Tolerant Computing, IEEE Computer Society, and Chairman, Technical Committee on Fault-Tolerant Systems, IECE Japan. He was Program Chairman of FTCS-10 and will be Chairman of Steering Committee for FTCS-18.

Author Index